Lecture Notes in Computer Science

Lecture Notes in Artificial Intelligence 16811

The series Lecture Notes in Artificial Intelligence (LNAI) was established in 1988 as a topical subseries of LNCS devoted to artificial intelligence.

The series publishes state-of-the-art research results at a high level. As with the LNCS mother series, the mission of the series is to serve the international R & D community by providing an invaluable service, mainly focused on the publication of conference and workshop proceedings and postproceedings.

Madalina Croitoru · Gerd Stumme ·
Domingo López-Rodríguez
Editors

Conceptual Knowledge Structures

Third International Joint Conference, CONCEPTS 2026
Montpellier, France, August 31 – September 4, 2026
Proceedings

Springer

Editors
Madalina Croitoru
University of Montpellier
Montpellier, France

Gerd Stumme
University of Kassel
Kassel, Germany

Domingo López-Rodríguez
University of Malaga
Málaga, Spain

ISSN 0302-9743 ISSN 1611-3349 (electronic)
Lecture Notes in Artificial Intelligence
ISBN 978-3-032-34741-1 ISBN 978-3-032-34742-8 (eBook)
https://doi.org/10.1007/978-3-032-34742-8

LNCS Sublibrary: SL7 – Artificial Intelligence

This Springer imprint is published by the registered company Springer Nature Switzerland AG
The registered company address is: Gewerbestrasse 11, 6330 Cham, Switzerland

Preface

The Third International Joint Conference on Conceptual Knowledge Structures (CONCEPTS 2026) continued a long tradition of research on conceptual structures, formal concept analysis, and conceptual learning. Emerging from the convergence of the International Conference on Conceptual Structures (ICCS), the International Conference on Formal Concept Analysis (ICFCA), and Concept Lattices and Their Applications (CLA), it brings together researchers interested in the representation, analysis, and use of concepts for knowledge discovery and reasoning.

This third Springer volume associated with CONCEPTS offers a snapshot of a field that continues to evolve while remaining firmly anchored in its foundational questions. Across the contributions collected here, a common concern emerges: how to represent, structure, and explore knowledge in ways that remain formally rigorous and meaningful in practice.

The volume reflects the vitality of research on conceptual structures. It reports on work concerning lattices, closure systems, implication bases, distributivity, and conceptual representations that sit alongside advances in concept mining, visualization, and interactive exploration. Together, these contributions reinforce the role of conceptual methods as tools for organizing and reasoning about complex information.

The range of applications represented is equally noteworthy. From cultural heritage and enterprise architecture to education, argumentation, social media, and human--robot interaction, the papers demonstrate the versatility of conceptual approaches across diverse domains. Several contributions also engage with contemporary challenges in artificial intelligence, including explainability, AI perception, and human--AI interaction.

The CONCEPTS 2026 conference featured two tracks, the LNAI Proceedings Track and the International Journal of Approximate Reasoning Track. The LNAI Proceedings Track received 42 submissions. Each submission underwent a single-blind peer review by at least three members of the Program Committee. Based on these reviews and subsequent discussion, the Program Committee accepted 18 long and 7 short papers for presentation and publication. This LNAI volume equally showcases ten abstracts of significant contributions recently published by members of the community. Last but not least the volume is complemented by supplementary proceedings.

Taken together, the papers in this volume illustrate a community that continues to bridge theory and application, formal reasoning and human understanding. We hope they will stimulate further advances and foster new connections across the broad landscape of conceptual structures research.

We thank all authors, reviewers, Program Committee members, and organizers whose efforts made this volume possible.

June 2026

Madalina Croitoru
Domingo López-Rodríguez
Gerd Stumme

Organization

Program Chairs

Madalina Croitoru	University of Montpellier, France
Domingo López-Rodríguez	University of Málaga, Spain
Gerd Stumme	University of Kassel, Germany

General and Conference Chair

Alexandre Bazin	University of Montpellier, France

Executive Board

Jaume Baixeries	Polytechnic University of Catalonia, Spain
Radim Belohlavek	Palacký University Olomouc, Czech Republic
Tanya Braun	University of Münster, Germany
Madalina Croitoru	University of Montpellier, France
Sergei Kuznetsov	HSE University, Moscow, Russia
Rokia Missaoui	Université du Québec en Outaouais, Canada
Amedeo Napoli	LORIA, Nancy, France
Sergei Obiedkov	TU Dresden, Germany
Manuel Ojeda-Aciego	University of Málaga, Spain
Uta Priss	Ostfalia University of Applied Sciences, Germany
Gerd Stumme	University of Kassel, Germany

Program Committee

Mohammad Abdulla	University of Kassel, Germany
Jaume Baixeries	Universitat Politècnica de Catalunya, Spain
Alexandre Bazin	LIRMM, Université de Montpellier, France
Mike Behrisch	Technische Universität Wien, Austria
Radim Belohlavek	Palacký University Olomouc, Czech Republic
Karell Bertet	L3I Laboratory, University of La Rochelle, France
Tanya Braun	University of Münster, Germany

Inma P. Cabrera	University of Málaga, Spain
Peggy Cellier	IRISA/INSA Rennes, France
Madalina Croitoru	LIRMM, Université de Montpellier, France
Christophe Demko	University of La Rochelle, France
Dominik Dürrschnabel	Baden-Württemberg Cooperative State University Mosbach, Germany
Tom Hanika	University of Hildesheim, Germany
Tobias Hille	University of Kassel, Germany
Marianne Huchard	LIRMM, Université de Montpellier, France
Mohamed-Hamza Ibrahim	École Polytechnique de Montréal, Canada
Dmitry Ignatov	National Research University Higher School of Economics, Moscow, Russia
Mehdi Kaytoue	INSA Lyon, France
Francesco Kriegel	Technische Universität Dresden, Germany
Sergei O. Kuznetsov	National Research University Higher School of Economics, Moscow, Russia
Leonard Kwuida	Bern University of Applied Sciences, Switzerland
Florence Le Ber	National School for Water and Environmental Engineering (ENGEES), France
Domingo López-Rodríguez	University of Málaga, Spain
Pierre Martin	French Agricultural Research Centre for International Development (CIRAD), France
Jesús Medina	University of Cádiz, Spain
Rokia Missaoui	Université du Québec en Outaouais, Canada
Amedeo Napoli	LORIA (CNRS, Inria, Université de Lorraine), France
Sergei Obiedkov	Technische Universität Dresden, Germany
Manuel Ojeda-Aciego	University of Málaga, Spain
Manuel Ojeda-Hernández	University of Málaga, Spain
Tim Pattison	Defence Science and Technology Organisation, Australia
Carmen Peláez-Moreno	Universidad Carlos III de Madrid, Spain
Uta Priss	Ostfalia University of Applied Sciences, Germany
Baris Sertkaya	Frankfurt University of Applied Sciences, Germany
Gerd Stumme	University of Kassel, Germany

Workshop Chair

Dominika Kotlárová	Pavol Jozef Šafárik University, Slovakia

Local Organizing Committee

Alexandre Bazin	University of Montpellier, France
Marianne Huchard	University of Montpellier, France
Imen Ben Sassi	University of Montpellier, France
Pierre Martin	French Agricultural Research Centre for International Development (CIRAD), France

Nectar Papers

The Nectar Papers highlight recent contributions from members of the conceptual structures community that have appeared in other venues. These papers provide an additional perspective on current developments in the field and illustrate the breadth and continued impact of research on conceptual structures, formal concept analysis, and related areas.

Adaricheva, Nourine, Vilmin. *Computing the D-base and D-relation in Finite Closure Systems*
Aragón, Medina, Molina-Ruiz. *Computing Bonds Between Formal Contexts*
Bazin, Kahn. *Distance between FCA Structures*
Cornejo Piñero, Medina, Ocaña. *Attribute Implication Bases from Galois Connection Structures*
Defrain, Ohana, Vilmin. *Enumerating the Irreducible Closed Sets of an Acyclic Implicational Base of Bounded Degree*
Espinosa-Aldama, Mendoza. *Multidimensional Representation of Physical Theories, Constants and Units Using Formal Concept Analysis*
Hodo, Balderas-Díaz, Guerrero-Contreras, Sertkaya. *Interactive Exploration of Concept Lattices with lattice.js: A Web-Based Visualization Library*
Sinclair-Desgagné. *Chasing Unknown Unknowns with the Available Data*
Stumme, Dürrschnabel, Hanika. *Towards Ordinal Data Science*
Valverde, Peláez-Moreno, Cabrera, Cordero, Ojeda-Aciego. *Formal Context Transforms and Their Affordances for Exploratory Data Analysis*

Contents

Data Analysis

Applications

Short Papers

Closing an Open Problem

Pseudo-Closed Family Verification is NP-Complete (Or: How Claude Helped Tackle Bernhard's Problem)

Sebastian Rudolph(✉)

TU Dresden and ScaDS.AI Dresden/Leipzig, Dresden, Germany
sebastian.rudolph@tu-dresden.de

Abstract. Every closure operator on a finite set admits a canonical minimum implication basis – the *stem base* or *Duquenne–Guigues base* – whose premises are the *pseudo-closed sets*. The *Pseudo-Closed Family* problem (PCF) asks whether a given family of sets equals the pseudo-closed sets of some closure operator. We prove that PCF is NP-complete, negatively answering a question posed by Bernhard Ganter at CONCEPTS'25, which essentially asked for "easy" ways to verify PCF.

As the large language model Claude Opus 4.6 was instrumental in establishing the NP-hardness part, this paper also discusses the methodology applied and observations made in the process.

1 Introduction

During the CONCEPTS'25 conference, Bernhard Ganter posed a problem to the audience. The problem revolved around one of the arguably most mysterious and misunderstood notions of FCA: a closure operator's *pseudo-closed sets*. Given that pseudo-closed sets are a key notion when it comes to describing and understanding the attribute logic of formal contexts, they have been a subject of intense research in FCA, in particular regarding their representational succinctness and computational properties [1,3,9–11,13,15,16,19,20].

The question posed was strikingly simple: Given a family of subsets of some finite set S, how can we find out if it corresponds to the pseudo-closed sets of some closure operator on S? While the problem is clearly decidable by brute-force methods (assuming a finite base set), it turned out surprisingly tricky to come up with necessary and sufficient conditions that can be easily checked. Ganter provided two necessary conditions (see Fig. 1), but the conjecture that they are also sufficient was refuted pretty much on the spot, by another attendee who provided a counterexample. Consequently, the matter remained unresolved.

In the aftermath of the conference, the author spent some time thinking about the problem from a complexity-theoretic perspective. Clearly, the existence of an easily verifiable characterization would require that the underlying

It is firm consensus among academic publishers and ethics organizations that large language models must not be listed as co-authors. If that weren't so, the author would have considered this – which would have raised the question of Claude's surname.

M. Croitoru et al. (Eds.): CONCEPTS 2026, LNAI 16811, pp. 3–19, 2027.
https://doi.org/10.1007/978-3-032-34742-8_1

Fig. 1. Impression of Bernhard Ganter presenting the problem discussed in this paper on 12 September 2025 during CONCEPTS'25 in Cluj-Napoca, Romania.

computational decision problem is tractable. Some tractable computational tools for related problems already exist, most notably closure computation [4] and "stembasification" [15] of an implication set. Yet, even with these at hand, the best the author could do was to show that the problem is in NP. Attempts to complement this upper complexity bound with a lower one by showing NP-hardness failed, putting the problem in tractability limbo between P and NP.

In view of the usual shortage of time available for uninterrupted research and made curious by the latest news about large language models solving non-trivial mathematical problems,[1] the author decided to try and solicit the help of a large language model (Claude Opus 4.6 by Anthropic) to tackle the problem. The ensuing exchange spanning a few days turned out to be an exciting journey with new insights into the opportunities and challenges of human-LLM collaboration in the mathematical domain. In the end it was possible with joint forces to settle the complexity problem by showing NP-hardness, which amounts to the insight that no easily (in the sense of tractably) verifiable conditions exist that would be both necessary and sufficient.

[1] cf. https://www-cs-faculty.stanford.edu/~knuth/papers/claude-cycles.pdf

The first part of the paper provides a full formal treatment of the established results, the second reflects on the experience of the unusual collaborative process.

2 Preliminaries

In this section, we set the stage by introducing the terminology relevant to our treatise. Notably, formal contexts and formal concepts – the foundational notions in Formal Concept Analysis – are not required at all, as the topic primarily revolves around closure operators.

Definition 1 (closure operator, closed set) *A* closure operator *on a finite set S is a function $\varphi\colon 2^S \to 2^S$ satisfying, for all $A, B \subseteq S$:*

- $A \subseteq \varphi(A)$ *(extensivity),*
- $A \subseteq B \implies \varphi(A) \subseteq \varphi(B)$ *(monotonicity),*
- $\varphi(\varphi(A)) = \varphi(A)$ *(idempotency).*

A set $C \subseteq S$ with $\varphi(C) = C$ is called closed.

While closure operators are often defined over arbitrary sets, in our investigation, we require S to be a finite set. This condition is justified by the fact that any complexity-theoretic consideration requires finite problem inputs; it also avoids some complications related to the recursive definitions of pseudo-closed sets.

The following straightforward consequence of monotonicity will be used repeatedly: If C is closed and $A \subseteq C$, then $\varphi(A) \subseteq C$.

Now we introduce implications as a key means of expressing closure operators.

Definition 2 (implication, closure under an implication set) *An* implication *on S is a pair $A \to B$ with $A, B \subseteq S$. A set $C \subseteq S$* respects *$A \to B$ if $A \subseteq C$ implies $B \subseteq C$.*

Given a finite set $\mathfrak{I}$ of implications on S, the $\mathfrak{I}$-closure *of $X \subseteq S$, denoted $X^{\mathfrak{I}}$, is the smallest superset of X respecting every implication in $\mathfrak{I}$.*

The term "$\mathfrak{I}$-closure" is justified by the fact that the map $X \mapsto X^{\mathfrak{I}}$ is a closure operator. The $\mathfrak{I}$-closure can be computed iteratively: Starting from $C = X$, whenever some $A \to B \in \mathfrak{I}$ satisfies $A \subseteq C$ whereas $B \not\subseteq C$, we replace C by $C \cup B$, repeating this process until C stabilizes. The time required for this naive approach is quadratic in the size of $\mathfrak{I}$, but with more elaborate algorithms a linear runtime can be achieved [4]. We now introduce the central notion of this paper. The definition seems to be notoriously hard to comprehend for students (and even some established researchers), due to its alleged circular nature.

Definition 3 (pseudo-closed set) *A set $P \subseteq S$ is* pseudo-closed *for a closure operator φ on S if:*

(i) $\varphi(P) \neq P$ (i.e., P is not closed), and
(ii) for every pseudo-closed $Q \subsetneq P$, we have $\varphi(Q) \subseteq P$.

This recursive definition is well-founded by strict inclusion.

One rather straightforward observation about pseudo-closed sets deserves to be made explicit, as it will be instrumental later on.

Fact 4 (sandwich property) *If φ is a closure operator with pseudo-closed sets Q and P such that $Q \subsetneq P$, then $Q \subsetneq \varphi(Q) \subsetneq P$.*

Note the sandwich property also immediately gives rise to the second necessary condition observed by Ganter (see Fig. 1): for any two pseudo-closed sets P and Q with $Q \subsetneq P$ we must have $|P \setminus Q| > 1$.

The first necessary condition of Ganter, essentially stating that the intersection of two inclusion-incomparable pseudo-closed sets must never be pseudo-closed, is justified by another easy observation presented next.

Fact 5 (intersection-free) *If φ is a closure operator with pseudo-closed sets P_1 and P_2 such that $P_1 \not\subseteq P_2$ and $P_2 \not\subseteq P_1$, then $P_1 \cap P_2$ is not pseudo-closed.*

The fact directly generalizes to intersections of more than two pseudo-closed sets. We proceed by providing another central notion, which in fact is the main reason for the existence of the notion of pseudo-closed sets: it warrants the definition of a canonical, minimal way of representing closure operators by means of implications.

Definition 6 (canonical base[2]) *Let φ be a closure operator. The* canonical base *$\mathfrak{S}_\varphi$ of φ is the implication set $\{P \to \varphi(P) \mid P$ pseudo-closed$\}$.*

Theorem 7 (Guigues & Duquenne [5,6]). *Given a closure operator φ, the canonical base $\mathfrak{S}_\varphi$ is a basis for φ, that is, it satisfies $(\cdot)^{\mathfrak{S}_\varphi} = \varphi$ and none of the implications of $\mathfrak{S}_\varphi$ follows from the others. Among all such bases, $\mathfrak{S}_\varphi$ has minimum cardinality.*

The StemBase algorithm [2,15] converts any finite set $\mathfrak{I}$ of implications on S into the canonical base of the closure operator $(\cdot)^{\mathfrak{I}}$ in polynomial time.

Algorithm StemBase($\mathfrak{I}$)
Input: A finite set $\mathfrak{I}$ of implications on S.
Output: The canonical base $\mathfrak{S}$ of $(\cdot)^{\mathfrak{I}}$.

1. Set $\mathfrak{S} := \emptyset$.
2. For every $A \to B \in \mathfrak{I}$: substitute $A \to B$ by $A \to (A \cup B)^{\mathfrak{I}}$.
3. As long as $\mathfrak{I} \neq \emptyset$:
   (a) select an $A \to B$ from $\mathfrak{I}$,
   (b) delete $A \to B$ from $\mathfrak{I}$,
   (c) if $A^{\mathfrak{I}\cup\mathfrak{S}} \neq B$ then add $A^{\mathfrak{I}\cup\mathfrak{S}} \to B$ to $\mathfrak{S}$.

[2] In the literature, the canonical base is also referred to as stem base or Duquenne–Guigues base. We follow Vincent Duquenne's wish to discontinue both terms in favor of *canonical base*, except for the already established name StemBase *algorithm*.

4. Output $\mathfrak{S}$ and terminate.

Theorem 8 (**[15, Theorem 2]**). *The algorithm* STEMBASE *computes a canonical base for* $(\cdot)^{\mathfrak{I}}$. *Specifically:*

(a) $(\cdot)^{\mathfrak{I}} = (\cdot)^{\mathfrak{S}}$ *(the closure operator is preserved), and*
(b) the premises of $\mathfrak{S}$*'s implications are exactly the pseudo-closed sets for* $(\cdot)^{\mathfrak{S}}$.

As computing the $\mathfrak{I}$-closure can be done in linear time [4], the algorithm runs in time quadratic in the size of $\mathfrak{I}$ (the naive implicational closure algorithm described above would yield cubic runtime, which is still polynomial). Crucially, the premises of $\mathfrak{S}$ thus computed are exactly the pseudo-closed sets of $(\cdot)^{\mathfrak{I}}$.

3 The Pseudo-Closed Family Problem

It is a worthwhile question how the definition of pseudo-closedness constrains the way in which pseudo-closed sets can co-exist. In particular, is it possible to capture such co-existence constraints in an exact way, so that for each family of subsets of some set S it can be straightforwardly verified if it corresponds to the pseudo-closed sets of some closure operator? These contemplations give rise to the computational problem at the core of this paper, which we now introduce.

Definition 9 (PCF) *An instance of the* Pseudo-Closed Family *problem (PCF) consists of a finite set* S *and a family* $\mathcal{F} \subseteq 2^S$ *of subsets of* S. *The question is whether there exists a closure operator on* S *whose pseudo-closed sets are exactly* $\mathcal{F}$. *If such a closure operator exists, we say* $(S, \mathcal{F})$ *is* valid. *If* S *is clear from the context, we may sometimes simply say* $\mathcal{F}$ *is* valid.

Example 1. Let us first consider the instance of PCF with $S_1 = \{a, b, c, d\}$ and $\mathcal{F}_1 = \{\{a\}, \{b\}, \{c\}, \{a, b, c\}\}$, noting that the instance satisfies both of Ganter's necessary conditions: $\mathcal{F}_1$ is intersection-free and any two comparable sets differ in more than one element. Still, $(S_1, \mathcal{F}_1)$ is not valid: Any fitting closure operator φ_1 would need to map each singleton element of $\mathcal{F}_1$ to a two-element subset of $\{a, b, c\}$. W.l.o.g. (exploiting symmetry), fix $\varphi_1(\{a\}) = \{a, b\}$, which forces $\varphi_1(\{b\}) = \{a, b\}$ by monotonicity and idempotency, because $\{b\} \subseteq \{a, b\} = \varphi_1(\{a, b\})$. But then, there is no appropriate choice left for $\varphi_1(\{c\})$: Picking $\varphi_1(\{c\}) = \{a, c\}$ would mean $\{a\} \subseteq \varphi_1(\{c\})$ which, by monotonicity and idempotency yields $\varphi_1(\{a\}) \subseteq \varphi_1(\varphi_1(\{c\})) = \varphi_1(\{c\})$, which contradicts the earlier choice of $\varphi_1(\{a\})$. Picking $\varphi_1(\{c\}) = \{b, c\}$ would produce the same issue. ◇

Example 2. To contrast the previous example, consider the PCF instance with $S_2 = \{a, b, c, d, e\}$ and $\mathcal{F}_2 = \{\{a\}, \{b\}, \{c\}, \{d\}, \{a, b, c, d\}\}$. We will argue that $(S_2, \mathcal{F}_2)$ is valid. In order to do so, we have to describe a corresponding closure operator φ_2. We choose to describe φ_2 by means of an implication set $\mathfrak{I}_2$, letting $\varphi_2 = (\cdot)^{\mathfrak{I}_2}$. Let now $\mathfrak{I}_2 = \{a \to ab,\ b \to ab,\ c \to cd,\ d \to cd,\ abcd \to abcde\}$ (using simplified notation for better readability). It can be verified, using the STEMBASE algorithm, that $\mathfrak{I}_2$ is already a canonical base and thus its premises are the pseudo-closed sets, which coincide with the elements of $\mathcal{F}_2$, as desired. ◇

In what follows, we are going to analyze the computational worst-case complexity of PCF. Sadly, our results imply that no polynomial time algorithm (thus: easily verifiable necessary and sufficient conditions) can exist, unless P = NP, since we will establish the following theorem:

Theorem 10. *PCF is* NP*-complete.*

We establish the easier result of NP-membership in Section 4 and the somewhat more involved NP-hardness in Section 5. The impacts of this complexity result on "easy expressibility" of necessary and sufficient conditions for PCF validity will be discussed in Section 6.

4 Membership in NP

As usual, to exactly pin down a problem's complexity class, one has to show membership and hardness. The former means that, using a certain underlying computational model, the problem can be solved within certain space or time bounds depending on the size of the input. The class NP contains all problems which can be solved in polynomial time on a nondeterministic Turing machine. A helpful alternative characterization of NP is through a "Guess and Verify" method: Using this model, the algorithm is allowed to "guess" a so called *certificate* – a piece of data the size of which is polynomially bounded by the size of the input. After guessing, the algorithm verifies the combined input and certificate in deterministic polynomial time. The crux here is that the algorithm will "guess right" whenever an appropriate certificate exists. For further and more formal treatment of the matter, we refer the interested reader to standard textbooks on complexity theory [14,21].

We will now proceed to establish NP-membership of PCF. While this falls short of establishing membership in P, it might also not be immediately clear why the complexity is not higher, say, further up in the polynomial hierarchy or even PSpace, if not ExpTime or NExpTime: The prime choice for a certificate would certainly be a "witnessing" closure operator φ, that is, one whose pseudo-closed sets are exactly the elements of the family $\mathcal{F}$ given as input. Yet, representing such a closure operator explicitly as a function $2^S \to 2^S$ would require exponential space (and hence too much to be of any use as an NP certificate). Luckily, as one might fathom upon studying the argument in Example 2, this issue can be overcome by representing φ by means of its canonical base, which both gives us direct access to the pseudo-closed sets and has size directly bounded by the size of S and $\mathcal{F}$.

Proposition 11 *PCF is in* NP.

Proof. Given an instance $(S, \mathcal{F})$ of PCF, we specify a "Guess and Verify" type algorithm consisting of four steps:

Guess. For each $P \in \mathcal{F}$, nondeterministically choose a set $B_P \subseteq S$ with $B_P \supsetneq P$. The intuitive goal is to guess, if possible, the appropriate right-hand side for the implication with P on the left in the canonical base.

Build. Form the implication set $\mathfrak{I} = \{P \to B_P \mid P \in \mathcal{F}\}$.
Compute. Run the StemBase algorithm (Theorem 8) on input $\mathfrak{I}$. This produces a canonical base $\mathfrak{S}$ for the closure operator $(\cdot)^{\mathfrak{I}}$ in quadratic time. By Theorem 8(b), the premises of $\mathfrak{S}$ are exactly the pseudo-closed sets of $(\cdot)^{\mathfrak{I}}$.
Verify. Accept exactly if the set of premises of $\mathfrak{S}$ equals $\mathcal{F}$.

We now argue that the algorithm is correct; it accepts if and only if $\mathcal{F}$ is valid. If the algorithm accepts, then $(\cdot)^{\mathfrak{I}}$ is a closure operator whose pseudo-closed sets are exactly $\mathcal{F}$, so $\mathcal{F}$ is indeed valid. Conversely, suppose $\mathcal{F}$ is valid, witnessed by some closure operator φ. By Theorem 7, the canonical base of φ is $\mathfrak{S}_\varphi = \{P \to \varphi(P) \mid P \in \mathcal{F}\}$. Guessing $B_P = \varphi(P)$ for each $P \in \mathcal{F}$ gives $\mathfrak{I} = \mathfrak{S}_\varphi$. Since $\mathfrak{I}$ is already a canonical base, the StemBase algorithm produces a canonical base with the same closure operator and hence the same pseudo-closed sets, namely $\mathcal{F}$. So this guess leads to acceptance.

Considering the complexity, we find that the guess has size $O(|\mathcal{F}| \cdot |S|)$, so it is clearly of polynomial size regarding the input. We now consider the time complexities of the three subsequent steps. Building $\mathfrak{I}$ is in $O(|\mathcal{F}| \cdot |S|)$. Running StemBase takes $O(|\mathcal{F}|^2 \cdot |S|)$ time and comparing the premises of $\mathfrak{S}$ with $\mathcal{F}$ takes $O(|\mathcal{F}| \cdot |S|)$ time. Therefore, the total is polynomial in $|S|$ and $|\mathcal{F}|$. □

This result also gives an (although certainly unsatisfactory) answer to Ganter's question: a necessary and sufficient condition for PCF is the existence of appropriate right-hand sides of the implications in the canonical base. Once they are provided, verification is easy. Clearly, a brute-force implementation checking all possibilities would be highly inefficient and much more goal-directed algorithms can be conceived, exploiting known properties of closure operators to reduce the search space and using highly optimized solvers for NP-complete problems (such as CSP or SAT solvers), but this would not improve the worst-case complexity of the problem (as shown by the hardness proof hereafter), and corresponding considerations are outside the scope of this paper.

The characterization of positive PCF instances as left-hand sides of canonical bases also gives rise to a noteworthy side observation: if $(S, \mathcal{F})$ is a positive PCF instance, then so is $(S, \mathcal{G})$ for every $\mathcal{G} \subseteq \mathcal{F}$. This follows from the insight that every subset of a canonical base is a canonical base (for another closure operator), since applying the StemBase algorithm would not lead to any changes.

5 NP-Hardness

We now turn to the NP-hardness part, essentially showing that PCF is intrinsically hard and no deterministic polynomial time algorithm can be found that solves it (unless P = NP). The common way to establish such a result is through reduction from another problem, whose NP-hardness has already been established. After identifying such an appropriate problem, one shows that any instance of said problem can be transformed in deterministic polynomial time into an acceptance-equivalent instance of the problem whose hardness is to be established. Intuitively, an easy way to solve the latter problem would imply existence of an easy way to solve the former, which would lead to a contradiction. Again we refer to the standard literature for more details [14,21].

In our case we need to identify a known NP-complete problem admitting a polynomial time translation to PCF, such that both acceptance and nonacceptance are preserved. The available options are plentiful, but there are some "usual suspects" to be tried first. One of these is *3SAT*, that is, checking satisfiability of a propositional formula that takes the form of a big conjunction over three-way disjunctions (called clauses) over literals (negated or unnegated atoms). Attempts to use this problem directly turned out to be unsuccessful. However, numerous variations of 3SAT have been discussed in the literature and classified complexity-wise. Among those is *NAE-3SAT* (where NAE stands for "not all equal"), refining 3SAT by requiring that the satisfying valuation must not evaluate all three literals of any clause to the same truth value simultaneously. A variant of NAE-3SAT is Monotone NAE-3SAT, which considers only negation-free formulas (that is, the only occurring literals are unnegated atoms).

Definition 12 (Monotone NAE-3SAT) *An instance Ψ of* Monotone NAE-3SAT *consists of a finite set $\{x_1, \dots, x_n\}$ of* variables *and a finite set $\{C_1, \dots, C_k\}$ of* clauses, *where each clause is a set $\{x_a, x_b, x_c\}$ of three distinct variables. We ask whether there exists a truth assignment $\sigma : \{x_1, \dots, x_n\} \to \{\mathbf{true}, \mathbf{false}\}$, such that $\{\sigma(x_\ell) \mid x_\ell \in C_i\} = \{\mathbf{true}, \mathbf{false}\}$ for every $i \in \{1, \dots, k\}$, i.e., every clause contains at least one* **true** *and at least one* **false** *variable.*

Schaefer proved that Monotone NAE-3SAT is NP-complete as part of his dichotomy theorem for generalized satisfiability [18].[3] In our investigations, it turned out that Monotone NAE-3SAT is best suited for establishing a reduction to PCF (to the best of our knowledge). Thus we will proceed as follows: First, we specify a translation from a Monotone NAE-3SAT instance Ψ into a PCF instance $(S_\Psi, \mathcal{F}_\Psi)$ (Section 5.1). Then we show that the translation preserves non-acceptance (Section 5.2) and acceptance (Section 5.3).

5.1 The Reduction

Let Ψ be a Monotone NAE-3SAT instance with variables $x_1, \dots, x_n$ ($n \geq 2$) and distinct clauses $C_1, \dots, C_k$. Let $C_j = \{x_{a_j}, x_{b_j}, x_{c_j}\}$, with pairwise distinct indices inside each clause. We define the corresponding PCF instance $(S_\Psi, \mathcal{F}_\Psi)$.

Ground set S_Ψ. For each variable x_i, we introduce a "complement element" y_i. Additionally, we introduce a fresh element z. Thus we define

$$S_\Psi = T \cup \{z\} \qquad \text{with} \qquad T = \{x_1, \dots, x_n, y_1, \dots, y_n\}.$$

[3] Interestingly, one of the reviewers pointed out that this problem is structurally equivalent to deciding whether a given 3-uniform hypergraph is 2-colorable, proven to be NP-complete by László Lovász [12] as early as 1973. The original publication seems to have a glitch that is easy to fix: https://cstheory.stackexchange.com/questions/39665/reduction-of-graph-chromatic-number-to-hypergraph-2-colorability

Elements x_i will be referred to as *x-type*; elements y_i as *y-type*.

Family $\mathcal{F}_\Psi$. We define three types of subsets of S_Ψ:

$$\begin{aligned} V_i &= T \setminus \{x_i, y_i\} && \text{for } 1 \le i \le n && \text{(assignment indicators)},\\ D_j^+ &= T \setminus \{x_{a_j}, x_{b_j}, x_{c_j}\} && \text{for } 1 \le j \le k && \text{(all-}\mathbf{true}\text{ detectors)},\\ D_j^- &= T \setminus \{y_{a_j}, y_{b_j}, y_{c_j}\} && \text{for } 1 \le j \le k && \text{(all-}\mathbf{false}\text{ detectors)}. \end{aligned}$$

Now we set $\mathcal{R} = \{V_i\} \cup \{D_j^+\} \cup \{D_j^-\}$ and let $\mathcal{F}_\Psi = \mathcal{R} \cup \{T\}$. Clearly, the reduction runs in polynomial time: $|\mathcal{F}_\Psi| = n + 2k + 1$ and $|S_\Psi| = 2n + 1$.

It might be helpful to provide some upfront intuition about the proposed reduction. Compared to T, each assignment indicator V_i misses the pair $\{x_i, y_i\}$. Then any witnessing closure operator must map V_i to a set strictly between V_i and T, adding exactly one of x_i or y_i. This choice is meant to encode the truth value of x_i. The detectors D_j^+ and D_j^- enforce the NAE condition: if all three variables in a clause receive the same truth value, the corresponding detector becomes closed, contradicting pseudo-closedness. We conclude this section with a straightforward observation.

Fact 13 (incomparability) *All sets in* $\mathcal{R}$ *are incomparable under inclusion.*

Proof. For each set $Q \in \mathcal{R}$, the "gap" $T \setminus Q$ has a characteristic type signature: $T \setminus V_i = \{x_i, y_i\}$ (one x-type, one y-type); $T \setminus D_j^+ = \{x_a, x_b, x_c\}$ (three x-type); $T \setminus D_j^- = \{y_a, y_b, y_c\}$ (three y-type). Containment $A \subseteq B$ requires $T \setminus B \subseteq T \setminus A$, which fails in every pair by comparing types and cardinalities. □

5.2 Backward direction: $\mathcal{F}_\Psi$ valid implies Ψ satisfiable

Now we prove that the translation from Monotone NAE-3SAT to PCF indeed preserves non-acceptance, that is, if Ψ does not have an NAE-satisfying variable assignment, then $\mathcal{F}_\Psi$ is not valid. We will show the contrapositive. To this end, assume $\mathcal{F}_\Psi$ is valid, witnessed by some closure operator φ. The following easily observed fact legitimizes the subsequent specification of a variable assignment.

Fact 14 (variable partition) *For each* i, $\varphi(V_i)$ *contains exactly one of* $\{x_i, y_i\}$.

Proof. $\mathcal{F}_\Psi$ being valid means V_i and T are pseudo-closed. Then, by the sandwich property: $V_i \subsetneq \varphi(V_i) \subsetneq T$. Since $T \setminus V_i = \{x_i, y_i\}$, the set $\varphi(V_i)$ contains at least one but not both of these elements. □

With this guarantee we can now define the variable assignment σ by letting $\sigma(x_i) = \mathbf{true}$ if $x_i \notin \varphi(V_i)$ (which is equivalent to $\varphi(V_i) = T \setminus \{x_i\}$), and **false** otherwise – in which case we have $y_i \notin \varphi(V_i)$, or equivalently $\varphi(V_i) = T \setminus \{y_i\}$.

Lemma 15 (NAE condition) σ *satisfies every clause of* Ψ *as required by Monotone NAE-3SAT.*

Proof. For any clause $C_j = \{x_a, x_b, x_c\}$ of Ψ, we verify that it contains at least one variable mapped to **true** and one to **false**, through a proof by contradiction.

Not all **true**. Suppose $\sigma(x_a) = \sigma(x_b) = \sigma(x_c) =$ **true**. Then $\varphi(V_i) = T \setminus \{x_i\}$ must hold for each $i \in \{a, b, c\}$. Now observe that for each such i we get $D_j^+ = T \setminus \{x_a, x_b, x_c\} \subseteq T \setminus \{x_i\} = \varphi(V_i)$. Since each $\varphi(V_i)$ is closed, we obtain $\varphi(D_j^+) \subseteq \varphi(V_i)$ by monotonicity and idempotency, as discussed earlier. Intersecting all these three upper bounds under set inclusion gives us:

$$\varphi(D_j^+) \subseteq \bigcap\nolimits_{i \in \{a,b,c\}} (T \setminus \{x_i\}) = T \setminus \{x_a, x_b, x_c\} = D_j^+.$$

Together with extensivity, we would obtain $\varphi(D_j^+) = D_j^+$, and therefore conclude that D_j^+ is closed. Yet, this contradicts pseudo-closedness of D_j^+.

Not all **false**. Assume $\sigma(x_a) = \sigma(x_b) = \sigma(x_c) =$ **false**. Then we obtain $\varphi(V_i) = T \setminus \{y_i\}$ for $i \in \{a, b, c\}$, and $D_j^- = T \setminus \{y_a, y_b, y_c\} \subseteq \varphi(V_i)$ for each such i. Thus, the analogous argument to the one above yields $\varphi(D_j^-) = D_j^-$, contradicting pseudo-closedness. □

We have thus shown that every valid $\mathcal{F}_\Psi$ (or rather the corresponding witnessing closure operator φ) gives rise to an assignment σ witnessing Ψ's satisfiability. By contraposition, our construction of $\mathcal{F}_\Psi$ from Ψ preserves non-acceptance.

5.3 Forward direction: Ψ satisfiable implies $\mathcal{F}_\Psi$ valid

What is left is to show that the proposed translation also preserves acceptance. To this end, assume Ψ is satisfiable and let σ be an NAE-satisfying assignment. We need to construct a closure operator whose pseudo-closed sets are exactly the elements of $\mathcal{F}_\Psi$. It will be convenient to describe said closure operator in terms of an implication set. The subsequent definition provides us with such an implication set, and also establishes the instrumental notion of witness elements.

Definition 16 *Given an NAE-satisfying assignment σ for Ψ, we construct an implication set $\mathfrak{I}$ over S_Ψ as follows. First, for each $Q \in \mathcal{F}_\Psi$, choose an element $s_Q \in S_\Psi \setminus Q$ such that:*

- $s_{V_i} = y_i$ *if* $\sigma(x_i) =$ **true**; $s_{V_i} = x_i$ *if* $\sigma(x_i) =$ **false**.
- $s_{D_j^+} = x_\ell$ *for some* x_ℓ *in clause* C_j *with* $\sigma(x_\ell) =$ **false** *(exists by NAE).*
- $s_{D_j^-} = y_h$ *for some* x_h *in clause* C_j *with* $\sigma(x_h) =$ **true** *(exists by NAE).*
- $s_T = z$.

Then define $\mathfrak{I} = \{Q \to Q \cup \{s_Q\} \mid Q \in \mathcal{F}_\Psi\}$ *and let* $\varphi = (\cdot)^{\mathfrak{I}}$.

Moreover, for each $i \in \{1, \ldots, n\}$, *we define the corresponding* witness w_i *such that* $w_i \in \{x_i, y_i\} \setminus \{s_{V_i}\}$, *that is, the witness is the element not chosen as* s_{V_i}. *Consequently,* $w_i = x_i$ *if* $\sigma(x_i) =$ **true** *and* $w_i = y_i$ *if* $\sigma(x_i) =$ **false**.

Note that there is a certain leeway in the construction of $\mathfrak{I}$ as the choices of s_Q are not all uniquely determined for the "detectors". The witness elements, on the other hand, are uniquely defined. A rough intuition behind the witnesses is to "shield" T from being "reached" by the closure of any of its subsets from $\mathcal{F}_\Psi$. The subsequent development of lemmas makes this intuition formal.

Lemma 17 (witnesses are never chosen) *For each $i \in \{1, \dots, n\}$ and every $Q \in \mathcal{R}$ we have $s_Q \neq w_i$.*

Proof. We consider any w_i and proceed by cases.
Case $\sigma(x_i) = \mathbf{true}$ (therefore $w_i = x_i$). We go through all choices for Q:

- For $Q = V_i$, we obtain $s_{V_i} = y_i \neq x_i$.
- Also, clearly for $Q = V_j$ with $j \neq i$, we have $s_{V_j} \in \{x_j, y_j\} \not\ni x_i$.
- For $Q = D_j^+$, we find that $s_{D_j^+} = x_\ell$ with $\sigma(x_\ell) = \mathbf{false}$, so $x_\ell \neq x_i$;
- For $Q = D_j^-$, we see that $s_{D_j^-} = y_h$ is y-type, so $s_{D_j^-} \neq x_i$.

Case $\sigma(x_i) = \mathbf{false}$ (therefore $w_i = y_i$). Again, we go through all choices for Q:

- For $Q = V_i$, we obtain $s_{V_i} = x_i \neq y_i$.
- Also, clearly for $Q = V_j$ with $j \neq i$, we have $s_{V_j} \in \{x_j, y_j\} \not\ni y_i$.
- For $Q = D_j^+$, we see that $s_{D_j^+} = x_\ell$ is x-type, so $s_{D_j^+} \neq y_i$.
- For $Q = D_j^-$, we find that $s_{D_j^-} = y_h$ with $\sigma(x_h) = \mathbf{true}$, which requires $h \neq i$ and hence implies $y_h \neq y_i$. □

Lemma 18 (witness complements are closed) *For each $i \in \{1, \dots, n\}$, the set $T \setminus \{w_i\}$ is a closed set of φ.*

Proof. Let $C = T \setminus \{w_i\}$. We check that C respects every implication in $\mathfrak{I}$. Thus we have to go through all $Q \in \mathcal{F}_\Psi$ with $Q \subseteq C$.

Obviously, the case $Q = T$ is impossible, since $w_i \in T$ but $w_i \notin C$.

If $Q \in \mathcal{R}$, we need to ensure that $s_Q \in C$, which just means that $s_Q \neq w_i$ must hold (all other possible s_Q are already trivially contained in T). And indeed, $s_Q \neq w_i$ holds by Lemma 17. □

Lemma 19 (no closure reaches T) *For every $Q \in \mathcal{R}$ we have $Q^{\mathfrak{I}} \subsetneq T$.*

Proof. For any such Q, we exhibit a witness w_i with $w_i \notin Q$, so that $Q \subseteq T \setminus \{w_i\}$. Since $T \setminus \{w_i\}$ is closed by Lemma 18, we can then conclude $Q^{\mathfrak{I}} \subseteq T \setminus \{w_i\} \subsetneq T$.

- For $Q = V_i$, we obtain $w_i \in \{x_i, y_i\} = T \setminus V_i$, so $w_i \notin V_i$.
- For $Q = D_j^+$, consider $C_j = \{x_a, x_b, x_c\}$. Since σ is an NAE-satisfying assignment, there must be some variable $x_i \in \{x_a, x_b, x_c\}$ with $\sigma(x_i) = \mathbf{true}$. But then $w_i = x_i \notin D_j^+$.
- For $Q = D_j^-$, again consider $C_j = \{x_a, x_b, x_c\}$. As σ is an NAE-satisfying assignment, there must also be some variable $x_i \in \{x_a, x_b, x_c\}$ with $\sigma(x_i) = \mathbf{false}$. Then we obtain $w_i = y_i \notin D_j^-$. □

Finally, the insights obtained through this chain of lemmas can be leveraged to make the final step and establish that the closure operator φ realized by the implication set $\mathfrak{I}$ has exactly the elements of $\mathcal{F}_\Psi$ as pseudo-closed sets.

Proposition 20 *The pseudo-closed sets of φ are exactly $\mathcal{F}_\Psi$.*

Proof. We show for each subset $F \subseteq S_\Psi$ the following correspondence: F is contained in $\mathcal{F}_\Psi$ if and only if it is pseudo-closed. We use strong induction on $|F|$. For the base case, $F = \emptyset \notin \mathcal{F}_\Psi$, the statement holds since $\varphi(\emptyset) = \emptyset$.

Now assume $F \in \mathcal{F}_\Psi$, whence we need to show that F is pseudo-closed. We show $\varphi(F) \neq F$ by observing $F^{\mathfrak{I}} \supseteq F \cup \{s_F\} \supsetneq F$. In order to show the second condition, let Q be pseudo-closed with $Q \subsetneq F$. By the induction hypothesis this means that $Q \in \mathcal{F}_\Psi$. In case $F = T$, we therefore get $Q \in \mathcal{R}$ and can indeed conclude $Q^{\mathfrak{I}} \subsetneq T$ thanks to Lemma 19. In case $F \in \mathcal{R}$ we know by Fact 13 that no element of $\mathcal{F}_\Psi$ is a proper subset of F, thus condition (ii) is vacuously true.

Now assume $F \notin \mathcal{F}_\Psi$. We need to show that F is not pseudo-closed. Toward a contradiction, suppose F were pseudo-closed. Then $F^{\mathfrak{I}} \supsetneq F$ would need to hold (due to F not being closed). Therefore, some $P \in \mathcal{F}_\Psi$ with $P \subseteq F$ must have $s_P \notin F$. Now since $P \neq F$ (due to $F \notin \mathcal{F}_\Psi$) we get $P \subsetneq F$. By the induction hypothesis, P must be pseudo-closed, so condition (ii) of pseudo-closedness for F requires $P^{\mathfrak{I}} \subseteq F$. However $s_P \in P^{\mathfrak{I}}$ which clearly contradicts $s_P \notin F$. □

This concludes our argument that for every satisfiable Monotone NAE-3SAT instance Ψ, the corresponding NAE-satisfying variable assignment can be exploited to create a closure operator – expressed through an implication set – whose pseudo-closed sets coincide with $\mathcal{F}_\Psi$'s elements, ensuring that $\mathcal{F}_\Psi$ is valid. Consequently, our construction of $\mathcal{F}_\Psi$ from Ψ preserves acceptance.

6 What This Means for Ganter's Original Question

The reader might (and, in fact, one of this paper's reviewers *did*) ask what the obtained result has to do with Ganter's original question, which did not ask for the complexity of PCF at all, but rather for necessary and sufficient conditions for it. Fortunately, the field of *descriptive complexity theory* [8] has established connections between computational complexity and expressivity which we can exploit to arrive at an answer that might be considered more informative.

Definition 21 (easy property) *Given an instance $(S, \mathcal{F})$ of PCF, let us define the corresponding first-order structure $\mathcal{I}_{(S,\mathcal{F})}$ as follows: The domain of $\mathcal{I}_{(S,\mathcal{F})}$ is set to $D = S \cup \mathcal{F} \cup \{S\} \cup \{\mathcal{F}\}$; that is, it contains all elements of S and all elements of $\mathcal{F}$ as first-class citizens, plus one element representing the full set S and one representing the family $\mathcal{F}$; we assume S does not itself contain sets as elements. Beyond that, $\mathcal{I}_{(S,\mathcal{F})}$ contains two constants* $\mathtt{S}$ *and* $\mathtt{F}$ *(interpreted by S and $\mathcal{F}$, respectively) as well as one binary predicate $\in$ (written in infix notation), which is interpreted in the obvious way: $\in^{\mathcal{I}_{(S,\mathcal{F})}} = \{(d, d') \mid d \in d'\}$.*

We call a property that a PCF instance may or may not have, easy, *if it is first-order expressible, that is, if there exists a first-order logic sentence χ such that $\mathcal{I}_{(S,\mathcal{F})} \models \chi$ exactly if $(S, \mathcal{F})$ has the property.*

Arguably, properties that are easy in the sense formalized above are preferable as structural conditions – they are both rather straightforward to grasp cognitively and computationally verifiable with low effort.

Example 3. Using the notational macros $t \notin s$ for $\neg(t \in s)$, as well as $t \subseteq s$ for $\forall w.(w \in t \Rightarrow w \in s)$, and $t \subset s$ for $t \subseteq s \wedge \neg(s \subseteq t)$, Ganter's two necessary conditions can be expressed by the following two first-order sentences:

$$\mathtt{S} \notin \mathtt{F} \wedge \forall y.\big(y \in \mathtt{F} \Rightarrow \exists x.x \notin y \wedge \forall z.(y \subset z \Rightarrow x \in z)\big)$$

$$\forall y,z.\big((y \in \mathtt{F} \wedge z \in \mathtt{F} \wedge y \subset z) \Rightarrow \exists x,x'.(x \neq x' \wedge x \in z \wedge x' \in z \wedge x \notin y \wedge x' \notin y)\big)$$

that is, both of these properties (and thus also their conjunction) are easy in the sense defined above. ◊

Theorem 22. *There is no easy property characterizing PCF validity.*

Proof (Sketch). For space reasons, we resort to a high-level argument and assume familiarity with circuit complexity. If PCF validity were first-order expressible over $\mathcal{I}_{(S,\mathcal{F})}$, it would be decidable in AC_0 via descriptive complexity theory [8]. On the other hand, it is easy to show that PCF is NP-complete even under AC_0 reductions. Since PARITY ∈ NP, composition would then yield AC_0 circuits for PARITY, contradicting the lower bound established by Håstad [7]. □

Note that this non-expressibility result is independent of the P vs. NP question. It essentially asserts that no first-order statement using the usual set operations and comparisons will work to characterize PCF validity, unless we allow to quantify over *all* subsets of S (which the definition of our setting excludes).

7 Contemplation: LLMs for Mathematical Research

Given that the methodology to arrive at the hardness result deviates from a mathematician's traditional working style "thinking hard while looking out of the window", the author finds it opportune to deliberate on his use of the large language model Claude Opus 4.6 accessed via `you.com` through a university-wide subscription. The full chat history of the exchange is made available online [17]. Note that the collaboration by itself was not a well-planned, controlled experiment, but rather an ad hoc attempt. Consequently, the reported observations and experiences have to be taken as anecdotal evidence and subjective impressions, which may include the tendency to anthropomorphize the used system, and be it only for the sake of a more relatable reporting.

The impression that the PCF problem might serve as a good test case to try this new approach arose from the consideration that

- the problem seemed easy to describe in a self-contained way,
- the type of argument needed (PTime algorithm or NP reduction) is quite standard and occurs frequently in the literature (ergo: the training data),
- a final argument would likely not be overly intricate, once discovered,
- the author had investigated the issue and thus developed a good intuition and capability of double checking, correcting, and steering the model's activities.

7.1 Method

To get started, the author provided Claude with a PDF of "Some Notes on Pseudo-Closed Sets" [15], providing many of the necessary formal preliminaries. To trigger engagement with the material, we let Claude create an in-depth summary of the technical content. Thereafter, the actual problem was presented, asking for an idea about the complexity. This being unsuccessful, Claude was presented the author's previously established argument for NP membership, which it[4] appeared to understand (and even to enthusiastically embrace). In the ensuing exchange on a rather scholarly level, the author deemed it useful to follow certain interaction patterns discussed next.

Enforcing rigor. The author repeatedly and persistently exhorted Claude to be rigorous and meticulous in its investigation and output. It was explicitly discouraged from using vague statements and hand-waving of any kind, and it was immediately called out whenever it did (way more harshly than the author would ever address a fellow human being). Whenever the model engaged in so-called *scratching* (indicated by phrases like "Hm...", "Wait!", "This does not work.", or "Let me try another approach."), it was afterwards told to produce a

[4] To withstand anthropomorphization, we use "it" rather than "he", "she" or "they".

clear and streamlined presentation of the findings obtained. At times, the model was asked to produce a full LaTeX document, for a technical and stylistic review.

Mode switching. For a long time in the process, it was unclear if PCF was indeed NP-hard, or if a PTIME algorithm did exist after all. The model repeatedly encountered problems establishing the hardness proof. In such cases, the author would switch the mode of investigation by asking Claude to leverage the obstacles encountered when trying to show NP-hardness for the creation of a PTIME algorithm. When after continued attempts to come up with such an algorithm Claude reported to have hit another barrier, it was asked to switch the mode again and exploit the insights gained for a hardness argument. Several such mode switches occurred in the course of the exchange, which seemed to result in "peeling off" peripheral problems and getting to the core of the issue.

Use of examples. Whenever Claude was of the opinion to have established a correct PTIME algorithm (which happened several times), the author advised it to verify the algorithm's correctness against several PCF instances – both positive and negative ones and both self-created ones as well as provided by the author. The same strategy was pursued whenever Claude was stuck trying to prove an important lemma towards the result. Very often glitches in the arguments could be found and assumed lemmas refuted by this technique.

Suggesting where to look. Occasionally, Claude had identified a subproblem which was crucial for the overall investigation. Sometimes the author was able to provide guidance and pointers to related problems or problem classes. Claude typically welcomed such suggestions and steered its investigation accordingly.

Pushing for Simplification. In the lengthy process of the theory development, many auxiliary notions were defined and helper lemmas proven. Some directions were abandoned. When asked to produce a coherent document, it became apparent that some of this material was irrelevant to the actual line of argumentation. For a clearer picture it was sometimes helpful to prompt Claude to critically verify which parts of the development were still necessary and which ones could be deleted. Likewise, toward the end of the exchange, Claude had established a twofold reduction: from Monotone NAE-3SAT to an intermediate problem (which Claude itself had created to describe the "hard core" of the task) and from there to PCF. While this was correct, it required another human intervention to turn this into a direct reduction, in the course of which another significant simplification and shortening of the material could be achieved.

Once a firm and reliable result was established and verified, Claude was prompted one last time to produce LaTeX output for a document. This document served as a starting point for this paper's technical part. What followed was a last in-depth check of all the arguments by the author and a very thorough rewrite, including re-arranging the material to follow a better narrative, adding "prose" to provide more intuition and smoothing out arguments in the proofs. Section 6 was added to the paper's final version (without any involvement of Claude) as a response to a concern brought up by one reviewer.

7.2 Observations regarding Claude

Claude makes errors on all levels. It may even occasionally confuse $\subseteq$ with $\supseteq$, but it seems such occurrences can be reduced by relentless appeal to mathematical rigor and the advice to continuously double-check itself. When called out on errors, it was usually quick in admitting and correcting them. On the other hand, Claude can be credited with a good knowledge of general proof strategies, as well as problem candidates for complexity reductions – it was indeed Claude which picked Monotone NAE-3SAT as appropriate "yardstick problem". Claude also sometimes surprised in providing good intuition and higher-level reasoning. It even verbalized encountered problems using catchy metaphors – Claude was the one to actually introduce certain names such as the "sandwich property" or "all-**true**-detector". Claude is not immune against the infamous phenomenon of reference fabrication; somewhat amusingly, it claimed the PCF problem had been posed in a 2024 technical report entitled "On pseudo-closed sets and their recognition" authored by a certain S. Krötzsch together with some H. Reiter.

7.3 Observations regarding Sebastian

One self-observation by the author is that the model somehow manages to keep the user "hooked", likely by conveying the impression that the final solution is just around the corner (using phrases like "the final solution" or "the breakthrough"), with the consequence of working extra hours unintentionally. This made the author wonder, if he could not have solved the problem just by himself with the same time investment – probably a clear case of *hindsight bias*.

An impression the author has mixed feelings about is that his role in the process felt quite "managerial" and thematically detached. This took away quite some of the usual fun of engaging with the matter in a hands-on fashion, and it also left the feeling of only having too loose a grasp of the matter, a feeling that only dissolved during the intense post-hoc reworking of the material.

8 Conclusion

Proving NP-completeness of the Pseudo-Closed Family problem, we negatively answered a question by Bernhard Ganter for straightforwardly verifiable necessary and sufficient criteria. The hardness result was established in the course of an intense mathematical exchange with Claude Opus 4.6, which also provided an initial draft of part of this paper's LaTeX sources. All technical results were carefully vetted by the (human) author, who also takes full responsibility for any remaining errors. The exchange has mellowed the author's sceptical stance toward the usefulness of large language models for serious mathematical work, but he would like to believe that the most impactful progress can be made only through collaborations between humans and AI agents.

Acknowledgments. We thank the anonymous reviewers of this paper for their valuable comments. This work was funded by BMFTR in ScaDS.AI and by BMFTR and DAAD in project 57616814 (SECAI).

References

1. Babin, M.A., Kuznetsov, S.O.: Recognizing pseudo-intents is conp-complete. In: Proc. 7th Int. Conf. on Concept Lattices and Their Applications (CLA). CEUR Workshop Proceedings, vol. 477, pp. 294–301. CEUR-WS.org (2010)
2. Day, A.: The lattice theory of functional dependencies and normal decompositions. Int. J. Algebra Comput. **2**(4), 409–432 (1992)
3. Distel, F.: Hardness of enumerating pseudo-intents in the lectic order. In: Proc. 8th Int. Conf. on Formal Concept Analysis (ICFCA). LNCS, vol. 5986, pp. 124–137. Springer (2010)
4. Dowling, W.F., Gallier, J.H.: Linear-time algorithms for testing the satisfiability of propositional horn formulae. J. Log. Program. **1**(3), 267–284 (1984)
5. Ganter, B., Wille, R.: Formal Concept Analysis - Mathematical Foundations, Second Editiontion. Springer (2024)
6. Guigues, J.L., Duquenne, V.: Familles minimales d'implications informatives résultant d'un tableau de données binaires. Math. Sci. Hum. **95**, 5–18 (1986)
7. Håstad, J.: Almost optimal lower bounds for small depth circuits. In: Proc. 18th Annual ACM Symposium on Theory of Computing. pp. 6–20. ACM (1986)
8. Immerman, N.: Descriptive complexity. Graduate texts in computer science, Springer (1999)
9. Kuznetsov, S.O.: On the intractability of computing the Duquenne-Guigues base. J. Univers. Comput. Sci. **10**(8), 927–933 (2004)
10. Kuznetsov, S.O., Obiedkov, S.A.: Counting pseudo-intents and #P-completeness. In: Proc. 4th Int. Conf. on Formal Concept Analysis (ICFCA). LNCS, vol. 3874, pp. 306–308. Springer (2006)
11. Kuznetsov, S.O., Obiedkov, S.A.: Some decision and counting problems of the Duquenne-Guigues basis of implications. Discret. Appl. Math. **156**(11), 1994–2003 (2008)
12. Lovász, L.: Coverings and colorings of hypergraphs. In: Proc. 4th Southeastern Conf. on Combinatorics. pp. 3–12. Utilitas Math. (1973)
13. Mannila, H., Räihä, K.J.: Design of Relational Databases. Addison-Wesley (1992)
14. Papadimitriou, C.H.: Computational complexity. Addison-Wesley (1994)
15. Rudolph, S.: Some notes on pseudo-closed sets. In: Proc. 5th Int. Conf. on Formal Concept Analysis (ICFCA). LNCS, vol. 4390, pp. 151–165. Springer (2007)
16. Rudolph, S.: Succinctness and tractability of closure operator representations. Theor. Comput. Sci. **658**, 327–345 (2017)
17. Rudolph, S.: Exchange with Claude Opus 4.6 towards proving NP-completeness of the Pseudo-Closed Family problem (PCF) (May 2026). https://doi.org/10.5281/zenodo.20307509
18. Schaefer, T.J.: The complexity of satisfiability problems. In: Proc. 10th Annual ACM Symposium on Theory of Computing (STOC). pp. 216–226 (1978)
19. Sertkaya, B.: Some computational problems related to pseudo-intents. In: Proc. 7th Int. Conf. on Formal Concept Analysis (ICFCA). LNCS, vol. 5548, pp. 130–145. Springer (2009)
20. Sertkaya, B.: Towards the complexity of recognizing pseudo-intents. In: Proc. 17th Int. Conf. on Conceptual Structures (ICCS). LNCS, vol. 5662, pp. 284–292. Springer (2009)
21. Sipser, M.: Introduction to the theory of computation. PWS Publishing (1997)

Theory

The Boolean Envelope of Finite Distributive Lattices

Mohammad Abdulla[1(✉)], Dominik Dürrschnabel[2], and Leonard Kwuida[3]

[1] Knowledge and Data Engineering Group, University of Kassel, Kassel, Germany
abdulla@cs.uni-kassel.de
[2] Baden-Württemberg Cooperative State University Mosbach, Mosbach, Germany
dominik.duerrschnabel@mosbach.dhbw.de
[3] School of Business, Bern University of Applied Sciences, Bern, Switzerland
leonard.kwuida@bfh.ch

Abstract. Distributive lattices arise naturally in order theory and logic, yet their lack of complements limits the logical operations they can support. A natural question is therefore whether a given distributive lattice can be canonically embedded into a Boolean algebra while preserving its order structure. In this paper, we study the Boolean envelope of a finite distributive lattice, defined as the minimal Boolean algebra into which the lattice can be embedded as a sublattice. We show that, in the finite case, the Boolean envelope is isomorphic to the power set algebra of the join-irreducible elements of the lattice. Using this characterization, we develop an explicit construction within Formal Concept Analysis (FCA). Using critical pairs and set-based representations of objects and attributes, we construct a conservative extension of the original formal context whose concept lattice realizes the Boolean envelope. Finally, we relate the Boolean envelope to the Birkhoff completion, characterizing precisely when the two constructions coincide.

Keywords: Distributive Lattices · Boolean Algebra · Formal Concept Analysis

1 Introduction

Distributive lattices enjoy strong structural properties that make them particularly useful in data analysis and knowledge representation. By Birkhoff's representation theorem, every finite distributive lattice is isomorphic to the lattice of order ideals of its join-irreducible elements, providing a rich structure that supports intuitive navigation of the concept lattice. Moreover, their implicational theory is given by particularly simple implications, as each of their premises consists of a single attribute only.

However, distributivity alone does not guarantee the existence of complements. In many applications – from logic and knowledge representation to circuit

M Abdulla, D. Dürrschnabel—Both authors have contributed equally to this work.

M. Croitoru et al. (Eds.): CONCEPTS 2026, LNAI 16811, pp. 23–38, 2027.
https://doi.org/10.1007/978-3-032-34742-8_2

design and database theory – the ability to negate or exclude is as fundamental as the ability to combine. Boolean algebras resolve this limitation completely: they are precisely the distributive lattices in which every element admits a unique complement. Their central importance is well established and their rich duality theory – most notably Stone's representation theorem [11] – underlies much of modern algebra and logic. A natural question therefore arises: given a distributive lattice, can one canonically extend it to a Boolean algebra while preserving its order structure?

In earlier work [1], we introduced the Birkhoff completion as the smallest distributive lattice in which a given finite lattice can be embedded as semilattice. This construction adjoins distributivity. Our present work investigates the next natural structural step: adjoining complements.

We study the *Boolean envelope* of a finite[1] distributive lattice as its canonical minimal Boolean extension – that is, the smallest Boolean algebra into which the lattice embeds via a lattice homomorphism preserving joins and meets. We show that it admits a concrete description: it is isomorphic to the powerset algebra $\mathcal{P}(\mathcal{J}(L))$, where $\mathcal{J}(L)$ denotes the set of join-irreducible elements of L. The canonical embedding maps each element to the set of join-irreducibles below it. While the Boolean envelope was introduced in [7] in the context of topological duality for distributive lattices – with related constructions appearing earlier in the representation-theoretic work of Priestley [9] and in the contextual setting of Kwuida [8] – an explicit algorithmic realization at the level of reduced formal contexts has not been systematically developed. We fill this gap by working entirely within the framework of Formal Concept Analysis. We introduce a base space of irreducible pairs and define object and attribute representations via non-incidence relation. By adjoining missing atomic singletons and defining incidence through disjointness in the base space, we obtain a conservative extension of the original context whose concept lattice is precisely the Boolean envelope. We note that the present construction is in a certain sense complementary to the work in [5], which locates Boolean structure inside a given concept lattice. Here, by contrast, we build the minimal Boolean algebra that contains the entire lattice from the outside. Finally, we show that the Birkhoff completion and the Boolean envelope together yield a two-step embedding of any finite lattice into a Boolean algebra, and characterize precisely when the two constructions coincide. The paper is organized as follows. Section 2 recalls preliminaries on lattices, Boolean algebras, and FCA. Section 3 introduces the Boolean envelope and establishes its universal property. Section 4 develops the explicit FCA-based construction. Section 5 relates the Boolean envelope to the Birkhoff completion. Section 6 concludes with directions for future work.

[1] Throughout this paper we assume that our data—the formal context—are finite.

2 Preliminaries

Here we briefly recall the basic notations. For more background on lattice theory and Formal Concept Analysis, we refer to [3,4,6]. We follow the notation of [6] whenever possible.

2.1 Ordered Sets and Lattices

An *order* (sometimes also called *partial order*) on a set P is a binary relation $\leq$ on P that is: reflexive , antisymmetric and transitive. $\boldsymbol{P} := (P, \leq)$ is then called an *ordered set* (poset for short). We call x and y *comparable* if $x \leq y$ or $y \leq x$. We call a comparable pair a *covering pair* and write $x \prec y$ if, for all $p \in$ P, $x \leq p < y$ implies $x = p$. Let $(P, \leq)$ be a poset. A subset $D \subseteq P$ is a *down-set* if $p \in D$ and $q \leq p$ imply $q \in D$. Dually, a subset $U \subseteq P$ is an *up-set* if $p \in U$ and $p \leq q$ imply $q \in U$. The collections of all down-sets and up-sets are denoted $D(P)$ and $U(P)$ respectively. For $p \in P$, the *principal down-set* and *principal up-set* are

$$\downarrow p = \{q \in P \mid q \leq p\}, \qquad \uparrow p = \{q \in P \mid p \leq q\}.$$

An ordered set $(L, \leq)$ is called a *lattice* if every pair of elements $x, y \in L$ admits a *meet* $x \wedge y$ (greatest lower bound) and a *join* $x \vee y$ (least upper bound). A lattice is called *bounded* if it has a least element $\bot$ and a greatest element $\top$. In a lattice with least element $\bot$, an *atom* is an element a such that $\bot \prec a$. If a is an element in a lattice, an element b is called a *complement* of a if $a \wedge b = \bot$ and $a \vee b = \top$. An element $x \in L$ is *join-irreducible* if it is not the join of a set of elements not containing x. It is *meet-irreducible* if it is not the meet of a set of elements not containing x. The set of all join-irreducible elements of L is denoted by $\mathcal{J}(L)$, and the set of all meet-irreducible elements of L is denoted by $\mathcal{M}(L)$. A lattice L is said to be *distributive* if for all $x, y, z \in L$, $x \wedge (y \vee z) = (x \wedge y) \vee (x \wedge z)$. A very important finding towards understanding distributivity in lattices came from Birkhoff and is illustrated by line-drawings in Fig. 1.

Theorem 1 (Birkhoff's characterization Theorem [2]). *A lattice L is distributive if and only if there exists no sublattice $A \subseteq L$ isomorphic to either M_3 or N_5.*

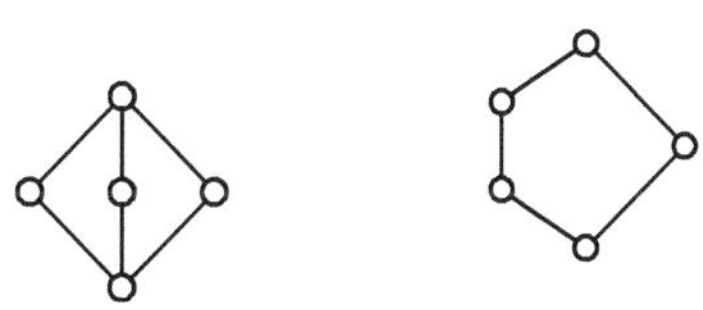

Fig. 1. The nondistributive lattices M_3 (left) and N_5 (right)

A function $f : L \to M$ is a *bounded lattice homomorphism* if $f(a \vee b) = f(a) \vee f(b), f(a \wedge b) = f(a) \wedge f(b), f(\bot_L) = \bot_M, f(\top_L) = \top_M$ for all $a, b \in L$. Lattice homomorphisms are always order-preserving. We call an injective homomorphism between lattices a *lattice embedding.* We call a bijective homomorphism between lattices a *lattice isomorphism.* Lattice homomorphisms and isomorphisms allow us to compare lattices structurally, raising the question of whether every finite distributive lattice admits a canonical representation. Birkhoff's Representation Theorem answers this completely.

Theorem 2 (Birkhoff's Representation Theorem [2]**).** *Any finite distributive lattice D is isomorphic to the lattice of down-sets of the partially ordered set of join-irreducible elements of D.*

2.2 Formal Contexts and Concept Lattices

In this section, we introduce the fundamental definitions and concepts from Formal Concept Analysis (FCA) used throughout this work. A *(formal) context* is a triple $\mathbb{K} := (G, M, I)$, where G and M are sets whose elements are called *objects* and *attributes*, resp., and $\mathrm{I} \subseteq G \times M$ is called *incidence relation.* For $A \subseteq G$, we define $A' := \{m \in M \mid \forall g \in A\ (g, m) \in I\}$. Dually, for $B \subseteq M$, we define $B' := \{g \in G \mid \forall m \in B\ (g, m) \in I\}$. A *(formal) concept* of $\mathbb{K}$ is a pair (A, B) such that $A \subseteq G$, $B \subseteq M$, $A' = B$, and $B' = A$. A is the *extent* and B the *intent* of the concept. The set of all concepts of $\mathbb{K}$, ordered by $(A_1, B_1) \leq (A_2, B_2) :\Longleftrightarrow A_1 \subseteq A_2$, forms a complete lattice, called the *concept lattice* of $\mathbb{K}$, and is denoted by $\underline{\mathfrak{B}}(\mathbb{K})$. A context is *clarified* if, for $g, h \in G$, $g' = h'$ implies $g = h$, and if for $m, n \in M$, $m' = n'$ implies $\mathrm{m} = n$. For $g \in G$, (g'', g') is an *object concept* and, for $m \in M$, (m', m'') is an *attribute concept.* A clarified context is *object-reduced* if every object concept is join-irreducible, it is *attribute-reduced* if every attribute concept is meet-irreducible. It is *reduced* if it is both.

2.3 Boolean Algebras

Definition 3. *A* Boolean algebra *is a tuple $(B, \wedge, \vee, \neg, \bot, \top)$ such that:*

1. *$(B, \wedge, \vee, \bot, \top)$ is a bounded distributive lattice.*
2. *For each $a \in B$, there exists a unique element $\neg a \in B$, called the* complement *of a, satisfying $a \wedge \neg a = \bot$ and $a \vee \neg a = \top$.*

In particular, the uniqueness of complements in a Boolean algebra ensures that the complement operation $\neg$ is well defined.

Proposition 4 (Representation Theorem for Finite Boolean Algebras [7,10]**).** *Let L be a finite distributive lattice. The following statements are equivalent:*

1. *L is a Boolean algebra.*

2. *Every join-irreducible element of L is an atom.*
3. *The order on $\mathcal{J}(L)$ is trivial, i.e., distinct elements are incomparable.*
4. *L is isomorphic to the power set $\mathcal{P}(\mathcal{J}(L))$.*

Proposition 5 (Homomorphisms via Join-Irreducibles [7]**).** *Let B be a finite Boolean algebra and L a finite distributive lattice. Then:*

1. *Any function $f\colon \mathcal{J}(B) \to \mathcal{J}(L)$ is automatically order-preserving.*
2. *The lattice homomorphisms $L \to B$ are precisely the inverse images of functions $\mathcal{J}(B) \to \mathcal{J}(L)$.*

3 Boolean Envelope

Distributive lattices are well-behaved in many ways, yet complements do not always exist. Boolean algebras resolve this limitation completely: every element has a unique complement. As a subclass of distributive lattices, they occupy a very special position – every distributive lattice has a minimal Boolean algebra sitting around it, called its *Boolean envelope.*

Definition 6 (Boolean envelope [7]**).** *Let L be a distributive lattice. A* Boolean envelope *of L is a Boolean algebra L^- together with a lattice embedding $\iota : L \hookrightarrow L^-$ such that, for every lattice homomorphism $h : L \to A$ into a Boolean algebra A, there exists a unique Boolean homomorphism $\bar{h} : L^- \to A$ satisfying $\bar{h} \circ \iota = h$.*

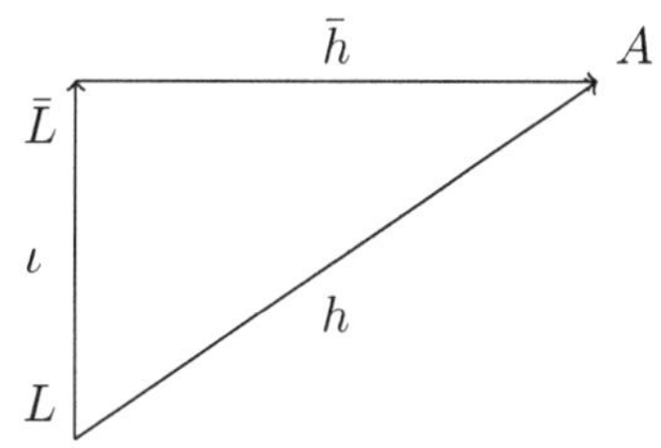

Proposition 7 (Properties of the Boolean Envelope). *Let L be a distributive lattice with Boolean envelope $\iota : L \hookrightarrow L^-$. Then the following hold:*

1. *The Boolean envelope is unique up to isomorphism.*
2. *If L is a finite Boolean algebra, then $L^- \cong L$.*
3. *An element $a \in L$ is complemented in L if and only if $\neg\iota(a) \in \iota[L]$.*

Proof. 1. Let $\iota_1 : L \hookrightarrow L_1^-$ and $\iota_2 : L \hookrightarrow L_2^-$ be two Boolean envelopes of L. By Definition 6 applied to (L_1^-, ι_1), there exists a unique Boolean homomorphism $\alpha : L_1^- \to L_2^-$ such that $\alpha \circ \iota_1 = \iota_2$. Interchanging the roles of L_1^- and L_2^-, there exists a unique Boolean homomorphism $\beta : L_2^- \to L_1^-$ such that $\beta \circ \iota_2 = \iota_1$. Hence, $\beta \circ \alpha \circ \iota_1 = \beta \circ \iota_2 = \iota_1$, so $\beta \circ \alpha$ is a Boolean homomorphism extending ι_1. By uniqueness , $\beta \circ \alpha = \mathrm{id}_{L_1^-}$. Dually, $\alpha \circ \beta = \mathrm{id}_{L_2^-}$. Thus, α is an isomorphism, and therefore $L_1^- \cong L_2^-$.

2. The identity map $\mathrm{id}_L : L \to L$ extends uniquely to a Boolean homomorphism $\bar{h} : L^- \to L$ with $\bar{h} \circ \iota = \mathrm{id}_L$, making $\bar{h}$ surjective. Since ι is an embedding, $|L| \leq |L^-|$, and surjectivity gives $|L^-| \leq |L|$. Therefore $L^- \cong L$.
3. Since ι is a bounded lattice homomorphism, it preserves meets, joins, $\bot$, and $\top$. Hence if $a \wedge b = \bot_L$ and $a \vee b = \top_L$ for some $b \in L$, then

$$\iota(a) \wedge \iota(b) = \iota(\bot_L) = \bot_{L^-}, \qquad \iota(a) \vee \iota(b) = \iota(\top_L) = \top_{L^-},$$

so $\iota(b) = \neg\iota(a)$ by uniqueness of complements in L^-, giving $\neg\iota(a) \in \iota[L]$. Conversely, if $\neg\iota(a) = \iota(b)$ for some $b \in L$, then

$$\iota(a \wedge b) = \iota(a) \wedge \neg\iota(a) = \bot_{L^-} = \iota(\bot_L), \qquad \iota(a \vee b) = \iota(a) \vee \neg\iota(a) = \top_{L^-} = \iota(\top_L),$$

and injectivity of ι gives $a \wedge b = \bot_L$ and $a \vee b = \top_L$.

3.1 Finite Representation and Conceptual Interpretation

If L is finite, its Boolean envelope admits a concrete and explicit description in terms of its join-irreducible elements. It can be identified with the powerset Boolean algebra $L^- \cong \mathcal{P}(\mathcal{J}(L))$, and the canonical embedding $\iota : L \longrightarrow \mathcal{P}(\mathcal{J}(L))$ is given by $\iota(a) = \{\, j \in \mathcal{J}(L) \mid j \leq a \,\}$. The following theorem makes this precise. The proof is only outlined in [7, Proposition 1.28]; we give a complete proof here for the sake of completeness.

Theorem 8. *Let L be a finite distributive lattice. The finite Boolean algebra $\mathcal{P}(\mathcal{J}(L))$, together with the canonical embedding $\iota : L \to \mathcal{P}(\mathcal{J}(L))$, is a Boolean envelope of L.*

Proof. Let $h : L \to A$ be a lattice homomorphism, where A is a Boolean algebra. By Birkhoff's representation theorem (Theorem 2), we may identify L with $D(P)$ for a finite poset P. Since every finite Boolean algebra is isomorphic to a powerset algebra (Proposition 4), we may identify A with $\mathcal{P}(X)$ for some finite set X. Under these identifications, Proposition 5 shows that h is the inverse image map of a function $f : X \to P$, i.e., $h = f^{-1}$. Define $\bar{h} : \mathcal{P}(P) \to \mathcal{P}(X)$ by

$$\bar{h}(u) = f^{-1}(u) \qquad (u \subseteq P).$$

Then $\bar{h}$ is a Boolean algebra homomorphism and $\bar{h}|_{D(P)} = h$, so $\bar{h}$ extends h.

Uniqueness. Suppose $k : \mathcal{P}(P) \to \mathcal{P}(X)$ is any Boolean homomorphism with $k|_{D(P)} = h$. We prove $k = \bar{h}$.

First note that for every $p \in P$ the principal down-set $\downarrow p \in D(P)$ and the principal up-set $\uparrow p \in U(P)$ satisfy: $\{\,p\,\} = \downarrow p \cap \uparrow p$ so each singleton $\{p\}$ is a meet of a down-set and an up-set. Since P is finite, every subset $u \subseteq P$ is a finite union of singletons,

$$u = \bigcup_{p \in u} \{p\},$$

hence every element of $\mathcal{P}(P)$ is obtained from elements of $D(P) \cup U(P)$ by finitely many joins and meets. In particular, $D(P) \cup U(P)$ generates $\mathcal{P}(P)$ as a

Boolean algebra (we use finiteness here to ensure only finite Boolean operations are needed). Now k agrees with $\bar{h}$ on $D(P)$ by hypothesis:

$$k(D) = h(D) = \bar{h}(D) \qquad (D \in D(P)).$$

Given any up-set $U \in U(P)$ we have $U = P \setminus D$ for some $D \in D(P)$, and because k and $\bar{h}$ preserve complements ,

$$k(U) = k(P \setminus D) = X \setminus k(D) = X \setminus \bar{h}(D) = \bar{h}(P \setminus D) = \bar{h}(U).$$

Thus k and $\bar{h}$ agree on $D(P) \cup U(P)$, and therefore on all of $\mathcal{P}(P)$ since this collection generates $\mathcal{P}(P)$. Hence $k = \bar{h}$. Together, the existence of $\bar{h}$ and its uniqueness show that every lattice homomorphism $h : L \to A$ into a Boolean algebra extends uniquely to a Boolean homomorphism $\bar{h} : \mathcal{P}(\mathcal{J}(L)) \to A$ satisfying $\bar{h} \circ \iota = h$. This is precisely the universal property of Definition 6, and therefore $\mathcal{P}(\mathcal{J}(L))$ together with the embedding ι is a Boolean envelope of L.

3.2 Example

Consider the three-element chain. The Boolean envelope is: $L^{-} \cong \mathcal{P}(\{x, y\})$, with the embedding $\iota : L \to \mathcal{P}(\{x, y\})$ given by:

$\bot \mapsto \emptyset$, $a \mapsto \{x\}$, $\top \mapsto \{x, y\}$, $\{y\}$ corresponds to the complement of a in L^{-}.

Although the Boolean envelope is unique up to isomorphism, the embedding need not be unique. For instance, the map $\iota'(a) = \{y\}$ also defines a valid embedding. The embeddings ι and ι' differ by the automorphism of $\mathcal{P}(\{x, y\})$ exchanging x and y (Fig. 2).

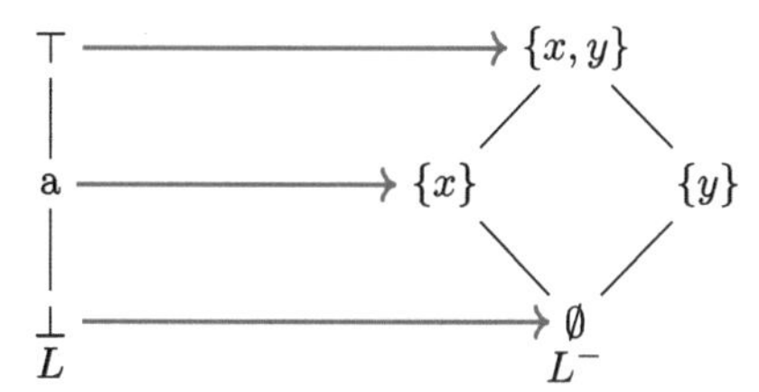

Fig. 2. The three-element chain L and its Boolean envelope $L^{-} \cong \mathcal{P}(\{x, y\})$. The element $\{y\} = \neg\iota(a)$ is the complement adjoined by the extension.

4 Formal Concept Analysis and the Boolean Envelope

In this section, we give a purely FCA-based interpretation of the Boolean envelope construction. Our starting point is the canonical formal context whose concept lattice is a finite distributive lattice. We then show how a simple modification of this context yields a new formal context whose concept lattice is the Boolean envelope of the original lattice.

4.1 Introduction and Theoretical Framework

Let L be a finite distributive lattice and let $\mathbb{K} = (G, M, I)$ be a *clarified and reduced* formal context such that $\mathfrak{B}(\mathbb{K}) \cong L$. Throughout this part, we naturally identify objects $g \in G$ and attributes $m \in M$ with their respective object and attribute concepts in L when evaluating lattice orders (e.g., $x \leq g$).

This section introduces an explicit algorithmic construction of the Boolean envelope. We demonstrate that by mapping objects and attributes to subsets of the irreducible base space, the Boolean envelope can be generated via a set-theoretic *disjointness rule*. Crucially, this algorithmic approach yields a conservative extension: it pads the context to generate the Boolean envelope without destroying the original incidence matrix.

Definition 9 (Double-arrow relation [6]**).** *Let $\mathbb{K} = (G, M, I)$ be a formal context. For $x \in G$ and $y \in M$ we define the double-arrow relation $x \swarrow\!\!\!\nearrow y$ if the following conditions hold:*

1. $(x, y) \notin I$,
2. $\forall h \in G : \ (h, y) \notin I \implies h' \subseteq x'$,
3. $\forall n \in M : \ (x, n) \notin I \implies n' \subseteq y'$.

In a distributive concept lattice, the double-arrow relation induces a bijection between join-irreducible objects and meet-irreducible attributes [6, Theorem 48].

Definition 10 (Critical pairs and base space). *A pair $(x, y) \in G \times M$ is called a* critical pair *if $x \swarrow\!\!\!\nearrow y$. The set of all critical pairs is called the* base space *and is denoted by*

$$P := \{(x, y) \in G \times M \mid x \swarrow\!\!\!\nearrow y\}.$$

Definition 11 (Base Space Representations). *We define the object representation $\rho : G \to \mathcal{P}(P)$ and the attribute representation $\sigma : M \to \mathcal{P}(P)$:*

$$\rho(g) = \{(x, y) \in P \mid (g, y) \notin I\},$$
$$\sigma(m) = \{(x, y) \in P \mid (x, m) \notin I\}.$$

In a Boolean context generating $\mathcal{P}(P)$, the fundamental incidence relation is no longer standard subset inclusion, but rather *disjointness*. Consequently, we no longer require distinct atoms and co-atoms; both missing objects and missing attributes are generated purely as singletons in P.

4.2 The Augmentation Algorithm

Algorithm 1 formalizes the construction of the Boolean envelope context $\mathbb{K}_\mathcal{B}$. The algorithm dynamically pads the matrix with pure singletons to preserve the original structure.

Algorithm 1: Construction of the Minimal Boolean Envelope $\mathbb{K}_\mathcal{B}$

Require: Reduced context $\mathbb{K} = (G, M, I)$ of a distributive lattice.
Ensure: Context $\mathbb{K}_\mathcal{B} = (G_\mathcal{B}, M_\mathcal{B}, I_\mathcal{B})$ such that $\mathfrak{B}(\mathbb{K}_\mathcal{B}) \cong \mathfrak{P}(P)$.

Compute the base space $P = \{(x, y) \in G \times M \mid x \nearrow y\}$.
Initialize $G_\mathcal{B} \leftarrow G$ and $M_\mathcal{B} \leftarrow M$.
Compute mappings $\rho(g)$ for all $g \in G$ and $\sigma(m)$ for all $m \in M$.
for all $p \in P$ **do**
  Let $S_p = \{p\}$ be the pure singleton.
  if $S_p \notin \{\rho(g) \mid g \in G_\mathcal{B}\}$ **then**
    Create new object g_p with $\rho(g_p) \leftarrow S_p$, and add to $G_\mathcal{B}$.
  end if
  if $S_p \notin \{\sigma(m) \mid m \in M_\mathcal{B}\}$ **then**
    Create new attribute m_p with $\sigma(m_p) \leftarrow S_p$, and add to $M_\mathcal{B}$.
  end if
end for
Define the incidence relation $I_\mathcal{B}$ on $G_\mathcal{B} \times M_\mathcal{B}$ via disjointness:
for all $g \in G_\mathcal{B}$ and $m \in M_\mathcal{B}$ **do**
  if $\rho(g) \cap \sigma(m) = \emptyset$ **then**
    $(g, m) \in I_\mathcal{B}$
  end if
end for
return $\mathbb{K}_\mathcal{B} = (G_\mathcal{B}, M_\mathcal{B}, I_\mathcal{B})$

4.3 Theoretical Results

Lemma 12 (Order-Theoretic Characterization of Representations). *In a distributive lattice, the base mappings ρ and σ represent principal down-sets (ideals) and up-sets (filters) of the irreducibles:*

$$\rho(g) = \{(x, y) \in P \mid x \leq g\},$$
$$\sigma(m) = \{(x, y) \in P \mid m \leq y\}.$$

Proof. For any object g, we have $(g, y) \notin I \iff g \not\leq y$. Because y is the maximal meet-irreducible not above x, the condition $g \not\leq y$ holds exactly when $x \leq g$. Thus, $(x, y) \in \rho(g) \iff x \leq g$. The statement for $\sigma(m)$ follows dually, proving the characterization for $\sigma(m)$.

Proposition 13 (Set-Theoretic Complementarity). *Let $g \in G$ and $m \in M$. If g and m generate the exact same formal concept in L (i.e., $g'' = m'$), then their representations are perfect set-theoretic complements in the base space P:*

$$\rho(g) = P \setminus \sigma(m).$$

Proof. By Lemma 12, $(x, y) \in \rho(g) \iff x \leq c$ and $(x, y) \in \sigma(m) \iff c \leq y$, where c is the generated concept. For any concept c, exactly one of the following must hold: either $x \leq c$ or $c \leq y$. They cannot be simultaneously true (as $x \not\leq y$), and they cannot be simultaneously false. Therefore, $\rho(g)$ and $\sigma(m)$ perfectly partition the base space P.

Remark 14. This complementarity directly illuminates the disjointness condition in Algorithm 1. Substituting $\sigma(m) = P \setminus \rho(m)$ into the incidence rule yields $\rho(g) \cap (P \setminus \rho(m)) = \emptyset$, which is the set-theoretic definition of subset inclusion $\rho(g) \subseteq \rho(m)$. Disjointness in P is therefore structurally equivalent to lattice subsumption.

Theorem 15 (Birkhoff Embedding via Representation). *The mapping $\rho : G \to \mathcal{P}(P)$ acts as a valid lattice embedding from L into $\mathcal{P}(P)$.*

Proof. By Lemma 12, $\rho(g)$ captures the down-set of join-irreducibles $\mathcal{J}(L)$ bounded by g. By Theorem 2, mapping an element of a distributive lattice to its generated down-set of join-irreducibles is a lattice isomorphism to a ring of sets, translating lattice joins and meets into set unions and intersections. Since ρ is precisely this map – restricted to the base space P – it follows that ρ is a lattice embedding of L into $\mathcal{P}(P)$.

Theorem 16 (Conservative Extension via Disjointness). *The generated incidence relation $I_{\mathcal{B}}$ is a conservative extension of I. For any $g \in G$ and $m \in M$ originally in $\mathbb{K}$:*

$$(g, m) \in I_{\mathcal{B}} \iff (g, m) \in I.$$

Proof. By Algorithm 1, $(g, m) \in I_{\mathcal{B}} \iff \rho(g) \cap \sigma(m) = \emptyset$.

($\Rightarrow$) Assume $(g, m) \notin I$. By standard distributive lattice properties, there exists a join-irreducible x and a meet-irreducible y separating them such that $x \swarrow\!\!\nearrow y$, where $x \leq g$ and $m \leq y$. By Lemma 12, $x \leq g \implies (x, y) \in \rho(g)$, and $m \leq y \implies (x, y) \in \sigma(m)$. Thus, $(x, y) \in \rho(g) \cap \sigma(m)$, meaning the intersection is not empty, and therefore $(g, m) \notin I_{\mathcal{B}}$.

($\Leftarrow$) Assume $(g, m) \in I$, which implies $g \leq m$. Suppose for contradiction there exists a pair $(x, y) \in \rho(g) \cap \sigma(m)$. By Lemma 12, $x \leq g$ and $m \leq y$. Transitively, $x \leq g \leq m \leq y$, which implies $x \leq y$. However, the definition of the double-arrow $x \swarrow\!\!\nearrow y$ strictly requires $(x, y) \notin I$, meaning $x \not\leq y$. This is a direct contradiction. Thus, $\rho(g) \cap \sigma(m) = \emptyset$, meaning $(g, m) \in I_{\mathcal{B}}$.

Theorem 17 (Minimal Boolean Envelope). *Let $\mathbb{K}_{\mathcal{B}}$ be the output of Algorithm 1. Then $\mathfrak{B}(\mathbb{K}_{\mathcal{B}}) \cong \mathcal{P}(P)$, representing the minimal Boolean envelope of $\mathfrak{B}(\mathbb{K})$.*

Proof. Since $|P| = |\mathcal{J}(L)|$, the context $\mathbb{K}_{\mathcal{B}}$ generates the powerset lattice $\mathcal{P}(P) \cong \mathcal{P}(\mathcal{J}(L))$, which has exactly $2^{|\mathcal{J}(L)|}$ elements. By Theorem 8, this is precisely the Boolean envelope, establishing minimality. By construction, the sets $\rho(G_{\mathcal{B}})$ and $\sigma(M_{\mathcal{B}})$ both contain every pure singleton $\{p\}$ for $p \in P$. The disjointness relation $\rho(g) \cap \sigma(m) = \emptyset$ evaluates equivalently to the canonical Boolean generating context $(P, P, \neq)$ [8], whose concept lattice is strictly the powerset lattice $\mathcal{P}(P)$.

Proposition 18 (Commutativity with Transposition). *Let $\mathfrak{B}(\mathbb{K})$ denote the application of Algorithm 1 to context $\mathbb{K}$. The construction of the Boolean envelope commutes with context transposition:*

$$(\mathbb{K}^T)_{\mathcal{B}} \cong (\mathbb{K}_{\mathcal{B}})^T.$$

Proof. Transposing the initial context $\mathbb{K} = (G, M, I)$ yields $\mathbb{K}^T = (M, G, I^T)$. In $\mathbb{K}^T$, the set of pairs P^T contains (y, x) if and only if $(x, y) \in P$. Because the definitions of ρ and σ are identical except for the order of arguments in the non-incidence tuple, applying the algorithm to $\mathbb{K}^T$ causes $\rho_{\mathbb{K}^T}$ to evaluate the same subsets as $\sigma_{\mathbb{K}}$, and $\sigma_{\mathbb{K}^T}$ to evaluate exactly as $\rho_{\mathbb{K}}$. Consequently, the objects and attributes are perfectly swapped, while the disjointness relation $\rho(\cdot) \cap \sigma(\cdot) = \emptyset$ evaluates identically. The resulting context is the transpose of $\mathbb{K}_{\mathcal{B}}$.

4.4 Example

To illustrate the mechanics of Algorithm 1, consider the formal context $\mathbb{K} = (G, M, I)$ where $G = \{1, 2, 3\}$ and $M = \{a, b, c\}$, specified by the incidence matrix below. This context generates a 5-element distributive lattice.

$\mathbb{K}$	a	b	c
1	×	×	
2	×		×
3			

Step 1: Base Space Calculation. We evaluate the double-arrow condition $x \swarrow\!\!\nearrow y$ across all non-incident pairs. This yields exactly three irreducible pairs:

$$p_1 = (1, c), \quad p_2 = (2, b), \quad p_3 = (3, a).$$

Other non-incident pairs, such as $(3, b)$, fail the required maximality conditions (e.g., $(2, b) \notin I$ but $2' \not\subseteq 3'$). Thus, the minimal base space is strictly $P = \{p_1, p_2, p_3\}$.

Step 2: Base Space Representations. We compute $\rho(g)$ and $\sigma(m)$ by testing non-incidence against the dual elements of P:

$$\rho(1) = \{p_1\} \qquad \sigma(a) = \{p_3\}$$
$$\rho(2) = \{p_2\} \qquad \sigma(b) = \{p_2, p_3\}$$
$$\rho(3) = \{p_1, p_2, p_3\} \qquad \sigma(c) = \{p_1, p_3\}$$

As dictated by Proposition 13, observe the strict set-theoretic complementarity: objects and attributes generating the same concept form exact partitions of P. For instance, object 1 and attribute b generate the identical formal concept, and indeed $\rho(1) = P \setminus \sigma(b)$.

Step 3: Augmentation. To construct the Boolean envelope generating $\mathcal{P}(P)$, Algorithm 1 requires every pure singleton of P to be explicitly present in both $\rho(G_{\mathcal{B}})$ and $\sigma(M_{\mathcal{B}})$.

- The current object representations contain $\{p_1\}$ and $\{p_2\}$, but lack $\{p_3\}$. We append a new object g_{p_3} uniquely defined by $\rho(g_{p_3}) = \{p_3\}$.
- The current attribute representations contain $\{p_3\}$, but lack $\{p_1\}$ and $\{p_2\}$. We append new attributes m_{p_1} and m_{p_2} uniquely defined by $\sigma(m_{p_1}) = \{p_1\}$ and $\sigma(m_{p_2}) = \{p_2\}$.

Step 4: Envelope Construction via Disjointness. We construct the final incidence relation $I_\mathcal{B}$ purely by evaluating $\rho(g) \cap \sigma(m) = \emptyset$. For example, object 1 is incident to m_{p_2} because $\rho(1) \cap \sigma(m_{p_2}) = \{p_1\} \cap \{p_2\} = \emptyset$.

The resulting minimal Boolean envelope $\mathbb{K}_\mathcal{B}$ evaluates to:

$\mathbb{K}_\mathcal{B}$	a	b	c	m_{p_1}	m_{p_2}
1	×	×			×
2	×		×	×	
3					
g_{p_3}				×	×

Notice that the top-left 3×3 submatrix perfectly preserves the original context $\mathbb{K}$, while the complete 4×5 augmented context fully generates the minimal 2^3 Boolean lattice $\mathcal{P}(P)$.

Fig. 3. The distributive lattice of Example 4.4 embedded as a sublattice of its Boolean envelope.

5 From Finite Lattices to Boolean Algebras

The Boolean envelope, as developed in the preceding sections, requires its input to be a distributive lattice. This raises two natural questions. First, can an arbitrary finite lattice—one that may fail distributivity—still be canonically embedded into a Boolean algebra? Second, and more ambitiously, can the definition of the Boolean envelope itself be extended to non-distributive lattices, yielding a minimal Boolean algebra with the same universal property? (Fig. 3)

The answer to the first question is yes, via a two-step procedure. We first recall a construction from [1] that embeds any finite lattice into a distributive one: the Birkhoff completion. Once distributivity is established, the Boolean envelope construction applies. The second question remains open; the two-step procedure described below provides a partial answer by reducing it to the distributive case.

We note that [1] introduces two dual completions—one via order ideals of join-irreducible elements, and one via filters of meet-irreducible elements. For consistency with the Boolean envelope construction developed in this paper, we work exclusively with the former.

Definition 19 (Birkhoff Completion [1]**).** *Let* $(L, \leq)$ *be a finite lattice. The* Birkhoff completion *of* L*, denoted* $\mathrm{BC}(L)$*, is the lattice of order ideals of join-irreducible elements of* L*:*

$$\mathrm{BC}(L) \cong (\mathcal{I}(\mathcal{J}(L)), \subseteq),$$

By construction, $BC(L)$ is a finite distributive lattice. Hence, the Boolean envelope construction applies to $BC(L)$. This shows that every finite lattice can be embedded into a Boolean algebra via the canonical two-step construction

$$L \longrightarrow BC(L) \longrightarrow BC(L)^{-}.$$

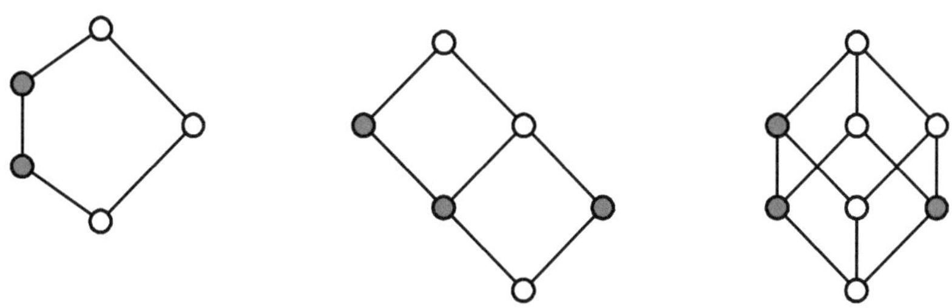

Fig. 4. The two-step embedding of N_5 into a Boolean algebra. Left: the nondistributive lattice N_5. Middle: its Birkhoff completion $\mathrm{BC}(N_5)$, which is distributive but not Boolean. Right: the Boolean envelope $\mathrm{BC}(N_5)^{-}$. Filled nodes ($\bullet$) mark the join-irreducible elements of N_5 and their images under each successive embedding.

Thus, the Birkhoff completion and the Boolean envelope together provide a systematic procedure for embedding an arbitrary finite lattice into a Boolean algebra. The relationship between the Birkhoff completion and its Boolean envelope can be understood more concretely. Since $BC(L) = \mathcal{I}(\mathcal{J}(L))$, it is naturally a lattice of subsets of $\mathcal{J}(L)$ and therefore embeds into the full powerset via inclusion (Fig. 4):

$$BC(L) = \mathcal{I}(\mathcal{J}(L)) \subseteq \mathcal{P}(\mathcal{J}(L)).$$

This inclusion raises a natural question: when do the Birkhoff completion of a finite distributive lattice L and its Boolean envelope L^{-} coincide ?

Proposition 20. *Let* L *be a finite lattice. The following are equivalent:*

1. *$BC(L)$ is a Boolean algebra.*
2. *The order on $\mathcal{J}(L)$ is trivial .*

In this case, $BC(L)$ coincides with its Boolean envelope.

Proof. Since $BC(L)$ is a finite distributive lattice, Proposition 4 applies. Thus, $BC(L)$ is a Boolean algebra if and only if every join-irreducible element of $BC(L)$ is an atom. Now, the join-irreducible elements of $BC(L) = \mathcal{I}(\mathcal{J}(L))$ are precisely the principal ideals $\downarrow j$ for $j \in \mathcal{J}(L)$, ordered by inclusion. Hence, each $\downarrow j$ is an atom if and only if $\downarrow j = \{j\}$, which holds exactly when no two distinct elements of $\mathcal{J}(L)$ are comparable. In this case, every subset of $\mathcal{J}(L)$ is an order ideal, and therefore $\mathcal{I}(\mathcal{J}(L)) = \mathcal{P}(\mathcal{J}(L))$. Thus, $BC(L)$ is Boolean if and only if the order on $\mathcal{J}(L)$ is trivial, and in that case it coincides with its Boolean envelope.

The next table summarizes the two constructions. While both are built from the join-irreducible elements of the input lattice, they operate under different assumptions and produce structurally distinct outputs (Table 1).

Table 1. Birkhoff completion vs. Boolean envelope

Property	Birkhoff Completion	Boolean Envelope
Input	finite lattice	finite distributive lattice
Output	distributive lattice	Boolean algebra
Construction	$\mathcal{I}(\mathcal{J}(L))$	$\mathcal{P}(\mathcal{J}(L))$
Preserves complements	no guarantee	yes
FCA representation	$\underline{\mathfrak{B}}(\mathcal{J}(L), \mathcal{J}(L), \ngeq)$	$\mathfrak{B}(\mathcal{J}(L), \mathcal{J}(L), \neq)$

6 Conclusion and Future Work

In this work, we studied the Boolean envelope of finite distributive lattices as the canonical minimal extension that adjoins complements. We showed that, in the finite case, this construction admits a concrete representation as the powerset algebra of join-irreducible elements, and we developed an explicit algorithmic realization within Formal Concept Analysis. The resulting construction yields a conservative extension of the original context, making the Boolean structure directly accessible from the incidence geometry via a disjointness-based rule.

A natural way to understand this construction is as part of a stepwise enrichment of lattice structure. Starting from an arbitrary finite lattice, the Birkhoff completion provides a canonical way to enforce distributivity. The Boolean envelope then continues this process by adjoining complements, passing from distributive lattices to Boolean algebras. In this way, the two constructions together yield a systematic passage from general finite lattices to Boolean algebras.

This perspective admits a natural categorical interpretation. Both constructions are canonical and functorial and are characterized by universal properties: the Birkhoff completion adjoins distributivity, while the Boolean envelope adjoins complementation in a minimal way. Their composition therefore yields a canonical embedding of any finite lattice into a Boolean algebra, explaining the uniqueness and minimality of the resulting extension.

Several directions remain open for future work. The finite setting was used essentially throughout—Birkhoff's representation theorem, the atom-based characterization of Boolean algebras, and the termination of Algorithm 1 all rely on finiteness. Extending the construction to infinite distributive lattices would require replacing the powerset algebra with a suitable topological or dual structure, connecting naturally to Priestley duality. The obstruction is concrete: the finite proof of Theorem 8 relies on $D(P) \cup U(P)$ generating $\mathcal{P}(P)$ via finitely many Boolean operations, which fails when P is infinite. It is also natural to ask whether Algorithm 1 can be adapted to accept non-distributive contexts directly, combining the Birkhoff completion and Boolean envelope into a single augmentation step. On the implicational side, while the conservative extension preserves all original implications, it remains open how the newly introduced singleton attributes interact with canonical bases. Finally, if a concept lattice of a context (G, M, I) has the same number of join-irreducible elements as meet-irreducible elements, then constructing the Boolean envelope via the Birkhoff completion using either join- or meet-irreducibles leads to two isomorphic Boolean algebras. For differing cardinalities, one instead obtains two Boolean algebras such that one embeds into the other. It would be interesting to find a natural interpretation of this isomorphism or embedding, analogous to the role played by critical pairs in Sect. 4.

References

1. Abdulla, M., Hirth, J., Stumme, G.: The Birkhoff completion of finite lattices. In: Conceptual Knowledge Structures, pp. 20–35. Springer, Cham (2024). https://doi.org/10.1007/978-3-031-67868-4_2
2. Birkhoff, G.: Lattice theory. In: Colloquium Publications, vol. 25, 3. edn. American Mathematical Society, Providence, RI (1967)
3. Caspard, N., Leclerc, B., Monjardet, B.: Fiinite Ordered Sets: Concepts, Results and Uses. Encyclopedia of Mathematics and its Applications, Cambridge University Press, Cambridge, UK (2012)
4. Davey, B.A., Priestley, H.A.: Introduction to Lattices and Order. Cambridge University Press, Cambridge, UK (2002)
5. Dürrschnabel, D., Koyda, M., Stumme, G.: Attribute selection using contranominal scales. In: Braun, T., Gehrke, M., Hanika, T., Hernandez, N. (eds.) ICCS 2021. LNCS (LNAI), vol. 12879, pp. 127–141. Springer, Cham (2021). https://doi.org/10.1007/978-3-030-86982-3_10
6. Ganter, B., Wille, R.: Formal Concept Analysis, 2 edn. Springer, Cham (2024). https://doi.org/10.1007/978-3-031-63422-2
7. Gehrke, M., van Gool, S.: Topological Duality for Distributive Lattices: Theory and Applications. Cambridge Tracts in Theoretical Computer Science, Cambridge University Press (2024)

8. Kwuida, L.: Dicomplemented Lattices: A Contextual Generalization of Boolean Algebras. Ph.D. thesis, Technische Universität Dresden, Dresden, Germany (2004)
9. Priestley, H.A.: Representation of distributive lattices by means of ordered stone spaces. Bull. Lond. Math. Soc. **2**, 186–190 (1970)
10. Stanley, R.P.: Enumerative Combinatorics. Cambridge University Press (2012)
11. Stone, M.H.: The theory of representations for boolean algebras. Trans. Am. Math. Soc. **40**(1), 37–111 (1936)

Sublattice Extensions of Moore Families

Christophe Demko(✉) and Karell Bertet

L3I - Laboratoire Informatique, Image et Interaction - EA 2118, Bâtiment Pascal
Avenue Michel Crépeau, F-17042 La Rochelle Cedex 1, France
christophe.demko@univ-lr.fr

Abstract. Moore families are fundamental structures in formal concept analysis and order theory, notably serving as lattices of closed sets. They play a crucial role in knowledge representation and conceptual data analysis. However, the practical computation and maintenance of complete Moore families remain challenging, particularly in dynamic contexts where new information continuously becomes available.

This paper presents a novel algorithm for completing Moore families by efficiently discovering missing closed sets and updating their fundamental elements (minimum, maximum, meet and join irreducibles, and principal closed sets) while maintaining the sublattice structure. Our approach builds upon prior work on generalized convex hulls applied to concepts and complements existing methods for reduced sub-context completion in concept lattices. Given a set of newly discovered closed sets, the algorithm iteratively produces missing closed sets, enabling on-the-fly intent discovery in description spaces.

We provide a complexity analysis of the algorithm and demonstrate its applicability to updating contexts when new concepts are added to existing description lattices. The work bridges the gap between formal concept analysis and practical applications in dynamic knowledge management systems.

Keywords: Moore family · Lattice · Completion

1 Introduction

In classical Formal Concept Analysis (FCA), a formal context is defined by a fixed set of objects and a fixed set of attributes. Concepts are then computed using the associated derivation operators, and the intent of each concept is obtained by intersecting the attribute sets of the corresponding objects. When contexts evolve, recomputing the full concept lattice is often too expensive, especially in pattern structures where descriptions involve costly predicate evaluation. In such settings, reusing previously discovered predicates and their extents is essential for incremental concept discovery.

Moore families [5], also known as closure systems [1], provide the natural formal framework: they are closed under intersection and correspond, in FCA [3], to families of closed sets. The practical question we address is how to complete

M. Croitoru et al. (Eds.): CONCEPTS 2026, LNAI 16811, pp. 39–54, 2027.
https://doi.org/10.1007/978-3-032-34742-8_3

a Moore sub-family when new closed sets are discovered, while preserving the sublattice structure needed for meet and join computations.

This issue is central in exploratory and dynamic settings, where relevant descriptions are discovered progressively rather than fixed in advance. In pattern FCA in particular, descriptions are derived from complex predicates; repeatedly recomputing them during lattice operations can be costly. Maintaining a compact closed-set representation and updating it incrementally is therefore crucial for practical scalability.

From an algorithmic perspective, the challenge is not only to insert newly discovered closed sets, but also to preserve the algebraic constraints that make subsequent meet/join reasoning correct. In particular, the completed family must remain compatible with the global lattice operations while avoiding unnecessary additions. This motivates the search for minimal completions that are structurally sound and efficiently enumerable.

Our previous work on reduced sub-context completion [2] maintains lattice structure when inserting new concepts. In this paper, we complement that line by handling the single-domain completion of Moore families, which yields the missing building block between reduced-lattice completion and concept-level incremental updates.

We study minimal complete sublattice completions and propose an algorithm that updates the fundamental elements of the family (minimum, maximum, irreducibles, principal closed sets) while enumerating only newly introduced closed sets. The enumeration uses a filtered variant of CloseByOne [4]. We also provide complexity bounds and an illustrative execution scenario.

The main contributions of this work can be summarized as follows. First, we formalize the completion problem as the computation of a minimal family that contains the initial sub-family and the newly discovered closed sets, while preserving the sublattice operations inherited from the global lattice. Second, we propose an incremental algorithm that updates the fundamental elements of the family directly, without materializing the full closed-set lattice at each step. Third, we provide a filtered enumeration strategy that focuses on newly generated closed sets and avoids traversing unchanged regions of the search space. Finally, we analyze memory usage and delay complexity, and we illustrate the behavior of the method on a representative completion scenario.

The scope of the paper is intentionally focused on structural completion under fixed lattice operations. We assume that meet and join are available as primitive operations from the global family, and we study how to maintain a compact sublattice representation when new closed sets arrive. This setting matches practical workflows where the global closure mechanism is known, but recomputing all closed sets is prohibitive. In this context, updating only fundamental elements and enumerating only genuinely new closed sets provides a good compromise between theoretical guarantees and computational efficiency.

The paper is organized as follows. Section 2 recalls closure operators, Moore families, and lattice notions. Section 3 presents the completion algorithm and its update procedures. Section 4 analyzes memory and time complexity. Finally, Conclusions concludes and outlines future work.

2 Mathematical Background

In this section, we recall the main mathematical notions used throughout the paper, including closure operators, Moore families, and their associated lattice structure.

2.1 Closure Operators and Closed Sets

Let X be a finite ground set. We denote by 2^X the power set of X, ordered by set inclusion.

Definition 1 (Closure operator). *A* ***closure operator*** *[1] on X is a mapping $\varphi : 2^X \to 2^X$ satisfying the following properties for all $A, B \subseteq X$:*

- *Extensivity:* $A \subseteq \varphi(A)$
- *Monotonicity:* $A \subseteq B \Rightarrow \varphi(A) \subseteq \varphi(B)$
- *Idempotency:* $\varphi(\varphi(A)) = \varphi(A)$

Definition 2 (Closed set). *A set $C \subseteq X$ is said to be* ***closed*** *(with respect to φ) if $\varphi(C) = C$*

Definition 3 (Family of all closed sets). *The family of all closed sets defined from φ and X is denoted $\mathcal{F}^{\varphi,X} := \{C \subseteq X \mid \varphi(C) = C\}$*

2.2 Moore Families

Definition 4 (Moore family). *A family $\mathcal{G} \subseteq 2^X$ is called a* ***Moore family*** *[5] (or closure system [1]) with ground set X if:*

- *It contains the whole set X:* $X \in \mathcal{G}$
- *It is closed under intersections:* $\forall \mathcal{C} \subseteq \mathcal{G}, \left(\bigcap \mathcal{C}\right) \in \mathcal{G}$

It is well known that every Moore family defines a closure operator, and conversely the family of all closed sets of any closure operator forms a Moore family through

$$\varphi(A) := \bigcap\{C \in \mathcal{G} \mid A \subseteq C\}$$

and

$$\mathcal{F}^{\varphi,X} := \mathcal{G}$$

Definition 5 (Moore sub-family). *A family $\mathcal{H} \subseteq 2^Y$ is called a Moore sub-family with a ground set Y of the Moore family $\mathcal{G} \subseteq 2^X$ if*

- *It is a Moore family defined on ground set $Y \subseteq X$*
- *It is included in $\mathcal{G}$: $\mathcal{H} \subseteq \mathcal{G}$*

Therefore, the closure operator associated with $\mathcal{H}$ is a sub-closure operator of $\mathcal{G}$, informally, it is a closure operator defined on a smaller ground set that preserves only a subset of the closed sets of the original one.

Definition 6 (Principal closed sets).
For each element $x \in X$, the ***principal closed set*** *[1] generated by x is defined as:*

$$\mathcal{F}_x^{\varphi,X} := \varphi(\{x\})$$

Principal closed sets are to Moore families what object-concepts and attribute-concepts are to concept lattices.

2.3 Lattice Structure of Closed Sets

Definition 7 (Complete lattice of closed sets). *Ordered by inclusion, the family $\mathcal{F}^{\varphi,X}$ of closed sets forms a complete lattice $\mathbb{L} = \langle \mathcal{F}^{\varphi,X}, \vee, \wedge \rangle$ where the meet and join are defined as follows:*

- *The* ***meet*** *is given by intersection: $\bigwedge \mathcal{C} := \bigcap \mathcal{C}$*
- *The* ***join*** *is given by the closure of the union: $\bigvee \mathcal{C} := \varphi\left(\bigcup \mathcal{C}\right)$*

This lattice structure plays a central role in Formal Concept Analysis, where closed sets correspond to concept **extents** on the set of objects, and concept **intents** on the set of attributes.

Recall that in a lattice, join-irreducible elements are precisely those with a unique predecessor, while meet-irreducible elements are those with a unique successor in the cover relation. It is worth noting that the join-irreducible elements of this lattice are included in the principal closed sets generated by singletons:

$$J_{\mathbb{L}} \subseteq \{\mathcal{F}_x^{\varphi,X} \mid x \in X\}$$

Definition 8 (Sublattice of closed sets). *A family $\mathcal{F}^{\psi,Y}$ of closed sets forms a* ***sublattice*** *[1] $\langle \mathcal{F}^{\psi,Y}, \vee, \wedge \rangle$ of $\langle \mathcal{F}^{\varphi,X}, \vee, \wedge \rangle$ if:*

- *It is a complete lattice of closed sets defined on ground set $Y \subseteq X$ and closure operator ψ*
- *It is included in $\mathcal{F}^{\varphi,X}$: $\mathcal{F}^{\psi,Y} \subseteq \mathcal{F}^{\varphi,X}$*
- *The meet and join operations of $\mathcal{F}^{\psi,Y}$ are the restrictions of those of $\mathcal{F}^{\varphi,X}$ to $\mathcal{F}^{\psi,Y}$*

For the sublattice $\langle \mathcal{F}^{\psi,Y}, \vee, \wedge \rangle$, $\mathcal{F}^{\psi,Y}$ is a Moore sub-family of $\mathcal{F}^{\varphi,X}$ (containing Y and closed under intersection), and closed under the closure of unions of its elements.

It is important to note that while every sublattice of closed sets is a Moore sub-family, not every Moore sub-family is a sublattice, as it may not be closed under the closure of unions (see Fig. 2b for an example of a Moore sub-family that is not a sublattice).

3 Contributions

In this section, we describe our algorithm for completing Moore families, emphasizing how it maintains the lattice structure and updates the fundamental elements of the family.

3.1 Problem Statement and Objectives

We consider a complete Moore family $\mathcal{F}^{\varphi,X}$ and the following completion problem: given a Moore sub-family $\mathcal{F}^{\psi,Y}$ of $\mathcal{F}^{\varphi,X}$, defined on a ground set $Y \subseteq X$ and a closure operator ψ, such that $\mathbb{L} := \langle \mathcal{F}^{\psi,Y}, \vee, \wedge \rangle$ forms a sublattice of $\langle \mathcal{F}^{\varphi,X}, \vee, \wedge \rangle$, and given a family of new closed sets $\mathcal{C} \subseteq \mathcal{F}^{\varphi,X}$, our goal is to compute a family $\mathcal{F}^{\psi^+,Y^+}$ such that: (i) $\mathcal{F}^{\psi,Y} \cup \mathcal{C} \subseteq \mathcal{F}^{\psi^+,Y^+}$, (ii) $\left\langle \mathcal{F}^{\psi^+,Y^+}, \vee, \wedge \right\rangle$ is a sublattice of $\langle \mathcal{F}^{\varphi,X}, \vee, \wedge \rangle$ (hence preserving the meet and join operations inherited from the global lattice), and (iii) $\mathcal{F}^{\psi^+,Y^+}$ is minimal for set inclusion among families satisfying (i) and (ii).

From an algorithmic point of view, we assume that the input lattice $\mathbb{L} := \langle \mathcal{F}^{\psi,Y}, \vee, \wedge \rangle$ is represented by its fundamental elements rather than by the full set of closed sets. In other words, these elements are part of the input specification: the minimum, the maximum, the join- and meet-irreducible elements (with their cover information), and the principal closed sets.

More formally, the input consists of a subset $\mathcal{C}$ of $\mathcal{F}^{\varphi,X}$ and a sub-family $\mathcal{F}^{\psi,Y}$ of $\mathcal{F}^{\varphi,X}$ described by the fundamental elements:

- $\bot_{\mathbb{L}}$: minimum element
- $\top_{\mathbb{L}}$: maximum element
- $\mathrm{Cov}_J(\mathbb{L}) := \{(j^-, j) \mid j \in J_{\mathbb{L}}\}$: its join irreducible elements and their predecessors in the cover relation of $\mathbb{L}$ (i.e., $j^- \prec j$ in $\mathbb{L}$)
- $\mathrm{Cov}_M(\mathbb{L}) := \{(m, m^+) \mid m \in M_{\mathbb{L}}\}$: its meet irreducible elements and their successors in the cover relation of $\mathbb{L}$ (i.e., $m \prec m^+$ in $\mathbb{L}$)
- $\mathrm{Prin}_{\mathbb{L}} := \{(x, \mathcal{F}_x^{\psi,Y}) \mid x \in Y\}$: the principal closed sets generated by each x in Y

The algorithm aims to construct a new Moore family $\mathcal{F}^{\psi^+,Y^+}$ such that $\left\langle \mathcal{F}^{\psi^+,Y^+}, \vee, \wedge \right\rangle$ is the smallest sublattice of $\langle \mathcal{F}^{\varphi,X}, \vee, \wedge \rangle$ containing $\mathcal{F}^{\psi,Y}$ and the family of newly added closed sets $\mathcal{C}$. The fundamental elements of $\mathcal{F}^{\psi^+,Y^+}$ are updated to reflect the newly added closed sets. Furthermore, we seek to identify only the new closed sets introduced by this completion (namely, the elements of $\mathcal{F}^{\psi^+,Y^+} \setminus \mathcal{F}^{\psi,Y}$) and enumerate them efficiently using a modified version of the CloseByOne algorithm adapted to traverse only the newly generated closed sets.

The output is a new Moore family $\mathcal{F}^{\psi^+,Y^+}$ forming a sublattice of $\langle \mathcal{F}^{\varphi,X}, \vee, \wedge \rangle$, described by its updated fundamental elements. Along with this output, we enumerate the elements of $\mathcal{F}^{\psi^+,Y^+} \setminus \mathcal{F}^{\psi,Y}$, that is, the new closed sets introduced by the completion.

This problem is similar to the one introduced in [2], where the objective was to complete a lattice by adding new elements while preserving the join and sup of an initial complete lattice. Two algorithms were proposed: the first completes a lattice by adding a new element x, while the second completes a concept lattice by adding a new concept $(\boldsymbol{A}, \boldsymbol{B})$. These two algorithms propose a completion of the reduced context, i.e., the irreducible elements. The first relies on traversing the irreducible elements of the lattice to add missing joins and meets, with exponential time complexity. The second restricts the traversal to the object-concepts associated with elements of $\boldsymbol{A}$ and to the attribute-concepts associated with elements of $\boldsymbol{B}$, with a polynomial-delay complexity per new concept. The algorithm we propose provides the missing building block between these two algorithms, in that it considers a Moore family defined on a single domain and completes it by updating its fundamental elements with polynomial delay per newly added closed set.

Example

To illustrate our problem statement, consider the Moore family $\mathcal{F}^{\varphi,X}$ on the ground set $X = \{a, b, c, d, e\}$ viewed as a complete lattice whose Hasse diagram is shown in Fig. 1a, with its fundamental elements. The input is:

- $\mathbb{L} := \langle \mathcal{F}^{\psi,Y}, \vee, \wedge \rangle$, a sublattice of this family whose Hasse diagram is shown in Fig. 1b, given by its fundamental elements;
- $\mathcal{C} = \{\mathtt{a}, \mathtt{ac}\}$, a family of new closed sets to add to $\mathcal{F}^{\psi,Y}$.

The MooreFamilyLatticeCompletion algorithm completes the sublattice $\mathbb{L}$ while preserving the lattice structure of $\mathcal{F}^{\varphi,X}$. The output is:

- $\left\langle \mathcal{F}^{\psi^+,Y^+}, \vee, \wedge \right\rangle$, the resulting sublattice in Fig. 2a, given by its fundamental elements;
- ($\emptyset$, `abcde`, `ac`, `acd`, `a`), the enumeration of new closed sets introduced by this completion.

The smallest Moore family containing the family of Fig. 1b and the elements `a` and `ac` is given in the Hasse diagram of Fig. 2b. This family is a Moore sub-family of $\mathcal{F}^{\varphi,X}$, but not a sublattice because it is missing `acd`, shown in red, required for the join `ac` $\vee$ `ad`. A minimal Moore family does not necessarily preserve the lattice structure. Our algorithm adds the extra closed set `acd` to maintain the original join.

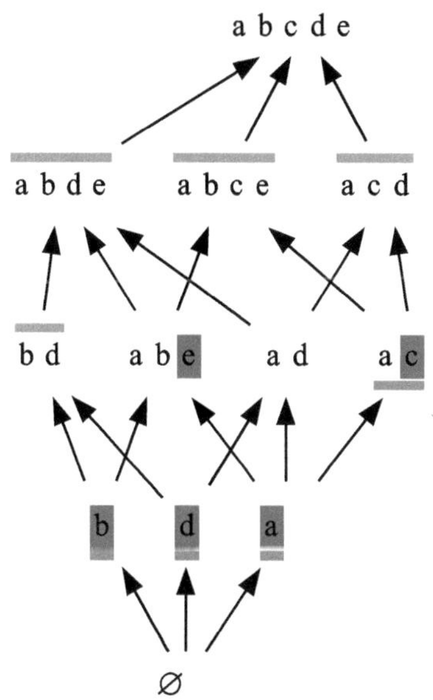

(a) The global Moore family

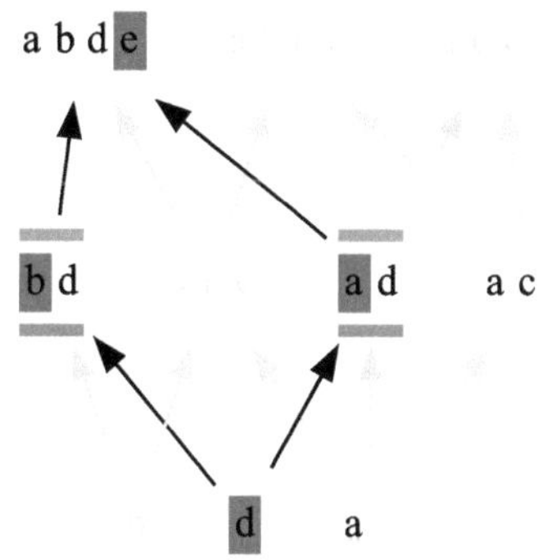

(b) A sublattice and elements to add.

Fig. 1. Hasse diagram of a Moore family and a sublattice of this family. Meet irreducible elements are overlined in orange, join-irreducible elements are underlined in green and principal elements are shown in magenta. (Color figure online)

3.2 Algorithm Description

To solve this problem, we first identify the new principal closed sets of the completed family $\mathcal{F}^{\psi^+,Y^+}$ from those of the initial family $\mathcal{F}^{\psi,Y}$ and the family of newly added closed sets $\mathcal{C}$. These newly introduced principal closed sets are the source of all additional closed sets generated by join operations in the completed family.

Once these new principal closed sets have been identified, we use a modified version of the CloseByOne algorithm to efficiently enumerate all newly introduced closed sets, by applying meet operations with the join-irreducible elements of the original family $\mathcal{F}^{\psi,Y}$.

To maintain readability, we assume that all algorithms have access to the following elements:

- $\vee, \wedge$, the join and meet operations of $\langle \mathcal{F}^{\varphi,X}, \vee, \wedge \rangle$
- $\mathbb{L} := \langle \mathcal{F}^{\psi,Y}, \vee, \wedge \rangle$ given by its fundamental elements:
  - $\bot_{\mathbb{L}}$, the minimum element of $\mathbb{L}$
  - $\top_{\mathbb{L}}$, the maximum element of $\mathbb{L}$
  - $\mathrm{Cov}_J(\mathbb{L})$, the join irreducible elements of $\mathbb{L}$ and their direct predecessors
  - $\mathrm{Cov}_M(\mathbb{L})$, the meet irreducible elements of $\mathbb{L}$ and their direct successors
  - $\mathrm{Prin}_{\mathbb{L}}$, the principal closed sets generated by each x in Y

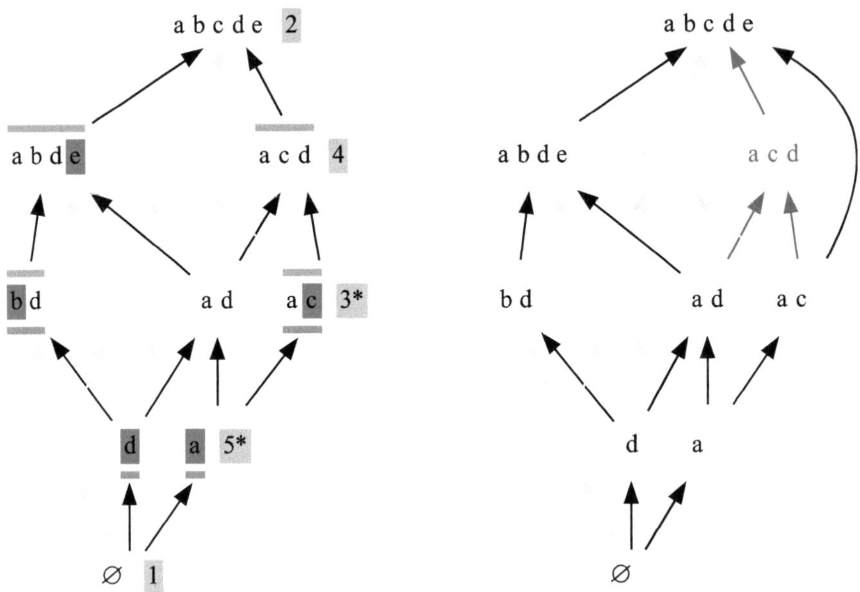

(a) The minimal sublattice containing the initial sublattice of Fig. 1b and the elements a and ac. New elements (∅, abcde, ac, acd, a) are shown in blue. A star indicates a new principal closed set.

(b) The minimal Moore family containing the initial sublattice of Fig. 1b and the elements a and ac – the element in red is not included.

Fig. 2. Hasse diagram of a completed sublattice and a Moore sub-family. (Color figure online)

- $\mathrm{Prin}^{+}_{\mathbb{L}}$, the newly introduced principal closed sets generated by $\mathcal{C}$, which are to be computed from $\mathrm{Prin}_{\mathbb{L}}$ and $\mathcal{C}$

3.3 Main Algorithm

Algorithm 1: MooreFamilyLatticeCompletion

```
Data: 𝒞, the family of new closed sets
Prin⁺_𝕃 ← ∅
foreach C ∈ 𝒞 :
    foreach x ∈ C : UpdateNewPrincipals(x, C)
end
while Prin⁺_𝕃 ≠ ∅ :
    (x, C) ← extract (Prin⁺_𝕃)
    if (x, C′) ∈ Prin_𝕃 : Prin_𝕃 \= {(x, C′)}
    Prin_𝕃 ∪= {(x, C)}
    if C < ⊥_𝕃 : Cov_M(𝕃) ∪= {(C, ⊥_𝕃)}; UpdateMinimum(C); yield C
    elif C > ⊤_𝕃 : Cov_J(𝕃) ∪= {(C, ⊤_𝕃)}; UpDateMaximum(C); yield C
    elif C ≠ ⊥_𝕃 :
        C′ ← ⊥_𝕃 ∧ C
        if C′ ≠ ⊥_𝕃 :
            UpdateMinimum(C′)
            foreach x′ ∈ C′ : UpdateNewPrincipals(x′, C′)
            yield C′
        end
        C′ ← ⊤_𝕃 ∨ C
        if C′ ≠ ⊤_𝕃 :
            UpDateMaximum(C′)
            foreach x′ ∈ C′ : UpdateNewPrincipals(x′, C′)
            yield C′
        end
        foreach (m, m⁺) ∈ Cov_M(𝕃) :
            C′ ← m ∧ C
            foreach x′ ∈ C′ : UpdateNewPrincipals(x′, C′)
        end
        J ← list ({j | (j⁻, j) ∈ Cov_M(𝕃), j ≮ C})
        foreach C′ ∈ FilteredCloseByOne(J, queue ().append((C, ∅, 0))) :
            UpdateMeet(C′)
            foreach x′ ∈ C′ : UpdateNewPrincipals(x′, C′)
            yield C′
        end
        UpdateJoin(C)
    end
end
```

The main loop of the algorithm[1] iteratively processes the newly introduced principal closed sets, updating the old principal closed sets and generating new

[1] To avoid unnecessarily complicating the algorithm, we did not describe how to handle the trivial case where the initial Moore family does not exist yet.

closed sets through meet and join operations. The UPDATENEWPRINCIPALS procedure ensures that the sets of principal closed sets are correctly maintained, while the UPDATEMINIMUM, UPDATEMAXIMUM, UPDATEJOIN, and UPDATEMEET procedures update the fundamental elements of the lattice as new closed sets are introduced. The FILTEREDCLOSEBYONE algorithm is used to efficiently enumerate the new closed sets generated by join operations with selected join-irreducible elements of the original family.

The MOOREFAMILYLATTICECOMPLETION algorithm operates as follows:

- Lines 2 to 4 are responsible for initializing the set of new principal closed sets based on the family of newly added closed sets $\mathcal{C}$.
- Lines 5 to 36 describe the main loop of the algorithm, which processes each new principal closed set, updating the old principal closed sets and generating new closed sets through meet and join operations.
- Lines 6 to 7 handle the extraction of a new principal closed set and the update of old principal closed sets.
- Lines 9 and 10 handle the cases where the current principal closed set is the new minimum or maximum element of the lattice, respectively.
- Line 11 handles the general case where the current principal closed set is neither the new minimum nor the new maximum.
- Lines 12 to 17 compute the meet of the current principal closed set with the minimum element and update the minimum if necessary.
- Lines 18 to 23 compute the join of the current principal closed set with the maximum element and update the maximum if necessary.
- Lines 24 to 27 compute the meet of the current principal closed set with each meet-irreducible element and update the new principal closed sets accordingly. This ensures that all new principal closed sets generated by meet operations with meet-irreducible elements are correctly identified and processed.
- Lines 28 to 33 apply the FILTEREDCLOSEBYONE algorithm to enumerate new closed sets generated by join operations with selected join-irreducible elements, and update the successors of meet irreducibles accordingly, and new principal closed sets.
- Line 34 updates the predecessors of the join irreducibles to reflect the new principal closed set and the new closed sets generated by join operations.

3.4 Auxiliary Procedures

The UPDATEMINIMUM and UPDATEMAXIMUM algorithms describe the auxiliary procedures used in the main algorithm to update the minimum and the maximum elements of the lattice and maintain the successors of the meet irreducibles and the predecessors of the join irreducibles.

UPDATENEWPRINCIPALS updates the set of new principal closed sets by merging the newly extracted principal closed set with any existing principal closed set generated by the same element x, whether it belongs to the set of new principal closed sets or to the set of old principal closed sets.

Algorithm 2: UPDATEMINIMUM

Data: C, the new minimum element of the completed family

$\mathsf{Cov}_J(\mathbb{L}) \cup= \{(C, \bot_{\mathbb{L}})\}$

$\bot_{\mathbb{L}} \leftarrow C$

Algorithm 3: UPDATEMAXIMUM

Data: C, the new maximum element of the completed family

$\mathsf{Cov}_M(\mathbb{L}) \cup= \{(\top_{\mathbb{L}}, C)\}$

$\top_{\mathbb{L}} \leftarrow C$

Algorithm 4: UPDATENEWPRINCIPALS

Data:
- x, an element of C,
- C, the new principal closed set generated by x

```
if (x, C') ∉ Prin⁺_L :
    if (x, C') ∈ Prin_L :
        if C' ≰ C : Prin⁺_L ∪= {(x, C ∧ C')}
    else
        Prin⁺_L ∪= {(x, C)}
    end
end
```

UPDATEJOIN and UPDATEMEET algorithms update the predecessors of the join irreducibles and the successors of the meet irreducibles, respectively, to reflect the new principal closed set and the new closed sets generated by join and meet operations.

Algorithm 5: UPDATEJOIN

Data: C, the new principal closed set

```
foreach (j⁻, j) ∈ Cov_J(L) :
    if C < j :
        Cov_J(L) \= {(j⁻, j)}
        j⁻ ← j⁻ ∨ C
        if j⁻ ≠ j : Cov_J(L) ∪= {(j⁻, j)}
    end
end
```

FILTEREDCLOSEBYONE algorithm is a modified version (line 3) of the classical CLOSEBYONE algorithm, adapted to traverse only the newly generated closed sets by join operations with selected join-irreducible elements of the original family.

Algorithm 6: UPDATEMEET

Data: C, the new principal closed set

foreach $(m, m^+) \in \mathrm{Cov}_M(\mathbb{L})$ **:**
  if $C > m$ **:**
    $\mathrm{Cov}_M(\mathbb{L}) \setminus= \{(m, m^+)\}$
    $m^+ \leftarrow m^+ \wedge C$
    if $m \neq m^+$ **:** $\mathrm{Cov}_M(\mathbb{L}) \cup= \{(m, m^+)\}$
  end
end
$m^+ \leftarrow \top_{\mathbb{L}} \wedge \bigwedge \{m \mid (m, m^+) \in \mathrm{Cov}_M(\mathbb{L}), C < m\}$
if $m \neq C$ **:** $\mathrm{Cov}_M(\mathbb{L}) \cup= \{(C, m^+)\}$

Algorithm 7: FILTEREDCLOSEBYONE

Data:
- J, the list of join-irreducible elements to consider for join operations with C,
- Q, the LIFO queue of triples (closed set, set of indices, start) to consider,

while Q **:**
  $C, I, s \leftarrow Q$.pop()
  if $C \notin \{\top_{\mathbb{L}}, \bot_{\mathbb{L}} \vee \bigvee \{j \mid (j^-, j) \in \mathrm{Cov}_J(\mathbb{L}), C \geq j\}\}$ **:**
    yield C
    for $k \in s..|J| - 1$ **do**
      if $k \notin I$ **:**
        $C' \leftarrow C \vee J_k$
        $I' \leftarrow I \cup \{i \mid i \in \complement_{0..|J|-1} I, C' \geq J_i\}$
        if $\forall i \in 0..k-1, i \notin I'$ **or** $i \in I$ **:**
          Q.append$((C', I', s+1))$
        end
      end
    end
  end
end

Example

Table 1 summarizes the execution of the MOOREFAMILYLATTICECOMPLETION algorithm on the example given in Fig. 1a and Fig. 1b, showing the updates of the fundamental elements of the family and the new closed sets generated at each step.

The first rows of the table correspond to the state of the initial sublattice $\mathcal{F}^{\psi,Y}$, given by its fundamental elements, and to the initialization of the set $\mathrm{Prin^+}_{\mathbb{L}}$ of new principal closed sets based on the newly added closed sets a and ac, respectively.

The following rows correspond to the iterations of the main loop of the algorithm, where the columns represent:

Table 1. Execution of the MOOREFAMILYLATTICECOMPLETION algorithm.

(x, C)	$\bot_{\mathbb{L}}$	$\top_{\mathbb{L}}$	$\mathrm{Cov}_J(\mathbb{L})$	$\mathrm{Cov}_M(\mathbb{L})$	$\mathrm{Prin}_{\mathbb{L}}$	$\mathrm{Prin}^{+}_{\mathbb{L}}$	Yielded
	Fundamental elements of the family $\mathcal{F}^{\psi,Y}$						
	d	abde	(d, bd)	(bd, abde)	(b, bd)		
			(d, ad)	(ad, abde)	(d, d)		
					(a, ad)		
					(e, abde)		
	Initialization of $\mathrm{Prin}^{+}_{\mathbb{L}}$						
						(a, a)	
						(c, ac)	
	Main while loop						
(c, ac)	∅	abcde	(d, bd)	(bd, abde)	(b, bd)	(a, a)	∅ (line 16)
			(d, ad)	(abde, abcde)	(d, d)		abcde (line 22)
			(∅, d)	(ac, acd)	(a, ad)		ac (line 32)
			(∅, ac)	(acd, abcde)	(e, abde)		acd (line 32)
					(c, ac)		
(a, a)	∅	abcde	(d, bd)	(bd, abde)	(b, bd)		a (line 32)
			(∅, d)	(abde, abcde)	(d, d)		
			(a, ac)	(ac, acd)	(a, a)		
			(∅, a)	(acd, abcde)	(e, abde)		
					(c, ac)		

- the current element x whose principal closed set C is being processed,
- the current fundamental elements $\bot_{\mathbb{L}}$, $\top_{\mathbb{L}}$, $\mathrm{Cov}_J(\mathbb{L})$, $\mathrm{Cov}_M(\mathbb{L})$ and $\mathrm{Prin}_{\mathbb{L}}$
- the new principal closed sets $\mathrm{Prin}^{+}_{\mathbb{L}}$ to consider in the next iterations of the main loop, and
- the new closed sets generated at each step of the algorithm, which are yielded on the fly.

4 Complexity Analysis

4.1 Memory Complexity

The algorithms have the following memory complexity:

- $O(|X|^2)$ for storing the principal closed sets, since there can be at most $|X|$ principal closed sets and each can contain at most $|X|$ elements.
- $O((2 \cdot |J_{\mathbb{L}}| + 2 \cdot |M_{\mathbb{L}}|) \cdot |X|) = O((|J_{\mathbb{L}}| + |M_{\mathbb{L}}|) \cdot |X|)$ for storing the join and meet irreducible elements and their predecessors/successors,
- $O(2 \cdot |X|) = O(|X|)$ for storing the minimum and maximum elements of the lattice.

Thus, the total memory complexity is

$$O\left(|X|^2 + \left(|J_{\mathbb{L}}| + |M_{\mathbb{L}}|\right) \cdot |X| + |X|\right) = O\left(|X| \cdot (|X| + |J_{\mathbb{L}}| + |M_{\mathbb{L}}|)\right)$$

In the case where we are calculating the completion of a family of attributes in classical formal concept analysis, we have (with M set of attributes and G set of objects):

- $|J_{\mathbb{L}}| \leq m = |M|$ since each join-irreducible element in the intent lattice corresponds to a meet-irreducible element in the concept lattice
- $|M_{\mathbb{L}}| \leq n = |G|$ since each meet-irreducible element in the intent lattice corresponds to a join-irreducible element in the concept lattice
- $|X| = m$

Therefore, the memory complexity of the algorithm in this case is

$$O\left(m \cdot (m + m + n)\right) = O\left(m \cdot (m + n)\right)$$

4.2 Time Complexity

The algorithms have the following time complexity:

UpdateMinimum and UpDateMaximum These procedures have a time complexity of $O(1)$, since they involve updating the minimum or maximum element.

UpdateNewPrincipals This procedure has a time complexity of $O(T_\wedge(|X|))$, where $T_\wedge(|X|)$ is the time complexity of the meet operation $\wedge$ in the global lattice $\langle \mathcal{F}^{\varphi,X}, \vee, \wedge \rangle$.

UpdateJoin and UpdateMeet These procedures have a time complexity of $O(|J_{\mathbb{L}}| \cdot T_\vee(|X|))$ and $O(|M_{\mathbb{L}}| \cdot T_\wedge(|X|))$ respectively. where $T_\vee(|X|)$ and $T_\wedge(|X|)$ are the time complexities of the join and meet operations $\vee$ and $\wedge$ in the global lattice $\langle \mathcal{F}^{\varphi,X}, \vee, \wedge \rangle$.

FilteredCloseByOne The time complexity of the production of one closed set is $O(|J_{\mathbb{L}}| \cdot (T_\vee(|X|) + |J_{\mathbb{L}}| \cdot |X|))$ in the worst case.

So, for each new closed set, the overall time complexity of the **MooreFamilyLatticeCompletion** algorithm is

$$O(|J_{\mathbb{L}}| \cdot T_{\vee}(|X|) + |M_{\mathbb{L}}| \cdot T_{\wedge}(|X|) + |J_{\mathbb{L}}| \cdot (T_{\vee}(|X|) + |J_{\mathbb{L}}| \cdot |X|))$$

which can be simplified to

$$O(|J_{\mathbb{L}}| \cdot T_{\vee}(|X|) + |M_{\mathbb{L}}| \cdot T_{\wedge}(|X|) + |J_{\mathbb{L}}|^2 \cdot |X|)$$

In the case where we are calculating the completion of a family of attributes in classical formal concept analysis with a set of objects G and a set of attributes M:

$$O(m^2 \cdot n + n \cdot m + m^3) = O(m^2 \cdot (m + n))$$

This is the *polynomial delay* time complexity, since the time between the production of two consecutive closed sets is polynomial in the size of the input. This is similar to the complexity of the original CloseByOne algorithm, which is $O(m^2 \cdot n)$

In practice, the constants hidden in these asymptotic bounds strongly depend on the representation of closed sets and on the implementation of meet/join operations. For example, bitset-based encodings typically provide efficient intersections and fast inclusion tests, which can significantly reduce the observed delay per generated closed set. Symmetrically, when joins require expensive closure computations, reducing the number of explored candidates becomes crucial. This is precisely the role of the filtered enumeration stage, which aims to avoid traversing regions that cannot produce new relevant closed sets.

Another practical aspect is memory locality: maintaining only fundamental elements (minimum/maximum, irreducibles with covers, and principal closed sets) avoids storing the entire completed family upfront. This incremental organization is particularly useful in dynamic pipelines, where new closed sets are integrated progressively and intermediate results must be available quickly for downstream FCA tasks.

5 Conclusions and Perspectives

This work introduced an algorithm for minimally completing Moore families while preserving the sublattice structure required for concept construction. Starting from an initial Moore sub-family and a set of newly discovered closed sets, the method updates the fundamental elements of the family (minimum, maximum, meet and join irreducibles, and principal closed sets) and enumerates only the new closed sets generated by the completion. In this way, the approach supports the incremental maintenance of description lattices without recomputing the whole structure from scratch.

Beyond the algorithm itself, the paper provides a structural characterization of these minimal sublattice completions, an illustrative example showing how the different fundamental elements evolve during the completion process, and a complexity analysis. This framework is particularly relevant in dynamic settings where attributes are progressively discovered and where it is important to reuse previously computed descriptions and stored extensions.

More broadly, the proposed completion mechanism strengthens the connection between formal concept analysis and practical knowledge-discovery workflows. It offers a principled way to maintain lattice-based representations in evolving description spaces, while remaining compatible with approaches based on generalized convex hulls and reduced sub-context completion, which combine multiple domains to handle complex concept lattices. The proposed algorithm has been implemented in a GitLab repository[2].

Future work includes:

i. A theoretical proof of the minimality of the produced family.
ii. Comparison of the proposed algorithm with an alternative suggested by a reviewer: first construct the smallest Moore family containing the new closed set, then construct the smallest complete sublattice containing this Moore family.
iii. An experimental time-complexity analysis, with output-sensitive and implementation optimizations.
iv. Integration into incremental formal concept analysis pipelines for dynamic knowledge discovery workflows.
v. Extensions of the framework to richer description spaces and more general update scenarios.

Acknowledgment. This study was funded by the ANR SmartFCA project (grant number ANR-21-CE23-0023).

Disclosure of Interests. The authors have no competing interests to declare that are relevant to the content of this article.

References

1. Birkhoff, G.: Lattice Theory. American Mathematical Society, 3rd edn. (1967)
2. Demko, C., Richard, J., Waffo Kemgne, M., Faucher, C., Bertet, K.: Reduced Sub-context completion in lattices and concept lattices. In: Lecture Notes in Computer Science. LNCS, vol. 15941, pp. 51–66. Springer, Cluj-Napoca, Romania (2025)
3. Ganter, B., Wille, R.: Formal Concept AnalysiâĂŕ: Mathematical Foundations. 2nd edn, Springer (2024)
4. Kuznetsov, S.O.: A fast algorithm for computing all intersections of objects in a finite semi-lattice. Autom. Doc. Math. Linguist. **27**(5), 11–21 (1993)
5. Moore, E.H.: Introduction to a form of general analysis. In: The New Haven Mathematical Colloquium, pp. 1–150. Yale University Press, New Haven, CT (1910)

[2] https://www.thegalactic.org/docs/algebras/closure/latest/.

Co-reflexivity in the Category of Double Boolean Algebras

Gael Tenkeu Kembang[1(✉)], Cyrille Nganteu[1], Leonard Kwuida[2], and Etienne Romuald Temgoua Alomo[3]

[1] Department of Mathematics, University of Yaounde 1, Yaounde, Cameroon
tenkeugael@gmail.com, nganteu2001@Yahoo.fr

[2] School of Business, Bern University of Applied Sciences, Bern, Switzerland
leonard.kwuida@bfh.ch

[3] Department of Mathematics, Ecole Normale Supérieure, University of Yaounde 1, Yaounde, Cameroon
retemgoua@gmail.com

Abstract. The present paper considers the category of double Boolean algebras and shows that the category of Boolean algebras and that of pure double Boolean algebras are co-reflexive subcategories. We also establish some concrete properties of the category of double Boolean algebras, among which certain limits like the equalizer, the product and the pull-back.

Keywords: Double Boolean algebra · Category · Co-reflexive subcategory

1 Introduction

Double Boolean algebras (dBas) were introduced by Rudolf Wille to capture the equational theory of the algebra of protoconcepts, which arises from the need of modeling negation on formal concepts [14]. They are defined by the equations in Definition 1 and therefore form a variety[1]. We denote by $\mathcal{DBA}$ the category of dBas. Pure double Boolean algebras (see Definition 2) form a subclass of double Boolean algebras that mimic the algebras of semi-concepts. Although pure double Boolean algebras do not form a subvariety of dBas (see Remark 3), they form a subcategory of the category of dBas denoted by $\mathcal{PDBA}$. Additional subclasses considered are the varieties of Boolean algebras denoted $\mathcal{BA}$ and of trivial double Boolean algebras (see Definition 2) denoted $\mathcal{TDBA}$. Their intersection is a singleton. Several papers are devoted to the study of the variety of dBas [6,9,11–13]. From this standpoint, all the subclasses mentioned above are completely different. Given a category $\mathcal{C}$ and a subcategory $\mathcal{D}$ of $\mathcal{C}$, the (co-)reflexivity of $\mathcal{D}$ in $\mathcal{C}$ allows replacing objects of $\mathcal{C}$ with those of $\mathcal{D}$ while

[1] In [10] the authors proposed a small and non redundant subset of equations defining double Boolean algebras.

M. Croitoru et al. (Eds.): CONCEPTS 2026, LNAI 16811, pp. 55–70, 2027.
https://doi.org/10.1007/978-3-032-34742-8_4

preserving certain structural properties. In [3], M. Erné conducted a study of the category of contexts and obtained that the category of complete lattices is a reflective subcategory of the category of contexts.

Our goal is to investigate the category of double Boolean algebras (resp. protoconcept algebras), including some of its prominent subcategories. A long term objective is the coalgebraic study of these categories as done in [8] for the category of BL-algebras. Our preliminary results included in this paper include

- the description of the initial and the terminal object, the equalizer, the product and the pullback in $\mathcal{DBA}$,
- the isomorphism between $\mathcal{BA}$ and some subcategories of $\mathcal{TDBA}$,
- the co-reflexivity of the categories $\mathcal{BA}$ and $\mathcal{PDBA}$ in $\mathcal{DBA}$,
- the co-reflexivity of the categories $\mathcal{CABA}$ of complete atomic Boolean algebras and $\mathcal{SCA}$ of semi-concept algebras in the category $\mathcal{PCA}$ of protoconcept algebras.

The rest of the paper is organized as follows: in Sect. 2, we recall some notions from double Boolean algebras and category theory, and use them to present our results in Sect. 3. The last section concludes the paper and gives some perspectives for future work.

2 Preliminaries

In this section, we recall some basic notions from double Boolean algebras and category theory useful to understand our contribution. We begin with the basic definitions and useful properties of double Boolean algebras.

Definition 1 ([14]) *An algebra* $\underline{D} := (D; \sqcap, \sqcup, \neg, \lrcorner, \bot, \top)$ *of type* $(2,2,1,1,0,0)$ *is called* ***double Boolean algebra (dBa)*** *if the following axioms are satisfied:*

$(1a)$ $(x \sqcap x) \sqcap y = x \sqcap y$	$(1b)$ $(x \sqcup x) \sqcup y = x \sqcup y$
$(2a)$ $x \sqcap y = y \sqcap x$	$(2b)$ $x \sqcup y = y \sqcup x$
$(3a)$ $x \sqcap (y \sqcap z) = (x \sqcap y) \sqcap z$	$(3b)$ $x \sqcup (y \sqcup z) = (x \sqcup y) \sqcup z$
$(4a)$ $x \sqcap (x \sqcup y) = x \sqcap x$	$(4b)$ $x \sqcup (x \sqcap y) = x \sqcup x$
$(5a)$ $x \sqcap (x \vee y) = x \sqcap x$	$(5b)$ $x \sqcup (x \wedge y) = x \sqcup x$
$(6a)$ $x \sqcap (y \vee z) = (x \sqcap y) \vee (x \sqcap z)$	$(6b)$ $x \sqcup (y \wedge z) = (x \sqcup y) \wedge (x \sqcup z)$
$(7a)$ $\neg\neg(x \sqcap y) = x \sqcap y$	$(7b)$ $\lrcorner\lrcorner(x \sqcup y) = x \sqcup y$
$(8a)$ $\neg(x \sqcap x) = \neg x$	$(8b)$ $\lrcorner(x \sqcup x) = \lrcorner x$
$(9a)$ $x \sqcap \neg x = \bot$	$(9b)$ $x \sqcup \lrcorner x = \top$
$(10a)$ $\neg\bot = \top \sqcap \top$	$(10b)$ $\lrcorner\top = \bot \sqcup \bot$
$(11a)$ $\neg\top = \bot$	$(11b)$ $\lrcorner\bot = \top$

$$(12)\ (x \sqcap x) \sqcup (x \sqcap x) = (x \sqcup x) \sqcap (x \sqcup x),$$

where $x \vee y := \neg(\neg x \sqcap \neg y)$ *and* $x \wedge y := \lrcorner(\lrcorner x \sqcup \lrcorner y)$.

On a dBa $\underline{D}$, a quasi-order relation $\sqsubseteq$ is defined as follows:

$$x \sqsubseteq y \text{ if and only if } (x \sqcap y = x \sqcap x \text{ and } x \sqcup y = y \sqcup y).$$

Let $\underline{D}$ be a dBa. We set $D_\sqcap := \{x \in D \mid x \sqcap x = x\}$, $D_\sqcup := \{x \in D \mid x \sqcup x = x\}$ and $D_p := D_\sqcap \cup D_\sqcup$.

Definition 2 ([7,14]) *A dBa $\underline{D}$ is called :*

1. ***Pure*** *if for all $x \in D$, either $x \sqcap x = x$ or $x \sqcup x = x$.*
2. ***Trivial*** *if $\top \sqcap \top = \bot \sqcup \bot$.*
3. ***Regular (or contextual)*** *if $\sqsubseteq$ is a partial order.*
4. ***Fully contextual*** *if it is contextual and for all $y \in D_\sqcap$ and $x \in D_\sqcup$ with $y \sqcup y = x \sqcap x$, there is a unique $z \in D$ with $z \sqcap z = y$ and $z \sqcup z = x$.*

Proposition 1. ([14, **Theorem 1, p. 6**])

1. *The algebra $\underline{D}_\sqcap := (D_\sqcap; \sqcap, \vee, \neg, \bot, \neg\bot)$ is a Boolean algebra whose order relation is the restriction of $\sqsubseteq$ to $\underline{D}_\sqcap$.*
2. *The algebra $\underline{D}_\sqcup := (D_\sqcup; \wedge, \sqcup, \lrcorner, \lrcorner\top, \top)$ is a Boolean algebra whose order relation is the restriction of $\sqsubseteq$ to $\underline{D}_\sqcup$.*
3. *The algebra $\underline{D}_p := (D_p; \sqcap, \sqcup, \neg, \lrcorner, \bot, \top)$ is the largest pure sub-algebra of $\underline{D}$.*

Example 1. 1. Let $(B; \wedge, \vee, ', 0, 1)$ be a Boolean algebra. Then the algebra $\underline{B} := (B; \wedge, \vee, ', ', 0, 1)$ is a pure double Boolean algebra.

2. **Algebra of protoconcepts**: Let $\mathbb{K} := (G, M, I)$ be a triple of sets with $I \subseteq G \times M$. For $A \subseteq G$ and $B \subseteq M$, define

$$A' := \{m \in M \mid (a, m) \in I, \forall a \in A\} \text{ and } B' := \{g \in G \mid (g, b) \in I, \forall b \in B\}.$$

A **protoconcept** of $\mathbb{K}$ is a pair (A, B) such that $A'' = B'$. Logical operations are defined on the set $\mathfrak{P}(\mathbb{K})$ of protoconcepts of $\mathbb{K}$ as follows:

$$\begin{aligned}
\textbf{meet}: (A,B) \sqcap (C,D) &:= (A \cap C, (A \cap C)'),\\
\textbf{join}: (A,B) \sqcup (C,D) &:= ((B \cap D)', B \cap D),\\
\textbf{negation}: \quad \neg(A,B) &:= (G \setminus A, (G \setminus A)'),\\
\textbf{opposition}: \quad \lrcorner(A,B) &:= ((M \setminus B)', M \setminus B),\\
\textbf{nothing}: \quad \bot &:= (\emptyset, M),\\
\textbf{all}: \quad \top &:= (G, \emptyset).
\end{aligned}$$

Then $\underline{\mathfrak{P}}(\mathbb{K}) := \big(\mathfrak{P}(\mathbb{K}); \sqcap, \sqcup, \neg, \lrcorner, \bot, \top\big)$ is a fully contextual double Boolean algebra. $\underline{\mathfrak{P}}(\mathbb{K})_\sqcap$ (resp. $\underline{\mathfrak{P}}(\mathbb{K})_\sqcup$) is isomorphic (resp. dual isomorphic) to the powerset algebra of G (resp. M). We set $\mathfrak{H}(\mathbb{K}) := \mathfrak{P}(\mathbb{K})_\sqcap \cup \mathfrak{P}(\mathbb{K})_\sqcup$. The algebra $\underline{\mathfrak{H}}(\mathbb{K}) := \big(\mathfrak{H}(\mathbb{K}); \sqcap, \sqcup, \neg, \lrcorner, \bot, \top\big)$ is the largest pure sub-algebra of $\underline{\mathfrak{P}}(\mathbb{K})$ and is called the **algebra of semi-concepts** of $\mathbb{K}$.

3. The algebra $\underline{D}_6 := (\{\bot, a, b, c, d, \top\}; \sqcap, \sqcup, \neg, \lrcorner, \bot, \top)$ where $D_{6_\sqcap} = \{\bot, a, b, c\}$ and $D_{6_\sqcup} = \{a, c, d, \top\}$ is a pure and regular dBa which is not trivial with the Hasse diagram and the Cayley tables given in Fig. 1.

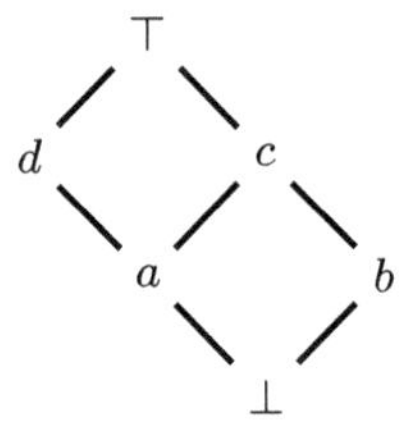

$\sqcap$	$\bot$	a	b	c	d	$\top$
$\bot$	$\bot$	$\bot$	$\bot$	$\bot$	$\bot$	$\bot$
a	$\bot$	a	$\bot$	a	a	a
b	$\bot$	$\bot$	b	b	$\bot$	b
c	$\bot$	a	b	c	a	c
d	$\bot$	a	$\bot$	a	a	a
$\top$	$\bot$	a	b	c	a	c

$\sqcup$	$\bot$	a	b	c	d	$\top$
$\bot$	a	a	c	c	d	$\top$
a	a	a	c	c	d	$\top$
b	c	c	c	c	$\top$	$\top$
c	c	c	c	c	$\top$	$\top$
d	d	d	$\top$	$\top$	d	$\top$
$\top$	$\top$	$\top$	$\top$	$\top$	$\top$	$\top$

x	$\neg x$	$\lrcorner x$
$\bot$	c	$\top$
a	b	$\top$
b	a	d
c	$\bot$	d
d	b	c
$\top$	$\bot$	a

Fig. 1. $\underline{D}_6$ and its Cayley tables.

Definition 3. *A map $f : \underline{D} \to \underline{E}$ between two dBas is a* ***homomorphism*** *if $f(\bot) = \bot$, $f(\top) = \top$ and for all $a, b \in D$, $f(a \sqcap b) = f(a) \sqcap f(b)$, $f(a \sqcup b) = f(a) \sqcup f(b)$, $f(\neg a) = \neg f(a)$ and $f(\lrcorner a) = \lrcorner f(a)$.*

Remark 1. If $f : \underline{D} \to \underline{E}$ is a homomorphism between two dBas $\underline{D}$ and $\underline{E}$, then $f(\bot \sqcup \bot) = \bot \sqcup \bot$, $f(\neg(\bot \sqcup \bot)) = \neg(\bot \sqcup \bot)$, $f(\top \sqcap \top) = \top \sqcap \top$, $f(\lrcorner(\top \sqcap \top)) = \lrcorner(\top \sqcap \top)$.

The following proposition is a useful characterization of homomorphisms of dBas.

Proposition 2. (**[12, Theorem 4.2]**) *Let $\underline{D}$ and $\underline{E}$ be two dBas and let $f : D \to E$ be a map. The following properties are equivalent:*

1. *f is a dBa homomorphism.*
2. *There exist $f_1 : D_\sqcap \to E_\sqcap$ and $f_2 : D_\sqcup \to E_\sqcup$ Boolean algebra homomorphisms and $f_3 : D \backslash D_p \to E$ a map such that*
$$f(x) = \begin{cases} f_1(x) \text{ if } x \in D_\sqcap, \\ f_2(x) \text{ if } x \in D_\sqcup, \\ f_3(x) \text{ if } x \in D \backslash D_p. \end{cases} \quad (\dagger)$$
and for all $x \in D$,
$$\begin{cases} x \in D_\sqcup \quad \Rightarrow \; f_1(x \sqcap x) = f_2(x) \sqcap f_2(x), \\ x \in D_\sqcap \quad \Rightarrow \; f_2(x \sqcup x) = f_1(x) \sqcup f_1(x), \\ x \in D \backslash D_p \Rightarrow \begin{cases} f_1(x \sqcap x) = f_3(x) \sqcap f_3(x), \\ f_2(x \sqcup x) = f_3(x) \sqcup f_3(x). \end{cases} \end{cases} \quad (\ddagger)$$

Now we recall some notions from category theory that can be found in [2].

Definition 4. *A* ***category*** *$\mathcal{C}$ consists of the following three entities:*

(i) a class $ob(\mathcal{C})$, whose elements are called objects;
(ii) a class $hom(\mathcal{C})$, whose elements are called morphisms. Each morphism f has a source object X and a target object Y. The expression $f : X \to Y$ would be verbally stated as "f is a morphism from X to Y". The expression $hom_{\mathcal{C}}(X, Y)$ denotes the hom-class of all morphisms from X to Y;

(iii) a binary operation $\circ$*, called composition of morphisms, such that for any three objects* X*,* Y *and* Z*, we have*

$$\circ\colon hom_{\mathcal{C}}(Y,Z) \times hom_{\mathcal{C}}(X,Y) \to hom_{\mathcal{C}}(X,Z)$$

governed by two axioms:

- *associativity: If* $f\colon X \to Y$*,* $g\colon Y \to Z$ *and* $h\colon Z \to T$*, then*

$$h \circ (g \circ f) = (h \circ g) \circ f;$$

- *identity: For every object* X*, there exists a morphism* $id_X : X \to X$*, called the identity morphism for* X*, such that for every morphism* $f\colon X \to Y$*, we have*

$$id_Y \circ f = f \circ id_X.$$

The **opposite category** $\mathcal{C}^{op}$ of a given category $\mathcal{C}$ is formed by reversing the morphisms, i.e., interchanging the source and the target of each morphism.

Definition 5. *A category* $\mathcal{D}$ *is said to be a* ***subcategory*** *of a category* $\mathcal{C}$ *provided that the following conditions are satisfied:*

(i) $Ob(\mathcal{D}) \subseteq Ob(\mathcal{C})$*,*
(ii) for each $X, Y \in Ob(\mathcal{D})$*,* $hom_{\mathcal{D}}(X,Y) \subseteq hom_{\mathcal{C}}(X,Y)$*,*
(iii) for each $\mathcal{D}$*-object* X*, the* $\mathcal{C}$*-identity on* X *is the* $\mathcal{D}$*-identity on* X*,*
(iv) the composition law in $\mathcal{D}$ *is the restriction of the composition law in* $\mathcal{C}$ *to the morphisms of* $\mathcal{D}$*.*

A subcategory $\mathcal{D}$ *of a category* $\mathcal{C}$ *is called a* ***full subcategory*** *if, for each* $X, Y \in Ob(\mathcal{D})$*,* $hom_{\mathcal{D}}(X,Y) = hom_{\mathcal{C}}(X,Y)$*.*

Definition 6. *Let* $\mathcal{C}$ *and* $\mathcal{D}$ *be two categories. A* ***(covariant) functor*** F *from* $\mathcal{C}$ *to* $\mathcal{D}$ *is a mapping that associates each object* X *in* $\mathcal{C}$ *to an object* $F(X)$ *in* $\mathcal{D}$ *and each morphism* $f\colon X \to Y$ *in* $\mathcal{C}$ *to a morphism* $F(f)\colon F(X) \to F(Y)$ *in* $\mathcal{D}$ *such that:*

(i) $F(id_X) = id_{F(X)}$ *for every object* X *in* $\mathcal{C}$*,*
(ii) $F(g \circ f) = F(g) \circ F(f)$ *for all morphisms* $X \xrightarrow{f} Y \xrightarrow{g} Z$ *in* $\mathcal{C}$*.*

A ***contravariant functor*** *from* $\mathcal{C}$ *to* $\mathcal{D}$ *is a functor from* $\mathcal{C}$ *to* $\mathcal{D}^{op}$*.*

We will denote by $\mathcal{SET}$ the category whose objects are sets and whose morphisms are maps.

The following example presents three particular functors that will help us in the presentation of our results (Theorem 2 and Theorem 3).

Example 2. Let $\mathcal{C}$ be a category.

1. There is the **identity functor** $id_{\mathcal{C}}\colon \mathcal{C} \to \mathcal{C}$ defined by: for each $f\colon Y \to Z$ morphism in $\mathcal{C}$, $id_{\mathcal{C}}(f) = f$.

2. For any $\mathcal{C}$-object X, there is the **covariant hom-functor** $hom_{\mathcal{C}}(X,-)\colon \mathcal{C} \to \mathcal{SET}$ defined by: for each $f\colon Y \to Z$ morphism in $\mathcal{C}$,

$$hom_{\mathcal{C}}(X,f)\colon hom_{\mathcal{C}}(X,Y) \to hom_{\mathcal{C}}(X,Z), g \mapsto f \circ g.$$

3. For any $\mathcal{C}$-object X, there is the **contravariant hom-functor** $hom_{\mathcal{C}}(-,X)\colon \mathcal{C} \to \mathcal{SET}$ defined by: for each $f\colon Y \to Z$ morphism in $\mathcal{C}$,

$$hom_{\mathcal{C}}(f,X)\colon hom_{\mathcal{C}}(Z,X) \to hom_{\mathcal{C}}(Y,X), g \mapsto g \circ f.$$

Definition 7. *Two categories $\mathcal{C}$ and $\mathcal{D}$ are* ***isomorphic*** *if there exist a functor $F : \mathcal{C} \to \mathcal{D}$ and a functor $G : \mathcal{D} \to \mathcal{C}$, such that $F \circ G = id_{\mathcal{D}}$ and $G \circ F = id_{\mathcal{C}}$.*

Definition 8. *Let $F : \mathcal{C} \to \mathcal{D}$ be a functor between two categories.*

(i) F is ***faithful*** *if for all $X, Y \in ob(\mathcal{C})$, the map $F_{X,Y} : Hom_{\mathcal{C}}(X,Y) \to Hom_{\mathcal{D}}(F(X), F(Y))$, $f \mapsto F_{X,Y}(f) = F(f)$ is one-to-one.*
(ii) F is ***conservative*** *if for any morphism f in $\mathcal{C}$, if $F(f)$ is an isomorphism in $\mathcal{D}$, then f is an isomorphism.*

The class of double Boolean algebras equipped with the class of homomorphisms of dBas forms a category which will be denoted by $\mathcal{DBA}$.

Sometimes in the rest of the work, we will denote a double Boolean algebra $\underline{D}$ simply by its underlying set D.

3 The Category $\mathcal{DBA}$

3.1 Some Properties of $\mathcal{DBA}$

In this subsection, we describe some special objects of the category $\mathcal{DBA}$, such as the initial and the terminal object. We also determine certain limits, such as the equalizer, the product, and the pullback. We end with some properties of the concrete category of double Boolean algebras.

Note that the results of this subsection are consistent with those known in the literature for categories of varieties in universal algebras.

Definition 9. *Let $\mathcal{C}$ be a category.*

1. *An object I in $\mathcal{C}$ is called* ***initial*** *if for every object X in $\mathcal{C}$, there exists exactly one morphism $f : I \to X$.*
2. *An object T in $\mathcal{C}$ is called* ***terminal*** *if for every object X in $\mathcal{C}$, there exists exactly one morphism $g : X \to T$.*

Notice that for the dBa $\underline{D}_6$ in Example 1, we have $a = \bot \sqcup \bot$, $c = \top \sqcap \top$, $b = \neg(\bot \sqcup \bot)$ and $d = \lrcorner(\top \sqcap \top)$. We denote by $\underline{\bot}$ the one-element double Boolean algebra on the set $\{\bot\}$.

Proposition 3. *The category $\mathcal{DBA}$ has an initial object which is the dBa $\underline{D}_6$ and a terminal object which is the dBa $\underline{\perp}$.*

Proof. Let $\underline{D}$ be a dBa. Let the correspondence $f\colon D_6 \to D$ defined as follows: $f(\perp) = \perp$, $f(a) = \perp \sqcup \perp$, $f(b) = \neg(\perp \sqcup \perp)$, $f(c) = \top \sqcap \top$, $f(d) = \lrcorner(\top \sqcap \top)$ and $f(\top) = \top$. Then $f(x) = \begin{cases} f_1(x) \text{ if } x \in D_{6_\sqcap} \\ f_2(x) \text{ if } x \in D_{6_\sqcup} \end{cases}$ where $f_1\colon D_{6_\sqcap} \to D_\sqcap$ with $f_1(\perp) = \perp$, $f_1(a) = \perp \sqcup \perp$, $f_1(b) = \neg(\perp \sqcup \perp)$, $f_1(c) = \top \sqcap \top$ and $f_2\colon D_{6_\sqcup} \to D$ with $f_2(a) = \perp \sqcup \perp$, $f_2(c) = \top \sqcap \top$, $f_2(d) = \lrcorner(\top \sqcap \top)$, $f_2(\top) = \top$. The maps f_1 and f_2 are Boolean algebra homomorphisms and it is easy to verify that: for all $x \in D_6$, $\begin{cases} x \in D_{6_\sqcup} \Rightarrow f_1(x \sqcap x) = f_2(x) \sqcap f_2(x) \\ x \in D_{6_\sqcap} \Rightarrow f_2(x \sqcup x) = f_1(x) \sqcup f_1(x) \end{cases}$, hence by Proposition 2 f is a dBa homomorphism. Let's show that f is unique. Let $g\colon D_6 \to D$ be another homomorphism of dBas. Then $g(\perp) = \perp = f(\perp)$, $g(a) = g(\perp \sqcup \perp) = \perp \sqcup \perp = f(a)$, $g(b) = g(\neg(\perp \sqcup \perp)) = \neg(\perp \sqcup \perp) = f(b)$, $g(c) = g(\top \sqcap \top) = \top \sqcap \top = f(c)$, $g(d) = g(\lrcorner(\top \sqcap \top)) = \lrcorner(\top \sqcap \top) = f(d)$ and $g(\top) = \top = f(\top)$. Therefore $f = g$. Hence f is the unique homomorphism of dBas from $\underline{D}_6$ to $\underline{D}$. We conclude that the category $\mathcal{DBA}$ has an initial object which is the dBa $\underline{D}_6$. Let $\underline{D}$ be a dBa. Then the unique dBa-homomorphism from $\underline{D}$ to $\underline{\perp}$ is the constant homomorphism. We conclude that the category $\mathcal{DBA}$ has a terminal object which is the dBa $\underline{\perp}$. ∎

Definition 10. *Let $\mathcal{C}$ be a category. Let $f : X \to Y$ and $g : X \to Y$ be two morphisms in $\mathcal{C}$. The* ***equalizer*** *of the pair (f, g) consists of an object E and a morphism $e : E \to X$ satisfying $f \circ e = g \circ e$, and such that, given any object O of $\mathcal{C}$ and morphism $m : O \to X$, if $f \circ m = g \circ m$, then there exists a unique morphism $u : O \to E$ such that $e \circ u = m$.*

Definition 11. *Let $\mathcal{C}$ be a category. Let $(X_i)_{i \in I}$ be a family of $\mathcal{C}$-objects. The* ***product*** *of the family $(X_i)_{i \in I}$ is an object X of $\mathcal{C}$ equipped with morphisms $\pi_i : X \to X_i$ in $\mathcal{C}$, such that for every $\mathcal{C}$-object Y and every I-indexed family of morphisms $f_i : Y \to X_i$ in $\mathcal{C}$, there exists a unique morphism $f : Y \to X$ in $\mathcal{C}$, such that for all $i \in I$, $f_i = \pi_i \circ f$.*

Definition 12. *Let $\mathcal{C}$ be a category. Let $X \xrightarrow{f} Z \xleftarrow{g} Y$ be two morphisms in $\mathcal{C}$. The* ***pullback*** *of f and g is an object P of $\mathcal{C}$ and two morphisms $p_1 : P \to X$ and $p_2 : P \to Y$ satisfying $f \circ p_1 = g \circ p_2$, and such that for every $\mathcal{C}$-object Q, and two morphisms $q_1 : Q \to X$ and $q_2 : Q \to Y$, if $f \circ q_1 = g \circ q_2$, then there exists a unique morphism $u : Q \to P$ in $\mathcal{C}$, such that $p_1 \circ u = q_1$ and $p_2 \circ u = q_2$.*

Proposition 4. *In the category $\mathcal{DBA}$,*

1. *the equalizer of the dBa-homomorphisms $D_1 \xrightarrow{f} D_2$ and $D_1 \xrightarrow{g} D_2$ is the embedding $E \xrightarrow{e} D_1$, where $E = \{x \in D_1 \mid f(x) = g(x)\}$,*
2. *the product of a family $(D_i)_I$ of dBas is the source $(P, P \xrightarrow{p_i} D_i)_I$ where*

$$P = \{I \xrightarrow{f} \cup_{i \in I} D_i \mid f(i) \in D_i \text{ for all } i \in I\}$$

and $P \xrightarrow{p_i} D_i$ is defined by $p_i(f) = f(i)$ for all $i \in I$,

3. *the pulback of the dBa-homomorphisms* $D_1 \xrightarrow{f} D \xleftarrow{g} D_2$ *is the triple* $(Pb(f,g), \pi_1, \pi_2)$ *where* $Pb(f,g) = \{(x,y) \in D_1 \times D_2 \mid f(x) = g(y)\}$ *and* π_i *is the projection on* D_i.

Proof. The proof is obtained by using standard computations as in [4]. ■

Definition 13. *Given a category* $\mathcal{X}$, *a* ***concrete category*** *over* $\mathcal{X}$ *is a pair* $(\mathcal{C}, U)$, *where* $U : \mathcal{C} \to \mathcal{X}$ *is a faithful functor. Sometimes,* U *is called the* ***forgetful (or underlying) functor*** *of the concrete category and* $\mathcal{X}$ *is called the* ***base category*** *of* $(\mathcal{C}, U)$.

Let $(\mathcal{C}, U)$ be a concrete category over $\mathcal{X}$. The **fibre** of an $\mathcal{X}$-object X is the preordered class consisting of all $\mathcal{C}$-objects A with $U(A) = X$ ordered by:

$$A \preceq B \Longleftrightarrow id_X : U(A) \to U(B) \text{ is (can be lifted to) a } \mathcal{C}\text{-morphism.}$$

Definition 14. *A concrete category* $(\mathcal{C}, U)$ *over* $\mathcal{X}$ *is said to be :*

(i) ***fibre-discrete*** *provided that its fibres are ordered by equality.*
(ii) ***(uniquely) transportable*** *provided that for every* $\mathcal{C}$*-object* A *and every* $\mathcal{X}$*-isomorphism* $U(A) \xrightarrow{f} X$, *there exists a (unique)* $\mathcal{C}$*-object* B *with* $U(B) = X$ *such that* $A \xrightarrow{f} B$ *is a* $\mathcal{C}$*-isomorphism.*

Remark 2. Let $(\mathcal{C}, U)$ be a concrete category over a category $\mathcal{X}$. A *lifting* of an $\mathcal{X}$-morphism $X \xrightarrow{f} Y$, whenever it exists, which will be denoted by $\overline{f}$ is a $\mathcal{C}$-morphism such that $U(\bar{f}) = f$. By the faithfulness of U, we have :

(i) the lifting $\overline{f}$ of an $\mathcal{X}$-morphism $U(A) \xrightarrow{f} U(B)$ is unique and $\overline{f}$ coincide with f in $U(A)$ if $\mathcal{X} = \mathcal{SET}$.
(ii) for any $\mathcal{X}$-morphisms $X \xrightarrow{g} Y \xrightarrow{f} Z$, $\overline{f \circ g} = \overline{f} \circ \overline{g}$, whenever $\overline{f}$ and $\overline{g}$ exist.

We consider the concrete category $(\mathcal{DBA}, U)$ over $\mathcal{SET}$, where U is the standard forgetful functor.

Theorem 1. *The concrete category* $(\mathcal{DBA}, U)$ *is fibre-discrete and uniquely transportable.*

Proof. Let X be a set and $\underline{D} := (X; \sqcap, \sqcup, \neg, \lrcorner, \bot, \top)$, $\underline{D'} := (X; \sqcap', \sqcup', \neg', \lrcorner', \bot', \top')$ be two dBas in the fibre of X. We assume that $\underline{D} \preceq \underline{D'}$. For $x, y \in X$, $x \propto y, \nabla x \in X$, where $\propto \in \{\sqcap, \sqcup\}$, $\nabla \in \{\neg, \lrcorner\}$ because $\underline{D}$ is a dBa. Thus by Remark 2 (i),

$$x \propto y = \overline{id_X}(x \propto y) \text{ and } \nabla x = \overline{id_X}(\nabla x).$$

Using the fact that $\overline{id_X}$ is a dBa-homomorphism, we obtain:

$$x \propto y = \overline{id_X}(x) \propto' \overline{id_X}(y) = x \propto' y \text{ and } \nabla x = \nabla' \overline{id_X}(x) = \nabla' x$$

where $\propto' \in \{\sqcap', \sqcup'\}$, $\nabla' \in \{\neg', \lrcorner'\}$. Hence $\underline{D} = \underline{D'}$. Conversely, if $\underline{D} = \underline{D'}$, then obviously $id_D = \overline{id_X}$. We conclude that $(\mathcal{DBA}, U)$ is fibre-discrete.

Now we show that $(\mathcal{DBA}, U)$ is uniquely transportable. Let $(D; \sqcap, \sqcup, \neg, \lrcorner, \bot, \top)$ be a dBa, X be a set and $D \xrightarrow{f} X$ be a bijective function. For $y_1, y_2 \in X$, define for $\propto' \in \{\sqcap', \sqcup'\}$, $\triangledown' \in \{\neg', \lrcorner'\}$,

$$y_1 \propto' y_2 = f(x_1 \propto x_2) \text{ and } \triangledown' y_1 = f(\triangledown x_1)$$

with $\propto \in \{\sqcap, \sqcup\}$, $\triangledown \in \{\neg, \lrcorner\}$, where $y_1 = f(x_1)$ and $y_2 = f(x_2)$. Then $D' := (X; \sqcap', \sqcup', \neg', \lrcorner', f(\bot), f(\top))$ is the unique dBa in the fibre of X such that $D \xrightarrow{f} D'$ is a dBa-isomorphism. Which proves that $(\mathcal{DBA}, U)$ is uniquely transportable. ■

3.2 Some Special Subcategories of $\mathcal{DBA}$

Two main results are stated in this subsection: the first shows that the category of Boolean algebras is isomorphic to two subcategories of the category of pure and trivial dBas. The second result shows that the category of Boolean algebras and that of pure dBas are co-reflexive subcategories of the category of dBas.

Remark 3. The class of pure double Boolean algebras doesn't form a subvariety of the variety of double Boolean algebras. In fact, we consider the dBas $\underline{D}_{2,I}$ and $\underline{D}_{2,II}$ defined by the tables of Table 1 and Table 2 respectively.

Table 1. Operations $\sqcap$, $\sqcup$, $\neg$ and $\lrcorner$ of $\underline{D}_{2,I}$.

$\sqcap$	$\bot$	$\top$
$\bot$	$\bot$	$\bot$
$\top$	$\bot$	$\top$

$\sqcup$	$\bot$	$\top$
$\bot$	$\top$	$\top$
$\top$	$\top$	$\top$

x	$\bot$	$\top$
$\neg x$	$\top$	$\bot$
$\lrcorner x$	$\top$	$\top$

Table 2. Operations $\sqcap$, $\sqcup$, $\neg$ and $\lrcorner$ of $\underline{D}_{2,II}$.

$\sqcap$	$\bot$	$\top$
$\bot$	$\bot$	$\bot$
$\top$	$\bot$	$\bot$

$\sqcup$	$\bot$	$\top$
$\bot$	$\bot$	$\top$
$\top$	$\top$	$\top$

x	$\bot$	$\top$
$\neg x$	$\bot$	$\bot$
$\lrcorner x$	$\top$	$\bot$

These dBas are pure but, the product dBa $\underline{D}_{2,I} \times \underline{D}_{2,II}$ is not pure since $(\top, \bot) \in D_{2,I} \times D_{2,II}$, but $(\bot, \top) \sqcap (\bot, \top) = (\bot \sqcap \bot, \top \sqcap \top) = (\bot, \bot) \neq (\bot, \top)$ and $(\bot, \top) \sqcup (\bot, \top) = (\bot \sqcup \bot, \top \sqcup \top) = (\top, \top) \neq (\bot, \top)$.

Definition 15. *We say that a dBa $\underline{D}$ is of **type I or II** if $D_{\sqcup} = \{\top\}$ or $D_{\sqcap} = \{\bot\}$, respectively.*

Example 3. The dBas $\underline{D}_{2,I}$ and $\underline{D}_{2,II}$ of Remark 3 are of type I and type II respectively.

Remark 4. Any double Boolean algebra of type I or II is a trivial double Boolean algebra.

The **ordinal sum** of two disjoint posets $(P; \leq_P)$ and $(Q; \leq_Q)$ is the poset $(P \cup Q; \leq)$ with $\leq := \leq_P \cup \leq_Q \cup P \times Q$. We denote it by $P \oplus Q$. If $(P; \leq_P)$ has a greatest element, say 1_P, and $(Q; \leq_Q)$ has a least element, say 0_Q, then the **glued sum** is obtained by identifying 1_P and 0_Q. We will denote the glued sum of $(P; \leq_p, 1_P)$ and $(Q; \leq_Q, 0_Q)$ by $P\dot{\oplus}Q$ (see [5]). In [6], the notion of glued sum was used to characterize pure and trivial dBas as follows:

Proposition 5. **([6, Theorem 3.5])** *A double Boolean algebra is pure and trivial if and only if it is a glued sum of two Boolean algebras.*

In the particular case of double Boolean algebras of type I or II, we have the following corollary:

Corollary 1. *Pure double Boolean algebras of type I (resp. type II) are exactly of the form* $\underline{B}\dot{\oplus}\underline{1_B}$ *(resp.* $\underline{0_B}\dot{\oplus}\underline{B}$*), where* $\underline{B}$ *is a Boolean algebra and* $\underline{1_B}$ *(resp.* $\underline{0_B}$*) is the one-element Boolean algebra on the set* $\{1_B\}$ *(resp.* $\{0_B\}$*).*

The double Boolean algebras in Proposition 5 and Corollary 1 arise from some exotic contexts as algebras of semi-concepts. These are the contexts $\mathbb{K}_1, \cdots, \mathbb{K}_5$ below with the corresponding algebra of semi-concept sketched on Fig. 2, from left to right, respectively, with the ellipses representing Boolean algebras. The last two are dBas of type I and II. They are all examples of trivial and pure double Boolean algebras.

$\mathbb{K}_1$	M
G	×

$\mathbb{K}_2$	m
G	×

$\mathbb{K}_3$	M
g	×

$\mathbb{K}_4$	$\emptyset$
G	·

$\mathbb{K}_5$	M
$\emptyset$	·

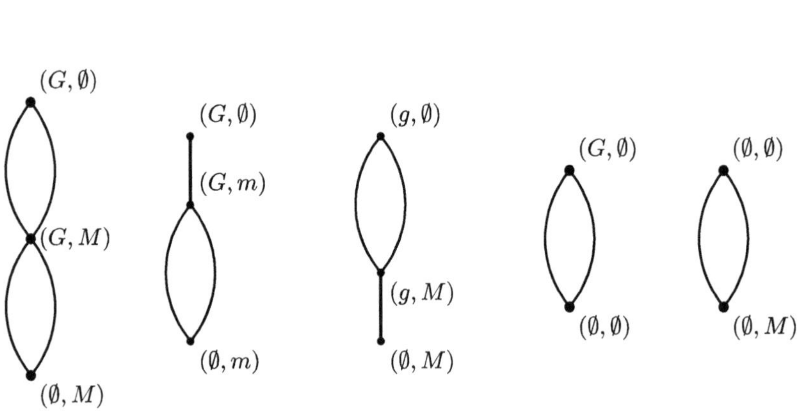

Fig. 2. Some algebras of semi-concept.

Let $\mathcal{BA}$ be the category of Boolean algebras, which has Boolean algebras as objects and Boolean algebra homomorphisms as morphisms.

Let $\mathcal{PDBA}$ be the category of pure double Boolean algebras, which has pure double Boolean algebras as objects and double Boolean algebra homomorphisms as morphisms.

Let $\mathcal{PDBA}I$ (resp. $\mathcal{PDBA}II$) be the category of pure double Boolean algebras of type I (resp. type II), which has pure double Boolean algebras of type I (resp. type II) as objects and double Boolean algebra homomorphisms as morphisms.

The morphisms in $\mathcal{BA}$, $\mathcal{PDBA}I$ (resp. $\mathcal{PDBA}II$) and $\mathcal{PDBA}$ are exactly dBa homomorphisms, thus $\mathcal{BA}$, $\mathcal{PDBA}I$ (resp. $\mathcal{PDBA}II$) and $\mathcal{PDBA}$ are full subcategory of $\mathcal{DBA}$.

Theorem 2. *The category $\mathcal{PDBA}I$ and $\mathcal{PDBA}II$ are both isomorphic to the category $\mathcal{BA}$.*

Proof. We consider the following correspondence $F\colon \mathcal{BA} \to \mathcal{PDBA}I$, such that for Boolean algebras $\underline{A}$ and $\underline{B}$ and for all Boolean algebra homomorphism $f\colon \underline{A} \to \underline{B}$, $F(\underline{A}) = \underline{A}\dot{\oplus}\underline{1_A}$ and $F(f)\colon \underline{A}\dot{\oplus}\underline{1_A} \to \underline{B}\dot{\oplus}\underline{1_B}$, $x \mapsto f(x)$. Then F is well defined by Corollary 1, and by easy computation, one can show that F is a functor. We also consider the correspondence $G\colon \mathcal{PDBA}I \to \mathcal{BA}$, such that for all pure dBas of type I $\underline{D}$ and $\underline{E}$, and all dBa homomorphism $f\colon \underline{D} \to \underline{E}$, $G(\underline{D}) = \underline{D}_\sqcap$ and $G(f)\colon \underline{D}_\sqcap \to \underline{E}_\sqcap$, $x \mapsto f(x)$. Then G is well defined by Proposition 1, and by easy computation we can show that G is a functor. Moreover, on the one hand, for all pure dBas of type I $\underline{D}$ and $\underline{E}$, and all dBa homomorphism $f\colon \underline{D} \to \underline{E}$, $F \circ G(\underline{D}) = F \circ G(\underline{D}_\sqcap\dot{\oplus}\underline{1_{D_\sqcap}}) = F(\underline{D}_\sqcap) = \underline{D}_\sqcap\dot{\oplus}\underline{1_{D_\sqcap}} = \underline{D}$ and $F \circ G(f) = F(f) = f$. On the other hand, for Boolean algebras $\underline{A}$ and $\underline{B}$ and for all Boolean algebra homomorphism $f\colon \underline{A} \to \underline{B}$, $G \circ F(\underline{A}) = G(\underline{A}\dot{\oplus}\underline{1_A}) = (\underline{A}\dot{\oplus}\underline{1_A})_\sqcap = \underline{A}$ and $G \circ F(f) = G(f) = f$. Hence $F \circ G = id_{\mathcal{PDBA}\mathrm{I}}$ and $G \circ F = id_{\mathcal{BA}}$. We conclude that F is an isomorphism and the categories $\mathcal{BA}$ and $\mathcal{PDBA}\mathcal{I}$ are isomorphic. Dually, we can show that the categories $\mathcal{BA}$ and $\mathcal{PDBA}II$ are isomorphic. ∎

Definition 16. *A full subcategory $\mathcal{D}$ of a category $\mathcal{C}$ is said* ***isomorphism-closed*** *if every object of $\mathcal{C}$ that is isomorphic to a $\mathcal{D}$-object is itself a $\mathcal{D}$-object.*

The following proposition will be useful in the proof of Proposition 7.

Proposition 6. (**[9, Theorem 3.2]**) *Any Boolean algebra $(B; \wedge, \vee, {}', 0, 1)$ forms a fully contextual as well as pure dBa $(B; \wedge, \vee, {}', {}', 0, 1)$. On the other hand, a dBa $(D; \sqcap, \sqcup, \neg, \lrcorner, \bot, \top)$ forms a Boolean algebra $(D; \sqcap, \sqcup, \neg, \bot, \top)$, if for all $a \in D$, $\neg a = \lrcorner a$ and $\neg\neg a = a$.*

Proposition 7. *The following are true:*

1. *The category $\mathcal{BA}$ is an isomorphism-closed subcategory of $\mathcal{DBA}$.*
2. *The category $\mathcal{PDBA}$ is an isomorphism-closed subcategory of $\mathcal{DBA}$.*

Proof. 1. Let D be a dBa isomorphic to a Boolean algebra B. Then there exists $f : B \to D$, dBa-isomorphism. Let us show that D is a Boolean algebra. Let $x \in D$, then there exists $a \in B$ such that $x = f(a)$. We have $\neg x = \neg f(a) = f(a') = \lrcorner f(a) = \lrcorner x$ and $\neg\neg x = \neg\neg f(a) = f(a'') = f(a) = x$, thus by Proposition 6, D is a Boolean algebra. We conclude that $\mathcal{BA}$ is an isomorphism-closed subcategory of $\mathcal{DBA}$.

2. Let D be a dBa isomorphic to a pure dBa E. Then there exists $f : E \to D$, dBa-isomorphism. Let us show that D is a pure dBa. Let $x \in D$, then there exists $y \in E$ such that $x = f(y)$. Since E is pure, then $y \sqcap y = y$ or $y \sqcup y = y$. If $y \sqcap y = y$, then $x \sqcap x = f(y) \sqcap f(y) = f(y \sqcap y) = f(y) = x$. If $y \sqcup y = y$, then similarly we have $x \sqcup x = x$. Hence D is a pure dBa. We conclude that $\mathcal{PDBA}$ is an isomorphism-closed subcategory of $\mathcal{DBA}$. ■

Lemma 1. *Let D and E be two dBas.*

1. *For all dBa-homomorphism $f : D_\sqcap \to E$, $Im(f) \subseteq E_\sqcap$.*
2. *For all dBa-homomorphism $f : D_\sqcup \to E$, $Im(f) \subseteq E_\sqcup$.*
3. *For all dBa-homomorphism $f : D_p \to E$, $Im(f) \subseteq E_p$.*

Proof. 1. Let $f : D_\sqcap \to E$ be a dBa-morphism. Let $y \in Im(f)$, then there exists $x \in D_\sqcap$ such that $y = f(x)$. We have $y \sqcap y = f(x) \sqcap f(x) = f(x \sqcap x) = f(x) = y$, that is $y \in E_\sqcap$. Hence $Im(f) \subseteq E_\sqcap$.

2. Dual to 1.
3. It comes from 1. and 2., and the fact that for every double Boolean algebra D, $D_p = D_\sqcap \cup D_\sqcup$. ■

Proposition 8. *1. The correspondence $\bigsqcap : \mathcal{DBA} \to \mathcal{BA}$ which assigns every dBa D to $D_\sqcap$ extends to a functor.*

2. The correspondence $\bigsqcup : \mathcal{DBA} \to \mathcal{BA}$ which assigns every dBa D to $D_\sqcup$ extends to a functor.

3. The correspondence $\mathbf{P} : \mathcal{DBA} \to \mathcal{PDBA}$ which assigns every dBa D its pure part D_p extends to a functor.

Proof. We just give the proof of the third statement and similarly, we can prove the first and the second statement.

Proof of 3. By Lemma 1, the correspondence $\mathbf{P}$ is well defined. Let $D \xrightarrow{f} E \xrightarrow{g} H$ be two dBa-homomorphisms. Then for all $x \in D_p$, $\mathbf{P}(g \circ f)(x) = (g \circ f)(x) = \mathbf{P}(g) \circ \mathbf{P}(f)(x)$ and $\mathbf{P}(1_D)(x) = x = 1_{D_p}(x) = 1_{\mathbf{P}(D)}(x)$. ■

In the sequel, the functors $\bigsqcap$, $\bigsqcup$ and $\mathbf{P}$ will be called the $\mathcal{BA}_\sqcap$-functor, the $\mathcal{BA}_\sqcup$-functor and the $\mathcal{PDBA}$-functor respectively.

Proposition 9. *The $\mathcal{BA}_\sqcap$-functor, the $\mathcal{BA}_\sqcup$-functor and the $\mathcal{PDBA}$-functor are neither faithful nor conservative.*

Table 3. Cayley tables of $D_{3,II}$.

$\sqcap$	$\bot$	a	$\top$
$\bot$	$\bot$	$\bot$	$\bot$
a	$\bot$	$\bot$	$\bot$
$\top$	$\bot$	$\bot$	$\top$

$\sqcup$	$\top$	a	$\top$
$\bot$	$\top$	$\top$	$\top$
a	$\top$	$\top$	$\top$
$\top$	$\top$	$\top$	$\top$

x	$\neg x$	$\lrcorner x$
$\bot$	$\top$	$\top$
a	$\top$	$\top$
$\top$	$\bot$	$\top$

Table 4. Cayley tables of D_4.

$\sqcap$	$\bot$	b	c	$\top$
$\bot$	$\bot$	$\bot$	$\bot$	$\bot$
b	$\bot$	$\bot$	$\bot$	$\bot$
c	$\bot$	$\bot$	$\bot$	$\bot$
$\top$	$\vert$	$\vert$	$\vert$	$\top$

$\sqcup$	$\top$	b	c	$\top$
$\bot$	$\top$	$\top$	$\top$	$\top$
b	$\top$	$\top$	$\top$	$\top$
c	$\top$	$\top$	$\top$	$\top$
$\top$	$\top$	$\top$	$\top$	$\top$

x	$\neg x$	$\lrcorner x$
$\bot$	$\top$	$\top$
b	$\top$	$\top$
c	$\top$	$\top$
$\top$	$\bot$	$\top$

Proof. We consider the dBas $\underline{D}_{3,II}$ defined on the set $\{\bot, a, \top\}$ and $\underline{D}_4$ defined on the set $\{\bot, b, c, \top\}$ by the tables of Table 3 and Table 4 respectively.

We have $D_{3,II_\sqcap} = D_{4_\sqcap} = \{\bot, \top\}$, $D_{3,II_\sqcup} = D_{4_\sqcup} = \{\top\}$, $D_{3,II} \setminus D_{3,II_p} = \{a\}$ and $D_4 \setminus D_{4_p} = \{b, c\}$. We also consider the maps $f, g : D_{3,II} \to D_4$ defined by: $f(\bot) = \bot$, $f(a) = b$, $f(\top) = \top$ and $g(\bot) = \bot$, $g(a) = c$, $g(\top) = \top$. Then

$$f(x) = \begin{cases} f_1(x) \text{ if } x \in D_{3,II_\sqcap} \\ f_2(x) \text{ if } x \in D_{3,II_\sqcup} \\ f_3(x) \text{ if } x \in D_{3,II} \setminus D_{3,II_p} \end{cases}$$

where $f_1 \colon D_{3,II_\sqcap} \to D_{4_\sqcap}$ with, $f_1(\bot) = \bot$, $f_1(\top) = \top$; $f_2 \colon D_{3,II_\sqcup} \to D_{4_\sqcup}$ with $f_2(\top) = \top$ and $f_3 \colon D_{3,II} \setminus D_{3,II_p} \to D_4$ with $f_3(a) = b$. Clearly, f_1 and f_2 are homomorphisms of Boolean algebras and f_3 is a map such that for all $x \in D_{3,II}$,

$$\begin{cases} x \in D_{3,II_\sqcup} & \Rightarrow \quad f_1(x \sqcap x) = f_2(x) \sqcap f_2(x), \\ x \in D_{3,II_\sqcap} & \Rightarrow \quad f_2(x \sqcup x) = f_1(x) \sqcup f_1(x), \\ x \in D_{3,II} \setminus D_{3,II_p} & \Rightarrow \begin{cases} f_1(x \sqcap x) = f_3(x) \sqcap f_3(x), \\ f_2(x \sqcup x) = f_3(x) \sqcup f_3(x). \end{cases} \end{cases}$$

Thus by Proposition 2, f is a homomorphism of dBas. In the same way, we can show that g is a homomorphism of dBas. In addition, $\bigsqcap(f) = \bigsqcap(g)$, $\bigsqcup(f) = \bigsqcup(g)$ and $\mathbf{P}(f) = \mathbf{P}(g)$, but $f \neq g$. Thus $\bigsqcap$, $\bigsqcup$ and $\mathbf{P}$ are not faithful. Moreover, $\bigsqcap(f)$, $\bigsqcup(f)$ and $\mathbf{P}(f)$ are dBa-isomorphism but it is not the case of f. Hence $\bigsqcap$, $\bigsqcup$ and $\mathbf{P}$ are not conservative. ■

Definition 17. *Let $L : \mathcal{C} \to \mathcal{D}$ and $R : \mathcal{D} \to \mathcal{C}$ be two functors. We say that R is the* ***right adjoint*** *of L if there exists a bijection*

$$\varphi_{A,B} : \mathrm{Hom}_{\mathcal{D}}(L(A), B) \to \mathrm{Hom}_{\mathcal{C}}(A, R(B))$$

which is natural in both arguments $A \in \mathrm{ob}(\mathcal{C})$ and $B \in \mathrm{ob}(\mathcal{D})$. That is, for a morphism $f : A \to A'$ in $\mathcal{C}$, and all morphism $g : B \to B'$ in $\mathcal{D}$, the following diagrams commute:

$$\begin{array}{ccc} \mathrm{Hom}_{\mathcal{D}}(L(A),B) & \xrightarrow{\varphi_{A,B}} & \mathrm{Hom}_{\mathcal{C}}(A,R(B)) \cdot \\ {\scriptstyle \mathrm{Hom}_{\mathcal{D}}(L(f),B)}\Big\uparrow & & \Big\uparrow{\scriptstyle \mathrm{Hom}_{\mathcal{C}}(f,R(B))} \\ \mathrm{Hom}_{\mathcal{D}}(L(A'),B) & \xrightarrow[\varphi_{A',B}]{} & \mathrm{Hom}_{\mathcal{C}}(A',R(B)) \end{array}$$

and

$$\begin{array}{ccc} \mathrm{Hom}_{\mathcal{D}}(L(A),B) & \xrightarrow{\varphi_{A,B}} & \mathrm{Hom}_{\mathcal{C}}(A,R(B)) \\ {\scriptstyle \mathrm{Hom}_{\mathcal{D}}(L(A),g)}\Big\downarrow & & \Big\downarrow{\scriptstyle \mathrm{Hom}_{\mathcal{C}}(A,R(g))} \\ \mathrm{Hom}_{\mathcal{D}}(L(A),B') & \xrightarrow[\varphi_{A,B'}]{} & \mathrm{Hom}_{\mathcal{C}}(A',R(B)) \end{array}$$

Definition 18. *Let $\mathcal{C}$ be a category. A full subcategory $\mathcal{D}$ of $\mathcal{C}$ is said* ***co-reflexive*** *if the inclusion functor $i : \mathcal{D} \hookrightarrow \mathcal{C}$ has a right adjoint R. In this case, R is called the* ***co-reflector****.*

We are ready to state our result on the co-reflexivity of the categories $\mathcal{BA}$ and $\mathcal{PDBA}$ into the category $\mathcal{DBA}$.

Theorem 3. *The categories $\mathcal{BA}$ and $\mathcal{PDBA}$ are co-reflexive subcategories of the category $\mathcal{DBA}$.*

Proof. The category $\mathcal{PDBA}$ is already a full subcategory of $\mathcal{DBA}$, so it remains to show that the inclusion functor $i\colon \mathcal{PDBA} \hookrightarrow \mathcal{DBA}$ has a right adjoint. For this, we will show that the $\mathcal{PDBA}$-functor is the right adjoint of the inclusion functor $i\colon \mathcal{PDBA} \hookrightarrow \mathcal{DBA}$. Let D be a pure dBa and E be a dBa. We consider the function

$$\begin{array}{rcl} \Phi_{D,E}\colon Hom_{\mathcal{DBA}}(i(D),E) & \to & Hom_{\mathcal{PDBA}}(D,\mathbf{P}(E)) \\ D \xrightarrow{f} E & \mapsto & \Phi_{D,E}(f) = \mathbf{P}(f). \end{array}$$

Recall that $\mathbf{P}(E) = E_p$. Since $\mathbf{P}(D) = D$, we obtain by Lemma 1 that $\Phi_{D,E}(f)$ is well defined. Let's show that $\Phi_{D,E}$ is a bijection. We set

$$\begin{array}{rl} \Psi_{D,E}\colon Hom_{\mathcal{PDBA}}(D,E_p) \to & Hom_{\mathcal{DBA}}(D,E) \\ D \xrightarrow{g} E_p & \mapsto \Psi_{D,E}(g)\colon D \to E,\ x \mapsto g(x). \end{array}$$

Then for all $D \xrightarrow{g} E_p$, $D \xrightarrow{f} E$ dBa-homomorphisms, we have $\Phi_{D,E} \circ \Psi_{D,E}(g) = g$ and $\Psi_{D,E} \circ \Phi_{D,E}(f) = f$, thus $\Phi_{D,E}$ is a bijection and its inverse is $\Psi_{D,E}$. Now we are going to show that $\Phi_{D,E}$ is natural in the first variable. Let $D \xrightarrow{f} D'$ be a homomorphism of pure dBas, $D' \xrightarrow{\alpha} E$ be a dBa-homomorphism and $x \in D$, then we have

$$\begin{aligned} Hom_{\mathcal{PDBA}}(f,E_p) \circ \Phi_{D',E}(\alpha)(x) &= \Phi_{D',E}(\alpha) \circ f(x) \\ &= \mathbf{P}(\alpha) \circ f(x) \\ &= \alpha \circ f(x) \\ &= \mathbf{P}(\alpha \circ f)(x) \\ &= \Phi_{D,E}(\alpha \circ f)(x) \\ &= \Phi_{D,E} \circ Hom_{\mathcal{DBA}}(f,E)(\alpha)(x) \end{aligned}$$

which proves the naturality of $\Phi_{D,E}$ in the first variable. With similar computations, one can show that $\Phi_{D,E}$ is also natural in the second variable. Thus the $\mathcal{PDBA}$-functor is the right adjoint of the inclusion functor i. Hence we have the result. Similarly, we can show that the $\mathcal{BA}_{\sqcap}$-functor (resp. $\mathcal{BA}_{\sqcup}$-functor) is the right adjoint of the inclusion functor $i\colon \mathcal{BA} \hookrightarrow \mathcal{DBA}$. ∎

Corollary 2. *The category $\mathcal{BA}$ is a co-reflexive subcategory of $\mathcal{PDBA}$.*

Proof. We just use the restriction of the $\mathcal{BA}_{\sqcap}$-functor (resp. $\mathcal{BA}_{\sqcup}$-functor) to $\mathcal{PDBA}$ and use the spirit of Theorem 3 to obtain the proof. ∎

Taking into account Theorem 2 and Theorem 3, we obtain the following corollary.

Corollary 3. *The categories $\mathcal{PDBA}I$ and $\mathcal{PDBA}II$ are co-reflexive subcategories of the category $\mathcal{DBA}$.*

After examining the category $\mathcal{DBA}$ of double Boolean algebras, we can apply similar methods to look at the category of protoconcept algebras and its semi-concept subcategory. Let $\mathcal{PCA}$ be the category of protoconcept algebras and $\mathcal{SCA}$ that of semi-concept algebras. It is well known that, for any protoconcept algebra $\underline{\mathfrak{P}}(\mathbb{K})$, the algebras $\underline{\mathfrak{P}}(\mathbb{K})_{\sqcap}$ and $\underline{\mathfrak{P}}(\mathbb{K})_{\sqcup}$ are complete atomic Boolean algebras[2]. We denote by $\mathcal{CABA}$ the category of complete atomic Boolean algebras. Replacing the categories $\mathcal{DBA}$, $\mathcal{PDBA}$ and $\mathcal{BA}$ by $\mathcal{PCA}$, $\mathcal{SCA}$ and $\mathcal{CABA}$ respectively, in Lemma 1 and Proposition 8 we get the analog of Theorem 3:

Theorem 4. *The categories $\mathcal{CABA}$ and $\mathcal{SCA}$ are co-reflexive subcategories of the category $\mathcal{PCA}$.*

The analog of Corollary 2 is:

Corollary 4. *The category $\mathcal{CABA}$ is a co-reflexive subcategory of $\mathcal{SCA}$.*

4 Conclusion

In this work, we have established some properties of the category of double Boolean algebras, such as the initial and the terminal object, the equalizer, the product, the pullback. We then showed that the categories $\mathcal{BA}$ and $\mathcal{PDBA}$ are co-reflexive subcategories of the category $\mathcal{DBA}$. In our future work, we plan to make a coalgebraic study of the category of double Boolean algebras/protoconcept algebras.

Acknowledgment. We thank anonymous referees for their constructive remarks and suggestions that help to improve this work. This article was prepared during a visit by the first author to Bern University of Applied Sciences, co-funded by Professor Hanamantagouda P. Sankappanavar and the institute of Applied Data Science & Finance, at Bern University of Applied Sciences.

[2] Complete Boolean algebras where every element is a supremum of atoms.

References

1. Burris, S., Sankappanaver, H: A Course in Universal Algebra. Springer Verlag.GTM78 (1981)
2. Adamek, J., Herrlich, H., Strecker, G.E.: Abstract and Concrete Categories. John Wiley and Sons Inc, New york/Chichester/Brisbane/Toronto/Singapore (1990)
3. Erné, M.: Categories of contexts. arXiv1407.0512 (2014)
4. Ghita, M.: Some categorical properties of Hilbert Algebras, pp. 95–104. Annals of University of Craiova, Craiova (2009)
5. Gratzer, G.: Lattice Theory: Foundation. Springer Basel AG, Berlin (2011)
6. Kembang, G.T., Kwuida, L., Temgoua, E.R.A, Tenkeu, Y.L.J: Simple and subdirectly irreducible double Boolean algebras. arXirv:2312.13686 (2023)
7. Kwuida, L.: Prime ideal theorem for double Boolean algebras. Discussiones Math. Gen. Algebra Appl. 263–275 (2007)
8. Nganteu, C., Kianpi, M., Lele, C.: On **MV**-coalgebras over the category of BL-algebras. Soft. Comput. **25**(20), 12805–12815 (2021). https://doi.org/10.1007/s00500-021-06082-9
9. Howlader, P., Banerjee, M.: Topological representation of double Boolean algebras. Algebra Univers. **84**(2), 1–32 (2023). https://doi.org/10.1007/s00012-023-00811-x
10. Howlader, P., Kwuida, L., Behrisch, M., Liau, C.J.: Towards a Simplified Theory of Double Boolean Algebras: Axioms and Topological Representation. Preprint https://doi.org/10.48550/arXiv.2601.01418
11. Tenkeu Jeufack, Y.L., Tenkeu Kembang, G., Temgoua Alomo, E.R., Kwuida, L.: Filters, ideals and power of double Boolean algebras. Discussiones Math. Gen. Algebra Appl. **44**(2), 451–478 (2024). https://doi.org/10.7151/dmgaa.1466
12. Tenkeu Kembang, G., Tenkeu Jeufack, Y.L., Temgoua Alomo, E.R., Kwuida, L.: Double Boolean algebras: Constructions, sub-structures and morphisms. Int. J. Approximate Reasoning **186** (2025). https://doi.org/10.1016/j.ijar.2025.109519
13. Tenkeu Kembang, G., Krebs, M., Kwuida, L., Temgoua Alomo, E.R., Tenkeu Jeufack, Y.L. : A Stone Duality for Pure and Trivial Double Boolean Algebras, In: Cellier, P., Ganter, B., Missaoui, R. (eds) Conceptual Knowledge Structures. CONCEPTS 2025. Lecture Notes in Computer Science, vol 15941. Springer, Cham. https://doi.org/10.1007/978-3-032-03364-2_26
14. Wille, R.: Boolean concept logic. In: Ganter, B., Mineau, G.W. (eds.) Conceptual Structures: Logical Linguistic, and Computational Issue, pp. 317–331. Springer, Berlin Heidelberg (2000)

Characterizing the Optimum Bases of a Convex Geometry Using Quasi-Closed Hypergraphs

Anthony Meunier[1], Lhouari Nourine[1], and Simon Vilmin[2(✉)]

[1] Université Clermont-Auvergne, CNRS, Clermont-Auvergne-INP, LIMOS, Clermont-Ferrand, France
{anthony.meunier,lhouari.nourine}@uca.fr
[2] Aix-Marseille Université, CNRS, LIS, Marseille, France
simon.vilmin@lis-lab.fr

Abstract. Optimizing an implicational base of a closure system consists in turning this implicational base into an equivalent one with premises and conclusions as small as possible. This task is known to be hard in general but tractable for a number of classes of closure systems. In particular, several classes of convex geometries are known to have tractable optimization, while the problem was recently claimed to remain hard in general convex geometries. Continuing this line of research, we give a characterization of the optimum bases of a convex geometry in terms of what we call quasi-closed hypergraphs. We then use this characterization to show that when each quasi-closed hypergraph has disjoint edges, any implicational base of the convex geometry can be optimized in polynomial time with existing minimization and reduction algorithms. Finally, we prove that this property applies to double-shelling, acyclic, affine and acceptant convex geometries, thus unifying the existing results regarding the tractability of optimization for the first three classes.

Keywords: closure systems · implicational bases · optimum bases · convex geometries

1 Introduction

Implications, also known as attribute implications in Formal Concept Analysis [18], functional dependencies in database theory [25,26], Horn clauses in logic [9,21], or join-covers in lattice theory [8] to cite a few, are a common representation of finite closure systems. Indeed, a closure system can always be represented by several (equivalent) implicational bases—i.e., collections of implications. Within the study of implicational bases, the task of turning an implicational base into a smaller one has been the topic of numerous research. Several

Due to space limitations, several proofs are omitted. They are given in the arXiv version of this paper: https://arxiv.org/abs/2603.14615v1.

M. Croitoru et al. (Eds.): CONCEPTS 2026, LNAI 16811, pp. 71–86, 2027.
https://doi.org/10.1007/978-3-032-34742-8_5

measures of the size of an implicational base have been defined and studied: the number of implications, the sum of sizes of the premises of its implications, of the conclusions, or both. An implicational base that minimizes the number of implications is *minimum*. It is *left-optimum* (resp. *right-optimum*) if the sum of sizes of its premises (resp. conclusions) is as small as possible. It is *optimum* if the sum of the sizes of all its premises and conclusions is minimum among all other equivalent bases. We refer to Sect. 2 for formal definitions.

In this paper we are interested in the *optimization* problem: given an implicational base of a closure system, find, or turn the implicational base into, an equivalent optimum implicational base. We briefly review the main results for this problem that has been studied from different perspectives such as database theory [4,25], propositional logic [9–11,20,21,24], or closure systems and lattices [1,2,6,28,30,31]. We redirect the reader to [13, section 6.7], [11,32] and to the long version of the paper for a more detailed overview of the results. The decision versions of optimization, left-optimization and right-optimization are well-known to be NP-complete [4,20,25]. These contributions also highlighted properties of optimum implicational bases, showing for instance that an optimum (or left-optimum) implicational base is minimum [25,26], that an implicational base is optimum if and only if it is both left- and right-optimum [4] (see also [2]) or that an implicational base is optimum if and only if all its equivalence classes are optimum [26]. The equivalence classes of an implicational base are the sets of implications whose premises share the same closure. This later result was recently reproved for right-optimization by Bichoupan [6, unpublished] with a different phrasing: the (right-)size of an equivalence class in any optimum implicational base is fixed. Besides, a consequent amount of works also studied the tractability of optimization in particular classes of closure systems or implicational bases. On the negative side, optimization remains hard for implicational bases with premises of size 2 [11,24] as well as in bounded closure systems [2]. On the positive side, optimization has been shown to admit polynomial time algorithms for simple binary matroids [30], modular closure systems [31], acyclic and quasi-acyclic Horn functions [21], and component quadratic Horn functions [9,10] that generalize acyclic and quasi-acyclic ones.

Convex geometries, i.e., closure systems with anti-exchange closure operator [16,27], also have recently received attention regarding optimization [1,6,28]. Kashiwabara and Nakamura [28] show that affine convex geometries, convex geometries arising from point configurations in $\mathbb{R}^d$, can be optimized in polynomial time. Since acyclic Horn functions turns out to be convex geometries known as acyclic convex geometries, poset-type convex geometries or G-geometries (see, e.g., [1,14,21,30]), the work of Hammer and Kogan [21] on acyclic Horn functions also fits the perspective of convex geometries. Both results on acyclic and affine convex geometries have been generalized by Adaricheva [1]. In that contribution, the author prove that convex geometries with the Carousel properties, generalizing affine convex geometries, D-geometries, generalizing acyclic convex geometries, and double-shelling convex geometries, convex geometries arising from convex subsets of posets [16,22], can all be optimized in polynomial time. Adaricheva leaves open the question of whether convex geometries can be optimized in polynomial time. Bichoupan [6, unpublished] recently answered negatively this question, proving that convex geometries are hard to optimize. Understanding what makes optimization tractable or not in convex geometries thus constitutes an interesting research question.

Our contribution more precisely follows this line. By associating to each essential set C (see Sect. 2 for definitions) of a given convex geometry $(X, \mathcal{C})$ a hypergraph $\mathcal{Q}(C)$, which we call the *quasi-closed hypergraph* of C, whose edges are the complement of the inclusion-wise maximal quasi-closed sets of C, we first propose a characterization of all the (left-)optimum bases of the convex geometry:

Theorem 1. *Let $(X, \mathcal{C})$ be a convex geometry. A pair (X, Σ) where Σ is a collection of valid implications of $(X, \mathcal{C})$ is a left-optimum (resp. optimum) implicational base of $(X, \mathcal{C})$ if and only if Σ is obtained by choosing, for each essential set C, exactly one implication of the form $\mathrm{ex}(C) \to T$ where T is a hitting set (resp. minimum hitting set) of $\mathcal{Q}(C)$.*

We then focus on the case where all the quasi-closed hypergraphs have pairwise disjoint edges. In this case, minimal and minimum hitting sets of these hypergraphs coincide. Therefore, based on Theorem 1, any greedy reduction of the conclusions of a left-optimum implicational base will produce an optimum implicational base. Since in convex geometries each closed set has a unique minimal spanning set, left-optimality is easily reached by a greedy reduction of the premises. Hence, any polynomial time algorithms such as in [25,29] that minimize and reduce an implicational base will in this case produce an optimum base, which yields our second theorem:

Theorem 2. *An implicational base of a convex geometry where each quasi-closed hypergraph has pairwise disjoint edges can be optimized in polynomial time.*

Finally, we prove that Theorem 2 applies to four different classes of convex geometries:

Theorem 3. *Each quasi-closed hypergraph of a convex geometry has pairwise disjoint edges whenever the convex geometry belongs to:*

(1) double-shelling convex geometries;
(2) acyclic convex geometries;
(3) affine convex geometries; or
(4) acceptant convex geometries.

Consequently, an implicational base of a convex geometry in any of these classes can be optimized in polynomial time.

As previously mentioned, the first three classes are already known to have tractable optimization [1,21,28]. Our approach connects and unifies these results, all the while adding a new class to the family of convex geometries with efficient optimization. This class, acceptant convex geometries, has been studied within the context of choice functions and stable matchings [3,12,15], where convex geometries are known as path-independent choice functions.

Paper Organization. We recall some definitions and give some notations in Sect. 2. In Sect. 3 we define quasi-closed hypergraphs and prove Theorem 1. In Sect. 4 we prove Theorems 2 and 3. Each class of Theorem 3 is discussed in a separate subsection: double-shelling convex geometries in Subsect. 4.1, acyclic ones in Subsect. 4.2, affine ones in Subsect. 4.3 and acceptant convex geometries in Subsect. 4.4. We conclude the paper in Sect. 5 with some discussions for further research.

2 Preliminaries

All the object we consider in this paper are finite. Let X be a set. We denote by $\mathcal{P}(X)$ its powerset and by $|X|$ its size. If $\mathcal{H}$ is a hypergraph, a *hitting set* of $\mathcal{H}$ is set of vertices that intersects every edge of $\mathcal{H}$. A hitting set T is *minimal* if it is inclusion-wise minimal among hitting sets, and *minimum* if it is cardinality minimum among hitting sets. Sometimes we write a set as the concatenation of its elements, i.e., abc instead of $\{a, b, c\}$. We also withdraw brackets for singletons when it is clear from the context. We proceed to recall definitions on closure systems, implicational bases, convex geometries.

Closure Operator, Closure Systems. A *closure operator* over a ground set X is a map $\phi : \mathcal{P}(X) \to \mathcal{P}(X)$ that satisfies, for all $A, B \subseteq X$: (1) $A \subseteq \phi(A)$, (2) $A \subseteq B$ entails $\phi(A) \subseteq \phi(B)$ and (3) $\phi(\phi(A)) = \phi(A)$. A set $C \subseteq X$ is *closed* w.r.t. ϕ if $\phi(C) = C$. The pair $(X, \mathcal{C})$ where $\mathcal{C} = \{C : C \subseteq X \text{ and } \phi(C) = C\}$ is a *closure system*. A closure system is a pair $(X, \mathcal{C})$ where $\mathcal{C}$ is a collection of subsets of X, called *closed sets*, such that $X \in \mathcal{C}$ and $C_1 \cap C_2 \in \mathcal{C}$ for every $C_1, C_2 \in \mathcal{C}$. Each closure system $(X, \mathcal{C})$ has an associated closure operator ϕ over X defined by $\phi(A) = \bigcap\{C : C \in \mathcal{C}, A \subseteq C\}$ for all $A \subseteq X$. Therefore, there is a one-to-one correspondence between closure operator and closure systems. If $(X, \mathcal{C})$ is a closure system, the poset $(\mathcal{C}, \subseteq)$ of closed sets ordered by inclusion form a *(closure) lattice* where, for any $C_1, C_2 \in \mathcal{C}$, $C_1 \wedge C_2 = C_1 \cap C_2$ and $C_1 \vee C_2 = \phi(C_1 \cup C_2)$. Let $C_1 \subseteq C_2$ be two closed sets. We say that C_1 is a *predecessor* of C_2 in $(\mathcal{C}, \subseteq)$, equivalently that C_2 *covers* C_1, if there is no $C_3 \in \mathcal{C}$ such that $C_1 \subset C_3 \subset C_2$.

Let $(X, \mathcal{C})$ be a closure system and let $A \subseteq X$. If $C \in \mathcal{C}$, we say that A is a *spanning set* of C if $\phi(A) = C$. For $x \in X$ with $x \notin A$, we say that A is a *(non-trivial) generator* of x if $x \in \phi(A)$. An *extreme point* of A is an element $x \in A$ such that $x \notin \phi(A \setminus \{x\})$. We denote by $\text{ex}(A)$ the extreme points of A. Note that for any $C \in \mathcal{C}$, $\text{ex}(C)$ is included in any (inclusion-wise) minimal spanning set of C. We now define quasi-closed, pseudo-closed, and essential sets.

Definition 1. *Let $(X, \mathcal{C})$ be a closure system and let $Q \subseteq X$. We say that Q is* quasi-closed *if it is not closed and for every $A \subseteq Q$, $\phi(A) \subset \phi(Q)$ implies*

$\phi(A) \subseteq Q$.[1] *A set* P *is* pseudo-closed *if it is an inclusion-wise minimal quasi-closed set among the spanning sets of* $\phi(P)$. *A closed set which is the closure of a quasi-closed (or pseudo-closed) set is* essential.

Note that for any closed set C, the quasi-closed sets of the closure system $(C, \{C' : C' \in \mathcal{C}, C' \subseteq C\})$ are exactly the quasi-closed sets of $(X, \mathcal{C})$ included in C. This holds in particular for pseudo-closed sets.

We finally define convex geometries. A closure system $(X, \mathcal{C})$ is a *convex geometry* if $\varnothing \in \mathcal{C}$ and for each closed set $C \subset X$, there exists $x \notin C$ such that $C \cup \{x\}$ is closed. Convex geometries can be characterized by their spanning sets: $(X, \mathcal{C})$ is a convex geometry if and only if every closed set C has a unique minimal spanning set being $\mathrm{ex}(C)$. As a consequence, we observe that the predecessors of each closed set $C \neq \varnothing$ are precisely the sets $C \setminus \{x\}$ for $x \in \mathrm{ex}(C)$.

Implicational Bases. We turn our attention to implications. We redirect the reader to [5,32] for a detailed introduction to the topic. An *implication* over X is an expression $A \to B$ where A, B are subsets of X. The set A is called the *premise* and B the *conclusion* of the implication. Given a collection Σ of implications over X, we call the pair (X, Σ) an *implicational base*. The number of implications in Σ is denoted by $|\Sigma|$. The *left-size* of Σ is defined as $||\Sigma||_\ell := \sum_{A \to B \in \Sigma} |A|$. Similarly, $||\Sigma||_r := \sum_{A \to B \in \Sigma} |B|$ denotes the *right-size* of Σ. The *total size* of Σ is defined as $||\Sigma|| := \sum_{A \to B \in \Sigma} |A| + |B|$. Note that we equivalently have $||\Sigma|| = ||\Sigma||_\ell + ||\Sigma||_r$.

We relate implications to closure systems. Let $A \to B$ be an implication and $C \subseteq X$. We say that C *satisfies* $A \to B$ if $A \subseteq C$ implies $B \subseteq C$. Let (X, Σ) be an implicational base. The set C satisfies Σ if it satisfies all the implications of Σ. The pair $(X, \mathcal{C})$ where $\mathcal{C}$ is the collection of subsets of X satisfying Σ is known to form a closure system. Its associated closure operator Σ can be computed in polynomial time from the pair (X, Σ) using the forward chaining procedure. For each $A \subseteq X$, this procedure builds a sequence $A = Y_0 \subseteq Y_1 \subseteq \cdots \subseteq Y_k = \Sigma(A)$ of sets defined by $Y_i = Y_{i-1} \cup \bigcup\{B : A \to B \in \Sigma, A \subseteq Y_{i-1}\}$. An *equivalence class* of (X, Σ) is a set of implications of Σ whose premises have the same closure. Any implicational base (X, Σ) is thus partitioned by its equivalence classes. Let $(X, \mathcal{C})$ be a closure system. An implication $A \to B$ over X is *valid* in $(X, \mathcal{C})$ if every closed set satisfies the implication. Note that $A \to B$ is valid in $(X, \mathcal{C})$ if and only if $B \subseteq \phi(A)$. An implicational base is a *(valid) implicational base* of $(X, \mathcal{C})$ if the closure system associated to (X, Σ) is precisely $(X, \mathcal{C})$. In general, an implicational base consisting only of valid implications of $(X, \mathcal{C})$ does not need to be an implicational base of $(X, \mathcal{C})$. A closure system can usually be represented by several different implicational bases. Two implicational bases with the same closure system are *equivalent*. Let (X, Σ) be an implicational base of $(X, \mathcal{C})$. We say that (X, Σ) is *minimum* if $|\Sigma| = \min\{|\Sigma'| : (X, \Sigma')$ is an implicational base of $(X, \mathcal{C})\}$. Similarly, we say that (X, Σ) is *optimum* (resp. *left-optimum*, *right-optimum*) if Σ minimizes $||\cdot||$

[1] Closed sets are often considered quasi-closed, but it will be more convenient for us to assume they are not.

(resp. $||\cdot||_\ell$, $||\cdot||_r$) among the implicational bases of $(X, \mathcal{C})$. We say that (X, Σ) is *left-reduced* if for every $A \to B \in \Sigma$ and every $A' \subset A$, $(\Sigma \setminus \{A \to B\}) \cup \{A' \to B\}$ is no longer an implicational base of $(X, \mathcal{C})$. Similarly, (X, Σ) is *right-reduced* if $(\Sigma \setminus \{A \to B\}) \cup \{A \to B'\}$ is no longer an implicational base of $(X, \mathcal{C})$ for every $B' \subset B$ and every $A \to B \in \Sigma$. Finally, (X, Σ) is *reduced* if it is both left- and right-reduced. Below we recall known results regarding optimum implicational bases. Notably, we recall that optimality can be achieved by optimizing each equivalence class of the implicational base independently from the others. In other words, the total sizes of the implicational bases of each equivalence class in an optimum base is fixed.

Theorem 4 (see, e.g., [4,6,25,26]). *Let $(X, \mathcal{C})$ be a closure system and let (X, Σ) be an implicational base of $(X, \mathcal{C})$. Then:*

(1) if (X, Σ) is (left-)optimum, it is also minimum;
(2) (X, Σ) is optimum if and only if it is both left- and right-optimum;
(3) (X, Σ) is optimum if and only if all its equivalence classes are optimum.

The *canonical base* of $(X, \mathcal{C})$ is the implicational base (X, Σ_c) where:

$$\Sigma_c := \{P \to \phi(P) \setminus P : P \text{ is pseudo-closed }\}$$

Theorem 5 (see, e.g., [17,19,30]). *Let $(X, \mathcal{C})$ be a closure system and let (X, Σ_c) be its canonical base. Then:*

(1) (X, Σ_c) is a minimum base of $(X, \mathcal{C})$ and every other implicational base (X, Σ) of $(X, \mathcal{C})$ contains for each pseudo-closed set P, an implication $A \to B$ such that $A \subseteq P$ and $\phi(A) = \phi(P)$.
(2) for each left-optimum base (X, Σ) of $(X, \mathcal{C})$ and for each pseudo-closed set P, Σ contains an implication $A \to B$ such that $A \subseteq P$, $\phi(A) = \phi(P)$ and $|A| = \min\{|Y| : Y \subseteq P, \phi(Y) = \phi(P)\}$.

3 Quasi-Closed Hypergraphs and Optimum Bases of Convex Geometries

In this section we give a characterization of the optimum bases of a convex geometry. This characterization relies on the minimum hitting sets of the hypergraphs of the quasi-closed sets that are, within a same equivalence class, inclusion-wise maximal.

The starting point of our approach lies in the more general context of arbitrary closure systems. Consider some closure system $(X, \mathcal{C})$ and let Σ be a collection of valid implications of $(X, \mathcal{C})$. In the next proposition, we observe that what makes (X, Σ) an implicational base of $(X, \mathcal{C})$ or not does only depend on its ability to make every quasi-closed set indeed non-closed using implications with premises from its equivalence class. Note that this has also been observed by Bichoupan [7, unpublished], although we propose a slightly stronger form.

Proposition 1 (Lemma 2 in [7]). *Let Σ be a collection of valid implications of $(X, \mathcal{C})$. The pair (X, Σ) is an implicational base of $(X, \mathcal{C})$ if and only if for every quasi-closed set Q of $\mathcal{C}$, there exists $A \to B \in \Sigma$ such that $A \subseteq Q$, $\phi(A) = \phi(Q)$, and B contains an element of $\phi(Q) \setminus Q$.*

Proof. We start with the only if part. Assume (X, Σ) is an implicational base of $(X, \mathcal{C})$ and let Q be a quasi-closed set of $\mathcal{C}$. Since (X, Σ) is an implicational base of $(X, \mathcal{C})$ and Q is not closed, there exists $A \to B \in \Sigma$ such that $A \subseteq Q$ but $B \nsubseteq Q$. As Q is quasi-closed, $\phi(A) \subset \phi(Q)$ would entail $B \subseteq \phi(A) \subset Q$, a contradiction with the fact that $B \nsubseteq Q$. We deduce that $\phi(A) = \phi(Q)$ and that B contains an element of $\phi(Q) \setminus Q$.

We move to the if part. It is sufficient to show that $\phi(Q) = \Sigma(Q)$ for each quasi-closed set Q. Since (X, Σ) contains only valid implications of $(X, \mathcal{C})$, we readily have $\Sigma(Q) \subseteq \phi(Q)$. Hence, it remains only to argue that $\phi(Q) \subseteq \Sigma(Q)$ for each quasi-closed set Q. Assume for contradiction this is not the case and let C be an inclusion-wise minimal closed set of $\mathcal{C}$ where such a Q exists. We thus have $\Sigma(Q) \subset \phi(Q)$. By assumption on Σ, $\Sigma(Q)$ cannot be quasi-closed in $(X, \mathcal{C})$ as otherwise there would exist an implication $A \to B$ in Σ such that $A \subseteq \Sigma(Q)$, A spans $\phi(Q)$ and $B \nsubseteq \Sigma(Q)$. Therefore, there exists $Y \subseteq \Sigma(Q)$ such that $\phi(Y) \subset \phi(\Sigma(Q)) = C$ and $\phi(Y) \nsubseteq \Sigma(Q)$. However, by minimality assumption on C, for every $C' \in \mathcal{C}$ such that $C' \subset C$ and any quasi-closed set Q' spanning C', $\Sigma(Q') = \phi(Q')$. This holds in particular for all pseudo-closed sets P such that $\phi(P) \subset C$. Therefore, $\phi(Y) = \Sigma(Y)$ must hold, and $\Sigma(Y) \subseteq \Sigma(Q)$ too as $Y \subseteq \Sigma(Q)$. This contradicts $\phi(Y) \nsubseteq \Sigma(Q)$, and concludes the proof.

Example 1. Let $X = \{a, \dots, f\}$ and consider the closure system $(X, \mathcal{C})$ depicted in Fig. 1. It has three essential sets being *ab*, *cdef*, *abcdef* and its canonical base (X, Σ_c) is given by:

$$\Sigma_c = \{a \to b, b \to a, f \to cde, ce \to df, de \to cf, abe \to cdf, abd \to cef\}$$

Consider for instance the quasi-closed sets of *cdef*. They coincide with its non-closed spanning sets: *ce*, *de*, *f* and every proper subset of *cdef* that includes at least one of these three sets. By Proposition 1, each quasi-closed set of *cdef* is non-closed in (X, Σ_c) due to an implication with a premise spanning *cdef*. For example, the quasi-closed sets *cf* and *ef* relate to the implication $f \to cde$.

Suppose that (X, Σ) is indeed an implicational base of $(X, \mathcal{C})$ and let C be an essential set of $\mathcal{C}$. From Proposition 1, we obtain that $T := \bigcup\{B : A \to B \in \Sigma \text{ and } \phi(A) = C\}$ is a hitting set of the hypergraph with vertex set C and edges the complements of the quasi-closed sets of C. Since some quasi-closed sets may be comparable, we can more simply observe that T is a hitting set of the hypergraph $\mathcal{Q}(C)$, which we call the *quasi-closed hypergraph of* C, having vertex set C and edge set:

$$\{C \setminus Q : Q \text{ is an inclusion-wise maximal quasi-closed set of } C\}.$$

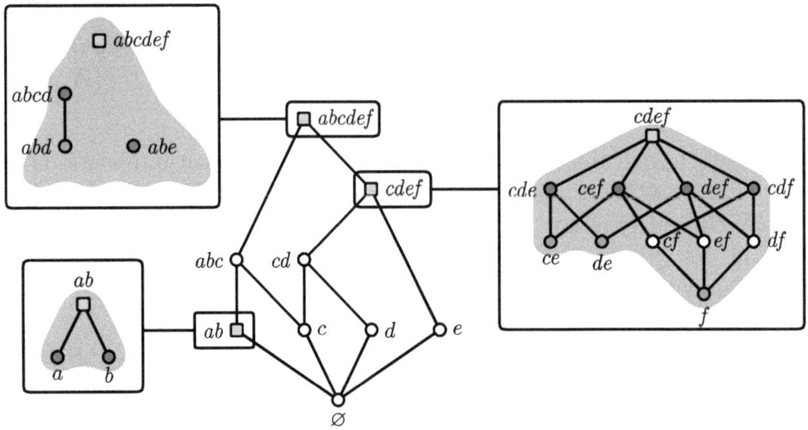

Fig. 1. The closure system of Example 1. It has three essential sets (yellow square nodes) being *ab*, *cdef*, *abcdef*. To each essential set is associated a box representing its quasi-closed sets (circle nodes) ordered by inclusion within its spanning sets (shaded zone). For instance the quasi-closed sets of *abcdef* are *abd*, *abe*, *abcd*. Minimal quasi-closed sets are green (e.g., *abd*), maximal ones red (e.g., *abcd*), and those that are both minimal and maximal purple (e.g., *abe*).(Color figure online)

Example 2 (continued). The maximal quasi-closed sets of *cdef* are *cde*, *cef*, *def*, *cdf*, so that $\mathcal{Q}(cdef) = \{f, d, c, e\}$. Similarly, the maximal quasi-closed sets of *abcdef* are *abcd*, *abe*. We thus have $\mathcal{Q}(abcdef) = \{ef, cdf\}$.

Proposition 1 now reads as follows: to build implicational bases of $(X, \mathcal{C})$, one has to select for each essential set C enough premises to subsume all quasi-closed sets of C and then a hitting set T of $\mathcal{Q}(C)$ to distribute over these premises. This applies in particular to minimum implicational bases of $(X, \mathcal{C})$ that can be obtained by applying the following steps to each essential set C:

1. choose a (unique) premise $A \subseteq P$ for each pseudo-closed set P of C;
2. choose a hitting set T of $\mathcal{Q}(C)$;
3. distribute T over the premises A so as to fulfill Proposition 1. Note that T needs not be partitioned over the premises.

The resulting (X, Σ) is indeed a minimum implicational base of $(X, \mathcal{C})$ due to Proposition 1 and Theorem 5. Besides, the fact that we indeed obtain all possible minimum implicational bases follows from as we choose for each essential set C and each pseudo-closed set of C all possible premises A and all possible hitting sets T of $\mathcal{Q}(C)$, where T can be any subset of C, that we distribute in all valid ways. In particular, the canonical base is built by taking each pseudo-closed set P as premise and repeating the trivial hitting set C of $\mathcal{Q}(C)$ in each conclusions, possibly withdrawing useless elements.

Example 3 (continued). We illustrate the construction of (X, Σ_c) in Example 1 by considering each essential set:

- $\mathcal{Q}(ab) = \{a, b\}$ with hitting set ab and pseudo-closed sets a, b. The implications thus are $a \to b$ and $b \to a$;
- $\mathcal{Q}(cdef) = \{f, d, c, e\}$ with hitting set $cdef$ and pseudo-closed sets ce, de, f. We obtain implications $f \to cde$, $ce \to df$, $de \to cf$;
- $\mathcal{Q}(abcdef) = \{ef, cdf\}$ with hitting set $abcdef$. The pseudo-closed sets being abe, abd, we obtain $abe \to cdf$, $abd \to cef$.

Let us restrict our attention to optimum bases, that are minimum by Theorem 4 (1), (2). By Theorem 4 (3), we can optimize the equivalence class of each essential set C independently from the others, and optimality is found by finding left- and right-optimality:

1. left-optimality is obtained by selecting for each pseudo-closed set P a minimal spanning set $A \subseteq P$ of $\phi(P)$ with minimum cardinality (item (2) in Theorem 5) ;
2. right-optimality is obtained by selecting a hitting set T of $\mathcal{Q}(C)$ that can be distributed over the premises of C in a minimum way.

For right-optimality in general, a given element of T might need to be repeated in conclusion of different implications. As a consequence, T does not need to be a minimum hitting set of $\mathcal{Q}(C)$ in general as we illustrate below:

Example 4 (continued). We construct an optimal implicational base (X, Σ) for the closure system of Example 1 by looking at each essential set. For ab, the unique possible choice is $a \to b$ and $b \to a$. For $cdef$, the left-optimum premises are its minimal spanning sets, f, ce, de. As for conclusions, $\mathcal{Q}(C)$ has a unique hitting set being $cdef$. However, the distribution of $cdef$ may produce right-reduced implications that are not optimum. For instance $f \to cde$, $ce \to f$, $de \to f$ cannot be reduced but is not optimum as we can reach 4 conclusions only with: $f \to ce$, $ce \to d$, $de \to f$. Finally for $abcdef$, optimum premises are for instance ad, ae. As for conclusions, $\mathcal{Q}(abcdef) = \{ef, cdf\}$ has hitting sets, e.g., f and ce which are of different size. Yet, since two implications are needed, both hitting sets produce optimum implications: one can take either $\{ad \to f, ae \to f\}$ or $\{ad \to e, ae \to c\}$. An example of optimum base is thus given by $\Sigma = \{a \to b, b \to a, f \to ce, ce \to d, de \to f, ad \to e, ae \to c\}$.

The situation simplifies for convex geometries. Let us then assume that $(X, \mathcal{C})$ is a convex geometry and let C be some essential set. Since C has a unique minimal spanning set, $\text{ex}(C)$, C plus the quasi-closed sets of C form a closure system. In particular, it follows that C has a unique pseudo-closed set and that each minimum implicational base of $(X, \mathcal{C})$ has a unique implication $A \to T$ for the equivalence class of C. This makes T on its own a hitting set of $\mathcal{Q}(C)$ by Proposition 1. Moreover, item (2) of Theorem 5 entails that $\text{ex}(C)$ is the unique choice of minimal spanning set for any left-optimum implicational base of $(X, \mathcal{C})$ (see also, e.g., [30, Corollary 13(b)], [1, Theorem 7]). We obtain the first part of Theorem 1 regarding left-optimality that we state in a separate lemma:

Lemma 1. *Let $(X, \mathcal{C})$ be a convex geometry. A pair (X, Σ) where Σ is a collection of valid implications of $(X, \mathcal{C})$ is a left-optimum implicational base of $(X, \mathcal{C})$ if and only if Σ is obtained by choosing, for each essential set C, exactly one implication of the form $\text{ex}(C) \rightarrow T$ where T is a hitting set of $\mathcal{Q}(C)$.*

Since optimum bases are left-optimum, we deduce that optimum bases of $(X, \mathcal{C})$ falls into the scope of Lemma 1. In particular, right-optimality is reached exactly when for each essential set C, the size of the chosen hitting set T of $\mathcal{Q}(C)$ is minimum. We thus obtain Theorem 1:

Theorem 1. *Let $(X, \mathcal{C})$ be a convex geometry. A pair (X, Σ) where Σ is a collection of valid implications of $(X, \mathcal{C})$ is a left-optimum (resp. optimum) implicational base of $(X, \mathcal{C})$ if and only if Σ is obtained by choosing, for each essential set C, exactly one implication of the form $\text{ex}(C) \rightarrow T$ where T is a hitting set (resp. minimum hitting set) of $\mathcal{Q}(C)$.*

For convex geometries, Theorem 1 shows that optimization amounts to identify a minimum hitting set T of $\mathcal{Q}(C)$ of each essential set C, possibly by explicitly computing $\mathcal{Q}(C)$, and then outputting $\text{ex}(C) \rightarrow T$. This strategy will not produce polynomial time algorithms in general as optimizing convex geometries is NP-hard [6, unpublished]. In the next section we use Theorem 1 to identify a property of convex geometries that makes optimization tractable and show this property applies to different classes of convex geometries.

4 Quasi-Closed Hypergraphs with Disjoint Edges

Drawing from Theorem 1, we investigate the case where each quasi-closed hypergraph of a convex geometry $(X, \mathcal{C})$ has pairwise disjoint edges. We prove that any implicational base of $(X, \mathcal{C})$ can be optimized in polynomial time (Theorem 2), and then that several classes of convex geometries do enjoy this property (Theorem 3).

For Theorem 2 we simply argue that, under our assumptions, any polynomial time algorithm that takes as input an implicational base (X, Σ) of $(X, \mathcal{C})$ and turns it into an equivalent minimum reduced base does in fact make it optimum. Minimization and reduction can be achieved in polynomial time by applying, say, Shock's algorithm [29], which turns an arbitrary implicational base into a minimum one in polynomial time, and then Maier's algorithm for reduction [25, Algorithm 5.7, p. 77] which first applies left-reduction and then right-reduction in a greedy fashion. Informally, assuming (X, Σ) is already minimum and considering some implication $A \rightarrow T$, left-reduction will turn A into $\text{ex}(C)$ where C is the essential set spanned by A while right-reduction will turn T into a minimal hitting set of $\mathcal{Q}(C)$ by Theorem 1. Given that the edges of $\mathcal{Q}(C)$ are disjoint this minimal hitting set is also minimum, which guarantees optimality again by Theorem 1.

Theorem 2. *An implicational base of a convex geometry where each quasi-closed hypergraph has pairwise disjoint edges can be optimized in polynomial time.*

We finally identify four classes of convex geometries to which Theorem 1 applies. Let us recall that the first three of them have been independently shown to have tractable optimization [1,21,28]. Our approach thus unifies all these results via the same optimization algorithm.

Theorem 3. *Each quasi-closed hypergraph of a convex geometry has pairwise disjoint edges whenever the convex geometry belongs to:*

(1) double-shelling convex geometries;
(2) acyclic convex geometries;
(3) affine convex geometries; or
(4) acceptant convex geometries.

Consequently, an implicational base of a convex geometry in any of these classes can be optimized in polynomial time.

The proof of Theorem 3 is divided in Subsects. 4.1 to 4.4, each subsection corresponding to one of the class mentioned in the Theorem.

4.1 Double-Shelling Convex Geometries

We prove that any convex geometry in the class of double-shelling convex geometries have quasi-closed hypergraphs with disjoint edges. Let $P := (X, \leq)$ be a poset and let $x, y \in X$. We write $x < y$ to denote that $x \leq y$ and $x \neq y$. If $x < y$, the *interval* of x, y is defined as $[x, y] := \{z : z \in X, x \leq z \leq y\}$. A set $C \subseteq X$ is called a *convex set* of P if for any $x, y \in C$ such that $x < y$, $[x, y] \subseteq C$ holds. Let $\mathcal{C}$ be the family of convex subsets of P. The pair $\mathrm{Co}(P) := (X, \mathcal{C})$ is known to be a convex geometry called the *double-shelling convex geometry* of P. Its closure operator thus maps any subset Y of X to the minimal convex set of P that includes Y. Its canonical base (X, Σ_c) is given by [1]:

$$\Sigma_c = \{xy \to [x, y] \setminus \{x, y\} : \exists z \in X, x < z < y \text{ in } P\}.$$

Observe that for any essential set C with pseudo-closed set xy, we have $\mathrm{ex}(C) = \{x, y\}$ as any singleton is convex. The *comparability graph* of P is the undirected graph G_P with vertex set $V(G_P) := X$ and edges $E(G_P) := \{xy : x < y\}$. For $x < y$, we define $G_P(x, y) := G_P[[x, y] \setminus \{x, y\}]$ where $G_P[Y]$ is the graph induced by Y. We illustrate these definitions in Example 5.

Example 5. Consider the poset P on ground set $X = \{a, \ldots, h, x, y\}$ on the left of Fig. 2. For instance, $[a, y] = \{a, f, g, y\}$. The canonical base (X, Σ_c) of the associated double-shelling convex geometry $\mathrm{Co}(P)$ is given by:

$$\Sigma_c = \left\{ \begin{array}{l} xf \to ab,\ xg \to ab,\ xe \to c,\quad xh \to ec,\ xy \to abcdefgh, \\ ay \to fg,\ by \to fg,\ cy \to eh,\ ey \to h,\ ch \to e \end{array} \right\}$$

The lemma below states that for any essential set C with extreme points x, y, $\mathcal{Q}(C)$ consists in the connected components of $G_P(x, y)$ (assuming without loss of generality $x < y$). This can be deduced from [1, Lemma 26].

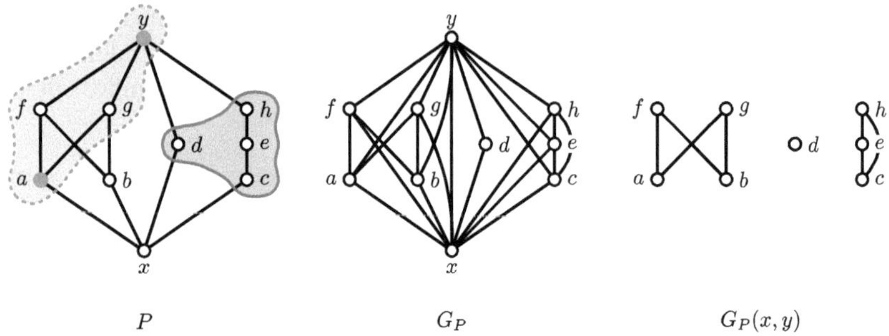

Fig. 2. On the left the poset P of Example 5. The set $cdeh$ (circled in purple, solid) is convex. The interval $[a, y]$ (circled in green, dotted) is $afgy$. It is also convex. The comparability graph G_P is pictured in the middle and the graph $G_P(x, y)$ on the right. It has three connected components: $abgf$, d, and ceh.

Lemma 2. *Let C be an essential set of $\mathcal{C}$ with $\text{ex}(C) = \{x, y\}$ and $x < y$ in P. Then, the edges of $\mathcal{Q}(C)$ are the connected components of $G_P(x, y)$, therefore they are disjoint.*

Example 6. We continue Example 5. According to Lemma 2 the edges of $\mathcal{Q}(X)$ are exactly the connected components of $G_P(x, y)$: $abgf$, d, and ceh (see Fig. 2). The set ade, also highlighted in the figure, is a minimal (hence minimum) hitting set of $\mathcal{Q}(X)$. This makes the implication $xy \to ade$ optimum for this equivalence class. An example of optimum base (X, Σ) for $\text{Co}(P)$ is:

$$\Sigma = \left\{ \begin{array}{l} xf \to ab,\ xg \to ab,\ xe \to c,\ xh \to c,\ xy \to ade, \\ ay \to fg,\ by \to fg,\ cy \to e,\ ey \to h,\ ch \to e \end{array} \right\}.$$

Hence the edges of $\mathcal{Q}(C)$ are indeed disjoint for any essential set C. More precisely, an optimum implication for C is obtained by picking one element in each connected component of the corresponding graph, as proved by Adaricheva [1, Lemma 26]. This proves item (1) of Theorem 3.

4.2 Acyclic Convex Geometries

We turn our attention to acyclic convex geometries. Let (X, Σ) be an implicational base. The *implication-graph* of (X, Σ) is the directed graph with vertex set X and arcs (a, b) if there exists $A \to B \in \Sigma$ such that $a \in A, b \in B$. We consider without loss of generality that $A \cap B = \varnothing$ to avoid loops. We say that (X, Σ) is *acyclic* if its implication-graph does not have directed cycles. An acyclic closure system is a closure system admitting an acyclic implicational base and acyclic closure systems are convex geometries, see e.g., [30,32].

Suppose that $(X, \mathcal{C})$ is an acyclic convex geometry and let C be essential. We show in the next lemma that each maximal quasi-closed set of C is of the form $C \setminus \{x\}$. This statement can be deduced from the connection between essential implicates, critical generators and quasi-closed sets drawn in earlier literature.

In [21], essential implicates are those implications $A \to x$ that belong to every possible implicational base with singleton conclusions of a given closure system $(X, \mathcal{C})$. The authors prove that if $(X, \mathcal{C})$ is an acyclic convex geometry, essential implicates do in fact constitute the unique optimum base of $(X, \mathcal{C})$ (once aggregated by premises). Then, Nourine et al. [14] observe that the essential implicates of an acyclic convex geometry coincide with the so-called critical generators of the convex geometry. In a convex geometry $(X, \mathcal{C})$, a minimal generator A of x is *critical* if $x \in \mathrm{ex}(\phi(A) \setminus \{a\})$ for every $a \in A$ [23]. Finally, Wild [30,32] noticed that A is a critical generator of x if and only if $\phi(A) \setminus \{x\}$ is quasi-closed which allows to derive the lemma below.

Lemma 3. *The maximal quasi-closed sets of an essential set C are of the form $C \setminus \{x\}$ with $x \in C$.*

The quasi-closed hypergraphs of $(X, \mathcal{C})$ thus consist of singleton edges that are trivially disjoint, which proves item (2) of Theorem 3. Note that in particular, each quasi-closed hypergraphs has a unique minimum hitting set. This entails that $(X, \mathcal{C})$ does indeed have a unique optimum base as showed in [21].

4.3 Affine Convex Geometries

We now consider affine convex geometries, i.e., convex geometries arising from point configurations in $\mathbb{R}^d$ [16]. If X is a set of points in $\mathbb{R}^d$, let $\phi(Y) = h(Y) \cap X$ where h is the usual convex hull operator in geometry. The operator ϕ is a closure operator and the associated closure system $(X, \mathcal{C})$ is a convex geometry called the *affine convex geometry* associated to X. Let $(X, \mathcal{C})$ be an affine convex geometry. To prove item (3) of Theorem 3, we first recall a Theorem of Kashiwabara and Nakamura [28], rephrased in our terminology.

Theorem 9 (Theorem 20 in [28]). *Let $P_1, \ldots, P_m$ be the pseudo-closed sets of $(X, \mathcal{C})$, and for each $1 \leq i \leq m$, let x_i be any element of $\phi(P_i) \setminus P_i$. Then, the pair (X, Σ) with $\Sigma = \{P_1 \to x_1, \ldots, P_m \to x_m\}$ is an optimum implicational base of $(X, \mathcal{C})$.*

From Theorem 9 and Theorem 1 we deduce that for each essential set C and each $x \in C \setminus \mathrm{ex}(C)$, x is a hitting set of $\mathcal{Q}(C)$. We obtain:

Lemma 4. *The unique maximal quasi-closed set of any essential set C is* $\mathrm{ex}(C)$.

The unique edge of $\mathcal{Q}(C)$ is thus $C \setminus \mathrm{ex}(C)$. It then vacuously holds that each quasi-closed hypergraph of $(X, \mathcal{C})$ has pairwise disjoint edges. This proves item (3) of Theorem 3.

4.4 Acceptant Convex Geometries

We finally study (q-)acceptant convex geometries. A convex geometry $(X, \mathcal{C})$ is *q-acceptant* for some $1 \leq q \leq |X|$ if for every $C \in \mathcal{C}$, $|\,\mathrm{ex}(C)| = \min(q, |C|)$. Observe that a convex geometry is acceptant for at most one q. Besides, the definition shows that a convex geometry $(X, \mathcal{C})$ is q-acceptant if and only if every subset of X with strictly less than q elements is closed and every closed set with at least q elements has precisely q extreme points. Moreover, we readily have that all minimal generators of a q-acceptant have size q. The trivial closed sets of a q-acceptant convex geometry thus are precisely all the closed sets of size at most q. Two 2-acceptant convex geometries are picture in Fig. 3. Much as affine convex geometries, an essential set C of a q-acceptant convex geometry has a unique maximal quasi-closed set.

Lemma 5. *Any essential set C has a unique maximal quasi-closed set.*

By Lemma 5, we have that $\mathcal{Q}(C)$ has, for every essential C, a unique edge. Its minimum hitting sets are therefore singletons, much as affine convex geometries, which finally proves item (4) of Theorem 3.

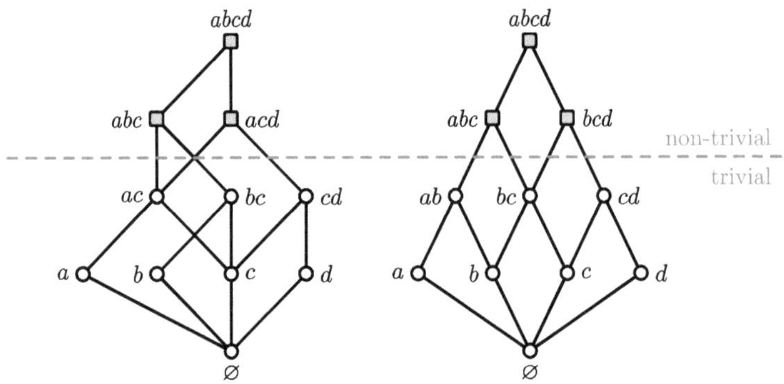

Fig. 3. Two 2-acceptant convex geometries. The dotted lines separate non-trivial and trivial closed sets. Essential sets are indicated by (yellow) square nodes. Closed sets with ≤ 2 elements are trivial, other ones are non-trivial and have 2 extreme points. (Color figure online)

Example 7. Consider the two 2-acceptant convex geometries of Fig. 3. Let us call $(X, \mathcal{C}_1)$ the left one and $(X, \mathcal{C}_2)$ the right-one. In both cases, non-trivial closed sets and essential sets coincide. For $\mathcal{C}_1$ we have $\mathcal{Q}(abc) = \mathcal{Q}(acd) = \{c\}$ and $\mathcal{Q}(abcd) = \{a\}$. For $\mathcal{C}_2$ we have $\mathcal{Q}(abc) = \{b\}$, $\mathcal{Q}(bcd) = \{c\}$ and $\mathcal{Q}(abcd) = \{bc\}$. We thus observe that $(X, \mathcal{C}_1)$ has a unique optimum base while $(X, \mathcal{C}_2)$ has two depending on which of b and c we choose as the conclusion associated to ad.

5 Discussion

In this paper, we proposed a characterization of the optimum bases of a convex geometry. This characterization relies on quasi-closed hypergraphs, the hypergraphs defined for each essential set by taking the complement of its inclusion-wise maximal quasi-closed sets. In the case where each quasi-closed hypergaph of the convex geometry has disjoint edges, we proved that using existing minimization and reduction algorithms was sufficient to produce, in polynomial time, an optimum base out of any other implicational base. This property of quasi-closed hypergraphs turns out to apply to double-shelling, acyclic, affine and acceptant convex geometries, which allows to unify existing results of the literature.

To conclude, we observe that using our approach to identify further classes of convex geometries for which optimization is tractable seems to be an intriguing problem for further research. Indeed, by Theorem 1, a convex geometry can be optimized efficiently if and only if for each quasi-closed hypergraph, some minimum hitting set can be computed in polynomial time. Thus, classifying convex geometries according to their quasi-closed hypergraphs may be a good yardstick to better understand the hardness of the optimization task in convex geometries. In particular, we may study whether other classes of convex geometries have quasi-closed hypergraphs with disjoint edges. Indeed, the next example shows that convex geometries with edge-disjoint quasi-closed hypergraphs properly contain the classes we studied in this paper:

Example 8. Let $X = \{a, \ldots, e\}$ and $\Sigma = \{ac \to b, bd \to c, ad \to bc, e \to ab\}$. The associated closure system is a convex geometry that does not belong to any of the classes of Theorem 3. It is not a (2-)acceptant, affine or double-shelling convex geometry as $\{e\} \notin \mathcal{C}$. It is not acyclic since b and c belongs to minimal generators of one another. The quasi-closed hypergraphs are $\mathcal{Q}(abe) = \{a, b\}$, $\mathcal{Q}(abc) = \{b\}$, $\mathcal{Q}(bcd) = \{c\}$ and $\mathcal{Q}(abcd) = \{bc\}$ and all have disjoint edges.

Convex geometries with the Carousel property and D-geometries are interesting candidates as they respectively generalize affine convex geometries and acyclic convex geometries being covered by Theorem 3 and have tractable optimization [1]. In particular, the proof of [1, Theorem 12] on convex geometries with the Carousel property seems to use an argument similar to [28, Theorem 9] that we used in Lemma 4. This suggests that the same holds true for convex geometries with the Carousel property.

References

1. Adaricheva, K.V.: Optimum basis of finite convex geometry. Discret. Appl. Math. **230**, 11–20 (2017)
2. Adaricheva, K.V., Nation, J.: On implicational bases of closure systems with unique critical sets. Discret. Appl. Math. **162**, 51–69 (2014)
3. Alkan, A.: On preferences over subsets and the lattice structure of stable matchings. Rev. Econ. Design **6**, 99–111 (2001)
4. Ausiello, G., D'Atri, A., Saccà, D.: Minimal representation of directed hypergraphs. SIAM J. Comput. **15**(2), 418–431 (1986)
5. Bertet, K., Demko, C., Viaud, J., Guérin, C.: Lattices, closures systems and implication bases: A survey of structural aspects and algorithms. Theor. Comput. Sci. **743**, 93–109 (2018)
6. Bichoupan, T.: Complexity results for implication bases of convex geometries. arXiv preprint arXiv:2211.08524 (2022). https://arxiv.org/abs/2211.08524

7. Bichoupan, T.: Independence of essential sets in finite implication bases. arXiv preprint arXiv:2304.06837 (2023), https://arxiv.org/abs/2304.06837
8. Birkhoff, G.: Lattice theory, vol. 25, American Mathematical Soc (1940)
9. Boros, E., Čepek, O., Kogan, A., Kučera, P.: A subclass of Horn CNFs optimally compressible in polynomial time. Ann. Math. Artif. Intell. **57**(3–4), 249–291 (2009)
10. Boros, E., Čepek, O., Kogan, A., Kučera, P.: Exclusive and essential sets of implicates of Boolean functions. Discret. Appl. Math. **158**(2), 81–96 (2010)
11. Boros, E., Čepek, O., Kučera, P.: A decomposition method for CNF minimality proofs. Theor. Comput. Sci. **510**, 111–126 (2013)
12. Chambers, C.P., Yenmez, M.B.: Choice and matching. Am. Econom. J.: Microeconom. **9**(3), 126–47 (2017)
13. Crama, Y., Hammer, P.L.: Boolean functions: Theory, algorithms, and applications, Cambridge University Press (2011)
14. Defrain, O., Nourine, L., Vilmin, S.: Translating between the representations of a ranked convex geometry. Discret. Math. **344**(7), 112399 (2021)
15. Doğan, B., Doğan, S., Yıldız, K.: On Capacity-Filling and Substitutable Choice Rules. Math. Oper. Res. **46**(3), 856–868 (2021)
16. Edelman, P.H., Jamison, R.E.: The theory of convex geometries. Geom. Dedicata. **19**(3), 247–270 (1985)
17. Ganter, B.: Two basic algorithms in concept analysis. In: Kwuida, L., Sertkaya, B. (eds.) ICFCA 2010. LNCS (LNAI), vol. 5986, pp. 312–340. Springer, Heidelberg (2010). https://doi.org/10.1007/978-3-642-11928-6_22
18. Ganter, B., Wille, R.: Formal Concept Analysis, vol. 150, Springer (1999)
19. Guigues, J.L., Duquenne, V.: Familles minimales d'implications informatives résultant d'un tableau de données binaires. Mathématiques et sciences humaines **95**, 5–18 (1986)
20. Hammer, P.L., Kogan, A.: Optimal compression of propositional horn knowledge bases: complexity and approximation. Artif. Intell. **64**(1), 131–145 (1993)
21. Hammer, P.L., Kogan, A.: Quasi-acyclic propositional horn knowledge bases: optimal compression. IEEE Trans. Knowl. Data Eng. **7**(5), 751–762 (1995)
22. Kashiwabara, K., Nakamura, M.: Characterizations of the convex geometries arising from the double shellings of posets. Discret. Math. **310**(15–16), 2100–2112 (2010)
23. Korte, B., Lovász, L., Schrader, R.: Greedoids. Springer Science & Business Media (2012)
24. Kučera, P.: Hydras: complexity on general graphs and a subclass of trees. Theor. Comput. Sci. **658**, 399–416 (2017)
25. Maier, D.: The Theory of Relational Databases, Computer Science Press (1983)
26. Mannila, H., Räihä, K.: On the relationship of minimum and optimum covers for a set of functional dependencies. Acta Informatica **20**, 143–158 (1983)
27. Monjardet, B.: A use for frequently rediscovering a concept. Order **1**(4), 415–417 (1985)
28. Nakamura, M., Kashiwabara, K.: The prime stems of rooted circuits of closure spaces and minimum implicational bases. Electron. J. Comb. **20**(1), 22 (2013)
29. Shock, R.C.: Computing the minimum cover of functional dependencies. Inf. Process. Lett. **22**(3), 157–159 (1986)
30. Wild, M.: A theory of finite closure spaces based on implications. Adv. Math. **108**(1), 118–139 (1994)
31. Wild, M.: Optimal implicational bases for finite modular lattices. Quaest. Math. **23**(2), 153–161 (2000)
32. Wild, M.: The joy of implications, aka pure horn formulas: Mainly a survey. Theoret. Comput. Sci. **658**, 264–292 (2017)

Updating a Base of Triadic Implications When Attributes Are Added or Removed

Romuald Kwessy Mouona[1], Blaise Blériot Koguep Njionou[2], Rokia Missaoui[3], Etienne Romuald Temgoua Alomo[1], and Leonard Kwuida[4](✉)

[1] University of Yaounde 1, Yaounde, Cameroon
romuald.kwessy@facsciences-uy1.cm
[2] University of Dschang, Dschang, Cameroon
blaise.koguep@univ-dschang.org
[3] University of Quebec in Outaouais (UQO), Gatineau, Canada
rokia.missaoui@uqo.ca
[4] Bern University of Applied Sciences, Bern, Switzerland
leonard.kwuida@bfh.ch

Abstract. We present a theoretical framework and algorithms for updating an implication base derived from a triadic context when attributes are added or removed. Starting with a context $\mathbb{K}_r$ of r attributes, we establish conditions under which a quasi-feature of $\mathbb{K}_r$ remains valid after attribute augmentation or reduction. For augmentation, we characterize stable and modified quasi-features that shape the new base. For reduction, the update primarily involves filtering and validating existing quasi-features. Two algorithms are proposed, and complexity analysis shows that our approach is significantly more efficient than full reconstruction.

Keywords: triadic context · triadic implication base · pseudo-features · optimal base

1 Introduction

Formal Concept Analysis (**FCA**) is a mathematical framework for analyzing data through concepts and hierarchies derived from binary object–attribute relations [3,8]. Since real-world data are often multi-dimensional, **Triadic Concept Analysis** (**TCA**) extends FCA by introducing ternary relations between objects, attributes, and conditions [12]. Therefore, a triadic context $\mathbb{K} := (G, M, C, I)$ models situations where an object is in relation with an attribute under specific conditions.

A central notion in this framework is that of conditional attribute implications (CAIs) defined by Ganter and Obiedkov [7], which express rules of the form "if an object has all attributes in A_1 under condition set C or any subset in C, then it also has all attributes in A_2 under the same conditions", which is

M. Croitoru et al. (Eds.): CONCEPTS 2026, LNAI 16811, pp. 87–102, 2027.
https://doi.org/10.1007/978-3-032-34742-8_6

denoted by $(A_1 \xrightarrow{C} A_2)$. One fundamental problem in both FCA and TCA is the extraction of implication bases—minimal sets of valid implications that logically entail all other implications. In the dyadic setting, the canonical (Duquenne–Guigues) base of attribute implications is constructed from pseudo-intents [9]. In TCA, Biedermann [4] studied another variant of triadic implications that we are using in this paper (see Sect. 2). Recent works have established an optimal base of CAIs [10,11]. This optimality occurs on a base $\mathcal{B}$ when for any other base of implications $\mathcal{B}_1$, one has $\|\mathcal{B}\| \leq \|\mathcal{B}_1\|$; where for any base of implications $\mathcal{B}$, $\|\mathcal{B}\| = \sum_{(A_1 \xrightarrow{C} A_2) \in \mathcal{B}} (|A_1| + |A_2| + |C|)$. The notation $\|\mathcal{B}\|$ not only defines minimality in terms of the number of implications in the base, but also in terms of the number of elements involved in each implication.

The construction of this optimal base relies on notions like features, quasi-features and pseudo-features: informally, a feature corresponds to the attribute-condition component of a triadic concept, while a quasi-feature is an attribute-condition set whose insertion in the context creates exactly one new feature. Among quasi-features, pseudo-features form a minimal generating family sufficient to construct an optimal base of implication base. These notions play a similar role to intents and pseudo-intents in FCA. Real-world data evolves over time. Attributes are added (e.g., new products in a sales database) or removed (e.g., discontinued products). When such changes occur, recomputing the implication base from scratch can be computationally expensive, as the number of candidate subsets grows exponentially with the attribute set size. Incremental algorithms that update the existing base rather than rebuilding it from scratch are therefore highly desirable. In FCA, incremental algorithms for updating the canonical implication base after adding attributes have been studied [17]. These algorithms exploit the properties of pseudo-intents to efficiently propagate changes. In the triadic setting, however, the presence of conditions adds a layer of complexity: implications are conditioned on subsets of C, and the notion of derivation involves all three dimensions, adding or removing an attribute may alter both attribute-condition interactions and the associated derivation operators. This motivates the need for dedicated update mechanisms in TCA.

This paper addresses the problem of updating an optimal base of CAI when an attribute is added to or removed from a triadic context. That is, given a triadic context $\mathbb{K}_r = (G, M_r, C, I_r)$ with $M_r = \{m_1, m_2, ..., m_r\}$ and its optimal base $\mathcal{B}_r$, we study how to derive the base of implications of the updated context $\mathbb{K}_{r+1}$ and $\mathbb{K}_{r-1}$ without rebuilding everything from scratch. Our contributions are as follows:

1. We provide a formal characterization of when a quasi-feature of the original context remains a quasi-feature after augmentation or reduction. Specifically, we introduce the notions of stable and modified sets and prove necessary and sufficient conditions for a quasi-feature to survive the context change.
2. We show how to construct the new pseudo-feature set $\mathcal{UP}_2(\mathbb{K}_{r+1})$ from the initial one $\mathcal{UP}_2(\mathbb{K}_r)$ when an attribute m_{r+1} is added. Our method distinguishes between m_{r+1}-stable pseudo-features (which remain valid), m_{r+1}-

modified pseudo-features (which must be re-evaluated), and new candidates containing m_{r+1}. For attribute removal, we prove that all pseudo-features of the context $\mathbb{K}_{r-1}$ are necessarily pseudo-features of the context $\mathbb{K}_r$ that do not contain the deleted attribute.
3. We present two algorithms: Algorithm 1 for updating an implication base after attribute augmentation and Algorithm 2 for updating after attribute removal. These algorithms leverage the theoretical results to avoid exhaustive enumeration of all subsets of $M_{r+1} \times C$.
4. We analyze the worst-case time complexity of our approach. Even though the problem remains exponential in general, we show that our update requires examining only $|\mathcal{UP}_2(\mathbb{K}_r)| + O(2^{|M_r|} \cdot |C|)$ candidates for augmentation, compared to $O(2^{|M_{r+1}|} \cdot |C|)$ for full recomputation. For deletion, the operation reduces to linear-time filtering in $\mathcal{UP}_2(\mathbb{K}_r)$.

To the best of our knowledge, this is the first work addressing the incremental update of implication bases in Triadic Concept Analysis under both attribute insertion and deletion. The remainder of the paper is organized as follows. Section 2 recalls the notions of TCA and introduces features, quasi-features, pseudo-features and CAI. Section 3 presents the theoretical results for updating CAI after attribute insertion or deletion. Section 4 describes the proposed algorithms and discusses their complexity. Finally, Sect. 5 concludes the paper and outlines future research directions.

2 Basic Notions

According to Peirce, a context is a set of categories (firstness, secondness, thirdness, etc.) linked by a **relationship of interdependence** [6]. For example, firstness can represent an object, secondness can represent certain properties common to that object, thirdness the mediation through which the first two categories are related. **Dyadic contexts** (G, M, I) consider only the first two categories, and **triadic contexts** $(G, M, \mathcal{C}, I)$ are an extension of dyadic contexts by taking the third category into account. We focus on triadic contexts.

A **triadic context** is a 4-tuple $\mathbb{K} := (G, M, \mathcal{C}, I)$ where $I \subseteq G \times M \times \mathcal{C}$ is a relation between objects in G, attributes in M and conditions in $\mathcal{C}$. Any restriction of I to subsets of G, M or $\mathcal{C}$ defines a **sub-context** of $\mathbb{K}$.

Example 1. The table on the left of Fig. 1 shows a triadic context that highlights relations between some clients (seen as objects: o_1, o_2, o_3, o_4, o_5), the ordered items (seen as attributes: a = *accessories*, b = *books*, c = *computers* and d = *digital cameras*) and suppliers (seen as conditions: P = *Peter*, N = *Nelson*, R = *Rick*, K = *Kevin* and S = *Simon*). We write $(o_1o_2$[1] $, a, P) \in I$ to mean that Customer o_1 and o_2 order *accessories* from *Peter*. The table on the right shows a subcontext.

[1] It refers to the set $\{o_1, o_2\}$.

A context may undergo deletion or augmentation of attributes or conditions. But, exchanging the positions of attributes and conditions does not change the relation of the context. Therefore, we will focus on solving the problem of deleting an attribute ($\mathbb{K}_r \rightsquigarrow \mathbb{K}_{r-1}$) or inserting an attribute ($\mathbb{K}_r \rightsquigarrow \mathbb{K}_{r+1}$).

$\mathbb{K}_4$	a	b	c	d
o_1	$PNRKS$	PNK	R	PN
o_2	RPK	NR	N	$PNRKS$
o_3	$PRKS$	RPK		PN
o_4	PRK	$PNRK$		PNS
o_5	$PNRKS$	KR	K	PNR

$\mathbb{K}_{4-1}$	a	b	c
o_1	$PNRKS$	PNK	R
o_2	RPK	NR	N
o_3	$PRKS$	RPK	
o_4	PRK	$PNRK$	
o_5	$PNRKS$	KR	K

Fig. 1. Our running context (left) and one of its sub-contexts (right).

Let $\mathbb{K}_r := (G, M_r, \mathcal{C}, I_r)$ be our initial triadic context with $M_r = \{m_1, m_2, \cdots, m_{r-1}, m_r\}$ where $m_1 < m_2 < \cdots < m_{r-1} < m_r$. Derivation operations are defined in dyadic contexts $\mathbb{K}_r^{(1)} := (G, M_r \times \mathcal{C}, I_r^{(1)})$, $\mathbb{K}_r^{(2)} := (M_r, G \times \mathcal{C}, I_r^{(2)})$ and $\mathbb{K}_r^{(3)} := (\mathcal{C}, G \times M_r, I_r^{(3)})$, where

$$(o,(a,c)) \in I_r^{(1)} \iff (a,(o,c)) \in I_r^{(2)} \iff (c,(o,a)) \in I_r^{(3)} \iff (o,a,c) \in I_r$$

and are called i-**derivation**, $i \in \{1,2,3\}$. For example, if $A \subseteq M_r$,

$$A^{(2)} = \{(o,c) \in G \times \mathcal{C} \mid (o,a,c) \in I_r, \text{ for all a} \in A\}.$$

Additionally, we can extract the following dyadic contexts: (G, M_r, I_C^{12}) with $C \subseteq \mathcal{C}$, $(G, \mathcal{C}, I_A^{13})$ with $A \subseteq M_r$ and $(M_r, \mathcal{C}, I_O^{23})$ with $O \subseteq G$, where

$$\begin{aligned} (o,a) \in I_C^{12} &:\iff (o,a,c) \in I, \quad \text{for all} \quad c \in C; \\ (o,c) \in I_A^{13} &:\iff (o,a,c) \in I, \quad \text{for all} \quad a \in A; \\ (a,c) \in I_O^{23} &:\iff (o,a,c) \in I, \quad \text{for all} \quad o \in O. \end{aligned}$$

Their derivations are: $(1,2,C)$-**derivation** for I_C^{12} with $C \subseteq \mathcal{C}$, $(1,3,A)$-**derivation** for I_A^{13} with $A \subseteq M_r$, $(2,3,O)$-**derivation** for I_O^{23} with $O \subseteq G$. For example, if $O \subseteq G$, then the set of attributes in M_r that can be derived from the pair (O, C) is given below.

$$O^{(1,2,C)} = \{a \in M_r : (o,a,c) \in I, \; \forall (o,c) \in O \times C\}.$$

For any X, Y subsets of G, M_r or $\mathcal{C}$ and $i \in \{1,2,3\}$, we have $X \subseteq X^{(i)(i)}$, and if $X \subseteq Y$, then $Y^{(i)} \subseteq X^{(i)}$. If $X_1 \subseteq Y_1$ and $X_2 \subseteq Y_2$, then $(Y_1 \times Y_2)^{(i)} \subseteq (X_1 \times X_2)^{(i)}$. These relations are valid if we replace the i-derivation by $(1,2,C)$-, $(1,3,A)$- or $(2,3,O)$-derivation. A **concept** of $\mathbb{K}_r$ [1,5,12] is a 3-tuple $(O, A, C) \in 2^G \times 2^{M_r} \times 2^{\mathcal{C}}$ such that $O = (A \times C)^{(1)}$, $A = (O \times C)^{(2)}$, $C = (O \times A)^{(3)}$. We call O, A, C and $A \times C$ respectively $\mathbb{K}_r$-**extent**, $\mathbb{K}_r$-**intent**, $\mathbb{K}_r$-**modus** and $\mathbb{K}_r$-**feature** of the $\mathbb{K}_r$-concept (O, A, C).

Example 2. In our running context (Fig. 1 left), one can verify that the triple $(o_1o_2o_3o_4o_5, ad, P)$ is a $\mathbb{K}_4$-concept. The $\mathbb{K}_4$-extent, $\mathbb{K}_4$-intent, $\mathbb{K}_4$-modus and the $\mathbb{K}_4$-feature are $o_1o_2o_3o_4o_5$, ad, P and $ad{\times}P$, respectively.

Since we frequently use the 1-derivation, we will very often adopt the notation $A^{(r)_C} := (A \times C)^{(1)}$ in the context $\mathbb{K}_r$. For any $\mathbb{K}_r$-concept $\mathfrak{c}$, we denote by $\text{ext}(\mathfrak{c})$, $\text{int}(\mathfrak{c})$, $\text{modus}(\mathfrak{c})$, $\text{feat}(\mathfrak{c})$ respectively its $\mathbb{K}_r$-extent, $\mathbb{K}_r$-intent, $\mathbb{K}_r$-modus and $\mathbb{K}_r$-feature. $\mathfrak{T}(\mathbb{K}_r)$ denotes the set of all $\mathbb{K}_r$-concepts and $\mathfrak{F}(\mathbb{K}_r)$ the set of all $\mathbb{K}_r$-features of $\mathbb{K}_r$. Note that each $\mathbb{K}_r$-feature defines a unique $\mathbb{K}_r$-concept.

Augmentation can also be applied to objects [10]. In fact, for $Z \subseteq M_r{\times}\mathcal{C}$, we can introduce in $\mathbb{K}_r$, a new object $o_Z \notin G$ such that $o_Z = Z^{(1)}$. Therefore, the context $\mathbb{K}_r$ augmented by Z is denoted $\mathbb{K}_r[Z] := (G \cup \{o_Z\}, M_r, \mathcal{C}, I_{r_Z})$ where $I_{r_Z} = I_r \cup (\{o_Z\}{\times}Z)$. **Quasi-features** are sub-sets of $M_r \times \mathcal{C}$ of the form $A \times C$ satisfying $A \times C \notin \mathfrak{F}(\mathbb{K}_r)$ and $|\mathfrak{F}(\mathbb{K}_r[A \times C])| = 1 + |\mathfrak{F}(\mathbb{K}_r)|$. The smallest set of quasi-features capable of generating all quasi-features of the same context is called the **pseudo-feature** set [10]. For example, the sets $c{\times}PS$ and $c{\times}P$ are both $\mathbb{K}_4$-quasi-features of our running context (Fig. 1 left) but $c{\times}P$ is a pseudo-feature while $c{\times}PS$ is not. This characterization is slightly different from that of a feature F which is $|\mathfrak{F}(\mathbb{K}_r[F])| = |\mathfrak{F}(\mathbb{K}_r)|$.

Pseudo-features are strongly related to the base generation of valid Biedermann's conditional attribute implications (BCAI) [10]. We recall that a valid BCAI is denoted by $(A_1 \rightarrow A_2)_C$ with $A_1, A_2 \subseteq M_r$, and $C \subseteq \mathcal{C}$ verifying $(A_1)^{(r)_C} \subseteq (A_2)^{(r)_C}$ ($\iff A_2 \subseteq A_1^{(r)_C(r)_C}$). In this context, $(A_1 \rightarrow A_2)_C$ is considered **valid**. A BCAI $(A_1 \rightarrow A_2)_C$ can be interpreted as follows: if an object of G has all attributes in A_1 under the whole condition set C, then it also has all attributes in A_2 under the same condition set [4]. Ganter and Obiedkov introduced **conditional attribute implications (CAI)** which is a compound form of BCAI denoted by $A_1 \xrightarrow{C} A_2$. These two forms are related to each other as follows: $A_1 \xrightarrow{C} A_2 \iff (A_1 \rightarrow A_2)_{C_1}$, for all $C_1 \subseteq C$ [7]. For example, in Fig. 1 left, the CAI $c \xrightarrow{PS} abd$ is equivalent to the following BCAI: $(c \rightarrow abd)_P$, $(c \rightarrow abd)_S$ and $(c \rightarrow abd)_{PS}$.

The optimal base $\mathcal{B}^{op}_{CAI}$ of CAI is generated from the set $\mathcal{UP}_2(\mathbb{K}_r)$ of the minimal cover of unit pseudo-features [11], i.e., those of the form $A \times \{c\}$:

$$\mathcal{B}^{op}_{CAI} = \{A \xrightarrow{\{c\}} A^{(r)_c(r)_c},\ A \times \{c\} \in \mathcal{UP}_2(\mathbb{K}_r)\}$$

Example 3. In [11], we proved for the context in Fig. 1 (left) that the optimal base with respect to the set of attributes is:

$$\mathcal{B}^{op}_{CAI} = \{\emptyset \xrightarrow{P} ad\ ;\ \emptyset \xrightarrow{N} d\ ;\ \emptyset \xrightarrow{KR} a\ ;\ c \xrightarrow{KPN} b\ ;\ d \xrightarrow{R} b\ ;\ b \xrightarrow{S} c\ ;\ c \xrightarrow{S} abd\}.$$

Obiedkov and Duquenne [17] studied **pseudo-intents** (a set P of attributes that differs from an intent and contains the closure of all pseudo-intents, subsets of P), showing that it is possible to deduce the **canonical base** of attribute implications of an augmented dyadic context from the canonical base of attribute implications of the initial dyadic context. In this work, we intend to extend this study to pseudo-features by proposing an update of the optimal CAI base, not only after an augmentation, but also after a deletion of new data. That is, we propose a study that allows us to deduce the $\mathbb{K}_{r+1}$-base (respectively, the $\mathbb{K}_{r-1}$-base) of CAI from the $\mathbb{K}_r$-base of CAI. The method will consist of constructing $\mathbb{K}_{r+1}$-pseudo-features (respectively, the $\mathbb{K}_{r-1}$-pseudo-features) from $\mathbb{K}_r$-pseudo-features.

3 Update of a Triadic Base of Implications

From our running context, we can consider that several customers are interested in a new product (for example $e := earphone$), and that a product may no longer be required by customers ($d := digital - camera$ for example), such a product may be carefully removed from the list of future purchases. Note that the unwanted product has certainly not erased all customers' old ordering habits. In contrast, the presence of the new product could encourage the emergence of new habits. What are these new habits? What impact do they have on suppliers' sales policies? These questions lead us to consider constructing a base of implications for the new contexts. To optimize this process, it would be essential to update the previous base of implications, rather than completely rebuild a new base from scratch.

To conform to the notations used in Sect. 2, we adopt the following changes to our running example: the elements of the condition set will remain unchanged, the object set will be denoted by $G = \{o_1, o_2, o_3, o_4, o_5\}$ and the attribute set will be denoted by $M_4 = \{m_1, m_2, m_3, m_4\}$, where $m_1 < m_2 < m_3 < m_4 = a < b < c < d$. We will occasionally write i for m_i. i.e., $1 = a,\ 2 = b,\ 3 = c,\ 4 = d$.

$\mathbb{K}_4$	1	2	3	4
o_1	$PNRKS$	PNK	R	PN
o_2	RPK	NR	N	$PNRKS$
o_3	$PRKS$	RPK		PN
o_4	PRK	$PNRK$		PNS
o_5	$PNRKS$	KR	K	PNR

Fig. 2. Our running context $\mathbb{K}_4$

3.1 Update After the Insertion of an Attribute

Assuming that the $\mathbb{K}_r$-pseudo-features are known, our aim is to determine the $\mathbb{K}_{r+1}$-pseudo-feature set, when the $(r+1)^{th}$ attribute is added to $\mathbb{K}_r$. The new set will contain $\mathbb{K}_r$-pseudo-features that remain **stable** in $\mathbb{K}_{r+1}$ and $\mathbb{K}_r$-pseudo-features that are **modified** since they contain the added attribute.

In the following, we define two key notions that characterize these situations.

Definition 1. *Let $C \subseteq \mathcal{C}$, $A \subseteq M_{r+1}$ and $B \subseteq M_r$. The set $A \times C$ is m_{r+1}-**modified** (after adding m_{r+1} to $\mathbb{K}_r$) if $m_{r+1} \in (A \backslash \{m_{r+1}\})^{(r+1)c(r+1)c}$. Otherwise, it is m_{r+1}-**stable**. Similarly, $B \times C$ is m_r-**modified** (after removing m_r from $\mathbb{K}_r$) if $m_r \in (B \backslash \{m_r\})^{(r)c(r)c}$. Otherwise, it is m_r-**stable**.*

$\mathbb{K}_{4+1}$	1	2	3	4	5
o_1	$PNRKS$	PNK	R	PN	$PNRKS$
o_2	RPK	NR	N	$PNRKS$	$PNRKS$
o_3	$PRKS$	RPK		PN	$PNRKS$
o_4	PRK	$PNRK$		PNS	
o_5	$PNRKS$	KR	K	PNR	$PNRKS$

$\mathbb{K}_{4-1}$	1	2	3
o_1	$PNRKS$	PNK	R
o_2	RPK	NR	N
o_3	$PRKS$	RPK	
o_4	PRK	$PNRK$	
o_5	$PNRKS$	KR	K

Fig. 3. Context $\mathbb{K}_{4+1}$ after augmenting $\mathbb{K}_4$ with $m_5 := e$ (left) and context $\mathbb{K}_{4-1}$ after removing $m_4 := d$ from the context $\mathbb{K}_4$ (right).

In this definition, we have two contexts: $\mathbb{K}_p \subsetneq \mathbb{K}_q$ with $p < q = p + 1$. An augmentation means that we add m_q to $\mathbb{K}_p$ and get $\mathbb{K}_q$, and a reduction means that we remove m_q from $\mathbb{K}_q$ and get $\mathbb{K}_p$. With $A \times C$ being m-modified, we refer to the attribute added or removed, m, and mean that m follows (in the large context) from $A \setminus \{m\}$. i.e. $(A \setminus \{m\} \to m)_C$ is valid in $\mathbb{K}_q$.

Example 4. In the context of Fig. 3 (left), $3{\times}S$ is 5-modified since the attribute 5 is in $3^{(4+1)_S(4+1)_S} = \emptyset^{(4+1)_S} = 12345$, and $25{\times}N$ is 5-stable since $5 \notin (\{2,5\}\setminus\{5\})^{(4+1)_N(4+1)_N} = 24$.

We can establish an interesting link between m_{r+1}-modified sets, m_{r+1}-stable sets, and implications of the form BCAI.

Definition 2. *$(A_1 \to A_2)_C$ is an m_r-**modified implication** if $A_1{\times}C$ is m_r-modified; otherwise it is an m_r-**stable implication**.*

Example 5. In Example 4, $3{\times}S$ is 5-modified while $25{\times}N$ is 5-stable. Thus, the implications $(3 \to 15)_S$ and $(25 \to 4)_N$ are 5-modified and 5-stable, respectively.

Remark 1. Let $A \subseteq M_r$ and $C \subseteq \mathcal{C}$ be non-empty sets. Note that $A \subseteq A_1$ implies $(A_1\setminus\{m_r\})^{(r)_C} \subseteq (A\setminus\{m_r\})^{(r)_C}$ and $(A\setminus\{m_r\})^{(r)_C(r)_C} \subseteq (A_1\setminus\{m_r\})^{(r)_C(r)_C}$.

- If $A{\times}C$ is m_r-stable, then for any set $A_1 \subseteq A$, $A_1{\times}C$ is m_r-stable.
- If $A{\times}C$ is m_r-modified, then for any set $A_1 \supseteq A$, $A_1{\times}C$ is m_r-modified.

These imply that

- If $A^{(r)_C(r)_C}{\times}C$ is m_r-stable then $A{\times}C$ is also m_r-stable.
- If $A{\times}C$ is m_r-modified then $A^{(r)_C(r)_C}{\times}C$ is also m_r-modified.

The next proposition presents the link between m_{r+1}-stable sets (respectively m_{r+1}-modified sets) and double derivation in $\mathbb{K}_r$ and $\mathbb{K}_{r+1}$.

Proposition 1. *Let $A \subseteq M_r$ and $C \subseteq \mathcal{C}$.*

i) $A^{(r+1)_C(r+1)_C} = A^{(r)_C(r)_C}$ *if and only if $A{\times}C$ is m_{r+1}-stable.*
ii) $A^{(r+1)_C(r+1)_C} = A^{(r)_C(r)_C} \cup \{m_{r+1}\}$ *if and only if $A{\times}C$ is m_{r+1}-modified.*

Proof. i) If $A^{(r+1)_{\mathcal{C}}(r+1)_{\mathcal{C}}} = A^{(r)_{\mathcal{C}}(r)_{\mathcal{C}}}$, then $m_{r+1} \notin A^{(r)_{\mathcal{C}}(r)_{\mathcal{C}}} = A^{(r+1)_{\mathcal{C}}(r+1)_{\mathcal{C}}} = (A\backslash\{m_{r+1}\})^{(r+1)_{\mathcal{C}}(r+1)_{\mathcal{C}}}$, i.e. $A{\times}C$ is m_{r+1}-stable. Reciprocally, if $A{\times}C$ is m_{r+1}-stable, then $m_{r+1} \notin (A\backslash\{m_{r+1}\})^{(r+1)_{\mathcal{C}}(r+1)_{\mathcal{C}}} = A^{(r+1)_{\mathcal{C}}(r+1)_{\mathcal{C}}}$ since $A \subseteq M_r$. Thus, $A^{(r+1)_{\mathcal{C}}(r+1)_{\mathcal{C}}} = A^{(r)_{\mathcal{C}}(r)_{\mathcal{C}}}$.

ii) Since $A \subseteq M_r$, we have $A^{(r+1)_{\mathcal{C}}} = A^{(r)_{\mathcal{C}}}$. If $A{\times}C$ is m_{r+1}-modified, then $m_{r+1} \in A^{(r+1)_{\mathcal{C}}(r+1)_{\mathcal{C}}}$, i.e. $A^{(r+1)_{\mathcal{C}}(r+1)_{\mathcal{C}}} = A^{(r)_{\mathcal{C}}(r)_{\mathcal{C}}} \cup \{m_{r+1}\}$. Reciprocally, if $A^{(r+1)_{\mathcal{C}}(r+1)_{\mathcal{C}}} = A^{(r)_{\mathcal{C}}(r)_{\mathcal{C}}} \cup \{m_{r+1}\}$, then $m_{r+1} \in A^{(r+1)_{\mathcal{C}}(r+1)_{\mathcal{C}}} = (A\backslash\{m_{r+1}\})^{(r+1)_{\mathcal{C}}(r+1)_{\mathcal{C}}}$, i.e. $A{\times}C$ is m_{r+1}-modified.

Remark 2. From the previous proposition, one can notice that for any sets $A \subseteq M_r$ and $C \subseteq \mathcal{C}$, $A^{(r)_{\mathcal{C}}(r)_{\mathcal{C}}} = A^{(r+1)_{\mathcal{C}}(r+1)_{\mathcal{C}}}\backslash\{m_{r+1}\}$.

Implications of $\mathbb{K}_{r+1}$ are of two types: those whose premises do not contain m_{r+1} and those whose premises contain m_{r+1}. For the first case, we present in what follows a characterization of stable and modified implications.

Proposition 2. *Let $A_1, A_2 \subseteq M_r$ and $C \subseteq \mathcal{C}$. The implication $(A_1 \to A_2)_C$ is valid in $\mathbb{K}_r$ if and only if it is also valid in $\mathbb{K}_{r+1}$.*

Proof. If $(A_1 \to A_2)_C$ is valid in $\mathbb{K}_r$, then $A_2 \subseteq (A_1)^{(r)_{\mathcal{C}}(r)_{\mathcal{C}}} \subseteq (A_1)^{(r+1)_{\mathcal{C}}(r+1)_{\mathcal{C}}}$, i.e. $(A_1 \to A_2)_C$ is valid in the context $\mathbb{K}_{r+1}$. If $(A_1 \to A_2)_C$ is valid in $\mathbb{K}_{r+1}$, then $(A_1)^{(r+1)_{\mathcal{C}}} \subseteq (A_2)^{(r+1)_{\mathcal{C}}}$, that is $(A_1)^{(r)_{\mathcal{C}}} \subseteq (A_2)^{(r)_{\mathcal{C}}}$ since $A_1, A_2 \subseteq M_r$. Thus, $(A_1 \to A_2)_C$ is valid in $\mathbb{K}_r$.

Proposition 3. *Let $A_1, A_2 \subseteq M_r$ and $Y \subseteq \mathcal{C}$. The implication $A_1 \xrightarrow{Y} (A_2 \cup \{m_{r+1}\})$ is valid in $\mathbb{K}_{r+1}$ if and only if $A_1 \xrightarrow{Y} A_2$ is valid in $\mathbb{K}_r$ and $A_1{\times}Y$ is m_{r+1}-modified.*

Proof. If $A_1 \xrightarrow{Y} (A_2 \cup \{m_{r+1}\})$ is valid in $\mathbb{K}_{r+1}$, then for any $C \subseteq Y$, $(A_1 \to A_2 \cup \{m_{r+1}\})_C$ is also valid in $\mathbb{K}_{r+1}$ and we have $A_1^{(r)_{\mathcal{C}}} = A_1^{(r+1)_{\mathcal{C}}} \subseteq (A_2 \cup \{m_{r+1}\})^{(r+1)_{\mathcal{C}}} \subseteq A_2^{(r+1)_{\mathcal{C}}} = A_2^{(r)_{\mathcal{C}}}$, i.e. $(A_1 \to A_2)_C$ is valid in the context $\mathbb{K}_r$. Furthermore, $A_2 \cup \{m_{r+1}\} \subseteq A_1^{(r+1)_{\mathcal{C}}(r+1)_{\mathcal{C}}} = (A_1\backslash\{m_{r+1}\})^{(r+1)_{\mathcal{C}}(r+1)_{\mathcal{C}}}$, i.e. $m_{r+1} \in (A_1\backslash\{m_{r+1}\})^{(r+1)_{\mathcal{C}}(r+1)_{\mathcal{C}}}$. This proves that $A_1{\times}C$ is m_{r+1}-modified.

If $A_1 \xrightarrow{Y} A_2$ is valid in $\mathbb{K}_r$ and $A_1{\times}C$ is m_{r+1}-modified, then $(A_1 \to A_2)_C$ is also valid in $\mathbb{K}_r$ for any $C \subseteq Y$, and we have $A_2 \subseteq A_1^{(r)_{\mathcal{C}}(r)_{\mathcal{C}}}$. That is, $A_2 \cup \{m_{r+1}\} \subseteq A_1^{(r)_{\mathcal{C}}(r)_{\mathcal{C}}} \cup \{m_{r+1}\} = A_1^{(r+1)_{\mathcal{C}}(r+1)_{\mathcal{C}}}$. Thus, $(A_1 \to (A_2 \cup \{m_{r+1}\}))_C$ is valid in $\mathbb{K}_{r+1}$.

Example 6. The implication $3 \xrightarrow{P} 125$ is valid in $\mathbb{K}_5$ (Fig 3) and one can verify that $3 \xrightarrow{P} 12$ is also valid in $\mathbb{K}_4$ (see Fig 2).

We have just covered all the implications of $\mathbb{K}_{r+1}$ that have premises in $M_r{\times}\mathcal{C}$. Among these, we want to distinguish those that are built from $\mathbb{K}_r$-quasi-features. The following proposition allows us to determine all m_{r+1}-stable implications of the context $\mathbb{K}_{r+1}$ built from $\mathbb{K}_r$-quasi-features.

Proposition 4. *Let $A \subseteq M_r$ and $C \subseteq \mathcal{C}$ such that $A \times C$ is m_{r+1}-stable. If $A \times C$ is a $\mathbb{K}_r$-quasi-feature, then $A \times C$ is necessarily a $\mathbb{K}_{r+1}$-quasi-feature.*

Proof. Let $A \subseteq M_r$ and $C \subseteq \mathcal{C}$ such that $A \times C$ is m_{r+1}-stable. If $A \times C$ is a $\mathbb{K}_r$-quasi-feature then $A \times C \notin \mathfrak{F}(\mathbb{K}_r)$ and $|\mathfrak{T}(\mathbb{K}_r[A \times C])| = |\mathfrak{T}(\mathbb{K}_r)| + 1$. Let us show that $A \times C \notin \mathfrak{F}(\mathbb{K}_{r+1})$ and $|\mathfrak{T}(\mathbb{K}_{r+1}[A \times C])| = |\mathfrak{T}(\mathbb{K}_{r+1})| + 1$. If $A \times C \in \mathfrak{F}(\mathbb{K}_{r+1})$, then $A = A^{(r+1)_{\mathcal{C}}(r+1)_{\mathcal{C}}}$. Since $A \times C$ is m_{r+1}-stable, $A^{(r+1)_{\mathcal{C}}(r+1)_{\mathcal{C}}} = A^{(r)_{\mathcal{C}}(r)_{\mathcal{C}}}$. Hence $A \times C \in \mathfrak{F}(\mathbb{K}_r)$, which is absurd because $A \times C$ is a $\mathbb{K}_r$-quasi-feature. Thus, $A \times C \notin \mathfrak{F}(\mathbb{K}_{r+1})$. Furthermore, since $A \times C$ is a $\mathbb{K}_r$-quasi-feature, we have $|\mathfrak{T}(\mathbb{K}_r[A \times C])| = |\mathfrak{T}(\mathbb{K}_r)| + 1$. Because $m_{r+1} \notin A \subseteq M_r$ and $A \times C$ is m_{r+1}-stable, we have $|\mathfrak{T}(\mathbb{K}_{r+1}[A \times C])| = |\mathfrak{T}(\mathbb{K}_{r+1})| + 1$.

We now want to determine all m_{r+1}-modified implications of the context $\mathbb{K}_{r+1}$ built from $\mathbb{K}_r$-quasi-features. First, we recall the following definition.

Definition 3. *A product $X \times Y \in S \subseteq 2^{M_r} \times 2^{\mathcal{C}}$ is minimal in S, if there is no element of S which is a strict subset of $X \times Y$.*

Proposition 5. *Let $A \subseteq M_r$ and $C \subseteq \mathcal{C}$ such that $A \times C$ is m_{r+1}-modified. If $A \times C$ is a $\mathbb{K}_r$-quasi-feature and is minimal among $\mathbb{K}_{r+1}[A \times C]$-features, then $A \times C$ is a $\mathbb{K}_{r+1}$-quasi-feature.*

Proof. If $A \times C$ is minimal among $\mathbb{K}_{r+1}[A \times C]$-features, then there is no feature $X \times Y$ of $\mathbb{K}_{r+1}[A \times C]$ such that $X \subseteq A$ and $Y \subseteq C$ with $X \times Y \neq A \times C$. Furthermore, if $A \times C$ is also a m_{r+1}-modified $\mathbb{K}_r$-quasi-feature, then $|\mathfrak{T}(\mathbb{K}_{r+1}[A \times C])| = |\mathfrak{T}(\mathbb{K}_{r+1})| + 1$. And since $A \times C$ is m_{r+1}-modified with $A \subseteq M_r$, we have $A \times C \notin \mathfrak{F}(\mathbb{K}_{r+1})$. Thus, $A \times C$ is a $\mathbb{K}_{r+1}$-quasi-feature.

We can now focus on $\mathbb{K}_{r+1}$-quasi-features $A \times C$ of $M_{r+1} \times \mathcal{C}$ such that $m_{r+1} \in A$. First, we will outline some interesting facts about quasi-features with one empty component.

Remark 3. [10] Let $c \in \mathcal{C}$. If there is a concept $\mathfrak{c}_c$ with non empty components such that $c \in modus(\mathfrak{c}_c)$ and $ext(\mathfrak{c}_c) = G$, then $\emptyset \xrightarrow{c} int(\mathfrak{c}_c)$ is a CAI.

In what follows, we will consider the notation :

$$\mathcal{Y} = \{c \in modus(\mathfrak{c}_c) : \mathfrak{c}_c \in \mathfrak{T}(\mathbb{K}_{r+1}),\ ext(\mathfrak{c}_c) = G,\ \emptyset \xrightarrow{c} int(\mathfrak{c}_c) \text{ is valid in } \mathbb{K}_{r+1}\}$$

For example, consider the concept $(o_1o_2o_3o_4o_5, 4, PN)$ in our running context. We can read that $c = P$ and $int(\mathfrak{c}_P) = 4$, so we have the valid CAI: $\emptyset \xrightarrow{P} 4$

Proposition 6. *Let $C \subseteq \mathcal{C}$. If $\{m_{r+1}\} \times C$ is m_{r+1}-modified, $\mathbb{K}_{r+1}$-quasi-feature, then C is a subset of $\mathcal{Y}$, where $\mathcal{Y}$ is the set of all such c described in Remark 3.*

Proof. Suppose that $\{m_{r+1}\} \times C$ is a $\mathbb{K}_{r+1}$-quasi-feature. To show that C is an element of $\mathcal{Y}$, we need to construct a concept $\mathfrak{c}_C$ as described in Remark 3. Since $\{m_{r+1}\} \times C$ is m_{r+1}-modified, we have $m_{r+1} \in \emptyset^{(r+1)_{\mathcal{C}}(r+1)_{\mathcal{C}}}$. Moreover, $\emptyset^{(r+1)_{\mathcal{C}}} = G$, it follows that the components of $(G, \{m_{r+1}\}, C)$ are respectively subsets of the extent, intent and modus of $\mathfrak{c}_C$. Thus, $\mathfrak{c}_C$ exists.

Let $A \subseteq M_{r+1}$ satisfy $m_{r+1} \in A$, $A \backslash \{m_{r+1}\} \neq \emptyset$, and $C \subseteq \mathcal{C}$. Note that the statements "$A \times C$ is m_{r+1}-modified and $\mathbb{K}_{r+1}$-quasi-feature" and "$(A \backslash \{m_{r+1}\}) \times C$ is a $\mathbb{K}_r$-quasi-feature" are not equivalent. In our running context, $3 \times N$ is 4-modified $\mathbb{K}_{4-1}$-quasi-feature, but $34 \times N$ is not a $\mathbb{K}_4$-quasi-feature. Similarly, $134 \times P$ is 4-modified and is also a $\mathbb{K}_4$-quasi-feature, but $13 \times N$ is not a $\mathbb{K}_{4-1}$-quasi-feature.

Finally, all $\mathbb{K}_{r+1}$-quasi-features $A \times C$ with $A \subseteq M_{r+1}$, $m_{r+1} \in A$ and $C \subseteq \mathcal{C}$ define new implications in $\mathbb{K}_{r+1}$.

Example 7. In this example, we want to update the set of $\mathbb{K}_4$-pseudo-features of the context in Fig. 2, to build the set of all $\mathbb{K}_{4+1}$-pseudo-features of the left context in Fig. 3. First, we recall from [11], the set of all $\mathbb{K}_4$-pseudo-features with respect to M_4:

$$\mathcal{UP}_2(\mathbb{K}_4) = \{\emptyset \times P;\ \emptyset \times N;\ \emptyset \times R;\ \emptyset \times K;\ 3 \times P;\ 4 \times R;\ 3 \times K;\ 3 \times N;\ 2 \times S;\ 3 \times S\}.$$

We already know all 5-stable, $\mathbb{K}_4$-pseudo-features from $\mathcal{UP}_2(\mathbb{K}_4)$ which are:

$$\emptyset \times P\ ;\ \emptyset \times N\ ;\ \emptyset \times R\ ;\ \emptyset \times K.$$

They will be recalled as $\mathbb{K}_{4+1}$-pseudo-features. Regarding 5-modified, $\mathbb{K}_4$-pseudo-features from $\mathcal{UP}_2(\mathbb{K}_4)$, it can be verified that they are also $\mathbb{K}_{4+1}$-quasi-features. We now have to verify if there exist any $\mathbb{K}_{4+1}$-pseudo-features containing the new attribute 5. The $\mathbb{K}_{4+1}$-quasi-features containing the new attribute 5 are:

$$5 \times P\ ;\ 5 \times N\ ;\ 5 \times R\ ;\ 5 \times K\ ;\ 5 \times S\ ;\ 1345 \times N\ ;\ 12345 \times P$$

However, none of these elements is a $\mathbb{K}_{4+1}$-pseudo-feature. Thus, all $\mathbb{K}_{4+1}$-pseudo-features are exactly $\mathbb{K}_4$-pseudo-features from $\mathcal{UP}_2(\mathbb{K}_4)$.

3.2 Update After the Removal of an Attribute

Let $\mathbb{K}_r = (G, M_r, \mathcal{C}, I_r)$ be our initial context. In this section, we want to give a necessary and sufficient condition for a $\mathbb{K}_r$-quasi-feature to be also a $\mathbb{K}_{r-1}$-quasi-feature; then state how to complete this sub-family so as to have all $\mathbb{K}_{r-1}$-pseudo-features. We will start the study with $\mathbb{K}_r$-quasi-features $A \times C$ with $A \subseteq M_{r-1}$.

Our first result is a corollary of Proposition 4. It concerns m_r-stable pairs and $\mathbb{K}_r$-quasi-features.

Corollary 1. *Let $A \times C$ be a $\mathbb{K}_r$-quasi-feature. If $r \notin A$ and $A \times C$ is m_r-stable, then $A \times C$ is a $\mathbb{K}_{r-1}$-quasi-feature.*

Proposition 7. *Let $A \times C$ be m_r-modified, and a $\mathbb{K}_r$-quasi-feature. If $r \notin A$, $A \times C \notin \mathfrak{F}(\mathbb{K}_{r-1})$ and $A \times C$ is minimal among the features in $\mathfrak{F}(\mathbb{K}_{r-1}[A \times C])$, then $A \times C$ is a $\mathbb{K}_{r-1}$-quasi-feature.*

Proof. Since $r \notin A$ and $A \times C \notin \mathfrak{F}(\mathbb{K}_{r-1})$, the augmentation by $A \times C$ produces at least one new feature in $\mathbb{K}_{r-1}[A \times C]$. Furthermore, $A \times C$ is minimal among all features of the context $\mathbb{K}_{r-1}[A \times C]$. Thus, $\mathfrak{F}(\mathbb{K}_{r-1}[A \times C])$ has only one new feature compared to $\mathfrak{F}(\mathbb{K}_{r-1})$. That is $A \times C$ is a $\mathbb{K}_{r-1}$-quasi-feature.

The following proposition explains how to complete the family of pseudo-features derived from Corollary 1 and Proposition 7 in order to obtain an implication base of $\mathbb{K}_{r-1}$.

Proposition 8. *All $\mathbb{K}_{r-1}$-pseudo-features are $\mathbb{K}_r$-pseudo-features.*

Proof. The presence of the attribute m_r in $\mathbb{K}_r$ does not invalidate any implication valid in $\mathbb{K}_{r-1}$ (see Proposition 2). Furthermore, $\mathbb{K}_{r-1}$-pseudo-features build the smallest set of $\mathbb{K}_{r-1}$-quasi-features capable of generating all valid implications. Thus, they are all essential in the construction of $\mathbb{K}_r$-pseudo-features.

From this last proposition, it follows that Corollary 1 and Proposition 7 are sufficient to describe how to build all $\mathbb{K}_{r-1}$-pseudo-features from $\mathbb{K}_r$-pseudo-features.

Example 8. In this example, we deduce all $\mathbb{K}_{r-1}$-pseudo-features from $\mathbb{K}_r$-pseudo-features. More specifically, we want to build $\mathbb{K}_{4-1}$-pseudo-features (the right context in Fig. 3) from $\mathbb{K}_4$-pseudo-features (our running context in Fig. 2).

First, we recall all unit $\mathbb{K}_4$-pseudo-features which are given by the set:

$$\mathcal{UP}_2(\mathbb{K}_4) = \{\emptyset \times P;\ \emptyset \times N;\ \emptyset \times R;\ \emptyset \times K;\ 3 \times P;\ 4 \times R;\ 3 \times K;\ 3 \times N;\ 2 \times S;\ 3 \times S\}.$$

Obviously, there is only one $\mathbb{K}_4$-pseudo-feature in $\mathcal{UP}_2(\mathbb{K}_4)$, containing the attribute 4. It cannot be found in the list of $\mathbb{K}_{4-1}$-pseudo-features. With respect to Corollary 1, Propositions 7 and 8, all unit $\mathbb{K}_{4-1}$-pseudo-features are therefore $\mathcal{UP}_2(\mathbb{K}_{4-1}) = \{\emptyset \times P;\ \emptyset \times N;\ \emptyset \times R;\ \emptyset \times K;\ 3 \times P;\ 3 \times K;\ 3 \times N;\ 2 \times S;\ 3 \times S\}$.

4 Incremental Construction of a CAI Base

In a context $\mathbb{K}_r$, updating a base of conditional attribute implications (CAIs) when a new attribute m_{r+1} is added (respectively, when an existing attribute m_r is removed) means augmenting (respectively, reducing) the initial context by one attribute to get the new context $\mathbb{K}_{r+1}$ (respectively, $\mathbb{K}_{r-1}$), its features $\mathfrak{F}(\mathbb{K}_{r+1})$ (respectively, $\mathfrak{F}(\mathbb{K}_{r-1})$) and its pseudo-features $\mathcal{UP}_2(\mathbb{K}_{r+1})$ (respectively, $\mathcal{UP}_2(\mathbb{K}_{r-1})$).

The update process after a context augmentation by one attribute is described as follows through Algorithm 1:

- First, we create K_{r+1}, then we build all concepts $\mathfrak{T}(\mathbb{K}_{r+1})$, leading to the set of features $\mathfrak{F}(\mathbb{K}_{r+1})$ of $\mathbb{K}_{r+1}$. It is done through Functions `CreateContext`$(m_{r+1}, \mathbb{K})$ and `Features(concepts)`. The function `Features(concepts)` extracts the $\mathbb{K}_{r+1}$-features from the set of $\mathbb{K}_{r+1}$-concepts by taking the Cartesian product of the intent and the modus of each concept.
- Next, the function `quasifeat`$_2(\mathbb{K}_{r+1}, \mathcal{N}, \mathfrak{F}(\mathbb{K}_{r+1}))$ performs a sort out on $\mathcal{N} = (2^{M_{r+1}} \times \mathcal{C}) - (\mathfrak{F}(\mathbb{K}_r) \cup 2^{M_r} \times \mathcal{C})$ to keep all $\mathbb{K}_{r+1}$-quasi-features in X.
- Finally, the function `mincover`$_2(\mathbb{K}_{r+1}, X)$ constructs the set $\mathcal{UP}_2(\mathbb{K}_{r+1})$ of $\mathbb{K}_{r+1}$-pseudo-features, useful for the implication base construction.

Algorithm 1: `UpdateAfterAugmentation` :
Input $\mathbb{K}_r = (G, M_r, \mathcal{C}, I)$; $\mathcal{UP}_2(\mathbb{K}_r)$ and $\mathfrak{F}(\mathbb{K}_r)$.
  $\mathcal{UP}_2(\mathbb{K}_{r+1}) \leftarrow \emptyset$
  $\mathbb{K}_{r+1} \leftarrow \texttt{CreateContext}(m_{r+1}, \mathbb{K}_r)$
  $concepts \leftarrow \texttt{ComputeConcepts}(\mathbb{K}_{r+1})$
  $\mathfrak{F}(\mathbb{K}_{r+1}) \leftarrow \texttt{Features(concepts)}$
  $\mathcal{N} \leftarrow 2^{M_{r+1}} \times \mathcal{C} - (2^{M_r} \times \mathcal{C} \cup \mathfrak{F}(\mathbb{K}_{r+1}))$
  $X \leftarrow \texttt{quasifeat}_2(\mathbb{K}_r, \mathcal{N}, \mathfrak{F}(\mathbb{K}_r))$
  $\mathcal{UP}_2(\mathbb{K}_{r+1}) \leftarrow \texttt{mincover}_2(\mathbb{K}_{r+1}, X \cup \mathcal{UP}_2(\mathbb{K}_r))$
Return $\mathcal{UP}_2(\mathbb{K}_{r+1})$

The following procedure describes $\texttt{quasifeat}_2(\mathbb{K}_r, \mathcal{N}, \mathfrak{F}(\mathbb{K}_r))$. It takes as input the context $\mathbb{K}_r$, the set $\mathcal{N}$ and all features of $\mathbb{K}_r$, i.e. $\mathfrak{F}(\mathbb{K}_r)$ and returns $\mathcal{UP}_2(\mathbb{K}_r)$ as the set of all **relevant quasi-features**[2] with respect to M_r.

Function $\texttt{quasifeat}_2(\mathbb{K}_r, \mathcal{N}, \mathfrak{F}(\mathbb{K}_r))$:
Input The context $\mathbb{K}_r$, $\mathcal{N}$ and $\mathfrak{F}(\mathbb{K}_r)$.

  $\mathcal{UP}_2(\mathbb{K}_r) = []$ *%Create a table to store all quasi-features of* $\mathbb{K}_r$
  i=1
  For all $Z \in \mathcal{N}$
    If $\texttt{feat}_2(Z, \mathbb{K}_r, \mathfrak{F}(\mathbb{K}_r))$ is true
      Add Z to the i-th cell of table $\mathcal{UP}_2(\mathbb{K}_r)$
      $i \leftarrow i + 1$
Return $\mathcal{UP}_2(\mathbb{K}_r)$

The function $\texttt{feat}_2(Z, \mathbb{K}_r, \mathfrak{F}(\mathbb{K}_r))$ verifies if the set $Z = A \times c \in \mathcal{N}$ is a relevant quasi-feature of $\mathbb{K}_r$ with respect to M_r. It takes as input the context $\mathbb{K}_r$, the set $Z = A \times c$, and all features of $\mathbb{K}_r$, i.e. $\mathfrak{F}(\mathbb{K}_r)$ and returns "true" if Z is a relevant quasi-feature of $\mathbb{K}_r$ with respect to M_r and "false" if not.

Function $\texttt{feat}_2(Z, \mathbb{K}_r, \mathfrak{F}(\mathbb{K}_r))$:
  Construct $\mathfrak{F}(\mathbb{K}_r[Z])$
  $\mathcal{D}(\mathbb{K}_r) \leftarrow \mathfrak{F}(\mathbb{K}_r[Z]) \setminus \mathfrak{F}(\mathbb{K}_r)$
  If $\mathcal{D}(\mathbb{K}_r) \neq \{Z\}$,
    return "false" and terminate.   *%If true, Z is already a quasi-feature*
    Else, if $(A)^{(1,2,c)(2,1,c)} \setminus A$ is empty   *%Verify if Z is relevant*
      return "false" and terminate.
      Else, Return "true" and terminate.

Procedure *mincover* computes the set of quasi-features of the minimal cover.

Function $\texttt{mincover}_2(\mathbb{K}_r, X)$:
Input The set $X \leftarrow \texttt{quasifeat}_2(\mathbb{K}_r, \mathcal{N}, \mathfrak{F}(\mathbb{K}_r))$ and the context $\mathbb{K}_r$.

[2] Quasi-features generating non-trivial implications.

$X_1, Store \leftarrow \emptyset$
For all $A{\times}C \in X$
  If $|A| = 0$
    $Store \leftarrow A{\times}C,$ *%Store has all quasi-features with one empty*
  If $|A| > 1$ *%component*
    $X_1 \leftarrow A{\times}C,$
$X \leftarrow X \backslash Store,$
For all $A{\times}C \in Store$
for all $A_1{\times}C_1 \in X$
  If $C = C_1$ and $(A)^{(1,2,C)(1,2,C)} = (A_1)^{(1,2,C_1)(1,2,C_1)}$
    $X \leftarrow X \backslash A_1{\times}C_1,$ *%Delete all elements of X whose implication*
$X_1 \leftarrow X \cap X_1,$ *%conveys the same information as those in Store*
$X \leftarrow X \backslash X_1,$
For all $A_1{\times}C_1 \in X_1$
for all $A{\times}C \in X$
  If $C = C_1$, $A \subseteq A_1$ and $(A)^{(1,2,C)(1,2,C)} = (A_1)^{(1,2,C_1)(1,2,C_1)}$
    $X_1 \leftarrow X_1 \backslash A_1{\times}C_1,$ *%Delete all elements of X_1 whose*
    %implication derives from elements in X
$X \leftarrow X \cup Store \cup X_1,$
Return X.

Example 9. In this example, we update the base of implications of context $\mathbb{K}_3$ (Fig 3 right) to obtain that of context $\mathbb{K}_{3+1}$ (Fig 2).

Input: context $\mathbb{K}_3$,
$\mathcal{UP}_2(\mathbb{K}_3) = \{\emptyset{\times}P;\ \emptyset{\times}R;\ \emptyset{\times}K;\ 2{\times}S;\ 3{\times}P;\ 3{\times}N;\ 3{\times}K;\ 3{\times}S\}$

Execution: The function `Createcontext`$(4, \mathbb{K}_3)$ produces $\mathbb{K}_{3+1}$,
$\mathcal{N} \leftarrow 2^{1234}{\times}\mathcal{C} - (2^{123}{\times}\mathcal{C} \cup \mathfrak{F}(\mathbb{K}_{3+1}))$

$$\texttt{quasifeat}_2(\mathbb{K}_{3+1}, \mathcal{N}, \mathfrak{F}(\mathbb{K}_{3+1})) = \{4{\times}P; 4{\times}N; 4{\times}R; 4{\times}K; 4{\times}S; 1234{\times}P; \emptyset{\times}N\}$$

$$X \leftarrow \texttt{quasifeat}_2(\mathbb{K}_{3+1}, \mathcal{N}, \mathfrak{F}(\mathbb{K}_{3+1}))$$

$$\begin{aligned} X \leftarrow X \cup \mathcal{UP}_2(\mathbb{K}_3) = &\{4{\times}P;\ 4{\times}N;\ 4{\times}R;\ 4{\times}K;\ 4{\times}S;\ 1234{\times}P;\ \emptyset{\times}N;\\ &\emptyset{\times}P;\ \emptyset{\times}R;\ \emptyset{\times}K;\ 2{\times}S;\ 3{\times}P;\ 3{\times}N;\ 3{\times}K;\ 3{\times}S\}\\ \texttt{mincover}_2(\mathbb{K}_{3+1}, X) = &\{\emptyset{\times}P;\ \emptyset{\times}N;\ \emptyset{\times}R;\ \emptyset{\times}K;\ 2{\times}S;\ 3{\times}P;\ 3{\times}N;\ 3{\times}K;\\ &3{\times}S;\ 4{\times}R\} \end{aligned}$$

$\mathcal{UP}_2(\mathbb{K}_{3+1}) \leftarrow \texttt{mincover}_2(\mathbb{K}_{3+1}, X)$.
Output:

$$\begin{aligned} \mathcal{UP}_2(\mathbb{K}_{3+1}) = &\{\emptyset{\times}P;\ \emptyset{\times}N;\ \emptyset{\times}R;\ \emptyset{\times}K;\ 2{\times}S;\ 3{\times}P;\ 3{\times}N;\ 3{\times}K;\\ &3{\times}S;\ 4{\times}R\} \end{aligned}$$

The following algorithm updates the set of pseudo-features of an initial $\mathbb{K}_r := (G, M_r, \mathcal{C}, I_r)$ once the last set T of t attributes is removed from M_r.

Algorithm 2: `UpdateAfterReduction` :
Input $\mathbb{K}_r = (G, M_r, \mathcal{C}, I_r)$, T and $\mathcal{UP}_2(\mathbb{K}_r)$.
  $\mathcal{UP}_2(\mathbb{K}_{r-t}) \leftarrow \emptyset$
  For all $A \times \{c\} \in \mathcal{UP}_2(\mathbb{K}_r)$
    If $T \cap A \neq \emptyset$ and $A \times \{c\}$ is a $(r-t)$-quasi-feature
      $\mathcal{UP}_2(\mathbb{K}_{r-t}) \leftarrow \mathcal{UP}_2(\mathbb{K}_{r-t}) \cup \{A \times \{c\}\}$
Return $\mathcal{UP}_2(\mathbb{K}_{r-t})$

Example 10. In this example, we update the implication base of context $\mathbb{K}_4$ (Fig 2) to obtain that of context $\mathbb{K}_{4-1}$ (Fig 3 right) after the deletion of attribute 4.

Input: context $\mathbb{K}_4$,
$\mathcal{UP}_2(\mathbb{K}_4) = \{\emptyset \times P;\ \emptyset \times N;\ \emptyset \times R;\ \emptyset \times K;\ 2 \times S;\ 3 \times P;\ 3 \times N;\ 3 \times K;\ 3 \times S;\ 4 \times R\}$

Execution: The function `Createcontext`$(3, \mathbb{K}_4)$ produces $\mathbb{K}_{4-1}$.

The pseudo-features of $\mathcal{UP}_2(\mathbb{K}_4)$ that do not contain Attribute 4 are

$$\{\emptyset \times P;\ \emptyset \times N;\ \emptyset \times R;\ \emptyset \times K;\ 2 \times S;\ 3 \times P;\ 3 \times N;\ 3 \times K;\ 3 \times S\}$$

In this set, the element $\emptyset \times N$ is a $\mathbb{K}_4$-pseudo-feature that is not a $\mathbb{K}_{4-1}$-quasi-feature. Thus,
Output: $\mathcal{UP}_2(\mathbb{K}_{4-1}) = \{\emptyset \times P;\ \emptyset \times R;\ \emptyset \times K;\ 2 \times S;\ 3 \times P;\ 3 \times N;\ 3 \times K;\ 3 \times S\}$

Note that a set X with n elements has 2^n subsets. Similarly, for an element $x \in X$, all the subsets of X containing x are 2^{n-1}. Thus, for a given context $\mathbb{K}_r$, the only $\mathbb{K}_r$-quasi-features that we need to verify if they are also $\mathbb{K}_{r+1}$-quasi-features are the m_{r+1}-modified elements. Therefore, to build all $\mathbb{K}_{r+1}$-quasi-features, we need about $(|2^r \times \mathcal{C}| + |m_{r+1} - modified,\ \mathbb{K}_r - quasi - features|)$-tests to select all $\mathbb{K}_{r+1}$-quasi-features, which will then be completed by m_{r+1}-stable, $\mathbb{K}_r$-quasi-features. Knowing that a test for us is the sum of operations that a set must undergo to be qualified as $\mathbb{K}_{r+1}$-quasi-features, we are forced to note that this number of tests is about half as expensive compared to the $|2^{r+1} \times \mathcal{C}|$-tests required to construct the $\mathbb{K}_{r+1}$-quasi-features if we were to start the whole process from scratch.

Regarding the algorithm that computes $\mathbb{K}_{r-1}$-pseudo-features from $\mathbb{K}_r$-pseudo-features, it should be noted that this process is nothing more than a restriction of $\mathbb{K}_r$-pseudo-features to $\mathbb{K}_r$-pseudo-features that do not contain the attribute m_r and are also $\mathbb{K}_{r-1}$-pseudo-features, i.e., subsets of $M_{r-1} \times \mathcal{C}$. Therefore, the execution time is significantly reduced compared to the possible exponential time needed for such computation.

5 Conclusion

This work proposes an efficient way to update Biedermann conditional attribute implication bases when attributes are added or removed. For augmentation, we introduced stable and modified quasi-features to capture how implications evolve, then completed them to form a base. We proved that updating requires only half the effort of full reconstruction. For reduction, we showed that updating pseudo-features amounts to filtering those unaffected by the removed attribute. Overall, the strategy significantly reduces candidate computation and execution time compared to total reconstruction.

One of our future studies is to design an alternative to the update of an implication base when a batch of attributes is added in one shot by adapting the approach defined in [23] to the Triadic Concept Analysis framework. Moreover, an empirical study will be conducted to compare a full reconstruction approach against our solution, focusing on performance and scalability issues (execution time and memory consumption) on large datasets.

References

1. Ananias, K.H.A., Missaoui, R., Ruas, P.H.B., Zarate, L.E., Song, M.A.J.: Triadic concept approximation. Inform. Sci. **572**, 126–146 (2021). ISSN 0020-0255. https://doi.org/10.1016/j.ins.2021.04.064
2. Armstrong, W.W.: Dependency structures of data base relationships. In: Information Processing, vol. 74, pp. 580–583., North-Holland (1974)
3. Belohlavek, R.: Introduction to Formal Concept Analysis, p. 47. Palacky University, Department of Computer Science, Olomouc (2008)
4. Biedermann, K.: How triadic diagrams represent conceptual structures. In: Lukose, D., Delugach, H., Keeler, M., Searle, L., Sowa, J. (eds.) ICCS-ConceptStruct 1997. LNCS, vol. 1257, pp. 304–317. Springer, Heidelberg (1997). https://doi.org/10.1007/BFb0027879
5. Cerf, L., Besson, J., Robardet, C., Boulicaut, J.F.: Data-Peeler: Constraint-based closed pattern mining in n-ary relations. In: Proceedings of the 2008 SIAM International Conference on Data Mining, pp. 37–48. Society for Industrial and Applied Mathematics (2008, April).
6. Everaert-Desmedt, N. The semiotic of Peirce, in Louis Hebert (dir.), Signo [on line]. Rimouski (Quebec) (2021). Available at: http://www.signosemio.com/peirce/semiotic.asp
7. Ganter, B., Obiedkov, S.: Implications in triadic formal contexts. In: Wolff, K.E., Pfeiffer, H.D., Delugach, H.S. (eds.) ICCS-ConceptStruct 2004. LNCS (LNAI), vol. 3127, pp. 186–195. Springer, Heidelberg (2004). https://doi.org/10.1007/978-3-540-27769-9_12
8. Ganter, B., Wille, R.: Formal concept analysis: mathematical foundations (2024). Springer. https://doi.org/10.1007/978-3-642-59830-2
9. Guigues, J.L., Duquenne, V.: Familles minimales d'implications informatives résultant d'un tableau de données binaires. Mathématiques et Sciences Humaines **95** 5-18 (1986). Available at: http://eudml.org/doc/94331

10. Kwessy Mouona, R., Koguep Njionou, B.B., Kwuida, L., Temgoua Alomo, E.R.: An optimal set of implications in triadic contexts. In: Panchenko, A., et al. Analysis of Images, Social Networks and Texts. AIST 2024. Lecture Notes in Computer Science, vol 15419. Springer, Cham (2025). https://doi.org/10.1007/978-3-031-88036-0_13
11. Mouona, R.K., Njionou, B.B.K., Alomo, E.R.T., Missaoui, R., Kwuida, L.: A construction of an optimal base for conditional attribute and attributional condition implications in triadic contexts [Preprint] (2026). arXiv. Available at: https://arxiv.org/abs/2601.01467
12. Lehmann, F., and Wille, R. (1995). A triadic approach to formal concept analysis. In Conceptual Structures: Applications, Implementation and Theory: Third International Conference on Conceptual Structures, ICCS'95 Santa Cruz, CA, USA, August 14–18, 1995 Proceedings 3 (pp. 32-43). Springer Berlin Heidelberg
13. Makhalova, T., Nourine, L.: An incremental algorithm for computing n-concepts. In: Formal Concept Analysis for Knowledge Discovery. Proceedings of International Workshop on Formal Concept Analysis for Knowledge Discovery (FCA4KD 2017), Moscow, Russia (2017 June)
14. Missaoui, R., Kwuida, L.: Mining triadic association rules from ternary relations. In: International Conference on Formal Concept Analysis, pp. 204–218. Berlin, Heidelberg: Springer Berlin Heidelberg (2011 May).
15. Missaoui, R., Ruas, P.H.B., Kwuida, L., Song, M.A.J.: Pattern discovery in triadic contexts. In: Alam, M., Braun, T., Yun, B. (eds.) ICCS 2020. LNCS (LNAI), vol. 12277, pp. 117–131. Springer, Cham (2020). https://doi.org/10.1007/978-3-030-57855-8_9
16. Missaoui, R., Ruas, P.H.B., Kwuida, L., et al.: Computing triadic generators and association rules from triadic contexts. Ann. Math. Artif. Intell. **90**(2022), 1083–1105 (2022). https://doi.org/10.1007/s10472-022-09784-4
17. Obiedkov, S., Duquenne, V.: Incremental construction of the canonical implication basis. In: Fourth International Conference Journée de l'Informatique messine, pp. 15–23 (2003). https://doi.org/10.1007/s10472-007-9057-2
18. Rodriguez-Lorenzo, E., Cordero, P., Enciso, M., Missaoui, R., Mora, Á.: An axiomatic system for conditional attribute implications in triadic concept analysis. Int. J. Intell. Syst. **32**(8), 760–777 (2017). https://doi.org/10.1002/int.21888
19. Rodrıguez-Lorenzo, E., Cordero, P., Enciso, M., Missaoui, R., Mora, Á.: Caisl: Simplification logic for conditional attribute implications. In: CLA, pp. 337–348 (2016)
20. Ruas, P.H., Missaoui, R., Song, M.A., Kwuida, L.: Mining the Groceries Database using Triadic Concept Analysis (2021). *RealDataFCA@ICFCA*
21. Rudolph, S.: Some notes on pseudo-closed sets. In: Kuznetsov, S.O., Schmidt, S. (eds.) ICFCA 2007. LNCS (LNAI), vol. 4390, pp. 151–165. Springer, Heidelberg (2007). https://doi.org/10.1007/978-3-540-70901-5_10
22. Valtchev, P., Missaoui, R., Lebrun, P.: A partition-based approach towards constructing Galois (concept) lattices. Discret. Math. **256**(3), 801–829 (2002)
23. Valtchev, P., Duquenne, V.: On the merge of factor canonical bases. In: Medina, R., Obiedkov, S. (eds.) ICFCA 2008. LNCS (LNAI), vol. 4933, pp. 182–198. Springer, Heidelberg (2008). https://doi.org/10.1007/978-3-540-78137-0_14
24. Wille, R.: The basic theorem of triadic concept analysis. Order **12**, 149–158 (1995)

Algorithms

GreCon2Compact: Memory-Efficient Evolution of the GreCon Algorithm for Boolean Matrix Factorization

Petr Krajča(✉) and Martin Trnecka

Department of Computer Science, Palacky University Olomouc, Olomouc, Czech Republic

petr.krajca@upol.cz

Abstract. Boolean matrix factorization (BMF) is a data analysis technique for discovering the latent structure in binary data. BMF is closely related to Formal Concept Analysis (FCA), as it can be viewed as the task of selecting a subset of formal concepts that covers all 1s (nonzero entries) in an input binary matrix. Based on this relationship, the GreCon and GreCon2 algorithms were proposed. Although these algorithms provide high-quality factorizations, they suffer from high computational and memory requirements. In this paper, we introduce GreCon2Compact, a novel algorithm that significantly reduces the memory demands of GreCon2 while improving its computational performance. The reduced memory footprint is achieved by employing space-efficient data structures during the selection of formal concepts. Consequently, GreCon2Compact is capable of processing datasets previously considered infeasible. Moreover, the reduced memory footprint enables further extensions of the algorithm, including a parallel implementation.

1 Introduction

Boolean Matrix Factorization (BMF) is a well-established technique for the analysis of binary data [10]. Its goal is to represent an input binary matrix as the product of two smaller binary matrices while preserving the essential information contained in the original data. Such a decomposition provides an interpretable representation of the data in terms of latent factors capturing underlying patterns [2].

A variety of algorithms for BMF have been proposed. Many of them exploit a close connection with Formal Concept Analysis (FCA) [5], which was established by Belohlavek and Vychodil in their seminal work [3]. FCA provides a principled framework for analyzing binary relations and extracting meaningful structures from binary datasets. In approaches exploiting this connection, formal concepts are typically used as factors; such methods are commonly referred to as *from-below* BMF [1].

Formally, the goal of from-below BMF is, for a given input binary matrix $\mathbf{I} \in \{0,1\}^{m\times n}$, to find two binary matrices $\mathbf{A} \in \{0,1\}^{m\times k}$ and $\mathbf{B} \in \{0,1\}^{k\times n}$

M. Croitoru et al. (Eds.): CONCEPTS 2026, LNAI 16811, pp. 105–121, 2027.
https://doi.org/10.1007/978-3-032-34742-8_7

such that

$$\mathbf{A} \circ \mathbf{B} \leq \mathbf{I},$$

where $\circ$ denotes the Boolean matrix product defined by

$$(\mathbf{A} \circ \mathbf{B})_{ij} = \bigvee_{l=1}^{k} (A_{il} \wedge B_{lj}),$$

with $\wedge$ and $\vee$ denoting the logical AND and OR, respectively. Equivalently, $(\mathbf{A} \circ \mathbf{B})_{ij} = 1$ if and only if there exists $l \in \{1, \ldots, k\}$ such that $\mathbf{A}_{il} = 1$ and $\mathbf{B}_{lj} = 1$.

Typically, the inner dimension k is much smaller than m and n and corresponds to the number of latent factors explaining the structure of the data. The aim of BMF is therefore to find matrices $\mathbf{A}$ and $\mathbf{B}$ providing a compact representation of $\mathbf{I}$ while minimizing the reconstruction error. An illustrative example of BMF follows.

Example 1. An exact decomposition of matrix $\mathbf{I}$ containing three factors.

$$\mathbf{I} = \begin{bmatrix} 1&1&1&1&0 \\ 0&0&0&1&1 \\ 0&1&1&1&0 \\ 1&1&0&0&0 \end{bmatrix} = \mathbf{A} \circ \mathbf{B} = \begin{bmatrix} 1&1&0 \\ 0&0&1 \\ 1&0&0 \\ 0&1&0 \end{bmatrix} \circ \begin{bmatrix} 0&1&1&1&0 \\ 1&1&0&0&0 \\ 0&0&0&1&1 \end{bmatrix} = \begin{bmatrix} 0&1&1&1&0 \\ 0&0&0&0&0 \\ 0&1&1&1&0 \\ 0&0&0&0&0 \end{bmatrix} \vee \begin{bmatrix} 1&1&0&0&0 \\ 0&0&0&0&0 \\ 0&0&0&0&0 \\ 1&1&0&0&0 \end{bmatrix} \vee \begin{bmatrix} 0&0&0&0&0 \\ 0&0&0&1&1 \\ 0&0&0&0&0 \\ 0&0&0&0&0 \end{bmatrix}.$$

In FCA-based approaches, the matrices $\mathbf{A}$ and $\mathbf{B}$ can be derived from a subset $\mathcal{F}$ of all formal concepts $\mathcal{B}$ of the input data, where $\mathcal{F}$ is referred to as the set of *factor concepts*. Recall that a *formal concept* is a pair $\langle C, D \rangle$, where C is a set of objects (called the *extent*) and D is a set of attributes (called the *intent*) such that C contains exactly the objects sharing all attributes in D, and D contains exactly the attributes common to all objects in C. In particular, the columns of $\mathbf{A}$ correspond to the extents of concepts in $\mathcal{F}$, represented by their characteristic vectors. Analogously, the rows of $\mathbf{B}$ correspond to the intents of the concepts in $\mathcal{F}$.

Based on this relationship, the GreCon and GreCon2 algorithms were proposed [3]. Although these algorithms produce high-quality factorizations, they suffer from substantial computational and memory requirements, which limits their applicability to larger datasets. This issue is partially addressed by the GreCon3 algorithm [8], which improves computational speed but reduces memory requirements only to a limited extent.

In this paper, we introduce GreCon2Compact, a novel algorithm designed to reduce the memory demands of GreCon2 while simultaneously improving its computational performance. The reduction in memory consumption is achieved by employing more space-efficient data structures during the selection and processing of formal concepts. As a result, the proposed algorithm is able to process datasets that were previously infeasible to handle with existing approaches. Moreover, the reduced memory footprint enables further extensions of the method, including a parallel implementation.

2 Algorithm

In [3] Belohlavek and Vychodil proposed the GreCon algorithm for BMF.[1] The algorithm uses a simple greedy strategy to find a matrix decomposition: (a) It enumerates all format concepts first, then (b) for each formal concept computes its *coverage* which is a number of 1s in the input matrix not covered by any factor concept discovered so far, (c) selects a concept with the highest coverage, (d) repeats steps (b) and (c) until all 1s in the input matrix are covered by some factor concept.

Steps (a) and (b) may be very time demanding, especially for large datasets. While the step (a) may be sped up with a suitable algorithm [6], possibly parallel [7], speeding up the step (b) requires a more fundamental change of the algorithm.

In [11] Trnecka and Vyjidacek propose the GreCon2 algorithm which uses auxiliary data structures to improve performance of the algorithm. These data structures are:

(i) the *covers* array maintaining information on how many uncovered 1s each concept covers,
(ii) the *cells* array that keeps a list of concepts covering each uncovered one in the input matrix.

Due to the *covers* array, the GreCon2 algorithm always has up-to-date information on how many 1s each concept covers. This information is used to discover the next factor concept. While the *cells* array provides list of concepts whose coverage has to be updated whenever a new factor concept is discovered. In consequence, it is no longer necessary to recompute coverage for each formal concept.

In fact, GreCon2 trades CPU time for memory. Consequently, available memory may become the bottleneck of this algorithm. To address this issue, in [8] Krajča and Trnecka propose the GreCon3 algorithm which initializes GreCon2's data structures incrementally. This, along with other optimizations, reduces CPU time and memory demands of the algorithm.

We now turn to the *cells* array. While it is the key component of the GreCon2 algorithm, it is also its the most memory-intensive structure. The GreCon2 algorithm assume that it is an array of size $m \times n$, i.e., for each cell in the input matrix $\mathbf{I}$ (no matter if 0 or 1), there is a corresponding cell in the *cells* array. If the cell of the *cells* array corresponds to an uncovered 1, it contains a list of concepts covering it, otherwise the cell is empty. Such representation is inefficient since it contains large amounts of empty cells for sparse datasets. Note that such data are often encountered in practice. Furthermore, access to a sparsely populated arrays is usually slow since the CPU can not utilize its cache to speed up memory access.

The GreCon3 algorithm uses a more compact data structure which avoids these issues. Basically, it is a data structure similar to a sparse matrix representation. For each row in the input matrix, it maintains a sequence of pairs

[1] In [3] it is denoted as *Algorithm 1*.

$\langle column, indexes \rangle$ whenever the cell in $\mathbf{I}_{row,column}$ contains an uncovered 1. See Fig. 1 for an illustrative example.

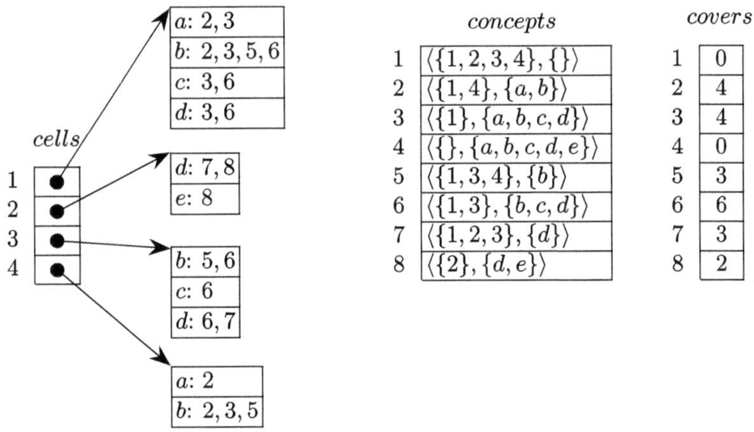

Fig. 1. Example of the *cells* data structure representation for the matrix in Example 1.

This improvement solves the high memory consumption issue only partially. Large amount of memory is allocated to store the lists of indexes referenced from the *cells* arrays. Therefore, when addressing the issue of high memory consumption, we must focus not only on the representation of the *cells* array itself, as GreCon3 does. We must also pay attention to the representation of the lists stored in the *cells* array.

2.1 Native List Encoding

Neither [11], nor [8] provide details on how the lists of indexes are supposed to be represented in GreCon2 and GreCon3. Therefore, it is reasonable to assume that implementations of the both algorithms would use a general list of integers. Straightforward representation of such list consists of an array of integers along with the number of values in the list. Note that reference implementations of these algorithms by their authors use this representation.

Since all values in the array are of a uniform size matching the processor's native data types (e.g., 32 bits), list manipulation operations are highly efficient. In what follows, we shall refer to this representation as *native encoding*.

2.2 Variable Length Encoding of Integers

The significant shortcoming of the native encoding in GreCon2 is its poor space efficiency. Clearly, not all values from the range of 32bit integers appear in the list of indexes. It is therefore natural to use a more space efficient integer encoding, for instance, *variable length quantity encoding* (VLQ). The VLQ encoding uses binary octets (bytes) to encode arbitrarily large integers. Basically, the most significant bit of each octet indicates if the encoding of a number is complete, or not. The remaining 7 bits of each octet are then concatenated to form an encoded value. For instance, values 13 and 863 are encoded as follows:

$$\phi_{VLQ}(13) = \mathbf{0}000\,1101, \phi_{VLQ}(863) = \mathbf{1}000\,0011\quad \mathbf{0}011\,1111.$$

Moreover, as GreCon2 stores indexes in ascending order, we can utilize delta encoding to further reduce the memory footprint by storing only the differences between consecutive values.

The size of the list should be represented as a fixed-size integer (32bit or 64bit). Each list grows during the GreCon2's initialization phase, thus we do not known in advance how many bits to allocate for the value representing the size of the list.

2.3 Custom Variable Length Encoding of Integers

The VLQ encoding has widespread applications, since it can be efficiently implemented and often provides significant improvement over fixed-size integer encoding. However, it has limits. Obviously, at least 8 bits is used to encode each value. Thus, in the best-case scenario the VLQ encoding can only be 4× more space efficient than the native encoding.

We observed that similar concepts often have similar indexes. This is a direct consequence of CbO-algorithms used to enumerate formal concepts.[2] The CbO-algorithms recursively extend each concept with a new attribute to form a new concept. In consequence, concepts listed close to each other tend to cover similar 1s in the input matrix. This reflects in the list of concept indexes if indexes are stored as deltas. The values are distributed non-uniformly in the lists; low values are prevailing, ones are often the most common values. Therefore, we propose our own encoding scheme tailored to exploit these observations.

In our custom variable length encoding (CVLQ) values are divided into four groups and encoded respectively:

- value 1 is encoded with a single bit 1;
- values from 2 to 17 (inclusive) are encoded using 6 bits in a form '01 $xxxx$' where is $xxxx$ is a 4bit unsigned integer which is increased by 2 to obtain the encoded value,
- values from 18 to 1041 (inclusive) are encoded using 13 bits as a sequence '001 xx $xxxx$ $xxxx$' where 10 least significant bits represent an unsigned integer which is increased by 18 to obtain the encoded value,
- all other values are represented as three bits '000' followed by 31 bits directly encoding the value.

[2] The CbO-algorithms are the state-of-the-art algorithms for enumerating formal concepts. Hence, we assume their use in conjunction with the GreCon algorithms.

Examples of the above-described CVLQ encoding:

$$\phi_{CVLQ}(1) = \mathbf{1}, \phi_{CVLQ}(13) = \mathbf{01}\underbrace{1011}_{11}, \phi_{CVLQ}(863) = \mathbf{001}\underbrace{11\,0100\,1101}_{845}.$$

2.4 GreCon2Compact Algorithm

With the aim to deal with high memory demands of the GreCon algorithms we propose a novel algorithm encompassing the following features:

- it is based on GreCon2 [11],
- uses a sparse representation of the *cells* data structure [8],
- uses a variable length encoding of lists in the *cells* data structure,
- optimizes discovery of the first factor.

This algorithm, named *GreCon2Compact*, has its pseudocode listed as Algorithm 1. It takes binary matrix $\mathbf{I}$ of size $m \times n$ and returns a set of factor concepts. The algorithm has two parts, (i) the initialization phase when all data structures are prepared, (ii) iterative step when new factors are discovered.

During the initialization phase, the algorithm obtains a set of all formal concepts (line 1) by arbitrary suitable algorithm (e.g., from the CbO family [6]). Then, the first factor concept is discovered (lines 2 and 3). The first factor concept has an exceptional feature. Its coverage is always the product of the sizes of its extent and intent. Therefore, it is sufficient to find the largest formal concept, i.e., the formal concept covering the largest number of 1s. This optimization not only reduces the time to discover the first factor concept, it also reduces time necessary to initialize the *cells* data structure. Indeed, we do not need initialize *cells* for 1s that are covered by the first factor. Moreover, the first factor often covers a large portion of 1s in the input data, hence, this simple optimization helps to reduce both memory and time demands of the algorithm. Therefore, the algorithm computes matrix $\mathbf{I}^0$ (line 4) which corresponds to the input matrix where all 1s covered by the first factor are turned to 0 s. The initialization concludes with construction of the *cells* data structure (line 5). For this purpose, we use an auxiliary procedure BuildCells taking a set of all concepts and the matrix $\mathbf{I}^0$ (indicating which 1s are still uncovered) as its arguments. Details on this procedure are provided later.

The main loop of the algorithm (lines 6 to 15), that takes care of discovery of factor concepts, is very similar to that of GreCon2. In each iteration, factor covering the largest portion of uncovered 1s is identified using the *covers* array and inserted into the set $\mathcal{F}$ of factor concepts (line 7 to 9). Afterwards, all covered 1s are removed from the *cells* data structure and values in the *covers* array are adjusted (lines 10 to 15). These steps have to be aligned with the actual representation of the *cells* data structure. Therefore, we iterate over all rows in the factor's extent. Then, we take all uncovered 1s in the given row (lines 11 to 15). If the given one is covered by the factor concept (line 12), it is removed

Algorithm 1: GRECON2COMPACT(**I**)

Input: Input matrix **I** of size $m \times n$.
Output: Set of factor concepts $\mathcal{F}$.

1 $concepts \leftarrow$ COMPUTEFORMALCONCEPTS($\mathbf{I}$);
2 $\langle A_0, B_0\rangle \leftarrow$ find concept $\langle A_0, B_0\rangle \in \mathcal{B}$ such that $|A| \times |B|$ is maximal;
3 $\mathcal{F} \leftarrow \{\langle A_0, B_0\rangle\}$;
4 $\mathbf{I}^0 \leftarrow \mathbf{I} - (\mathbf{A}_\mathcal{F} \circ \mathbf{B}_\mathcal{F})$;
5 $cells, covers \leftarrow$ BUILDCELLS($concepts, \mathbf{I}^0$);
6 **while** $\mathbf{A}_\mathcal{F} \circ \mathbf{B}_\mathcal{F} \neq \mathbf{I}$ **do**
7     $l \leftarrow$ find index l in covers such that $covers[l]$ is maximal;
8     $\langle A_l, B_l\rangle \leftarrow concepts[l]$;
9     $\mathcal{F} \leftarrow \mathcal{F} \cup \{\langle A_l, B_l\rangle\}$;
10   **foreach** $i \in A_l$ **do**
11   **foreach** $\langle j, indexes\rangle \in cells[i]$ **do**
12   **if** $j \in B_l$ **then**
13                 $cells[i] \leftarrow cells[i] - \{\langle j, indexes\rangle\}$;
14   **foreach** $k \in indexes$ **do**
15                     $covers[k] \leftarrow covers[k] - 1$;
16 **return** $\mathcal{F}$;

from *cells* (line 13). Further, coverage of all formal concepts covering this one, is reduced by 1 (lines 14 to 15).

The algorithm stops when all 1s are covered (line 6) and set of factors is returned (line 16).

It remains to clarify the auxiliary procedure BUILDCELLS that takes care of the *cells* data structure initialization, see pseudocode in Algorithm 2. This procedure takes a set of formal concepts to initialize the data structure with and the matrix $\mathbf{I}^0$ indicating uncovered ones.

First, the procedure creates an empty *cells* array (line 1) of size m (number of lines in the input matrix). Then, for each uncovered one $\mathbf{I}_{ij}$ in each row i creates a pair $\langle j, \{\}\rangle$. The first part of the pair is a column, the latter part is a set of concept indexes covering the entry on coordinates i, j (lines 3 to 8).

Afterwards, the procedure iterates over all formal concepts (lines 9 to 17) and computes its coverage (lines 10, 16, and 17). For each one covered by this concept an index is inserted to the corresponding list (lines 13 to 16). This part of the procedure reflects the layout of the *cells* data structure. We iterate over all rows in the extent of the concept (lines 11 to 16), then for each one in the given row (lines 12 to 16) we check if it is covered by the concept (lines 13). If so, index of the concept is placed in the list and coverage of the concept is increased by one.

In the description of the *cells* data structure we use a set notation to denote collection of pairs $\langle j, indexes\rangle$. In practical implementation any appropriate data structure can be used, for instance, an array.

Algorithm 2: BuildCells($concepts, \mathbf{I}^0$)

Input: Array *concepts* of all formal concepts. Matrix $\mathbf{I}^0$ of size $m \times n$ with uncovered 1s.

Output: The *cell* data structure; the *covers* array with coverage of each formal concept.

```
cells ← empty array of size m;
covers ← empty array of size |concepts|;
for i from 1 to m do
    row ← {};
    for j from 1 to n do
        if I⁰_ij = 1 then
            row ← row ∪ {⟨j, {}⟩};
    cells[i] ← row;
foreach ⟨A_l, B_l⟩ ∈ 𝓑 do
    c ← 0;
    foreach i ∈ A_l do
        foreach ⟨j, list⟩ ∈ cells[i] do
            if j ∈ B_l then
                cells[i] ← cells[i] − {⟨j, list⟩};
                cells[i] ← cells[i] ∪ {⟨j, list ∪ {l}⟩};
                c ← c + 1;
    covers[l] ← c;
return cells, covers;
```

Similarly, we use a set notation to describe lists of indexes referencing to concepts covering entries in the input matrix. This is the place where one of the aforementioned encoding schemes is applied. Since encodings of these lists is an implementation aspect, it is not explicitly mentioned in the pseudocode and its up to the implementor's decision which encoding is to be used.

Remark 1. In the both cases each value in the list appears upmost once, thus, both collections can be seen as sets, even though they are represented as arrays or lists in the memory of computer.

2.5 Parallel Variant of the Algorithm

Reduced memory footprint of the algorithm allows to increase the size of data the algorithm can processed. Consequently, with the increasing size of data also increases time spent within the BuildCells procedure. To reduce this time one may utilize modern multi-core hardware to initialize the *cells* data structure in parallel. The parallel variant of the BuildCells procedure works as follows:

1. For each thread an empty independent *cells* data structure is build.

2. All formal concepts are split into small batches, e.g., by 1,000 or 10,000 concepts (depending on overall number of concepts). These batches are placed in a single shared working queue.
3. Each thread picks a batch from the queue and places all concepts from the batch in its *cells* data structure.
4. This repeats until all batches are processed.
5. Finally, all *cells* data structures from all threads are merged into a single data structure *cells* used by Algorithm 1.

Remark 2. It is also possible to parallelize the step of the GreCon2 algorithm which finds the concept with the maximal coverage, see Algorithm 1, line 7. From our observations parallelization of this step is beneficial when dealing with high volumes of concepts, approximately millions or more. Otherwise, the effect of the parallelization of this step is negligible or negative. Therefore, in our implementation we do not parallelize this step.

3 Experimental Results

We experimentally evaluated the proposed encodings—native, VLQ, and CVLQ—in terms of memory usage and computational speed. The GreCon2Compact algorithm was implemented in the Java programming language. Note that the native encoding serves as a baseline, as it represents algorithm very close the original GreCon2 algorithm.

All experiments were performed on otherwise idle computer equipped with AMD Ryzen Threadripper 3960X (24 cores × 2 threads), 188 GB RAM, running Ubuntu Linux and Java 25. For the purposes of our experiments the heap size of Java Virtual Machine was set to 100 GB.

3.1 Datasets

In the experimental evaluation, we used standard real-world benchmark datasets from UCI ML Dataset Repository [9], FIMI Dataset Repository,[3] [4].[4] All of them are commonly employed in BMF research.

The characteristics of the datasets are shown in Table 1. Specifically, the number of objects, the number of attributes, the density of non-zero entries in the data (in percents), and the number of concepts.

3.2 Memory Footprint

The main goal of the GreCon2Compact is to reduce the memory footprint of the algorithm. To validate this goal, we have to be able to quantify amount of consumed memory. Unlike in case of CPU-time we can not simply measure the

[3] http://fimi.uantwerpen.be/data/.

[4] Binarized versions of several datasets used in the paper are available on the web page https://phoenix.inf.upol.cz/~konecnja/fcalad/.

memory the process has allocated to run the algorithm. For instance, (i) running process usually allocates more RAM than it actually needs at the given moment, (ii) in case of languages with a garbage collector, there may be unused

Table 1. Datasets and their characteristics.

dataset	objects	attributes	density (%)	concepts
T10I4D100K	100,000	1,000	1.01	2,347,376
advertisement	3,279	1,557	0.88	9,192
americas_large	10,127	3,485	52.50	36,992
americas_small	3,477	1,587	1.91	2,764
apj	2,044	1,164	0.29	798
customer	10,961	277	1.50	47,848
dna	4,590	392	1.47	4,483
inter10crx_nomissing	653	139	44.10	10,199,818
inter3magic04	19,020	52	40.39	1,006,553
inter5bikesharing_day	731	93	36.26	3,023,326
inter5crx_nomissing	653	79	39.80	348,428
inter5shuttle	43,500	88	42.09	333,783
inter6shuttle	43,500	106	43.44	381,636
mushroom	8,124	119	17.65	221,525
nfs	12,841	4,894	89.82	24,303,286
nom10bikesharing_day	731	100	12.71	52,697
nom10crx_nomissing	653	85	15.81	51,078
nom10shuttle	43,500	97	10.31	2,931
nom10x10magic04	19,020	102	10.79	583,386
nom15magic04	19,020	152	7.24	1,149,717
nom20magic04	19,020	202	5.45	1,376,212
nom5bikesharing_day	731	65	19.57	61,853
nom5bikesharing_hour	17,379	90	15.23	1,868,205
nom5crx_nomissing	653	55	24.44	29,697
nom5shuttle	43,500	52	19.23	1,461
ord10bikesharing_day	731	93	41.66	664,713
ord10crx_nomissing	653	79	71.78	1,547,971
ord10shuttle	43,500	88	48.34	97,357
ord5bikesharing_day	731	58	35.18	81,277
ord5bikesharing_hour	17,379	83	31.73	2,174,964
ord5crx_nomissing	653	49	60.78	139,752
ord5magic04	19,020	42	66.98	821,796
ord5shuttle	43,500	43	46.45	4,068

objects in the memory, memory can be reclaimed undeterministically, (iii) each allocated object is accompanied with its header which may differ by processor, operating system, or even by configuration of the runtime environment.

In order to suppress technical complexities related to memory allocation, we decided not to measure the memory assigned to the running process, but rather to compute the amount of memory required to encode data in the memory of a computer. We primarily focus on the encoding of indexes in the *cells* data structure and the formal concepts since these data occupy the major part of the memory.

Let L be a set of n values $L = \{a_1, a_2, \ldots, a_n\}$. To encode this set with the native encoding, we need $4+4 \cdot n$ bytes, i.e., 4 bytes per each value and additional 4 bytes to hold information on size of the set. For variable length encodings we assume that we need to allocate byte array to store all bits of the encoding and additional four bytes to represent size of this array and four bytes for number of values in the set, i.e., we need

$$8 + \left\lceil \frac{|\phi(a_1)| + \sum_{i=2}^{n} |\phi(a_i - a_{i-1})|}{8} \right\rceil$$

bytes in total. Note that $|\phi(x)|$ denotes number of bits to encode number x.

For the sake of comparison we include also the sizes of concepts that are stored in the memory (see column "concepts" in Table 2). Albeit various encoding can be used to encode concepts, we assume that extent is encoded as a list of integers, i.e., the native encoding is used, and intents are encoded as bit vectors aligned to the size of the machines native word sizes, i.e., bit vector aligned to 64 bits. This means, a formal concept $\langle A, B \rangle$ in a matrix $m \times n$ is encoded with

$$4 + 4 \cdot |A| + 8 \cdot \left\lceil \frac{n}{64} \right\rceil$$

bytes. This combination of encodings was selected since it is commonly used by algorithms for computing formal concepts.

During the computation, memory is gradually released, since parts of the *cells* data structure are no longer needed. We analyzed in detail how memory usage decreases during the computation of individual factors. The results for selected datasets are shown in Fig. 2.

Generally, we can observe from results in Table 2 that in some cases storing the formal concepts alone already requires a substantial amount of memory. The native encoding typically needs several times more memory for storing the cell structure than is required to store the concepts themselves. The VLQ encoding provides an average reduction of about 70%, while CVLQ achieves a reduction of approximately 80%, exceeding 90% for several large datasets.

Note that for the datasets inter5shuttle, inter6shuttle, and ord5magic04, the native encoding does not allow the factorization to be computed due to insufficient memory. The dataset inter6shuttle, which has the largest number of concepts, cannot be factorized even using the VLQ encoding.

The results indicate that VLQ and CVLQ provide significant memory savings.

Table 2. Comparison of memory requirements, in megabytes (MB), where 1 MB = 2^{20} bytes, for different encodings. Symbol "–" indicates that the algorithm was unable to compute the factorization due to insufficient memory. The column "concepts" indicates how many megabytes are required to store all formal concepts.

dataset	concepts	native	VLQ	CVLQ
T10I4D100K	386,365	247,928	92,796	102,593
advertisement	2,449	3,167	1,209	1,199
americas_large	49,488	270,886	69,550	24,103
americas_small	960	15,471	4,244	1,935
apj	161	78	64	91
customer	4,663	8,814	2,814	2,596
dna	759	1,603	666	635
inter10crx_nomissing	3,275,883	29,822,894	7,494,042	2,161,511
inter3magic04	3,928,194	18,261,378	4,612,626	2,479,863
inter5bikesharing_day	771,541	6,074,039	1,527,415	454,658
inter5crx_nomissing	120,666	739,987	186,556	62,037
inter5shuttle	42,977,107	–	16,549,390	4,959,124
inter6shuttle	43,151,930	–	–	8,723,342
mushroom	92,518	556,689	146,249	84,865
nfs	15,450,658	1,403,877	453,131	446,347
nom10bikesharing_day	2,535	5,527	1,601	1,306
nom10crx_nomissing	5,315	18,307	4,753	2,549
nom10shuttle	76,393	141,123	37,517	19,667
nom10x10magic04	102,193	370,162	104,025	89,261
nom15magic04	122,704	402,393	115,927	99,485
nom20magic04	125,642	322,487	94,796	84,207
nom5bikesharing_day	3,855	11,259	3,048	2,032
nom5bikesharing_hour	264,152	1,117,953	297,467	203,239
nom5crx_nomissing	5,166	18,747	4,829	2,309
nom5shuttle	68,191	123,817	32,611	18,974
ord10bikesharing_day	204,156	1,696,737	426,537	105,497
ord10crx_nomissing	897,054	5,979,904	1,502,910	446,707
ord10shuttle	13,335,365	29,713,035	7,445,853	2,018,210
ord5bikesharing_day	15,332	74,541	18,966	6,356
ord5bikesharing_hour	2,652,883	13,343,420	3,363,586	774,816
ord5crx_nomissing	76,357	380,087	95,805	32,546
ord5magic04	10,601,244	–	12,150,122	6,461,726
ord5shuttle	521,025	576,037	146,188	55,797

Table 3. Minimal running times of GreCon2Compact for the initialization phase and the total time (in milliseconds) using a single thread.

dataset	initial phase			total time		
	native	VLQ	CVLQ	native	VLQ	CVLQ
T10I4D100K	4,463	4,617	7,250	12,285	12,503	17,892
advertisement	22	23	21	119	118	121
americas_large	1,265	2,079	1,435	2,290	3,253	2,778
americas_small	57	52	57	112	108	126
apj	1	0	0	14	16	14
customer	61	59	67	115	133	161
dna	11	10	11	26	26	29
inter10crx_nomissing	–	13,780,260	226,713	–	13,808,737	282,207
inter3magic04	471,253	789,445	460,666	481,230	808,851	500,964
inter5bikesharing_day_cut	42,727	466,509	40,290	44,740	470,376	48,918
inter5crx_nomissing	9,919	41,294	6,226	10,773	42,185	8,699
inter5shuttle	–	7,802,713	3,787,801	–	7,856,671	3,892,893
inter6shuttle	–	11,558,313	6,493,276	–	11,630,546	6,664,898
mushroom	4,137	4,324	3,968	4,519	4,859	5,276
nfs	26,786	31,628	32,432	207,217	178,937	191,295
nom10bikesharing_day	32	33	37	57	62	80
nom10crx_nomissing	83	93	90	115	140	162
nom10shuttle	2,376	1,748	1,987	2,598	1,987	2,327
nom10x10magic04	2,307	2,506	2,643	2,827	3,145	3,882
nom15magic04	2,328	2,483	2,457	2,911	3,713	4,011
nom20magic04	1,869	2,276	2,222	2,564	3,267	3,776
nom5bikesharing_day	55	73	57	82	107	112
nom5bikesharing_hour	6,568	8,299	6,346	7,560	9,646	9,706
nom5crx_nomissing	81	115	99	109	149	160
nom5shuttle	2,253	1,722	2,306	2,413	1,902	2,571
ord10bikesharing_day	17,241	75,486	10,578	18,481	76,767	13,258
ord10crx_nomissing	76,317	1,126,723	63,912	79,193	1,132,714	76,573
ord10shuttle	–	2,045,000	1,746,497	–	2,068,204	1,794,466
ord5bikesharing_day	394	528	392	431	599	534
ord5bikesharing_hour	232,640	463,461	157,177	237,406	472,952	177,051
ord5crx_nomissing	3,601	10,186	2,697	3,820	10,509	3,497
ord5magic04	–	14,980,599	2,322,031	–	15,053,936	2,416,622
ord5shuttle	22,935	25,531	18,446	23,486	26,337	19,643

Table 4. Minimal running times of GreCon2Compact for the initialization phase and the total time (in milliseconds) using 20 threads.

dataset	initial phase			total time		
	native	VLQ	CVLQ	native	VLQ	CVLQ
T10I4D100K	2,330	2,478	1,108	20,320	20,190	9,646
advertisement	29	31	40	159	164	190
americas_large	725	913	879	3,849	3,900	3,865
americas_small	199	152	189	475	394	768
apj	15	22	32	53	66	90
customer	29	31	42	156	177	222
dna	18	18	22	50	50	61
inter10crx_nomissing	–	637,798	10,641	–	685,955	94,205
inter3magic04	46,404	48,293	37,558	71,634	77,293	87,255
inter5bikesharing_day	3,939	16,143	1,787	10,718	23,777	15,393
inter5crx_nomissing	657	470	207	2,191	1,489	2,041
inter5shuttle	–	417,179	296,494	–	512,459	416,838
inter6shuttle	–	688,331	481,652	–	825,679	662,290
mushroom	448	373	409	1,612	1,506	2,241
nfs	3,829	2,459	3,013	195,550	155,625	173,385
nom10bikesharing_day	9	8	12	60	53	73
nom10crx_nomissing	17	14	18	88	81	113
nom10shuttle	1,626	2,695	3,710	2,295	3,557	4,887
nom10x10magic04	327	248	304	1,624	1,632	2,345
nom15magic04	566	581	309	3,794	3,895	2,673
nom20magic04	269	469	717	2,223	3,594	5,149
nom5bikesharing_day	15	18	14	93	93	104
nom5bikesharing_hour	854	642	1,049	3,415	4,716	7,551
nom5crx_nomissing	18	22	19	89	97	113
nom5shuttle	5,572	1,268	1,608	6,290	1,663	2,152
ord10bikesharing_day	1,421	2,214	743	3,883	4,683	4,329
ord10crx_nomissing	4,066	19,699	1,909	10,459	27,113	14,639
ord10shuttle	–	216,213	188,686	–	257,900	252,540
ord5bikesharing_day	45	52	60	189	203	279
ord5bikesharing_hour	19,567	22,305	12,555	35,722	39,091	38,724
ord5crx_nomissing	353	385	228	1,222	1,241	1,711
ord5magic04	–	496,360	176,129	–	575,149	293,325
ord5shuttle	19,919	6,997	18,155	22,008	8,235	21,041

3.3 Computational Performance

We also evaluated the computational performance of the algorithm. Table 3 reports the minimal times[5] required for the initialization phase (i.e., time spent in the BuildCells procedure) and the total time needed to compute the factorization, including both concept computation and the initialization phase, when a single thread is used.

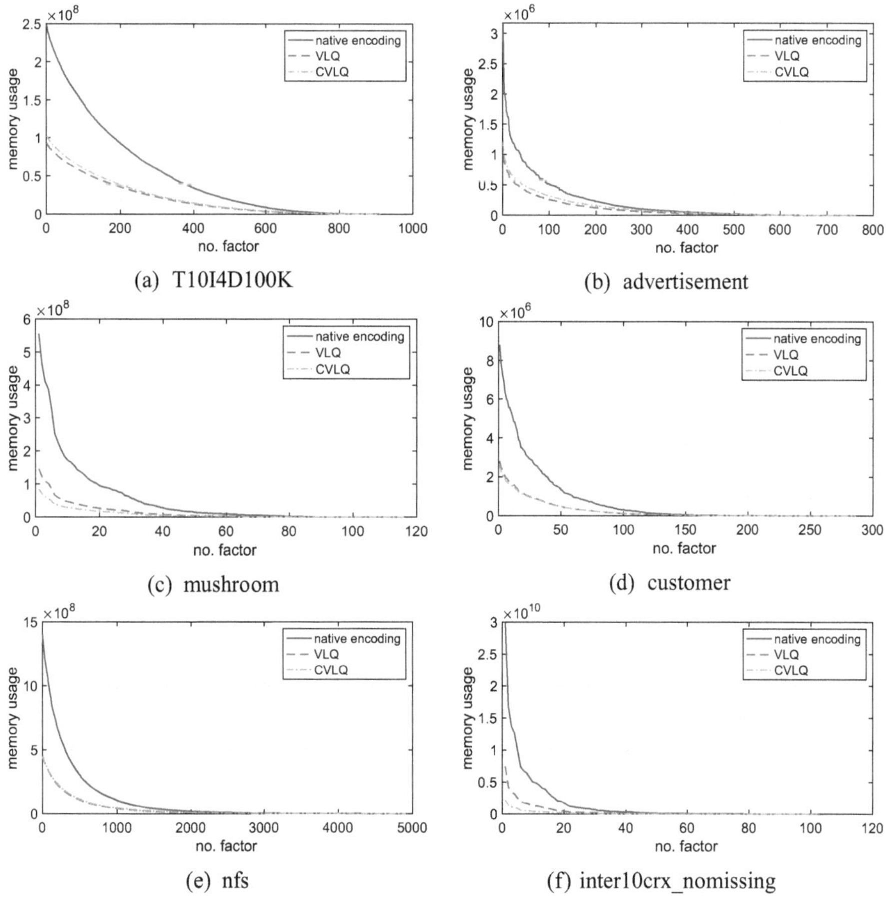

(a) T10I4D100K
(b) advertisement
(c) mushroom
(d) customer
(e) nfs
(f) inter10crx_nomissing

Fig. 2. Memory footprint of GreCon2Compact during the computation on selected datasets.

[5] The algorithm is implemented in Java. In our experience, Java provides performance comparable to C or C++ for this type of algorithms. Since Java uses just-in-time compilation, the first runs may be slower; therefore, we report the minimal running time.

We can observe that VLQ and CVLQ increase the computation time compared to the native encoding, which is particularly noticeable for larger datasets. For smaller datasets, the results are comparable or even slightly better. With a few exceptions, CVLQ provides better performance than VLQ, which is again more apparent for larger datasets.

Table 4 reports the same statistics when 20 threads are used. In this case, the time savings become more apparent. The total factorization time is comparable to the native encoding and in many cases even better. The slight slowdown observed for some datasets compared to the single-threaded version (e.g., T10I4D100K or apj) is likely caused by the overhead associated with thread management, which may outweigh the benefits of parallelization.

Overall, we can observe that the proposed encoding schemes, which bring substantial memory savings, have only a minor negative impact on the computation time.

Remark 3. We decided not to include a comparison with GreCon3 even though it has a similar aim and shares features with GreCon2Compact. GreCon3 maintains data in the *cells* data structure in a different way (the structure is initialized incrementally) and the encodings proposed in the present paper cannot be directly applied to it. Consequently, such a comparison would not provide meaningful insight. In fact, integrating the memory-efficient encodings from GreCon2Compact into GreCon3 will be the subject of our follow-up research.

4 Conclusion

We introduced GreCon2Compact, a memory-efficient variant of the GreCon2 algorithm for Boolean matrix factorization based on formal concepts. The proposed approach reduces the memory footprint by employing more compact data encodings.

We proposed and experimentally evaluated two alternative encodings, VLQ and CVLQ, and compared them with the native representation used in GreCon2. The experimental results demonstrate that both encodings significantly reduce memory consumption. In particular, VLQ achieves an average reduction of approximately 70%, while CVLQ reduces memory usage by roughly 80% on average and often exceeds 90% on larger datasets. These reductions allow the algorithm to process datasets that cannot be factorized using the original encoding due to memory limitations.

The proposed algorithm is an evolutionary step towards more efficient GreCon algorithms that can process larger data sets while providing high quality Boolean matrix factorization. Optimizations proposed in the paper are not fully compatible with optimizations proposed in [8]. Therefore, for the future research we are to investigate how to combine GreCon2Compact and GreCon3 to a faster algorithm. We are to investigate how to efficiently encode formal concepts in the memory to reduce memory footprint of the algorithm even further. Other possible research direction includes offloading non-essential parts of data from the *cells* and *concepts* data structures to a secondary storage (e.g., hard drive) that would entirely removed memory constraints of this family of algorithms.

References

1. Belohlavek, R., Trnecka, M.: From-below approximations in boolean matrix factorization: Geometry and new algorithm. J. Comput. Syst. Sci. **81**(8), 1678–1697 (2015). https://doi.org/10.1016/j.jcss.2015.06.002
2. Belohlavek, R., Trnecka, M.: Semantic explorations in factorizing boolean data via formal concepts. Int. J. Approx. Reason. **173**, 109247 (2024). https://doi.org/10.1016/j.ijar.2024.109247
3. Belohlavek, R., Vychodil, V.: Discovery of optimal factors in binary data via a novel method of matrix decomposition. J. Comput. Syst. Sci. **76**(1), 3–20 (2010). https://doi.org/10.1016/J.JCSS.2009.05.002
4. Ene, A., Horne, W.G., Milosavljevic, N., Rao, P., Schreiber, R., Tarjan, R.E.: Fast exact and heuristic methods for role minimization problems. In: Proceedings of SACMAT, pp. 1–10 (2008). https://doi.org/10.1145/1377836.1377838
5. Ganter, B., Wille, R.: Formal Concept Analysis: Mathematical Foundations, 2th edn. Springer (2024)
6. Konecny, J., Krajca, P.: Systematic categorization and evaluation of cbo-based algorithms in FCA. Inf. Sci. **575**, 265–288 (2021). https://doi.org/10.1016/J.INS.2021.06.024
7. Krajca, P., Outrata, J., Vychodil, V.: Parallel algorithm for computing fixpoints of galois connections. Ann. Math. Artif. Intell. **59**(2), 257–272 (2010). https://doi.org/10.1007/S10472-010-9199-5
8. Krajca, P., Trnecka, M.: GreCon3: mitigating high resource utilization of GreCon algorithms for Boolean matrix factorization. arXiv:2603.13772 (2026)
9. Lichman, M.: UCI machine learning repository (2013). http://archive.ics.uci.edu/ml
10. Miettinen, P., Neumann, S.: Recent developments in Boolean matrix factorization. In: Proceedings of IJCAI, pp. 4922–4928. (2020). https://doi.org/10.24963/ijcai.2020/685
11. Trnecka, M., Vyjidacek, R.: Revisiting the GreCon algorithm for Boolean matrix factorization. Knowl. Based Syst. **249**, 108895 (2022). https://doi.org/10.1016/J.KNOSYS.2022.108895

Lattice-Based Approaches for Enumerating Stable Extensions in Abstract Argumentation Frameworks

Sergei Obiedkov[1,2(✉)] and Barış Sertkaya[3]

[1] Knowledge-Based Systems Group, TU Dresden, Dresden, Germany
sergei.obiedkov@tu-dresden.de

[2] Center for Scalable Data Analytics and Artificial Intelligence (ScaDS.AI) Dresden, Dresden, Germany

[3] Frankfurt University of Applied Sciences, Frankfurt, Germany
sertkaya@fra-uas.de

Abstract. We investigate two approaches for computing stable extensions in abstract argumentation frameworks. The first represents stable extensions using Formal Concept Analysis (FCA), where they form an antichain in the concept lattice of a formal context derived from the framework. To improve the performance of this approach on sparse frameworks, we combine it with a dynamic-programming strategy based on decomposition into strongly connected components. The second approach transforms the attack relation into an implicational system such that the complements of stable extensions are among its models. FCA algorithms can then be used to explore the corresponding lattice and enumerate stable extensions. We experimentally evaluate the proposed techniques.

Keywords: Abstract Argumentation · Stable Extensions · FCA · Strongly Connected Components · Implications

1 Introduction

Argumentation provides formal tools for representing and analyzing conflicting information. In abstract argumentation [5], arguments are represented as vertices of a directed graph and attacks between arguments as edges. Different semantics characterize acceptable sets of arguments, giving rise to computational tasks such as deciding acceptance or enumerating extensions [3].

This paper extends our previous FCA-based approach for computing stable extensions [16]. While the method performed well on dense frameworks, its efficiency decreased on sparse ones. To address this, we investigate two complementary directions. The first decomposes the argumentation framework into connected components and combines solutions of the resulting subproblems. The second is based on the implicational characterization from [7], where complements of stable extensions appear among the closed sets of the corresponding closure system.

M. Croitoru et al. (Eds.): CONCEPTS 2026, LNAI 16811, pp. 122–137, 2027.
https://doi.org/10.1007/978-3-032-34742-8_8

The remainder of the paper is organized as follows. Section 2 recalls the required background on abstract argumentation and FCA. Section 3 reviews the FCA-based method from our previous work. Section 4 presents the decomposition approaches, and Sect. 5 describes the implicational one. Section 6 reports experimental results, and Sect. 7 concludes the paper.

2 Preliminaries

2.1 Abstract Argumentation Frameworks

We briefly recall the notions from abstract argumentation needed in this paper; for a general introduction see [5]. An *abstract argumentation framework* (AF) is a pair $F = (A, R)$, where A is a finite set of arguments and $R \subseteq A \times A$ is the attack relation. If $(a, b) \in R$, then a is said to *attack* b.

For a set $S \subseteq A$, we write $R(S)$ for the set of arguments attacked by elements of S and $R^{-1}(S)$ for the set of arguments attacking at least one element of S. For a singleton $\{a\}$, we simply write $R(a)$ and $R^{-1}(a)$. A set S attacks an argument a if $a \in R(S)$, and an argument a attacks a set S if $a \in R^{-1}(S)$. Furthermore, S is said to *defend* an argument a if every attacker of a is itself attacked by some argument from S.

A pair (A_1, R_1) is called a *subframework* of $F = (A, R)$ whenever $A_1 \subseteq A$ and $R_1 \subseteq R$.

Example 1. Fig. 1, borrowed from [16], shows an AF over the argument set $A = \{a, b, c, d, e\}$. In this framework, argument a attacks b and c, while $\{b, c\}$ attacks both a and d. The argument d attacks c and e, and therefore also any set containing one of these arguments. The set $\{a, e\}$ defends d, since both attackers of d are attacked by at least one of its elements.

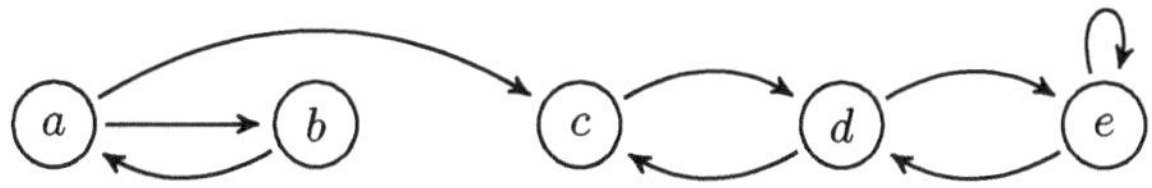

Fig. 1. Example of an argumentation framework.

A set $S \subseteq A$ is *conflict-free* if no two arguments in S attack each other. The family of all conflict-free sets of an AF F is denoted by $cf(F)$:

$$cf(F) = \{S \subseteq A \mid \forall a, b \in S : (\{a, b\} \times \{a, b\}) \cap R = \varnothing\}.$$

Let $F = (A, R)$ be an AF, and let $S \in cf(F)$. Then:

- S is *admissible* if it defends each of its elements;
- S is a *preferred extension* if it is inclusion-maximal among admissible sets;

– S is a *stable extension* if every argument outside S is attacked by some argument in S.

Every stable extension is preferred, since a stable extension necessarily defends all its elements. Stable extensions also coincide with independent dominating sets of the directed graph underlying the AF, i.e., sets of vertices that are pairwise non-adjacent and such that every vertex outside the set has an incoming edge from some vertex in the set. For the framework in Fig. 1, the preferred extensions are $\{a, d\}$, $\{b, c\}$, and $\{b, d\}$, while the stable extensions are $\{a, d\}$ and $\{b, d\}$.

A central computational task in abstract argumentation is to determine extensions under a given semantics. This is computationally difficult for many semantics of practical interest [6,11]. Many state-of-the-art systems tackle them by translating AF reasoning problems into other well-studied formalisms, such as SAT or answer-set programming, and then applying optimized external solvers. Examples include μ-toksia [14], taas-fudge [19], pyglaf [1], and Scalop [13]. Other approaches rely on algorithms developed specifically for argumentation. A survey of these methods is given in [4]. Benchmark comparisons are regularly provided by the International Competition on Computational Models of Argumentation (ICCMA).

2.2 Formal Concept Analysis

Formal Concept Analysis (FCA) [9] provides mathematical tools for describing dependencies and hierarchical structures in data. In FCA, data are represented by a *formal context* $\mathbb{K} = (G, M, I)$, where G is a set of *objects*, M a set of *attributes*, and $I \subseteq G \times M$ the *incidence relation*. An incidence $(g, m) \in I$ means that object g has attribute m.

For $A \subseteq G$ and $B \subseteq M$, define

$$A^{\uparrow} = \{m \in M \mid \forall g \in A: \ (g, m) \in I\},$$

$$B^{\downarrow} = \{g \in G \mid \forall m \in B: \ (g, m) \in I\}.$$

The operators $(\cdot)^{\uparrow\downarrow}$ and $(\cdot)^{\downarrow\uparrow}$ are closure operators on G and M, respectively.

A *formal concept* of $\mathbb{K}$ is a pair (A, B) such that

$$A^{\uparrow} = B \qquad \text{and} \qquad B^{\downarrow} = A.$$

Here, A is the *extent* and B the *intent* of the concept. Formal concepts ordered by extent inclusion (equivalently, reverse intent inclusion) form a complete lattice called the *concept lattice* of $\mathbb{K}$.

For every $A \subseteq G$, the pair $(A^{\uparrow\downarrow}, A^{\uparrow})$ is a formal concept, and $A^{\uparrow\downarrow}$ is the smallest extent containing A. Hence, extents are precisely the subsets of G closed under $(\cdot)^{\uparrow\downarrow}$, and intents are precisely the subsets of M closed under $(\cdot)^{\downarrow\uparrow}$. Since arbitrary intersections of extents and intents are again extents and intents, they form closure systems on G and M [9].

Several algorithms for enumerating formal concepts are known, including polynomial-delay [10] algorithms; see [12] for a comparison.

Implications provide another description of concept intents. For $A, B \subseteq M$, the implication $A \to B$ is *valid* in $\mathbb{K}$ if $A^{\downarrow} \subseteq B^{\downarrow}$. A set $X \subseteq M$ satisfies $A \to B$ if either $A \not\subseteq X$ or $B \subseteq X$. Given a set $\mathcal{L}$ of implications, we write $X \models \mathcal{L}$ if X satisfies every implication in $\mathcal{L}$.

Any implication set $\mathcal{L}$ over M induces a closure operator

$$X \mapsto \mathcal{L}(X),$$

where

$$\mathcal{L}(X) = \bigcap \{Y \mid X \subseteq Y \subseteq M, \quad Y \models \mathcal{L}\}.$$

The models of $\mathcal{L}$ form a lattice. In particular, if $\mathcal{L}$ is the set of implications valid in $\mathbb{K}$, then its models are exactly the intents of $\mathbb{K}$ and

$$\mathcal{L}(X) = X \iff X^{\downarrow\uparrow} = X.$$

We also allow implications of the form $A \to \bot$. A set $X \subseteq M$ satisfies such an implication iff $A \not\subseteq X$. Such implications exclude M from the model set, so the resulting structure is generally only a semilattice. Moreover, if $A \subseteq X$ for some implication $A \to \bot \in \mathcal{L}$, we define $\mathcal{L}(X) = \bot$.

3 Stable Extensions as Concept Intents

In [16], following the ideas from [2], we have presented a characterization of AFs as formal contexts. In this characterization, stable extensions of the original AF are concept intents of the constructed formal context. Using algorithms for enumerating concept intents, we have shown how stable extensions can be enumerated. We briefly recall this approach.

Given an AF $F = (A, R)$, the *induced formal context* of (A, R) is

$$\mathbb{K}(A, R) = (A, A, (A \times A) \setminus R).$$

In this context, for $S \subseteq A$,

$$S^{\uparrow} = \{t \in A \mid \forall s \in S \colon (s, t) \notin R\}$$

is the set of arguments not attacked by S and

$$S^{\downarrow} = \{t \in A \mid \forall s \in S \colon (t, s) \notin R\}$$

is the set of arguments that do not attack S. Then

- S defends $x \in A$ iff $S^{\uparrow} \subseteq \{x\}^{\downarrow}$;
- S is conflict-free iff $S \subseteq S^{\uparrow}$ or, equivalently, $S \subseteq S^{\downarrow}$;
- S is an admissible set iff $S \subseteq S^{\uparrow} \subseteq S^{\downarrow}$;
- if S is a preferred extension, then $S = S^{\downarrow\uparrow}$;

- S is a stable extension iff $S = S^{\uparrow}$.

The stable and preferred extensions are thus concept intents of $\mathbb{K}(A, R)$. Moreover, the concepts whose intents are conflict-free form an order filter in the concept lattice of $\mathbb{K}(A, R)$, and the antichain of preferred extensions constitutes the border of this filter containing the stable extensions. As an example, Fig. 2 shows the concept lattice of the formal context induced by the argumentation framework in Fig. 1.

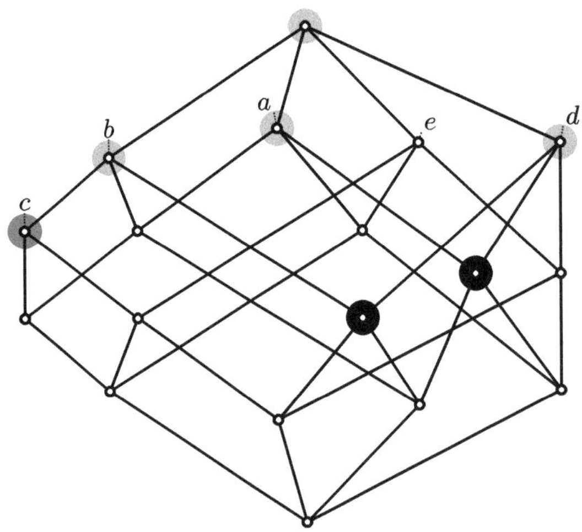

Fig. 2. The concept lattice of the formal context induced by the argumentation framework in Fig. 1. Object labels are omitted. The stable extensions correspond to the intents of the concepts depicted as black circles; the only preferred extension that is not stable, $\{b, c\}$, is depicted as a dark-gray circle; and the remaining conflict-free intents are depicted as light-gray circles.

In [16], we use FCA lattice-construction algorithms to enumerate all conflict-free concept intents. When a maximal conflict-free intent is encountered, the current computation branch is pruned. If this intent is stable, we output it.

We adapted two lattice construction algorithms in this way: Next Closure [8] and the incremental algorithm proposed in [15]. Next Closure enumerates all concept intents with a polynomial delay. It lists intents included in intent S before it produces S, thus being suitable for exploring the order filter of the concept lattice. Its other advantage is that it needs memory that is only linear in the number of arguments. Finally, it can be used to enumerate closed sets of an arbitrary closure operator, which will be important for Sect. 5.

The incremental algorithm processes attributes of the input formal context one by one and stores all generated concepts to ease generation of new concepts. This means that it may need exponential amount of memory, but, when it is available, the algorithm is usually faster than Next Closure.

As can be seen from the experimental results presented in [16], enumerating stable extensions with concept-generation algorithms is efficient for dense frameworks. However, sparse frameworks are only feasible when they are small. This suggests that, to scale these algorithms to sparse frameworks, one could try to first decompose the input framework into smaller parts.

4 Scaling Up with Connected Components

In this section, we present two approaches to argumentation framework decomposition. The first approach yields a simple divide-and-conquer algorithm based on decomposing the framework into weakly connected components. The second approach subsumes the first by using strongly connected components instead. In this case, we propose a dynamic-programming approach in which stable extensions of individual components induce smaller subproblems in the remaining part of the framework, which are then solved recursively. Both approaches assume that another algorithm is used to compute stable extensions in the base case. In our experiments, we use lattice-based algorithms for this purpose, although other algorithms could also be used.

4.1 Weakly Connected Components

An immediate option is to decompose the framework into *weakly connected components* (WCC), i.e., components of the underlying undirected graph.

Proposition 1. *Let $F = (A, R)$ be an argumentation framework and $F_1 = (A_1, R_1), \ldots, F_k = (A_k, R_k)$ be all its weakly connected components. Then $S \subseteq A$ is a stable extension of F if and only if $S \cap A_i$ is a stable extension of F_i for every $1 \leq i \leq k$.*

Proof. Since there are no attacks among arguments from different components, S is conflict-free if and only if $S \cap A_i$ is conflict-free for every $1 \leq i \leq k$. For the same reason, S attacks $a \in A_i \setminus S$ if and only if $S \cap A_i$ attacks a. As $A = \bigcup_i A_i$, the statement follows.

Example 2. Consider the argumentation framework shown in Fig. 3. It comprises two WCCs induced by argument subsets $\{a, b\}$ and $\{c, d, e\}$. The first component has two stable extensions, $\{a\}$ and $\{b\}$, while the second component has only one, $\{d\}$. The stable extensions of the entire framework are obtained by forming all possible unions of stable extensions from different components, resulting in $\{a, d\}$ and $\{b, d\}$.

Proposition 1 suggests a straightforward divide-and-conquer approach: decompose the argumentation framework into WCCs, compute stable extensions in each component using any available algorithm, and then form the unions of extensions resulting from different components. If a component has no stable extension, then the entire framework has none either. If we are only interested

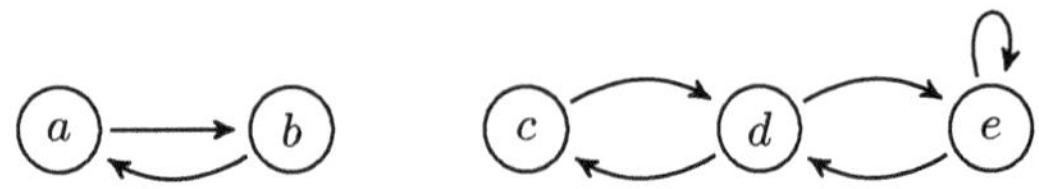

Fig. 3. An argumentation framework with two weakly connected components.

in finding a single extension, it is sufficient to find a single extension in each component and then form their union.

Since decomposition into WCCs can be achieved in linear time, this approach incurs very little overhead. However, its applicability is limited to frameworks that are not weakly connected, i.e., have multiple WCCs.

4.2 Strongly Connected Components

In this section, we present an approach applicable to a much wider category of argumentation frameworks: those with multiple *strongly connected components* (SCC), i.e., maximal subgraphs where there is a directed path between every two vertices.

As an example, the directed graph in Fig. 1 has one WCC, but two SCCs, coinciding with the WCCs of the graph in Fig. 3: $G_1 = (\{a, b\}, \{(a, b), (b, a)\})$ and $G_2 = (\{c, d, e\}, \{(c, d), (d, c), (d, e), (e, d), (e, e)\})$. SCCs of a directed graph can be computed in linear time using Tarjan's algorithm [18].

Decomposing frameworks into SCCs and computing stable extensions independently in each component, as we did for weakly connected components, is not sufficient, since there may be attacks between different components. A subtler approach is needed.

Definition 1. *A strongly connected component (A_1, R_1) of an argumentation framework (A, R) is called its* source component *if $(a, b) \notin R$ for all $a \in A \setminus A_1$ and $b \in A_1$.*

An argumentation framework can have multiple source components.

Definition 2. *Let $F = (A, R)$ be an argumentation framework, $F_1 = (A_1, R_1)$ be its subframework, and $S \subseteq A_1$. The* residual (sub)framework *of F w.r.t. F_1 and S, denoted by $F \mid (F_1, S)$, is the subframework of F obtained by removing from A the arguments in A_1, as well as the arguments attacked by S:*

$$F \mid (F_1, S) = (B, (B \times B) \cap R),$$

where $B = A \setminus (A_1 \cup R(S))$.

Theorem 1. *Let $F = (A, R)$ be an argumentation framework, and let C be any of its source components. $E \subseteq A$ is a stable extension of F if and only if $E = E_1 \cup E_2$, where E_1 is a stable extension of C and E_2 is a stable extension of the residual framework $F \mid (C, E_1)$.*

Algorithm 1. SCC-STABLE-EXTENSIONS(F)

Input: Argumentation framework $F = (A, R)$
Parameter: A base procedure STABLEEXTENSIONS(H) computing stable extensions for its input framework H
Output: The stable extensions of F

1. Find a source component C in F.
2. Compute its stable extensions with the base procedure: $\mathcal{E} :=$ STABLEEXTENSIONS(C).
3. For each extension $E_1 \in \mathcal{E}$:
   (a) Form the residual framework $F_r := F \mid (C, E_1)$.
   (b) Recursively compute stable extensions $\mathcal{E}_r$ of F_r: $\mathcal{E}_r :=$ SCC-STABLE-EXTENSIONS(F_r)
   (c) For every $E_2 \in \mathcal{E}_r$, output $E_1 \cup E_2$.

Proof. Suppose that E_1 is a stable extension of C and E_2 is a stable extension of $F_r = F \mid (C, E_1)$, and let $E = E_1 \cup E_2$. Arguments from E_1 do not attack E_2, since the residual framework F_r contains no arguments attacked by E_1. Arguments from E_2 do not attack E_1, since arguments from E_1 belong to a source component of F and those from E_2 belong to a different component. Therefore, given that E_1 and E_2 are both conflict-free, so is E.

Take an argument $a \in A \setminus E$. We know that E_1 attacks all arguments in C. Hence, if a is not attacked by E_1, it is in F_r, and then it is attacked by E_2. Thus, E attacks every argument in $A \setminus E$ and, since it is conflict-free, it is a stable extension.

Conversely, assume that E is a stable extension of F and let $E_1 = E \cap C$, $E_2 = E \setminus E_1$, and $F_r = F \mid (C, E_1)$. As subsets of the conflict-free set E, both E_1 and E_2 are conflict-free, too.

Since C is a source component, arguments outside C cannot attack C. Hence, for E to be a stable extension, it is necessary that E_1 attacks all other arguments in C. Therefore, E_1 is a stable extension of C.

By the definition of a residual framework, arguments of F_r are not attacked by E_1. Still, they are all attacked by E, and this must be due to E_2, which is then a stable extension of F_r.

Theorem 1 gives rise to Algorithm 1, which enumerates all stable extensions of an argumentation framework $F = (A, R)$. This recursive algorithm is parameterized with a procedure STABLEEXTENSIONS(H), which is used to compute stable extensions in the base case, i.e., for the source component of F. Residual frameworks are then formed w.r.t. the component and each of its stable extensions, and the extensions in the residual frameworks are computed recursively.

Theorem 2. *Algorithm 1 outputs only stable extensions of F. It outputs every stable extension of F exactly once.*

Proof. Theorem 1 guarantees that Algorithm 1 outputs all and only the stable extensions of F. It may generate a stable extension E more than once only if there are at least two ways to represent E as the union of stable extensions of respective subframeworks: $E_1 \cup E_2 = E = E_1' \cup E_2'$, where E_1 and E_1' are stable extensions of the same source component C, while E_2 and E_2' are stable extensions of the residual frameworks $F \mid (C, E_1)$ and $F \mid (C, E_1')$. Note that, $E_1 = E_1'$ if and only if $E_2 = E_2'$, since each of E_1 and E_1' is disjoint with both E_2 and E_2'.

If $E_1 \neq E_1'$, there must be $a \in C$ that belongs to only one of E_1 and E_1'. Without loss of generality, assume that $a \in E_1$. From $E_1 \cup E_2 = E_1' \cup E_2'$, it then follows that $a \in E_2'$, which is impossible, since $E_2' \cap C = \varnothing$. Therefore, $E_i = E_i'$ for $i \in \{1, 2\}$ and, hence, every stable extension of F is produced exactly once.

Example 3. Consider the framework F in Fig. 1. It has only one source component, C, induced by $\{a, b\}$. This component has two stable extensions: $\{a\}$ and $\{b\}$.

Since c is the only argument outside C attacked by a, the residual framework $F \mid (C, \{a\})$ is obtained from F by removing c, along with a and b. Hence, it is induced by $\{d, e\}$. This framework is strongly connected, so its stable extensions are computed using the base algorithm. Its only stable extension is $\{d\}$, which yields the stable extension $\{a, d\}$ of F.

Similarly, the component extension $\{b\}$ gives rise to the residual framework induced by $\{c, d, e\}$. This framework is also strongly connected, and its only stable extension is again $\{d\}$. Consequently, we obtain another stable extension of F, namely $\{b, d\}$.

As formulated, Algorithm 1 may have to process the same residual framework more than once, since it may happen that $F \mid (C, E_1) = F \mid (C, E_2)$ for some stable extensions $E_1 \neq E_2$ of C. Identical residual frameworks can also occur at different levels of recursion. In recursive implementations of dynamic-programming algorithms, such unnecessary computation is usually avoided by memoizing solutions for subproblems. Here, we store sets of stable extensions computed for residual frameworks in a hashtable. The key used to retrieve the stable extensions for a residual framework is its set of arguments. Before issuing a recursive call in step 3b, we check if the hashtable already contains the stable extensions of F_r and, if so, use them in subsequent computations.

5 Stable Extensions via Implication Systems

In this section, we present quite a different approach extending the results from [7]. While our FCA-based approach represents stable extensions as elements of the lattice of concept intents of a formal context derived from the argumentation framework, here the idea is to translate the framework into a set of implications and explore the lattice of its models.

Elaroussi et al. [7] focus on admissible sets. Recall that an admissible set is a conflict-free set that defends all its elements. Consider two arguments x and

y such that $(x, y) \in R$. If $(y, x) \in R$, then y defends itself against x. Otherwise, every self-defending set S containing y must contain an attacker of x. In other words, if S contains no attacker of x, it cannot contain y, which means that $A \setminus S$ is a model of the implication $R^{-1}(x) \to \{y\}$. This leads to the following result from [7]:

Theorem 3. *Let $F = (A, R)$ be an argumentation framework. Define*

$$\mathcal{SD}(F) := \{R^{-1}(x) \to \{y\} \mid (x, y) \in R \text{ and } (y, x) \notin R\}.$$

$S \subseteq A$ is a self-defending set if and only if $A \setminus S$ is a model of $\mathcal{SD}(F)$.

Example 4. Consider again the framework F in Fig. 1. There is only one attack that does not reciprocate, (a, c). Thus, $\mathcal{SD}(F) = \{\{b\} \to \{c\}\}$. Self-defending sets are those that contain b or do not contain c.

As defined, $|\mathcal{SD}(F)| \leq |R|$. Note that $\mathcal{SD}(F)$ can be equivalently defined as follows:

$$\mathcal{SD}(F) := \{R^{-1}(x) \to R(x) \mid x \in A\}.$$

This representation contains $|A|$ implications; those with $R(x) \subseteq R^{-1}(x)$ can be removed.

To compute admissible sets, one can enumerate the models of $\mathcal{SD}(F)$ with Next Closure, consider their complements, and output those that are conflict-free.

However, we are interested in stable extensions. Every stable extension is admissible, but not vice versa. The difference is that a stable extension must attack all other arguments and not just attackers of its elements. Put differently, in addition to being self-defending, a stable extension must be a dominating set. We define an implication set $\mathcal{D}(F)$ that captures this condition.

Theorem 4. *Let $F = (A, R)$ be an argumentation framework. Define*

$$\mathcal{D}(F) := \{\{x\} \cup R^{-1}(x) \to \bot \mid x \in A\}.$$

$S \subseteq A$ is a self-defending dominating set if and only if $A \setminus S$ is a model of $\mathcal{SD}(F) \cup \mathcal{D}(F)$.

Proof. Given Theorem 3, it is sufficient to show that being a model of $\mathcal{D}(F)$ is equivalent to being the complement of a dominating set. Indeed, S is a dominating set if and only if, for every $x \in A$, it contains either x or an attacker of x and, therefore, $\{x\} \cup R^{-1}(x) \not\subseteq A \setminus S$.

Example 5. For the framework in Fig. 1, $\mathcal{D}$ consists of the following implications:

$$\begin{aligned} \{a, b\} &\to \bot \text{ (from } a \text{ and } b) \\ \{a, c, d\} &\to \bot \text{ (from } c) \\ \{c, d, e\} &\to \bot \text{ (from } d) \\ \{d, e\} &\to \bot \text{ (from } e) \end{aligned}$$

The implications obtained from a and b coincide, since a and b are the only attackers of each other. The implication resulting from d is entailed by the one resulting from e and can be removed.

Theorem 4 makes it possible to enumerate the complements of self-defending dominating sets with NEXT CLOSURE. For any two listed sets $X \subsetneq Y$, the algorithm lists X before Y. Thus, the algorithm starts with the complements of large self-defending dominating sets, moving towards those of smaller ones. As soon as the algorithm encounters the complement of a conflict-free set S, it should output S as a stable extension and the current computation branch can be pruned, since subsets of S cannot be stable extensions.

This is an important difference from the concept-based algorithms: those algorithms explore the conflict-free part of the lattice of concept intents, while here we explore the non-conflict-free part of the semi-lattice of self-defending dominating sets. This suggests that concept-based algorithms may be more efficient on dense frameworks, with a relatively small conflict-free part, while the implication-based approach is more appropriate for sparse frameworks, with relatively few conflicts.

Still, it is desirable to reduce the search space by removing from it at least some of the non-conflict-free sets—or, rather, their complements. In [7], it is suggested to add or strengthen implications to capture some type of conflicts. The simplest type is the self-conflict: if $(x, x) \in R$, the implication $\varnothing \to \{x\}$ is added. Since a conflict-free set cannot contain such x, its complement must satisfy this implication.

The intuitive meaning of the implication $R^{-1}(x) \to \{y\}$ is that arguments from $R^{-1}(x)$ defend y against x, and, therefore, every self-defending set with y must contain at least one of these. However, if $(z, y) \in R$ or $(y, z) \in R$ for some $z \in R^{-1}(x)$, then z is useless as a defender of y in a conflict-free set, since y is itself in conflict with z. Therefore, if we are interested only in conflict-free sets, the implication can be strengthened to

$$R^{-1}(x) \setminus (R^{-1}(y) \cup R(y)) \to \{y\}. \tag{1}$$

Similarly, $z \in R^{-1}(x)$ is not a suitable defender of y against x if it is in conflict with every defender of y against some other argument x', i.e., if

$$(x', y) \in R \text{ and } R^{-1}(x') \subseteq R(z) \cup R^{-1}(z). \tag{2}$$

Therefore, the implication $R^{-1}(x) \to \{y\}$ can be strengthened by removing z from its premise.

In the latter case, z is in indirect conflict with y: although neither attacks the other, they cannot belong to the same conflict-free set. The strengthening rules described above can be generalized by replacing the attack relation R with a gradually constructed symmetric *indirect conflict relation.* The conflict relation C initially contains pairs (x, y) such that $\{x, y\}$ is not conflict-free, i.e., either x attacks y, y attacks x, or one of them attacks itself. The implication set $\mathcal{L}$ includes implications from $\mathcal{SD}(\mathcal{F})$ strengthened according to (1), as well as those from the set $\mathcal{D}(F)$ and $\{\varnothing \to \{x\} \mid (x, x) \in R\}$. The following two steps are then repeated until both the conflict relation and the implication set stabilize.

First, the conflict relation is updated. For every $x \in A$, the closure D of $C(x)$ under $\mathcal{L}$ is computed and C is updated with $(\{x\} \times D) \cup (D \times \{x\})$. The reason for this is as follows. Since D is the closure of $C(x)$ under the implications, every stable extension disjoint with $C(x)$ must be disjoint with D. On the other hand, a conflict-free set containing x must be disjoint with $C(x)$ and, hence, with D. Thus, arguments from D are in (indirect) conflict with x.

Second, the implications from $\mathcal{L}$ are strengthened: implication $X \to \{y\}$ is replaced by $X \setminus C(y) \to \{y\}$. This is similar to (1) but using the indirect conflict relation instead of the attack relation. Due to the conflict-update step, this also covers case (2).

As soon as neither step results in updates, the implication set $\mathcal{L}$ is used to enumerate stable extensions as described above.

6 Experimental Results

To evaluate the performance of the approaches described in Sects. 4 and 5, we implemented them in our FCA-based argumentation solver AFCA[1], introduced in [16]. We report evaluation results for the SCC-based algorithm from Sect. 4.2, using our adaptation of the incremental algorithm proposed by Norris in [15] (see Sect. 3) and the implication-based algorithm from Sect. 5 as base procedures.

For comparison, we used the solvers μ-toksia[2], taas-fudge[3], and an earlier version of scalop known as crustabri[4]. Only μ-toksia supports enumeration of stable extensions, but all three support computing a single stable extension (or detecting that no such extension exists). We therefore ran all three solvers in single-extension mode, while our algorithms were used to enumerate all stable extensions. Note that this is to our disadvantage, as our algorithms were tasked with a computationally harder problem.

To measure the effect of the number of connected components in an argumentation framework, we generated test data with varying numbers of arguments and components, and with varying densities within the components. More precisely, we generated random frameworks with n arguments and at least k strongly connected components using a parameter p with $0 < p < 1$ as follows. We first assigned n arguments to k components uniformly at random, ensuring that every component receives at least one argument. Then, for every argument x in component i and argument y in component j, we added an attack between x and y with probability p: the attack (x, y) if $i \leq j$ and the attack (y, x) otherwise. Thus, p corresponds to the expected density of attacks within components, while attacks between components are oriented so that the component order is respected. This guarantees that no two of the k subsets of arguments are merged into a single component. However, for smaller values of p, there may not be enough attacks within a subset to ensure that it is strongly connected. Therefore, the resulting framework may contain more than k strongly connected components.

The generated test data are available in the AFCA repository.

[1] https://github.com/sertkaya/afca.
[2] https://bitbucket.org/andreasniskanen/mu-toksia.
[3] https://github.com/aig-hagen/taas-fudge.
[4] https://github.com/crillab/crustabri.

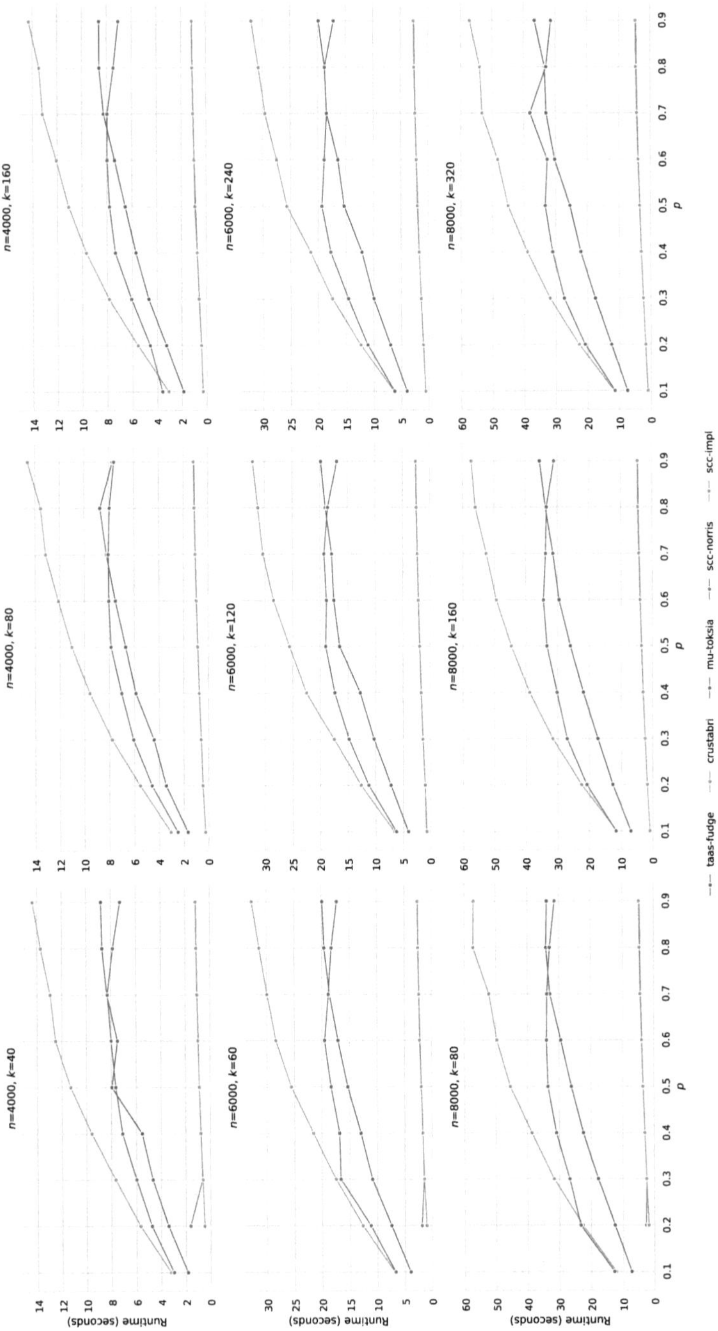

Fig. 4. Runtime comparison of algorithms.

We performed the tests on a Linux machine with a 32-core CPU running at 2.9 GHz and 256 GB of main memory. We used a time limit of five minutes but did not impose any limit on memory usage. The runtimes are presented in Fig. 4 for a total of 81 argumentation frameworks with 4000, 6000, and 8000 arguments. The minimal number k of connected components took the values 1%, 2%, and 4% of the number of arguments, and p varied from 0.1 to 0.9. Both scc-norris and scc-impl (shown in Fig. 4) implement Algorithm 1, but differ in the base procedures: scc-norris uses the Norris-based algorithm, whereas scc-impl uses the algorithm from Sect. 5. For values of k between 80 and 320, the performances of scc-norris and scc-impl are so close to each other that the corresponding lines in Fig. 4 cannot be distinguished.

For $k = n/100$ and $p = 0.1$, both scc-norris and scc-impl timed out for all three values of n (hence, there are no corresponding points in the plots), even though these instances were among the easiest for the other three solvers. This is consistent with what we observed in [16]: lattice-based algorithms are not usually efficient on sparse datasets even of moderate size. With $k = n/100$ and $p = 0.1$, we deal with components containing on average 100 arguments each with attack density of 0.1. This is still hard for lattice-based algorithms.

However, when we reduce the component size to 50 by increasing k to $n/50$, scc-norris and scc-impl become the fastest algorithms even when $p = 0.1$. When $p \geq 0.2$, scc-norris and scc-impl are the fastest already for $k = n/100$, although, in our experiments from [16], the density 0.2 was typically beyond the reach of the Norris-based algorithm used on its own. This is precisely the effect we hoped to achieve by decomposing sparse frameworks into smaller parts.

7 Conclusion

In our earlier work, we observed that FCA-based concept-enumeration algorithms are effective for enumerating stable extensions in dense frameworks, which induce sparse contexts with relatively few concepts and even fewer conflict-free intents. In this paper, we proposed a decomposition strategy that extends the applicability of these algorithms to sparser frameworks containing multiple dense or moderately sized connected components. As another approach, we presented an algorithm based on enumerating a closure system induced by an implication set, building on ideas from [7]. Both approaches were evaluated experimentally against existing solvers for stable extensions.

The experiments show that the SCC-based decomposition substantially improves the performance of concept-enumeration algorithms. In frameworks with many stable extensions, they tend to outperform existing tools by a large margin. Moreover, the approach is naturally parallelizable, which may lead to additional performance gains.

Although we evaluated the SCC decomposition only in combination with lattice-based algorithms, other algorithms for enumerating stable extensions can also be used to handle the base case. Investigating such combinations is part of our future work.

Although we tested the SCC approach only in combination with lattice-based algorithms, other algorithms for enumerating stable extensions can be used to handle the base case. We plan to investigate the performance of various combinations in the future.

We also plan to adapt the proposed techniques to other semantics, in particular preferred semantics. Related directions have recently been explored in our work on computing single complete, stable, and preferred extensions through enumeration of closed sets [17].

Acknowledgements. This work is partly supported by the Federal Ministry of Research, Technology and Space of Germany and by Sächsische Staatsministerium für Wissenschaft, Kultur und Tourismus in the program Center of Excellence for AI-research "Center for Scalable Data Analytics and Artificial Intelligence Dresden/Leipzig" (ScaDS.AI); by Deutsche Forschungsgemeinschaft (DFG, German Research Foundation) in project 389792660 (TRR 248, Center for Perspicuous Systems); and in DAAD project 57616814 (SECAI, School of Embedded Composite AI) as part of the program Konrad Zuse Schools of Excellence in Artificial Intelligence.

References

1. Alviano, M.: The pyglaf argumentation reasoner (ICCMA2021) (2021). CoRR abs/2109.03162
2. Amgoud, L., Prade, H.: A formal concept view of abstract argumentation. In: van der Gaag, L.C. (ed.) ECSQARU 2013. LNCS (LNAI), vol. 7958, pp. 1–12. Springer, Heidelberg (2013). https://doi.org/10.1007/978-3-642-39091-3_1
3. Baroni, P., Caminada, M., Giacomin, M.: An introduction to argumentation semantics. Knowl. Eng. Rev. **26**(4), 365–410 (2011)
4. Cerutti, F., Gaggl, S.A., Thimm, M., Wallner, J.P.: Foundations of implementations for formal argumentation. FLAP **4**(8), (2017)
5. Dung, P.M.: On the acceptability of arguments and its fundamental role in nonmonotonic reasoning, logic programming and n-person games. Artif. Intell. **77**(2), 321–358 (1995)
6. Dunne, P.E., Wooldridge, M.J.: Complexity of abstract argumentation. In: Simari, G.R., Rahwan, I. (eds.) Argumentation in Artificial Intelligence, pp. 85–104. Springer (2009)
7. Elaroussi, M., Nourine, L., Radjef, M.S.: Lattice point of view for argumentation framework. Ann. Math. Artif. Intell. **91**(5), 691–711 (2023)
8. Ganter, B.: Two basic algorithms in concept analysis. Technical Report, Preprint-Nr. 831, Technische Hochschule Darmstadt, Darmstadt, Germany (1984)
9. Ganter, B., Wille, R.: Formal Concept Analysis – Mathematical Foundations. 2 edn. Springer. Cham (2024)
10. Johnson, D.S., Yannakakis, M., Papadimitriou, C.H.: On generating all maximal independent sets. Inf. Process. Lett. **27**(3), 119–123 (1988)
11. Kröll, M., Pichler, R., Woltran, S.: On the complexity of enumerating the extensions of abstract argumentation frameworks. In: Sierra, C. (ed.) Proceedings of the Twenty-Sixth International Joint Conference on Artificial Intelligence, IJCAI 2017, Melbourne, Australia, 19–25 August 2017. pp. 1145–1152. ijcai.org (2017)

12. Kuznetsov, S.O., Obiedkov, S.: Comparing performance of algorithms for generating concept lattices. J. Exp. Theor. Artif. Intell. **14**(2–3), 189–216 (2002)
13. Lagniez, J.M., Lonca, E., Mailly, J.G.: Counterexample-guided abstraction refinement for assumption-based argumentation. In: Proceedings of the 22nd International Conference on Principles of Knowledge Representation and Reasoning, pp. 694–706 (10 2025)
14. Niskanen, A., Järvisalo, M.: μ-toksia: an efficient abstract argumentation reasoner. In: Calvanese, D., Erdem, E., Thielscher, M. (eds.) Proceedings of the 17th International Conference on Principles of Knowledge Representation and Reasoning, KR 2020, Rhodes, Greece, 12–18 September 2020. pp. 800–804 (2020)
15. Norris, E.M.: An algorithm for computing the maximal rectangles in a binary relation. Rev. Roumaine Math. Pures Appl. **23**(2), 243–250 (1978)
16. Obiedkov, S., Sertkaya, B.: Computing stable extensions of argumentation frameworks using formal concept analysis. In: Gaggl, S.A., Martinez, M.V., Ortiz, M. (eds.) Logics in Artificial Intelligence - 18th European Conference, JELIA 2023, Dresden, Germany, 20–22 September 2023, Proceedings. LNCS, vol. 14281, pp. 176–191. Springer (2023)
17. Obiedkov, S., Sertkaya, B.: Computing extensions of abstract argumentation frameworks by enumerating closed sets. In: Mugnier, M.L., Baader, F. (eds.) Proceedings of the 23rd International Conference on Principles of Knowledge Representation and Reasoning, KR 2026, Lisbon, Portugal (2026). (To appear)
18. Tarjan, R.: Depth-first search and linear graph algorithms. SIAM J. Comput. **1**(2), 146–160 (1972)
19. Thimm, M., Cerutti, F., Vallati, M.: Fudge: a light-weight solver for abstract argumentation based on SAT reductions. CoRR **abs/2109.03106** (2021)

Using JRL Order to Shape Spanning Trees for Interactive FCA

Tim Pattison[1(✉)], Dominik Dürrschnabel[2], and Mohammed Abdullah[3]

[1] Defence Science & Technology Group, 13/205 Maritime Ave, Edinburgh, South Australia 5111, Australia
tim.pattison@defence.gov.au

[2] Baden Württemberg Cooperative State University Mosbach, Lohrtalweg 10, Mosbach, Baden Württemberg 74821, Germany
dominik.duerrschnabel@mosbach.dhbw.de

[3] University of Kassel, Wilhelmshöher Allee 73, Kassel, Hesse 34121, Germany
mabdullah@cs.uni-kassel.de

Abstract. The navigation of various ordered trees computed as by-products of Formal Concept Analysis has been demonstrated or proposed to simplify and scale exploratory user interaction with the resultant concept lattice. Examples include the Concept Trees traversed by Close-by-One algorithms and the K&O Spanning Trees constructed by modified versions of the top-down and bottom-up algorithms of Bordat and Lindig respectively. This paper explores pre-processing of the formal context to ensure that Concept Trees span the lattice digraph and examines the viability of simultaneous user interaction with top-down and bottom-up K&O Spanning Trees.

To assist the user in coordinating their navigation, both K&O Spanning Trees should be simultaneously overlaid on a drawing of the lattice digraph, which in turn requires that they be topologically consistent. Anecdotal evidence has suggested that their topological consistency can be improved by appropriately permuting the rows and columns of the input context matrix to shape the auxiliary, ordered trees constructed by the chosen Formal Concept Analysis algorithm. In particular, permuting the matrix into Jointly Reverse Lectic (JRL) order – for which an efficient algorithm exists – showed some promise not only for this purpose, but also for coercing the Concept Tree to span the lattice digraph. However, a more systematic study of whether JRL order reliably confers the benefits sought, and if so, whether JRL orders are alone in doing so, was hampered by our inability to efficiently generate *all* JRL orders for a given context.

In a companion paper, we have developed the Dominus algorithm for this purpose which is efficient in its use of both computation and memory, and is provably correct. In this paper, we provide a definition of topological consistency which is readily computable, and apply the Dominus algorithm to contexts in the FCA Repository to demonstrate that: JRL ordering guarantees neither topologically-consistent K&O Spanning Trees nor digraph-spanning Concept Trees; and post-order traversals of the top-down and bottom-up K&O Spanning Trees often but not always

M. Croitoru et al. (Eds.): CONCEPTS 2026, LNAI 16811, pp. 138–148, 2027.
https://doi.org/10.1007/978-3-032-34742-8_9

yield concepts in the Reverse Lectic Orders of intents and extents, respectively.

Keywords: Formal Concept Analysis · Jointly Reverse Lectic order · Computational study · Empirical corpus · Topological consistency · Bypass arc · Concept Tree · K&O Spanning Tree

1 Introduction

Formal Concept Analysis [5] transforms a bigraph represented by its bi-adjacency matrix into a digraph whose vertices represent a partially-ordered set (poset) of formal concepts and whose arcs represent the cover relation between them. This poset forms a complete lattice which constitutes a multiple inheritance hierarchy amongst formal concepts. In the worst case, the number of formal concepts scales exponentially with the smaller dimension of the bi-adjacency matrix, challenging our ability to draw the lattice digraph, let alone support the user in meaningful interactive exploration [13].

Andrews and Hirsch [2] proposed the Concept Tree traversed by Close-by-One algorithms as a proxy for interaction with the lattice digraph and demonstrated the resultant interaction using the FCA Tree Tool. However this tree contains so-called *bypass* arcs – defined as those between concepts which are not adjacent in the digraph – and hence does not span the lattice digraph [10]. Bypass arcs interfere with the user's ability to form an integrated mental model of the lattice digraph through interaction with the Concept Tree. Permuting the context bi-adjacency matrix into Jointly Reverse Lectic (JRL) order showed some promise in mitigating but not eliminating such bypass arcs [10], but has not been systematically explored. The remaining bypass arcs can be efficiently detected and remediated [11] to produce the corresponding Spanning Concept Tree.

Top-down and bottom-up K&O Spanning Trees [11] are produced and exploited as auxiliary data structures by the algorithms of Bordat [4] and Lindig [9], respectively, as modified by Kuznetsov and Obiedkov [7]. Since these trees each span the lattice digraph, they do not require remediation of bypass arcs in order to prevent disruption of the user's mental model. Pattison [11] proposed their simultaneous use as joint proxies for interaction with the lattice digraph. In addition to the obvious benefit of collectively representing more of the arcs of the lattice digraph, the simultaneous use of both trees constitutes a compromise between: the simplicity of backtracking only to the lattice ancestor corresponding to the tree parent; and the disorientation potentially induced by structural navigation of the full multiple inheritance hierarchy. Its symmetrical treatment of intents and extents also reinforces the Galois connection between their partial orders.

Pattison [11] emphasised the importance of topological consistency between the two ordered K&O Spanning Trees for the user's construction of a consistent mental model of the lattice digraph. Topological consistency allows both trees to be presented as superimposed on a drawing of the lattice digraph, provided the latter is suitably small, but remains important even when superimposed drawing becomes infeasible due to increasing lattice size. Preliminary observations have suggested that JRL order may mitigate but not always eliminate topological inconsistency between the top-down and bottom-up variants of Concept Trees, Spanning Concept Trees and K&O Spanning Trees [10,11]. Such observations can be rationalised for the former two tree types as follows: post-order traversals of the top-down and bottom-up trees yield the concepts in Reverse Lectic Order of intents and extents respectively [10], while Jointly Reverse Lectic Order can be defined as consistency between the Reverse Lectic Orders over the object intents and attribute extents. While consistent ordering of all pairs of *concrete* concepts might therefore be expected, this need not extend to pairs in which at least one concept is abstract. The connection between Reverse Lectic Ordering of concepts and post-order traversal of either K&O Spanning Tree is also unclear [11].

A systematic study of whether JRL order reliably mitigates or frequently eliminates topological inconsistency between top-down and bottom-up spanning trees, or bypass arcs in either Concept Tree, has been hampered by our inability to efficiently generate *all* JRL orders for a given context. In a companion paper [12], we have developed the Dominus algorithm for this purpose which is not only provably correct, but also efficient in its use of both computation and memory. In this paper, we use the Dominus algorithm to enumerate all JRL orders of contexts in the FCA Repository [6], and apply a readily computable definition of topological consistency and an efficient test for bypass arcs [11] to demonstrate empirically that JRL ordering guarantees neither topologically-consistent K&O Spanning Trees nor digraph-spanning Concept Trees. We also demonstrate that post-order traversals of the top-down and bottom-up K&O Spanning Trees often but not always yield concepts in Reverse Lectic Order of their intents and extents, respectively. This systematic investigation qualifies an earlier anecdotal observation [11] regarding this necessary condition for the (Spanning) Concept and K&O Spanning Trees to coincide.

This paper is structured as follows. In Sect. 2 we: consider two possible definitions of topological consistency; choose the one which is more readily computable; review an efficient test for bypass arcs in the Concept Tree; and examine two notions of consistency between the orders of object intents and attribute extents in a JRL-ordered context. In Sect. 3.1, we discuss the methods used to empirically survey the prevalence of bypass arcs and topological consistency for JRL-ordered formal contexts, and to compare post-order traversals of the top-down and bottom-up K&O Spanning Trees with the Reverse Lectic Orders of concept intents and extents respectively. The results are tabulated and discussed in Sect. 3.2. Section 4 summarises and draws conclusions from those results, as well as identifying potential future work required to strengthen the conclusions.

2 Theory and Algorithms

2.1 Topological Consistency

Pattison [10] implicitly defined topological consistency between a top-down and a bottom-up tree as the ability to overlay both on a drawing of the lattice digraph without edge crossings within either tree. This definition is deficient in that it does not explicitly constrain the drawing of the lattice digraph to preserve in its left-right ordering the topological order [10] of the incomparable pairs within either tree, let alone both. It is also difficult to operationalise because it requires that we either find a suitable drawing of the lattice digraph or rule out its existence. While such a drawing should be constrained by convention to be upward, it need not be layered or involve only straight-line arcs. The space of drawings which must be exhausted to establish inconsistency is therefore infeasibly large.

Pattison [10] defined the topological order of an ordered tree such that a tree descendant is less than its ancestor and the order of each pair of vertices which are not comparable in the tree is determined by that of the children of the least common ancestor from which the vertices are respectively descended. A "top-down" tree is an in-tree rooted at the lattice top, while a "bottom-up" tree is an in-tree rooted at the lattice bottom. Since top-down and bottom-up trees respect and reverse, respectively, the lattice order, they necessarily disagree on the relative topological order of pairs which are ancestor and descendant in both trees.

We arbitrate this discrepancy in favour of the lattice order – and the upward drawing convention for the lattice digraph – and limit our definition of topological consistency to pairs of concepts which are incomparable in the lattice digraph – and hence also in both trees. This excludes not only all pairs which are comparable in either tree, but also those which are comparable in the lattice digraph but rendered incomparable by the omission from either tree of one or more digraph arcs. This choice is vindicated in the case of Concept Trees, for which the top-down and bottom-up trees are ordered such that their post-order traversals yield the concepts in RLO of intents and extents respectively [10]. Since superset must precede subset in any Reverse Lectic Order, the top-down and bottom-up Concept Trees must disagree on the relative order of all lattice-comparable concept pairs.

Definition 1 (Topological consistency). *A top-down and a bottom-up tree are topologically consistent if each lattice-incomparable pair is assigned the same relative topological order by both trees.*

Definition 1 ensures that for each pair of lattice-incomparable concepts, there exists a left-right order in a drawing of the lattice digraph which respects their relative topological order in both the top-down and bottom-up trees. A lattice drawing which respects in its left-right ordering that of all *all* such pairs may not however be optimally compact, since it entails left-right separation between the entire subtrees rooted at each tree sibling. As we will see in Sect. 3.1, Definition 1 is readily decidable with the aid of one traversal of each tree to enumerate and order each incomparable pair.

For each JRL order of a given context, we can construct – using the algorithm of Kuznetsov and Obiedkov [7] – and traverse the top-down and bottom-up K&O Spanning Trees, enumerating and ordering each lattice-incomparable pair, and counting the number of pairs on whose order the two trees disagree. If this count is zero, the count of JRL orders for the context which are (completely) topologically consistent is incremented.

2.2 Ordering Lattice-Incomparable Pairs

A depth-first traversal suffices to identify and order all pairs of lattice-incomparable concepts in a K&O Spanning Tree. Traversal of the subtree rooted at vertex x compiles a list of both its individual concepts and its incomparable pairs. Iteration over its children performs two functions: it accumulates both the concepts and incomparable pairs of the corresponding subtrees; and adds to the accumulated pairs those lattice-incomparable pairs whose least common ancestor in the tree is x. Updating these novel pairs for child vertex z involves calculating the Cartesian product between concepts in the subtree rooted at each sibling $y < z$ and those in the subtree rooted at z, and retaining those pairs which are incomparable in the concept lattice.

Traversal of the tree structure serves not only to topologically order each lattice-incomparable pair, but also to omit – and hence avoid testing the known lattice comparability of – pairs consisting of tree ancestor and descendant. Since the topological order over the K&O Spanning Tree is a topological sort over the lattice digraph [11], the first concept in each tree-incomparable pair is a candidate sub-concept but not super-concept of the second, allowing the use of a one-sided subsumption test for computational efficiency. We used bitsets for efficient storage and comparison of intents or extents.

2.3 Detecting Bypass Arcs

Let (G, M, I) be a formal context with object set G, attribute set M, binary relation $I \subseteq G \times M$, and formal concept set $\mathfrak{B}(G, M, I)$ obtained using the usual derivation operator(s) $'$. Denote by $\leq$ the order relation between concepts corresponding to the inclusion relation $\subseteq$ between their extents, and by $\langle \mathfrak{B}, \leq \rangle$ the concept lattice. Pattison [11] applied a result of Lindig [8] to produce an efficient test for bypass arcs in a Concept Tree. The test involves comparing either the rows or columns – whichever is fewer – of a typically small sub-matrix of the context bi-adjacency matrix I. The required computation can be aborted with a positive result as soon as a difference is detected. The test can be applied to every arc during a traversal of the Concept Tree with a total of $\mathcal{O}(|\mathfrak{B}||G||M|)$ bit comparisons.

For each JRL order of a given context, we can construct – using any Close-by-One variant such as In-Close 2 [1] – and traverse the top-down and bottom-up Concept Trees, counting the number of bypass arcs. If this count is zero, the count of JRL orders for the context which yield no bypass arcs is incremented.

2.4 Reverse Lectic Order of Intents and Extents

Post-order traversals of the top-down and bottom-up K&O Spanning Trees each yield total orders over the concepts of a JRL-ordered formal context, and hence also over their intents and extents respectively. The Reverse Lectic Orders over these same intents and extents are alternative total orders which can be obtained using post-order traversals of the top-down and bottom-up Concept Trees respectively [10] – if available – or computed using the MAXMODPARTITION algorithm [3]. The corresponding total orders can be compared element-wise, and the comparison aborted if and when they first disagree.

2.5 "Consistency" in JRL Order

JRL ordering of a context matrix orders the attribute extents and object intents – and hence also the corresponding attributes and objects respectively – "consistently" in the sense that the attribute order induces the RLO of object intents and the object order induces the RLO of attribute extents. An alternative notion of consistent ordering is that the relative orders amongst the extents and intents of those formal concepts which are both an attribute concept and an object concept should be consistent. Here we provide a simple construction which demonstrates that JRL ordering is not sufficient to achieve such consistency. In particular, this construction transforms any standardised context to preserve its lattice structure while ensuring that none of its JRL orders is consistent in this sense.

A standardised formal context can be augmented by adding an attribute for each concept which is not already an attribute concept and an object for each concept which is not already an object concept. This yields a clarified but no longer reduced formal context in which the extent of each concept is an attribute extent, and the intent of each concept is an object intent. While the resultant concept lattice is intentionally isomorphic to that for the original context, the benefit of this construction is that the augmented context contains the intents and extents of *every* concept, so that permuting it into JRL order imposes simultaneous Reverse Lectic Orders over both.

Since each concept now corresponds to both an object and an attribute, we might naively expect the attribute and object orders to respect this correspondence. In particular, we might expect that the intent and extent of a concept have the same ordinal positions in the RLO of (object) intents and the RLO of (attribute) extents, respectively. However, any JRL order for this augmented formal context must place the attribute extent for the lattice top first in the RLO of extents and its object intent last in the RLO of intents. Similarly any such JRL order must place the object intent for the lattice bottom first in the RLO of intents and its attribute extent last in the RLO of extents. More generally, the intent of a sub-concept must precede that of all of its super-concepts, whereas the extent of a super-concept must precede that of all of its sub-concepts. For this augmented, JRL-ordered formal context, therefore, the Reverse Lectic Orders of object intents and attribute extents must disagree on the relative order of every lattice-comparable concept pair, and hence also reverse every lattice chain.

3 Experiment

3.1 Method

The DOMINUS algorithm [12] efficiently enumerates all JRL orders of a given formal context. For each JRL order, the top-down and bottom-up Concept and K&O Spanning Trees were constructed and traversed depth-first, and counts compiled of the number of bypass arcs and topologically inconsistent pairs respectively. If either count was zero, the corresponding counter of JRL orders for which there are no bypass arcs or no topologically inconsistent pairs was incremented. Since the top-down and bottom-up Concept Trees may differ in the number of bypass arcs, the corresponding counts were compiled separately. In contrast, topological consistency between the top-down and bottom-up K&O Spanning Trees involved *comparison* of the two trees, yielding only a single count per JRL order. Post-order traversals of the top-down and bottom-up K&O Spanning Trees were also compared with the Reverse Lectic Orders over concept intents and extents, respectively, and the proportion of JRL orders for which they agreed was tabulated.

This procedure was iterated over all formal contexts in the FCA Repository [6] for which $\max(|G|, |M|) \leq 18$ and the results tabulated in Tables 1, 2 and 3. The English variant of each context was used in cases where two contexts differed only in the language – English (EN) or German (DE) – used for their labels. The DOMINUS algorithm returns all JRL orders for even the two largest formal contexts in the FCA Repository in reasonable timeframes [12]. However, these were excluded from the current study using the above constraint on the context size because the cost of computing top-down and bottom-up Concept and K&O Spanning Trees for every JRL order became prohibitive. While the efficiency of the code which constructs these trees could certainly be improved, the remaining 11 formal contexts proved sufficient for the current purposes.

3.2 Results

Table 1 reports the results for topological consistency between top-down and bottom-up K&O Spanning Trees, Table 2 examines the prevalence of bypass arcs in Concept Trees, and Table 3 focuses on whether post-order traversals of the K&O Spanning Trees yield corresponding Reverse Lectic Orders.

For each formal context whose name appears in the first column of Table 1, the number of JRL orders is listed in the second, and the number of lattice-incomparable pairs in the third. The number of lattice-incomparable pairs is the same regardless of whether it is derived using the top-down or the bottom-up K&O Spanning Trees, and is accordingly recorded in a single column of Table 1. The count of topologically inconsistent concept pairs between the top-down and bottom-up K&O Spanning Trees is shown in column 4, averaged over all JRL orders. The number of JRL orders yielding no pairs whose topological order is inconsistent between top-down and bottom-up K&O Spanning Trees is listed in column 5 of Table 1. While most (8 out of 11) contexts averaged a moderate proportion of topologically inconsistent lattice-incomparable pairs, three of the contexts (`New Zealand Leisure`, `Office Supplies` and `Planets`) had one or more JRL orders for which there were none.

Table 1. Average number of topologically inconsistent pairs, and number of JRL orders which lack any, for contexts in the FCA Repository [6].

Context	JRL orders	Incomparable pairs	Inconsistent pairs (avg)	Consistent orders
`Animals`	151	401	112	0
`Bodies of water (DE)`	48	253	46	0
`Bodies of water (EN)`	9	21	4	0
`Drive Concepts`	48	147	34	0
`Famous Animals`	12	35	4	0
`Living Beings and Water`	18	91	17	0
`Miss Marple murder methods`	16	39	5	0
`New Zealand Leisure`	4	6	1	2
`Office Supplies`	2	2	0	2
`Planets`	18	27	3	4
`Tea Ladies`	540	1471	349	0

Table 2. Average number of bypass arcs in the top-down (TD) and bottom-up (BU) Concept Trees, and proportion of JRL orders for which these trees lack any, for contexts in the FCA Repository [6].

Context	JRL orders	TD bypass arcs (avg)	Bypass-free TDs (%)	BU bypass arcs (avg)	Bypass-free BUs (%)
`Animals`	151	2	13	1	44
`Bodies of water (DE)`	48	0	100	0	100
`Bodies of water (EN)`	9	0	100	0	100
`Drive Concepts`	48	0	79	0	83
`Famous Animals`	12	0	100	0	100
`Living Beings and Water`	18	0	100	0	100
`Miss Marple murder methods`	16	0	100	0	100
`New Zealand Leisure`	4	0	100	0	100
`Office Supplies`	2	0	100	0	100
`Planets`	18	0	100	0	100
`Tea Ladies`	540	0	77	0	92

Table 3. Proportion of JRL orders for which post-order traversal of top-down (TD) or bottom-up (BU) K&O Spanning Trees yields concepts in Reverse Lectic Order (RLO) of intents or extents respectively for contexts in the FCA Repository [6].

Context	JRL orders	TD RLO intents (%)	BU RLO extents (%)
`Animals`	151	38	96
`Bodies of water (DE)`	48	100	100
`Bodies of water (EN)`	9	100	100
`Drive Concepts`	48	100	100
`Famous Animals`	12	100	100
`Living Beings and Water`	18	100	100
`Miss Marple murder methods`	16	100	100
`New Zealand Leisure`	4	100	100
`Office Supplies`	2	100	100
`Planets`	18	100	100
`Tea Ladies`	540	72	98

The first two columns of Table 1 are repeated in Tables 2 and 3. Table 2 then lists in columns 3 and 5 the number of bypass arcs for the top-down and bottom-up Concept Trees, averaged over all JRL orders, and in columns 4 and 6 the proportion of JRL orders for which these trees lack bypass arcs. All JRL orders for most (8 out of 11) contexts yielded both top-down and bottom-up Concept Trees which were free of bypass arcs; some JRL orders for the contexts `Animals`, `Drive Concepts` and `Planets` contained bypass arcs which the JRL ordering had failed to remediate.

Columns 3 and 4 of Table 3 list the proportions of all JRL orders for each context for which post-order traversals of the top-down and bottom-up K&O Spanning Trees yield the concepts ordered in Reverse Lectic Order of intents and extents, respectively. While all JRL orders for 9 of the 11 contexts examined yielded the conjectured Reverse Lectic Orders, the remaining 2 contexts (`Animals` and `Tea Ladies`) yielded significantly lower rates of Reverse Lectic Ordering, especially for the top-down trees. The reason for the apparent asymmetry between the top-down and bottom-up trees was not further investigated.

4 Conclusions and Future Work

The results in Sect. 3.2 demonstrate that JRL ordering guarantees neither topologically-consistent K&O Spanning Trees nor digraph-spanning Concept Trees. The prevalence of topological inconsistency between the top-down and bottom-up K&O Spanning Trees appears fatal for the proposed simultaneous user interaction with both trees, since without additional measures it will compromise the integrity of the user's mental model. Even judicious selection amongst the JRL orders would eliminate topological inconsistency in only 3 of the 11 contexts examined. If this proposal is to be salvaged, it would require a relaxation of the stringent definition of topological consistency provided in Sect. 2 while retaining fidelity to the requirement for integrity of the mental model induced by interaction with the two trees. Whilst JRL ordering appears more successful in reducing and mostly eliminating bypass arcs in Concept Trees, it cannot be relied on to produce a Spanning Concept Tree without also screening for bypass arcs and remediating as per [11] any which are detected.

Importantly, this study was not designed to assess the effectiveness of JRL ordering in mitigating bypass arcs and topological inconsistency. To do so would require a baseline assessment of the prevalence of these conditions amongst randomly-selected permutations of the formal context – both JRL and non-JRL – for comparison. JRL ordering does however provably prevent bypass arcs to the supremum from non-coatomic attribute concepts in the top-down, and to the infimum from non-atomic object concepts in the bottom-up, Concept Trees; such arcs are introduced in the top-down tree as a consequence of the attribute order recommended by Andrews [1] for computational efficiency.

The children of a concept in the top-down K&O Spanning Tree are in Reverse Lectic Order of *extents* [11], which seems unlikely to coincide with the RLO of intents. Noting that such a coincidence is a necessary condition for post-order traversal of the top-down tree to yield the concepts in RLO of intents, it does, however, occur in a surprising proportion – 100% in 9 of 11 cases – of the JRL orders of the contexts examined. Nevertheless, the exceptions demonstrate that this property cannot be assumed for a randomly-selected JRL order of an arbitrary formal context. We conclude that despite anecdotal counter-examples [11], the top-down K&O Spanning Tree does not in general coincide with the top-down Spanning Concept Tree. Future work might seek to: characterise the circumstances under which such an assumption may be valid; and relate instances where it is not to topological (in)consistency between the top-down and bottom-up K&O Spanning Trees.

References

1. Andrews, S.: A 'best-of-breed' approach for designing a fast algorithm for computing fixpoints of Galois connections. Inf. Sci. **295**, 633–649 (2015). https://doi.org/10.1016/j.ins.2014.10.011
2. Andrews, S., Hirsch, L.: A tool for creating and visualising formal concept trees. In: Andrews, S., Polovina, S. (eds.) Proc. 5th Conceptual Structures Tools & Interoperability Wkshp (CSTIW). pp. 1–9 (2016). http://ceur-ws.org/Vol-1637/
3. Berry, A., Bordat, J.P., Sigayret, A.: A local approach to concept generation. Ann. Math. Artif. Intell. **49**(1–4), 117–136 (2007). https://doi.org/10.1007/s10472-007-9063-4
4. Bordat, J.: Calcul pratique du trellis de Galois d'une correspondance. Math. Inform. Sci. Hum. **24**(94), 31–47 (1986)
5. Ganter, B., Wille, R.: Formal Concept Analysis: Mathematical Foundations. Springer (1999). https://doi.org/10.1007/978-3-642-59830-2
6. Hanika, T., Jäschke, R.: A repository for formal contexts. In: Cabrera, I., Ferré, S., Obiedkov, S. (eds.) Conceptual Knowledge Structures. pp. 182–197. Springer Nature Switzerland, Cham (2024).https://doi.org/10.1007/978-3-031-67868-4_13
7. Kuznetsov, S.O., Obiedkov, S.A.: Comparing performance of algorithms for generating concept lattices. J. Exp. Theor. Artif. Intell. **14**(2–3), 189–216 (2002). https://doi.org/10.1080/09528130210164170
8. Lindig, C.: Algorithmen zur Begriffsanalyse und ihre Anwendung bei Softwarebibliotheken. Ph.D. thesis, Technischen Universität Braunschweig (1999). https://www.st.cs.uni-saarland.de/publications/files/lindig-phd-1999.pdf
9. Lindig, C.: Fast concept analysis. In: Stumme, G. (ed.) Working With ConceptualStructures - Contributions to ICCS 2000, pp. 152–161. Shaker Verlag (2000)
10. Pattison, T.: Spanning concept trees: algorithms and interaction. In: Cabrera, I.P., Ferré, S., Obiedkov, S. (eds.) Conceptual Knowledge Structures. CONCEPTS 2024. LNCS, vol. 14914, pp. 166–181. Springer (2024).https://doi.org/10.1007/978-3-031-67868-4_12
11. Pattison, T., Dürrschnabel, D., Abdullah, M.: Selected Papers from the Third International Joint Conference on Conceptual Knowledge Structures (CONCEPTS 2026). Int. J. Approximate Reasoning **197** (2026)
12. Pattison, T., Dürrschnabel, D., Abdullah, M.: Enumerating jointly reverse lectic orders for bi-adjacency matrices. Int. J. Approximate Reasoning Spec. Issue Int. Joint Conf. Conceptual Knowl. Struct. (2026). https://doi.org/10.1016/j.ijar.2026.109725. in press
13. Pattison, T., Enciso, M., Mora, A., Cordero, P., Weber, D., Broughton, M.: Scalable visual analytics in FCA. In: Complex Data Analytics with Formal Concept Analysis. Springer (2022). https://doi.org/10.1007/978-3-030-93278-7_8

Data Analysis

Degrees of Distributivity: Quantifying Structural Deviations in Real World Data

Mohammad Abdulla[1,2](✉), Jannik Nordmeyer[1,2], and Tom Hanika[3]

[1] Knowledge & Data Engineering Group, University of Kassel, Kassel, Germany
[2] Interdisciplinary Research Center for Information System Design, University of Kassel, Kassel, Germany
abdulla@cs.uni-kassel.de
[3] Information Systems and Machine Learning Lab, University of Hildesheim, Hildesheim, Germany

Abstract. We introduce complementary indices for quantifying non-distributivity in finite lattices. These indices include pointwise deviation indices, which are based on forbidden-triple counting, and global deviation distances, which are derived from Birkhoff's completion theorem.

Experiments on 18 real-world datasets shows that the indices yield largely consistent severity rankings while each captures distinct structural aspects, revealing, e.g., that non-distributivity is predominantly of the M_3-type and that well-supported concepts behave more distributively.

Keywords: Distributive Lattices · Dismantlable Lattices · FCA

1 Introduction

Lattices arising from empirical data rarely satisfy ideal algebraic properties. In Formal Concept Analysis (FCA), concept lattices derived from real-world datasets often violate classical conditions such as distributivity. While lattice theory provides precise structural characterizations of distributive lattices, these are purely qualitative: a lattice either satisfies the distributive laws or it does not. For empirical applications, however, such binary classifications are often insufficient. Concept lattices obtained from data may exhibit only mild violations of distributivity, and a graded assessment of these deviations can provide substantially more insight than a simple yes-or-no decision.

In this paper we introduce *Structural Deviation Indices* (SDIs) that quantify the degree of non-distributivity in finite lattices. The proposed indices fall into two complementary categories:

- **Pointwise Deviation Indices (PDI)**, which measure how frequently distributive laws are violated in local lattice configurations, and
- **Global Deviation Distances (GDD)**, which quantify the distance to distributive lattices using completion and dismantling constructions.

M. Croitoru et al. (Eds.): CONCEPTS 2026, LNAI 16811, pp. 151–167, 2027.
https://doi.org/10.1007/978-3-032-34742-8_10

We analyze the theoretical properties of these indices and evaluate them on 18 real-world FCA benchmark datasets. Despite their different constructions, the indices produce largely consistent severity rankings while capturing distinct structural aspects of non-distributivity.

The remainder of the paper is organized as follows. Section 2 reviews related work. Section 3 recalls basic notions from lattice theory and FCA. Section 4 introduces the proposed indices and presents their empirical evaluation. Section 5 compares the measures, and Sect. 6 concludes the paper.

2 Related Work

Research on distributivity in lattices has a long tradition in order theory and Formal Concept Analysis. Existing work can be grouped into three main directions: structural characterizations of distributivity, quantitative measures of non-distributivity in FCA, and algorithmic approaches for transforming lattices into distributive ones. From the perspective of classical lattice theory, distributivity has been studied through a variety of structural refinements. Jakubík investigated higher degrees of distributivity in lattices and lattice-ordered groups, analyzing generalizations of the classical distributive laws and their interaction with algebraic properties of ordered groups and Boolean algebras [16,17]. Related work by Huhn introduced the notion of n-distributivity as a hierarchy of weakening conditions for distributivity [15]. These approaches classify lattices by how closely they satisfy distributive identities but do not provide explicit numerical measures of deviation. Within FCA, several authors have proposed quantitative approaches to assess distributivity in concept lattices derived from empirical data. Buzmakov et al. proposed a complementary dataset-level perspective that assesses structural complexity through properties of intents, pseudo-intents, keys, and minimal implication bases [5]. Their empirical results demonstrate that lattices derived from real-world data tend to be closer to distributive behavior than randomized datasets. Another line of research focuses on algorithms for checking or enforcing distributivity. Gély et al. studied methods for embedding arbitrary concept lattices into distributive sublattices via prime ideals and formal contexts, and proposed procedures for transforming non-distributive lattices into distributive representations [11]. In later work, Gély et al. further investigated algorithmic connections between distributive lattices, median graphs, and FCA representations [12].There are one-sided relaxations of the distributive laws, such as meet- and join-distributivity, are closely connected to antimatroids and convex geometries [8], as well as (practically) to knowledge and learning spaces [7]. Both connections demonstrate that partial distributivity still preserves highly structured and interpretable semantic properties. Furthermore, quantifying deviation can also be viewed through the lens of extracting regular substructures from complex data. Wille observed the frequent occurrence of truncated distributive lattices in everyday conceptual thinking, explicitly connecting them to simple-implicational theories [20]. Finally, more abstract viewpoints have connected distributivity to the problem of assigning consistent numerical valuations to lattices. Knuth investigated how distributive symmetries constrain possible quantifications of lattices, linking algebraic structure to numeric representations [18].

Fig. 1. The nondistributive lattices M_3 (left) and N_5 (right).

3 Basics

We assume the reader is familiar with the standard notions of order theory, lattice theory [4,6], and Formal Concept Analysis [10]. In the following, we briefly establish the notation used throughout this work.

For a partially ordered set P, the principal down-set and up-set of an element $x \in P$ are denoted by $\downarrow x := \{a \in P \mid a \leq x\}$ and $\uparrow x := \{a \in P \mid a \geq x\}$, respectively. The family of all order ideals of P is denoted by $\mathcal{I}(P)$, and the family of its order filters by $\mathcal{F}(P)$. For a lattice L, the set of all meet-irreducible elements is denoted by $\mathcal{M}(L)$, and the set of all join-irreducible elements by $\mathcal{J}(L)$. The set of doubly irreducible elements (both join- and meet-irreducible) is denoted by $Irr(L)$. We call $S \neq \emptyset$ a *sublattice* of L if $(a, b \in S \Rightarrow a \vee b \in S$ and $a \wedge b \in S)$ holds. A lattice L is said to be *modular* if for all $x, y, z \in L$, $x \leq z \Rightarrow x \vee (y \wedge z) = (x \vee y) \wedge z$, we call this property **M1** in the following. Analogously, a lattice is *distributive* if for all $x, y, z \in L$, $x \wedge (y \vee z) = (x \wedge y) \vee (x \wedge z)$, a property in the following denoted by **D1**.

A very important finding towards understanding distributive laws in lattices came from Birkhoff and is illustrated by line-drawings in Fig. 1.

Theorem 1 (Birkhoff Theorem [4]**).** *A lattice L is distributive if and only if there exists no sublattice $A \subseteq L$ isomorphic to either M_3 or N_5.*

With respect to Formal Concept Analysis (FCA), we denote a formal context by $\mathbb{K} = (G, M, I)$. The standard derivation operators for $A \subseteq G$ and $B \subseteq M$ are denoted by A' and B'. The set of all formal concepts of $\mathbb{K}$ ordered by extent inclusion forms the concept lattice, denoted by $\underline{\mathfrak{B}}(\mathbb{K})$. We call a context *clarified* [10] if $g' = h'$ implies $g = h$ for all $g, h \in G$, and $m' = n'$ implies $m = n$ for all $m, n \in M$. Furthermore, a context is *object-reduced* if every object concept is join-irreducible, *attribute-reduced* if every attribute concept is meet-irreducible, and *reduced* if it is both.

4 Distributivity Measures

Let $\mathcal{L}$ denote the class of all finite lattices. A *Structural Deviation Index* (SDI) is a function $D : \mathcal{L} \to [0, 1]$ that assigns to each lattice $L \in \mathcal{L}$ a numerical value representing its deviation from an algebraic property, such as distributivity.

It can be helpful to normalize such a function to a unit interval in order to establish comparability, especially for lattices of the same size. In the cases of distributivity, for example, we say a lattice L with $D(L) = 0$ is distributive, and any lattice L with $D(L) > 0$ is non-distributive. Larger values shall indicate stronger violations of the respective algebraic property. We specify what 'stronger' is supposed to mean in the following.

Whenever we do not specify the underlying structure to which we want to measure the deviation in this work, it can be assumed that we mean distributivity.

4.1 Classes of Structural Deviation

All of the structural deviation indices considered in this study naturally fall into one of two categories, each of which offers a different perspective.

1. **Pointwise Deviation Indices (PDI)** Instances of this kind quantify how frequently distributive laws are violated within lattice. They are typically based on triples of elements or individual nodes and therefore reflect the proportion of *local structure violations*.
2. **Global Deviation Distance (GDD)** SDI functions in this category aim to quantify how far a lattice is from fulfilling a necessary algebraic property, such as the distributive laws. They typically rely on constructions such as completions or structural transformations and quantify the difference in size or structure between the original lattice and a related distributive lattice.

Together, these different perspectives provide complementary insights into the degree of structural deviation within a given lattice.

4.2 Pointwise Deviation Indices

As the first representative of the PDI, we would like to mention the counting of **non-distributive triples**. It is arguably the most natural one when studying distributivity. The line of reasoning here is that because deciding distributivity requires checking all three-element subsets of L in different permutations to see whether the distributivity laws (**D1**) apply, it is natural to count how many triples violate these laws. This leads to a simple counting-based SDI: we compute the set of triples of elements of L that fail to be distributive within L and compare the cardinality of this set with $|L|$. In this sense, the resulting index is a normalized counting that quantifies how frequently non-distributive triples occur within the lattice L. We specify this idea as follows.

Let L be a finite lattice and $a, b, c \in L$. A triple (a, b, c) is *distributive* if the sublattice it generates, $\langle a, b, c\rangle_L$ is distributive and the lattice L is distributive if and only if this holds for all triples [4].

Definition 1 (Triple Count Distributivity Index) *Let L be a finite lattice. The* triple count distributivity index *(TCDI) of L is*

$$I_{distr}(L) := \frac{\left|\{(a, b, c) \in L^3 \mid \langle a, b, c\rangle_L \text{ is not distributive}\}\right|}{|L^3|}$$

This index can also be interpreted as the probability that three randomly chosen elements of the lattice generate a non-distributive sublattice.

Given this first index we can already shed some light on the properties of the SDI in general and on PDI in particular. One might assume that SDIs should satisfy a sublattice inclusion monotonicity property, i.e., if L_1 is a sublattice of L, then $D(L_1) \leq D(L)$. However, this is not the case for the Triple Count Distributivity Index, as illustrated in Fig. 2. Due to the local nature of PDIs, any monotony as described above will be difficult to achieve. Since we consider the PDI introduced in Definition 1 very important, we refrain from demanding such monotonicity restrictions from require structural deviation indices .

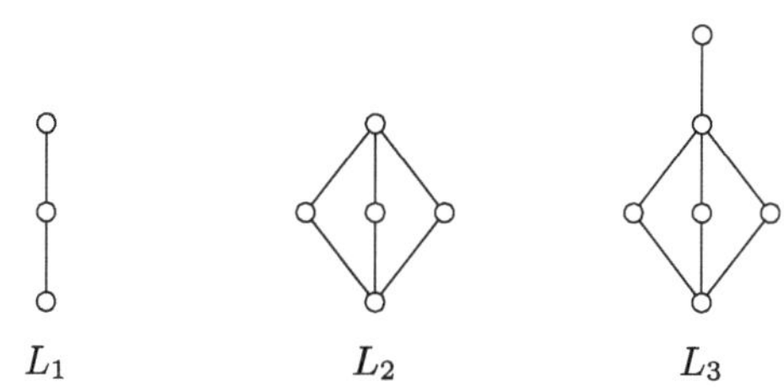

$I_{\text{distr}}(L_1) = 0$ $\quad I_{\text{distr}}(L_2) = 1/10$ $\quad I_{\text{distr}}(L_3) = 1/20$

Fig. 2. Example lattices illustrating different local distributivity behaviour.

Analogously to Definition 1, we can find an index for the deviation from modularity (**M1**).

Definition 2 (Triple Count Modularity Index) *The* triple count modularity index *(TCMI) of a finite lattice L is the proportion of triples that fail the modular property (**M1**). We denote this index by $I_{mod}(L)$.*

For structural investigations, it can be very useful to identify lattice elements that more frequently obstruct an algebraic property than others. The PDIs introduced so far naturally also allow a view on individual elements and their influence on the breaking of algebraic association properties.

Definition 3 (Element-TCDI/TCMI) *Let L be a finite lattice and $e \in L$. The elemenent-TCDI/TCMI of e in L is*

$$I_{distr/mod}(L, e) := \frac{|\{(a,b,c) \in L^3 \mid e \in \{a,b,c\} \text{ and } \langle a,b,c\rangle_L \text{ is not distr/mod}\}|}{|\{(a,b,c) \in L^3 \mid e \in \{a,b,c\}\}|}$$

So far, the introduced PDIs only use properties of the lattice order of L. In a concept lattice $\mathfrak{B}(\mathbb{K})$ of some formal context $\mathbb{K}$, even more information is available, which we want to capture with the following index.

Since a formal concept is defined by a set of objects and set of their shared attributes, and vice versa, one might consider concepts with large extents to represent a more significant portion of the dataset. Therefore, the *importance* of such a concept within the order structure might be considered higher than of a concept with an extent of smaller size. Hence, we propose an extent-weighted adaptation of the Element-TCDI of a concept lattice.

Definition 4 (Extent-Weighted-TCDI) *Given a concept lattice $L := \underline{\mathfrak{B}}(\mathbb{K})$ for some formal context $\mathbb{K}$, the extent-weighted TCDI is defined by*

$$\widetilde{I_{distr}}(L) = \frac{1}{|L|} \sum_{e \in L} I_{distr}(L, e) \cdot \frac{|\operatorname{Ext}(e)|}{|G|}$$

It is perfectly clear that behind this definition lies a much more general notion of weighted lattice elements. In this sense, weighting by extent can be replaced not only by weighting by intent, but also by any weighting function. It would be particularly interesting to examine how lattice valuations behave in this regard. However, since a theoretical investigation of this would take us too far away from the current topic, we would like to postpone this discussion to a future work.

Distributivity Index Based on Non-Unit Rises

The PDIs so far quantify the number of violations of the distributive laws with respect to three element triples in L and the corresponding order relation $\leq$. In this section we turn to *non-unit meet-rises* and *non-unit join-rises* [1] and their capacity to capture structural irregularities along the covering relation with respect to $(L, \leq)$. To assess the usefulness of this approach for the pointwise deviation index, we will first review the relevant definitions. In the following, for any given lattice L and $x \in L$ we will use the notations $m^L(x) := |\{m \in \mathcal{M}(L) \mid x \leq m\}|$ and $j^L(x) := |\{j \in \mathcal{J}(L) \mid j \leq x\}|$.

Definition 5 (Non-Unit Rises (Meet-Rise / Join-Rise) [1]) *Let L be a finite lattice, and let $\prec$ denote the covering relation on L. For any covering pair (x, y) in L (i.e., $x \prec y$), we define the* meet-rise / join-rise *as*

$$\Delta_m^L(x, y) := m^L(x) - m^L(y) \qquad \Delta_j^L(x, y) := j^L(y) - j^L(x).$$

We call a meet/join-rise between covering elements unit *if its value is one, otherwise we call it non-unit*

With respect to distributivity there is an important characterization: a finite lattice is distributive if and only if all rises are unit [1, Cor. 10]. We want to take advantage of this characterization to measure the deviation from distributivity for our purpose and define the following quantities.

Definition 6 (Non-Unit Meet/Join-Rises Index (NUMRI / NUJRI)) *The number of* non-unit meet-rises *in L is*

$$\mathrm{nur}^{\wedge}(L) := \left|\left\{(x,y) \in L^2 \,\middle|\, x \prec y,\ \Delta_m^L(x,y) > 1\right\}\right|$$

and dually, the number of non-unit join-rises *is*

$$\mathrm{nur}^{\vee}(L) := \left|\left\{(x,y) \in L^2 \,\middle|\, x \prec y,\ \Delta_j^L(x,y) > 1\right\}\right|.$$

After normalization via the cardinality of the covering relation $|\prec|$, we call

$$\widetilde{\mathrm{nur}}^{\wedge}(L) = \frac{\mathrm{nur}^{\wedge}(L)}{|\prec|}, \quad \widetilde{\mathrm{nur}}^{\vee}(L) = \frac{\mathrm{nur}^{\vee}(L)}{|\prec|}$$

the non-unit meet-rise index *and* non-unit join-rise index *of L respectively.*

These indices measure how frequently covering relations exhibit non-unit rises. This quantifies deviations from the characteristic behavior of distributive lattices along the edges of the line diagram.

4.3 Experimental Analysis of PDIs

All introduced PIDs could be derived from the underlying algebraic equations (M1/D1) using theoretical considerations. In doing so, we also incorporated FCA specifications into the designs, i.e., practical data-based requirements in particular. In order to study the behavior of the various PIDs on real-world data, we conducted experiments in this and the next section on 18 real-world data sets that we took from the testing data of *conexpl-clj* [14]. The data sets used are described in more detail in Table 1, i.e., their properties when represented as a formal context.

The results for all PIDs are shown in Table 2 and are now discussed.

Observations. We have identified several structural observations in the data, which we will present in the following categories.

Consistent and Rare The very first observation is that $I_{\mathrm{mod}}(L)$ and $I_{\mathrm{distr}}(L)$ are small but never zero. Hence, real-world data is not expected to be distributive in its representation as a concept lattice. Yet, the amount they deviate from being distributive seems small. Across all datasets, $I_{\mathrm{mod}}(L) \ll I_{\mathrm{distr}}(L)$ holds without exception. Since every distributive lattice is modular, but not conversely,

Table 1. Summary of the used data sets.

Context	$\|L\|$	$\|\prec\|$	$\|G\|$	$\|M\|$	$\frac{\|I\|}{\|G\|\cdot\|M\|}$
triangles	18	31	7	7	0.469
living-beings-and-water	19	32	8	9	0.472
Seasoning-Planner	532	1593	56	37	0.199
drive-concepts-for-motorcars	24	50	5	25	0.376
digits	48	120	10	7	0.671
bodiesofwater	12	18	17	5	0.576
Wood-Properties	315	924	29	28	0.284
Southern-Woman	65	148	18	14	0.353
Forum-Romanum	19	31	14	7	0.449
Dolphins	282	752	62	62	0.083
Dirichlet-1	308	1086	198	10	0.389
Diagnosis	88	210	120	17	0.471
Cointoss-2	411	1324	200	15	0.209
california	21	35	19	8	0.520
Brunson-Club	62	136	25	15	0.253
Bird-Diet	16	27	10	8	0.300
ben-and-jerrys-allergens	9	12	7	7	0.571
ben-and-jerrys-flavors	16	26	7	9	0.381

each triple whose generated sublattice is non-modular also generates a non-distributive sublattice, while the converse does not hold.

It is important to recall that triples that generate an M_3-type sublattice do contribute to I_{distr} but not to I_{mod}. When looking into the ratio $I_{\text{mod}}/I_{\text{distr}}$, this value ranges from approximately 0.05 (Brunson-Club) to 0.37 (bodiesofwater). The consistently small ratios indicate that the non-distributivity in these real-world lattices is predominantly of the M_3-type, i.e., modular but not distributive.

Non-distributivity is not well supported For all datasets, $\widetilde{I_{\text{distr}}}(L) < I_{\text{distr}}(L)$. The reduction factor $\widetilde{I_{\text{distr}}}/I_{\text{distr}}$ ranges from 0.11 (Brunson-Club) to 0.47 (living-beings-and-water). This clearly indicates that concepts with large extents, which represent a larger portion of the object set, tend to participate less frequently in non-distributive triples than concepts with small extents.

The rise indices exhibit pronounced asymmetry The NUMRI $\widetilde{\text{nur}}^{\wedge}(L)$ and the NUJRI $\widetilde{\text{nur}}^{\vee}(L)$ can differ substantially within the same lattice. For example, drive-concepts-for-motorcars shows $\widetilde{\text{nur}}^{\wedge} = 0.240$ versus $\widetilde{\text{nur}}^{\vee} = 0.040$, while bodiesofwater exhibits the opposite pattern with $\widetilde{\text{nur}}^{\wedge} = 0.056$ versus $\widetilde{\text{nur}}^{\vee} = 0.333$. Bird-Diet is notable in that both indices coincide at 0.407.

Rise vs triple-based Ranking the data sets by I_{distr} does not generally agree with the ordering induced by the rise indices. This might indicate that the rise indices capture structural irregularities along covering relations that are not fully reflected in triple-based counting. Despite the ranking disagreements, the datasets with the highest TCDI values (Brunson-Club (0.495), Diagnosis (0.355), and Southern-Woman (0.269)) also exhibit elevated rise indices. The Diagnosis data set has the second-highest values for both $\widetilde{\text{nur}}^{\wedge}$ (0.405) and $\widetilde{\text{nur}}^{\vee}$ (0.476), while Brunson-Club attains the highest $\widetilde{\text{nur}}^{\vee}$ (0.515). This suggests that severe non-distributivity, as measured by triple violations, is typically accompanied by widespread non-unit rises along the covering relation.

Table 2. Pointwise deviation indices for the evaluated concept lattices.

Context	$\lvert L\rvert$	$\lvert\prec\rvert$	I_{distr}	I_{mod}	$\widetilde{I_{distr}}$	$\widetilde{\text{nur}}^{\wedge}$	$\widetilde{\text{nur}}^{\vee}$
triangles	18	31	0.082	0.014	0.023	0.129	0.355
living-beings-and-water	19	32	0.159	0.031	0.074	0.250	0.344
drive-concepts-for-motorcars	24	50	0.047	0.008	0.020	0.240	0.040
digits	48	120	0.062	0.008	0.024	0.117	0.167
bodiesofwater	12	18	0.027	0.010	0.012	0.056	0.333
Southern-Woman	65	148	0.269	0.034	0.054	0.209	0.324
Forum-Romanum	19	31	0.030	0.009	0.019	0.098	0.226
Diagnosis	88	210	0.355	0.028	0.080	0.405	0.476
california	21	35	0.058	0.016	0.025	0.229	0.371
Brunson-Club	62	136	0.495	0.025	0.056	0.338	0.515
Bird-Diet	16	27	0.231	0.027	0.053	0.407	0.407
ben-and-jerrys-allergens	9	12	0.079	0.012	0.012	0.250	0.333
ben-and-jerrys-flavors	16	26	0.146	0.017	0.041	0.423	0.269

Discussion. These observations raise numerous points for discussion. Above all, it should be noted that the low values of the PDIs indicate that distributivity, and modularity in particular, can serve as important "ideal models" for the analysis of real-world data using lattices.

The difference $I_{\text{distr}}(L) - I_{\text{mod}}(L)$ isolates the proportion of triples that violate distributivity while still satisfying modularity. In the evaluated datasets, this gap accounts for the large majority of all distributivity violations, with $I_{\text{mod}}/I_{\text{distr}}$ never exceeding 0.37. This has practical implications: methods that assume or exploit modularity may remain approximately valid for these lattices, even though distributivity cannot be assumed. Moreover, the ratio $I_{\text{mod}}/I_{\text{distr}}$ may serve as an indicator of whether the non-distributivity in a given dataset is predominantly of the M_3-type (modular but not distributive) or involves N_5-type violations (non-modular). In the datasets studied here, M_3-type violations clearly dominate.

The consistent inequality $\widetilde{I_{\text{distr}}}(L) < I_{\text{distr}}(L)$ implies that concepts representing many objects tend to occupy more structurally regular positions in the lattice. Hence, the most important, well-supported concepts behave more distributively, while non-distributive structure is concentrated among concepts with small extents that capture more specific or peripheral phenomena in the data. This observation motivates the use of the extent-weighted procedures (such as TITANIC [19]) when analyzing data. However, it also highlights the fact that concepts that break distributivity (and therefore potentially important facts) will be discarded by the aforementioned procedures.

The observed asymmetry between $\widetilde{\text{nur}}^{\wedge}$ and $\widetilde{\text{nur}}^{\vee}$ can be interpreted as reflecting the structural asymmetry between the object and attribute sides of the underlying formal context. For instance, drive-concepts-for-motorcars has few objects ($|G| = 5$) but many attributes ($|M| = 25$), and its meet-rise index substantially exceeds its join-rise index. Conversely, bodiesofwater has many objects ($|G| = 17$) relative to attributes ($|M| = 5$), and its join-rise index dominates. This makes the pair of rise indices particularly informative for identifying whether non-distributivity in a concept lattice originates from the object side or the attribute side of the data.

We can conclude the discussion of this section by noting that the proposed PDIs provide complementary perspectives on non-distributivity within a data set. The triple-based indices quantify the global frequency of algebraic law violations and allow to some extent a probabilistic interpretation, while the rise indices localize structural deviations along the edges of the line diagram. The partial disagreement in dataset rankings demonstrates that neither perspective subsumes the other. For a comprehensive assessment of non-distributivity in a given lattice, we therefore recommend reporting both types of indices. The index I_{distr} together with I_{mod} reveals the qualitative nature of the violations, $\widetilde{I_{\text{distr}}}$ assesses their relevance with respect to the underlying data, and the rise indices identify whether the structural irregularities are concentrated on the object or attribute side.

4.4 Global Deviation Distance

While the previous indices quantify pointwise deviations from distributivity, it is also natural to ask for a global quantification that answers the question: *How far away is a given lattice from the closest distributive one?* This type of analysis is very common in graph theory, for example, where the splitance [13] is a global measure of how far a graph is from being a split graph. Similarly, we want to introduce several global views, particularly with regard to distributivity. Of course, it's not clear what is meant by "closest" and "distance" per se. We will clarify both of these points below.

Let us start with recalling a crucial notion in the domain of distributive lattices that was recently introduced.

Definition 7 (Birkhoff Completion [2]) *Let L be a finite lattice. The* Upset Birkhoff completion *of L, denoted* $\text{BC}^{\uparrow}(L)$, *is the smallest distributive lattice in* *which L can be embedded as a join-semilattice. Equivalently,* $\mathrm{BC}^{\uparrow}(L)$ *is isomorphic to the lattice of order filters* $(\mathcal{F}(\mathcal{M}(L)), \supseteq)$. *The* Downset Birkhoff completion $\mathrm{BC}^{\downarrow}(L)$ *is defined dually.*

To confirm that this definition is well-defined, we refer the reader to the original paper, in which the uniqueness of the Birkhoff completion was shown [2].

So the idea behind the Birkhoff completion is to embed a finite lattice L into a distributive lattice $\hat{L}$ that is generated by the irreducible elements of L. Comparing L and $\hat{L}$, i.e., the original lattice and its Birkhoff completion, reflects the necessary structural extension that is required to represent L within a distributive lattice. This comparison can now be done on different levels. The simplest, but also the most obvious, approach is to compare the cardinalities of the base sets of the lattices. Yet, since there are two potential candidates (upsets and downsets), we need to give two indices.

Definition 8 (Birkhoff Distributivity Index (BDI)) *Let L be a finite lattice. The* Birkhoff Distributivity Indices *of L, are defined as:*

$$\mathcal{I}_B^{\uparrow}(L) = \frac{|\mathrm{BC}^{\uparrow}(L)| - |L|}{|\mathrm{BC}^{\uparrow}(L)|} \qquad \mathcal{I}_B^{\downarrow}(L) = \frac{|\mathrm{BC}^{\downarrow}(L)| - |L|}{|\mathrm{BC}^{\downarrow}(L)|}$$

Dismantling-Based Approach

The following approach is intended to present a completely different method for quantifying globally the distance to a distributive structure. It is based on the idea of dismantling.

A finite lattice L is called *dismantlable* if it can be reduced to a single element by successively deleting doubly-irreducible elements [10]. Formally, for a lattice with $|L| = n$ there exists a sequence of sublattices L_i with $|L_i| = i$ such that $L = L_n \supset L_{n-1} \supset \cdots \supset L_1$, where each $L_{i-1} = L_i \setminus \{x_i\}$ and x_i is doubly irreducible in L_i.

There is a natural way to assess non-distributivity based on the dismantlable property: if a dismantalable lattice becomes distributive after fewer deletions of doubly irreducible elements, it should be regarded as closer to distributivity than a lattice requiring more deletions. Since a one-element lattice is trivially distributive, any dismantlable lattice admits at least one sequence of removals that eventually yields a distributive lattice. This leads to the central question: *How large a distributive sublattice of L can be obtained solely by removing doubly-irreducible elements?* The order of deletions may influence the size of the resulting distributive sublattice. For this reason, we formulate the problem as an optimization task and introduce indices based on all possible dismantling sequences.

In the following, we say for a finite dismantlable lattice L, that a sublattice $K \leq L$ is *reachable by dismantling* if there exists a sequence of removal steps, beginning with L and terminating in K.

Definition 9 (Dismantlable Distributive Reachability Set) *For a finite dismantlable lattice L, we let*

$$\mathcal{R}_{dis}(L) := \{\, K \leq L \mid K \text{ is distributive and reachable from } L \text{ by dismantling} \,\},$$

be called the dismantlable distributive reachability set.

It is clear, that $\mathcal{R}_{\text{dis}}(L)$ cannot be empty as long as L is not empty. The question of whether there is a single largest element in $\mathcal{R}_{\text{dis}}(L)$ is not well-posed, but we can ask about the largest cardinality in there. This allows us to explain the following global deviation distances.

Definition 10 (Max-Reach / Min-Delete Index (MRI/MDI)) *Let L be a finite dismantlable lattice. The* max-reach index *of L is defined as*

$$MRI(L) := \max\{\, |K| \mid K \in \mathcal{R}_{dis}(L) \,\},$$

and the min-delete index *is the minimal number of deletions required to reach distributivity, i.e.,*

$$MDI(L) := \min\{\, k \mid \exists \text{ a sequence of } k \text{ removal steps leading to a distr. lattice} \,\}.$$

Both quantities are well defined for every dismantlable lattice and do not require any assumption about the uniqueness of reachable sublattices(Table 3).

4.5 Experimental Analysis of GDDs

We evaluate the two global deviation distances introduced above on the same 18 real-world datasets described in Table 1. For the BDI, we computed both the upset and downset Birkhoff completions $\text{BC}^{\uparrow}(L)$ and $\text{BC}^{\downarrow}(L)$ and derived the normalized indices $\mathcal{I}_B^{\uparrow}(L)$ and $\mathcal{I}_B^{\downarrow}(L)$. For the dismantling-based approach, we computed via an exhaustive algorithm all possible dismantling sequences to find the largest reachable distributive sublattice. The results are shown in Table 4.

Observations. We find that the novel indices seem to uncover several different structural aspects of the data. First of all, we see that the Birkhoff indices vary considerably across datasets: from $\mathcal{I}_B^{\uparrow} = 0.143$ (bodiesofwater) to 0.994 (Brunson-Club), and from $\mathcal{I}_B^{\downarrow} = 0.250$ (drive-concepts-for-motorcars) to 0.999 (Brunson-Club). For Brunson-Club and Diagnosis, both indices approach 1, indicating that the Birkhoff completion is orders of magnitude larger than the original lattice.

Asymmetry of values For most datasets, $\mathcal{I}_B^{\downarrow}(L) > \mathcal{I}_B^{\uparrow}(L)$, indicating that the downset Birkhoff completion tends to be larger. However, for Bird-Diet (0.800 vs 0.833), ben-and-jerrys-flavors (0.733 vs 0.789), and drive-concepts-for-motorcars (0.250 vs 0.333), the upset completion is larger. The direction of the asymmetry reflects the relative complexity of $\mathcal{J}(L)$ and $\mathcal{M}(L)$: the downset completion is generated by the join-irreducibles, while the upset completion is generated by the meet-irreducibles.

Table 3. Birkhoff Distributivity Indices for the evaluated concept lattices.

Context	$\vert L\vert$	$\vert\prec\vert$	$\mathcal{I}_B^{\downarrow}$	$\mathcal{I}_B^{\uparrow}$
triangles	18	31	0.667	0.419
living-beings-and-water	19	32	0.763	0.672
drive-concepts-for-motorcars	24	50	0.250	0.333
digits	48	120	0.500	0.333
bodiesofwater	12	18	0.333	0.143
Southern-Woman	65	148	0.972	0.894
Forum-Romanum	19	31	0.406	0.367
Diagnosis	88	210	0.995	0.983
california	21	35	0.571	0.475
Brunson-Club	62	136	0.999	0.994
Bird-Diet	16	27	0.800	0.833
ben-and-jerrys-allergens	9	12	0.550	0.400
ben-and-jerrys-flavors	16	26	0.733	0.789

Exponential growth The absolute sizes of the Birkhoff completions reveal dramatic growth for several datasets. Brunson-Club has $|L| = 62$ but $|BC^{\uparrow}(L)| = 10\,560$ and $|BC^{\downarrow}(L)| = 565\,248$. For Diagnosis ($|L| = 88$), the upset completion already reaches $|BC^{\uparrow}(L)| = 5\,040$, while the downset completion could not be computed. For several of the larger lattices (Seasoning-Planner, Wood-Properties, Dolphins, Cointoss-2), neither completion was computable within reasonable resource limits.

Dismantling is limited Of the 18 datasets, 10 have $|\mathrm{Irr}(L)| = 0$, i.e., no doubly irreducible elements exist. For those data sets the dismantling approach is rendered entirely inapplicable. Among the remaining 8 datasets with $|\mathrm{Irr}(L)| > 0$, the exhaustive algorithm reaches a distributive sublattice in only 5 cases (triangles, bodiesofwater, Forum-Romanum, ben-and-jerrys-allergens, ben-and-jerrys-flavors). In the remaining 3 cases (living-beings-and-water, california, Bird-Diet), dismantling terminates without reaching distributivity, despite removing all available doubly irreducible elements.

Finally, we observe that the BDI is not a useful index for the applicability of the dismantling approach.

Discussion. The direction in which the two Birkhoff indices differ reflects the relative structure of the join- and meet-irreducible elements of L. Since $\mathrm{BC}^{\downarrow}(L) \cong (\mathcal{I}(\mathcal{J}(L)), \subseteq)$ and $\mathrm{BC}^{\uparrow}(L) \cong (\mathcal{F}(\mathcal{M}(L)), \supseteq)$, the downset completion is governed by the poset of join-irreducibles and the upset completion by the poset of meet-irreducibles. When $\mathcal{I}_B^{\downarrow} > \mathcal{I}_B^{\uparrow}$, the join-irreducible poset generates a disproportionately large family of order ideals relative to the lattice size, indicating a

Table 4. Dismantling results and Birkhoff completion sizes. The column *ex. size* displays the size of the sublattice resulting from exhaustively removing doubly irreducible elements in all possible orders, until either a maximal reachable distributive sublattice is reached, or all doubly irreducible elements are removed. The column *distr.?* indicates whether a distributive sublattice was reached. An entry of – indicates that the value could not be computed.

Context	$\lvert L\rvert$	$\lvert\prec\rvert$	$\lvert\mathrm{Irr}\rvert$	**ex. size**	**distr.?**	$\lvert BC^{\uparrow}\rvert$	$\lvert BC^{\downarrow}\rvert$
triangles	18	31	3	13	Y	31	54
living-beings-and-water	19	32	2	17	N	58	80
Seasoning-Planner	532	1593	0	532	N	–	–
drive-concepts-for-motorcars	24	50	0	24	N	36	32
digits	48	120	0	48	N	72	96
bodiesofwater	12	18	2	10	Y	14	18
Wood-Properties	315	924	0	315	N	–	–
Southern-Woman	65	148	0	65	N	616	2358
Forum-Romanum	19	31	4	15	Y	30	32
Dolphins	282	752	4	278	N	–	–
Dirichlet-1	308	1086	0	308	N	1024	–
Diagnosis	88	210	0	88	N	5040	–
Cointoss-2	411	1324	0	411	N	–	–
california	21	35	2	18	N	40	49
Brunson-Club	62	136	0	62	N	10560	565248
Bird-Diet	16	27	1	14	N	96	80
ben-and-jerrys-allergens	9	12	3	5	Y	15	20
ben-and-jerrys-flavors	16	26	3	12	Y	76	60

more complex join-irreducible structure. Hence, any asymmetry provides structural information beyond what a single scalar index can convey.

Theoretically, the dismantling approach was very promising. Yet, the practical evaluation on the real-world data sets sheds a different light. The datasets where dismantling successfully reaches distributivity (triangles, bodiesofwater, Forum-Romanum, ben-and-jerrys-allergens, ben-and-jerrys-flavors) share the property that their non-distributivity is, in a precise sense, peripheral: it is concentrated at a small number of doubly irreducible elements whose removal restores distributivity. In contrast, the majority of datasets (including all of the larger ones) have $|\mathrm{Irr}(L)| = 0$, meaning that every element is either join-reducible or meet-reducible. For these lattices, the non-distributivity is distributed across the entire structure and cannot be resolved by local element removal. The dismantling approach is therefore best understood as a diagnostic tool for identifying lattices with localized non-distributivity, rather than as a general-purpose measure applicable to all lattices.

Finally, due to the exponential growth of the Birkhoff completion, it application to larger lattices is limited as well. In our experiments, the completion could not be computed for 5 of the 18 datasets. This computational limitation is inherent to the global nature of the BDI: measuring how far a lattice is from a distributive one requires constructing or at least estimating the size of that distributive lattice, which can be exponentially larger, which opens up interesting questions, particularly in combinatorics.

5 Comparison of the Distributivity Indices

Having introduced pointwise deviation indices and global deviation distances in the previous sections, we now compare all indices jointly. To this end, we compute Pearson correlation coefficients between all pairs of indices across the 13 datasets for which all measures could be evaluated, and additionally examine their dependence on lattice size (Table 5).

Table 5. Correlation matrix of the different distributivity metrics (Pearson).

	$\mathcal{I}_B^{\downarrow}(L)$	$\mathcal{I}_B^{\uparrow}(L)$	$\widetilde{\text{nur}}^{\wedge}(L)$	$\widetilde{\text{nur}}^{\vee}(L)$	I_{distr}	I_{mod}	$\widetilde{I_{distr}}$
$\mathcal{I}_B^{\downarrow}(L)$	1.0						
$\mathcal{I}_B^{\uparrow}(L)$	0.94	1.0					
$\widetilde{\text{nur}}^{\wedge}(L)$	0.63	0.80	1.0				
$\widetilde{\text{nur}}^{\vee}(L)$	0.76	0.62	0.41	1.0			
I_{distr}	0.88	0.90	0.64	0.7	1.0		
I_{mod}	0.88	0.86	0.55	0.63	0.75	1.0	
$\widetilde{I_{distr}}$	0.83	0.87	0.65	0.55	0.77	0.89	1.0
$\lvert L\rvert$	0.65	0.63	0.28	0.35	0.73	0.50	0.61
$\lvert\prec\rvert$	0.61	0.59	0.26	0.31	0.70	0.47	0.59

The most surprising feature of the correlation matrix is the strong agreement between the PDIs and the GDDs: I_{distr} correlates at 0.88–0.90 with the Birkhoff indices, confirming that local triple violations and global completion size yield largely consistent severity rankings despite their fundamentally different constructions. The two BC indices are the most strongly correlated pair (0.94).

The unit rise indices stand apart as the most independent measures. Their mutual correlation is only 0.41, and each aligns selectively with the Birkhoff index governed by the same irreducible structure: $\widetilde{\text{nur}}^{\wedge}$ correlates more strongly with $\mathcal{I}_B^{\uparrow}$ (0.80), while $\widetilde{\text{nur}}^{\vee}$ correlates more strongly with $\mathcal{I}_B^{\downarrow}$ (0.76). This is consistent with the theoretical construction, as meet-rises are governed by $\mathcal{M}(L)$ and join-rises by $\mathcal{J}(L)$.

The rise indices also exhibit the weakest dependence on lattice size (0.28 and 0.35 with $|L|$), whereas I_{distr} shows the strongest (0.73). This makes the rise indices the most suitable choice for cross-size comparisons and suggests that the TCDI values for larger lattices should be interpreted with some caution. When the Birkhoff completion is too large to compute, as occurred for 5 of our 18 datasets, the TCDI serves as a reliable proxy ($r \geq 0.88$).

6 Conclusion and Future Work

We introduced complementary indices to quantify non-distributivity in finite lattices. These indices span pointwise deviation indices and global deviation distances. Despite their fundamentally different constructions, the experimental evaluation on 18 real-world datasets showed that these indices yield largely consistent severity rankings ($r \geq 0.83$), while each captures distinct structural aspects, e.g., the ratio $I_{\text{mod}}/I_{\text{distr}}$ reveals that non-distributivity is predominantly of the M_3-type, the extent-weighted index shows that well-supported concepts behave more distributively, and the rise indices localize irregularities along the object or attribute side.

This work opens several directions for future research. The strong empirical correlations between PDIs and the Birkhoff indices raise the question of whether formal bounds relating triple violation proportions to completion size can be established. The extent-weighted TCDI naturally generalizes to other weighting functions, including intent-based weights and lattice valuations, whose effect on the index merits investigation. Since the dismantling approach was inapplicable for the majority of datasets, extending it to interval dismantling [3,9] could yield a more broadly applicable optimization-based index. Finally, the consistently small ratio $I_{\text{mod}}/I_{\text{distr}}$ across all datasets suggests that real-world concept lattices are close to being modular, a pattern whose structural causes and generality deserve further study, and the SDI framework developed here can be adapted to other algebraic properties such as semi-distributivity or n-distributivity.

References

1. Abdulla, M., Hille, T., Dürrschnabel, D., Stumme, G.: Rises for measuring local distributivity in lattices. In: Conceptual Knowledge Structures. pp. 392–407. Springer (2025). https://doi.org/10.1007/978-3-032-03364-2_25
2. Abdulla, M., Hirth, J., Stumme, G.: The Birkhoff completion of finite lattices. In: Conceptual Knowledge Structures. pp. 20–35. Springer, Cham (2024). https://doi.org/10.1007/978-3-031-67868-4_2
3. Adaricheva, K., Hyndman, J., Lempp, S., Nation, J.B.: Interval dismantlable lattices. Order **35**(1), 133–137 (2017). https://doi.org/10.1007/s11083-017-9422-7
4. Birkhoff, G.: Lattice theory. In: Colloquium Publications, vol. 25. American Mathematical Society, 3. edn. (1967)
5. Buzmakov, A., Kuznetsov, S.O., Makhalova, T., Napoli, A., Dudyrev, E.: Data complexity: an FCA-based approach (2023). https://doi.org/10.1016/j.ijar.2023.109084

6. Davey, B.A., Priestley, H.A.: Introduction to Lattices and Order. Cambridge University Press (2002). https://doi.org/10.1017/cbo9780511809088
7. Doignon, J.P., Falmagne, J.C.: Knowledge Spaces. Springer (1999). https://doi.org/10.1007/978-3-642-58625-5
8. Edelman, P.H.: Meet-distributive lattices and the anti-exchange closure. Algebra Univers. **10**(1), 290–299 (1980).https://doi.org/10.1007/BF02482912
9. Felde, M., Koyda, M.: Interval-dismantling for lattices. Int. J. Approx. Reason. **159**, 108931 (2023). https://doi.org/10.1016/J.IJAR.2023.108931
10. Ganter, B., Wille, R.: Formal Concept Analysis - Mathematical Foundations. Second Editiontion. Springer (2024). https://doi.org/10.1007/978-3-031-63422-2
11. Gély, A., Couceiro, M., Napoli, A.: Steps towards achieving distributivity in formal concept analysis. In: Kuznetsov, S.O., Napoli, A., Rudolph, S. (eds.) CLA 2018. vol. 2123, pp. 105–116. CEUR-WS.org (2018). http://ceur-ws.org/Vol-2123/paper9.pdf
12. Gély, A., Couceiro, M., Miclet, L., Napoli, A.: A study of algorithms relating distributive lattices, median graphs, and formal concept analysis. Int. J. Approximate Reasoning **142**(3), 370–382 (2022). https://doi.org/10.1016/j.ijar.2021.12.011
13. Hammer, P.L., Simeone, B.: The splittance of a graph. Combinatorica **1**(3), 275–284 (1981). https://doi.org/10.1007/BF02579333
14. Hanika, T., Hirth, J.: Conexp-Clj — a research tool for FCA. In: Cristea, D., Ber, F.L., Missaoui, R., Kwuida, L., Sertkaya, B. (eds.) ICFCA (Supplements). vol. 2378, pp. 70–75. CEUR-WS.org (2019). https://ceur-ws.org/Vol-2378/shortAT8.pdf
15. Huhn, J.: n-distributive lattices. Algebra Univers. **10**, 388–398 (1980)
16. Jakubík, J.: Higher degrees of distributivity in lattices and lattice-ordered groups. Czechoslovak Math. J **18**(2), 356–376 (1968). https://doi.org/10.21136/cmj.1968.100836
17. Jakubík, J.: Convergences and higher degrees of distributivity of lattice ordered groups and of boolean algebras. Czechoslovak Math. J **40**(3), 453–458 (1990). https://doi.org/10.21136/cmj.1990.102397
18. Knuth, K.H.: Lattices and their consistent quantification, (2017). arXiv:1711.07358
19. Stumme, G., Taouil, R., Bastide, Y., Pasquier, N., Lakhal, L.: Computing iceberg concept lattices with T. Data Knowl. Eng. **42**(2), 189–222 (2002). https://doi.org/10.1016/S0169-023X(02)00057-5
20. Wille, R.: Truncated distributive lattices: Conceptual structures of simple-implicational theories. Order **20**(3), 229–238 (2003).https://doi.org/10.1023/b:orde.0000026494.22248.85

Revisiting Attribute Ordering for Concept Mining

Fernand Adam[1(✉)] and Tobias Hille[1,2]

[1] Knowledge & Data Engineering Group, University of Kassel, Kassel, Germany
fernandadam@posteo.de , hille@cs.uni-kassel.de

[2] Interdisciplinary Research Center for Information System Design, University of Kassel, Kassel, Germany

Abstract. Formal Concept Analysis (FCA) is a central method for knowledge processing in cross-tables or binary matrices. Since concept mining is a #P-complete problem and the number of concepts can grow exponentially, research has produced various optimized algorithms to handle these complexities. While existing algorithms typically focus on reducing redundant calculations through canonicity tests, this work suggests that optimizing attribute ordering is an area where further optimization can be particularly useful, especially as it can be added to most concept mining algorithms with ease. The study examines how different sequences influence the efficiency of common algorithms such as Next Closure, CbO, FCbO, and IC5. To this end, three sorting heuristics Number of Non-Zeroes (NNZ), Maximum Entropy (ME), and Diagonalization (DIAG) - were analyzed. The results indicate that attribute ordering has a measurable impact on performance, with the NNZ order seeming to be the most effective heuristic. Furthermore, we argue that the number of intent calculations serves as a more reliable metric for comparing algorithms than raw time measurements.

Keywords: Formal Concept Analysis · Concept Mining Algorithms · Attribute Ordering · Performance Evaluation · Benchmarking

1 Introduction

Formal Concept Analysis (Formal Concept Analysis (FCA)) provides a mathematical framework for analyzing relational data represented as binary incidence tables called *formal contexts*. From such contexts, *formal concepts* can be derived, and the collection of all concepts forms a concept lattice. Enumerating all formal concepts is a central computational task in FCA,, but the number of concepts can grow exponentially and the problem is known to be #P-complete [8]. Numerous algorithms have been proposed to address this task, including (NC), Close-By-One (CBO), Fast Close-By-One (FCBO), and In-Close 5 (IC5), which primarily focus on reducing redundant computations during enumeration. However, the impact of the attribute ordering used in these algorithms has received comparatively little systematic attention.

M. Croitoru et al. (Eds.): CONCEPTS 2026, LNAI 16811, pp. 168–175, 2027.
https://doi.org/10.1007/978-3-032-34742-8_11

In this paper we investigate how different attribute ordering heuristics affect the performance of concept mining algorithms. Using the number of closure computations as a machine-independent performance measure, we experimentally evaluate several ordering strategies on both real-world and synthetic contexts. Our results indicate that attribute ordering can significantly influence computational effort and that the NNZ heuristic performs best on average.

2 Related Work

That rearrangement of formal contexts influences the runtime of concept mining is widely known [3, p.80], but no scientifically based heuristic finding the optimal ordering seems to be found yet [9]. The most recent study compares the runtime of several concept mining algorithms on sorted formal contexts. Although that work also evaluates fuzzy formal contexts, the following work focuses exclusively on binary attributes. Moreover, concept mining can be reduced to constraint satisfaction problems, thereby relating it to the generally #P-complete #CSP framework [1]. Therefore, heuristics developed for CSPs, such as those discussed by Knuth [6], may also improve concept mining. For instance, the Minimum Remaining Values (MRV) heuristic is similar to the NNZ ordering, while other variable-ordering strategies can be determined dynamically during the search, such as WTD (weighted) or FailureRate Based (FRB) heuristics.

A comparison of algorithms apart from NC analyzes pruning techniques of concept mining algorithms from the In-Close family and FCBO.. Using FCBO. and IC5 covers the most relevant pruning strategies, while CBO serves as the base algorithm [7].

3 Theoretical Basis

We briefly recap the foundations of formal context analysis referenced in this work and direct interested readers to the standard introductory textbook by Ganter and Wille [3].

Definition 1. *Let G be a set of objects, M a set of attributes, and $I \subseteq G \times M$ an incidence relation between objects and attributes. The tuple $\mathbb{K} = (G, M, I)$ is called a* ***Formal Context****.*

To find the set of shared attributes (or objects) of an object (or attribute) set, we use the so called *derivation* operator.

Definition 2. *The* ***derivation*** *of an object set $A \subseteq G$ and an attribute set $B \subseteq M$ is given by:*

$$A' := \{m \mid \forall g \in A : (m, g) \in I\} \quad B' := \{g \mid \forall m \in B : (m, g) \in I\}$$

Definition 3. *$\langle A, B\rangle \in \mathcal{P}(G) \times \mathcal{P}(M)$ is called a* ***formal concept*** *if and only if $A' = B \wedge B' = A$. A is called the extent and B the intent.*

The derivation operator has the property $A''' = A'$ which is useful to create formal concepts. Formal contexts and formal concepts are further called shortly contexts and concepts. For simplicity, we represent objects and attributes in contexts by their respective index sets.

3.1 Algorithms

Concept mining Algorithms compute the set of all concepts $\mathbb{B}$ of a given formal context. The Next Closure algorithm computes them by lexicographically iterating over the power set of attributes. The attribute order determines the sequence in which attributes are considered during iteration, thereby directly affecting the execution flow. While lexicographical ordering is used here, it is essentially arbitrary; any other permutation maintains the correctness of the result. Alternatively, the CBO algorithm follows a recursive structure, employing a depth-first search strategy to traverse the concept space. Although both algorithms utilize an identical condition to prune the search tree and avoid redundant calculations, CBO's recursive nature fundamentally differs from the iterative approach of Next Closure in its traversal logic. In addition, the FCBO algorithm refines the recursive approach by introducing a "combined sweep" strategy and a multiset N of indices to store previously computed intents allowing enhanced pruning. Finally, the IC5 algorithm represents the most efficient approach by utilizing a simplified set of attributes $N \subseteq M$ to store information from previous closure computations enabling other pruning techniques as FCBO.

4 Experimental Setup

To measure the computational effort of the concept mining algorithms, a unified code base[1] written in Rust was used to enable direct comparisons, such as counting function calls. This was done to prevent the unreliable and inaccurate time measurements that would have resulted from different implementations. The main focus of our investigations is measuring the computational effort by the number of computed closures, since this is the most expensive step in determining concepts. To make the experiment completely deterministic, context generation is seeded and function calls in the closure computation are counted.

4.1 Contexts

The evaluation is performed on both real-world and synthetically generated formal contexts. Since only a limited number of established benchmark contexts are publicly available, synthetic data is required to obtain more general and statistically meaningful results.

Contexts of real world data: We use the collection by Hanika and Jäschke [4], containing contexts with $5 \leq |G| \leq 35$ objects and $5 \leq |M| \leq 14$ attributes, including the well-known *"living-in-water"* [3] context. These datasets provide realistic and structurally heterogeneous test cases. Measuring closure computations instead of runtime ensures hardware-independent and reproducible results, especially for small contexts.

Synthetic Contexts: We create contexts with two random generators Coin-Toss and Dirichlet. The first model is parameterized by an probability p of the

---

[1] accessible via https://codeberg.org/Fernand/concept-miner-attribute-order-study.

independently identically distributed incidence occurrence, whereas the behavior of the later model only depends on the targeted context dimensions by defining an underlying Dirichlet distribution with concentration parameter $\alpha\beta$, with $\alpha = \nu/\|\nu\|$, $\nu = (1, \ldots, 1) \in [0,1]^{|M|}$, and $\beta = |M| + 1$ [2].

4.2 Orders

The algorithms use an order $\leq$ on the attribute set M, which is defined via the usual "smaller than" $\leq_{\mathbb{R}}$ relation on real numbers. Figure 1 visualizes all orders.

Definition 4 ([9]). *Let $\mathbb{K} = (G, M, I)$ be a context. The size of an attribute $m \in M$ is defined as $\mathit{SIZE}(m) := |\{g \in G \mid (g, m) \in I\}|$. Then the NNZ-ordering $\leq$ for all attributes $m_1, m_2 \in M$ is defined by*

$$m_1 \leq m_2 \iff \mathit{SIZE}(m_1) \leq_{\mathbb{R}} \mathit{SIZE}(m_2).$$

Definition 5 ([5]). *Let $\mathbb{K} = (G, M, I)$ be a context. The ME-ordering $\leq$ for all attributes $m_1, m_2 \in M$ is defined by*

$$m_1 \leq m_2 \iff H(m_1) \leq_{\mathbb{R}} H(m_2),$$

where $p_1 = \frac{|\{m\}'|}{|G|}$, $p_0 = 1 - p_1$ and $H(m) = -(p_1 \cdot \log_2(p_1) + p_0 \cdot \log_2(p_0))$.

Definition 6. *The DIAG ordering of a context $\mathbb{K} = (G, M, I)$ is defined as the following procedure iterated until convergence. The function AVG receives a list of numbers and returns their arithmetic mean.*

1. *Calculate the mean $\mathit{AVG}(\{m\}') = \sum_{g \in \{m\}'} \frac{g}{|\{m\}'|}$ for each attribute m such that:*
   $\forall m_1, m_2 \in M : m_1 \leq m_2 \iff \mathit{AVG}(\{m_1\}') \leq_{\mathbb{R}} \mathit{AVG}(\{m_2\}')$.
2. *Calculate the mean $\mathit{AVG}(\{g\}') = \sum_{m \in \{g\}'} \frac{m}{|\{g\}'|}$ for each object g such that:*
   $\forall g_1, g_2 \in G : g_1 \leq g_2 \iff \mathit{AVG}(\{g_1\}') \leq_{\mathbb{R}} \mathit{AVG}(\{g_2\}')$.

We indicate the inversion of an ordering by the suffix -*i* added to the name.

5 Results

Our experimental evaluation reveals several key insights regarding the computational efficiency of the implemented algorithms. A primary finding is that CBO requires exactly the same number of closure computations as NC. In terms of overall computational effort, measured by the number of intent calculations shown in Fig. 2, the algorithms follow a clear hierarchy:

$$FCBO \leq IC5 \leq NC = CBO$$

Figure 3 presents the computational effort of three types of contexts generated by Bernoulli chains and the Dirichlet distribution; in the right-hand

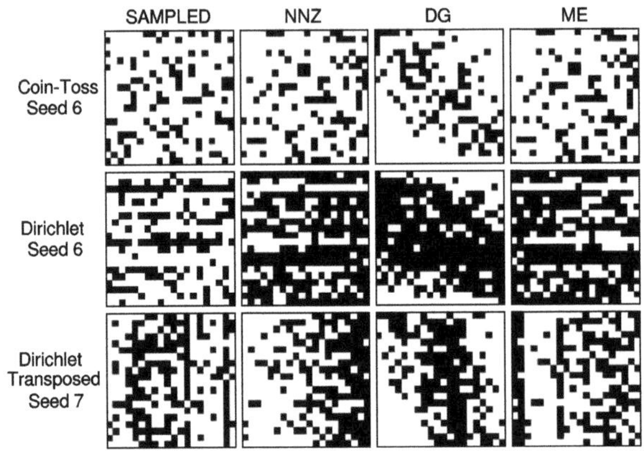

Fig. 1. Context generators and the application of different attribute orderings investigated in this work. The example contexts are of size $|G| = |M| = 20$.

diagram, the incidence relation of the Dirichlet contexts is inverted. Although Dirichlet and transposed Dirichlet contexts are based on the same $\mathbb{K}_i = (G, M, I)$ and differ only by the inversion $\tilde{\mathbb{K}}_i = (M, G, I^{-1})$, the transposed contexts exhibit a clearer ordering and a more uniform distribution of data points, suggesting that the incidence direction significantly affects computational efficiency.

Figure 4 shows the relative effort $\frac{|\text{computed intents}|-|\mathbb{B}|}{|\mathbb{B}|}$ for concept generation. Diagram (a) presents real-world contexts, and (b) transposed Dirichlet contexts. Real-world contexts exhibit substantial variance depending on attribute ordering. While contexts such as *bodiesofwater_de* show little order dependence, others like *livingbeings* vary strongly, indicating a significant structural influence. For transposed Dirichlet contexts, no clear correlation between relative effort and the number of concepts is observed. A value of 0 represents the optimal case without redundant intents, and both context structure and incidence direction significantly affect computational cost. Based on our empirical results of Fig. 4b, the ordering heuristics follow the hierarchy of efficiency:

$$NNZ \leq \text{ME-i} \leq ME \leq \text{Diag} \leq \text{Diag-i} \leq \text{NNZ-i}$$

6 Discussion

Our analysis of the runtime performance reveals a hierarchy of $IC5 \leq FCBO \leq CBO \leq NC$, which seemingly contradicts the results obtained from counting closure computations. This discrepancy highlights that while algorithms may be equivalent in terms of high-level intent calculations, the overhead of maintaining state information and managing variables in memory also significantly influences actual execution time. Furthermore, the observed alignment between NC and CBO performance initially appears to conflict with previous studies [9], where NC demonstrated significantly slower runtimes than CBO. However, this

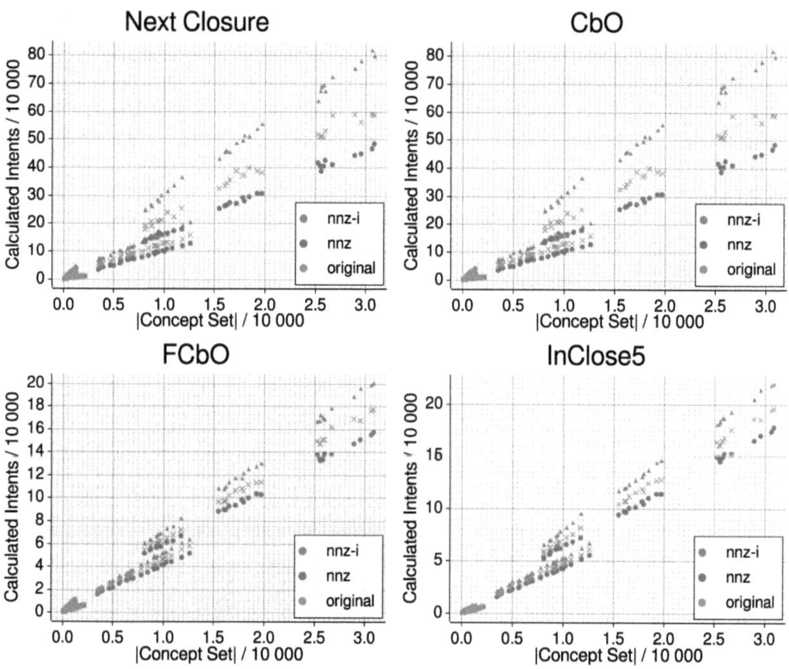

Fig. 2. Number of calculated intents for 10 coin-toss contexts of various sizes ($|M| \in \{25, 50, 75\}$, $|G| \in \{75, 100, 125\}$) and densities ($p \in \{0.1, 0.25\}$), comparing NNZ, NNZ-i, and the generated attribute orderings.

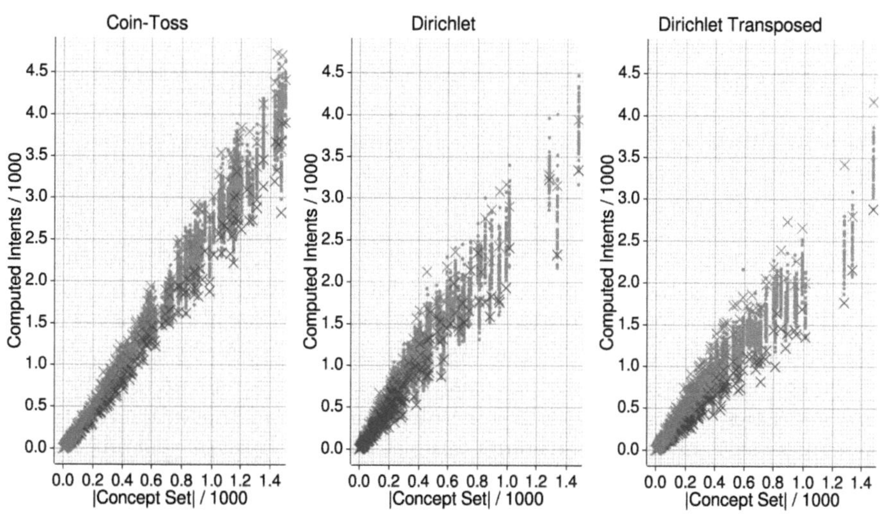

Fig. 3. Number of intents calculated on NNZ, (red), NNZ-i (green) and random permutations (gray) by IC5 for contexts generated by Coin-Toss (left) or Dirichlet models (standard: middle, transposed: right). (Color figure online)

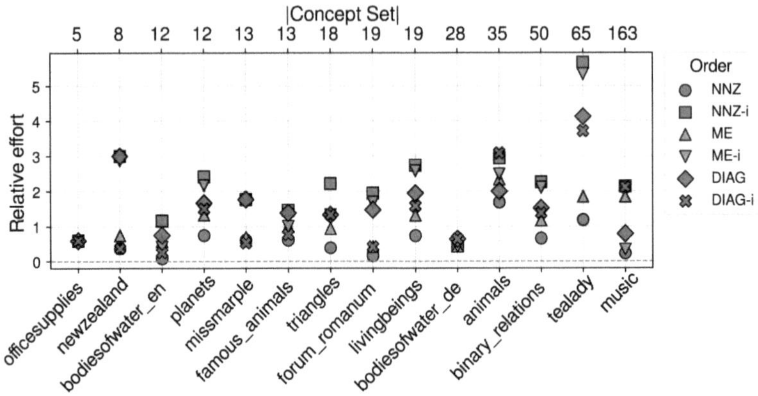

(a) Existing contexts applied to NC

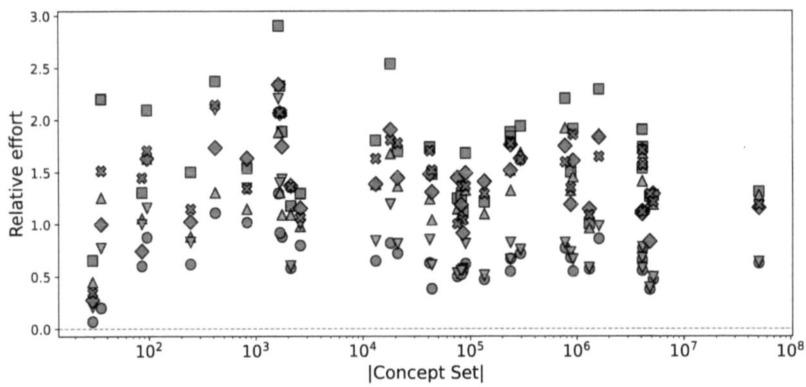

(b) Transposed Dirichlet contexts with
$n \in \{y \mid \forall x \in \{1, \ldots, 35\}, \exists y \in \mathbb{N} : y = 2 \cdot x + 10\}$ and $|M| = |G| = n$ applied to IC5.

Fig. 4. Relative effort $\frac{|\text{calculated intents}| - |\mathbb{B}|}{|\mathbb{B}|}$ when applied with NC for different context types.

can be attributed to the unified implementation used in our study; by employing a consistent method for calculating the double derivation $D \leftarrow (B \cup \{m\})''$, the inherent algorithmic equivalence in search space traversal becomes evident. Finally, the presence of superior random permutations in Fig. 3 suggests that for certain contexts, optimal orderings exist that are not yet captured by the standard heuristics evaluated here. The results demonstrate that attribute ordering significantly influences the computational effort of concept generation algorithms. While optimized algorithms reduce this dependency, the NNZ ordering consistently achieves the lowest effort and can be regarded as the most effective heuristic among those studied. The absolute impact of ordering increases with the size of the concept lattice, whereas for Dirichlet-generated contexts the relative effect appears largely independent of the number of concepts. Generated contexts exhibit clearer structural patterns, while real-world contexts show higher variance, suggesting that Dirichlet models do not fully represent practically relevant structures. Among alternative orderings, ME behaves inconsistently and DIAG is generally less efficient than NNZ. Regarding methodology, runtime measurements are only partially reproducible due to hardware and system influences. The number of computed intents provides a more robust and comparable efficiency measure, and could be refined further by incorporating low-level operation counts such as memory accesses [6].

References

1. Bulatov, A.A.: The complexity of the counting constraint satisfaction problem. J. ACM **60**(5) (2013)
2. Felde, M., Hanika, T.: Formal context generation using Dirichlet distributions. In: Endres, D., Alam, M., Şotropa, D. (eds.) Graph-Based Representation and Reasoning, pp. 57–71. Springer International Publishing, Cham (2019)
3. Ganter, B., Wille, R.: Order-theoretic foundations, chap. 2, pp. 77–115 (2024)
4. Hanika, T., Jäschke, R.: A repository for formal contexts. In: Cabrera, I.P., Ferré, S., Obiedkov, S. (eds.) Conceptual Knowledge Structures, pp. 182–197. Springer Nature Switzerland, Cham (2024)
5. K., Ch, S., Li, A.K., J.: Concept compression in FCA using entropy-based attribute priority. Appl. Artif. Intell. **31**(3), 251–278 (2017)
6. Knuth, D.E.: The art of computer programming. 4, Fascicle 7 constraint statisfaction. pp. 65–69. chap. 7.2.2.3 (2025)
7. Konecny, J., Krajča, P.: Systematic categorization and evaluation of CBO-based algorithms in FCA. Inf. Sci. **575**, 265–288 (2021)
8. Krolak-Schwerdt, S., Orlik, P., Ganter, B.: Tripat: a model for analyzing three-mode binary data. In: Bock, H.H., Lenski, W., Richter, M.M. (eds.) Information Systems and Data Analysis, pp. 298–307. Springer, Berlin Heidelberg (1994)
9. Ojeda-Hernández, M., López-Rodríguez, D.: Enhancing performance of FCA algorithms via rearrangement of formal contexts. In: 2024 IEEE International Conference on Fuzzy Systems, pp. 1–6. FUZZ-IEEE (2024)

Hierarchical Background Knowledge in FCA via Must-Link-Before Constraints

Klara M. Gutekunst[1(✉)], Dominik Dürrschnabel[2], Stefan Schneider[3], and Martin Potthast[4]

[1] University of Kassel and hessian.AI, Kassel, Germany
klara.gutekunst@uni-kassel.de
[2] Baden-Wuerttemberg Cooperative State University Mosbach, Mosbach, Germany
dominik.duerrschnabel@mosbach.dhbw.de
[3] Otto-von-Guericke-Universität Magdeburg, Magdeburg, Germany
stefan.schneider@sschneider.de
[4] ScaDS.AI, University of Kassel, hessian.AI, ScaDS.AI, Kassel, Germany
martin.potthast@uni-kassel.de

Abstract. Formal Concept Analysis (FCA) enables the construction of concept hierarchies from formal contexts without requiring expert ontologies. Hierarchical expert knowledge can additionally be encoded through Must-Link-Before (MLB) constraints in constrained clustering. However, when hierarchies are derived from different knowledge sources, it remains unclear how their agreement can be quantified systematically.

In this work, we prove that MLB constraints induce a valid closure operator, providing a theoretical foundation for incorporating hierarchical expert knowledge into FCA. Building on this result, we introduce a method for comparing concept lattices derived from MLB constraints and from data-driven topic models. Using the BankSearch dataset, we compare concept lattices derived from expert-defined MLB constraints and a Latent Dirichlet Allocation-based document-topic context. We analyze their agreement through *consistency* and *coherence* lattice intersections at different levels of coherence. Our analysis reveals distinct structural differences between both hierarchies, highlighting the need for relaxed coherence measures when integrating heterogeneous knowledge sources.

Keywords: Formal Concept Analysis · Constraints · Topic Modeling

1 Introduction

Ontologies provide formal and explicit specifications of concepts and their relationships within a domain [36]. They support knowledge retrieval, reuse, and rule formulation [11,42], and communication through shared conceptualizations [35,36]. While manual ontology construction is often regarded as the gold standard, it is costly and typically reflects only a snapshot of evolving knowledge [26]. Automatic concept hierarchy generation therefore aims to reduce time

M. Croitoru et al. (Eds.): CONCEPTS 2026, LNAI 16811, pp. 176–191, 2027.
https://doi.org/10.1007/978-3-032-34742-8_12

and cost [2,33] and extends coverage of domains not represented in existing ontologies.

Existing automatic approaches operate on both structured and unstructured data sources. Structured linguistic resources, such as the semantic dictionary Roget's Thesaurus [28,30,32], lexical databases such as WordNet [15,30,31] and FrameNet [38], and morphological feature systems [29,34], can be represented as formal contexts. For unstructured text corpora, formal contexts must first be derived from textual information using methods ranging from pattern-based extraction [20,24] to multi-step Natural Language Processing pipelines that construct binary object-attribute contexts [11], as well as approaches using phrases directly as attributes [9,12].

FCA-based concept hierarchy generation can be viewed as a form of conceptual clustering [10] that yields intensional descriptions of abstract concepts through their intents [11]. Since each concept is characterized by an explicit set of shared attributes, the resulting hierarchy provides transparent, attribute-based explanations of the relationships between concepts, making FCA-based hierarchies inherently interpretable compared to similarity-based clustering methods.

Despite their scalability, automatically generated hierarchies may conflict with established expert ontologies, potentially reducing trust in either source. Ensuring consistency with hierarchical background knowledge therefore requires mechanisms that guide and constrain the generation process. Existing approaches (Sect. 2) include human-in-the-loop strategies [42], the use of Large Language Models (LLMs) [23,44], constrained FCA [6–8,21,27], and hierarchical constraints in similarity-based settings [3,5].

To date, the systematic integration of hierarchical background knowledge into FCA-based concept hierarchy generation through MLB constraints has received limited attention. We address this gap by incorporating MLB constraints into the FCA framework (Sect. 4),[1] thereby extending prior work that incorporates pairwise constraints [6]. In addition, we present a case study (Sect. 5) comparing concept lattices derived from expert-defined MLB constraints and from a data-driven topic model through *consistency* and *coherence* lattice intersections at different coherence levels.

2 Related Work

Automatic concept hierarchy generation from text corpora has been approached in various ways. Hierarchical text classification assigns documents one or more labels organized in a taxonomy [43], implicitly creating a hierarchical structure of documents. Approaches range from regularization-based classifiers [18], embedding-based document-label matching [25] to neural sequence models [33,43] and LLM-assisted taxonomy enrichment [44].

Beyond classification-based approaches, research has explored deriving concept hierarchies directly from textual data using FCA. Since FCA-based hierarchy generation can be viewed as conceptual clustering that yields intensional

[1] The code is available at github.com/KlaraGtknst/fca-constrained-clustering.

descriptions of abstract concepts via their intents [11], text corpora can be represented as a formal contexts in which documents form the objects and extracted features serve as attributes. Feature sources include semantic dictionaries [28,30,32], lexical databases [15,30,31,38], morphological structures [29,34], bag-of-words representations capturing the presence of phrases [9,12], and latent topics derived from topic models [2,19,22,40,41].

In constrained clustering, prior knowledge is expressed through constraints rather than derived from data. Conventional constrained clustering methods typically operate on a single level of granularity [39]. However, pairwise *must-link* and *cannot-link* constraints become ambiguous in hierarchical clustering settings, where objects may belong to the same cluster at one hierarchy level but not at another [5]. To address this limitation, Bade et al. [3,4] introduce MLB constraints for hierarchical agglomerative clustering (HAC). These constraints encode relative hierarchical relationships through the order in which objects should be merged during agglomeration [3–5]. Existing approaches incorporate MLB constraints by modifying similarity measures during merging [3], delaying merges until constraint violations are resolved [45], or integrating them into matrix-based approaches [46].

Several works also investigate incorporating constraints or expert knowledge directly into FCA. Constraints have been used to encode mutually exclusive attributes [21] and to prune concept lattices by retaining only concepts whose intents satisfy relevance criteria. These criteria have been defined through attribute properties [6,8,21], constraints on the closure operator [7], or additional operators [27]. Research has also extended Attribute Exploration to settings with multiple, potentially contradictory or incomplete experts, aiming to derive implications shared across different subsets of experts [13,14].

However, prior work has incorporated hierarchical MLB constraints mainly into traditional clustering methods rather than hierarchy construction via FCA. To the best of our knowledge, no comparison exists between concept lattices derived from probabilistic topic models and those derived from constraints.

3 Foundations

In Sect. 3.1, we present the background on FCA, and subsequently, in Sect. 3.2, we discuss MLB constraints in constrained HAC.

3.1 FCA

The mathematical theory of FCA [16] is a method to analyze relational data in a hierarchical structure. The triple $\mathbb{K} := (G, M, I)$ defines the *formal context*. G is the set of *objects*, M is the set of *attributes*, and $I \subseteq G \times M$ is the *incidence relation*, which describes when an object g has an attribute m. The object derivation $(\cdot)' : \mathcal{P}(G) \to \mathcal{P}(M)$ defines for any subset $A \subseteq G$ as $A' := \{m \in M \mid \forall g \in A : (g, m) \in I\}$. The attribute derivation $(\cdot)' : \mathcal{P}(M) \to \mathcal{P}(G)$ is defined for any subset $B \subseteq M$ as $B' := \{g \in G \mid \forall m \in B : (g, m) \in I\}$. The same notation $(\cdot)'$ is used for both derivation operators. A formal concept of $\mathbb{K}$ is a pair (A, B) where $A \subseteq G$ and $B \subseteq M$ satisfy the conditions $A' = B$ and $B' = A$. The set $\mathfrak{B}(\mathbb{K})$ denotes all formal concepts of $\mathbb{K}$. The concept lattice $\underline{\mathfrak{B}}(\mathbb{K}) := (\mathfrak{B}(\mathbb{K}), \leq)$ is defined by the set of all formal concepts with the order relation $(A, B) \leq (C, D)$ if and only if $A \subseteq C$ [19].

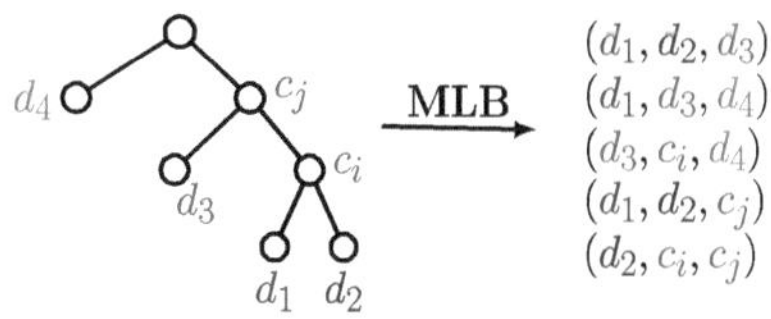

Fig. 1. Valid MLB constraints given a document hierarchy

3.2 Must-Link-Before Constraints

Clustering structures unlabeled data, which is particularly useful in real-world applications where labeled data is scarce and annotation is costly. Clustering algorithms group data points according to a similarity criterion, typically minimizing intra-cluster distances while maximizing inter-cluster distances. Prior knowledge about the dataset can be incorporated through constraints. The simplest forms are pairwise *must-link* and *cannot-link* constraints, enforcing that two instances must or must not belong to the same cluster. However, pairwise constraints generally apply only at one level of granularity.

Hierarchical clustering instead organizes data into nested groups at different levels of granularity [5]. To incorporate prior knowledge in this setting, MLB constraints specify the relative agglomeration order of three data points d_x, d_y, d_z. An MLB constraint $MLB_{xyz} = (d_x, d_y, d_z)$ states that d_x and d_y should be merged before either is merged with d_z, where d_x and d_y are symmetric. The cluster hierarchy H is defined by $(C, \prec, \text{root})$, where C is a set of clusters, $\prec$ is a strict partial order over C representing the parent-child relation, and root $\in C$ is the root cluster [5]. Definitions (1) and (2) formalize the idea that d_x and d_y are more closely related in the hierarchy than d_x and d_z. Figure 1 illustrates valid MLB constraints for a toy example.

Definition 1 (MLB Implication).
Given MLB constraint MLB_{xyz}*:* $\forall c \in H : d_x \in c \wedge d_z \in c \rightarrow d_y \in c$

Definition 2 (MLB Counter Example).
Given MLB constraint MLB_{xyz}*:* $\exists c \in H : d_x \in c \wedge d_y \in c \wedge d_z \notin c$

4 Method

The core of our methodology relies on the insight that both the structural MLB constraints provided by expert knowledge (Subsection 4.1) and the statistical patterns derived from topic models (Subsection 4.2) can be formalized as closure operators. By computing the intersection of their respective closure systems (Subsection 4.3), we derive the *consistency*-lattice, i.e., a concept lattice that respects both MLB constraints and empirical data.

4.1 Hierarchical Constraints for Concept Lattices

This section establishes that MLB constraints induce a valid closure operator and that the resulting lattice represents the search space of valid dendrograms.

Theoretical Analysis of MLB Constraints. Let G be the set of documents. A set of MLB constraints is given as $\Sigma \subseteq G \times G \times G$. A constraint $MLB_{xyz} = (d_x, d_y, d_z) \in \Sigma$ expresses a hierarchical dependency: whenever documents d_x and d_z occur together in a cluster, d_y must also belong to that cluster.

MLB Constraints as a Closure Operator. To utilize FCA, we must first establish that these constraints define a closure system.

Definition 3 *(Σ-Consistency). A subset $A \subseteq G$ is called Σ-consistent (or valid) if for all $(d_x, d_y, d_z) \in \Sigma$, the condition $\{d_x, d_z\} \subseteq A \implies d_y \in A$ holds.*

Theorem 1. *The mapping $\phi_\Sigma : \mathcal{P}(G) \to \mathcal{P}(G)$, which maps any set A to the smallest Σ-consistent set containing A, is a closure operator.*

Proof. Let $\mathcal{S}_\Sigma$ be the family of all Σ-consistent subsets of G. The set G itself is trivially Σ-consistent (as it contains all elements). Furthermore, the intersection of any family of Σ-consistent sets is also Σ-consistent: Let $\{C_i\}_{i \in I}$ be a family of sets where each $C_i \in \mathcal{S}_\Sigma$. Let $D = \bigcap_{i \in I} C_i$. Suppose $\{d_x, d_z\} \subseteq D$ for some constraint $(d_x, d_y, d_z) \in \Sigma$. By definition of intersection, $\{d_x, d_z\} \subseteq C_i$ for all $i \in I$. Since each C_i is Σ-consistent, $d_y \in C_i$ for all $i \in I$. Consequently, $d_y \in D$. Thus, D is Σ-consistent.

Since $\mathcal{S}_\Sigma$ is closed under arbitrary intersection, it forms a *closure system*. The associated operator defined by $\phi_\Sigma(A) = \bigcap\{S \in \mathcal{S}_\Sigma \mid A \subseteq S\}$ satisfies the axioms of a closure operator (extensivity, monotonicity, and idempotence [16]). □

Structural Constraint Saturation. MLB constraints inherently define a hierarchical (ultrametric) relationship, where (d_x, d_y, d_z) implies that d_x and d_y are more closely related to each other than to d_z. However, standard FCA closure operators operate on flat propositional implications (as formalized in Definition (1), $d_x \wedge d_z \to d_y$). To bridge this gap, we must translate the structural transitivity of the MLB hierarchy into a complete set of implication rules before applying ϕ_Σ.

We perform a structural saturation step on Σ by exhaustively applying transitive inference rules. For instance, if two constraints $(d_{x_1}, d_{y_1}, d_{z_1})$ and $(d_{x_2}, d_{y_2}, d_{z_2})$ overlap in their sets of strictly closer elements, we dynamically derive and add the implied MLB constraints (e.g., if d_a, d_b merge before d_c, and d_b, d_c merge before d_e, it implies d_a, d_b must merge before d_e). This deductive closure ensures that all indirect hierarchical dependencies are explicitly encoded as implications, allowing the FCA closure operator to natively process the complete underlying tree structure.

The Lattice as the Search Space of Valid Clusters. A hierarchical clustering (i.e., dendrogram) is traditionally defined as a nested sequence of clusters. In the presence of constraints, we define a valid hierarchy $\mathcal{V}$ as follows:

Definition 4 (Valid Hierarchy). *A collection of subsets $\mathcal{V} \subseteq \mathcal{P}(G)$ is a valid hierarchy with respect to Σ if:*

1. *$G \in \mathcal{V}$ and $\emptyset \in \mathcal{V}$.*
2. *For all $A, B \in \mathcal{V}$, either $A \cap B = \emptyset$ or $A \subseteq B$ or $B \subseteq A$ (Nested property).*
3. *Every $A \in \mathcal{V}$ is Σ-consistent.*
4. *For every $(d_x, d_y, d_z) \in \Sigma$, there exists $C \in \mathcal{V}$ such that $d_x, d_y \in C$ and $d_z \notin C$.*

Condition 3 and 4 of (4) corresponds to Definitions (1) and (2), respectively. While the closure operator ϕ_Σ strictly enforces the implication part (Condition 3), it does not natively enforce the strict structural separation required by Condition 4. However, we claim that the resulting concept lattice provides the exact *search space* containing all admissible building blocks (clusters) for any valid hierarchy.

Theorem 2. *Let $\mathfrak{B}_\Sigma$ be the lattice of all closed sets under ϕ_Σ. For any valid hierarchy $\mathcal{V}$, it holds that $\mathcal{V} \subseteq \mathfrak{B}_\Sigma$.*

Proof. Let $C \in \mathcal{V}$ be an arbitrary cluster in a valid hierarchy. By the Condition 3 of (4), C must be Σ-consistent. By the definition of our closure system $\mathcal{S}_\Sigma$, a set is closed if and only if it is Σ-consistent. Therefore, $C \in \mathcal{S}_\Sigma$. Since $\mathfrak{B}_\Sigma$ is the lattice formed by all elements of $\mathcal{S}_\Sigma$, it follows that $C \in \mathfrak{B}_\Sigma$.

This theorem demonstrates that while $\mathfrak{B}_\Sigma$ itself contains overlapping concepts, it encompasses every valid cluster of every possible hierarchy that respects the constraints. This implies that the concept lattice $\underline{\mathfrak{B}}(\mathbb{K}_\Sigma)$ constitutes the exact search space for constrained hierarchical clustering. A particular dendrogram can be derived by selecting a sub-order that satisfies Condition 2 of (4), for instance by prioritizing concepts with higher stability or topic coherence.

4.2 Topic Model

The data-driven topic model-based approach comprises three steps: (i) constructing a LDA topic model, (ii) deriving a constrained document-topic incidence relation, and (iii) filtering concepts using the TITANIC algorithm [19].

Topic Model Construction. We employ gensim's implementation of LDA[2] [1], a widely used generative probabilistic model that represents documents as mixtures of T latent topics. To ensure comparability with the manually annotated BankSearch taxonomy, the number of latent topics is fixed to the number of ground-truth categories ($T = 11$). For a corpus of D documents, LDA produces a document-topic probability matrix $\Theta \in \mathbb{R}^{D \times T}$, where θ_{dt} denotes the probability that document d is associated with topic t. To derive a binary formal context from Θ, document-topic probabilities are thresholded using a minimum topic probability δ_t. The threshold is selected empirically using the elbow criterion on the resulting incidence density, as illustrated in Fig. 2.

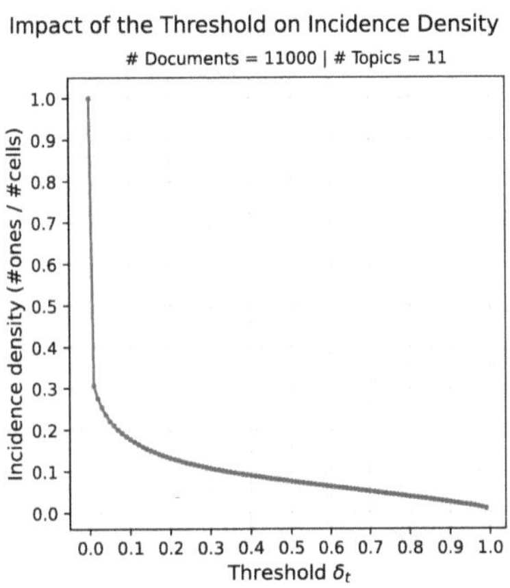

Fig. 2. LDA document-topic incidence density for varying thresholds δ_t on the BankSearch dataset. The elbow criterion selects $\delta_t = 0.07$, yielding a density slightly above 0.2.

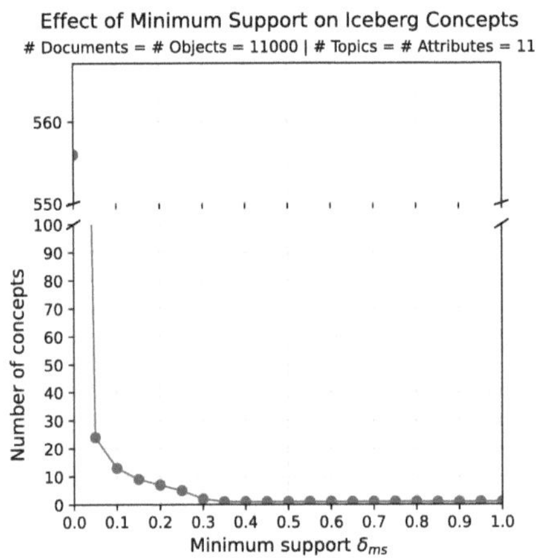

Fig. 3. Number of iceberg concepts for varying minimum support thresholds on the BankSearch dataset. The selected threshold $\delta_{ms} = 0.05$ results in 24 concepts.

Document-Topic Incidence. Given a threshold δ_t, a document d is assigned topic t if $\theta_{dt} \geq \delta_t$. This produces a binary incidence relation $I \subseteq D \times T$, where $(d, t) \in I$ indicates that topic t sufficiently characterizes document d. Lower threshold values yield denser contexts with more document-topic associations, whereas higher values retain only the most dominant topics. If no topic exceeds the threshold, the highest-probability topic is assigned to ensure that each document remains associated with at least one topic.

The resulting binary incidence relation $I \subseteq D \times T$ defines the formal context $\mathbb{K} = (G, M, I)$, where G denotes the set of documents (objects), M the set of topics (attributes), and I the document-topic incidence relation.

[2] https://radimrehurek.com/gensim/models/ldamodel.html (30.12.2025).

Concept Filtering via TITANIC. Computing the complete concept lattice of $\mathbb{K}$ can be computationally challenging, as the number of concepts may grow exponentially with the size of the context. Moreover, large lattices often hinder interpretability. To address this issue, Stumme et al. [37] introduced the TITANIC algorithm, which computes *iceberg concept lattices*. These lattices contain only concepts whose intents correspond to frequent attribute sets.

Let $\delta_{ms} \in [0, 1]$ denote a minimum support threshold. An attribute set $B \subseteq M$ is considered frequent if $\text{supp}(B) = \frac{|B'|}{|G|}$ meets or exceeds δ_{ms}. A concept (A, B) is retained in the iceberg concept lattice if its intent B is frequent.

Intuitively, this restriction preserves only those topic combinations that characterize at least $\delta_{ms} \times 100\%$ documents of the corpus. The choice of δ_{ms} directly influences the granularity of the resulting hierarchy [19]. Figure 3 shows the relationship between the minimum support threshold δ_{ms} and the number of extracted concepts for the BankSearch dataset.

4.3 Consistency-Lattice

To integrate the background knowledge from the MLB constraints with the latent knowledge from the LDA topic model, we construct the intersection of their respective closure systems. Let $\mathbb{K}_{TM} = (G, M_{TM}, I_{TM})$ be the formal context derived from the LDA topic model. This context induces a standard FCA closure operator $\phi_{TM}(X) = X''$.

We seek the closure system containing those sets of documents that are closed under *both* the MLB constraints and the topic model logic:

$$\mathcal{C}_\cap = \mathcal{C}_\Sigma \cap \mathcal{C}_{TM} = \{A \subseteq G \mid \phi_\Sigma(A) = A \wedge \phi_{TM}(A) = A\} \tag{1}$$

Alternating Closure Composition. The closure operator $\phi_\cap$ corresponding to this intersection is the limit of the alternating composition of ϕ_Σ and ϕ_{TM}. For any set $X \subseteq G$, we define a sequence $X_0 = X$, $X_{k+1} = \phi_{TM}(\phi_\Sigma(X_k))$. Since G is finite and closure operators are extensive and monotone, this sequence converges to a fixpoint: $\phi_\cap(X) = \lim_{k\to\infty}(\phi_{TM} \circ \phi_\Sigma)^k(X)$. This combined operator ensures that any generated concept is valid with respect to the expert constraints while also being statistically supported by the topic model.

On-The-Fly Computation of Irreducible Concepts. Generating the full lattice for large datasets is computationally expensive. This challenge is further exacerbated by the preceding saturation step, which significantly increases the number of implications and thus the density of the closure system. However, to define a new, reduced formal context representing the merged knowledge, we only require the $\cap$-irreducible (meet-irreducible) elements of the lattice. An extent $A \in \mathcal{C}_\cap$ is $\cap$-irreducible if it cannot be represented as the intersection of its strict supersets.

Instead of generating all closed sets and filtering them post-hoc, we employ an optimized version of Ganter's Next-Closure algorithm. During the canonical generation of closed sets, for a current closed set A, we perform an *on-the-fly irreducibility check*. We inspect the immediate upper neighbors by tentatively adding elements $g \in G \setminus A$:

$$I_{sup}(A) = \bigcap_{g \in G \setminus A} \phi_{\cap}(A \cup \{g\}) \tag{2}$$

If $I_{sup}(A) = A$, then A is the intersection of its upper neighbors and thus **reducible**. If $I_{sup}(A) \supsetneq A$, then A is **irreducible**.

This approach is crucial to our methodology: while constraint saturation ensures structural completeness, the on-the-fly irreducibility check effectively manages the resulting complexity. It discards redundant combinations immediately upon generation, leaving only the essential, structurally significant clusters. The resulting set of irreducible extents $\{E_1, \ldots, E_k\}$ forms the attribute set of the final, knowledge-integrated formal context:

$$\mathbb{K}_{merged} = (G, \{m_1, \ldots, m_k\}, I_{merged}),$$

where $g\, I_{merged}\, m_i \iff g \in E_i$. We denote the concept lattice derived from $\mathbb{K}_{merged}$ as the *consistency*-lattice, as it represents the hierarchy of concepts that are consistent with both the expert and data-driven knowledge.

5 Case Study

We apply our method to the BankSearch dataset (Subsect. 5.1), for which we map topic-level MLB constraints to document-level constraints (Subsect. 5.2). The resulting MLB-constrained concept lattice is then compared with a topic model-based iceberg lattice (Subsect. 5.3 and 5.4).

5.1 Banksearch Dataset

We obtained the Banksearch dataset from Carnegie Mellon University.[3] Each document is associated with exactly one topic, and the documents themselves are not hierarchically structured. Bade et al. [4] introduced a topic hierarchy to organize these topics. Although the reported hierarchy contains 14 categories, only 11 topics are represented in the documents of the dataset. This topic hierarchy organizes them into four main domains: *Finance* (Commercial Banks, Building Societies, Insurance Agencies), *Science* (Astronomy, Biology), *Programming* (C/C++, Java, Visual Basic), and *Sport* (Soccer, Motor Racing). Topics without associated documents in the dataset are omitted.

[3] http://lib.stat.cmu.edu/datasets/ (29.12.2025).

5.2 Topic-Document Constraint Mapping

We extract MLB constraints at the topic level and map them to document-level constraints using the topic assignments. Since each document belongs to exactly one topic, documents sharing the same topic form an equivalence class. Instead of translating constraints for every document individually, we select one representative document per topic and map the topic-level MLB constraints to these representatives. This reduces the number of constraints while preserving the structure induced by the topic hierarchy. We omit MLB constraints involving categories that have no associated documents. For example, if documents d_x, d_y, and d_z belong to topics x, y, and z, respectively, the topic-level constraint (x, y, z) translates to the document-level constraint (d_x, d_y, d_z). For the BankSearch dataset, this procedure yields 81 MLB constraints.

5.3 Comparison of Resulting Concept Lattices

The two lattices are constructed over the same object set of 11 000 documents. The MLB-constrained lattice in Fig. 4 contains all concepts, the topic model-based lattice in Fig. 5 is computed as an iceberg lattice, retaining only concepts whose intents satisfy a minimum support δ_{ms} threshold. This restriction is necessary because the complete topic model-based lattice contains more than 550 concepts (Fig. 3), which would hinder visualization and interpretation.

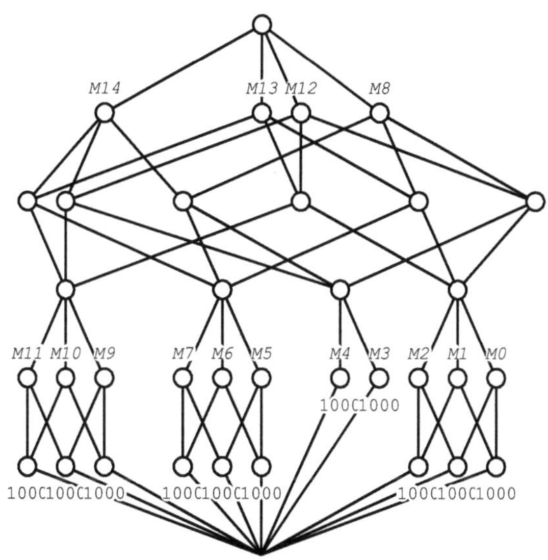

Fig. 4. MLB-constrained concept lattice. Top labels denote attributes; bottom labels indicate the number of documents in the corresponding concept extent. Evaluation against manually annotated ground-truth labels indicates that numbered nodes correspond to document clusters sharing the same topic.

In the MLB-constrained concept lattice (Fig. 4), attributes are labeled M_i as generated by the script constructing the formal context from the MLB constraints. The lattice contains 15 attributes, of which only $M3$ and $M4$ correspond directly to ground-truth topics (`Biology` and `Astronomy`). This correspondence was identified by matching concept extents to the original topic assignments. Most remaining topics emerge as intersections of attributes; for example, `Sport` corresponds to $M0 \cap M1$. In the lattice, most ground-truth topics are located near the bottom. The following attribute intersections correspond exactly to ground-truth topics:

- $\{M3\}$: `Biology`
- $\{M4\}$: `Astronomy`
- $\{M0, M2\}$: `Motor Racing`
- $\{M1, M2\}$: `Soccer`
- $\{M0, M1\}$: `Sport`
- $\{M5, M7\}$: `C/C++`
- $\{M6, M7\}$: `Java`
- $\{M5, M6\}$: `Visual Basic`
- $\{M10, M11\}$: `Commercial Banks`
- $\{M9, M10\}$: `Insurance Agencies`
- $\{M9, M11\}$: `Building Societies`

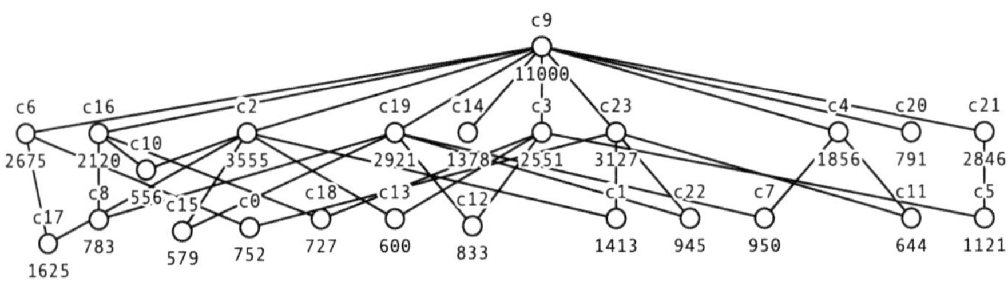

Fig. 5. Iceberg concept lattice derived from the topic model. Top labels denote cluster IDs in the concept intent; bottom labels indicate the number of documents in the concept extent.

The topic model-based lattice (Fig. 5) contains 24 concepts with support of at least $\delta_{ms} = 0.05$. Unlike the MLB-constrained lattice, the original dataset topics are not explicitly represented as individual concepts. Due to the pruning effect of the iceberg constraint, the topic model lattice contains only two non-trivial levels besides the top and bottom concepts, yielding substantially less hierarchical depth than the MLB-constrained lattice.

To compare both lattices, we compute the Jaccard similarity [17] between all pairs of concept extents. For extents A and B, the similarity is defined as $J(A, B) = \frac{|A \cap B|}{|A \cup B|}$. Figure 6 shows that most similarities are close to zero, indicating minimal overlap between document clusters. Excluding the trivial similarity of the top concepts, only five concept pairs reach a similarity above 0.5 (Table 1). Only two of the five high-similarity pairs correspond directly to ground-truth topics (`Astronomy` and `Sport`, `Soccer`); for the remaining pairs, semantic correspondence can be inferred indirectly from lower neighbors and representative LDA topic words. Overall, the scarcity of highly similar concepts indicates limited structural agreement between the lattices.

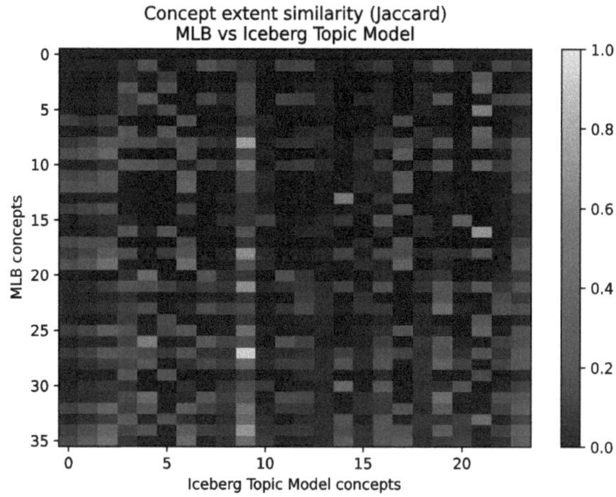

Fig. 6. Pairwise Jaccard similarities between concept extents of the MLB-constrained lattice and the topic model-based iceberg lattice. Apart from the trivial similarity of the top concepts, most pairs exhibit near-zero similarity.

Table 1. Concept pairs with $J(A, B) > 0.5$, where A' denotes an MLB-constrained concept intent and B' a topic model-based concept intent. Ground-truth topics are reported only for exact matches of A'. Representative LDA topic words are shown for B'.

A'	B'	$J(A, B)$	Topics A'	Topic words B'
$\{M12, M13, M14\}$	$\{c7\}$	0.77		Account, Rate, Mortage
$\{M1, M8, M12, M13\}$	$\{c9\}$	0.65	Soccer, Sport	Team, Player, Cup
$\{M4, M8, M12, M14\}$	$\{c10\}$	0.64	Astronomy	Galaxy, Universe, Star
$\{M8, M13, M14\}$	$\{c4\}$	0.56		Java, com, Visual
$\{M8, M12, M13\}$	$\{c0\}$	0.53		Race, Car

5.4 Consistency-Lattice Vs. Coherence-Lattice

The consistency lattice in Fig. 7 (left) is computed by intersecting the MLB-constrained lattice with the lattice derived from the topic model, following the procedure described in Sect. 4.3. Formally, $\mathcal{C}_\cap = \mathcal{C}_\Sigma \cap \mathcal{C}_{TM}$. In our case, this intersection is near-trivial, containing only the top and bottom concepts. To investigate partial overlaps, we define the *coherence-lattice* $\mathfrak{B}(\mathbb{K}_{coh})$. We construct a new formal context $\mathbb{K}_{coh} = (G, M_{coh}, I_{coh})$, where the attributes M_{coh} are derived from pairs of concepts (A, B) with $A \in \mathcal{C}_\Sigma$ and $B \in \mathcal{C}_{TM}$ that satisfy a Jaccard threshold θ:

$$M_{coh} = \{A \cap B \mid A \in \mathcal{C}_\Sigma, B \in \mathcal{C}_{TM}, J(A, B) > \theta\} \quad (3)$$

We set $\theta = 0.5$ as a moderate threshold, enabling the visualization of coherence relationships beyond exact matches while excluding weakly overlapping concepts. Since the top node of the coherence lattice contains 11 000 documents the resulting lattice covers the complete corpus.

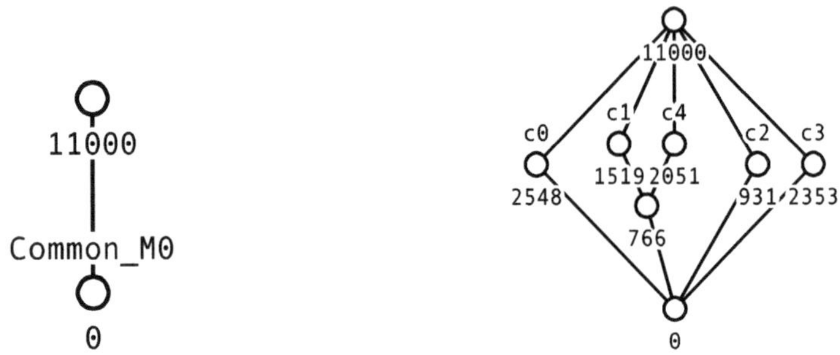

Fig. 7. The *consistency* lattice (left) and *coherence* lattice (right) from the MLB-constrained lattice and the topic model-based lattice for the BankSearch dataset.

6 Conclusion, Limitations, and Future Work

Our study provides two main contributions. First, we showed that MLB constraints can be integrated natively into the FCA framework through a fixpoint-based closure operator. Second, experiments on the BankSearch dataset demonstrated that exact consistency between expert-defined hierarchies and data-driven topic models is rarely observed in real-world corpora, motivating the need for relaxed coherence-based integration strategies.

The consistency-lattice retains only concepts whose extents coincide exactly in both the MLB-constrained and the topic model-based lattices. In our experiments, only trivial concepts were shared exactly, indicating that strict consistency is often too restrictive for heterogeneous knowledge bases.

In principle, pruning low-support concepts that could potentially form exact overlaps can yield an incomplete consistency-lattice. However, the empty consistency-lattice in our experiments primarily reflects semantic differences between the two knowledge bases rather than an artefact of pruning: The MLB-constrained lattice is derived from manual annotations and thus reflects human expertise and annotation decisions, whereas the topic model-based lattice is data-driven and captures latent statistical regularities in the corpus.

Instead of requiring identical extents, the coherence-lattice identifies partially overlapping document clusters and thereby enables the analysis of meaningful semantic alignments between heterogeneous knowledge bases.

Future work will investigate the integration of more than two knowledge bases, methods for selecting similarity thresholds for coherence-lattices, and alternative overlap measures beyond Jaccard similarity for comparing concept extents across multiple lattices.

References

1. Alghamdi, R., Alfalqi, K.: A survey of topic modeling in text mining. Int. J. Adv. Comput. Sci. Appl. **6**(1), 147–153 (2015)
2. Aznag, M., Quafafou, M., Jarir, Z.: Leveraging Formal Concept Analysis with Topic Correlation for Service Clustering and Discovery pp. 153–160 (2014). https://doi.org/10.1109/ICWS.2014.33

3. Bade, K., Nürnberger, A.: Personalized hierarchical clustering. In: 2006 IEEE / WIC / ACM International Conference on Web Intelligence (WI 2006), 18-22 December 2006, Hong Kong, China. pp. 181–187. IEEE Computer Society (2006). https://doi.org/10.1109/WI.2006.131
4. Bade, K., Nürnberger, A.: Creating a cluster hierarchy under constraints of a partially known hierarchy. In: Proceedings of the SIAM International Conference on Data Mining, SDM 2008, April 24-26, 2008, Atlanta, Georgia, USA. pp. 13–24. SIAM (2008). https://doi.org/10.1137/1.9781611972788.2
5. Bade, K., Nürnberger, A.: Hierarchical constraints - providing structural bias for hierarchical clustering. Mach. Learn. **94**(3), 371–399 (2014). https://doi.org/10.1007/S10994-013-5397-9
6. Belohlávek, R., Macko, J.: Selecting important concepts using weights. In: Valtchev, P., Jäschke, R. (eds.) Formal Concept Analysis - 9th International Conference, ICFCA 2011, Nicosia, Cyprus, May 2-6, 2011. Proceedings. Lecture Notes in Computer Science, vol. 6628, pp. 65–80. Springer (2011). https://doi.org/10.1007/978-3-642-20514-9_7
7. Belohlávek, R., Vychodil, V.: Formal concept analysis with constraints by closure operators. In: Schärfe, H., Hitzler, P., Øhrstrøm, P. (eds.) Conceptual Structures: Inspiration and Application, 14th International Conference on Conceptual Structures, ICCS 2006, Aalborg, Denmark, July 16-21, 2006, Proceedings. Lecture Notes in Computer Science, vol. 4068, pp. 131–143. Springer (2006). https://doi.org/10.1007/11787181_10
8. Belohlávek, R., Vychodil, V.: Formal concept analysis with background knowledge: attribute priorities. IEEE Trans. Syst. Man Cybern. Part C **39**(4), 399–409 (2009). https://doi.org/10.1109/TSMCC.2008.2012168
9. Cigarrán, J., Castellanos, Á., García-Serrano, A.: A step forward for topic detection in twitter: an FCA-based approach. Expert Syst. Appl. **57**, 21–36 (2016). https://doi.org/10.1016/J.ESWA.2016.03.011
10. Cimiano, P., Hotho, A., Staab, S.: Comparing conceptual, divise and agglomerative clustering for learning taxonomies from text. In: de Mántaras, R.L., Saitta, L. (eds.) Proceedings of the 16th Eureopean Conference on Artificial Intelligence, ECAI'2004, including Prestigious Applicants of Intelligent Systems, PAIS 2004, Valencia, Spain, August 22-27, 2004. pp. 435–439. IOS Press (2004)
11. Cimiano, P., Hotho, A., Staab, S.: Learning concept hierarchies from text corpora using formal concept analysis. J. Artif. Intell. Res. **24**, 305–339 (2005). https://doi.org/10.1613/JAIR.1648
12. Elzinga, P., Poelmans, J., Viaene, S., Dedene, G.: Detecting domestic violence - showcasing a knowledge browser based on formal concept analysis and emergent self organizing maps. In: Cordeiro, J., Filipe, J. (eds.) ICEIS 2009 - Proceedings of the 11th International Conference on Enterprise Information Systems, Volume AIDSS, Milan, Italy, May 6-10, 2009. pp. 11–18 (2009)
13. Felde, M., Stumme, G.: Triadic exploration and exploration with multiple experts. In: Braud, A., Buzmakov, A., Hanika, T., Ber, F.L. (eds.) Formal Concept Analysis - 16th International Conference, ICFCA 2021, Strasbourg, France, June 29 - July 2, 2021, Proceedings. Lecture Notes in Computer Science, vol. 12733, pp. 175–191. Springer (2021). https://doi.org/10.1007/978-3-030-77867-5_11
14. Felde, M., Stumme, G.: Attribute exploration with multiple contradicting partial experts. In: Braun, T., Cristea, D., Jäschke, R. (eds.) Graph-Based Representation and Reasoning - 27th International Conference on Conceptual Structures, ICCS 2022, Münster, Germany, September 12-15, 2022, Proceedings. Lecture Notes in

Computer Science, vol. 13403, pp. 51–65. Springer (2022). https://doi.org/10.1007/978-3-031-16663-1_5
15. Galán-Páez, J., Borrego-Díaz, J.: Discovering new sentiments from the social web. CoRR **abs/1407.0374** (2014). http://arxiv.org/abs/1407.0374
16. Ganter, B., Wille, R.: Formal Concept Analysis: Mathematical Foundations. Springer Nature (2024)
17. Glückstad, F.K., Herlau, T., Schmidt, M.N., Mørup, M.: Unsupervised Knowledge Structuring: Application of Infinite Relational Models to the FCA Visualization pp. 233–240 (2013). https://doi.org/10.1109/SITIS.2013.48
18. Gopal, S., Yang, Y.: Recursive regularization for large-scale classification with hierarchical and graphical dependencies. pp. 257–265. ACM (2013). https://doi.org/10.1145/2487575.2487644
19. Gutekunst, K.M., Dürrschnabel, D., Hirth, J., Stumme, G.: Conceptual topic aggregation. In: Cellier, P., Ganter, B., Missaoui, R. (eds.) Conceptual Knowledge Structures. Lecture Notes in Computer Science, vol. 15941, pp. 3–18. Springer (2025). https://doi.org/10.1007/978-3-032-03364-2_1
20. Hearst, M.A.: Automatic acquisition of hyponyms from large text corpora. In: COLING 1992, Nantes, France, August 23-28, 1992. pp. 539–545 (1992). https://aclanthology.org/C92-2082/
21. Hidayat, T., bin Ahmad, A., Ngo, H.C.: Non-redundant implicational base of formal context with constraints using SAT. PeerJ Comput. Sci. **10**, e1806 (2024).https://doi.org/10.7717/PEERJ-CS.1806
22. Hirth, J., Horn, V., Stumme, G., Hanika, T.: Ordinal motifs in lattices. Inf. Sci. **659**, 120009 (2024). https://doi.org/10.1016/J.INS.2023.120009
23. Kommineni, V.K., König-Ries, B., Samuel, S.: From human experts to machines: An LLM supported approach to ontology and knowledge graph construction. CoRR **abs/2403.08345** (2024). https://doi.org/10.48550/ARXIV.2403.08345
24. Le, M., Roller, S., Papaxanthos, L., Kiela, D., Nickel, M.: Inferring concept hierarchies from text corpora via hyperbolic embeddings. In: Korhonen, A., Traum, D.R., Màrquez, L. (eds.) Proceedings of the 57th Conference of the Association for Computational Linguistics, ACL 2019, Florence, Italy, July 28- August 2, 2019, Volume 1: Long Papers. pp. 3231–3241. Association for Computational Linguistics (2019). https://doi.org/10.18653/V1/P19-1313
25. Li, K., Li, S., Yavuz, S., Zha, H., Su, Y., Yan, X.: HierCon: Hierarchical Organization of Technical Documents Based on Concepts. pp. 379–388. ICDM (2019). https://doi.org/10.1109/ICDM.2019.00048
26. Li, K., Zha, H., Su, Y., Yan, X.: Unsupervised neural categorization for scientific publications. In: Ester, M., Pedreschi, D. (eds.) Proceedings of the 2018 SIAM International Conference on Data Mining, SDM 2018, May 3-5, 2018, San Diego Marriott Mission Valley, San Diego, CA, USA. pp. 37–45. SIAM (2018). https://doi.org/10.1137/1.9781611975321.5
27. Mao, H.: Formal concept analysis with constraints by em operators. J. Indonesian Math. Soc., 13–26 (2017)
28. Old, L.J.: Unlocking the semantics of rogets? Thesaurus using formal concept analysis. In: Eklund, P.W. (ed.) Concept Lattices, Second International Conference on Formal Concept Analysis, ICFCA 2004, Sydney, Australia, February 23-26, 2004, Proceedings, pp. 244–251. Lecture Notes in Computer Science, Springer (2004). https://doi.org/10.1007/978-3-540-24651-0_22
29. Petersen, W.: A Set-Theoretical Approach for the Induction of Inheritance Hierarchies pp. 296–308 (2001). https://doi.org/10.1016/S1571-0661(05)82590-3

30. Priss, U.: The Formalization of WordNet by Methods of Relational Concept Analysis (1996). https://api.semanticscholar.org/CorpusID:60160807
31. Priss, U.: Relational Concept Analysis: Semantic Structures in Dictionaries and Lexical Databases. Ph.D. thesis, Darmstadt University of Technology, Germany (1998). https://d-nb.info/955153514
32. Priss, U., Old, L.J.: Modelling lexical databases with formal concept analysis. J. Univers. Comput. Sci. **10**(8), 967–984 (2004)
33. Risch, J., Garda, S., Krestel, R.: Hierarchical document classification as a sequence generation task. In: Huang, R., Wu, D., Marchionini, G., He, D., Cunningham, S.J., Hansen, P. (eds.) JCDL'20: Proceedings of the ACM/IEEE Joint Conference on Digital Libraries in 2020, Virtual Event, China, August 1-5, 2020. pp. 147–155. ACM (2020). https://doi.org/10.1145/3383583.3398538
34. Sporleder, C.: A galois lattice based approach to lexical inheritance hierarchy learning. In: OLT 2002 (2002)
35. Storey, V.C., Dey, D., Ullrich, H., Sundaresan, S.: An ontology-based expert system for database design. Data Knowl. Eng. **28**(1), 31–46 (1998)
36. Studer, R., Benjamins, V.R., Fensel, D.: Knowledge engineering: principles and methods. Data Knowl. Eng. **25**(1–2), 161–197 (1998)
37. Stumme, G., Taouil, R., Bastide, Y., Pasquier, N., Lakhal, L.: Computing iceberg concept lattices with titanic. Data Knowl. Eng. **42**(2), 189–222 (2002)
38. Valverde-Albacete, F.J.: Explaining the structure of framenet with concept lattices. In: Ganter, B., Godin, R. (eds.) ICFCA 2005. LNCS (LNAI), vol. 3403, pp. 79–94. Springer, Heidelberg (2005). https://doi.org/10.1007/978-3-540-32262-7_6
39. Wagstaff, K., Cardie, C., Rogers, S., Schrödl, S.: Constrained K-means clustering with background knowledge. In: ICML, pp. 577–584 (2001)
40. Wang, F., Wang, N., Cai, S., Zhang, W.: Dynamically constructing semantic topic hierarchy through formal concept analysis. Multim. Tools Appl. **82**(5), 7267–7292 (2023). https://doi.org/10.1007/S11042-022-13640-2
41. Wang, K., Wang, F.: Topic-feature lattices construction and visualization for dynamic topic number. JSSI **9**(5), 558–574 (2021)
42. Yang, H.: Personalized concept hierarchy construction. Doctoral dissertation, Pittsburgh, PA (2012)
43. Yu, C., Shen, Y., Mao, Y.: Constrained sequence-to-tree generation for hierarchical text classification. pp. 1865–1869. ACM SIGIR (2022). https://doi.org/10.1145/3477495.3531765
44. Zhang, Y., Yang, R., Xu, X., Li, R., Xiao, J., Shen, J., Han, J.: TELEClass: taxonomy enrichment and LLM-enhanced hierarchical text classification with minimal supervision. pp. 2032–2042. ACM (2025). https://doi.org/10.1145/3696410.3714940
45. Zhao, H., Qi, Z.: Hierarchical agglomerative clustering with ordering constraints. In: Third International Conference on Knowledge Discovery and Data Mining, WKDD 2010, Phuket, Thailand, 9-10 January 2010. pp. 195–199. IEEE Computer Society (2010). https://doi.org/10.1109/WKDD.2010.123
46. Zheng, L., Li, T.: Semi-supervised hierarchical clustering. pp. 982–991. ICDM (2011). https://doi.org/10.1109/ICDM.2011.130

On the Limits of Information Transmission in Concept Lattices

Emma Reyner-Fuentes[1(✉)], Carmen Peláez-Moreno[1], and Francisco J. Valverde-Albacete[2]

[1] Depto. Teoría de Señal y Comunicaciones, Univ. Carlos III de Madrid, Madrid, Spain
emma.reyner@alumnos.uc3m.es, carmen@tsc.uc3m.es

[2] Depto. Teoría de Señal y Comunicaciones y Sistemas Telemáticos y Computación, Univ. Rey Juan Carlos, Madrid, Spain
francisco.valverde@urjc.es

Abstract. In this paper we study which regions of entropy triangles are *structurally attainable* when binary formal contexts are randomized, providing a combinatorial baseline for FCA-based information mappings. For each size we generate 5,000 contexts with different densities, process them through the FCA pipeline, and compute entropy coordinates from the resulting extent and intent distributions to obtain Source and Channel Multivariate Entropy triangles (SMET and CMET). Across all tested sizes, occupancy is highly non-uniform. In the SMET, points concentrate along a small number of narrow radial trajectories ("rays"), revealing a robust geometric signature induced by closure-based transformation. In these randomized experiments, SMET triangles computed from intents and extents are empirically indistinguishable. Dimensional effects are governed mainly by the minimum of the cardinals of objects and attributes: increasing the larger dimension while keeping the smaller fixed saturates the occupied support, whereas increasing the smaller dimension unlocks additional rays and extends accessible regimes toward more extreme regions. In parallel, CMET occupancy remains concentrated on the right-hand axis, as expected in ordinary formal contexts where extents and intents are mutually determined and residual variation is minimal. Its spread is nevertheless size-dependent: depending on context shape, the occupied region along that axis expands or contracts, reflecting how dimensionality constrains the range of attainable transmission regimes. These findings characterize the feasible geometry of lattice-to-entropy mappings and establish a baseline against which non-random organization can be assessed.

1 Introduction

The use of information theoretical metrics in connection with FCA lattices has been found relevant to measure similarities between concepts [2] in a framework of finding semantic similarities in taxonomies [3]. Entropy Triangles (ET) are an

M. Croitoru et al. (Eds.): CONCEPTS 2026, LNAI 16811, pp. 192–209, 2027.
https://doi.org/10.1007/978-3-032-34742-8_13

example of said metrics, which provide a compact geometric representation of how information is distributed across a system. In recent work they have proved useful for reading FCA-derived structures as information channels [7], making it possible to compare families of formal contexts through the geometry of their entropy-based embeddings. However, before assigning interpretive meaning to any observed pattern, a more basic question must be addressed: *which regions of the triangle are structurally reachable at all?*

This question arises naturally in our own work on the sensorium of *Caenorhabditis elegans*, where we model odorant stimuli as formal objects and sensory neurons as formal attributes. In that setting, we are interested both in the information content of the source side and in the transmission of information from objects to attributes. Entropy triangles provide a natural way to visualize these quantities, but their interpretation quickly raises a methodological difficulty: which geometric features reflect distinctive properties of the empirical data, and which are induced by the FCA pipeline itself?

In our setting, the mapping is not a direct transformation from data to entropy coordinates. A context is first processed through the FCA pipeline (binary context $\rightarrow$ closure operators $\rightarrow$ formal concepts $\rightarrow$ extent- and intent-membership matrices), yielding dual closure systems of extents and intents, bound as formal concepts [4]. Entropic coordinates are then computed from the comparison of closure systems. This procedure can impose purely structural constraints: distinct random incidence patterns may collapse into the same closure-derived descriptions, and the resulting entropy points may occupy only restricted regions of the simplex even when the original contexts are unstructured.

For this reason, a null reference baseline is needed before empirical geometries can be interpreted. The aim of this work is to characterize the support and organization of entropy-triangle occupancies generated by *randomized* binary formal contexts of controlled size and density. This provides a combinatorial baseline for the FCA-to-entropy mapping itself, against which empirical deviations can later be assessed.

2 Methods

2.1 *C. Elegans* case study and empirical triangles

To compare the randomized baselines with empirical entropy triangles, we briefly recall the biological setting from which the empirical contexts are obtained. Following previous $\mathcal{K}$-FCA analyses of the *C. elegans* sensorium, we consider a graded data table relating 23 odorants, taken as objects, and 11 bilateral chemosensory neuron pairs, taken as attributes. Its entries represent stimulus-response associations extracted from functional imaging data [6]. In this setting, extents correspond to odorant-side descriptions and intents to neuron-side descriptions.

The empirical formal contexts are not given directly as binary tables. They are obtained from graded $\mathcal{K}$-FCA contexts by sweeping a threshold parameter φ.

For each value of φ, the graded odorant-neuron relation is binarized by retaining only those associations whose value exceeds the threshold. Thus, low values of φ produce denser contexts, in which many odorant-neuron associations are retained, whereas high values of φ produce sparser contexts, containing only the strongest associations. This threshold sweep yields a family of binary contexts and their associated concept lattices.

In the present paper, these empirical contexts are used only as a point of comparison for the randomized baselines developed here. In particular, each empirical SMET or CMET point corresponds to one thresholded context from the φ-sweep, processed through the same FCA-to-entropy pipeline as the randomized contexts. A fuller account of the biological data, the $\mathcal{K}$-FCA construction, and the interpretation of the resulting ETs can be found in [7], where this odorant-neuron sensory system was analysed in terms of a family of concept lattices acting as information channels.

2.2 Entropy Triangles for FCA-Derived Representations

Entropy triangles are quantitative and visual tools for representing Shannon-type entropy decompositions. Their basic idea is to split a finite entropy budget into three non-negative components that add to one, so that each system can be represented as a point in a 2-simplex [8,11]. In this paper we use two multivariate variants: the Source Multivariate Entropy Triangle (SMET), which describes how information is organized within a multivariate source [9], and the Channel Multivariate Entropy Triangle (CMET), which describes how information is transmitted between two multivariate descriptions [7,10].

For a multivariate source $\overline{X} = (X_i)_{i \in I}$, the SMET decomposes the normalized contribution of each marginal X_i as

$$\Delta H'_{P_{X_i}} + M'_{P_{X_i}} + VI'_{P_{X_i}} = 1. \tag{1}$$

The three axes of the SMET correspond to: $\Delta H'_{P_{X_i}}$, the normalized distance from uniformity; $M'_{P_{X_i}}$, the normalized bound or shared information among variables; and $VI'_{P_{X_i}}$, the normalized privative information associated with individual variables. Thus, regions dominated by $\Delta H'$ correspond to low effective uncertainty or nearly deterministic behaviour, regions dominated by M' indicate strongly shared or redundant structure, and regions dominated by VI' indicate information that remains comparatively variable-specific.

The CMET applies the same geometric principle to a channel relating an input random vector $\overline{X}$ and an output random vector $\overline{Y}$. In its full form, the entropy budget is decomposed into marginal non-uniformity, transmitted information, and remanent entropy:

$$\Delta H_{P_{\overline{XY}}} + 2I_{P_{\overline{XY}}} + VI_{P_{\overline{XY}}} = H_{U_{\overline{X}}} + H_{U_{\overline{Y}}}. \tag{2}$$

In practice, we use the split CMET representation, in which the two sides of the channel are normalized separately. The apical coordinate represents transmitted or shared information, the remanent-entropy coordinate measures information that remains unexplained by the opposite side of the channel, and the non-uniformity coordinate measures the departure of the corresponding marginal distribution from uniformity. Points close to the transmitted-information vertex indicate strong mutual determination between input and output; points close to the remanent-entropy region indicate weak or incomplete transmission; and points close to the non-uniformity vertex indicate highly constrained marginal structure.

In this paper, the triangles are computed after applying FCA to each context, not directly from the raw incidence matrix. The resulting geometry is therefore the output of a lattice-to-entropy mapping: the context is first transformed into closure-derived extent and intent representations, and the entropy coordinates are then computed from those representations.

2.3 Randomized-Context Ensembles and *lattice-to-Entropy* pipeline

To characterize which regions of the ETs are structurally attainable, we generated randomized binary formal contexts of controlled size and density. Controlling density is natural in FCA, since the sparsity/density of the underlying context is a classical parameter affecting the behaviour of concept-generation algorithms [5]. For each tested size $(n \times m)$, we sampled $n_{\text{ctx}} = 5000$ contexts by independently drawing each entry of the incidence matrix from a Bernoulli distribution with parameter p. This Bernoulli coin-toss scheme defines a simple and analytically convenient null model for formal contexts, although richer null-model generators have been proposed to capture a broader variety of context ensembles [1]. Here we deliberately adopt the minimal version, with no imposed row- or column-wise structure, so that any regularity observed in the ETs can be attributed to the combinatorics of closure and the entropy mapping rather than to latent patterns in the data. To cover both sparse and dense regimes, we swept p across 20 values distributed symmetrically around 0.5: 10 values geometrically spaced in $(p_{\min}, 0.5)$ and 10 in $(0.5, p_{\max})$, with $p_{\min} = 0.01$ and $p_{\max} = 0.99$, excluding 0.5 itself. An equal number of contexts was generated for each p level. We explored several dimensional families in order to separate the effect of total size from that of the smaller or bigger dimension. These included square contexts (e.g., 10×10, 20×20, 40×40), rectangular families with fixed $\min(n, m)$ while increasing the other dimension (e.g., 10×20, 10×30, 10×40), families in which the smaller dimension increases (e.g., 10×30, 20×30, 30×30), transposed pairs $(n \times m)$ and $(m \times n)$, and an extreme rectangular case 10×400.

Each sampled context $\mathbb{K}$ was processed through the standard FCA pipeline to obtain its formal concepts $\{(A_k, B_k)\}_{k=1}^{|\mathbb{B}(\mathbb{K})|}$.

From these, we constructed the system extents and intents co-ocurrence matrices, whose rows correspond to concepts and whose columns encode object and attribute memberships, respectively. These matrices provide the closure-derived representations on which entropy calculations are based.

For SMET, the rows of the extent/intent matrix were treated as the empirical population, with one equally weighted observation per concept. On the intent side, each attribute defines a binary variable over the concept set, producing one

SMET point per attribute; analogously, the extent side produces one point per object. For CMET, each concept provides a paired description across the object and attribute sides, and the corresponding concept-level empirical distributions define the channel quantities. The goal is to characterize the geometry induced by the *lattice-to-entropy* transformation itself.

3 Results

3.1 Findings for Randomized Contexts with the SMET

In all SMET figures, points are coloured by the density parameter p used to generate each randomized context. This makes it possible to track how sparse and dense regimes redistribute mass within the feasible region. Across all tested sizes, SMETs computed from extents and from intents are empirically indistinguishable: they occupy the same region of the simplex. In view of this and to simplify the presentation, the randomized-context results are reported using a single SMET representation, namely the system of intents side.

A Robust Ray Geometry Induced by the lattice-to-Entropy Mapping. For all randomized context sizes, triangle occupancy is highly non-uniform: points do not form a diffuse cloud but concentrate along a few narrow radial trajectories ("rays"). This organization is stable across dimensions and therefore cannot be ascribed to any particular dataset. Rather, it reflects a structural signature of the lattice-to-entropy mapping: randomized incidences are first transformed into closure-derived objects, and the entropy coordinates are then computed from those closure-derived representations. The resulting combinatorial constraints restrict the set of attainable statistics in the simplex and naturally produce ray-like families.

Figure 1 shows that this qualitative ray structure is preserved across sizes, while the maximal reach of the rays and the density of points along them vary with (n, m). The presence of rays must therefore be regarded as part of the randomized baseline itself, not as evidence of domain-specific organization.

The Smaller Dimension Governs the Accessible Support. A striking observation is that increasing the total number of entries $n \cdot m$ does *not* necessarily expand the accessible region of the ET. When one dimension is small, enlarging the other dimension produces only minor changes in support. For example, the SMET for 10×20, 10×30, and 10×40 are visually almost indistinguishable: the same rays appear with comparable extent and coverage (Fig. 2). This indicates a strong saturation effect when $\min(n, m)$ is small.

In contrast, increasing the smaller dimension produces substantial changes. Moving from 10×30 to 20×30 markedly increases both the number of visible rays and their length, and extends occupancy toward more extreme regions of the simplex (Fig. 3). Increasing the smaller dimension further continues this expansion. Together, these observations support a bottleneck interpretation: the

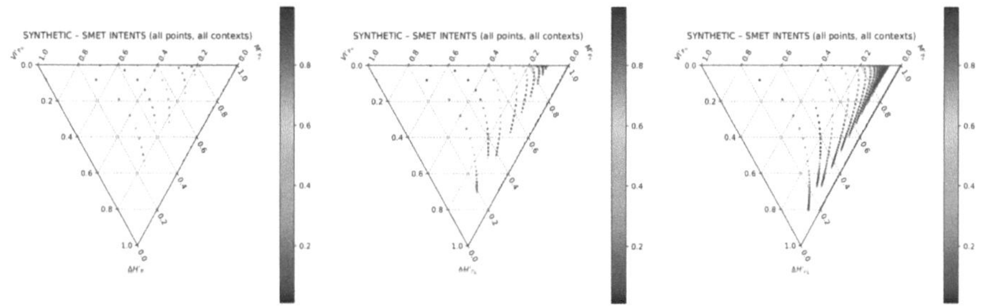

(a) 10 × 10. (b) 20 × 20. (c) 40 × 40.

Fig. 1. Robust ray geometry in randomized contexts. Representative SMET triangles for three sizes show a stable ray-like organization under randomization.

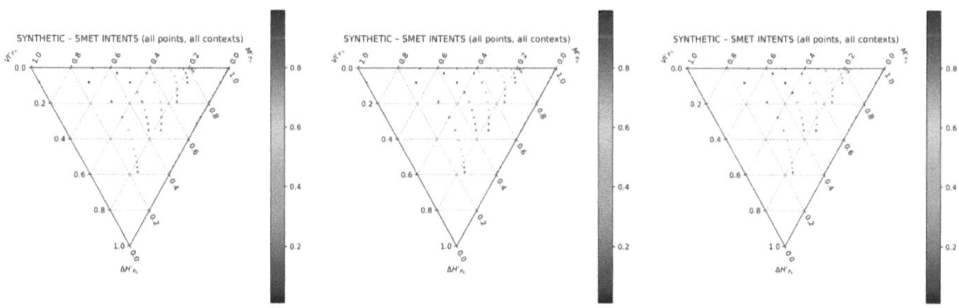

(a) 10 × 20. (b) 10 × 30. (c) 10 × 40.

Fig. 2. Saturation when the minimum dimension is small. Increasing the larger dimension while keeping $\min(n, m) = 10$ leaves the occupied support largely unchanged.

geometry of the randomized baseline is governed primarily by $\min(n, m)$ rather than by the total number of cells.

Approximate Symmetry Under Transposition. Transposed pairs such as 10×20 and 20×10 are globally very similar: they occupy essentially the same region and exhibit the same ray structure. Nonetheless, small and reproducible differences in point density and ray reach are observed. Since SMET is computed on a specific side—here, intents—transposition changes the number and identity of the summarized variables, and therefore changes the normalization budgets and empirical pattern counts entering the triangle coordinates. The observed asymmetry is thus consistent with an approximate invariance of the feasible region under transposition, modulated by representation-dependent normalization and finite-size effects.

Large and Extreme-Aspect-Ratio Cases. At the largest square size tested (40×40), rays become longer and in some cases more numerous, indicating increased accessibility of extreme regimes. At the same time, the upper portion

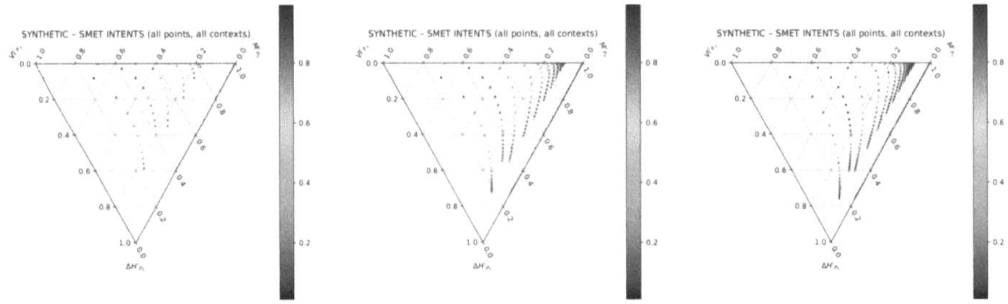

(a) 10 × 30. (b) 20 × 30. (c) 30 × 30.

Fig. 3. Bottleneck effect: increasing the smaller dimension unlocks new regimes. Increasing $\min(n, m)$ substantially increases the number and length of rays and extends occupancy toward more extreme regions.

of the occupied region appears comparatively less populated, suggesting a redistribution of mass toward more boundary-dominated regimes as both dimensions grow.

To stress-test the saturation regime, we also considered an extreme rectangular case with $\min(n, m) = 10$, namely 10×400. The resulting SMET does not open new portions of the simplex; instead, the occupancy becomes more concentrated, with most points collapsing onto a reduced subset of the previously available structures, especially the right boundary and one dominant interior ray (Fig. 4). This provides an illustrative limit of the saturation phenomenon: once the smaller dimension is fixed and small, increasing the larger one does not expand the feasible support and instead mainly redistributes mass along already accessible structures.

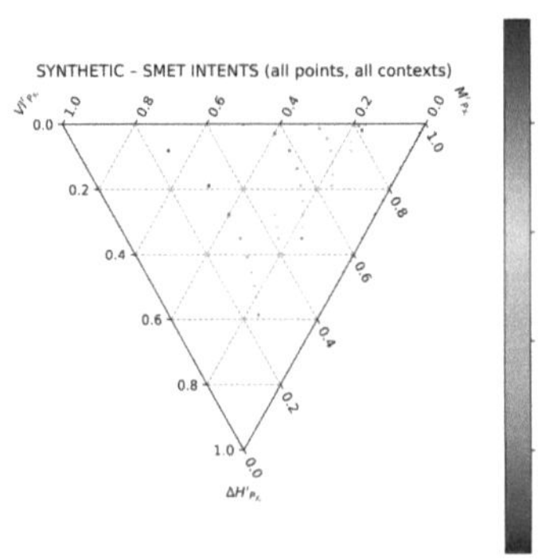

Fig. 4. Extreme aspect-ratio case (10×400): the accesible area does not expand but becomes more concentrated.

3.2 Implications for Interpreting Empirical SMET Triangles

These randomized-context experiments provide a reference baseline for interpreting empirical triangles. First, they show that the ray-like organization and the presence of unoccupied regions arises from the lattice-to-entropy transformation itself under randomization, rather than from biological structure. Second, they reveal strong dimensional effects: triangle occupancy is largely governed by bottlenecks associated with the smaller dimension, while the larger dimension mainly modulates how probability mass is distributed along the occupied region. Consequently, empirical results should be evaluated relative to this baseline: departures such as a more continuous filling between rays, systematic occupation of restricted subregions rather than the whole structurally feasible support, or dimensional trends that do not follow the bottleneck behavior are indicative of structured (non-random) organization in the underlying data.

In Fig. 5 we compare this randomized baseline with the empirical SMET triangles of intents (neurons) and extents (odorants). The three panels share a broadly similar feasible region and, importantly, the empirical triangles remain compatible with the randomized baseline in the sense that they lie within regions that are structurally attainable under randomization. However, the comparison also reveals differences in density and organization. Relative to the baseline, the empirical triangles appear to populate the feasible region more selectively. In particular, they do not fill all structurally available rays and remain confined to a more restricted portion of the simplex. They also exhibit a more coherent progression as φ varies, with a clearer trajectory-like organization along the occupied rays. The intent- and extent-side empirical triangles are themselves very similar, but some subtle differences can be observed. The odorant-side triangle shows a clearer φ progression along the rays, the second ray from the left appears more populated on the neuron side, and the odorant-side triangle seems to occupy the right axis somewhat more strongly.

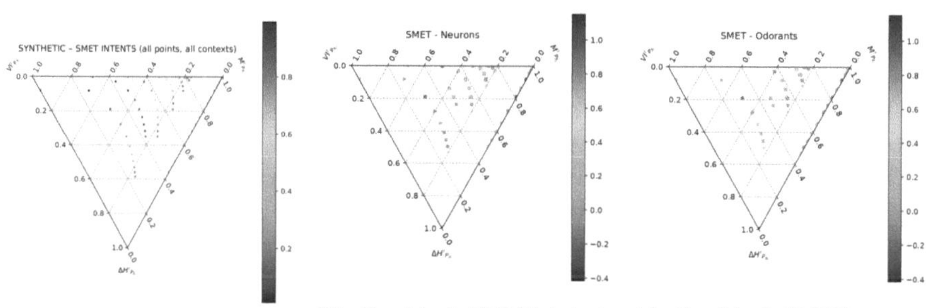

(a) SMET baseline (b) Empirical SMET intents (neurons) (c) Empirical SMET extents (odorants)

Fig. 5. Randomized baseline vs. empirical SMET for the 23×11 case. Since randomized SMET triangles computed from extents and intents are empirically indistinguishable, only the baseline for intents is shown.

3.3 Findings for Randomized Contexts with the CMET

In all CMET figures, points are displayed in the channel entropy triangle and coloured by the density parameter p used to generate each randomized context.

CMET Collapses Onto the Right-Hand Axis. Across all tested sizes, CMET points lie essentially on the right-hand axis of the triangle. This is a structural consequence of the ordinary binary formal-context setting. Hence, for that specific context, the relation is fully fixed: extents are determined by their intents and vice-versa. In channel terms, this yields total mutual determination and therefore minimal remanent entropy. Geometrically, this forces the CMET occupancy onto the right-hand side of the simplex.

This restriction is robust across all randomized ensembles considered here. Changing the context size does not open up a two-dimensional CMET support; instead, dimensional effects are expressed as expansions, contractions, and redistributions of density along the right-hand axis.

Dimensional Effects Are Split-Dependent. For rectangular contexts, the X and Y split CMET are not directly comparable, because the two split representations are normalized by different budgets: in an $(n \times m)$ context, the X split is normalized on the object side by $\log n$ and the Y split on the attribute side by $\log m$. As a consequence, changing only one dimension affects the two splits differently.

This is already visible in the comparison between 10×5 and 10×10 (Fig. 6). On the X split, both cases occupy very similar segments of the right-hand axis, with only minor differences in density. On the Y split, however, the 10×10 case extends further than 10×5. Thus, increasing one dimension does not produce a uniform change in CMET as a whole; rather, it mainly affects the split normalized by that dimension.

A natural interpretation of this phenomenon is that enlarging one side increases the variety of normalized channel balances that can be expressed from that side, even though the global support remains confined to the same axis.

The same split dependence appears in the comparisons among 10×10, 10×20, and 20×10 (Fig. 7). Relative to 10×10, the 10×20 case is nearly unchanged in the X split but more extended in the Y split, Conversely, 20×10 remains close to 10×10 in the Y split but expands in the X split, especially in the lower part of the axis. Moreover, transposed pairs become nearly equivalent once the normalization is matched: the X split for 10×20 is almost indistinguishable from the Y split for 20×10, and the Y split for 10×20 closely mirrors the X split for 20×10. Hence, the transpose asymmetry is largely a normalization effect rather than a change in the underlying channel geometry.

Intermediate Sizes Broaden the Occupied Segment but Generate Empty Intervals. The 20×20 case (Fig. 7 e and f) is particularly informative. Relative to 10×10, the occupied segment extends further downward, so that

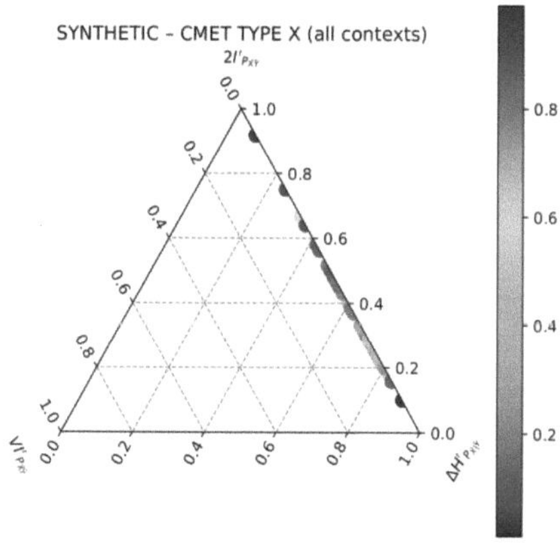

(a) 10 × 5, CMET-X.

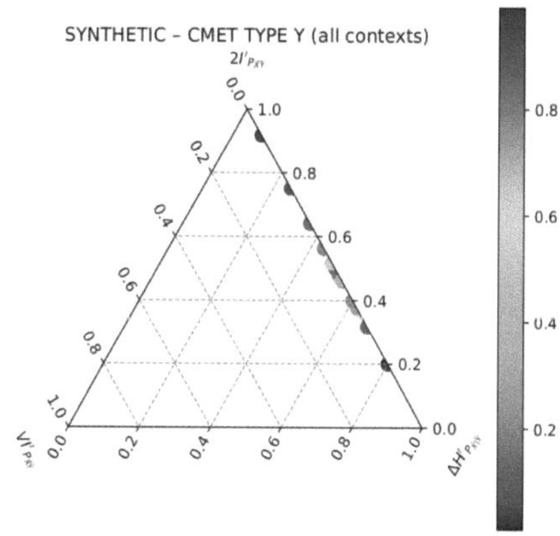

(b) 10 × 5, CMET-Y.

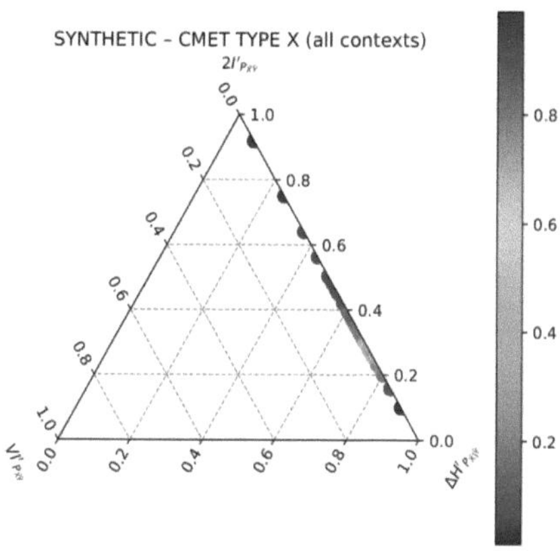

(c) 10 × 10, CMET-X.

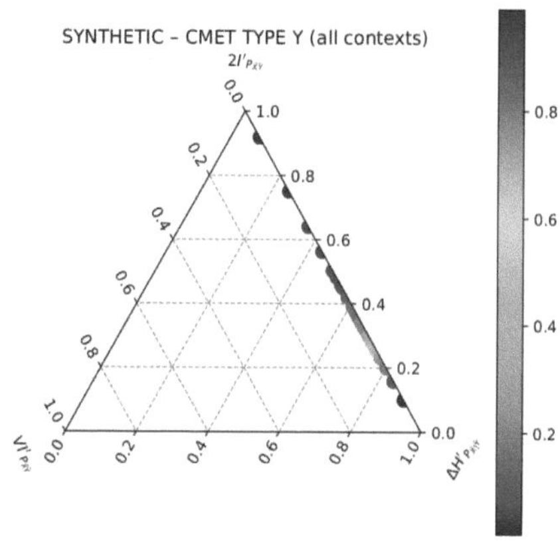

(d) 10 × 10, CMET-Y.

Fig. 6. CMET for 10 × 5 and 10 × 10 randomized contexts.

lower values of transmitted information become accessible without losing the upper part entirely. At the same time, the axis is no longer filled continuously: a clear empty interval appears just below the 0.4 level of transmitted information.

This empty interval is unlikely to be a plotting artifact. Rather, it indicates that the randomized lattice-to-entropy mapping does not generate all intermediate channel balances continuously. After the closure step, many randomized contexts collapse onto similar concept-level structures, so the resulting CMET values concentrate in separated structural regimes instead of filling the axis smoothly. In this sense, even though the CMET support is one-dimensional, its occupancy is still combinatorially constrained.

As context size increases further, the same empty interval persists but moves downward along the axis. This suggests that the inaccessible band is not fixed,

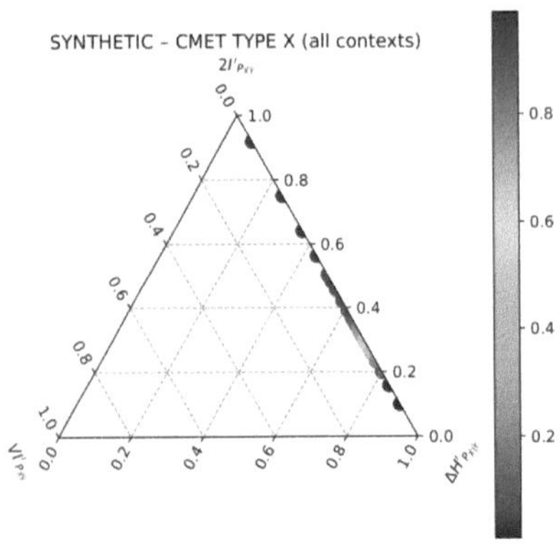

(a) 10 × 20, CMET-X.

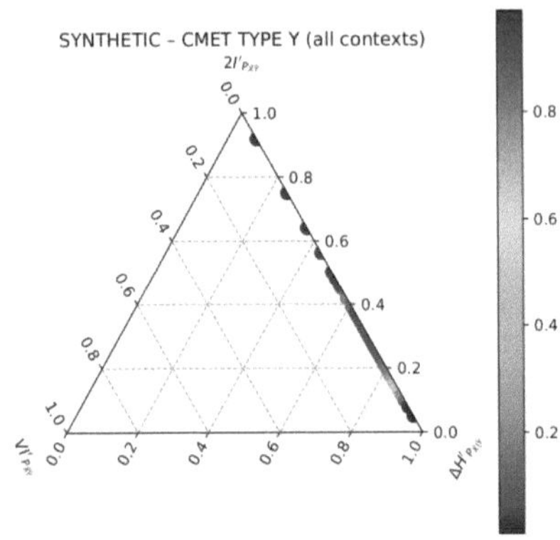

(b) 10 × 20, CMET-Y.

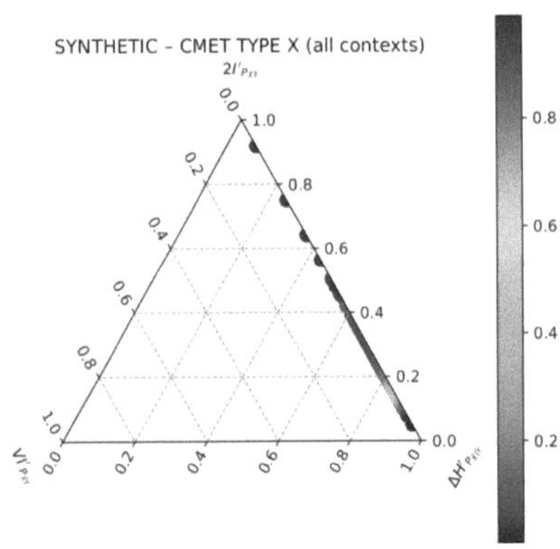

(c) 20 × 10, CMET-X.

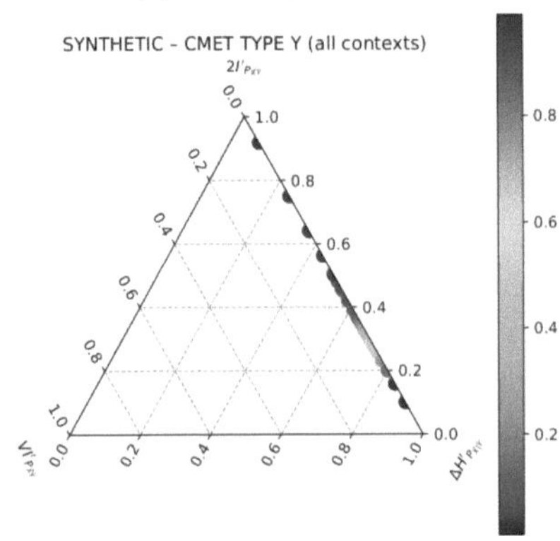

(d) 20 × 10, CMET-Y.

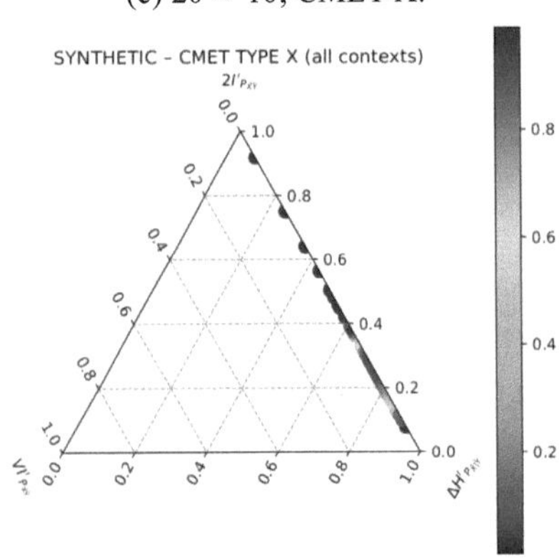

(e) 20 × 20, CMET-X.

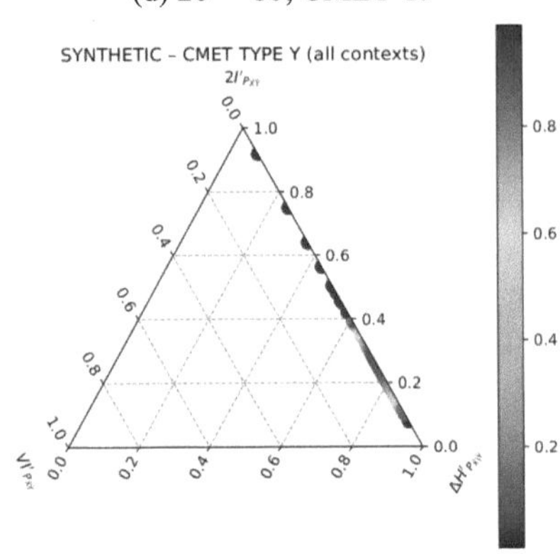

(f) 20 × 20, CMET-Y.

Fig. 7. CMET comparison for 10×20, 20×10, and 20×20 randomized contexts.

but depends systematically on context dimensions and on the corresponding normalization.

For Larger Contexts, Occupancy Shifts Downward. Beyond approximately the 20×20 regime, a second size effect becomes visible. As both dimensions continue to grow, the upper part of the occupied segment becomes progressively less populated, while the lower part gains density. This can be observed in the progression from 20×20 to 30×30 and 40×40. Figures 7 e and f and 8, where only the X variant is shown due to the fact that, for square contexts, the split X and Y CMETs are equal.

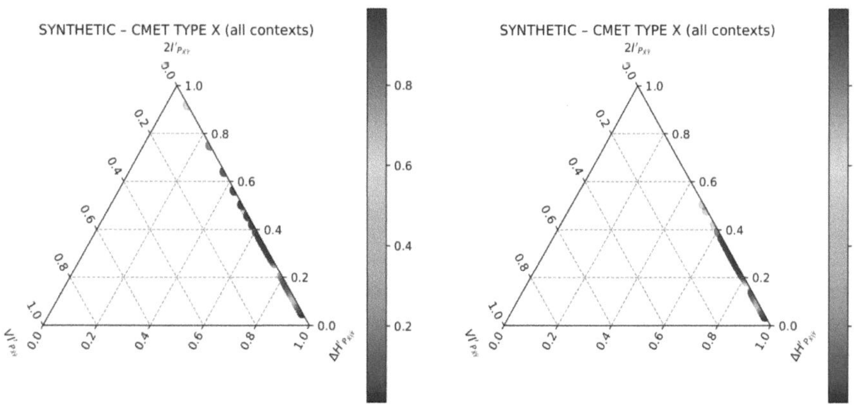

(a) 30 × 30, CMET-X.

(b) 40 × 40, CMET-X.

Fig. 8. CMET for 30×30 and 40×40 randomized contexts.

As the context size increases, the occupied CMET segment progressively shifts downward along the right-hand axis. In geometric terms, this means that larger contexts place a greater proportion of their points in regimes with lower *normalized* transmitted information and higher non-realized information. This should be read as a relative effect, not as the complete disappearance of transmission. The issue is not that larger contexts contain no structure, but that, after the FCA step and the subsequent normalization, transmitted information accounts for a smaller fraction of the total channel balance than it does in smaller or intermediate-sized contexts. In other words, with bigger contexts there is more room for potential information that ends up not being consolidated as realized or transmitted information.

The same interpretation helps explain the behaviour of the empty interval. As the whole occupied segment moves downward with increasing size, the empty interval also appears at lower positions on the axis. Thus, the downward drift of the empty interval and the progressive depopulation of the upper part of the axis are two manifestations of the same global effect: increasing context size shifts the CMET points toward lower normalized transmitted-information regimes.

The Density Parameter Orders the Channel Regimes. A second robust feature is the strong colour ordering along the occupied segment. Sparse contexts (small p, blue/purple points) accumulate near the lower-right corner, whereas denser contexts (large p, orange/red points) occupy the upper part of the axis.

At first sight, one might expect both very sparse and very dense contexts to yield low transmitted information, since both are close to uniform configurations. However, this intuition does not carry over directly to the present setting because CMET is not computed from the raw binary matrix, but from the concept-level representation obtained after FCA. Under this pipeline, near-empty and near-full contexts are not symmetric. Very sparse contexts produce little effective coupling between both sides (objects and attributes) and are therefore dominated by non-realized information. Near-full contexts, by contrast, still induce a highly coherent concept-level pairing between objects and attributes: most incidences are realized and the few missing ones generate structured deviations that remain strongly coupled across both sides. As a result, dense contexts occupy the upper part of the right-hand axis rather than collapsing downward.

Extreme Aspect Ratios Show that both Dimensions Matter. The extreme cases 10×400, 400×10, and 400×400 (Fig. 9) show that CMET cannot be characterized from only one dimension. For instance, the split X CMET for 400×10 and 400×400 are not the same, even though both are normalized on a side of size 400: the 400×400 case is much more compressed. Likewise, on the Y side, the 400×10 case still reaches around 0.4 transmitted information, whereas in 400×400 the occupied segment remains very close to zero. This indicates that the dimension of the normalized side sets the reference scale, but the opposite side still constrains how much of that scale can be expressed as transmitted information. A small opposite dimension can still sustain a non-trivial occupied segment, whereas when both dimensions are very large the CMET collapses toward the lower-right corner.

3.4 Implications for Interpreting Empirical CMET Triangles

The randomized-context CMET experiments provide a baseline for interpreting the empirical channel triangles, and the comparison between the two is presented in Fig. 10. Although points in the empirical CMETs remain in the same right-hand sector of the triangle, they are no longer confined to the axis. In the randomized baseline, this axial collapse is the structural expectation for ordinary binary formal contexts: after the FCA step, each concept couples an extent and an intent, so the two sides are mutually determined and remanent entropy is minimal. Thus, the empirical geometry is less extreme than the baseline, but also more structured. This difference is consistent with the nature of the data. In a single randomized context, each object–attribute relation is fixed once and

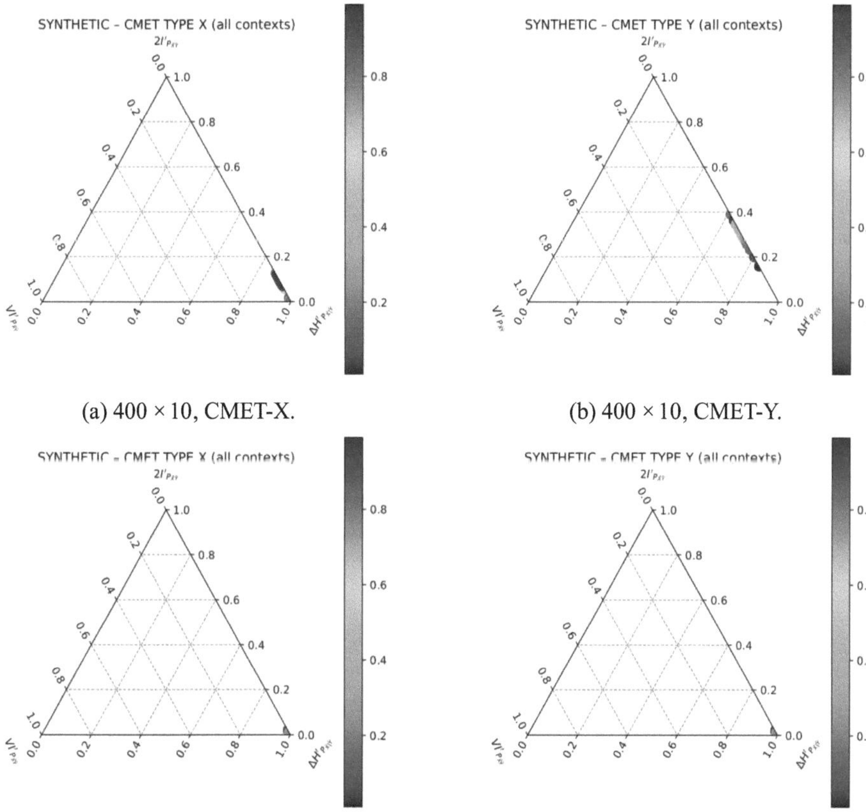

(a) 400 × 10, CMET-X.

(b) 400 × 10, CMET-Y.

(c) 400 × 400, CMET-X.

(d) 400 × 400, CMET-Y.

Fig. 9. CMET for extreme-aspect-ratio and large randomized contexts.

for all, so mutual determination is total. In the empirical setting, however, the same odorant–neuron relation is observed across multiple worms and activation levels. A given pair may therefore be active in some observations and inactive in others, introducing genuine channel variability. This reduces perfect mutual determination and allows the empirical CMET to move away from the axis.

The colour ordering is also informative, but it differs across the two empirical sides. In these figures, colour encodes the threshold parameter φ, with low φ producing denser contexts and higher, stricter φ producing sparser ones. On the neuron side, represented by the split Y CMET, the progression is broadly monotone, apart from a few small negative values attributable to numerical or estimation noise. These negative values correspond to what we call hallucinated structure in the information-theoretic sense: apparent output-side organization that is not sufficiently supported by the input side of the channel, rather than a biological claim about the animal. Lower-φ points lie higher, whereas stricter thresholds shift the points downward. Biologically, this suggests that

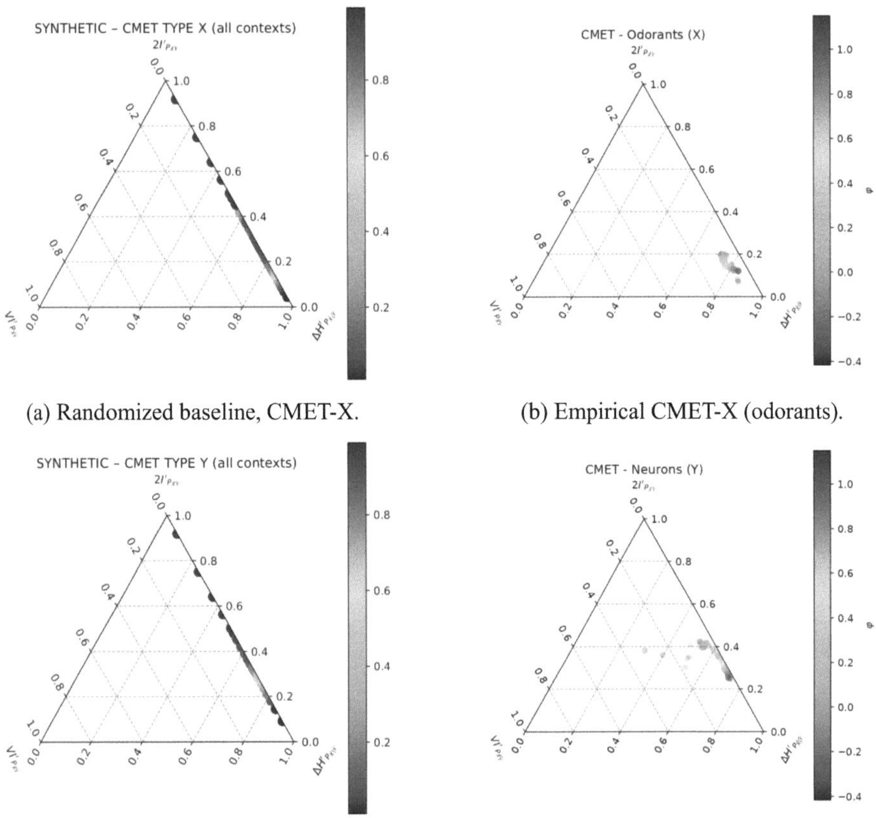

(a) Randomized baseline, CMET-X.

(b) Empirical CMET-X (odorants).

(c) Randomized baseline, CMET-Y.

(d) Empirical CMET-Y (neurons).

Fig. 10. Randomized baseline vs. empirical CMET for the 23×11 case.

as φ becomes more restrictive, less information effectively reaches the neuron side of the channel. On the odorant side, in the X split CMET, in contrast, the progression is non-monotone: the trajectory starts near the lower-right corner, moves through an intermediate band, and returns close to the same corner. This suggests that odorants transmit comparatively little information both at very low and at very high φ, with a more informative regime only at intermediate thresholds. A plausible explanation is that low φ yields overly dense contexts, where odorants become less discriminative because many induce similar neuronal patterns, whereas high φ yields overly sparse contexts, where too little structure remains to sustain effective transmission.

Overall, the randomized 23×11 CMET baseline shows the structural expectation for the FCA pipeline: collapse onto the right-hand axis with density-driven ordering. The empirical CMETs remain compatible with that baseline, but deviate from it in a meaningful way. Therefore, they are not explained solely by the combinatorics of the FCA pipeline, but also reflect the particularities and nature of the data.

4 Discussion

The main outcome of this work is that entropy-triangle occupancies obtained from FCA-derived representations are strongly constrained by the combinatorics of the pipeline. Even when the incidence tables are fully randomized, the resulting SMET and CMET geometries are far from uniform. This confirms that entropy triangles should not be interpreted directly as free geometric summaries of the data: part of their structure is already imposed by the closure transformation and by the subsequent entropy mapping.

For SMET, the randomized baseline reveals a rich but highly constrained geometry. The most prominent feature is the appearance of narrow radial trajectories, or rays, which persist across all tested sizes. Their robustness shows that this ray-like organization is not a distinctive signature of any empirical dataset, but a structural consequence of the lattice-to-entropy mapping under randomization. At the same time, the support is not determined simply by the total number of cells $n \cdot m$. Instead, the smaller dimension $\min(n, m)$ acts as the main bottleneck: increasing the larger dimension alone produces strong saturation, whereas increasing the smaller one opens new rays and extends the feasible region. In this sense, the randomized SMET baseline shows that accessibility in the simplex is governed primarily by dimensional constraints on the closure system.

For CMET, the randomized baseline is much more rigid. Across all tested sizes, occupancy collapses onto the right-hand axis, reflecting the fact that in an ordinary binary formal context each object–attribute relation is instantiated only once and is therefore fully fixed. The interesting structure in CMET does not come from a two-dimensional support, but from how occupancy is distributed along that axis. Here again, size matters, but in a different way: the effect is split-dependent in rectangular contexts, transposed pairs become nearly equivalent once normalization is taken into account, and beyond intermediate sizes the occupied segment shifts downward, indicating a relative loss of transmitted information in normalized terms. The appearance and displacement of empty intervals further suggest that even this one-dimensional support is not filled continuously, but is itself combinatorially constrained.

Taken together, these results provide a null reference for interpreting empirical entropy triangles. In the *C. elegans* case study, the empirical SMETs remain compatible with the randomized feasible region, but occupy it more selectively and exhibit clearer, more coherent trajectories as φ varies. The CMET comparison is even more informative: while the randomized baseline for a 23×11 context remains confined to the right-hand axis, the empirical CMETs move into the interior of the triangle. This shows that the multi-worm setting introduces a form of channel variability that is absent from single randomized binary contexts, reducing perfect mutual determination and producing genuinely non-trivial transmission regimes.

From a methodological perspective, this study highlights the importance of distinguishing between *structurally attainable* and *empirically occupied* regions of entropy triangles. Without such a baseline, one could easily misinterpret rays, empty regions, or density gradients as domain-specific, when in fact they arise from the FCA-based construction. The baseline therefore plays the same role as a null model in other areas of data analysis: it establishes which geometric features should be regarded as expected, and which departures deserve biological or domain-specific interpretation.

Beyond the specific randomized ensembles considered here, the broader contribution of this work is methodological. It shows that entropy-triangle geometries obtained from FCA-derived representations must be read against an explicit structural baseline: some features, such as SMET rays or the one-dimensional collapse of CMET, are generic consequences of the FCA-to-entropy pipeline, whereas others reflect the particular organization of the data. Future work should relate the observed SMET rays and CMET empty intervals more explicitly to properties of the underlying closure systems and compare this minimal Bernoulli baseline with richer null models. For the *C. elegans* case study, this will make it possible to identify more precisely which threshold-dependent triangle features exceed the geometry imposed by FCA itself.

Acknowledgements. This work was funded by Grants PID2021-125780NB-I00 and PID2024-158251NB-C31 funded by MICIU/AEI/10.13039/501100011033 and, by "ERDF/EU".

References

1. Felde, M., Hanika, T., Stumme, G.: Null models for formal contexts. Information **11**(3), 135 (2020). https://doi.org/10.3390/info11030135
2. Formica, A.: Concept similarity in formal concept analysis: an information content approach. Knowl.-Based Syst. **21**(1), 80–87 (2008)
3. Formica, A., Taglino, F.: An Enriched Information-Theoretic Definition of Semantic Similarity in a Taxonomy. IEEE Access **9**, 100583–100593 (2021). https://doi.org/10.1109/ACCESS.2021.3096598. https://ieeexplore.ieee.org/abstract/document/9483871
4. Ganter, B., Wille, R.: Formal Concept Analysis: Mathematical Foundations. Springer, Berlin, Heidelberg (1999)
5. Kuznetsov, S.O., Obiedkov, S.A.: Comparing performance of algorithms for generating concept lattices. J. Exp. Theoretical Artif. Intell. **14**(2–3), 189–216 (2002). https://doi.org/10.1080/09528130210164170
6. Lin, A., et al.: Functional imaging and quantification of multineuronal olfactory responses in C. elegans. Sci. Adv. **9**(9), eade1249 (2023). https://doi.org/10.1126/sciadv.ade1249
7. Reyner-Fuentes, E., Peláez-Moreno, C., Valverde-Albacete, F.J.: Qualitative and quantitative analyses of C. elegans' perception with concept lattices as information channels. In: Cellier, P., Ganter, B., Missaoui, R. (eds.) Conceptual Knowledge Structures: Second International Joint Conference, CONCEPTS 2025, Cluj-Napoca, Romania, 8–12 September 2025, Proceedings, pp. 264–280. Lecture Notes

in Computer Science, Springer, Cham (2025). https://doi.org/10.1007/978-3-032-03364-2_17
8. Shannon, C.E.: A mathematical theory of Communication. Bell Syst. Tech. J. XXVI **I**(3), 379–423 (1948). https://doi.org/10.1002/j.1538-7305.1948.tb00917.x
9. Valverde-Albacete, F.J., Peláez-Moreno, C.: The evaluation of data sources using multivariate entropy tools. Expert Syst. Appl. **78**, 145 – 157 (2017). https://doi.org/10.1016/j.eswa.2017.02.010
10. Valverde-Albacete, F.J., Peláez-Moreno, C.: Assessing information transmission in data transformations with the channel multivariate entropy triangle. Entropy **20**(7), 498 (2018). https://doi.org/10.3390/e20070498
11. Valverde-Albacete, F.J., Peláez-Moreno, C.: A framework for supervised classification performance analysis with information-theoretic methods. IEEE Trans. Knowl. Data Eng. **32**(11), 2075–2087 (2020). https://doi.org/10.1109/TKDE.2019.2915643

Themes and Variations in Integrating Clustering in FCA

Jaume Baixeries[1], Alexandre Bazin[2], Jérome David[3], and Amedeo Napoli[4](✉)

[1] Computer Science Department, Universitat Politécnica de Catalunya, Barcelona 08034, Catalonia
jbaixer@cs.upc.edu
[2] Université de Montpellier, CNRS, LIRMM, 34095 Montpellier, France
alexandre.bazin@lirmm.fr
[3] Inria, CNRS, Grenoble INP, LIG, Université Grenoble Alpes, 38000 Grenoble, France
jerome.david@inria.fr
[4] Université de Lorraine, CNRS, LORIA, 54000 Nancy, France
amedeo.napoli@loria.fr

Abstract. In this paper, we apply "Agglomerative Hierarchical Clustering" (AHC) to construct a compact and representative set of concept clusters, given an initial concept lattice. This representative set can be used for various purposes, e.g., interactive navigation and interpretation of the components of a possibly large concept lattice. The results of the AHC process depend on the choice of its parameters and other decisions in the design of the algorithm which is detailed below. Actually we continue in this paper an on-going research work started in previous papers, where we presented an original AHC algorithm. Here, we study in depth specific aspects that were not discussed and analyzed previously, namely: (i) the dissimilarity measure, (ii) the linkage criterion, and (iii) constraints about the content of a cluster. The results that are presented in this paper extend and complete our previous proposal and open the way to further open questions concerning a relevant problem in the field of FCA: the compact and comprehensive representation of complex structures like concept lattices.

Keywords: Formal Concept Analysis · Concept Lattice Representation · Agglomerative Hierarchical Clustering · Representative Set of Concepts · Preservation of the Lattice Ordering · Lattice Reduction

1 Introduction

The general objective of this paper is to analyze different ways of applying Agglomerative Hierarchical Clustering (AHC [14,16]) in Formal Concept Analysis (FCA) for reducing a concept lattice into a set of clusters of concepts, allowing an analyst interactive navigation, information retrieval, and cluster interpretation. The content of this paper is both theoretical and practical, where the final

M. Croitoru et al. (Eds.): CONCEPTS 2026, LNAI 16811, pp. 210–225, 2027.
https://doi.org/10.1007/978-3-032-34742-8_14

ambition is to provide an operational zooming facility for exploring a possibly large concept lattice.

This paper is a follow-up of preceding papers about the discovery of identity links in RDF datasets [1,2,4]. Below we briefly recall the history of the paper, going back to the discovery of link keys in RDF data. A link key can be seen as a rule for identifying pairs of individuals that represent the same real-world entity in two different RDF datasets. Link keys are based on "maximal sets of conditions" that can be discovered thanks to FCA [10], where they correspond to concept intents in a specific concept lattice. The conditions related to a link key are materialized by the intent of the corresponding concept while the pairs of identified individuals constitute the extent of the concept. As in every data mining problem, the number of link keys can be very large and makes their interpretation quite hard. Then the natural question of compacting the results arises, stated as the design of a representative set of link keys preserving a maximal number of identity links and providing interpretation capabilities to a domain analyst. A first lattice reduction solution was proposed in [1], where a concept lattice representing link keys was built and reduced thanks to partition pattern structures and crisp set equality. Then an alternative solution relaxing crisp set equality and replacing it by a similarity was proposed to build a partition of concept subsets [2,4].

Here we start a systematic review of the main constraints related to a reference AHC algorithm to be applied to the splitting of a concept lattice into a set of clusters composed of concepts. This algorithm constitutes a basis for discussion and allow us to examine the possible and admissible variations of the algorithm with respect to our goal. Following the tracks presented in [4], the AHC process supports the construction of a compact and representative set of concept clusters for offering interactive data analysis and interpretation capabilities. Finding such a representative set relies on various constraints related to the particularities of the data, here a concept lattice, and to the AHC process. As input the clustering algorithm takes a concept lattice, a dissimilarity or a distance measure, and a linkage criterion or linkage function. As output the algorithm returns a set of clusters from which a representative set can be issued in fulfilling a number of constraints, mainly related to the preservation of the original data, i.e., minimization of information loss and in particular of the original individuals and their attributes, and preservation of the lattice ordering.

The present approach relates AHC and FCA in a simple and practical way, and outputs a reliable and interpretable condensed representation of a concept lattice. Among the possible applications, we can list data exploration with variable precision, concept lattice reduction, concept interpretation, and knowledge representation in a particular domain. In a more general setting, such a clustering process can be considered as a general method for building a condensed representation of a collection of subsets of elements organized into an ordinal structure, depending on the links existing between these subsets.

The organization of the paper is as follows: in Sect. 2 we discuss the different choices and constraints that are analyzed in this paper. In Sect. 3 we discuss the nature of the output generated by our algorithm and we also present and characterize different dissimilarity measures that are used in our algorithm. Section 4 presents and discusses the experiments that have been performed according to the considerations explained in this paper.

2 Themes and Variations

In our preceding study [4], we proposed a number of choices and constraints related to the clustering process that were not sufficiently discussed and justified. Here we would like to more deeply study and discuss these choices, to evaluate their relevance, and to propose alternatives that could provide different results and open the road to novel interpretations and generalizations. Before listing the main themes and related variations that are developed in this paper, we would like to recall what are the parameters of the AHC process that are questionable.

A clustering process based on AHC takes as inputs a dataset D, a dissimilarity or distance function, and a linkage function that is defined in terms of the dissimilarity [9]. The clustering process begins with all elements in D considered as singleton clusters, at level 0 in the output, actually a dendrogram or binary tree. Then the process searches for pairs of clusters X and Y achieving the lowest linkage ℓ, select –in case of a tie– and merge one pair X and Y, and create a new cluster $X \cup Y$ at level ℓ in the output. The clustering process continues until all elements in the dataset are in one final cluster and returns the dendrogram with the linkage levels being constructed. Moreover, a dissimilarity table recording the dissimilarity between data elements at initialization or the linkage between those elements, should be updated after every merge. Thus there are three main degrees of freedom that can be varied, the dissimilarity measure, the linkage function, and the global constraints related to the clustering process such as the management of ties or the preservation of objects or of an ordering between elements.

- In the present case, the input of the AHC process is a concept lattice, while a sublattice or a poset of concepts could be acceptable.
- The dissimilarity measure is based on the Jaccard similarity score applied to objects sets. Here there are many variations, in particular involving both objects and attributes, contrasting preceding choices, e.g., $\alpha \times diss(extents) + (1-\alpha) \times diss(intents)$ or the area of a concept, i.e., $|extents| \times |intents|$ where $|X|$ denotes the cardinality of set X. These two measures can be normalized. Other interesting variations are proposed and discussed in [8].
- Moreover, a dissimilarity measure may respect *interval monotonicity* –restricting dissimilarity to an element between two other elements does not increase the dissimilarity– and thus minimizing the updates of the dissimilarity table at each step of the AHC process. This gain of efficiency should be kept and ensured with alternative dissimilarity measures.
- Several linkage criteria are available, among them complete linkage, single linkage, average linkage, and Ward linkage. The complete linkage was selected in [4] and was well suited to the minimization of the updates of the dissimilarity table. Here we would like to check other possibilities and provide if possible a comparative study.

- In a clustering process, one often has to deal with ties at the aggregation step. In our case, the ties are randomly selected but alternatives exist as presented in [19], where ties are all agglomerated at the same time. Again, we would like to discuss this aspect and propose a more disciplined way of dealing with ties. For example, the agglomeration of ties could be related to the preservation needs attached to the clustering process.

An important constraint that we would like to impose is respecting the lattice ordering inside a cluster and among the clusters in the final cluster hierarchy. First of all, we have to make clear the meaning of respecting the lattice ordering inside and outside the clusters. Moreover, for having a correspondence between clusters and sublattices, one should use a dissimilarity measure based on a *congruence relation*. Recall that an equivalence relation θ on a lattice L is a congruence relation on L if for all $a, b, x, y \in L$, $a\theta x$ and $b\theta y$ imply $(a \wedge b)\theta(x \wedge y)$ and $(a \vee b)\theta(x \vee y)$. In particular, this is not necessarily the case for dissimilarity based on the Jaccard measure (see among others [10–12]).

The AHC process outputs a set of clusters, each one composed of a subset of concepts, that can be hierarchically organized within a dendrogram. Then, a cut level should be set for determining a final set of clusters from which a representative cluster set is determined. In addition, a cluster consists of a subset of concepts, where one specific concept may be selected as the "medoid", i.e., the barycenter minimizing the dissimilarities to all other concepts in the cluster. For example, when a cluster is composed of a chain the medoid is a concept located "in the middle" of the chain, while when the cluster is a diamond, two choices can be made, the upper or lower bound of the diamond.

As the representative cluster set is based on the selection of a cut level, it is not unique, but it may be characterized by several properties such as, (i) the size in terms of medoids, possibly related to a compression rate, (ii) the preservation involved in terms of objects and attributes, (iii) the quality of the retained clusters using for example the "Silhouette score", i.e., a kind of internal inertia [9,14]. However, these properties may be orthogonal such as size minimization and object preservation, and their concurrent optimization relies on an acceptable compromise to be reached.

3 Dissimilarity Measures

The output of the AHC algorithm is a dendrogram, a tree-like hierarchical diagram that represents the arrangement into clusters based on similarity. A horizontal cut across the dendrogram produces a partition of the data set. In our setup, this is a partition of the set of formal concepts, where each vertical branch that the cut line crosses represents a cluster. Therefore, a dendrogram over a finite set X can be seen as a family of partitions $\{\mathcal{P}_t\}_{t\geq 0}$ of X:

1. At initialization of AHC, $i = 0$ and $\mathcal{P}_0 = \big\{\{x\} \mid x \in X\big\}$, i.e., all clusters are singletons and $\mathcal{P}_0$ is the finer partition.

2. At each next step, AHC merges clusters while it never splits any cluster. When i is increasing, $\mathcal{P}_i$ is coarser than $\mathcal{P}_j$ whenever $i \geq j$.
3. There are finitely many distinct partitions or finitely many mergings.
4. At the end, all formal concepts are grouped into one single cluster $\mathcal{P}_N = \{X\}$, i.e., everything merges.

3.1 Dissimilarity Measures and Basic Equivalence Relation Properties

We now discuss the relationship between a dissimilarity measure and the structure of the equivalence relation generated by the measure in trying to answer the question: *To what extent may a dissimilarity measure predict the structural properties of the equivalence relation computed at each step by the AHC algorithm?* If we can find dissimilarity measures that *naturally* guarantee certain properties of the output, then, it is not necessary that the AHC algorithm enforces them, saving computation time and side effects.

Moreover, *what would be the optimal structural properties that these partitions should verify in order to ease their interpretation*? We would like to turn these partitions into structurally faithful views of a concept lattice and preserve as much as possible the lattice structure or, at least, an ordering over the set of clusters allowing us to reason as we do within a lattice. In order to enforce the output of the AHC algorithm, at each step we could: (a) check whether the equivalence relation determines a lattice otherwise modify it accordingly, (b) try to find a dissimilarity measure ensuring that some structural properties will be maintained along the execution of the algorithm, or (c) use both strategies, i.e., use a dissimilarity measure that is likely to maintain some structural properties in the equivalence class. In case this is not possible to maintain such structure properties, then the algorithm should modify the equivalence relation accordingly.

One possible way to ensure that the quotient space of an equivalence relation is a lattice is to force the relation to be a congruence [7,18], by trying to find distances compatible with the properties of congruences. However, this strategy has two main drawbacks. Firstly the characterization of a congruence implies that all equivalence classes have to be convex sublattices and that the quadrilateral property holds (Th. 9.5 in [3,18]). Finding dissimilarity measures compatible with these two conditions may be too difficult. Secondly, congruences are very restrictive relations for ensuring the presence of a lattice or an order, even using the same order as defined in the quotient lattice of the congruence.

For example, let us consider the following equivalence relation δ:

$$C_1 \leq C_2 \text{ if and only if there exist } x \in C_1 \text{ and } y \in C_2 \text{ with } x \leq y.$$

δ is not a congruence while its quotient space is a lattice, as shown in Fig. 1.

Can we find properties less restrictive than those of a congruence that, yet, allow us to obtain a lattice or an order? In most of the frameworks for building quotients of ordered structures in [20], *convexity* of the equivalence classes is

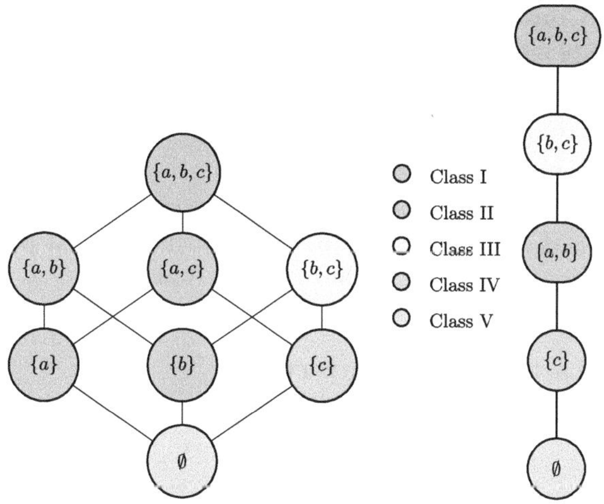

Fig. 1. Example of an equivalence relation δ that is not a congruence whose quotient set $\mathcal{P}(\{a,b,c\})/\delta$ is a chain.

either assumed as an axiom or derived as a necessary consequence. The reason is probably that, without convexity, the induced order on classes fails to be antisymmetric. Therefore, we now explore two properties that may be compatible with the idea of maintaining an order in the clustering generated by the AHC algorithm: (i) building equivalence classes that (ii) are *convex.*

Definition 1 (Ultrametric inequality).
A metric distance D satisfies the ultrametric inequality if, for all $a, b, c \in L$*:*

$$D(a,c) \leq \max\big(D(a,b),\ D(b,c)\big).$$

Firstly, the generation of equivalence relations based on distances satisfying the *ultrametric inequality* is presented in, e.g., [6]. Although the ultrametric inequality is a sufficient condition for a dissimilarity measure to generate an equivalence relation, it is not a necessary condition. An ultrametric measure ensures transitivity while this may not be the case for any generic measure. However, transitivity may be forced by considering connected components, which is exactly what single-linkage clustering does [5]. Therefore, having a dissimilarity measure that complies with the ultrametric inequality may be desirable, but not mandatory.

Given an equivalence relation, either because the dissimilarity measure satisfies the ultrametric inequality or because the linkage function forces it, let us now examine another desiderable property, i.e., interval convexity. In particular, in e.g., [17], this property is characterized as a "monometric function" with respect to an order-induced betweenness relation.

Definition 2 (Convexity).
A dissimilarity measure δ on L generates convex clusters if, for all $a, b, c \in L$, whenever $a \leq b \leq c$, we have

$$\delta(a,b) \leq \delta(a,c) \quad \textit{and} \quad \delta(b,c) \leq \delta(a,c).$$

Finally, we add an additional desirable property to the two preceding ones, called "lattice-based contractivity". This property ensures that the closest neighbor of a concept is another comparable concept. It also allows us to optimize the AHC algorithm, as shown in Sect. 4.

Definition 3 (Lattice-based contractivity).
A dissimilarity measure D on L satisfies lattice-based contractivity if, for all $a, b \in L$:

$$D(a,\ a \wedge b) \leq D(a,b) \quad \textit{and} \quad D(a,\ a \vee b) \leq D(a,b).$$

Given two incomparable elements a, b, the property states that the distance with respect to D between a and b is always larger than the distance between a and the meet $a \wedge b$ or the join $a \vee b$. For comparable elements the conditions are straightforward and impose no constraint. If $a \leq b$, then $a \wedge b = a$ and $a \vee b = b$, so $D(a,\ a \wedge b) = D(a,a) = 0$ and $D(a,\ a \vee b) = D(a,b)$; the two inequalities become $0 \leq D(a,b)$ and $D(a,b) \leq D(a,b)$ (the case $b \leq a$ is symmetric).

Above we reviewed three *desirable* and *useful* conditions that a general dissimilarity measure may have in order to generate an equivalence relation over lattice elements such that the generated classes are convex sublattices.

In [4], the AHC algorithm ensures the generation of an equivalence relation over a lattice such that equivalence classes are convex sublattices by *forcing* it, regardless of the measure that we are using. This is a mechanism that is forced every time two different clusters are merged. However, having a measure that is compliant with some of the properties reviewed above, in particular convexity, allows the algorithm not to recompute the merge of classes at each step. Thus a new question now arises: *Which dissimilarity measures can be used for ensuring that the AHC is compliant with some desirable properties introduced above?*

3.2 Jaccard-Based Distances

We start by presenting a dissimilarity measure between concepts that is popular in FCA [8], i.e., the Jaccard dissimilarity measure, where x and y denotes either both set of objects or both sets of attributes:

$$D_J(x,y) \;=\; 1 - \frac{|x' \cap y'|}{|x' \cup y'|}.$$

However popular, this measure does not verify the ultrametric property. For example, let us consider the following formal context with three objects g_1, g_2, g_3, and four attributes, m_1, m_2, m_3, and m_4.

	m_1	m_2	m_3	m_4
g_1	×	×		
g_2		×	×	
g_3			×	×

We have $D_J(g_1, g_2) = D_J(g_2, g_3) = \frac{2}{3}$, and, $D_J(g_1, g_3) = 1$. If we check the ultrametric inequality for the triple (g_1, g_2, g_3), we observe that the D_J measure does not satisfy the ultrametric inequality:

$$D_J(g_1, g_3) = 1 \not\leq \max\{D_J(g_1, g_2), D_J(g_2, g_3)\} = \max\left\{\frac{2}{3}, \frac{2}{3}\right\} = \frac{2}{3}.$$

By contrast, while the ultrametric property is not verified, lattice-based contractivity property is verified in this example.

3.3 Valuation-Based Distances

A distance between concepts can be defined using valuation functions. Below we analyze two valuation functions, namely the size of the extent and the size of the intent. Given a concept $c = (A, B)$ from a formal context (G, M, I), we consider the following valuation functions:

$$v_e(c) = |A| \qquad v_i(c) = |B|$$

Based on the Basic Theorem on Concept lattices [10], the following inequalities hold for any pair of concepts c, d:

$$\begin{aligned} v_e(c) + v_e(d) &\leq v_e(c \vee d) + v_e(c \wedge d) \\ v_i(c) + v_i(d) &\leq v_i(c \vee d) + v_i(c \wedge d) \end{aligned}$$

For example, the first inequality for concepts $c = (A, B)$ and $d = (C, D)$ reads as follows $|A| + |C| \leq |(A \cup C)''| + |A \cap C|$, and the second as $|B| + |D| \leq |B \cap D| + |(B \cup D)''|$. The extent of the join of two concepts, say c_1 and c_2, is the closure of the union of the extents of c_1 and c_2, and the intent of the meet is the closure of the union of the intents of c_1 and c_2. It is therefore possible to define the following normalized distances [13]:

$$\begin{aligned} \delta_e(c, d) &= 1 - \frac{v_e(c \wedge d)}{v_e(c) + v_e(d) - v_e(c \wedge d)} \\ \delta_i(c, d) &= 1 - \frac{v_i(c \vee d)}{v_i(c) + v_i(d) - v_i(c \vee d)} \end{aligned}$$

The metrics δ_e and δ_i do not verify the ultrametric property and they only satisfy one of the conditions of lattice-based contractivity (see Definition 3):

$$\begin{aligned} \delta_e(c, c \wedge d) &\leq \delta_e(c, d) \\ \delta_i(c, c \vee d) &\leq \delta_i(c, d) \end{aligned}$$

However, δ_e and δ_i satisfy the convexity property (Definition 2) and for any pair of concepts c, d it comes:

$$\delta_e(c,d) \leq \delta_e(c \vee d, c \wedge d) \quad \text{and} \quad \delta_i(c,d) \leq \delta_i(c \vee d, c \wedge d)$$

The convexity property guarantees that the distance between two concepts within a lattice L is bounded by the distance between the supremum and the infimum of the two concepts in L.

The fact that δ_e and δ_i satisfy one of the conditions of lattice-based contractivity and also the convexity property implies that the closest concept of a concept is in its upper or lover cover. This allows to optimize the AHC algorithm by reducing the number of dissimilarity values to compute as shown in [4].

Moreover, the lattice-based contractivity can be enforced if the metrics δ_e and δ_i are replaced by the following functions:

$$\delta_{e\vee}(c,d) = \delta_e(c \vee d, c \wedge d) = 1 - \frac{v_e(c \wedge d)}{v_e(c \vee d)}$$
$$\delta_{i\wedge}(c,d) = \delta_i(c \vee d, c \wedge d) = 1 - \frac{v_i(c \vee d)}{v_i(c \wedge d)}$$

The functions $\delta_{e\vee}$ and $\delta_{i\wedge}$ are dissimilarity measures but not metrics because they do not satisfy triangle inequality. Moreover, these measures are still compatible with the AHC algorithm and $\delta_{e\vee}$ was used in [4].

3.4 Combining Intent-Based and Extent-Based Dissimilarity

For comparing concepts comparing it can be useful to examine both their intent and their extent. This can be achieved by combining measures working on intents and on extents. However, in such a case, which properties of the underlying measures are still preserved? We will introduce below two ways combining either the pair of measures $(\delta_1, \delta_2) = (\delta_e, \delta_i)$ or the pair $(\delta_1, \delta_2) = (\delta_{e\vee}, \delta_{i\wedge})$:

$$\Delta_{\cup}^{\delta_1,\delta_2}(c,d) = \delta_1(c,d) + \delta_2(c,d) - \delta_1(c,d) \times \delta_2(c,d) \quad \text{(probabilistic union)}$$
$$\Delta_{L^2}^{\delta_1,\delta_2}(c,d) = \sqrt{\frac{\delta_1(c,d)^2 + \delta_2(c,d)^2}{2}} \quad (\text{L}^2\text{-norm})$$

When δ_e and δ_i are combined together with some function or norm, none of the conditions for lattice-based contractivity can be guaranteed. The combination of metrics based on a L^p-norm is still a metric while the probabilistic union does not preserve triangle inequality. In addition, as L^p-norms are additive, they preserve the convexity property.

Combining measures based on extent and intent thanks to probabilistic union allows one to define a dissimilarity measures over the maximal rectangles related to concepts. Figure 2 shows the maximal rectangles of concepts c and d, their meet $c \wedge d$ and their join $c \vee d$. $\Delta_{\cup}^{\delta_e,\delta_i}$ uses the ratio of the area common to the

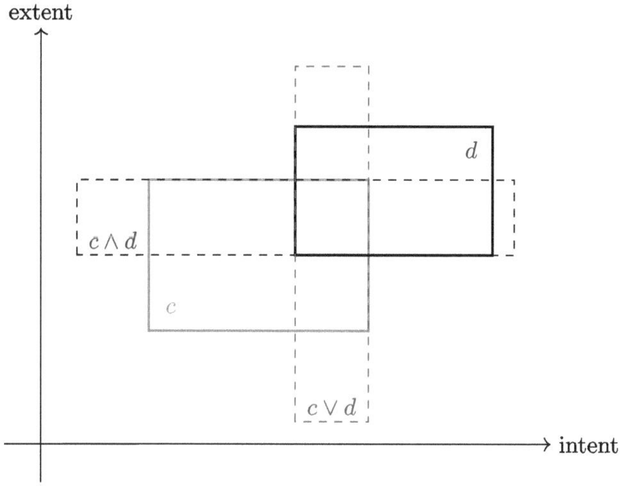

Fig. 2. Maximal rectangles involving two formal concepts c and d, their meet and their join.

rectangles associated with concepts c and d to the area of the minimal rectangle enclosing those of c and d. $\Delta_{\cup}^{\delta_{e\vee},\delta_{i\wedge}}$ divides the area of the common rectangle by the area of the rectangle containing $c \vee d$ and $c \wedge d$.

It can be shown that $\Delta_{\cup}^{\delta_e,\delta_i}$ preserves the convexity property:

Proposition 1. *For $a \leq b \leq c$, we have that:*
(i) $\Delta_{\cup}^{\delta_e,\delta_i}(a,b) \leq \Delta_{\cup}^{\delta_e,\delta_i}(a,c)$, and (ii) $\Delta_{\cup}^{\delta_e,\delta_i}(b,c) \leq \Delta_{\cup}^{\delta_e,\delta_i}(a,c)$.

Proof. For concepts $x \leq y$ we have $x \wedge y = x$ and $x \vee y = y$, thus

$$1 - \delta_e(x,y) = \frac{v_e(x)}{v_e(y)} \text{ and } 1 - \delta_i(x,y) = \frac{v_i(y)}{v_i(x)}.$$

Therefore, we obtain:

$$1 - \Delta_{\cup}^{\delta_e,\delta_i}(x,y) = (1 - \delta_e(x,y)) \times (1 - \delta_i(x,y)) = \frac{v_e(x)}{v_e(y)} \times \frac{v_i(y)}{v_i(x)}.$$

Now, given concepts $a \leq b \leq c$, we have to prove

$$1 - \Delta_{\cup}^{\delta_e,\delta_i}(a,c) = \frac{v_e(a)}{v_e(c)} \times \frac{v_i(c)}{v_i(a)} \leq \frac{v_e(a)}{v_e(b)} \times \frac{v_i(b)}{v_i(a)} = 1 - \Delta_{\cup}^{\delta_e,\delta_i}(a,b).$$

This inequality holds because from the increasing concepts $b \leq c$ we obtain decreasing intents, i.e., $v_e(a) \times v_i(c) \leq v_e(a) \times v_i(b)$, and increasing extents, i.e., $v_e(c) \times v_i(a) \geq v_e(b) \times v_i(a)$.

The other inequality can be shown analogously. □

Table 1. Statistics about the datasets considered in the experiments.

dataset	#concepts	#attributes	#objects
abalone	254	9	64
atom-sites	1,034	12	41
bridges	1,266	12	63
fd-reduced-250k-30	351	26	313
flight-1k-30c	3,058	19	288
flights-20-500k	490	12	23
glass	134	10	36
iris	27	5	10
page-blocks	254	11	27
wine	117	14	76

4 Experiments

In this section, dissimilarity measures and two linkage criteria are experimentally compared. The objective is to evaluate and analyze their ability to preserve some properties within the clusters produced by the AHC algorithm, namely that a cluster is convex, is a sublattice, and is a convex sublattice.

4.1 Datasets, Algorithms and Protocol

The experiments are performed over 10 different datasets from the UC Irvine Machine Learning Repository[1] which are displayed in Table 1. Every dataset is transformed into a reduced and clarified context, possibly leading to a reduction of the initial sets of objects and attributes. The AddIntent algorithm [15] is used to compute the concept lattices whose concept count is shown in column `#concepts` in Table 1. Moreover, all experiments were conducted on a laptop equipped with an Intel(R) Core(TM) i7-10875H CPU @ 2.30GHz and 8GB of memory dedicated to the JVM.

In the experiments, the AHC algorithm for clustering concepts is based on Algorithm 1. This is a basic version of AHC that makes no assumption about the properties of the dissimilarity measure. The algorithm takes as input a lattice L, a dissimilarity measure δ, and a linkage criterion *dclust*. It calculates all dissimilarity values between all pairs of concepts (lines 4–6), then uses a greedy approach to iteratively construct the cluster hierarchy (lines 7–19).

4.2 Results and Synthesis

Comparing Dissimilarity Measures. Below we analyze results obtained over datasets for a given dissimilarity measure with complete linkage criterion. For

[1] https://archive.ics.uci.edu/.

Algorithm 1. The function FCACLUST iteratively builds the hierarchy of clusters.

```
function FCACLUST(L : a lattice, δ : a dissimilarity measure, dclust : a linkage criterion)
    values ← createMinPriorityQueue()
    ▷ Computing dissimilarity between every pairs of concepts ◁
    for {x, y} ⊆ L do
        d ← δ(x, y)
        add(values, ⟨{x}, {y}⟩, d)
    while size(values) > 1 do
        ▷ Select and merge the clusters with the smallest dissimilarity ◁
        ⟨X, Y⟩, d ← extractMin(values)
        clust ← createClust(x, y, d)
        Z ← X ∪ Y
        ▷ Update the dissimilarity values based on linkage criterion dclust ◁
        for all (⟨X′, Y′⟩, d′) ∈ values do
            if ( X = X′ or Y = X′ ) then
                add(values, ⟨Z, Y′⟩, dclust(δ, Z, Y′))
                remove(values, ⟨X′, Y′⟩)
            else if ( X = Y′ or Y = Y′ ) then
                add(values, ⟨Z, X′⟩, dclust(δ, Z, X′))
                remove(values, ⟨X′, Y′⟩)
    return extractMin(values)
```

every dissimilarity measure and every dataset, Algorithm 1 is applied to build a dendrogram, which is cut w.r.t. A threshold varying between 0 and 1 with increments of 0.1. For each cut, the proportions of convex clusters, sublattice clusters, and convex sublattice clusters are calculated. As expected, the clustering preserves the convexity and sublattice property when the cutting level is low, but the preservation declines when the clusters become larger. Convexity is generally better preserved than the sublattice property.

The charts in Figs. 3 and 4 show, for each considered dissimilarity measure, the deviations from the metric achieving the best value in the case under study (cut level, dataset). These deviations have been averaged across all datasets. The lower the curve, the closer the dissimilarity measure is to the best performer.

Figure 3 displays the results for valuation-based measures that take either the extents or the intents into account. Figure 4 focuses on metrics that combine both extents and intents. The charts on the left show the results of measures defined in terms of the union of the extents (δ_e) and the intents (δ_i), whilst those on the right show the results of measures defined in terms of the extents of the supremums ($\delta_{e\vee}$) or the intents of the infimums ($\delta_{i\wedge}$).

The most effective dissimilarity measure is $\delta_{e\vee}$ across all three criteria examined. Dissimilarity measures based on extents perform better than those based on intents. One possible explanation is that datasets under study always contain more objects than attributes. Measures using $\delta_{e\vee}$ and/or $\delta_{i\wedge}$ outperform those based on δ_e and/or δ_i. The fact that these measures satisfy both conditions of lattice-based contractivity (Definition 3) has undoubtedly a beneficial effect on the preservation of convexity and sublattices.

Measures that combine extents and intents tend to follow the behavior of the worst-performing measure, i.e., the intent-based ones. Combining them with probabilistic union ($\Delta_{\cup}$) appears to be even more sensitive than L^2-norm (Δ_{L^2}).

We also carried out the same evaluation using single linkage. As single linkage generates larger clusters more quickly, the convexity and sublattice ratios decline sooner than with complete linkage. We observed fewer differences between measures based on extent and those based on intent. Measures based on intent even perform better than those based on extent. It is interesting to notice that there is no difference between δ_e and $\delta_{e\vee}$, nor between δ_i and $\delta_{i\wedge}$.

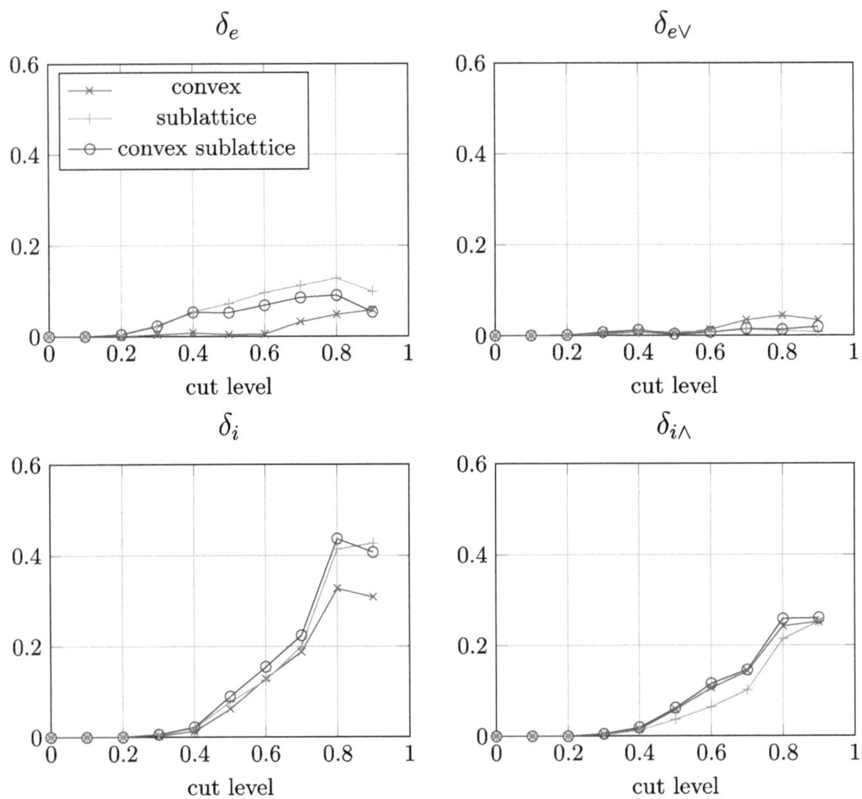

Fig. 3. Valuation-based measures: deviations from the best-performing measure (average across all datasets), the lower the better.

For summarizing, the properties of the measures influence the preservation of convexity and the sublattice property during clustering. However, the fact that the measures satisfy the convexity property and/or lattice-based contractivity is not sufficient. If we wish to guarantee convexity and the sublattice property, these criteria must therefore be incorporated into the clustering algorithm.

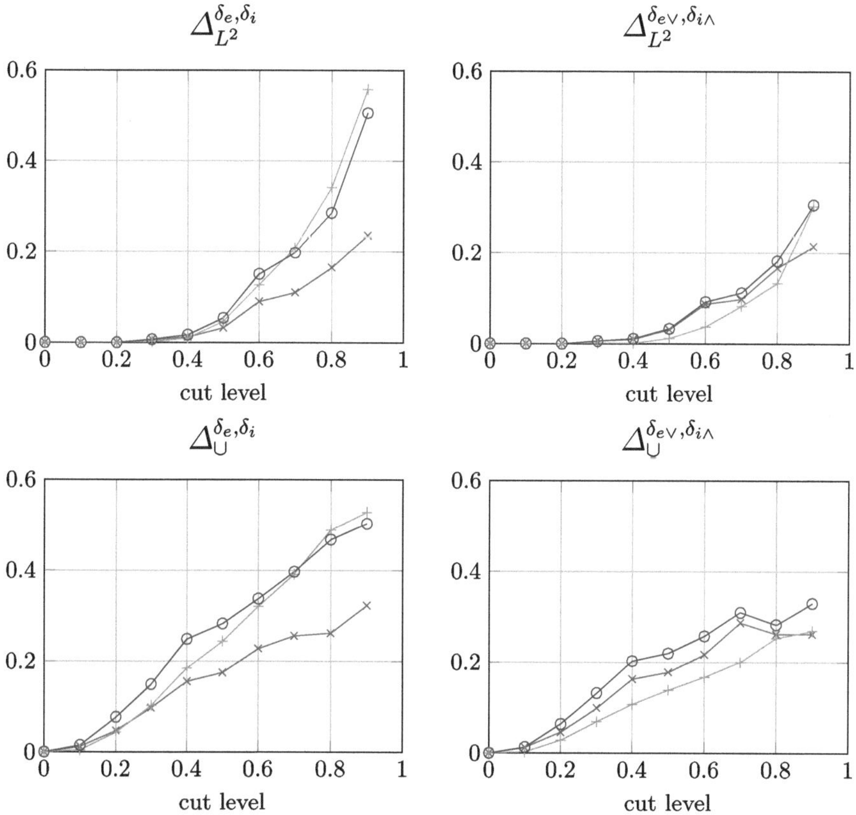

Fig. 4. Combined measures: deviations from the best-performing measure (average across all datasets), the lower the better.

Comparing Linkage Criteria. The first observation is that the dendrograms based on single linkage are more compact than those based on complete linkage, as shown in Figs. 6(a) and 6(b).

Single linkage merges elements at low thresholds and favors large clusters. Complete linkage builds more compact clusters. In Fig. 5, the chart represents the differences between the convexity rate, the sublattice preservation rate, and the convex sublattice preservation rate, calculated as averages across all datasets. Single linkage preserves convexity better than complete linkage, whereas the sublattice condition is satisfied in a better way by complete linkage. With a high cut level and the measure $\delta_{i\wedge}$, the single linkage outperforms the complete linkage on all three criteria. Indeed, at high cut levels, simple linkage builds large clusters, enabling the straightforward reconstruction of sublattices.

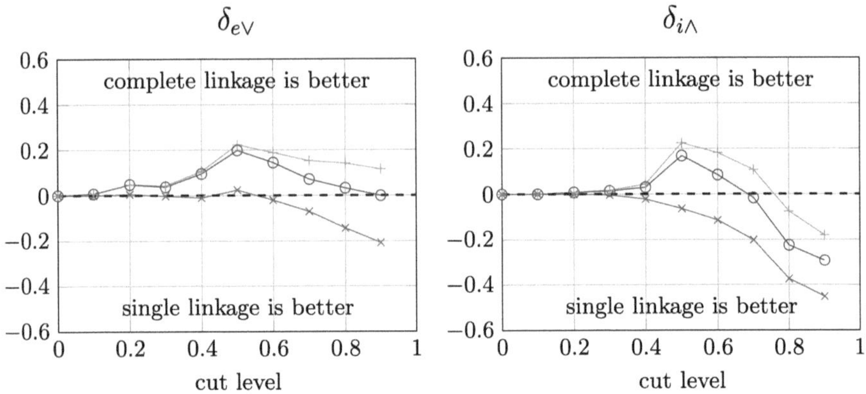

Fig. 5. Differences between complete and single linkage (average across all datasets)

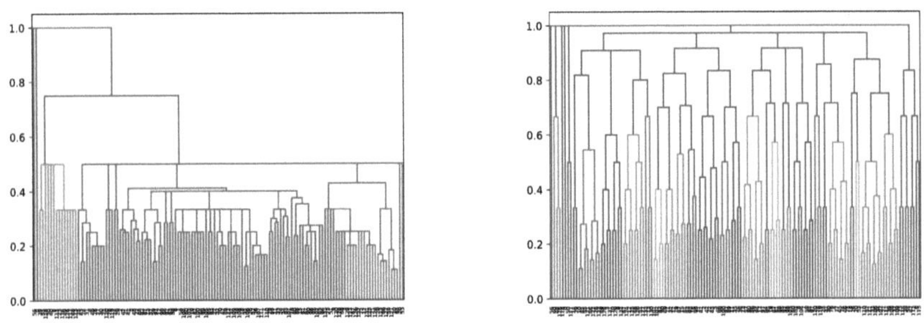

(a) Single linkage (b) Complete linkage

Fig. 6. Dendrograms obtained with $\delta_{e\vee}$ measure on Glass dataset.

Acknowledgements. Jaume Baixeries is supported by a recognition 2021SGR-Cat (01266 LQMC) from AGAUR (Generalitat de Catalunya) and the grants AGRUPS-2022 and AGRUPS-2023 from Universitat Politècnica de Catalunya. Alexandre Bazin and Amedeo Napoli are carrying out this research work as part of the French ANR-21-CE23-0023 SmartFCA Research Project.

References

1. Abbas, N., Bazin, A., David, J., Napoli, A.: Discovery of link keys in resource description framework datasets based on pattern structures. Int. J. Approximate Reasoning **161**, 108978 (2023)
2. Abbas, N., Bazin, A., David, J., Napoli, A.: Discovering a Representative Set of Link Keys in RDF Datasets. In: Proceedings of the 24th International Conference EKAW, pp. 53–68. Lecture Notes in Computer Science 15370, Springer (2024)
3. Aragón, R.G., Medina, J., Ramírez-Poussa, E.: Reducing concept lattices by means of a weaker notion of congruence. Fuzzy Sets Syst. **418**, 153–169 (2021)

4. Baixeries, J., Bazin, A., David, J., Napoli, A.: A Proposal for Building a Compact and Tunable Representation of a Concept Lattice Based on Clustering. In: Proceedings of CONCEPTS, pp. 161–177. Lecture Notes in Computer Science 15941, Springer (2025)
5. Bakkelund, D.: Order preserving hierarchical agglomerative clustering. Mach. Learn. **111**(5), 1851–1901 (2022)
6. Carlsson, G., Mémoli, F.: Characterization, stability and convergence of hierarchical clustering methods. J. Mach. Learn. Res. **11**, 1425–1470 (04 2010)
7. Davey, B.A., Priestley, H.A.: Introduction to Lattices and Order. Cambridge University Press, Cambridge (1990)
8. Domenach, F.: Similarity Measures of Concept Lattices. In: Data Science, Learning by Latent Structures, and Knowledge Discovery, pp. 89–99. Springer (2015)
9. Flach, P.A.: Machine Learning. Cambridge University Press (2012)
10. Ganter, B., Wille, R.: Formal Concept Analysis. Springer (1999)
11. Grätzer, G.: General Lattice Theory (Second Edition). Birkhäuser (2003)
12. Grätzer, G.: The Congruences of a Finite Lattice, A Proof-by-Picture Approach (Third Edition) (2023). https://arxiv.org/abs/2104.06539
13. Grimonprez, G., Van Dorpe, J.C.: Distance définie par une application monotone sur un treillis. Mathématiques et Sciences Humaines **56**, 47–62 (1977)
14. Kaufman, L., Rousseeuw, P.J.: Finding Groups in Data: an Introduction to Cluster Analysis. Wiley (2009)
15. van der Merwe, D., Obiedkov, S.A., Kourie, D.G.: AddIntent: A New Incremental Algorithm for Constructing Concept Lattices. In: Proceedings of tICFCA, pp. 372–385. Lecture Notes in Computer Science 2961, Springer (2004)
16. Murtagh, F., Contreras, P.: Algorithms for hierarchical clustering: an overview. Wiley Data Min. Knowledge Discovery **2**(1), 86–97 (2012)
17. Pérez-Fernández, R., Baets, B.D.: On the role of monometrics in penalty-based data aggregation. IEEE Trans. Fuzzy Syst. **27**(7), 1456–1468 (2019)
18. Roman, S.: Lattices and Ordered Sets. Springer (2008)
19. Siff, M., Reps, T.W.: Identifying modules via concept analysis. IEEE Trans. Software Eng. **25**(6), 749–768 (1999)
20. Williams, N.J.: A survey of congruences and quotients of partially ordered sets (2025). https://arxiv.org/abs/2303.03765

On Exhaustive Enumeration of Redescriptions

Naomi Lefrançois(✉) and Justine Reynaud

UMR 6072, Université Caen Normandie, ENSICAEN, CNRS, Normandie Univ, GREYC, 14000 Caen, France

naomi.lefrancois@unicaen.fr; justine.reynaud@unicaen.fr

Abstract. Redescription mining is a data mining task aiming at finding multiple descriptions of the same set of objects. Many methods and algorithms to mine redescriptions have been developed, most of them making use of heuristics in order to get few rules quickly. However, for certain tasks which require not only a good precision but also a high recall, it can be interesting to mine redescriptions exhaustively. In this paper, we take advantage of the Charm-L algorithm to perform this task. The Charm-L algorithm allows the exhaustive extraction of exact redescriptions. We make use of Formal Concept Analysis (FCA) to extend the Charm-L algorithm in order to mine both exact and approximate redescriptions in an exhaustive manner (with regards to given frequency and similarity thresholds), introducing pruning methods to handle the mining of approximate redescriptions without compromising on exhaustivity. We show that this task is possible in a reasonable time even for large datasets, and discuss how it can be extended.

Keywords: Redescription Mining · Rule Mining · Formal Concept Analysis · Concept Lattice

1 Introduction

Redescription mining [8,15] is a data mining task aiming at finding multiple descriptions of the same set of objects. A classic example of such a task is searching for bio-climatic niches: localities (the objects) are characterised both by climatic conditions and presence-absence records of various animal species. In this case, a redescription identifies climatic conditions (in terms of ranges of climatic variables) and groups of species, such that both are found in the same localities. The climate description helps understand the bio-climatic niche of the species.

One of the most popular algorithm to mine redescriptions is ReReMi [6]. This algorithm allows to mine redescriptions where each pattern is a linearly parsable query. Along with a few others, this algorithm can be used in Siren [7], a graphical interface which allows to mine and visualize redescriptions. Currently, redescriptions are discovered either with tree-based approaches [15], or with

M. Croitoru et al. (Eds.): CONCEPTS 2026, LNAI 16811, pp. 226–241, 2027.
https://doi.org/10.1007/978-3-032-34742-8_15

greedy-extension approaches [6]. In both cases, these methods cannot provide an exhaustive enumeration. While the exhaustive enumeration of redescriptions can be performed *ad hoc*, to the best of our knowledge, there is no work on the best way to extract them. The current strategy consists in mining patterns and then pairing the ones with a similar support. However, this approach is costly in term of time and performances, especially when it comes to complex patterns.

One of the reasons this problem has never been addressed is that most of the time, data analysts are not interested in being exhaustive: most of the research focuses on reducing the number of patterns extracted. However, in some cases, it can be useful to exhaustively enumerate exact and approximate redescriptions. This is especially justified when the data available is not very voluminous, and when domain experts require not only high precision, but also a very high recall. In humanities, for example, some corpuses are manually built by experts of the field, who find rare patterns very important (for instance, the use of a particular term in a text, even if it only appears once or twice). Therefore, in this paper, we investigate exhaustive enumeration of redescriptions.

The paper is structured as follows: in Sect. 2 we introduce basic notions of Formal Concept Analysis and Redescription Mining, along with the CHARM-L algorithm. Then we develop our main contribution in Sect. 3. We explain how we adapted CHARM-L to exhaustively enumerate redescriptions. Experimental results of our approach are presented in Sect. 4: we use seven datasets to discuss the performance and the number of redescriptions extracted. We compare our approach with the state of the art in Sect. 5. Finally, we conclude that exhaustive redescription enumeration is computationally reasonable for many datasets, and that the method can be expanded upon to allow the mining of semantically richer redescriptions in Sect. 6.

2 Formal Concept Analysis and Redescription Mining

In this work, we take advantage of the Formal Concept Analysis (FCA) [10] formalism in order to introduce Redescription Mining (RM) [15]. In this section, we briefly recall basic notions of these two frameworks.

2.1 Formal Concept Analysis

We consider datasets composed of a set of objects and a set of attributes, and a binary relation between these two sets. In this article, objects will be represented by the letter o and attributes by the letter a. If an object o is in relation with an attribute a, this means that "the object o has the attribute a" or dually that "the attribute a describes the object o". As shown in Fig. 1, we can represent such a dataset as a two column table where each row contains an object as well as the set of attributes that this object has or as a formal context.

Definition 1 (Formal context). *A formal context* $\mathbb{K}$ *is a triple* $(\mathcal{O}, \mathcal{A}, \mathcal{R})$ *where* $\mathcal{O}$ *is a set of objects,* $\mathcal{A}$ *is a set of attributes and* $\mathcal{R} \subseteq \mathcal{O} \times \mathcal{A}$ *is a binary relation.*

Object	Attributes
o_1	$a_1a_2a_3a_4$
o_2	a_3a_5
o_3	$a_1a_2a_3a_4$
o_4	$a_1a_3a_4a_5$
o_5	$a_1a_2a_3a_4a_5$
o_6	a_2

(a) Toy dataset

	a_1	a_2	a_3	a_4	a_5
o_1	×	×	×	×	
o_2			×		×
o_3	×	×	×	×	
o_4	×		×	×	×
o_5	×	×	×	×	×
o_6		×			

(b) Formal context of 1a

Fig. 1. Toy dataset with 6 objects and 5 attributes, and the associated formal context. This dataset is a slightly simplified version of the one found in [19].

Example 1. Figure 1 is a toy example of a dataset with 6 objects and 5 attributes. Looking at this dataset, we can say that the object o_2 has the attributes a_3 and a_5. We can also observe that o_2, o_4 and o_5 are all the objects that have the attribute a_5.

Definition 2 (Derivation operators). *Let $O \subseteq \mathcal{O}$ and $A \subseteq \mathcal{A}$. The derivation operators are:*

$$O' = \{a \in \mathcal{A} \mid (\forall o \in O)\ o\,\mathcal{R}\,a\} \quad \textit{and}$$
$$A' = \{o \in \mathcal{O} \mid (\forall a \in A)\ o\,\mathcal{R}\,a\};$$

O' is the set of attributes that all of the objects from O have in common while A' is the set of objects that all have the itemset A. A' is also called the **support** of the itemset A (sometimes denoted $supp(A)$) and its cardinality $|A'|$ is called the **frequency** of A. In this article, we use the letter A for itemsets and O for supports. We also simplify the notation as follows: $A = a_1a_4$ and $O = supp(A) = o_1o_3o_4o_5$.

The composition of the two derivations operators, denoted by $(.)''$ hereafter, define a relation that is reflexive, symmetric and transitive, and therefore is an equivalence relation. This relation is true for two itemsets A_1, A_2 if and only if they share the same support. This relation defines an equivalence class which groups the set of itemsets $\{A \subseteq \mathcal{A} \mid A' = O\}$ that are supported by O. Moreover, the composition of the two derivations are **closure operators**. The itemset A'' is the greatest itemset having the same support as A and is called a **closed itemset**. We can now define formal concepts.

Definition 3 (Formal concept). *A formal concept in a formal context $\mathbb{K} = (\mathcal{O}, \mathcal{A}, \mathcal{R})$ is a pair $C = (O, A)$ where $O \subseteq \mathcal{O}$, $A \subseteq \mathcal{A}$, $O' = A$ and $A' = O$. O is called the **extent** (or **support**, denoted $supp(C)$) of the concept, and A is its **intent**. We set the **frequency** as $|supp(C)| = |O|$.*

Example 2. Let us consider the itemset $A_1 = a_2a_4$. Its support is $supp(A_1) = A_1' = \{a_2a_4\}' = o_1o_3o_5$, which means that the 3 objects o_1,o_3 and o_5 are all described by the itemset a_2a_4 and that the frequency of A_1 is $|supp(A_1)| = 3$.

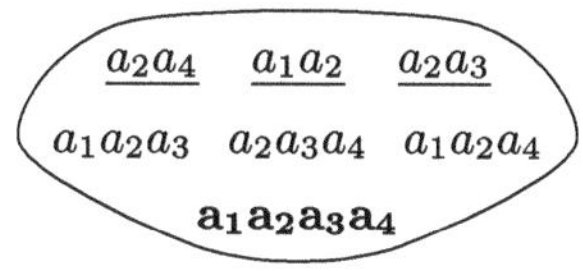

Fig. 2. Equivalence class of the formal concept $C = (o_1o_3o_5, a_1a_2a_3a_4)$, showing every itemset of the class. The closed itemset is in bold and the minimal generators are underlined.

The itemset A_1 belongs to the equivalence class $\{A \subseteq \mathcal{A} \mid A' = o_1o_3o_5\}$. Several other itemsets such as $A_2 = a_1a_2a_3a_4$ and $A_3 = a_1, a_2, a_3$ belong to the same equivalence class because they are also supported by $o_1o_3o_5$. This equivalence class is depicted in Fig. 2.

Since $A_2'' = A_2$, A_2 is the closed itemset of the equivalence class $\{A \subseteq \mathcal{A} \mid A' = o_1o_3o_5\}$. We have $supp(A_2) = supp(a_1a_2a_3a_4) = o_1o_3o_5$ and $(o_1o_3o_5)' = a_1a_2a_3a_4$. Therefore, the pair $(O_2, A_2) = (supp(A_2), A_2)$ is a formal concept.

The formal concepts can be ordered into a concept lattice. The concept lattice of the toy dataset is depicted in Fig. 3.

Definition 4 (Concept lattice). *Given two different concepts $C_1 = (E_1, I_1)$ and $C_2 = (E_2, I_2)$, we say that C_1 is a* ***subconcept*** *of C_2 iff $E_1 \subseteq E_2$ (which is equivalent to $I_2 \subseteq I_1$). Reciprocally, we say that C_2 is a* ***superconcept*** *of C_1 iff $E_1 \subseteq E_2$ (which is equivalent to $I_2 \subseteq I_1$). These relations define a partial order on formal concepts.*

The ordered set of all concepts of a formal context $\mathbb{K} = (\mathcal{O}, \mathcal{A}, \mathcal{R})$ is called the ***concept lattice*** *of $\mathbb{K}$ and is denoted $\mathcal{B}(\mathcal{O}, \mathcal{A}, \mathcal{R})$.*

A closed itemset is the maximal generator of the intent of a formal concept. We can also consider the minimal elements of a formal concept, which there can be several for a single formal concept. We will see later that they are good candidates for forming redescriptions.

Definition 5 (Generator, minimal generator). *Let A_0 be a closed itemset. The itemset A is a* ***generator*** *of A_0 if and only if $A'' = A_0$. Said otherwise, any member of the equivalence class $eq(A_0)$ is a generator of A_0.*

A generator A_1 is said ***minimal*** *if there exists no itemset A_2 such that $A_2'' = A_0$ and $A_2 \subset A_1$.*

In this article, we often consider the relation between a formal concept and the minimal generators from the same equivalence class. For the sake of simplicity, hereafter, we refer to "minimal generators of the formal concept" instead of minimal generators of the equivalence class given by the extent of this formal concept.

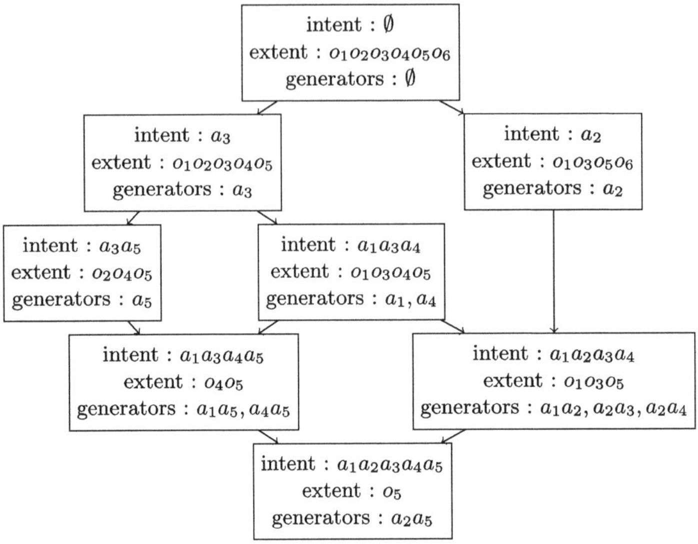

Fig. 3. Concept lattice from dataset from Fig. 1, along with the minimal generators of each formal concept

2.2 Redescription Mining

Redescription mining was introduced in 2004 by [15]. This task resembles the more known association rule mining task, as introduced by [1] in 1993. The goal of association rule mining is to mine rules in a dataset under the form $A \rightarrow B$, or "A implies B", where A and B are two itemsets.

In redescription mining, the goal is also to mine rules, but the nature of the rules are different. Intuitively, a redescription is a pair of descriptions that describe *almost the same* objects. That is, we are looking for equivalences ("A is equivalent to B") rather than implications. A redescription, denoted $A \equiv B$, means that $A \rightarrow B$ and $B \rightarrow A$, where A and B are two itemsets.

Definition 6 (Redescription). *Let $A_1 = \{a_1^1, ..., a_1^n\}$ and $A_2 = \{a_2^1, ..., a_2^l\}$ be two itemsets where $A_1 \neq A_2$, θ_s a similarity threshold and θ_f a frequency threshold. The pair $R = (A_1, A_2)$ is a* ***redescription*** *iff $sim(A_1, A_2) \geq \theta_s$ and $freq(A_1, A_2) \geq \theta_f$, where $sim(A_1, A_2) = \frac{|supp(A_1) \cap supp(A_2)|}{|supp(A_1) \cup supp(A_2)|}$ is the* ***similarity*** *of (A_1, A_2) and $freq(A_1, A_2) = |supp(A_1) \cap supp(A_2)|$ is its* ***frequency****. We write $A_1 \equiv A_2$.*

This definition of the similarity of a redescription corresponds to the **Jaccard index** of their respective supports, a statistic commonly used to measure the accuracy of a redescription. Its range is $[0, 1]$. If $J(R) = 1$, R is an **exact** redescription, which means that all the objects described by the itemset A_1 are also described by the itemset A_2. Otherwise, R is an **approximate** redescription. Based on this definition, we also define the similarity between two formal concepts $C_1 = (O_1, A_1)$ and $C_2 = (O_2, A_2)$ as the Jaccard index of their extent: $sim(C_1, C_2) = \frac{|O_1 \cap O_2|}{|O_1 \cup O_2|}$.

Example 3. Let us consider the itemsets $A_1 = a_1a_3$ and $A_2 = a_2$. We have $J(A_1, A_2) = \frac{|o_1o_3o_5|}{|o_1o_3o_4o_5o_6|} = \frac{3}{5}$, which means that three fifths of the objects that are described by either the itemset A_1 or the itemset A_2 are described by both of the itemsets.

It worth noting that in this paper, we consider a simpler definition of redescriptions than in the state of the art (see Sect. 5). Indeed, each side of our version of a redescription is a simple conjunction of attributes, whereas we can find other approaches where (i) more complex data (numerical or nominal) is handled, (ii) descriptions are expressed in propositional logic (with the conjunction, disjunction and negation connectors) and (iii) attributes are partitioned into views, meaning there are restrictions on which side of the redescription an attribute can be.

2.3 The CharmL Algorithm

The CHARM-L [19] algorithm combines itemsets in order to efficiently build the concept lattice and extract exact redescriptions from it. To do so, CHARM-L uses Depth First Search and makes use of the notion of closed itemset to prune the search space. The algorithm can be divided into three steps: (i) building a concept lattice, (ii) finding minimal generators and (iii) building redescriptions. We describe each step below; the algorithm is explained in more details in [18] and [19].

Firstly, CHARM-L builds the concept lattice of the data. Each time it finds a new closed itemset, it adds its corresponding formal concept to a partial concept lattice. The full concept lattice is obtained after every closed itemset has been found. Secondly, CHARM-L uses the lattice in order to compute the minimal generators of every formal concept. To do so, CHARM-L computes the set differences between the intent of a concept and the intent of its direct superconcepts. It obtains several sets containing the attributes present in that concept but not in the corresponding superconcept. By computing the minimal hitting sets of those sets, CHARM-L obtains sets of attributes present in that concept but not in its direct superconcepts: those sets of attributes are minimal generators. This process is explained in more details in [19]. Finally, CHARM-L iterates over every concept one at a time, and forms every possible pair of minimal generators within that concept in order to form exact redescriptions.

Example 4. Let us consider the formal concept $C = (o_1o_3o_5, a_1a_2a_3a_4)$. Its minimal generators are $A_1 = a_1a_2$, $A_2 = a_2a_3$ and $A_3 = a_2a_4$ (*cf.* Fig. 3). The possible pairs of minimal generators are (A_1, A_2), (A_2, A_3) and (A_1, A_3), meaning we can create 3 exact redescriptions : $a_1a_2 \equiv a_2a_3$, $a_2a_3 \equiv a_2a_4$ and $a_1a_2 \equiv a_2a_4$. They are all conditional redescriptions, as at least one attribute appears in each side of the redescription. They can be denoted as follows: $a_1 \equiv a_3 \mid a_2$, $a_3 \equiv a_4 \mid a_2$

and $a_1 \equiv a_4 \mid a_2$. They mean that, if we observe a_2, then the attributes a_1 and a_3 appear in exactly the same set of objects. The same goes for a_3 and a_4 on the one hand and a_4 and a_1 on the other hand.

3 Adapting CHARM-L to Enumerate Redescriptions

We saw that CHARM-L offers a method to find exact redescriptions by pairing minimal generators within each formal concept. However, it does not handle approximate redescriptions.

In this section, we present our adaptation of CHARM-L in order to find approximate redescriptions. That is, we aim to find *every* redescription with a similarity above a given threshold. We denote this threshold θ_s.

The intuition is the following: instead of looking for pairs of generators from the same equivalence class, we are looking for two generators from different equivalence classes. This means that the two generators do not have the same support, therefore this is an approximate redescription. We pair generators from all possible pairs of concepts, whether identical or different, in order to find both exact and approximate redescriptions.

This intuition is quite trivial, and has already been depicted in [14] (although the authors do not use generators). The difficulty comes from the best way to compare equivalence classes together. We discuss two techniques to perform this task. The first consists in comparing concepts instead of generators, and the second consists in taking advantage of bounding similarity to reduce the search space.

3.1 Comparing Concepts Instead of Generators

The Jaccard index of a pair of itemsets is based on their supports. If two itemsets have the same support, then (i) they are in the same equivalence class and (ii) their Jaccard index is 1. Consequently, two generators of the same formal concept (i.e. in the same equivalence class) necessarily form an exact redescription. On a wider scale, a redescription $A \equiv B$ has the same support and the same similarity for any A_i in the same equivalence class of A and for any B_j in the same equivalence class of B. Therefore, we can consider only one representative itemset for each equivalence class.

Example 5. Let $C_1 = (o_4o_5, a_1a_3a_4a_5)$ and $C_2 = (o_1o_3o_5, a_1a_2a_3a_4)$. We can see from the concept lattice in Fig. 3 that the minimal generators of C_1 are a_1a_5 and a_4a_5, and the minimal generators of C_2 are a_1a_2, a_2a_3 and a_2a_4. Thus, we have $sim(a_1a_5, a_1a_2) = sim(a_1a_5, a_2a_3) = sim(a_1a_5, a_2a_4) = sim(a_4a_5, a_1a_2) = sim(a_4a_5, a_2a_3) = sim(a_4a_5, a_2a_4) = sim(C_1, C_2) = \frac{|E_1 \cap E_2|}{|E_1 \cup E_2|} = \frac{1}{4} = 0.25$.

So it is more efficient to create pairs of formal concepts, prune the pairs that don't satisfy the similarity threshold, and only then enumerate pairs of minimal generators from each pair of formal concepts.

3.2 Similarity Upper Bound

We can notice, based on their frequency alone, that some pairs of formal concepts cannot meet the similarity threshold.

Theorem 1. *The Jaccard index of two concepts C_1 and C_2 with a frequency of f_1 and f_2, respectively, is bounded as follows:*

$$J(C_1, C_2) \leq \frac{min(f_1, f_2)}{max(f_1, f_2)}$$

Proof. Let us consider $C_1 = (O_1, A_1)$ and $C_2 = (O_2, A_2)$, two formal concepts, and f_1 and f_2 their respective frequency.

Since $O_1 \cap O_2 \subseteq O_1$ we have that $|O_1 \cap O_2| \leq |O_1|$ and since $O_1 \cap O_2 \subseteq O_2$ we have that $|O_1 \cap O_2| \leq |O_2|$. Therefore, $|O_1 \cap O_2| \leq min(|O_1|, |O_2|)$. In a similar way, since $O_1 \cup O_2 \supseteq O_1$, we have $|O_1 \cup O_2| \geq |O_1|$, and since $O_1 \cup O_2 \supseteq O_2$, we get $|O_1 \cup O_2| \geq |O_2|$. Therefore, $|O_1 \cup O_2| \geq max(|O_1|, |O_2|)$. So (greater numerator, lower denominator):

$$J(C_1, C_2) = \frac{|O_1 \cap O_2|}{|O_1 \cup O_2|} \leq \frac{min(|O_1|, |O_2|)}{max(|O_1|, |O_2|)} = \frac{min(f_1, f_2)}{max(f_1, f_2)}$$

This means that, if we know the frequency of the concepts, we can prune the search space according to this upper bound: for every pair of concepts, if the upper bound is lower than the similarity threshold, we can ignore the candidate redescription.

Considering the dataset from Fig. 1 and using a similarity threshold $\theta_s = \frac{2}{3}$, this upper bound allows us to consider 21 pairs of concepts instead of the 36 possible pairs (a concept can be paired with itself). We show in Sect. 4 that the number of pairs of concepts strongly decreases as the similarity threshold increases.

Let $\mathcal{G}$ be the set of all formal concepts in a given lattice $\mathcal{B}(\mathcal{O}, \mathcal{A}, \mathcal{R})$[1]. Let $f_i \in \mathbb{N}$ be a frequency, e.g., one appearing among the concepts of $\mathcal{G}$. We define $G_i \subseteq \mathcal{G}$ as the set of all concepts $C \in \mathcal{G}$ satisfying $|supp(C)| = f_i$. In other words, G_i is the set of all concepts of frequency f_i.

Instead of considering every pair of formal concepts, we can consider every pair of groups (G_1, G_2). If the similarity upper bound of f_1 and f_2 is lower than the similarity threshold θ_s, we know that no pair of concepts (C_1, C_2) can meet the similarity threshold. So we only need to consider every pair of groups whose similarity upper bound is higher than the given similarity threshold. For each of those pairs of groups, we can then consider every pair of concepts, compute their similarity, and check whether this similarity meets the threshold θ_s.

[1] This set can also be defined as the carrier set, or underlying set of $\mathcal{B}$.

3.3 Implementation

Algorithm 1: Similar concepts using concept frequency

Data: A similarity threshold θ_s, a frequency threshold θ_f and all formal concepts grouped by support: $\mathcal{G} = \{G_1, \dots G_n\}$ where G_i is the set of formal concepts $C = (O, A)$ of frequency f_i

Result: A set $\mathcal{P}$ of triples $(C_i, C_j, sim(C_i, C_j))$ where $sim(C_i, C_j) \geq \theta_s$

1. $\mathcal{P} \leftarrow \emptyset$
2. **foreach** $G_i \in \mathcal{G}$ *where* $f_i > \theta_f$ **do**
3. $f_{min} = \lceil f_i * \theta_s \rceil$
4.   **foreach** $G_j \in \mathcal{G}$ *where* $f_i \geq f_j \geq max(f_{min}, \theta_f)$ **do**
5.   **foreach** $C_k = (O_k, A_k) \in G_j$ **do**
6.   **foreach** $C_l = (O_l, A_l) \in G_k$ **do**
7.   **if** $|O_k \cap O_l| \geq \theta_f$ **then**
8. $s \leftarrow sim(C_k, C_l)$
9.   **if** $s \geq \theta_s$ **then**
10.   Add (C_k, C_l, s) to $\mathcal{P}$
11. **return** $\mathcal{P}$

Based on the considerations of the previous section, we detail our algorithm. Its implementation is publicly available at https://git.unicaen.fr/lefranc226/enumerating-redescriptions.

The first step consists in building the concept lattice. While our algorithm is meant to build the concept lattice the same way CHARM-L does, our implementation is only a reproduction from the pseudo-code included in [19]. The original CHARM-L algorithm is freely available online[2] and implemented in C++ whereas our implementation is written in Python. Because parts of the pseudo-code for the CHARM-L algorithm are not shown in [19], we modified some aspects of the algorithm while still obtaining the complete concept lattice of the data. In particular, CHARM-L uses "cidsets", which are the sets of direct supersets of an itemset, to determine whether a candidate itemset is actually closed or not. We did not implement lattice construction the same way. The groups as presented in the previous section are stored in a hash table and used to check whether a candidate itemset has the same support as an already discovered closed itemset.

The second step consists in finding all the pairs of formal concepts from the lattice that meet the similarity threshold. The pseudo-code is written in Algorithm 1. We start by selecting distinct pairs of groups (lines **2**–**4**). Based on the similarity upper bound, we compute f_{min} , a lower bound for the frequency of the second group G_j. If the frequency of G_j is inferior to f_{min}, we know for sure that the similarity between any concept from G_i and any concept of G_j will be below the similarity threshold. Once we have a pair of groups, we compare formal concepts from each group pairwise (lines **5**–**6**). We check whether the frequency of the pair of formal concepts is higher than the frequency threshold at line **7**, although a first pruning is done on groups of concepts at line **2**. Then,

[2] https://github.com/zakimjz/CHARM-L/tree/master.

the similarity of the pair is computed, and the pair is added to the result (lines **8–11**).

Our implementation of the algorithm uses the bitsets[3] package to represent itemsets. However, the python built-in frozensets could have been used instead, and might offer a similar or better performance.

4 Experiments

4.1 Datasets

We tested our algorithm on seven datasets of various size and domains (see Table 1). Three of them (`Wine`, `Yeast` and `Abalone`) are datasets from the UCI Machine Learning Repository [12]. The other four (`Turing`, `Smartphone`, `Sports_cars` and `French_films`) are dataset built from DBpedia [2].

The datasets from UCI consists of heterogeneous data. Therefore, we transformed them in order to build a formal context. This conversion of numerical and categorical data into Boolean data is based on the methodology of [13]. Numerical data is converted into categorical data by splitting the values into five bins of equal size, and categorical data is converted into Boolean data by creating a binary attribute for every possible value.

The datasets from DBpedia come from [16]. A transformation of the data (detailed in the original article) is done in order to convert the (graph) data into a formal context. The original data consists of a list of (subject, predicate, complement) triples. It is processed in the following way: the set of objects is obtained from the set of every subject appearing in the data, and the set of attributes is obtained from all existing (predicate, complement) pairs in the data.

Table 1. Descriptive statistics of the datasets tested.

Dataset	Objects	Attributes	Density
`Wine`	178	68	0.206
`Yeast`	1484	50	0.180
`Abalone`	4177	58	0.115
`Turing`	65	1360	2.99e-2
`Smartphone`	598	2089	6.74e-3
`Sports_cars`	604	2730	5.49e-3
`French_films`	6039	25487	7.89e-4

[3] https://github.com/xflr6/bitsets.

4.2 Results

Experiments were performed on a Linux computer (Ubuntu 24) with 32Gb RAM and an Intel Core Ultra 7 265H processor. The Table 2 shows the number $N_{Concepts}$ of formal concepts in the concept lattice, as well as the number N_{Pairs} of pairs of concepts that meet the frequency and similarity thresholds, and the number N_{Rd} of redescriptions found. This number covers both usual and conditional redescriptions as defined in [19]. The number N_{dRd} is the number of non-conditional redescriptions, which are redescriptions (A_1, A_2) whose sides are disjoint: $A_1 \cap A_2 = \emptyset$.

We also record, for every dataset, the time $T_{Lattice}$ the algorithm took to build the concept lattice and find the minimal generators of every concept, the time $T_{PairsRd}$ the algorithm took to find pairs of formal concepts that meet the similarity threshold and extract redescriptions from it, and the total time T_{Total}, which is the addition of the last two. The time it takes to import data is negligible and is therefore ignored.

Table 2. Information and runtime on the different datasets tested, using a frequency threshold $\theta_f = 10$ and a similarity threshold $\theta_s = 0.5$. Time is given in seconds.

Dataset	$N_{Concepts}$	N_{Pairs}	N_{Rd}	N_{dRd}	$T_{Lattice}$	$T_{PairsRd}$	T_{Total}
Wine	14555	93135	114764	1426	9.380	1.216	10.596
Yeast	18946	10809	6072	6	16.514	1.399	17.913
Abalone	61882	470675	466004	3768	115.042	75.296	190.338
Turing	1811	3640	3601	403	0.578	0.023	0.601
Smartphone	5610	75386	296022	80600	3.625	1.324	4.948
Sports_cars	7054	2014	1624	142	5.071	0.433	5.504
French_films	87969	26908	33281	3629	4034.381	177.434	4211.815

We extracted redescriptions for those datasets in a reasonable time, which shows that exhaustive enumeration of redescriptions is possible for many datasets. The number of found redescriptions is sometimes lower than the number of similar concepts. This can happen when many concepts only have one minimal generator. Because there are (C_i, C_i) pairs in the similar concepts, if the C_i concept only has one minimal generator, no pairs of distinct minimal generators are created, so no redescription will be obtained from that pair of similar concepts. Moreover, most pairs of different similar concepts will only have one possible pair of minimal generators and therefore form only one redescription. As a result, the number of similar concepts may be close to, if not lower than the number of redescriptions obtained.

The number of obtained redescriptions is usually high, with over 10 000 redescriptions, which is too many to read. Though obtaining a reasonable number of redescriptions is not the focus of this article, we can notice that the number of non-conditional redescriptions can be reasonable (less than 500) for several datasets. For the other datasets, additional methods of pruning the redescriptions or allowing efficient exploration of them could be considered. The `Smartphone` dataset is symptomatic of this problem, with 80 600 redescriptions extracted (296 022 with conditional redescriptions).

We observe that density seems to play an important role in execution time, as a dense dataset with few objects and attributes like `Wine` has a longer runtime than datasets like `Smartphones`. This reflects the fact that dense datasets require going through more itemsets and have more concepts in their corresponding concept lattice, increasing the amount of computation.

An implementation of the algorithm in a lower level language is likely to speed up execution by at least one order of magnitude. In comparison, running the original C++ CHARM-L implementation on the `Smartphones` dataset without a frequency threshold gives us a $T_{Lattice}$ time of 0.2 s (against 6 s for our approach). With a frequency threshold $\theta_f = 10$, CHARM-L takes less than 0.01 s (against 3.6 s for our approach). On the contrary, our approach takes surprisingly less time to find redescriptions than [13].[4] The two approaches are very different: we only look for redescriptions, whereas [13] also looks for associations rules, which are more numerous. We also rely on a concept lattice, whereas [13] uses the Minimum Description Length (MDL) approach.

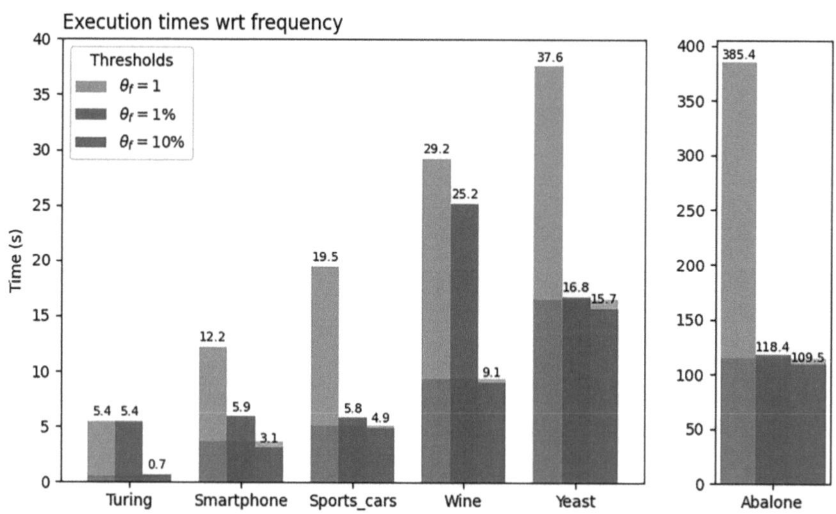

Fig. 4. Execution times $T_{Lattice}$ and $T_{PairsRd}$ for $\theta_s = 0.5$ and three different frequency thresholds θ_f (1, 1% and 10%). $T_{Lattice}$ is shown in darker $T_{PairsRd}$ is the lighter part of the bar.

[4] Running the original algorithm on our machine gives times of roughly half of what is given in the original article.

Figure 4 reports the execution times $T_{Lattice}$ and $T_{PairsRd}$ for 3 different frequency thresholds θ_f (1, 1% and 10%) and $\theta_s = 0.5$. As $T_{Lattice}$ is the same for all thresholds of a given dataset, it is depicted in light gray behind the bars. To deal with the different time scales, we chose not to show the French_Films dataset and we used a different y-axis for the Abalone dataset.

The figure reads as follows: for the Abalone dataset, the execution time for building the lattice is $T_{Lattice} = 115.0s$ (this value, not displayed in the figure, is reported in Table 2) and it is 385.4 s for finding the pairs with $\theta_f = 1$ ($T_{PairsRd}$ is twice as long than $T_{Lattice}$). For $\theta_f = 1\%$, the execution time is 118.4 s, and we can see by the size of the bar that this represents about the same execution time obtained for $\theta_f = 10\%$ (109.5 s).

Building the concept lattice usually takes most of the execution time, except for low ($\leqslant 1\%$) frequency thresholds. For a frequency threshold $\theta_f = 10\%$ (or higher), computing the pairs of similar concepts seems to become a negligible part of the execution time.

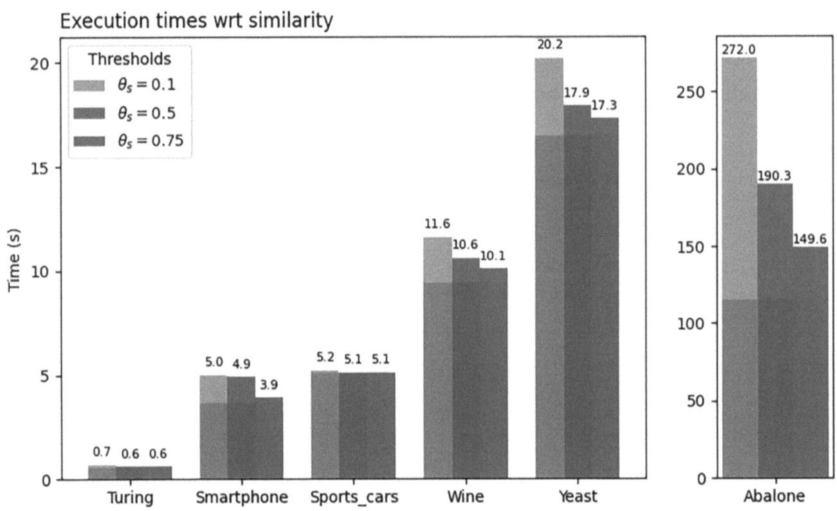

Fig. 5. Execution times $T_{Lattice}$ and $T_{PairsRd}$ for $\theta_f = 10$ different similarity thresholds θ_s. $T_{Lattice}$ is shown in darker $T_{PairsRd}$ is the lighter part of the bar.

Figure 5 reports the execution times $T_{Lattice}$ and $T_{PairsRd}$ for 3 different similarity thresholds θ_s (0.1, 0.5 and 0.75), with $\theta_f = 0.5$. We observe that while similarity doesn't have a noticeable influence on the total execution time on a dataset, it has a large influence on the time required to compute pairs of similar concepts. Indeed, the datasets where the total time doesn't vary much are ones where the lattice construction takes most of the time already. This shows the effectiveness of the similarity upper bound. We can also evaluate the effectiveness of this upper bound by looking at the number of pairs of concepts considered: for the Yeast dataset, using a similarity threshold $\theta_s = 0.5$ allows us to consider

71 330 825 pairs of concepts, or about 40% of the 179 484 931 possible pairs. For the `Smartphones` dataset, we consider 6 348 996 pairs of concepts, or also about 40% of the 15 738 855 possible pairs.

5 State of the Art and Discussion

5.1 State of the Art

FCA and its Extensions. FCA has been widely studied and numerous extensions and applications have been proposed. A lot of them rely on pattern structures [9]. Some of the generalisations allows to take into account different kinds of data, like numerical data [11]. Other extensions proposed to take into account a more complex structure of the data like relational data [4]. In [3], the authors define pattern structures allowing to combine heterogeneous contexts.

Rule Mining. While there is not much work combining FCA and redescription mining, there is a prolific literature on association rule mining. In [17], the author developed and adapted algorithms for finding *minimal non-redundant association rules* and introduced *Closed Rules*. This thesis [17] also introduced a typology of association rule bases.

Redescription Mining. In [6], the authors define a way to consider numerical and categorical data, together with propositional logic connectors. That is, it is possible to find redescriptions like $[A = 1.8] \sqcup B \equiv [C = \text{"mod1"}]$, for example. In [5] redescription mining is used on relational data. However, in both cases, these methods cannot provide an exhaustive enumeration. In [16], the authors compare redescriptions extracted by the ReReMi algorithm [6] and redescriptions built from an exhaustive extraction of association rules. The experiment, which aimed to define DBpedia categories, showed that while the heuristic used in ReReMi reduces duplicates in the extracted redescriptions and offers quite high precision, the recall is not as good (the competitor, based on association rules, allows to define on average twice as many categories).

5.2 Discussion

Performance of the Algorithm. Our algorithm can be adapted to consider the frequency threshold and build a partial concept lattice with frequent concepts only (i.e. an *iceberg lattice*), which would reduce execution time. The frequency threshold influences both parts of the algorithm, requiring minimal generators to be computed for fewer concepts in the lattice construction part, and removing the need to consider pairs of concepts where one of the concepts is not frequent. This threshold has a greater influence for computing pairs of similar concepts.

Views. One of the main differences between usual redescription mining algorithms like ReReMi and our approach is the use of *views*. Views consist in a partition of the attributes which constrain the mining of the redescription. For example, if we consider a dataset with attributes partitioned into two views $\mathcal{A} = V_1 \cup V_2, V_1 \cap V_2 = \emptyset$, then a redescription $A_i \equiv A_j$ is valid if all the attributes of A_i belong to the same view, and all the attribute of A_j belong to the same other view. The partition is usually based either on the source of the data or on a choice of the data analyst regarding a specific task. We are currently exploring how views can be taken into account in our approach, and a future work is to qualify how views influence the redescriptions extracted (both quantitatively and qualitatively).

6 Conclusion

In this paper, we laid the foundations for exhaustive redescription mining based on the formal concept analysis framework. We adapted Charm-L to perform this task and showed that being exhaustive is possible in a reasonable time and that the number of redescriptions extracted is smaller that one can expect, even more so when we do not mine conditional redescriptions. Further experiments should be performed to confirm this observation.

The first stop of our future work is to strengthen our approach by (i) improving our algorithm, for example, by avoiding to build the full lattice if we already know the frequency threshold or by replacing bitsets with frozensets in the implementation; and (ii) go more in depth with the experiments to characterize more precisely both the execution time variations and the diversity of redescriptions found, and the impact of views.

Subsequently, we will generalize our approach in order to mine more complex data. While taking into account numerical and categorical data may look straightforward (at least with a naive approach consisting in transforming input data), it raises some challenges concerning the notion of equivalence class. Indeed, the generalisation of FCA like Pattern Structures for numerical data [11] or graphs [4] allow to easily compute the closed itemsets, but the computation of minimal generators may be more complex, and their number may be far more important than with Boolean attributes.

Finally, we should adapt the algorithm to be able to deal with redescriptions expressed in propositional logic. Along with the computation complexity, one of the main challenge of this task is probably to deal with the number of redescriptions extracted.

Acknowledgments. The PhD position of the first author is funded by the Normandy Region.

Disclosure of Interests. The authors have no competing interests to declare that are relevant to the content of this article.

References

1. Agrawal, R., Imieliński, T., Swami, A.: Mining association rules between sets of items in large databases. In: Proceedings of the 1993 ACM SIGMOD International Conference on Management of Data, vol. 22, pp. 207–216 (1993)
2. Auer, S., Bizer, C., Kobilarov, G., Lehmann, J., Cyganiak, R., Ives, Z.: DBpedia: a nucleus for a web of open data. In: Proceedings of the 6th International Semantic Web Conference. ISWC (2007)
3. Codocedo, V., Napoli, A.: A proposition for combining pattern structures and relational concept analysis. In: Glodeanu, C.V., Kaytoue, M., Sacarea, C. (eds.) Proceedings of ICFCA. LNCS. Springer (2014)
4. Ferré, S.: Graph-FCA Meets Pattern Structures. In: Dürrschnabel, D., López-Rodríguez, D. (eds.) Proceedings of ICFCA. LNCS. Springer (2023)
5. Galbrun, E., Kimmig, A.: Finding relational redescriptions. Mach. Learn. **96**(3) (2014)
6. Galbrun, E., Miettinen, P.: From black and white to full color: extending redescription mining outside the Boolean world. Stat. Anal. Data Min.: ASA Data Sci. J. **5**(4), 284–303 (2012)
7. Galbrun, E., Miettinen, P.: SIREN: an interactive tool for mining and visualizing geospatial redescriptions. Knowl. Discov. Data Min., 1544–1547 (2012)
8. Galbrun, E., Miettinen, P.: Redescription Mining. SpringerBriefs in Computer Science. Springer (2017)
9. Ganter, B., Kuznetsov, S.O.: Pattern structures and their projections. In: Delugach, H.S., Stumme, G. (eds.) Proceedings of ICCS. LNCS. Springer (2001)
10. Ganter, B., Wille, R.: Formal Concept Analysis. Springer, Berlin, Heidelberg (1999)
11. Kaytoue, M., Kuznetsov, S.O., Napoli, A.: Revisiting Numerical pattern mining with formal concept analysis. In: Walsh, T. (ed.) Proceedings of IJCAI (2011)
12. Kelly, M., Longjohn, R., Nottingham, K.: The UCI Machine Learning Repository. https://archive.ics.uci.edu
13. van Leeuwen, M., Galbrun, E.: Association discovery in two-view data. IEEE Trans. Knowl. Data Eng. **27**(12) (2015)
14. Parida, L., Ramakrishnan, N.: Redescription mining: structure theory and algorithms. In: Proceedings of the AAAI (2005)
15. Ramakrishnan, N., Kumar, D., Mishra, B., Potts, M., Helm, R.: Turning CARTwheels: an alternating algorithm for mining redescriptions. In: Proceedings of the 10th ACM SIGKDD International Conference on Knowledge Discovery and Data Mining, pp. 266–275 (2004)
16. Reynaud, J., Toussaint, Y., Napoli, A.: Using redescriptions and formal concept analysis for mining definitions linked data. In: Cristea, D., Le Ber, F., Sertkaya, B. (eds.) Proceedings of ICFCA. LNCS. Springer (2019)
17. Szathmary, L.: Symbolic Data Mining Methods with the Coron Platform. PhD Thesis in Computer Science, Univ. Henri Poincaré – Nancy 1, France (2006)
18. Zaki, M.J., Hsiao, C.J.: CHARM: an efficient algorithm for closed itemset mining. In: Proceedings of the 2002 SIAM International Conference on Data Mining. SDM (2002)
19. Zaki, M.J., Hsiao, C.J.: Efficient algorithms for mining closed itemsets and their lattice structure. IEEE Trans. Knowl. Data Eng. **17**, 462–478 (2005)

Applications

Conceptual Patterns in Teachers' AI Perception

Veronika Pavlikova[1(✉)], Martin Trnecka[1], Ján Guniš[2], Lubomír Šnajder[2], Dominika Kotlárová[2], Stanislav Krajči[2], L'ubomír Antoni[2], and Peter Eliaš[3]

[1] Department Computer Science, Palacký University Olomouc, 17. listopadu 12, Olomouc, Czech Republic
veronika.pavlikova@upol.cz

[2] Faculty of Science, Institute of Computer Science, Pavol Jozef Šafárik University in Košince, Jesenná 5, Košice 04001, Slovak Republic

[3] Slovak Academy of Sciences, Mathematical Institute, Grešákova 6, Košice 04001, Slovak Republic

Abstract. Understanding teachers' perceptions and usage patterns of artificial intelligence (AI) is important for the responsible integration of AI technologies into education. In this paper, we analyze survey responses from 338 teachers from primary, secondary, and tertiary education in Slovakia and the Czech Republic. After binarizing selected categorical and ordinal variables, we construct a binary incidence matrix with 86 attributes describing AI information sources, teaching use cases, attitudes, recognition abilities, demographic characteristics, and reported AI tool usage. We apply two Boolean matrix decomposition methods: Greedy Concept on Demand (GreConD), grounded in Formal Concept Analysis, and an association rule-based Boolean matrix factorization method (ASSO). GreConD identifies clear and well-defined groups of teachers, while ASSO highlights both the most common patterns in the data and more detailed profiles associated with specific AI tools. Both methods reveal a strong preference for internet-based sources of AI information, practical classroom-oriented uses of AI (particularly for lesson preparation and material creation), and a cautious attitude toward AI. In particular, teachers do not fully trust AI outputs and are not always confident in recognizing AI-generated content. The comparison shows that GreConD produces clearer and more structured groups, whereas ASSO provides a more detailed and flexible description of the data.

Keywords: Formal Concept Analysis · Boolean Matrix Decomposition · Artificial Intelligence in Education · Teacher Perception

1 Introduction

Artificial intelligence is increasingly influencing educational practice, affecting teaching methods, learning processes, and assessment strategies. Generative AI

M. Croitoru et al. (Eds.): CONCEPTS 2026, LNAI 16811, pp. 245–259, 2027.
https://doi.org/10.1007/978-3-032-34742-8_16

systems, automated evaluation tools, and adaptive learning environments are becoming widely accessible to teachers. However, the integration of AI into formal education depends not only on technological availability, but also on teachers' perceptions, trust, attitudes, and actual usage patterns. Understanding these latent conceptual structures is therefore essential for responsible and evidence-based innovation in education [5,7,9].

Recent research on AI in education has primarily relied on statistical analysis, clustering, and regression-based methods to examine teachers' and students' attitudes [8,14]. While such approaches can identify correlations and group differences, they often fail to reveal deeper structural regularities inherent in categorical or multi-select survey data.

Survey responses of this type naturally form binary incidence matrices. In this setting, Boolean matrix decomposition (BMD), also referred to as Boolean matrix factorization, provides a principled framework for extracting latent factors from binary data [10]. In particular, Formal Concept Analysis (FCA) offers a mathematically grounded approach to identifying maximal rectangles of ones in binary contexts, known as formal concepts [6,13]. Concept-based decomposition methods such as GreConD interpret factors as formal concepts that exactly cover portions of the data matrix [4]. Although several other BMD algorithms based on FCA have been proposed [3,4,12], GreConD remains one of the principal approaches, as recent results show that it can identify meaningful natural patterns in data [2].

In contrast, general approximate BMD methods allow factors that are not necessarily complete submatrices of ones. Among the most widely used representatives of these methods is the ASSO algorithm [10]. These approaches trade exactness for compactness and often achieve lower reconstruction error in noisy real-world datasets [11]. The methodological comparison between exact concept-based decompositions and approximate rectangle-based approaches is particularly relevant for social science and educational data, where responses often exhibit only partial consistency.

Despite the rapid growth of AI-related educational research, the application of FCA-based and Boolean decomposition techniques to teachers' perception data remains limited. Most existing studies do not exploit the algebraic and lattice-theoretic structure inherent in binarized survey data.

In this paper, we analyze responses from 338 teachers from Slovakia and the Czech Republic. After selecting relevant variables and binarizing categorical responses, we obtain a binary matrix with 86 attributes describing AI information sources, usage contexts, attitudes toward AI, recognition abilities, demographic characteristics, and reported AI tool usage. We apply two Boolean matrix decomposition methods, namely GreConD and ASSO, to study teachers' perceptions of AI. The contributions of this paper are threefold:

- We provide a concept-oriented analysis of teachers' AI perception data using Boolean matrix decomposition.

- We compare exact concept-based decomposition (GreConD) with approximate decomposition (ASSO) in terms of interpretability and structural properties.
- We identify latent conceptual teacher profiles and discuss their educational implications.

By combining formal concept theory with empirical educational data, the paper contributes both to applied concept mining and to the methodological discussion on interpretable Boolean matrix decomposition in social science contexts.

2 Survey Design and Data Preparation

This section briefly describes the survey design and data preparation. It presents the selected variables and the preprocessing steps used to transform the responses into a binary matrix suitable for Boolean matrix decomposition.

2.1 Survey Description

We created the survey instrument as part of the KEGA project[1] focused on the integration of artificial intelligence into education and the analysis of teachers' perceptions and experiences with AI technologies. The questionnaire was designed based on previous research on AI literacy, educational technology adoption, and teacher attitudes toward AI-assisted tools. The development of the questionnaire included survey conceptualization, formulation of the questionnaire items, data collection, and subsequent statistical analysis. The survey was administered online and distributed among teachers from Slovakia and the Czech Republic. The data collection was conducted in two phases: in Slovakia from October 23, 2024 to November 18, 2024, and in the Czech Republic from November 7, 2024 to December 10, 2024.

The target population consisted of teachers of primary, secondary and higher education institutions in both countries. For the purpose of this study, only teacher responses were considered, resulting in a dataset of 338 respondents.

The questionnaire consisted of 15 items, with minor differences depending on the language version, and included multiple response formats:

- demographic variables (age, school type, locality, country),
- multiple-choice questions with single selection,
- multiple-choice questions with multiple selections,
- ordinal Likert-type scales,
- open-ended questions (not included in the present analysis).

[1] The use of artificial intelligence in the teaching of school informatics in secondary schools.

The instrument covered topics such as sources of AI-related information, perceived possibilities of AI use in education, general attitudes toward AI in society, self-assessed ability to recognize AI-generated content, and reported usage of AI-based products.

For the present study, only closed-ended categorical and ordinal responses were considered, as these allow a principled transformation into a binary formal context suitable for Boolean matrix decomposition.

2.2 Selected Variables

A subset of relevant variables was selected from the original questionnaire and transformed into binary attributes. For clarity and reproducibility, the full formulation and the English variable names used in the dataset are provided. The selected variables are as follows:

(V1) AI Information Sources (AI Sources) Original question: "Which sources do you use to obtain information about artificial intelligence?"
Options (multiple selection):

- Trainings (courses, seminars, webinars)
- Professional literature (books, journals, electronic journals)
- Internet sources (blogs, videos, tutorials, discussion forums, social media)
- Radio and television
- None

(V2) Perceived AI Use in Teaching (AI Use) Original question: "Where do you see opportunities for the use of artificial intelligence in education?"
Options (multiple selection):

- Lesson planning (preparation for teaching)
- Creation of teaching materials and student resources
- Direct classroom use (as a tool)
- AI as a teaching topic
- Student assessment and grading
- Evaluation of overall teaching effectiveness

(V3) School Type Options (single selection):

- Primary school – lower stage
- Primary school – upper stage
- Vocational secondary school
- Four-/five-year grammar school
- Six-/eight-year grammar school – lower stage (Czech Republic only)
- Six-/eight-year grammar school – upper stage (Czech Republic only)
- Eight-year grammar school – lower stage (Slovakia only)
- Eight-year grammar school – upper stage (Slovakia only)
- College/university

Note that a more standardized categorization of school type would improve the interpretability and comparability of the results. In future iterations of the survey, we plan to adopt a unified classification framework based on official educational levels and institutional categories. In the current study, however, we preserved the original labels reported by respondents to avoid information loss caused by the aggregation of heterogeneous school categories.

(V4) Country Options (single selection):

- Slovakia
- Czech Republic

(V5) School Locality Options (single selection):

- Regional capital
- District capital
- City
- Rural village

(V6) General Perception of AI (AI Perception)
Original question: "How do you perceive artificial intelligence and its role in society?"
Options (multiple selection):

- AI as a helper replacing humans in some activities
- Useful technology requiring regulation
- Dangerous technology
- Insignificant technology/temporary hype

Originally ordinal scale (strongly disagree, disagree, neutral, agree, strongly agree). The wording of item V6, particularly the option "Insignificant technology," may be perceived as non-neutral. However, we decided to preserve the original wording to maintain consistency with the collected data and comparability of the results. In future versions of the questionnaire, we plan to use more neutral formulations.

(V7) Recognition Ability Originally two questions:

- "Can you tell the difference between a photo generated by artificial intelligence and a photo taken by a human with a camera?"
- "Can you tell the difference between text generated by artificial intelligence and text written by a human?"

Originally ordinal scale (never, sometimes, always). Although audio deepfakes are highly relevant today and represent an important and rapidly growing area of generative AI, they were not included in the original version of question V7. At the time the survey was designed, the focus was placed primarily on text- and image-based AI content, which were the most commonly discussed forms. Audio deepfakes will be considered in future extensions of the questionnaire.

(V8) Trust in AI Output (AI Trust)
Original question: "If we formulate the request sufficiently precisely, can artificial intelligence generate a response that we can trust?"
Originally ordinal scale (never, sometimes, always).

(V9) AI Product Categories (AI Products) Reported AI tools included: *ChatGPT*, *Copilot*, *Gemini*, *DALL-E*, *Canva*, *DeepL*, *Perplexity*, *MagicSchool*, *Teachable Machine*, *Socrative*, *Google Translate*, *Google Lens*, *Curipod*, *Mizou*, *Dream by WOMBO*, general *AI assistants*, *image generators*, *recommendation systems*, *AI-enabled browsers*, *navigation systems*, *translation systems*, and the option *none reported.*

(V10) Age Age of the respondent.

(V11) Time Total time spent completing the questionnaire.

2.3 Binarization

In order to apply Boolean matrix decomposition methods, all selected variables (V1–V11) were transformed into a binary representation.

Categorical variables with nominal values (V3, V4, V5) were transformed using one-hot encoding. For each possible category value, a binary attribute was created indicating whether the respondent selected that category.

For multiple-selection questions (V1, V2, V9) each possible answer option was directly encoded as a separate binary attribute.

Ordinal Likert-type variables (V6, V7, V8) were transformed using one-hot encoding. For each ordinal scale with ordered values $\{v_1 < v_2 < \cdots < v_k\}$, a separate binary attribute was introduced for each response category, i.e., "respondent's answer $= v_i$". This approach preserves all individual response levels and provides a finer-grained representation, while maintaining compatibility with Boolean formal contexts. Note that six attributes were created from V7, as it contains two questions, each with three possible answers.

Variable V10, representing age, was divided into quartiles: $age < 38$, $38 \leq age < 47$, $47 \leq age < 53$, and $age \geq 53$. Variable V11 was divided into two groups according to the median of the entire dataset (411 s).

After preprocessing, the resulting dataset forms a binary incidence matrix

$$I \in \{0,1\}^{338 \times 86},$$

where rows correspond to teachers and columns correspond to derived binary attributes.

The matrix serves as a formal context in the sense of Formal Concept Analysis, where teachers are interpreted as objects and binarized attributes as properties. This representation enables the application of both exact concept-based decomposition (GreConD) and general approximate Boolean matrix decomposition (ASSO).

The choice of binarization strategy can significantly influence the resulting formal concepts and factorization outputs. In this study, we primarily employed one-hot encoding due to its simplicity, interpretability, and compatibility with standard Boolean matrix factorization methods. This approach may partially suppress ordinal relationships between some variables. More advanced approaches, such as conceptual scaling or ordinal scaling techniques, could better preserve order information and may lead to richer conceptual structures. However, since the primary goal of this work is to provide an initial exploratory analysis of teachers' perceptions of AI, we opted for a simpler and more interpretable preprocessing pipeline.

3 Survey Results

This section presents the evaluation of the survey data using the GreConD and ASSO algorithms.

The GreConD algorithm produces a Boolean matrix decomposition interpretable within the framework of Formal Concept Analysis (FCA). In this setting, each factor corresponds to a formal concept (A, B) (i.e., a closed itemset with respect to the Galois connection) of the binarized survey matrix I, where the *extent* A represents a set of teachers (rows) and the *intent* B denotes the set of binary attributes (columns) shared by all teachers in A. Consequently, the factors identified by GreConD can be directly interpreted as *conceptually coherent teacher profiles* characterized by the attributes that describe them.

Unlike GreConD, the ASSO algorithm is less restrictive and can therefore produce both very broad factors capturing dominant marginal patterns and more specific multi-attribute patterns.

3.1 Experimental Results: GreConD

The GreConD algorithm produced 131 factors. The coverage quality curve [1], which illustrates how these factors progressively explain the data (i.e., the coverage of the original data by the factors), is shown in Fig. 1. The curve exhibits a typical coverage pattern, with the first 50 factors explaining approximately 90% of the data.

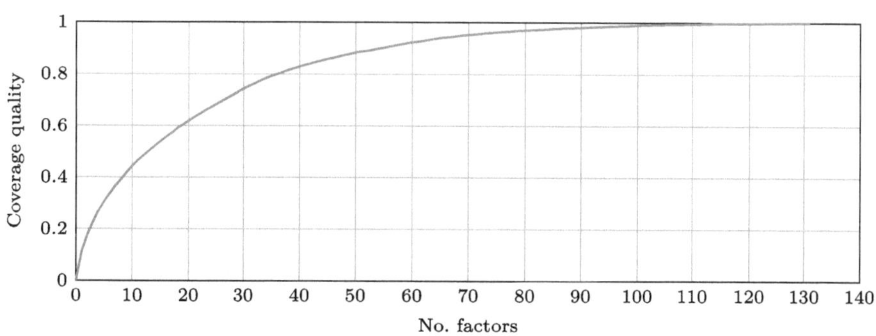

Fig. 1. Coverage quality curve for the factors obtained by the GreConD algorithm.

General Structure of the Extracted Factors. Across the extracted factors, several dimensions were observed: (i) *AI information sources* (most frequently internet-based sources, sometimes combined with formal training), (ii) *AI use cases in education* (especially lesson preparation and creation of teaching materials), (iii) *attitudes and level of trust in AI* (perception of AI as a useful technology vs. insignificant or dangerous; trust in AI-generated outputs), (iv) *self-assessed recognition ability* of AI-generated content (recognizing AI-generated images or texts, typically expressed as "sometimes"), and (v) *tool adoption* (explicit mention of product categories such as ChatGPT or other AI tools). In addition, several factors reflected *contextual variables* (country, school type, locality, age group), which serve primarily as cohort descriptors rather than behavioral profiles.

Representative GreConD Concepts. Table 1 summarizes a selection of the first five GreConD factors together with their interpretations. We emphasize concepts that combine (a) engagement and usage attributes with (b) attitudinal and recognition-related attributes, as these are the most informative for profiling teachers' AI adoption and perceptions. Purely demographic concepts (e.g., country × school-type cohorts) are treated as contextual baselines and are therefore not central to the qualitative interpretation.

Table 1. Selected GreConD factors (formal concepts), including the number of teachers covered by each factor, the shared attributes, and the interpretation of the factor.

Factor	Teachers	Intent (shared attributes)	Interpretation
F1	118	*AI sources: training, AI sources: internet, AI use: lesson preparation, AI use: material creation, AI use: in-class teaching, Recognize AI-generated photos: sometimes*	Active engagement and practical adoption; moderate confidence in AI-image recognition
F2	145	*AI sources: internet, AI use: material creation, Recognize AI-generated text: sometimes, AI can generate trustworthy answers: sometimes*	Pragmatic material-focused use; cautious trust and moderate text recognition
F3	113	*Country: Slovakia, AI sources: training, AI use: material creation, AI use: AI as a topic*	Training-supported "AI as topic" subgroup (Slovakia)
F4	113	*AI use: lesson preparation, Tool category: ChatGPT, AI is insignificant: strongly disagree*	Adoption profile: practical use + strong perceived relevance
F5	118	*Total time: long, Recognize AI-generated photos: sometimes, Recognize AI-generated text: sometimes*	Deliberative response pattern; moderate self-assessed recognition

A first factor (F1) groups teachers who report *active information seeking* (AI sources: training and internet) and simultaneously use AI for *practical classroom-related tasks* (lesson preparation, material creation, and in-class teaching). Interestingly, this engagement co-occurs with only *moderate confidence* in recognizing AI-generated photographs ("sometimes"), suggesting that practical adoption does not automatically imply high confidence in recognition.

Factor (F2) captures a *pragmatic use pattern*: teachers rely on internet sources and primarily associate AI with *creating teaching materials*, while their recognition of AI-generated text and their trust in AI-generated answers are both expressed as "sometimes". Methodologically, this concept is important because it demonstrates how GreConD naturally extracts factors that combine behavioral and epistemic dimensions into a single interpretable pattern.

A country-linked factor (F3) illustrates a subgroup of teachers from Slovakia whose shared attributes include participation in AI-related training, use of AI for material creation, and addressing AI explicitly as a *teaching topic*. This factor supports the interpretation that formal training may co-occur with the "educational adaptation" of AI (i.e., not only using AI as a tool, but also incorporating AI as curricular content).

We also observe clear *technology adoption* factors. For instance, a factor combining lesson preparation with explicit mention of the tool category ChatGPT and a strong rejection of the statement that AI is an "insignificant technology" (F4) can be interpreted as an adoption-oriented profile emphasizing both practical use and perceived relevance. Such factors are valuable because they link attitudes (perceived significance) with reported practice (use of a specific AI product category).

Finally, GreConD also obtains factors centered around *response behavior and self-assessment* (F5), such as the co-occurrence of longer questionnaire completion time with "sometimes" responses in recognition tasks. We do not claim that this shows a cause-and-effect relationship. However, it is still an interesting pattern that may indicate more careful answering or lower confidence in recognizing AI-generated content.

Overall, the dominant GreConD factors highlight strong reliance on internet-based AI information sources, practical teaching-related AI use cases (lesson preparation, material creation, in-class usage), a more careful attitude toward AI, where trust and recognition are often expressed as "sometimes", and distinct patterns of tool adoption, most notably the use of ChatGPT.

The extracted factors should not be interpreted as isolated final results, but rather as an exploratory representation of latent structures present in the dataset. In the case of GreConD, the factors are ordered according to the decomposition process, and the first factors typically cover larger and more representative groups of teachers.

The remaining factors were also generally interpretable and semantically meaningful. However, many of them represented smaller or more specific teacher subgroups with lower coverage. Therefore, we included only a subset of representative factors corresponding to larger and more illustrative groups of teachers.

3.2 Experimental Results: ASSO

The ASSO algorithm produced 85 factors. The coverage quality curve, which illustrates how these factors progressively explain the data, is shown in Fig. 2. The curve again exhibits the typical coverage pattern for this algorithm, with the first 35 factors explaining approximately 90% of the data.

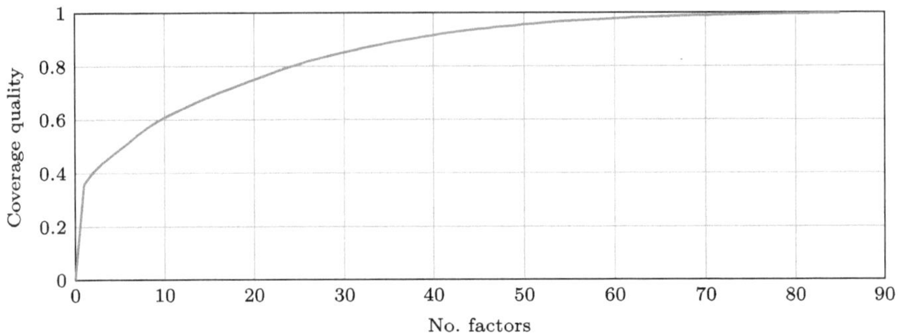

Fig. 2. Coverage quality curve for the factors obtained by the ASSO algorithm.

General Structure of the Extracted Factors. The ASSO output exhibited three characteristic types of factors:

- **High-support single-attribute factors.** Several factors consist of a single frequently occurring attribute (e.g., *AI sources: internet* or *tool category: ChatGPT*). Such factors may arise because their support exceeds that of smaller, more complex multi-attribute factors.
- **Cohort/context factors.** Some factors reflect demographic or contextual intersections (e.g., *country* together with a *school type*). These factors are helpful for describing the composition of the sample, but they are not necessarily behavioral profiles.
- **Behavioral/adoption micro-profiles.** ASSO also produced richer factors combining multiple dimensions: learning sources (training, literature, internet, media), concrete classroom use cases (preparation, material creation, in-class teaching, AI as a topic, assessment, and evaluation), attitudes toward AI (AI as helper, AI as a meaningful technology, perceived danger), self-assessed recognition of AI-generated text and images, perceived trustworthiness of generated answers, and explicit tool categories (e.g., Copilot, Canva, Gemini, DALL-E, Perplexity, DeepL, etc.). These factors provide a fine-grained view of teacher practices and perceptions.

Representative ASSO Factors. Table 2 lists selected representative factors from the ASSO output. Since many of the initial ASSO factors consisted of only a single attribute and therefore provided limited interpretative value, we manually reviewed the extracted factors and selected those that were considered the most semantically meaningful and interesting from an educational perspective. The presented factors therefore emphasize interpretability and coherence rather than purely statistical coverage.

Table 2. Selected Asso factors, including the number of teachers covered by each factor, the shared attributes, and the interpretation of the factor.

Factor	Teachers	Attributes (factor content)	Interpretation
G1	262	*AI sources: training, AI use: lesson preparation, AI use: material creation, AI use: in-class teaching, AI use: AI as a topic, Country: Slovakia, AI as a technology: agree, AI as dangerous: disagree, Recognize AI-generated photos: sometimes, Recognize AI-generated text: sometimes, AI can generate trustworthy answers: sometimes, Tool category: recommendation systems, Total time: long*	Training-backed adoption with cautious trust/recognition; Slovak subgroup
G13	95	*AI sources: training, AI use: lesson preparation, Tool category: Copilot*	Copilot-oriented preparation profile
G29	51	*AI sources: training, AI use: lesson preparation, AI use: material creation, Tool category: Canva*	Canva used for preparation/materials
G66	6	*AI sources: internet, AI use: material creation, AI use: in-class teaching, AI as an insignificant technology: strongly disagree, Recognize AI-generated photos: sometimes, AI can generate trustworthy answers: sometimes, Tool category: AI assistants*	"Assistant" tools for materials + in-class use
G38	36	*AI use: lesson preparation, AI use: material creation, Tool category: Gemini*	Gemini adoption in preparation/material creation
G67	6	*AI sources: internet, AI use: material creation, Recognize AI-generated photos: sometimes, Recognize AI-generated text: sometimes, Tool category: DALL-E*	Image-generation tools linked to teaching materials

Among the more informative multi-attribute factors, ASSO extracted a large profile (G1) combining: *AI sources: training*; multiple teaching-related applications (*preparation*, *material creation*, *in-class teaching*, and *AI as a topic*); *country: Slovakia*; a generally positive but careful attitude (*AI as a technology: agree* together with *AI as dangerous: disagree*); moderate self-assessed recognition of AI-generated photo/text (*sometimes*); moderate trust in generated answers (*sometimes*); and a longer completion time. This factor is particularly valuable because it links adoption (use cases + training) with careful attitude toward AI (recognition and trust at the "sometimes" level), i.e., a mixed profile that is often hard to capture using purely demographic grouping.

ASSO additionally revealed tool-specific adoption patterns. Examples include factors joining *training* and *preparation* with *tool category: Copilot* (G13), *preparation + material creation* with *tool category: Canva* (G29), *preparation + material creation* with *tool category: Gemini* (G38), and *material creation* with *tool category: DALL-E* (G67). The presence of these micro-profiles indicates that ASSO is sensitive to smaller co-occurrences that may be too sparse or not sufficiently "closed" to appear as prominent GreConD concepts.

ASSO complements GreConD by revealing both broad, high-support patterns (single-attribute factors capturing dominant marginals) and fine-grained groups connecting specific tool categories with concrete teaching use cases. The most informative ASSO factors consistently combine practical usage (preparation materials, in-class) with a careful attitude toward AI (recognition and trust frequently at the "sometimes" level), while also highlighting a diversity of tool ecosystems (ChatGPT, Copilot, Canva, Gemini, DALL-E, Perplexity, DeepL, MagicSchool, etc.).

4 Discussion

When comparing the concrete outputs reported in Sect. 3, the most visible difference concerns the *structure and granularity* of the extracted factors. Although GreConD produced more factors than ASSO, the extracted concepts were more structurally coherent and semantically interpretable.

These concepts typically combine information sources (training, internet), practical classroom uses (lesson preparation, material creation, and in-class use), and a cautious attitude toward AI, where recognition and trust are often expressed at the "sometimes" level. In contrast, ASSO generated a more heterogeneous set of factors, including both broad high-support attributes (e.g., *AI sources: internet*) and patterns centered on specific tools (e.g., Copilot, Canva, Gemini, DALL-E).

A second difference lies in how behavioral and attitudinal dimensions are coupled. In GreConD, engagement and epistemic caution frequently appear within the same closed concept, forming interpretable profiles (e.g., active classroom use together with moderate trust in AI outputs). ASSO confirms the same empirical tendency, but often decomposes it into overlapping approximate factors. Instead of a single closed profile, multiple partially intersecting patterns emerge, some focused on usage, others on trust or recognition, indicating that ASSO captures the same structure in a more fragmented form. The observed differences between ASSO and GreConD should not be interpreted purely semantically. They are also influenced by structural properties of the dataset and by the different optimization and factor-construction mechanisms employed by the two methods.

The role of specific AI tools is more pronounced in the ASSO results. While GreConD highlights tool adoption primarily when it is strongly integrated with broader patterns of practice and attitudes (e.g., lesson preparation + ChatGPT + strong perceived relevance), ASSO reveals a wider range of tools connected to particular use cases. This suggests that GreConD emphasizes stable groups, whereas ASSO is more sensitive to fine-grained variation in tool selection.

Overall, the result sets produced by GreConD and ASSO are substantively consistent but structurally different. Both approaches identify internet-based information seeking as dominant, practical teaching-oriented AI use as central, and a moderate level of confidence (often expressed as "sometimes" in recognition and trust) as a characteristic feature. However, GreConD presents these patterns as compact formal teacher profiles, whereas ASSO distributes them across a richer and more diverse set of approximate factors.

These observations suggest that the two approaches provide complementary perspectives on the same structure. GreConD emphasizes stable and interpretable conceptual groups of teachers, making it particularly suitable for identifying coherent behavioral profiles. In contrast, ASSO offers a more flexible representation of the data, revealing finer-grained patterns and tool-specific variations that may not appear within strictly closed concepts. Together, the two methods provide a richer understanding of teachers' AI perception and usage patterns.

The relevance of our study (i.e., teachers' perceptions and practices related to AI) is emphasized by recent reviews showing the rapid expansion of AI applications in education and the need to better understand how these technologies are adopted and interpreted by educators in real teaching contexts [14].

5 Conclusions

This paper presented a concept-oriented analysis of teachers' perceptions and usage patterns of artificial intelligence in education using Boolean matrix decomposition methods. By transforming survey responses from 338 teachers in Slovakia and the Czech Republic into a binary formal context with 86 attributes, we enabled the application of two complementary matrix decomposition techniques: the concept-based GreConD algorithm and the general approximate ASSO method.

The results demonstrate that both approaches reveal substantively consistent patterns. Across methods, three dominant dimensions emerge: a strong reliance on internet-based sources of AI information, practical classroom-oriented uses of AI, particularly for lesson preparation and the creation of teaching materials, and a moderate level of confidence, with recognition ability and trust in AI-generated outputs frequently expressed at the "sometimes" level.

At the same time, the structural properties of the extracted factors differ significantly. GreConD provides compact and formally closed teacher profiles that combine behavioral, attitudinal, and contextual attributes into coherent conceptual units. In contrast, ASSO produces a richer and more heterogeneous decomposition, capturing both high-support marginal patterns and fine-grained tool-specific groups. In particular, ASSO highlights the diversity of the AI tool ecosystem (ChatGPT, Copilot, Canva, Gemini, DALL-E, and others) and its association with specific instructional practices.

From a methodological perspective, the study illustrates the value of Formal Concept Analysis and Boolean matrix decomposition for analyzing binarized survey data in educational research. The comparison shows that the two methods do not compete with each other but rather offer complementary advantages: one produces clearer and more structured profiles that are easier to interpret, while the other provides a more detailed and flexible description of the data.

From an educational perspective, the results suggest that teachers primarily use AI in a practical manner, focusing on everyday teaching tasks. At the same time, they do not trust AI outputs uncritically but approach them with a certain degree of caution. These insights may inform teacher training programs, policy decisions, and future research on the responsible integration of AI in education.

Future work may extend the analysis by incorporating open-ended responses, longitudinal data, or cross-country comparative modeling. It may also explore the stability and robustness of extracted concept structures under alternative binarization strategies or fuzzy approaches.

Acknowledgments. This work was supported by the Slovak Research and Development Agency under contract No. APVV-21-0468 (L. Antoni). This article was partially supported by the project KEGA 010-UPJS-4/2024 (J. Gunis, L. Snajder, D. Kotlarova) and Grants No. IGA_PrF_2025_18 and IGA_PrF_2026_26 of the Internal Grant Agency of Palacký University Olomouc.

Disclosure of Interests. The authors have no competing interests to declare that are relevant to the content of this article.

References

1. Belohlavek, R., Outrata, J., Trnecka, M.: Toward quality assessment of Boolean matrix factorizations. Inf. Sci. **459**, 71–85 (2018). https://doi.org/10.1016/j.ins.2018.05.016
2. Belohlavek, R., Trnecka, M.: Semantic explorations in factorizing Boolean data via formal concepts. Int. J. Approx. Reason. **173**, 109247 (2024). https://doi.org/10.1016/j.ijar.2024.109247
3. Belohlavek, R., Trnecka, M.: From-below approximations in Boolean matrix factorization: geometry and a new algorithm. J. Comput. Syst. Sci. **81**(8), 1678–1697 (2015). https://doi.org/10.1016/j.jcss.2015.06.002
4. Belohlavek, R., Vychodil, V.: Discovery of optimal factors in binary data via a novel method of matrix decomposition. J. Comput. Syst. Sci. **76**(1), 3–20 (2010). https://doi.org/10.1016/j.jcss.2009.05.002
5. Cabero-Almenara, J., Palacios-Rodríguez, A., Loaiza-Aguirre, M.I., Andrade-Abarca, P.S.: The impact of pedagogical beliefs on the adoption of generative AI in higher education: predictive model from UTAUT2. Front. Artif. Intell. **7**, 1497705 (2024). https://doi.org/10.3389/frai.2024.1497705
6. Ganter, B., Wille, R.: Formal Concept Analysis: Mathematical Foundations, 2nd edn. Springer (2024)
7. Granström, M., Oppi, P.: Assessing teachers' readiness and perceived usefulness of AI in education: an Estonian perspective. Front. Educ. **10**, 1622240 (2025). https://doi.org/10.3389/feduc.2025.1622240
8. Holmes, W., Bialik, M., Fadel, C.: Artificial Intelligence in Education: Promise and Implications for Teaching and Learning, Center for Curriculum Redesign (2019)
9. Kizilcec, R.F.: To advance AI use in education, focus on understanding educators. Int. J. Artif. Intell. Educ. **34**(1), 12–19 (2024). https://doi.org/10.1007/s40593-023-00351-4
10. Miettinen, P., Mielikäinen, T., Gionis, A., Das, G., Mannila, H.: The discrete basis problem. IEEE Trans. Knowl. Data Eng. **20**(10), 1348–1362 (2008). https://doi.org/10.1109/TKDE.2008.53
11. Miettinen, P., Neumann, S.: Recent developments in Boolean matrix factorization. In: Proceedings of the IJCAI 2020, Survey Track, pp. 4922–4928 (2020). https://doi.org/10.24963/ijcai.2020/685
12. Trnecka, M., Vyjidacek, R.: Revisiting the GreCon algorithm for Boolean matrix factorization. Knowl.-Based Syst. **249**, 108895 (2022). https://doi.org/10.1016/j.knosys.2022.108895

13. Wille, R.: Formal concept analysis as applied lattice theory. In: Proceedings of the International Conference on Concept Lattices and Their Applications (CLA 2006), pp. 42–67. Springer, Berlin, Heidelberg (2006)
14. Zhai, X., et al.: A review of artificial intelligence (AI) in education from 2010 to 2020. Complexity, Article ID 8812542 (2021). https://doi.org/10.1155/2021/8812542

Visual Exploration of Boolean Factors

Veronika Pavlikova(✉) and Martin Trnecka

Department Computer Science, Palacký University Olomouc, Olomouc, Czech Republic
veronika.pavlikova@upol.cz

Abstract. Boolean matrix factorization (BMF) is a widely used technique for discovering latent patterns in binary data, offering high interpretability due to its Boolean nature. However, current analyses of BMF results are often limited to quantitative measures such as reconstruction error, leaving interpretability and relationships between factors largely unexplored. In this work, we investigate the qualitative aspects of the factors and propose a visualization-based approach for exploratory analysis that supports the interpretation of individual factors. Moreover, we introduce a novel method for visualizing factors that preserves their mutual relationships, facilitates the interpretation of individual factors, and provides a global view of the obtained factorization and, consequently, of the analyzed data. The method employs proximity-based representations derived from similarities over attributes, objects, or their combinations, together with multidimensional scaling to produce a low-dimensional overview of the factorization. We further introduce a software tool, BFLens, that enables interactive exploration of BMF results.

Keywords: Boolean matrix factorization · Visualization of factors · Factor evaluation · Factor exploration

1 Introduction

Boolean matrix factorization (BMF) is a well-established and widely used data mining technique that reveals fundamental patterns implicitly present in data, thereby helping to explain the underlying structure of data [12].

The main aim of BMF is to describe the input Boolean matrix $\mathbf{I}$ with m rows $(x_1, \ldots, x_m)$, n columns $(y_1, \ldots, y_n)$, and potentially (if available) an additional column c representing the class label, via two Boolean matrices $\mathbf{A}$ and $\mathbf{B}$, as outlined in Fig. 1.

The matrix $\mathbf{A}$ represents an object–factor matrix and captures the relationship between the original objects of matrix $\mathbf{I}$ and the new variables called factors $(f_1, \ldots, f_k)$. Analogously, matrix $\mathbf{B}$ represents a factor–attribute matrix and captures the relationship between the factors and the original attributes of $\mathbf{I}$.

The Boolean nature of the method is particularly advantageous when it comes to data interpretation. Boolean factors are upon a permutation of rows and

M. Croitoru et al. (Eds.): CONCEPTS 2026, LNAI 16811, pp. 260–276, 2027.
https://doi.org/10.1007/978-3-032-34742-8_17

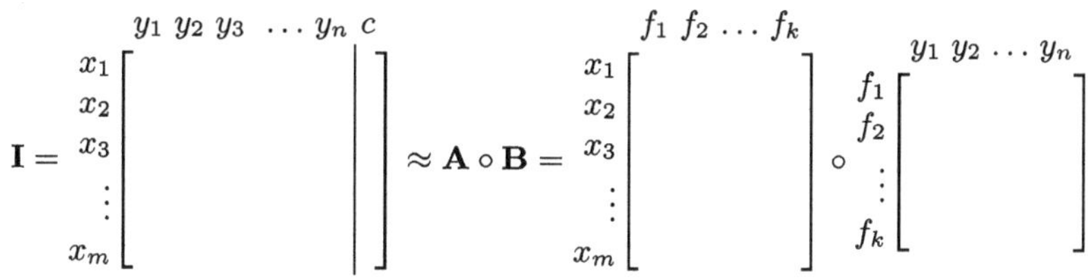

Fig. 1. Basic Boolean matrix factorization model considered in this paper. The operation $\circ$ denotes Boolean matrix multiplication. The symbol $\approx$ indicates that the factorization need not be exact, i.e., $\mathbf{I}$ and $\mathbf{A} \circ \mathbf{B}$ may differ in some entries.

columns, rectangular areas—rectangles for short—in the input matrix containing ones and, if desired, a reasonably small number of zeros, which represent fundamental patterns in the data. Thus, a factor is defined by the attributes that constitute its manifestation (this information is contained in the rows of matrix $\mathbf{B}$) and by the objects to which it applies (this information is contained in the columns of matrix $\mathbf{A}$). Boolean nature simplifies the interpretation to yes-no, i.e., a particular attribute is a manifestation of a given factor or not, similarly for the objects.[1]

Many BMF algorithms, as well as practical applications of BMF, build upon Formal Concept Analysis (FCA) [11]. In its simplest form, formal concepts can serve as factors, and FCA more generally provides a framework for BMF—most notably, factors can in certain situations be seen as formal concepts [1], which is advantageous from the viewpoint of interpretability.

Unfortunately, the actual interpretation of obtained factors—determining their meaning—is often reduced to a tedious manual inspection of the attributes and objects involved in a particular factor [4]. This process is particularly disadvantageous when BMF is used for exploratory data analysis. Moreover, relationships between factors—such as similarities—that may carry valuable information and facilitate the interpretation of individual factors are often overlooked.

Graphics provide an excellent approach for exploring data and are essential for presenting results. Although graphics—especially for result presentation—have been used in BMF for a long time, there is still no substantive theory on the topic. Moreover, visualization is typically limited to quantitative aspects. The most commonly presented characteristic is the so-called coverage quality curve [3]. There exist several variants of this curve. All of them share the property that they capture reconstruction error, i.e., the number of entries that are either not explained or incorrectly explained. A typical coverage quality curve is shown in Fig. 2.

From the coverage quality curve, one can observe how much of the data is explained by the factors, as well as the cumulative contribution of individual factors. Although coverage quality provides useful information—since BMF can

[1] Note that the model can also be extended to ordinal data, i.e., data containing degrees (or grades) on a given scale, without affecting interpretability; see, e.g., [5].

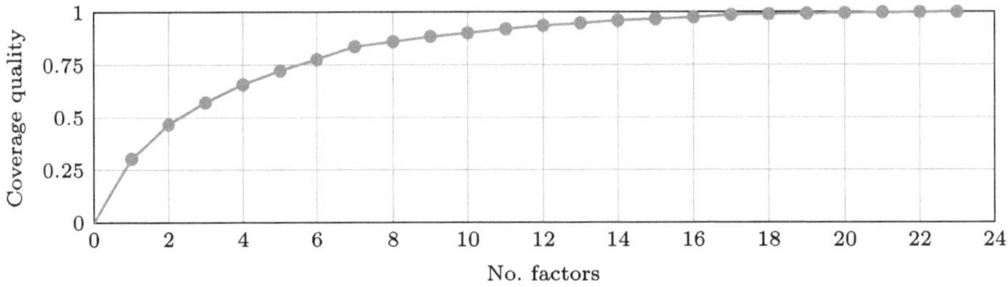

Fig. 2. An example of a coverage quality curve. The value indicates the proportion of the data explained by the factors; for example, 0.75 means that 75% of the input entries are explained.

essentially be viewed as a set cover problem [12]—important aspects remain hidden. For example, the curve does not reveal the number of attributes constituting individual factors; factors defined by a single attribute are clearly of limited importance. Similarly, the diversity of the associated objects affects interpretability, which varies depending on whether the objects are heterogeneous or homogeneous. Finally, similarities between factors are not captured: some factors may be similar, yet this potentially valuable information is not captured.

There are differences between graphics for presentation and graphics for exploration. Presentation graphics are generally used to summarize the information being presented and should be of high quality, including complete definitions and explanations of both the variables shown and the form of the graphic. In contrast, exploratory graphics are used to search for results. Many may be generated, and they should be quick to read and informative rather than precise. They are not intended for presentation; detailed legends and captions are therefore unnecessary. While a single presentation graphic may be viewed by thousands of readers, thousands of exploratory graphics may be produced to support the data investigation of a single analyst [8]. Another important difference is that presentation graphics are typically static, whereas exploratory graphics benefit greatly from interactivity.

Motivated by our experience with the practical use of BMF, the main aim of this work is to demonstrate how BMF results can be visualized to emphasize their informative value, primarily in exploratory tasks, but also—although this is not our primary focus—in presentation scenarios. We argue that suitable visualization can facilitate the interpretation of factors. Furthermore, we introduce a novel method for factor visualization that captures relationships between factors and provides a global view of the data. Finally, we present a software tool that enables interactive exploration of BMF results.

The rest of the paper is organized as follows. Section 2 discusses the analysis of individual factors and presents visualization techniques that facilitate their interpretation and reduce the number of factors considered for further analysis. Section 3 introduces a novel visualization approach. Section 4 provides illustrative examples of analyses utilizing the proposed approach. Section 5 presents the BFLens tool for exploratory analysis of factorization results. Finally, Sect. 6 concludes the paper and outlines directions for future research.

2 How to Recognize a Good Factor

We consider the factorization model shown in Fig. 1. Royce [14] defines a factor in terms of the attributes constituting its manifestation. This idea, rooted in classical factor analysis, is justified because attributes play a key role in data explanation. The analyzed data capture only a part of the real world, represented by a limited set of observed objects. A factor that provides an explanation of the data is therefore applicable not only to the analyzed data but also to other data that are not present in analyzed data (generalization). From this perspective, BMF can be viewed as a projection from the attribute space to the factor space [1], where factor provides a different—more fundamental—description of observed world [4].

In some situations, however, the enumeration of attributes alone may not be sufficient for an intuitive explanation of a factor. In such cases, one may also consider the objects to which the factor applies. Although this set of objects is incomplete due to the data limitations, it can still be helpful for understanding the nature of the factor. This perspective is particularly justified when factorization is utilized as a form of clustering or in supervised machine learning tasks, where a class label (attribute c in Fig. 1) is present. Note that in such cases, the class label provides additional information that can be exploited in the interpretation of factors.

In general, factors can be evaluated in terms of (i) their attributes, (ii) their objects, possibly augmented by class labels, and (iii) both attributes and objects. To illustrate these perspectives, we present several ways of capturing and visualizing factorization, primarily for the exploratory task. In the following, we consider results obtained by analyzing the Zoo dataset [9] using the GreConD algorithm [1]. The Zoo dataset contains 101 animals described by 16 attributes and a single class attribute. The class attribute assigns each animal to one of seven categories: mammal, bird, reptile, invertebrate, bug, fish, and amphibian.

2.1 Attributes Manifested by Factors

A key characteristic of each factor is the number of attributes that constitute its manifestation. Clearly, factors with either too few or too many attributes are more difficult to interpret. Therefore, in exploratory analysis, it is highly useful to be able to assess this characteristic quickly. Following the basic principles of data visualization [16], a simple bar chart appears to be the most suitable choice, as illustrated in Fig. 3a. Based on this, one may filter out irrelevant concepts and thereby reduce the number of factors to be further analyzed.

Closely related is another key indicator reflecting how large a portion of the occurrences of a given attribute is represented by a factor. For example, the significance of a factor differs substantially depending on whether an attribute

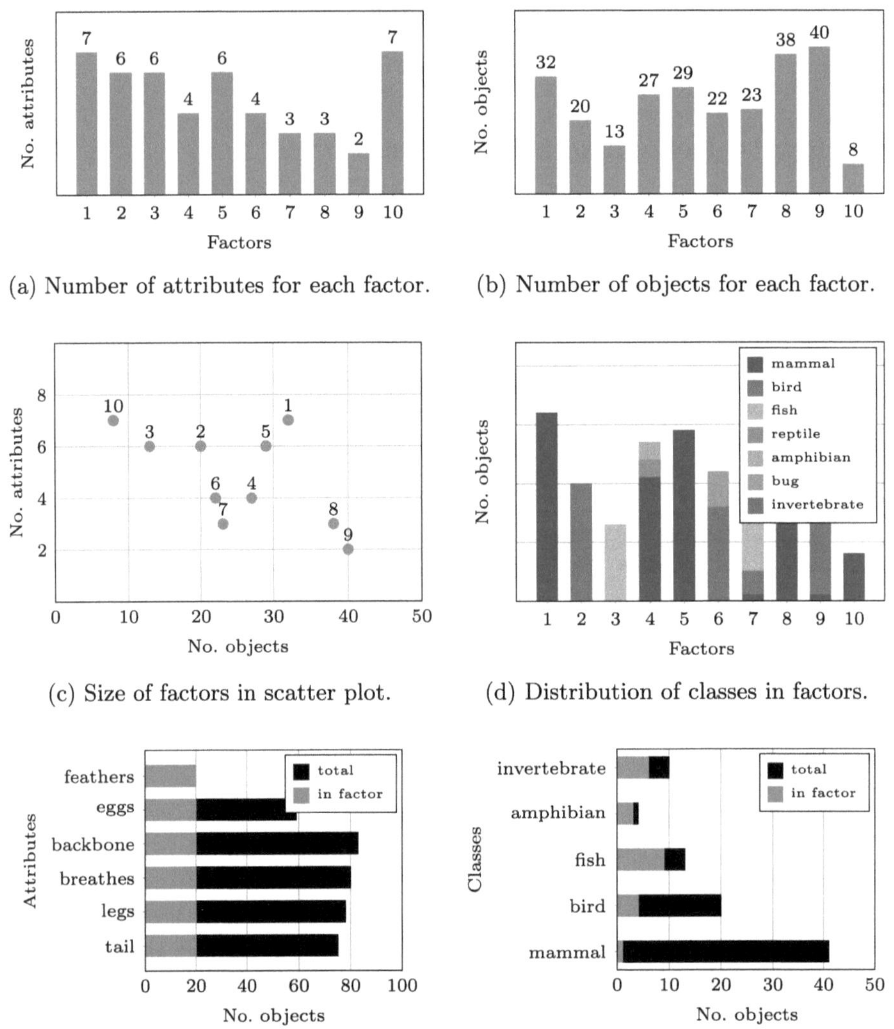

(a) Number of attributes for each factor. (b) Number of objects for each factor.

(c) Size of factors in scatter plot. (d) Distribution of classes in factors.

(e) Distribution of attributes in one factor. (f) Distribution of classes in one factor.

Fig. 3. Different characteristics of the BMF of the Zoo dataset. For readability, only the top 10 factors are shown.

occurs in 75% of objects and the factor covers 90% of these occurrences, or only 10%. This can be quickly observed from the chart depicted in Fig. 3e.

2.2 Objects to Which Factors Apply

Analogously to attributes, one may wish to quickly assess the number of objects to which each factor applies. Clearly, factors applying to either too few or too many objects are difficult to interpret. Again, a simple bar chart (Fig. 3b) is a suitable choice.

The number of attributes and the number of objects involved in a factor can be examined jointly. A comprehensive overview can be obtained using a scatter plot that displays the number of objects on one axis and the number of attributes on the other; this visualization is shown in Fig. 3c. From this plot, one can easily identify factors that cover a large portion of the data (points located in the upper-right part of the graph), as well as factors that exhibit sufficiently large numbers of objects or attributes from the perspective of analysis. This plot, together with the charts in Fig. 3a and Fig. 3b, can also be presented with axes showing relative (percentage) proportions instead of absolute counts.

The interpretation of a factor can be significantly facilitated by analyzing the classes, if available, to which the corresponding objects belong. Clearly, factors dominated by a single class are much easier to interpret than very general factors that cover multiple classes. For a quick overview, a bar chart showing the class distribution within individual factors is again useful, as illustrated in Fig. 3d. Also useful is information indicating how large a portion of the occurrences of a given class is represented by a factor (see Fig. 3f).

Overall, Fig. 3 provides a concise overview of the analyzed factorization. For example, the second extracted factor contains a relatively large number of attributes and objects and thus belongs to the larger factors (see Figs. 3a, 3b, and 3c). It is exclusively associated with birds and includes all objects possessing the attribute *feathers*, as well as approximately one third of those with the attribute *eggs* (see Fig. 3e). Similarly, factor 7 is comparatively smaller and predominantly describes amphibians, fish, and invertebrates (see Fig. 3d). An analysis of its attributes (not shown in Fig. 3 due to space limitations) suggests that this factor corresponds to a predator that lives in or hunts near water.

3 Big Picture

So far, we have considered only the properties of individual factors. In BMF, however, multiple factors form a whole. When interpreting the factorization as a whole, not only the aforementioned characteristics of individual factors play a role, but also properties of the factorization itself.

In classical factor analysis, the interpretability of factorization is guided by the law of parsimony, commonly known as Occams razor—namely, that the simplest explanation is preferred. Such an explanation is selected according to the parsimony principle and is referred to as a simple structure. In 1947, Thurstone formalized five criteria for simple structure in his work [15]. Later, Cattell [7] argued that factors exhibiting simple structure are usually easy to interpret. Unfortunately, Thurstones formalization of good factors is informal, vague, and described only verbally.

According to Thurstone, interpretable factors satisfy the following five conditions, which we translate into BMF terminology:

1. Each row of matrix **B** should contain at least one zero.

2. Each row of matrix **B** should contain at least as many zeros as there are factors.
3. For every pair of rows of matrix **B**, there should be attributes with zeros in one factor and ones in the other.
4. For every pair of rows of matrix **B**, a large proportion of attributes should be zero in both rows, particularly when the number of factors is large.
5. For every pair of rows of matrix **B**, there should be only a few attributes with ones in both rows.

Thurstones definition of good factorization adopts the Royce model of a factor. Among the five criteria, the third and the fifth are of overriding importance, i.e., in a good factorization, factors share only a small number of attributes.[2]

To provide a big picture—a global view of the data and the factorization—we propose the following approach based on Multi Dimensional Scaling (MDS) [13]. MDS is a dimensionality reduction technique that represents objects in a low-dimensional space while preserving their pairwise dissimilarities as faithfully as possible. By projecting factors into a two- or three-dimensional space, we obtain a visual representation reflecting their mutual similarities and differences, thereby providing an intuitive overview of the factorization structure. In our case, the specific meaning of the dimensions is not essential, as the projection primarily serves as a map of relationships between factors. Although the dimensions do carry meaning, their interpretation is non-trivial and difficult to determine explicitly.

Note that the idea of visualizing factors was already outlined in [10], where, similarly to classical factor analysis, results were visualized for two factors without additional quantitative measures. In contrast, the method proposed in this paper captures relationships among all factors and is based on similarity measures.

MDS takes as input a matrix of pairwise dissimilarities or similarities—commonly referred to as proximities—between factors and computes their coordinates in a low-dimensional space such that the distances between points approximate the original proximities as closely as possible. Consequently, similar factors are placed close to each other, whereas dissimilar factors appear further apart. The quality of the low-dimensional embedding is typically assessed using a stress function

$$\text{stress} = \sqrt{\frac{\sum_{i<j} \left(d_{ij} - \hat{d}_{ij}\right)^2}{\sum_{i<j} d_{ij}^2}}$$

where d_{ij} denotes the original distances (or dissimilarities) between factors i and j, and $\hat{d}_{ij}$ denotes the corresponding distances between the same factors in the low-dimensional embedding. The stress function quantifies how well the embedding preserves the original relationships in the data, with lower values indicating better preservation.

[2] Note that the first and second criteria take into account the number of attributes that constitute the manifestation of a factor. This aspect was addressed in Sect. 2.1.

Although general guidelines for acceptable stress values exist, in our case MDS is employed primarily for visualization. The stress value therefore indicates whether a two- or three-dimensional representation is sufficient or whether the data cannot be adequately represented in such low-dimensional spaces. The latter case is itself informative, as high stress values may reflect the intrinsic complexity of the factorization rather than merely poor visualization quality.

3.1 Similarity Matters

The proximity matrix represents relationships between factors, thereby providing a richer characterization of them. Accordingly, the MDS outcome is determined by the similarity or dissimilarity measure used to construct the matrix.

In general, a suitable similarity measure should increase with the number of shared attributes and decrease with increasing differences, while appropriately emphasizing shared positive features. For binary data, it is often desirable to downweight shared absences. Moreover, psychological studies suggest that human similarity judgments are feature-based and need not satisfy metric axioms [17]. Although MDS can, in principle, handle various types of similarities, in standard settings it typically assumes metric properties.

In [2], 69 practically applicable similarity measures for Boolean data were identified. In the following, we consider three variants for assessing similarity between factors, namely similarity based on their attributes, similarity based on their objects, and similarity based on both their attributes and objects. Each variant allows the use of various similarity measures.

For the first two variants, one may employ the standard scheme: for two binary vectors x and y representing sets of attributes or objects, let a denote the number of elements common to both x and y, b the number of elements present in x but not in y, c the number of elements present in y but not in x, and d the number of elements absent from both x and y.

In the case of the last variant, one may compare the rectangles corresponding to the compared factors; that is, let a denote the number of overlapping entries, b the number of entries present in the first rectangle but not in the second, c the number of entries present in the second rectangle but not in the first, and d the number of entries absent from both rectangles. Furthermore, relationships between factors may also be considered. For example, two factors can be regarded as similar even without overlapping entries, provided they share certain objects or attributes.

The selection of a similarity measure is a key step in data analysis. However, since our primary goal is to illustrate the usefulness of the proposed approach, we employ a basic measure satisfying the previously stated properties, namely the Jaccard distance

$$D_J(x, y) = 1 - \frac{a}{a + b + c}$$

for first two variants and the overlapping distance

$$D_O(x, y) = 1 - \frac{a}{\min(a + b,\ a + c)}$$

for the last variant.

4 Illustrative Examples of Analysis

We select three datasets to demonstrate how the proposed approach can facilitate analysis of factors: the Zoo dataset, already described in Sect. 2; the Congressional voting records dataset [18]; and the Pokémon dataset.[3] Prior to applying our method, all datasets were binarized. In the Zoo dataset, the categorical attribute *legs* was converted into a binary distinction, namely *has legs* versus *does not have legs*. In the Congressional voting records dataset, missing values were handled by duplicating each attribute into separate *yes* and *no* variants. For the Pokémon dataset, we adopted the binarization proposed in [6].

We applied MDS to the factors obtained by the GRECOND algorithm, using the Jaccard-based dissimilarity D_J, computed over both intents and extents, and the overlap-based dissimilarity D_o.

4.1 Zoo Data

For this dataset, we obtained 22 factors. Given this relatively small number, all factors were retained for subsequent visualization.

After projection into two-dimensional space (Fig. 4), several clusters of factors can be observed across all visualizations, easily identifiable even without detailed inspection of the coordinates. We refer to these as reference clusters. This is consistent with the underlying logic of MDS algorithms, which aim to position the most distinctive entities first.

Analysis of the clusters reveals clear patterns corresponding to major animal classes. Specifically, clusters represent mammals (cluster C_1), birds (cluster C_2), and fish (cluster C_3). Remaining factors are positioned according to their proximity to these reference clusters, and the clusters remain recognizable across all similarity measures.

Cluster C_1 contains factors 1, 5, 10, and 21, all describing mammals exclusively. These factors share defining characteristics, notably *hair* and *milk production.*

The bird-dominated cluster C_2 contains factor 2, describing only birds. The main shared attribute is *eggs*, although a few insects also appear due to traits such as *eggs*, *legs*, *breathing*, or *flight*. These inclusions reflect functional rather than phylogenetic similarities.

The last cluster C_3 is dominated by *fish* and associated with traits such as an *aquatic habitat*, *eggs*, *backbone*, *fins*, *tail*, *teeth*, and *predator*. Atypical aquatic mammals and birds, including *dolphins* and *penguins*, also appear nearby. Their relative rarity within their classes places them closer to *fish* in the embedding, reflecting shared ecosystemic and physiological traits.

The strong correspondence between clusters, animal classes, and defining physiological traits is exemplified by factor 17, representing aquatic mammals,

[3] https://www.kaggle.com/datasets/rounakbanik/pokemon.

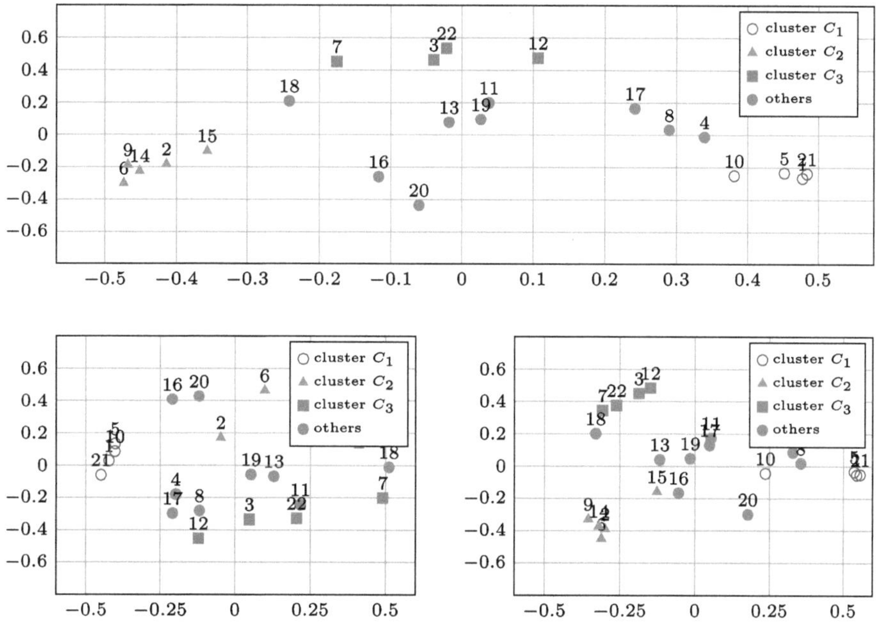

Fig. 4. MDS projections of the Zoo dataset for: overlapping coefficient (top), Jaccard over intents (bottom left), and Jaccard over extents (bottom right).

which consistently occupies an intermediate position between the *fish* and *mammal* clusters across all visualizations.

In all cases, the stress value was low, suggesting that the factors are well differentiated and that the obtained embedding is informative.

4.2 Pokémon Data

The Pokémon dataset comprises 801 Pokémon from seven generations, each described by 73 binary attributes encoding type membership (allowing multiple types), effectiveness against other types at different intensity levels, and legendary status. We restricted our analysis to the first generation (151 Pokémon). The resulting factorization produced 51 factors; however, this number proved impractical for visual interpretation. Therefore, only the first 25 factors, covering 90% of the data, were retained for subsequent analysis.

The resulting projections reveal less distinct cluster structures compared to the other datasets. Across the considered similarity measures, clusters are generally weaker and less clearly separated.

For the overlapping coefficient (see Fig. 5, top), two large clusters can be observed in the central part of the graph. Although these clusters contain several overlapping factors, their internal cohesion is not particularly strong. What these factors share is that they are highly dissimilar to most of the remaining factors; however, each of them differs in a distinct way.

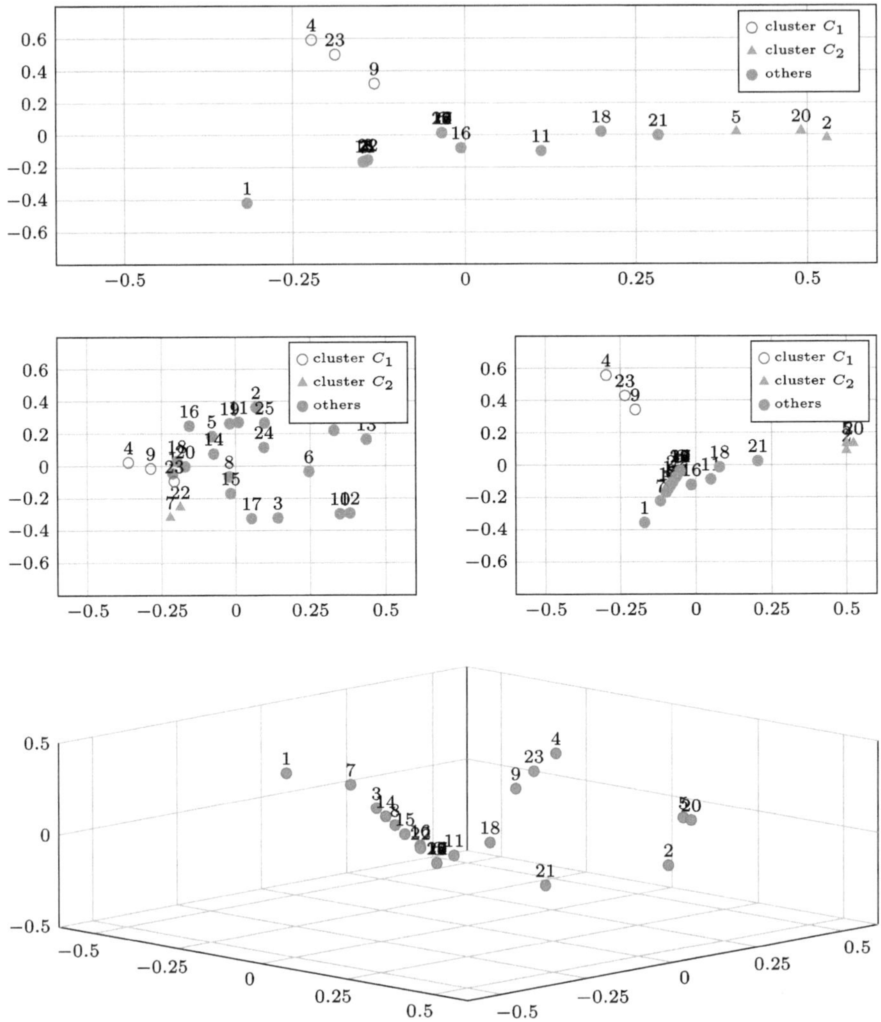

Fig. 5. MDS projections of the Pokémon dataset for: overlapping coefficient (top), Jaccard over intents (middle left), Jaccard over extents (middle right) and Jaccard over extents in 3D.

Cluster C_1 consisting of factors 4, 9, and 23 appears consistently across all visualizations; this cluster represents *ground-* and *rock-type* Pokémon.

When using the overlapping coefficient and Jaccard similarity over extents, another cluster emerges, grouping factor 5 (*grass-type* Pokémon) with factors 2 (*poison-type* Pokémon) and 20 (mainly *grass-* and *poison-type*), see C_2 in Fig. 5 (top and middle right). This indicates that *grass-type* Pokémon share similarities with a subset of *poison-type* Pokémon. This is consistent with the well-known overlap between *grass-* and *poison-type* Pokémon in the first generation, where many *grass-type* also possess the *poison-type*.

A similarly interesting cluster appears when using Jaccard over intents. In the lower-left region of the graph, factors 7 and 22 form a cluster, see C_2 in Fig. 5 (middle left). Factor 7 corresponds to a subset of *water-type* Pokémon, while factor 22 represents *ice-* and *water-type* Pokémon. This grouping indicates that *ice-type* Pokémon share notable similarities with many *water-type* Pokémon. This reflects the underlying design of Pokémon type system as in early generations where most *ice-type* Pokémon simultaneously possess the *water-type*.

Using Jaccard similarity over extents results in a projection with a relatively high stress value (0.72). Increasing the embedding dimension to three, see Fig. 5 (bottom), improves the representation, as reflected by a lower stress value (0.64).

Overall, the Pokémon dataset exhibits relatively high structural complexity. As a result, cluster structures are less pronounced; nevertheless, meaningful relationships between factors can still be identified in the visualizations.

4.3 Congressional Voting Records Data

The Congressional voting records data captures the voting behavior of 435 members of the U.S. House of Representatives on 16 key legislative issues in 1984. Each congressman is described by binary attributes indicating their votes, together with a class label specifying party affiliation (Democrat or Republican).

The BMF of the voting data yielded 76 factors. For subsequent analysis, we retained the first 33 factors, covering 90% of the data.

After plotting the projections, three clearly distinguishable clusters emerge across all graphs (see Fig. 6). Factors in cluster C_1 predominantly contain objects labeled Democrat, whereas factors in cluster C_2 group objects labeled Republican. Cluster C_3 comprises factors whose objects belong to both the Democrat and Republican classes, with class ratios varying but typically close to 50:50.

Within clusters C_1 and C_2, the factors exhibit high mutual similarity. In contrast, the factors in cluster C_3 are not necessarily similar to one another; however, they share some degree of similarity with other factors.

Democratic representatives in cluster C_1 are characterized by factors with "yes" votes on the adoption of the budget resolution and aid to the Nicaraguan Contras. These votes reflect core Democratic positions of the era, emphasizing government spending and selective foreign intervention.

Republican representatives in cluster C_2 are characterized by voting in favor of crime-related measures, approval of foreign aid to El Salvador, and specific positions on education spending. They overwhelmingly voted "yes" on these issues. In contrast, Democrats generally voted oppositely, highlighting a clear separation between the parties.

4.4 Discussion

The resulting projections provide a concise overview of the factorization as a whole. This overview makes it possible to identify groups of related factors, as

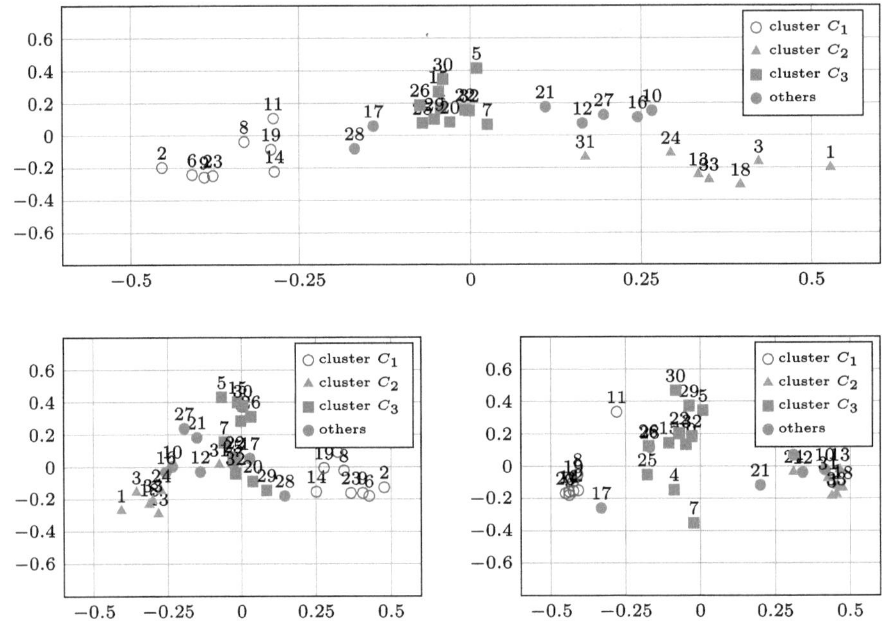

Fig. 6. MDS results on the Congressional Voting Records dataset for three similarity measures: overlap coefficient (top), Jaccard over intent (bottom left), and Jaccard over extent (bottom right).

well as factors that are clearly separated from the others, thereby highlighting potentially significant and interpretable factors (cf. the second and third Thurstone criteria). Moreover, the similarity between certain factors significantly facilitates their interpretation. Once one factor has been interpreted, the meaning of related factors can be inferred more easily from their mutual relationships.

During subsequent analysis, attention may be restricted to selected clusters, or a representative factor may be chosen from each cluster. This strategy is particularly suitable when working with many factors or heterogeneous data. It is especially useful when a class attribute is available, as objects from the same class may naturally form subcategories not explicitly encoded in the original attributes and not immediately apparent in the data. In the visualization, factors associated with a single class may therefore appear in distinct clusters, revealing meaningful differences between these subcategories. This reduction simplifies interpretation by enabling analysis of individual substructures before integrating them into the broader context. Importantly, the same approach remains applicable even without an explicit class attribute. Overall, the resulting visualization provides a valuable tool for analyzing and interpreting BMF results.

4.5 Practical Notes

The proposed approach is limited by the properties of MDS. As the number of factors increases, projection into two- or three-dimensional space becomes less accurate. Since we employ classical MDS, it is also possible in our case to assess how well the original data are approximated in a lower-dimensional space. In general, this issue can be addressed by focusing only on the first l factors instead of considering all factors.

5 BFLens

BFLens[4] is a web-based application developed as part of this work that enables interactive exploration of BMF results through the visualization techniques presented in this paper, as well as additional views such as the coverage quality curve, similarity matrices, and interactive inspection of individual factors. The tool aims to simplify the otherwise time-consuming process of factor exploration, which has so far largely relied on manual analysis.

The software is implemented as a web-based visualization tool using the Next.js framework. Its monolithic design allows execution as a standalone application without reliance on external services, enabling local deployment. In addition, the application can be deployed on a server, facilitating presentation and sharing of results through a web interface. The use of Next.js supports efficient rendering, flexible deployment strategies, and a unified codebase for both local execution and web-based presentation.

The user interface, optimized for desktop use, is divided into four sections, each highlighting a different aspect of the factorization results: (i) the general overview, presenting the data and extracted factors, including factor size and coverage; (ii) the class distribution, summarizing class occurrences across factors when available; (iii) the factor overlap, examining shared attributes and classes between factors and the original data; and (iv) the factor similarity section, visualizing relationships and similarities among factors. An example of the user interface is shown in Fig. 7.

For performance reasons, we chose to precompute all statistics using an external script rather than calculating them within the application. The script takes the factorization as input—namely the input matrix **I** and matrices **A** and **B**—and outputs the processed data in JSON format, which are subsequently visualized by the application. This design choice is motivated by computational efficiency, as computing all characteristics for larger datasets can be time-consuming and is better handled by technology optimized for numerical processing. In future work, we plan to integrate this preprocessing step directly into the application.

[4] The source code of the application is publicly available on GitHub at https://github.com/PavlikovaVeronika/BFLens.

Fig. 7. BFLens tool.

6 Conclusion

In this paper, we addressed the problem of interpreting BMF results from a qualitative and exploratory perspective. While existing approaches typically emphasize quantitative measures such as reconstruction error, we focused on structural relationships between factors and their role in interpretation. We discussed key characteristics of individual factors and proposed visualization techniques that support exploratory analysis, facilitate interpretation, and reduce the number of factors considered in subsequent investigation.

To capture the overall structure of a factorization, we introduced a similarity-based approach combined with multi dimensional scaling, enabling simultaneous visualization of relationships among all factors. The resulting projections provide an intuitive global overview, reveal clusters of related factors, and highlight distinctive or particularly interpretable factors. The approach is designed primarily as an exploratory tool, supporting interactive investigation rather than formal statistical inference.

We demonstrated the proposed methodology on datasets with different structural properties and showed that it uncovers meaningful patterns even in structurally complex data. Finally, we presented BFLens, a web-based tool for interactive exploration of BMF results that integrates the proposed visualizations into a unified analytical framework.

Future research will pursue several directions. First, the results of the proposed analysis depend on the chosen similarity measure. Although preliminary experiments with alternative similarities revealed substantial differences, some clusters remained stable across measures. A natural continuation of this work is a more extensive experimental study of the similarity measures discussed in [2], including their systematic comparison with respect to suitability for visualization and exploratory analysis. Furthermore, the proposed approach can be extended to support direct comparison of different factorizations, a task frequently required in practice. Another promising direction is the incorporation of interactive zooming mechanisms. In particular, a selected region of the projection could be re-visualized using an alternative similarity measure, potentially revealing finer-grained relationships between factors and facilitate their interpretability.

Acknowledgments. This work was supported by Grant No. IGA_PrF_2025_18 and IGA_PrF_2026_26 of the Internal Grant Agency of Palacký University Olomouc.

References

1. Belohlavek, R., Vychodil, V.: Discovery of optimal factors in binary data via a novel method of matrix decomposition. J. Comput. Syst. Sci. **76**(1), 3–20 (2010). https://doi.org/10.1016/j.jcss.2009.05.002
2. Belohlavek, R., Mikula, T.: Similarity metrics vs human judgment of similarity for binary data: which is best to predict typicality? Appl. Soft Comput. **153**, 111270 (2024). https://doi.org/10.1016/j.asoc.2024.111270
3. Belohlavek, R., Outrata, J., Trnecka, M.: Toward quality assessment of Boolean matrix factorizations. Inf. Sci. **459**, 71–85 (2018). https://doi.org/10.1016/j.ins.2018.05.016
4. Belohlavek, R., Trnecka, M.: Semantic explorations in factorizing Boolean data via formal concepts. Int. J. Approx. Reasoning **173**, 109247 (2024). https://doi.org/10.1016/j.ijar.2024.109247
5. Belohlavek, R., Krmelova, M.: Factor analysis of ordinal data via decomposition of matrices with grades. Ann. Math. Artif. Intell. **72**, 23–44 (2014). https://doi.org/10.1007/s10472-014-9398-6
6. Brazdilova, K., Trnecka, M., Trneckova, M.: Data preprocessing using banded structure and image morphology enhancing Boolean matrix factorization. Knowl.-Based Syst. **329**(B), 114366 (2025). https://doi.org/10.1016/j.knosys.2025.114366
7. Cattell, R.B.: The Scientific Use of Factor Analysis in Behavioral and Life Sciences. Springer, US (1978)
8. Chen, C.-H., Härdle, W.K., Unwin, A. (eds.): Handbook of Data Visualization. Springer, Berlin (2008)
9. Forsyth, R.: Zoo [Dataset]. UCI Mach. Learn. Repos. (1990). https://doi.org/10.24432/C5R59V
10. Ganter, B., Glodeanu, C.V.: Ordinal factor analysis. In: Domenach, F., Ignatov, D.I., Poelmans, J. (eds.) Formal Concept Analysis (ICFCA 2012),Lecture Notes in Computer Science, vol. 7278, pp. 128–139. Springer, Berlin (2012). https://doi.org/10.1007/978-3-642-29892-9_15
11. Ganter, B., Wille, R.: Formal Concept Analysis: Mathematical Foundations, 2nd edn. Springer (2024)
12. Miettinen, P., Neumann, S.: Recent developments in Boolean matrix factorization. In: Proceedings of the IJCAI 2020, Survey Track, pp. 4922–4928 (2020). https://doi.org/10.24963/ijcai.2020/685
13. Borg, I., Groenen, P.J.F.: Modern Multidimensional Scaling: Theory and Applications, 2nd edn. Springer, New York (2005)
14. Royce, J.R.: Factors as theoretical constructs. Am. Psychol. **18**(8), 522 (1963)

15. Thurstone, L.L.: Multiple-Factor Analysis: A Development and Expansion of the Vectors of Mind. University of Chicago Press (1947)
16. Tufte, E.R.: The Visual Display of Quantitative Information, 2nd edn. Graphics Press, Cheshire (2001)
17. Tversky, A.: Features of similarity. Psychol. Rev. **84**(4), 327–352 (1977). https://doi.org/10.1037/0033-295X.84.4.327
18. Congressional Voting Records [Dataset]. UCI Mach. Learn. Repos. (1987). https://doi.org/10.24432/C5C01P

Exploring Cultural Heritage Corpus Using Formal Concept Analysis

Olivier Bruneau[2], Prunelle D. Treuil[1], Jean Lieber[1], Emmanuel Nauer[1](✉), and Laurent Rollet[2]

[1] LORIA, Université de Lorraine, Nancy, France
{prunelle.daudre-treuil,jean.lieber,emmanuel.nauer}@loria.fr
[2] AHP-PReST, Université de Lorraine, Université de Strasbourg, Strasbourg, France
{olivier.bruneau,laurent.rollet}@univ-lorraine.fr

Abstract. This paper presents Harold, a system based on formal concept analysis (FCA) to access and explore a cultural heritage corpus. The application focuses on the correspondence of the French mathematician Henri Poincaré, comprising more than 2,000 letters written in French, which have been digitized and semantically annotated using RDF. The objective of Harold is to provide a conversational interface that enables historians to explore and navigate the corpus interactively. To this end, the system organizes the documents into a hierarchical conceptual structure derived through FCA, offering a synthetic and structured view of the collection. The formal concepts generated by FCA provide analytical insights that can guide further retrieval steps, enabling users to discover new documents relevant to their research questions. Users can interact with the resulting concept lattice to progressively refine their focus, identifying relevant documents while excluding irrelevant ones. Beyond document navigation, the concept hierarchy highlights candidate terms that historians can curate into a folksonomy—i.e., a user-defined hierarchy of terms connected by heterogeneous, untyped relations—through a dedicated knowledge management interface. In this way, the system supports users in structuring and managing research-related concepts while simultaneously conducting their investigation. The resulting folksonomy is also subsequently reintegrated in the FCA process to enhance the hierarchical organization of documents.

Keywords: formal concept analysis · hierarchical access · folksonomy and terminology management · conversational system · textual corpus exploration

1 Introduction

This paper addresses a conversational system based on formal concept analysis (FCA) whose goal is to explore the correspondence of Henri Poincaré, and textual corpus in general. Henri Poincaré (1854-1912) is a famous French mathematician who has contributed to various domains (mathematics, philosophy of science, theoretical physics, and astrophysics), exchanging with numerous other scholars. The main goal of historians working in the AHP-PReST laboratory is to study the correspondence of Henri Poincaré containing more than 2,000 letters sent by or received by Henri Poincaré.[1]

[1] https://poincare.univ-lorraine.fr.

M. Croitoru et al. (Eds.): CONCEPTS 2026, LNAI 16811, pp. 277–291, 2027.
https://doi.org/10.1007/978-3-032-34742-8_18

One of their works consists in analyzing the letters to gather them into thematic volumes (e.g., letters to mathematicians [9] or letters to geodesists [14]).

These letters have been digitized, transcribed in plain text, and annotated with general metadata, with the objective of being queried through a SPARQL endpoint. These metadata are represented using RDFS, an extension of RDF providing a basic vocabulary description language for defining classes, properties, and hierarchical relationships between resources on the Semantic Web [3]. So, electronic resources are available and can be used by a web site access[2] or by a SPARQL endpoint access which a restricted access for authenticated users. However, there are three main difficulties: (1) the use of SPARQL for historians and, more generally, users that are not computer scientists, is difficult; (2) the historians need to know the vocabulary used in the annotations; and (3) solving a precise search problem is usually based on the assumption that the user has a clear and formal idea of the query at the start of the process. But for historians who want to answer a historical research question (e.g., what has Henri Poincaré written about mathematics for physics?), the objective is more general and has to be made precise for querying the system. At the same time, historians need to take into account new pieces of knowledge they will acquire about concepts (mathematical functions, institutions, people, etc.) relevant to the research question.

These difficulties have led to the implementation of a conversational query system, called Harold, to query and explore the corpus through a more iterative process. The users will, step by step, refine their search and find the data that interest them, without the requirement of having to write a SPARQL query themselves. Harold implements an exploration process, organizing letters hierarchically (and not in a mere list) using FCA [6] on the properties of the letters, highlighting at the same time frequent sets of properties (and therefore links between properties) associated with sets of letters. Users can interact with Harold to specify their needs based on the clustering of properties, and thus iteratively search the corpus to discover links between different elements in the letters. Therefore, this approach helps overcome the difficulties listed above. Moreover, studying a given historical research problem involves knowledge about the research topic. Harold provides an interface in which the historian can organize their knowledge in a folksonomy (a hierarchy of terms organized, without a well-defined semantics). The terms extracted from the letters and displayed in the hierarchical organization of sets of letters are good candidate terms to identify and organize, in the first step, a folksonomy of Henri Poincaré correspondence. For this, specific functionalities allow the user to manage and organize the terms hierarchically. Harold uses this folksonomy to extend the term annotation by associating more general terms with a letter. This affects the hierarchical structure built using FCA by gathering letters in more general sets of letters, e.g., if the user has indicated that *physics* is more general than *heat propagation*, then a letter related to *heat propagation* is also related to *physics*. Moreover, every time letters about *physics* are searched, those about *heat propagation* will also be retrieved. This back and forth between the user, the corpus, and the folksonomy facilitates the generation of new pieces of knowledge.

The paper is organized as follows. Section 2 presents the preliminaries. Section 3 highlights the motivations. Section 4 describes the Harold system: the main functional-

[2] https://henripoincare.fr/.

ities are illustrated by a running example and the way FCA is used is detailed. Section 5 describes the folksonomy management the system offers to the users. Section 6 gives the related work. Section 7 concludes the paper.

2 Preliminaries

This section describes previous work to exploit the Henri-Poincaré correspondence, the available data, and the tools that will be used for this work.

2.1 The Henri Poincaré Corpus and the Henri Poincaré Ontology

The Henri Poincaré correspondence corpus contains more than 2, 000 letters exchanged by the French mathematician Henri Poincaré with more than 300 correspondents. The letters use five languages (French, English, German, Sami, and Swedish), but only letters in French (around 1, 500 letters) are considered in this work. These letters were written between the start of the mathematician's study at *École polytechnique* (a famous French school) in 1873 and his death in 1912. All these documents have been collected, digitized, transcribed, and annotated semantically with general metadata and additional information produced by historians for over 30 years. These additional pieces of information produced by historians are of various types (e.g., context of the letter, information about a person or a place mentioned in the letter) and constitute the so-called critical apparatus of the corpus.

The letters are available in three formats: hardback thematic books (e.g., [9, 12]), a website[2], and a SPARQL endpoint, currently accessed with a login and a password. The website uses Omeka-S [8], a content management system for cultural heritage collection with some additional tools to manage ontologies. This website proposes a simple search engine with limited functionalities. In fact, the engine only scans the raw text for the searched keywords and does not allow the user to express more complex and nuanced queries. The SPARQL endpoint has been recently added to allow for a direct and more precise query to the knowledge base, but requires in-depth knowledge of the SPARQL language and the ontology vocabulary.

Each letter is described by semantic annotations using RDF triples, as illustrated in Fig. 1. Triples use properties of the Henri Poincaré ontology (`ahpo` prefix), such as the sender (`ahpo:sentBy`), the recipient (`ahpo:sentTo`), the written place (`ahpo:writtenAt`), the language (`ahpo:language`), and the date (`ahpo:writingDate`).

The Henri Poincaré ontology has been developed by the Henri Poincaré Archives to organize all metadata related to the Henri Poincaré correspondence. It contains the properties required to describe the letters, the person exchanging these letters or simply cited in it, but also information about the archiving (archiving place, copyrights, etc.) and about the various books and web articles published by the Archives (presented letters, cited persons, etc.). Numerous other documents related to the life of Henri Poincaré are also described by this ontology: scientific articles and journals, books published by the mathematician, theses, etc.

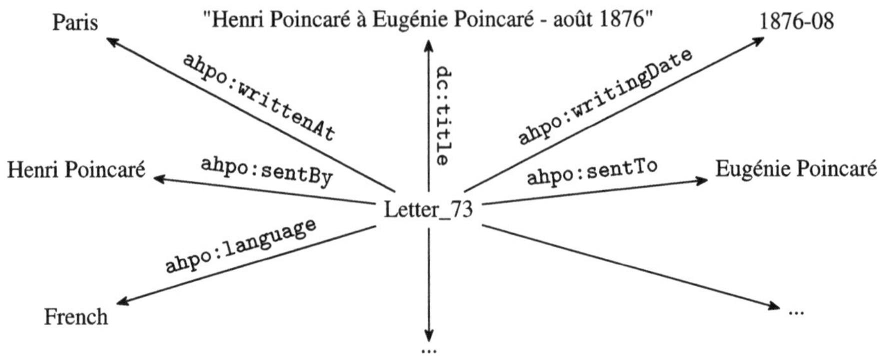

Fig. 1. RDF triples associated to the letter *"Henri Poincaré to Eugénie Poincaré - August 1876."*

2.2 Formal Concept Analysis

FCA is a mathematical approach to data analysis based on lattice theory. A *formal context* is a triple $\mathcal{K} = (O, A, R)$, where O is a set of objects, A is a set of attributes, R is the relation on $O \times A$ stating that an object is described by an attribute property [6]. Fig. 2 (a) gives an example of formal context: O is a set of 6 letters ($\{\mathtt{l}_1,...,\mathtt{l}_6\}$) and A is the set of 7 properties that annotate the letters. A *formal concept* is a pair (E, I) (with $E \subseteq O$, $I \subseteq A$), such that (1) it is a *rectangle* of $\mathcal{K}$ (for every $o \in E$ and $a \in I$, oRa) and (2) it is maximal in the sense that if (F, J) is a rectangle such that $E \subseteq F$ and $I \subseteq J$, then $F = E$ and $J = I$. E is called the *extent* and I is called the *intent* of the formal concept. For example, $(\{\mathtt{l}_1, \mathtt{l}_4\}, \{\mathtt{physics}, \mathtt{differential\ equation}\})$ is a concept. Furthermore, the set $\mathcal{C}_\mathcal{K}$ of all formal concepts of the context $\mathcal{K} = (O, A, R)$ is partially ordered by extent inclusion, also called *specialization* (denoted by $\leq_\mathcal{K}$) between concepts. $\mathcal{L} = \langle \mathcal{C}_\mathcal{K}, \leq_\mathcal{K} \rangle$ is a complete lattice, called the *concept lattice*. The lattice $\mathcal{L}$ can be drawn as a Hasse diagram where the nodes are concepts and the arrows are specialization links, as illustrated in Fig. 2 (b). In this illustration, the top concept contains all the letters; its intent is empty because there is no common property shared by all the letters. By contrast, the bottom concept is defined by the set of all properties, and its extent is empty because none of the letters is described by all the properties. Several algorithms have been proposed for the construction of concept lattices; see [6]. For Harold, CORON is used,[3] where CORON is a software platform that implements a wide set of algorithmic methods for symbolic data mining, including concept lattice construction algorithms [13].

3 Motivations

If the existing interfaces (website and SPARQL endpoint interface) provide easier ways to access the data, there still remains the difficulty of exploring and analyzing the corpus even if the goal of the current study of the user is well defined. Let us take, for example,

[3] http://coron.loria.fr.

	physics	mathematics	three – body problem	differential equation	abelian function	analitic function	Physics Nobel Commitee
l_1	×	×	×	×	×		
l_2	×	×	×				
l_3	×	×	×				
l_4	×			×			
l_5		×	×			×	×
l_6		×	×				

(a)

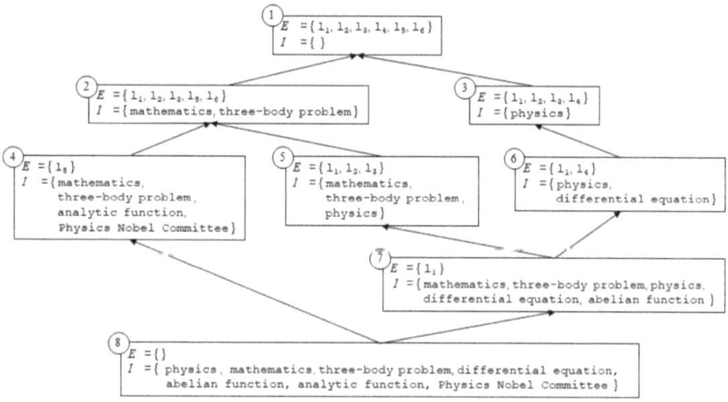

(b)

Fig. 2. A binary context (a) and the corresponding concept lattice (b).

the question of "Mathematics for physics". The objective is well defined but studying what Henri Poincaré has exchanged about this topic requires more than simple queries on metadata: (1) in addition to RDF annotations, the full text content must be also taken into account; (2) a set of queries covering this topic is difficult to establish because some letters may not contain the words "mathematics" or "physics" but may contain more precise terms linked to these two terms (such as, for example, "heat propagation" for "physics" and "equation" for "mathematics"); (3) the whole vocabulary belonging to a given concept is most of the time not established, especially if the addressed concept is a new aspect of what the historians want to study; and (4) usually, when starting a study, the historian does not have a clear and formal idea of what exactly to search but more a general or vague idea that has to be made precise.

All these points have motivated the implementation of a conversational query system to help historians with their task. Natural Language Processing (NLP) has been used to automatically extract terms (simple controlled terms, nominal groups, named entities) to enrich the description of a letter by new properties coming from its full text. The use of FCA on letter properties (including new properties automatically extracted from full texts) provides a way to explore the set of letters, to highlight regularities in these letters, and to organize and group letters according to the properties they share. The users can interact with this system to specify their needs on the basis of the clustering of properties, and thus iteratively search the corpus to discover links between different elements in the letters. Finally, the new knowledge emerging during the exploration process (concepts related to a particular research question) must be capitalized to improve the exploration. That is why a specific interface allows the historian to manage terminology organized in a folksonomy in parallel with the exploration of the letters.

4 The Harold System

The Harold system has been designed to help historians explore the Henri Poincaré correspondence through functionalities for retrieving letters, analyzing their content, and acquiring knowledge, i.e., discovering knowledge units related to their historical research questions from properties appearing conjointly and frequently in formal concepts, as well as the facility to manage these knowledge units through a dedicated knowledge management interface. In order to propose the exploitation of the full text of the letters and of the critical apparatus, an NLP step for the identification of terms in full texts has been developed. Section 4.1 explains how the letters have been annotated from the full text, Sect. 4.2 introduces a running example followed, in the next sections, by the description and illustration of Harold functionalities on this running example.

4.1 Exploiting Full Texts Using NLP

The work of historians analyzing the Henri Poincaré correspondence requires the exploitation of the full text of the letters and/or of the critical apparatus, and not only the exploitation of the basic metadata produced during the transcription and stored in the SPARQL endpoint. In order to do so, a list of terms has been extracted from every letter and from their critical apparatus. This was done in two ways: both by using an already existing list of predefined terms to check their presence in texts and by automatically extracting noun phrases.

This allows the system to use different types of information found in the letter. First, all scientific terms are mainly found by automatic extraction of noun phrases, completed by a list of terms established by the historians. Second, many institutes such as Nobel committees or scientific academies are also extracted as noun phrases. Several terms coming from the social environment of Henri Poincaré are also used, such as those of the polytechnic slang. This list was established by the historians of the Henri Poincaré Archive, since many words have completely different meanings in different settings. For example, *rat* is used to indicate a person who is late instead of referring to the animal. Since these terms are one-word only and could be seen as not important by non-specialists, keeping them in a list is primordial. Finally, a last list of terms created by the historians is the list of all the cultural and scientific works cited in the letters and critical apparatus (e.g., theater play, book, scientific article).

4.2 Running Example

Let us take as running example the study about the impact of the mathematician's work on the physics research. The historian can use Harold to search for letters related to this research problem. As a starting point, they could look for letters exchanged with the physicists Henri Poincaré knew. Terms linked to *mathematical physics* could be used for a keyword search (e.g., *mathematics*, *physics* or more precise concepts such as *differential equation*, *three-body problem*, etc.). Solving this historical research problem is not a one-step process and requires many searches and analysis of the content of the letters. Based on the first result, the historian can query again the system on different terms linked to their search (e.g., more specific terms of physics and mathematics, scientific circles, institutes). In contrast, some results may appear to be irrelevant for the research problem and require to be excluded from the search scope.

During this step-by-step access to the letters and their content, some knowledge can progressively emerge, especially the vocabulary of the search scope (i.e., terms) and, by extension, the concepts described by these terms. Managing these concepts, in particular organizing them into a folksonomy, is helpful for such a type of search and can furthermore be exploited to improve the search.

Section 4.3 presents the search form used to explore the corpus. In Sect. 4.4, we explain how the results are displayed. Section 4.5 illustrates different types of interactions with Harold and shows the benefit of an interactive and iterative exploration process. Section 4.6 gives a formal description of how user interactions are linked to the FCA process that computes the hierarchical organization of letters.

4.3 Searching Letters by Properties

Harold allows to search, in the Henri Poincaré correspondence, letters that have some properties using a specific search form illustrated in Fig. 3. In this screenshot, the historian searches for the letters that contain the term *physique* (French for: *physics*). This form also allows the user to indicate which properties are useful to examine for the research problem. The checkboxes on the right-hand side of the textual input indicate that the property has to be taken into account by the FCA (if checked) or not (if not checked). In the illustration, the historian has mentioned that they are interested in knowing who exchanged on this subject (i.e., `Sender` and `Recipient` properties), and what terms appear in both the letters and their critical apparatus (`Containing` properties). The content of this form is transformed into a SPARQL query in order to search for letters that have the desired properties.

Finding all the letters useful to answer a given research problem in one attempt is rare, so some back-and-forth between the user and the system is required. In this way, Harold manages, for a given research problem, a set of letters related to this problem. The idea is that the set of letters evolves, being established progressively by adding new letters (e.g., with additional queries) or by removing irrelevant letters. In the interface, *Start a new search* refers to the creation of a new set of letters and *Complete the current search* refers to the addition of new letters to the current set of letters of the research problem.

4.4 Visualizing the Results

Instead of showing the letters retrieved from the search form through a simple list, Harold triggers FCA on the retrieved letters and the properties selected by the historian. The objective is to build a synthetic view, gathering letters according to the properties they share, and highlighting their common properties, as explained and illustrated in Sect. 4.6. The lattice resulting from the FCA on letter properties is hierarchically displayed using a depth-first search, as shown in Fig. 4. The sign ⌄, at the beginning of the lines, indicates that the set of letters is detailed by displaying its subsets, while the sign › indicates that the subsets are not displayed. The description of a subset contains only properties that are not inherited from the more general set already displayed. For example, in Fig. 4, the 96 letters sent to *Henri Poincaré* are letters that also contain *physique* in the letter. The user can interact with these two signs to open or close some parts of the hierarchy according to what is interesting or not. The minimal size of the sets displayed is a parameter of the search. The user can modify it. In the illustration, it

Fig. 3. The search form filled with a search on *physique*, looking for the people involved and the content of the letters.

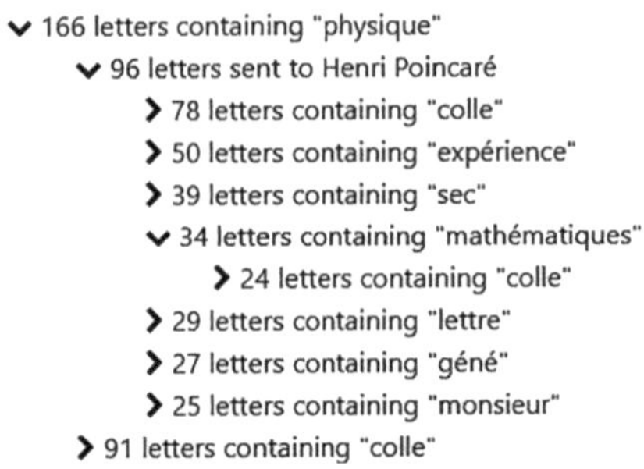

Fig. 4. Hierarchical presentation of the results after starting a new search on *physique* (as illustrated in Fig. 3).

has been fixed to 24, but will be fixed to 40 in the following figures to better showcase the resulting hierarchy.

In this illustration, it can be seen, from the 166 letters containing *physique*, that 96 of these letters have been sent to *Henri Poincaré* and, since this group of 96 letters is detailed, some additional characteristics are also displayed. Interestingly, many of the terms extracted from the letters containing *physique* come from polytechnic slang. The terms *mathématiques* (French for: *mathematics*) and *expérience* (French for: *experiment*) are also potentially interesting to solve the research problem of the running example.

4.5 Interacting with the Results

As expected, to find all the letters related to the topic *"Mathematics for physics"*, a search for letters containing *physique* is not enough, in particular because most of the letters do not contain this term. The idea, with the interaction functionalities provided by Harold, is that, from the letters found at a given step, and in particular with a first query, the user could trigger new queries to search for additional letters, and provide other feedbacks to improve the hierarchical organization of letters provided by the FCA process, e.g., by removing irrelevant letters, by expressing that a property is not relevant according to the research question, and by managing knowledge that will be embedded in the FCA process.

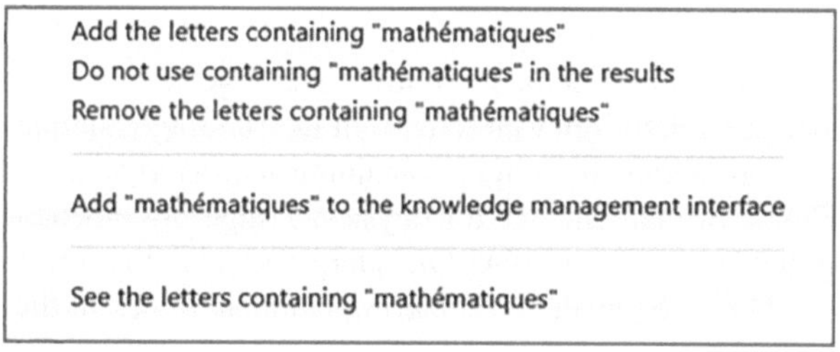

Fig. 5. Actions associated to the 34 letters *contains "mathématiques"* of Fig. 4.

As illustrated in Fig. 5, several actions associated to each letter group are available (in the screenshot, the actions concern the 34 letters containing the term *mathématiques*). The three first possible actions are related to the analysis of the letters, the fourth one is linked to the ontology management (see Sect. 5) and the last one provides access to the letters themselves. The actions are now detailed:

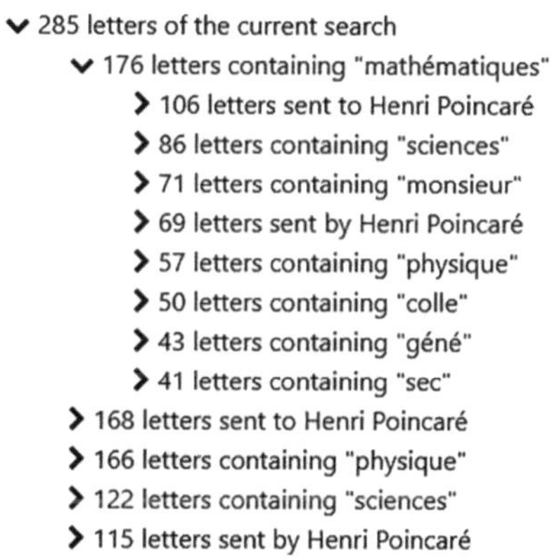

Fig. 6. The results after adding the letters containing the term *"mathématiques"*.

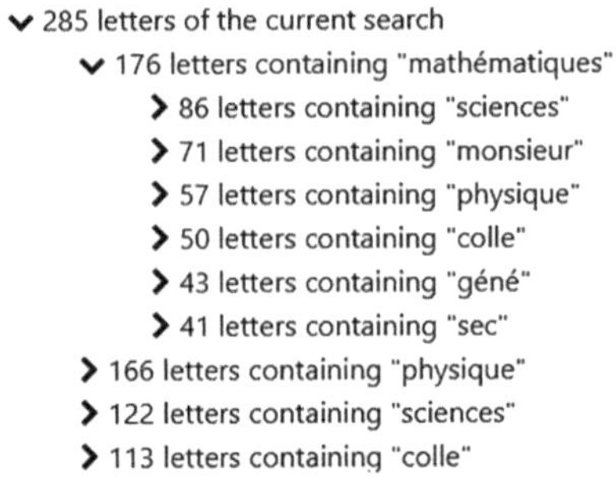

Fig. 7. The results after removing properties `sent by` and `sent to` Henri Poincaré.

- *Add the letters containing "mathématiques"*: The objective of this functionality is to retrieve other potentially relevant letters. In the running example, the user could want to know more about the letters containing *mathématiques* as they could be related to the topic of mathematics for physics. Triggering this action retrieves the corresponding letters by a new SPARQL query and adds them to the set of letters to be analyzed. This is equivalent to entering *mathématiques* in the **Containing in the letters** field of the search form and clicking on *Complete the current search.* Figure 6 shows the result after using this action. 119 letters have been added, and the subsets of these letters reveal new formal concept properties.
- *Do not use containing "mathématiques" in the results*: The objective of this functionality is to not take into account the property for grouping letters using FCA and to clean the hierarchical result from group of letters not useful for the research problem. In the running example, it is not used on *mathématiques*, because this set of letters is interesting for the current research problem. However, this functionality could be interesting to avoid generating sets of letters *sent by* or *sent to* Henri Poincaré, which are not helpful for the research problem of the running example. Figure 7 shows the results after having removed these two properties from the formal context used to build the hierarchy.
- *Remove the letters containing "mathématiques"*: The objective of this functionality is to eliminate letters that are not interesting at all for the research problem. For the running example, removing the letters containing *mathématiques* is not adequate, but sometimes letters that are not helpful for a given research problem appear, and this functionality allows removing them from the analysis. Compared to the previous functionality which removes properties (attributes) in the formal context, this functionality will remove documents (objects).
- *Add "mathématiques" to the knowledge management interface*: The objective of this functionality is to help the user acquire knowledge about the content of the letter. The term *mathématiques* is added to the set of unlabeled concepts of the knowledge management interface, waiting to be placed in the folsksonomy hierarchy.

4.6 Formal Description of the Hierarchy Computation Using FCA

The resolution of a historical research problem requires many interactions with Harold. These interactions have a direct impact on the hierarchical organization of the documents because they modify the way the formal context is built. At the beginning (i.e., before the first action of the user), the formal context is $K = (\emptyset, \emptyset, \emptyset)$: no object, no attribute, and so no relation between the set of objects and the set of attributes. At a given time, the formal context can be computed by a synthesis of the documents the user wants and does not want, as well as the properties or property/value the user wants and does not want. Let Q be a user query. Q is a non-empty set of property/value (p,v): $Q = \{(p_i, v_i)\}_i$ with $|Q| \geq 1$, where p_i is an RDF property and v_i a value. Let $D(Q) = \{d_j\}_j$ with $|D(Q)| \geq 0$ be the set of documents returned by the SPARQL endpoint to the query Q, i.e., the set of documents (RDF resource) having all the property/value of Q. In the context of the Henri Poincaré application, a document is a letter. For example, for $Q = \{(contains, \text{“physique”})\}$, $D(Q)$ is the set of letters returned by the SPARQL query `SELECT {?LetterId contains"physique".}`. Let Q^+ (resp. Q^-) be a query related to documents the user wants (resp. does not want).

Formal Context Object Set Computation. Let D^+ be the set of documents the user wants: $D^+ = \bigcup_i D(Q_i^+)$, the union of documents returned by the set $\{Q_i^+\}_i$ of queries. D^+ increases when the user triggers a new query. Let D^- be the set of documents the user does not want: $D^- = \bigcup_i D(Q_i^-)$, the union of documents returned by the set $\{Q_i^-\}_i$ of queries. When the user triggers “Start a new search”, “Complete the current search” or “Add the letters with a given property/value”, D^+ increases. When the user triggers “Remove the letters with a given property/value”, D^- increases. Finally, the set of objects O of the formal context at a given step is computed as $O = D^+ \setminus D^-$.

Formal Context Attribute Set Computation. Let $P_h = \{p_i\}_i$ be the set of properties that the user wants to explore (e.g., `sendBy`, `contains`). Let $P_d = \{(d, p, v)\}$ be the set of triples where p is a property linking the document d (i.e. a RDF resource) to a value v. The set of attributes A of the formal context K is computed according to the objects of O. Every property/value pairs linked to the documents of O are used to form A. Formally, $A = \cup_{d \in O}\{pv \mid (d, p, v) \in P_d\}$, with pv the concatenation of the property name p with the string representing v to build an attribute for the formal context.

The relation R between O and A is built from A and O: $R = \{(d_j, pv_k) \mid (d_j \in O, pv_k \in A, (d_j, p, v_k) \in P_{d_j}\}$.

5 Knowledge Management

A specific embedded knowledge management interface allows the manual creation of concepts related to the historical research problem. Currently, it manages primitive concepts, primitive properties, and their links. At this point, as well as in RDF, the primitive concepts and properties are seen as simple strings which can be organized hierarchically in groups, and constitute a folksonomy. As shown in Fig. 8, it has three main parts:

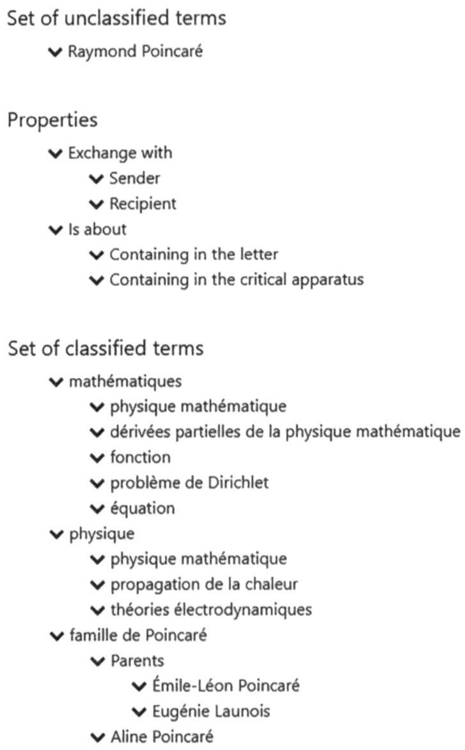

Fig. 8. Knowledge hierarchy management interface.

- a *set of unclassified termes*, containing candidate terms added by the user or retrieved from the *Add to the knowledge management interface* functionality or created by typing in a dedicated input field,
- a *set of classified terms*, organized hierarchically, and
- a *set of properties*, organized hierarchically as well.

For example, *Raymond Poincaré* is in the unclassified set of terms, while the classified set of terms includes *mathématiques*, *physique*, and *famille de Poincaré* (French for Henri Poincaré family) with their respective subterms (e.g., the parents and name of members of the Henri Poincaré family). Hierarchy management, including moving terms, is done by drag-and-drop. Here, *Raymond Poincaré* can be moved under *famille de Poincaré*.

The relation between two concepts is not well defined at this point, implying various types of relation in regard to an ontological point of view. For example, the type of relation between "Eugénie Launois" (Henri Poincaré's mother) and "Famille de Poincaré" is not the same as between "fonction" and "mathématiques". The first example of relation is related to an `isInstanceOf` property and the second one to a `subconceptOf` property. However, this non-well-defined relationships is not a problem for our application, as the goal of the hierarchy is to reflect specific/generic relationships w.r.t. a set (i.e., class) of letters. This means that if *fonction* is a child of *mathématiques* in the hierarchy, it has to be interpreted as "a letter about *fonction* will also be about *mathématiques*." Formally, using description logic notation, this means that the following formula could be added to a future ontology:

$$\texttt{Letter} \sqcap \exists \texttt{isAbout}.\{\texttt{"fonction"}\} \sqsubseteq \texttt{Letter} \sqcap \exists \texttt{isAbout}.\{\texttt{"mathématiques"}\}$$

6 Related Work

FCA has been used for a long time for conceptual structuring across domains. In the context of textual corpora, FCA has been applied to structure and navigate collections of documents by mapping documents and lexical features (such as terms, syntactic dependencies, or semantic entities) into formal contexts. Concept lattices derived from such contexts provide a semantic organization of the corpus, enabling hierarchical browsing, clustering of related documents, and identification of relevant terms [11]. In some work, the structure of the concept lattice is exploited to present a graphical view to access the corpus, e.g., [2]. In Harold, FCA is used to provide a hierarchical access to the corpus (by transformation of the concept lattice into a tree access) by contrast to an individual letter access. The fact that a research problem requires many steps and, therefore, interaction with the search system, has conducted to an approach in which the concept lattice is not built only once, but every time the user interacts with the system. Thus, Harold follows the approach of the CreChainDo system [10], an iterative and interactive information retrieval system that organizes Google web answers in a hierarchy using FCA. Navigation in the hierarchy helps the user explore a structured and synthetic result, and the user can interact with the result to indicate concepts that are relevant or irrelevant for a given information retrieval task. These user choices have an impact on the hierarchy: some concepts are removed if they are irrelevant, and new ones appear by triggering additional web queries about relevant concepts. All user interactions are taken into account by modifying the formal context, making the hierarchical access structure evolve. This approach is typically the one implemented by Harold.

The folksonomy building process presented in Sect. 5 is inspired by some of the many approaches that can be found in the literature (see [1] for a survey of ontology learning techniques). The folksonomy building is helped by candidate concepts resulting from an NLP process associated with the use of FCA to highlight frequent terms. So, it addresses four layers of the *"Ontology Learning Layer Cake"* proposed in [4]: identifying terms, identifying synonyms (this is not detailed in this paper but has been implemented in Harold), identifying concepts, and organizing concepts into a concept hierarchy. The folksonomy building process proposed in this work is also based on [5] for the interactive and interactive approach. Even if our objective in this work is not to build definitions of concepts as in [5], we share the idea of progressively building the folksonomy thanks to a sequence of steps guided by the domain expert who provides additional useful knowledge, in a given step, to find other relevant pieces of knowledge (new concepts related to their research problem) in the next step.

Finally, numerous works address the problem of interrogating knowledge bases, especially represented in RDFS or accessible through a SPARQL endpoint. A classification of approaches that address this problem, from the most informal (natural language) to the most formal (SPARQL), can be found in [7]. In our work, providing a way to navigate, thanks to the hierarchical structure using FCA, is a way to implement a user friendly access on a SPARQL endpoint.

7 Conclusion

This paper has presented Harold, an iterative and interactive system to explore the Henri Poincaré correspondence without requiring knowledge of semantic web technologies. The system enables analysis of both metadata and full text, using FCA to gather letters by shared properties. Terminology management through a folksonomy, integrated with the exploration system, improves knowledge discovery by organizing concepts and properties hierarchically, which improves both letter organization and retrieval. The principles used to explore the Henri Poincaré correspondence are applicable to other corpora or other data types. For example, Harold could be applied to scientific publications, with metadata that include authors, year, keywords, and textual data that include title and abstract.

Future work includes evaluating the system. Experiments will be carried out with the objective of estimating the benefit of using Harold instead of the usual tools historians have the habit of using (the Henri Poincaré web site). An experiment session will concern historical research questions of the form *"What can I find in Henri Poincaré letters about T?"*, with T a given theme randomly chosen, for example, a mathematical concept, a personal aspect (e.g., travels), etc. For each experiment session, two historians have to solve a given research question, one with Harold, the other without it, in a limited amount of time. At the end of the session, they will have to answer a questionnaire with (1) open questions about their difficulties to solve the research question (technical difficulties and difficulties related to their knowledge background about T), (2) specific questions about Harold, about its usefulness, its usability, its suitability, its strengths and limits. Another type of evaluation will also be made on the search synthesis produced by historians during the experiment about the related pieces of knowledge they find, the letters they find, and the people involved they find. This evaluation will simply consists in counting how many elements of each type they have found.

References

1. Asim, M.N., Wasim, M., Khan, M.U.G., Mahmood, W., Abbasi, H.M.: A survey of ontology learning techniques and applications. Database: J. Biol. Databases Curation (2018)
2. Boissier, F., Rychkova, I., Le Grand, B.: Using formal concept analysis for corpus visualisation and relevance analysis. In: 16th International Conference on Knowledge Management and Information Systems, pp. 120–129. SCITEPRESS - Science and Technology Publications, Porto, Portugal (2024)
3. Brickley, D., Guha, R.V.: Rdf schema 1.1. w3C Recommendation, World Wide Web Consortium (W3C) (2014). https://www.w3.org/TR/rdf-schema/
4. Buitelaar, P., Cimiano, P., Magnini, B.: Ontology Learning from Text: An Overview, vol. 123, pp. 3–12. IOS Press, Amsterdam (2005)

5. d'Aquin, M.: TaBIIC: taxonomy building through iterative and interactive clustering. In: Formal Ontology in Information Systems, pp. 155–168. IOS Press (2023)
6. Ganter, B., Wille, R.: Formal Concept Analysis: Mathematical Foundations. Springer, Berlin (1999). https://doi.org/10.1007/978-3-031-63422-2
7. Kaufmann, E., Bernstein, A.: Evaluating the usability of natural language query languages and interfaces to Semantic Web knowledge bases. J. Web Semant. **8**(4), 377–393 (2010)
8. Meunier, J.M., Szoniecky, S., Berthereau, D.: Utilisation d'Omeka-S pour la conception et le partage de ressources pédagogiques. In: Zotero & Omeka-des outils pour les humanités numériques. Poitiers, France (2019)
9. Nabonnand, P., et al.: La correspondance entre Henri Poincaré et les mathématiciens. Publication des Archives Henri Poincaré, Birkhäuser, Cham (2024)
10. Nauer, E., Toussaint, Y.: CreChainDo: an iterative and interactive web information retrieval system based on lattices. Int. J. General Syst. **38**, 363–378 (2009)
11. Poelmans, J., Elzinga, P., Viaene, S., Dedene, G., Kuznetsov, S.: Text Mining Scientific Papers: A Survey on FCA-Based Information Retrieval Research, pp. 82–96 (2011)
12. Rollet, L.: La correspondance de jeunesse d'Henri Poincaré. Publication des Archives Henri Poincaré, Birkhäuser, Cham (2017)
13. Szathmary, L., Napoli, A.: CORON: a framework for levelwise itemset mining algorithms. In: Supplementary Proceedings of The Third International Conference on Formal Concept Analysis (ICFCA '05), pp. 110–113., Lens, France (2005)
14. Walter, S.A., Nabonnand, P., Krömer, R., Schiavon, M.: La correspondance entre Henri Poincaré, les astronomes, et les géodésiens. Publication des Archives Henri Poincaré, Birkhäuser, Cham (2016)

Short Papers

n-Dimensional Hypercontexts

Alexandre Bazin(✉)

LIRMM, Université de Montpellier, CNRS, Montpellier, France
alexandre.bazin@lirmm.fr

Abstract. Polyadic concept analysis is the generalisation of formal concept analysis in which more than two dimensions are considered. Little is known about how adding dimensions impacts the formation of concepts. In this paper, we observe that concepts are not monotonous w.r.t dimensions and propose a modification of the framework in which they are. We argue that this monotonicity is fundamental in polyadic concept analysis, and that it allows for the study of dimensions and how they produce concepts.

1 Introduction

We start by presenting notions of formal and polyadic concept analysis before introducing the problem.

Formal Concept Analysis. In formal concept analysis (FCA), a *formal context* (or *context*) is a triple $(\mathcal{O}, \mathcal{A}, \mathcal{I})$ where $\mathcal{O}$ is a set of objects, $\mathcal{A}$ is a set of attributes and $\mathcal{I} \subseteq \mathcal{O} \times \mathcal{A}$ is a *binary relation* between objects and attributes. It can be depicted as a crosstable. For instance, Fig. 1 depicts a formal context representing the types of meals (attributes) proposed by three restaurants (objects).

	Vegan	Meat	Fish
Duality	×	×	
The Cannibal		×	
Fish & Chips	×		×

Fig. 1. A formal context describing three restaurants with the type of dishes they offer.

In a formal context, a *formal concept* is a pair (E, I) where $E \subseteq \mathcal{O}$, $I \subseteq \mathcal{A}$ and such that both E and I are inclusion-maximal such that $E \times I \subseteq \mathcal{I}$. This corresponds to a maximal rectangle of crosses, up to permutation of rows and columns, in the crosstable representation of the context. Note that this is not

M. Croitoru et al. (Eds.): CONCEPTS 2026, LNAI 16811, pp. 295–305, 2027.
https://doi.org/10.1007/978-3-032-34742-8_19

the usual (but equivalent) definition of formal concepts. We refer the interested reader to the handbook [3]. In the Fig. 1 context, the formal concepts are

({Duality, Fish & Chips},{Vegan}) ({Duality, The Cannibal},{Meat})
({Duality},{Vegan, Meat}) ({Fish & Chips},{Vegan, Fish})
(∅,{Vegan, Meat, Fish}) ({Duality, The Cannibal, Fish & Chips},∅)

The concept ({Duality, Fish & Chips},{Vegan}) is interpreted as "the restaurants that offer a Vegan option", to which both Duality and Fish & Chips belong. The concept ({Duality},{Vegan, Meat}) is interpreted as "the restaurants that offer both a Vegan and a Meat options", to which only Duality belongs. Hence, the former is more general than the latter. For two concepts (E_1, I_1) and (E_2, I_2), we say that $(E_1, I_1) \leq (E_2, I_2)$ if and only if $I_2 \subseteq I_1$. Then, the set of all concepts in a context, ordered by $\leq$, forms a complete lattice called the *concept lattice* of the context.

Polyadic Concept Analysis. Polyadic concept analysis (PCA) is the generalisation of FCA in which more than two dimensions are involved in the relation. The notions of contexts, concepts and lattices are inherited with an additional "n-" in front of them to denote the number of dimensions. In PCA, an n-context is a tuple $(D_1, \ldots, D_n, \mathcal{I})$ where the D_i are dimensions and $\mathcal{I} \subseteq \prod_{i=1}^{n} D_i$ is an n-ary relation between elements of said dimensions. It can be depicted as an n-dimensional crosstable. Let us go back to our previous restaurant example and observe the situation a bit more closely by also considering their opening hours. The Cannibal is open only in the evening, Fish & Chips opens for both lunch and dinner with no change in its menu, and Duality decided to offer Vegan dishes for lunch and Meat dishes for dinner. Figure 2 represents this as a 3-context.

	Vegan	Meat	Fish	Vegan	Meat	Fish
Duality	×				×	
The Cannibal					×	
Fish & Chips	×		×	×		×
	Lunch			Dinner		

Fig. 2. A 3-context representing three restaurants with the types of dishes they offer at different times.

An n-concept is then a tuple $(C_1, \ldots, C_n)$ for which the $C_i \subseteq D_i$ are inclusion-maximal such that $\prod_{i=1}^{n} C_i \subseteq \mathcal{I}$. Again, there exists a closure-based definition for these objects that can be found in [8]. Let $\mathcal{C}$ be an n-context and $\mathcal{L}(\mathcal{C})$ denote the set of its n-concepts. Let $\lesssim_i$ be the quasi-order on $\mathcal{L}(\mathcal{C})$ such that $(A_1, \ldots, A_n) \lesssim_i (B_1, \ldots, B_n)$ if and only if $A_i \subseteq B_i$, $i \in \{1, \ldots, n\}$. Then, $(\mathcal{L}(\mathcal{C}), \lesssim_1, \ldots, \lesssim_n)$ forms a complete n-lattice called the *concept n-lattice* of $\mathcal{C}$.

The Problem. In the Fig. 2 3-context, the 3-concepts are

({Duality, Fish & Chips},{Vegan},{Lunch})
({Fish & Chips},{Vegan, Fish},{Lunch, Dinner})
({Duality, The Cannibal},{Meat},{Dinner})
(∅,{Vegan, Meat, Fish},{Lunch, Dinner})
({Duality, The Cannibal, Fish & Chips},∅,{Lunch, Dinner})
({Duality, The Cannibal, Fish & Chips},{Vegan, Meat, Fish},∅)

The 3-concept ({Fish & Chips},{Vegan, Fish},{Lunch, Dinner}) is interpreted as "the restaurants that offer both Vegan and Fish dishes at Lunch and Dinner". These concepts are valid and perfectly represent the situation as they could be used to reconstruct 3-context. Since the 3-context is a refinement of the Fig. 1 context, the information in the original 2d context is also in the 3-concepts. However, the conceptual knowledge extracted from the context has been changed by the observation of the third dimension: there is no 3-concept corresponding to restaurants offering both Vegan and Meat dishes. This is because the 2-concept ({Duality},{Vegan, Meat}) has been split by the introduction of time.

In this paper, we argue that this non-monotonicity of concepts with regard to dimensions is a problem, not only for knowledge extraction but also for more profound mathematical reasons. Indeed, the literature already proposes a construction that allows 2-concepts and 3-concepts to coexist in the same structure – a concept n-lattice –, and that seems to be fundamentally important in that it is needed to generalise many FCA results to PCA [1,2]. Let $\mathcal{C} = (D_1, \ldots, D_n, \mathcal{I})$ be an n-context and $\mathcal{C}^+$ be the n-context $(D_1 \cup \{\cdot_1\}, \ldots, D_n \cup \{\cdot_n\}, \mathcal{I}^+)$ with $\mathcal{I}^+ = \bigcup_{i=1}^{n} \mathcal{I}^i$ where

$$\mathcal{I}^0 = \mathcal{I}$$

and

$$\mathcal{I}^j = \{(d_1, \ldots, d_{k-1}, \cdot_k, d_{k+1}, \ldots, d_n) \mid (d_1, \ldots, d_n) \in \mathcal{I}^{j-1}, k \in \{1, \ldots, n\}\}$$

when $1 \leq j \leq n$. In other words, a new element $\cdot_i$ is added to the dimension D_i to represent the fact that D_i is not used and the incidence relation is projected over the remaining dimensions. Figure 3 depicts this construction for the Fig. 2 3-context.

	Vegan	Meat	Fish	$\cdot_2$	Vegan	Meat	Fish	$\cdot_2$	Vegan	Meat	Fish	$\cdot_2$
Duality	×			×		×		×	×	×		×
The Cannibal						×		×		×		×
Fish & Chips	×		×	×	×		×	×	×		×	×
$\cdot_1$	×		×	×	×	×	×	×	×	×	×	×
	Lunch				Dinner				$\cdot_3$			

Fig. 3. The 3-context $\mathcal{C}^+$ where $\mathcal{C}$ is the Fig. 2 3-context.

Note that the Fig. 1 2-context is included in the $\cdot_3$ slice of $\mathcal{C}^+$, where the mealtime dimension is represented as omitted. The 3-concepts of $\mathcal{C}^+$ are then

({Duality, Fish & Chips,$\cdot_1$},{Vegan,$\cdot_2$},{Lunch,$\cdot_3$})
({Fish & Chips,$\cdot_1$},{Vegan, Fish,$\cdot_2$},{Lunch, Dinner,$\cdot_3$})
({Duality,$\cdot_1$},{Meat,$\cdot_2$},{Dinner,$\cdot_3$})
({Duality,$\cdot_1$},{Vegan, Meat,$\cdot_2$},{$\cdot_3$})
({Duality, Fish & Chips,$\cdot_1$},{$\cdot_2$},{Lunch, Dinner, $\cdot_3$})
($\emptyset$,{Vegan, Meat, Fish,$\cdot_2$},{Lunch, Dinner,$\cdot_3$})
({Duality, The Cannibal, Fish & Chips,$\cdot_1$},$\emptyset$,{Lunch, Dinner,$\cdot_3$})
({Duality, The Cannibal, Fish & Chips,$\cdot_1$},{Vegan, Meat, Fish,$\cdot_2$},$\emptyset$)

The resulting concepts are, admittedly, poorly readable so let us remove the $\cdot_i$ elements as well as the components in which they appear as singletons:

({Duality, Fish & Chips},{Vegan},{Lunch})
({Fish & Chips},{Vegan, Fish},{Lunch, Dinner})
({Duality},{Meat},{Dinner})
({Duality},{Vegan, Meat})
({Duality, Fish & Chips},{Lunch, Dinner})
($\emptyset$,{Vegan, Meat, Fish},{Lunch, Dinner})
({Duality, The Cannibal, Fish & Chips},$\emptyset$,{Lunch, Dinner})
({Duality, The Cannibal, Fish & Chips},{Vegan, Meat, Fish},$\emptyset$)

The 3-concepts are all present and there are two additional tuples that correspond to 2-concepts: ({Duality},{Vegan, Meat}) and ({Duality, Fish & Chips},{Lunch, Dinner}). The first one is the missing 2-concept representing restaurants that offer both Vegan and Meat-based dishes while the second is a 2-concept representing restaurants that are open for both Lunch and Dinner, i.e. a 2-concept that does not involve the dish-type dimension. These 3- and 2-concepts all coexist within a 3-lattice.

The $\mathcal{C}^+$ construction appears, at the time of writing, in the polyadic generalisations of Relational Concept Analysis [1,7] and the fact that the covering relation of a concept lattice forms a base of association rules [2,4,6]. Indeed, the covering relation of the concept n-lattice of an n-context is not sufficient to obtain a base of n-dimensional association rules and it is the covering relation of this particular construction that is instead needed. It also seems to be involved in the polyadic generalisation of implications. These problems have in common the need to isolate and manipulate subsets of dimensions. Therefore, we believe that the resulting structure combining concepts of different dimensionalities is fundamental in PCA. For this reason, we begin its study in this paper.

In Sect. 2, we provide a reformulation/generalisation of the $\mathcal{C}^+$ constructions called hypercontexts, without the added elements impeding readability. In Sect. 3, we show that the set of hypercontexts preserving arbitrary concept sets form lattices. This enables the comparison of contexts/lattices of different dimensionalities and represents the beginning of a theory of dimensionality in concept analysis. In Sect. 4, we discuss how these new structures allow us to perform polyadic concept analysis on any number of contexts of any dimensionality, whether they share dimensions or not.

2 Hypercontexts

In the remainder of this paper, we use set-theoretic notations on tuples. For instance, we write $(a, c) \subseteq (a, b, c)$. For a tuple X, we use $X^{\downarrow} = \{Y \mid Y \subseteq X\}$ to denote the set of its subtuples. For a set of tuples $\mathcal{X}$, we use $\mathcal{X}^{\downarrow} = \bigcup_{X \in \mathcal{X}} X^{\downarrow}$.

Let $\mathcal{E}$ be a ground set and $\mathcal{D} = \{D_1, \ldots, D_n\}$ a partition of $\mathcal{E}$ into n *dimensions*.

Definition 1 (Hypercontext). *A* hypercontext *over dimensions $\mathcal{D}$ is a tuple $(D_1, \ldots, D_n, \mathcal{R}^{\downarrow})$ where $\mathcal{R} \subseteq \bigcup_{D \subseteq \mathcal{D}} \prod_{D_i \in D} D_i$.*

In other words, $\mathcal{R}$ is the union of k-ary relations, $k \in \{1, \ldots, n\}$, between dimensions of $\mathcal{D}$ and $\mathcal{R}^{\downarrow}$ is the projection of these relations on subsets of their dimensions. To represent hypercontexts graphically, we use crosstables with unlabeled slices to indicate that a dimension is not in the relation. Figure 4 illustrates this on the hypercontext $(\{1, 2\}, \{a, b\}, \{\alpha, \beta\}, \mathcal{R}^{\downarrow})$ with $\mathcal{R} = \{(2, b, \alpha), (a, \beta), (1, \beta), (2, \beta)\}$. Notice that it is similar to the representation of $\mathcal{C}^+$ without the added $\cdot_i$ elements.

However, not all hypercontexts correspond to $\mathcal{C}^+$ constructions as $\mathcal{R}$ is not necessarily a subset of $\prod_{i=1}^{n} D_i$.

A "concept" in a hypercontext then corresponds, as usual, to a maximal subset of the incidence relation that forms a box. However, since all dimensions need not be involved in a "concept", maximality cannot be defined through the inclusion relation and instead requires new orders. Let X and Y be two tuples of subsets of dimensions, i.e. $X, Y \in \bigcup_{D \subseteq \mathcal{D}} \prod_{D_i \in D} 2^{D_i}$. We use $dim(X)$ to denote the set of all the dimensions of which a subset is a component of X. For a dimension $D_i \in dim(X)$, we use $X \cap D_i$ to denote the component of X that is

	a	b		a	b		a	b	
1						×			×
2		×	×			×		×	×
		×	×	×		×	×	×	×
		α			β				

Fig. 4. Hypercontext over dimensions $\{\{1,2\},\{a,b\},\{\alpha,\beta\}\}$ and incidence relation $\mathcal{R}^{\downarrow}$ with $\mathcal{R} = \{(2,b,\alpha),(a,\beta),(1,\beta),(2,\beta)\}$.

included in D_i. Note that $X \cap D_i$ can be the empty set if X contains it as a component. Then, we define $\leq_i$ on the set of aforementioned tuples such that $X \leq_i Y$ if and only if

$$D_i \in dim(X) \text{ and } X \cap D_i = \emptyset$$

or

$$D_i \notin dim(X), D_i \in dim(Y) \text{ and } Y \cap D_k \neq \emptyset$$

or

$$D_i \in dim(X), D_i \in dim(Y) \text{ and } \emptyset \subset X \cap D_i \subseteq Y \cap D_i.$$

By basing maximality on $\leq_i$, we can now define "concepts".

Definition 2 *(k-**Concept**). In a hypercontext $(D_1,\ldots,D_n,\mathcal{R}^{\downarrow})$, a k-concept is a tuple $(C_{j_1},\ldots,C_{j_k}) \in \bigcup_{D\subseteq\mathcal{D}} \prod_{D_i\in D} 2^{D_i}$ such that*

1. *$\prod_{i=1}^{k} C_i \subseteq \mathcal{R}^{\downarrow}$*
2. *it is maximal in $\bigcap_{i=1}^{n} \leq_i$ among the tuples that respect 1).*

The Fig. 4 example possesses

- one 1-concept $(\{a,b\})$
- three 2-concepts $(\{1,2\},\{\beta\})$, $(\{a\},\{\beta\})$ and $(\{2\},\{\alpha,\beta\})$
- four 3-concepts $(\{2\},\{b\},\{\alpha\})$, $(\emptyset,\{a,b\},\{\alpha,\beta\})$, $(\{1,2\},\emptyset,\{\alpha,\beta\})$ and $(\{1,2\},\{a,b\},\emptyset)$

It is quite straightforward to show that the k-concepts of a hypercontext form an n-lattice.

Theorem 1. *Let $\mathcal{H} = (D_1,\ldots,D_n,\mathcal{R}^{\downarrow})$ be a hypercontext and $\mathcal{L}(\mathcal{H})$ be the set of its k-concepts, $k \in \{0,\ldots,n\}$. Then, $(\mathcal{L}(\mathcal{H}),\leq_1,\ldots,\leq_n)$ forms an n-lattice.*

Proof. We show that $(\mathcal{L}(\mathcal{H})),\leq_1,\ldots,\leq_n)$ is isomorphic to the concept n-lattice of an n-context analogous to the $\mathcal{C}^+$ construction discussed in the introduction.

First, it is easy to see that $\mathcal{H}$ itself is isomorphic to the construction described in the introduction, i.e. $(d_{j_1},\ldots,d_{j_k}) \in \mathcal{R}^{\downarrow} \Leftrightarrow (d_1,\ldots,d_n) \in \mathcal{I}$ where $\mathcal{I}$ is the incidence relation of the construction and $(d_1,\ldots,d_n)$ is constructed from $(d_{j_1},\ldots,d_{j_k})$ by adding the element $\cdot_i$ for every $i \notin \{j_1,\ldots,j_k\}$.

Then, if $(C_{j_1}, \ldots, C_{j_k})$ is a k-concept in $\mathcal{H}$, then by definition $\prod_{i=1}^{k} C_i \subseteq \mathcal{R}^{\downarrow}$. Therefore, there exists a tuple $(C_1, \ldots, C_n)$ such that $\prod_{i=1}^{n} C_i \subseteq \mathcal{I}$ where $C_i = C_{i_j} \cup \{\cdot_{i_j}\}$ when $i = i_j$ and $C_i = \{\cdot_{i_j}\}$ otherwise. Furthermore, the maximality of $(C_{j_1}, \ldots, C_{j_k})$ for this property implies the maximality $(C_1, \ldots, C_n)$. Hence, $(C_{j_1}, \ldots, C_{j_k})$ being a k-concept of $\mathcal{H}$ implies that $(C_1, \ldots, C_n)$ is an n-concept of the construction. The converse is proved analogously.

Finally, for two pairs $((C_{j_1}, \ldots, C_{j_k}), (C_1, \ldots, C_n))$ and $((C_{j_1}, \ldots, C_{j_k})', (C_1, \ldots, C_n)')$ of corresponding concepts as described above, we have $(C_{j_1}, \ldots, C_{j_k}) \leq_i (C_{j_1}, \ldots, C_{j_k})' \Leftrightarrow (C_1, \ldots, C_n) \lesssim_i (C_1, \ldots, C_n)'$. Consequently, the n-lattices formed by the k-concepts of $\mathcal{H}$ is isomorphic to the concept n-lattice of the construction. □

Let $\mathcal{C} = (D_1, \ldots, D_n, \mathcal{R})$ be an n-context. We use $\mathcal{C}^{\downarrow} = (D_1, \ldots, D_n, \mathcal{R}^{\downarrow})$ to denote the hypercontext generated by $\mathcal{C}$. Hypercontexts $\mathcal{C}^{\downarrow}$ seem to be of particular importance in polyadic concept analysis as the concept n-lattice of $\mathcal{C}^{\downarrow}$ is required to produce a base of association rules of $\mathcal{C}$ [2] when $n > 2$. When $n = 2$, it is well-known that the concept 2-lattice of $\mathcal{C}$ is sufficient [4,6]. We remark, however, that the concept 2-lattices of $\mathcal{C}$ and $\mathcal{C}^{\downarrow}$ are isomorphic when $\mathcal{C}$ does not contain empty rows or columns. Figure 5 illustrates this.

	Vegan	Meat	Fish	
Duality	×	×		×
The Cannibal		×		×
Fish & Chips	×		×	×
	×	×	×	×

Fig. 5. The hypercontext generated by the Fig. 1 2-context.

The k-concepts, $k \in \{1, \ldots, n\}$, of this hypercontext are

({Duality, Fish & Chips},{Vegan}) ({Duality, The Cannibal},{Meat})
({Duality},{Vegan, Meat}) ({Fish & Chips},{Vegan, Fish})
({Vegan, Meat, Fish}) ({Duality, The Cannibal, Fish & Chips})

The isomorphism with the concepts in the Fig. 1 2-context is straightfoward as only the top and bottom concepts are changed, replaced by ({Vegan, Meat, Fish}) and ({Duality, The Cannibal, Fish & Chips}). Therefore, it can be said that the hypercontext $\mathcal{C}^{\downarrow}$ is fundamental to association rules mining in any number of dimensions.

3 Structuring Hypercontexts

Hypercontexts allow concepts of different dimensionalities to coexist in an n-lattice. We now take an interest in the situation in which all the concepts in an

n-lattice are preserved in an $(n+m)$-lattice in the sense that they are either found unchanged or extended along the new dimensions. This corresponds to the situation in which the observation of a new dimension does not invalidate conceptual knowledge. For instance, the concepts in the Fig. 5 hypercontext are all preserved in the Fig. 6 hypercontext generated by the Fig. 2 3-context (corresponding to the Fig. 3 construction).

	Vegan	Meat	Fish		Vegan	Meat	Fish		Vegan	Meat	Fish	
Duality	×			×		×		×	×	×		×
The Cannibal						×		×		×		×
Fish & Chips	×		×	×	×		×	×	×		×	×
	×		×	×	×	×	×	×	×	×	×	×
	Lunch				Dinner							

Fig. 6. Hypercontext generated by the Fig. 2 3-context.

Given two hypercontexts $\mathcal{H}_1$ and $\mathcal{H}_2$, we say that

$$\mathcal{H}_1 \leq_d \mathcal{H}_2$$

$$\Updownarrow$$

$$\forall C_1 \in \mathcal{L}(\mathcal{H}_1), \exists C_2 \in \mathcal{L}(\mathcal{H}_2) \text{ such that } C_1 =_i C_2, \forall D_i \in dim(C_1), \text{ and } C_1 \leq_j C_2, \forall D_j \in dim(C_2) \backslash dim(C_1).$$

We read this as "all the concepts in $\mathcal{H}_1$ are represented in $\mathcal{H}_2$". We extend the notation to concept n-lattices by writing $\mathcal{L}(\mathcal{H}_1) \leq_d \mathcal{L}(\mathcal{H}_2)$ when $\mathcal{H}_1 \leq_d \mathcal{H}_2$.

For a hypercontext $\mathcal{H} = (D_1, \ldots, D_n, \mathcal{I})$ and a subset $D = \{D_{i_1}, \ldots, D_{i_k}\}$ of its dimensions, we note $\mathcal{H}^D = (D_{i_1}, \ldots, D_{i_k}, \mathcal{I} \cap (\prod_{j=1}^{j} D_{i_j})^{\downarrow})$ the hypercontext in which only the dimensions in D have been observed.

Let us take as an example $\mathcal{H}$ the hypercontext depicted in Fig. 4. The different $\mathcal{H}^D$ are then:

$\mathcal{H}^{\emptyset} =$

×

$\mathcal{H}^{\{D_1\}} =$

1	2	
×	×	×

$\mathcal{H}^{\{D_1,D_2\}} =$

	a	b	
1			×
2		×	×
	×	×	×

$\mathcal{H}^{\{D_2\}} =$

a	b	
×	×	×

$\mathcal{H}^{\{D_1,D_3\}} =$

	α	β	
1		×	×
2	×	×	×
	×	×	×

$\mathcal{H}^{\{D_3\}} =$

α	β	
×	×	×

$\mathcal{H}^{\{D_2,D_3\}} =$

	α	β	
a		×	×
b	×		×
	×	×	×

$\mathcal{H}^{\{D_1,D_2,D_3\}} =$

	a	b		a	b		a	b	
1						×			×
2		×	×			×		×	×
		×	×	×		×	×	×	×
	α			β					

The hypercontext $\mathcal{H}^{\emptyset} = (\emptyset)$ does not contain any dimension and has an empty relation.

For any two $\mathcal{H}_1 = (D_1^1, \ldots, D_n^1, \mathcal{I}^1)$, $\mathcal{H}_2 = (D_1^2, \ldots, D_m^2, \mathcal{I}^2)$, we note

$$\mathcal{H}_1 \sqcup \mathcal{H}_2 = (D_1^1, \ldots, D_n^1, D_1^2, \ldots, D_m^2, \mathcal{I}^1 \cup \mathcal{I}^2)$$

the union of $\mathcal{H}_1$ and $\mathcal{H}_2$. For instance, $\mathcal{H}^{\{D_1,D_2\}} \sqcup \mathcal{H}^{\{D_2,D_3\}}$ is:

	a	b		a	b		a	b	
1									×
2								×	×
		×	×	×		×	×	×	×
		α			β				

We now use $\mathbb{H}_{\mathcal{H}}$ to denote the $\sqcup$-closure of the set $\{H^D \mid D \subseteq \{D_1, \ldots, D_n\}\}$.

Proposition 1. *Let $\mathcal{H}_1, \mathcal{H}_2 \in \mathbb{H}_{\mathcal{H}}$. Then, $\mathcal{H}_1 \sqcup \mathcal{H}_2 = \mathcal{H}_2 \Leftrightarrow \mathcal{H}_1 \leq_d \mathcal{H}_2$.*

Proof. Let $\mathcal{H}_1 = (D_1^1, \ldots, D_n^1, \mathcal{I}^1)$ and $\mathcal{H}_2 = (D_1^2, \ldots, D_m^2, \mathcal{I}^2)$.

Let us start with $\Rightarrow$.Let C be a k-concept in $\mathcal{H}_1$. Since $\mathcal{H}_1 \sqcup \mathcal{H}_2 = \mathcal{H}_2$, we have $\{D_1^1, \ldots, D_n^1\} \subseteq \{D_1^2, \ldots, D_m^2\}$ and $\mathcal{I}^1 \subseteq \mathcal{I}^2$. Furthermore, $\mathcal{I}^1 = \mathcal{I}^2 \cap \prod_{i=1}^n D_i^1$. Hence, either C is an n-concept in $\mathcal{H}_2$ or there is a k'-concept C' in $\mathcal{H}_2$ that extends C on $k' - k$ dimensions in $\{D_1^2, \ldots, D_m^2\} \setminus \{D_1^1, \ldots, D_n^1\}$. Therefore, $\mathcal{H}_1 \leq_d \mathcal{H}_2$.

We now treat $\Leftarrow$. If $\mathcal{H}_1 \leq_d \mathcal{H}_2$, then $\{D_1^1, \ldots, D_n^1\} \subseteq \{D_1^2, \ldots, D_m^2\}$ and $\mathcal{I}^1 \subseteq \mathcal{I}^2 \cap \prod_{i=1}^n D_i^1$. Therefore, $\mathcal{I}^1 \subseteq \mathcal{I}^2 \downarrow$. Consequently, since both dimensions and relations are included, $\mathcal{H}_1 \sqcup \mathcal{H}_2 = \mathcal{H}_2$. □

Corollary 1. *$(\mathbb{H}_{\mathcal{H}}, \leq_d)$ is a complete lattice.*

This lattice structures the different observations of dimensions that are, in a sense, compatible with in each others as they do not invalidate concepts.

4 Discussion

An obvious application of hypercontexts is in performing concept analysis on multiple contexts simultaneously. For instance, the two following formal contexts

	a	b
1	×	×
2		×

	α	β
□		×
△	×	

can be merged through the $\sqcup$-union of their respective hypercontexts to obtain the following 4-dimensional hypercontext

	a	b		a	b		a	b		a	b		a	b		a	b		a	b		a	b		a	b	
1																									×	×	×
2																										×	×
						×			×			×						×			×			×	×	×	×
		α			β						α			β						α			β				
					$\square$									$\triangle$													

Its concept 4-lattice then contains both the concept lattices of the formal contexts.

Such operation is perhaps more useful when the contexts share some of their dimensions, such as in redescription mining [5] where objects are described by different sets of attributes in two (or more) independent datasets. For instance, the two following descriptions of objects 1, 2 and 3

	a	b	c
1	×		
2		×	×
3			×

	α	β	γ
1		×	
2	×		
3			×

produce the following 3-dimensional hypercontext

	a	b	c		a	b	c		a	b	c		a	b	c	
1								×					×			×
2				×										×	×	×
3												×			×	×
				×				×				×	×	×	×	×
		α				β				γ						

whose concepts are

$$(\emptyset, \{a,b,c\}, \{\alpha,\beta,\gamma\}) \quad (\{1,2,3\}, \emptyset, \{\alpha,\beta,\gamma\}) \quad (\{1,2,3\}, \{a,b,c\}, \emptyset)$$
$$(\{1\}, \{a\}) \quad (\{2\}, \{b,c\}) \quad (\{2,3\}, \{c\})$$
$$(\{1\}, \{\beta\}) \quad (\{2\}, \{\alpha\}) \quad (\{3\}, \{\gamma\})$$
$$(\{1,2,3\}) \quad (\{a,b,c\}) \quad (\{\alpha,\beta,\gamma\})$$

The two attribute quasi-orders are isomorphic to the original intent lattices while both original extent lattices can be embedded in the object quasi-order.

Beyond this immediate practicality, we believe that hypercontexts open the way to a theory of dimensionality in concept analysis that allows for the study of unobserved dimensions/variables. The lattice described in Proposition 1 could be used as a framework for this: the currently observed dimensions produce an element of the lattice and the observation of new dimensions correspond to join operations on this element.

References

1. Bazin, A., Galasso, J., Kahn, G.: Polyadic relational concept analysis. Int. J. Approx. Reason. **164**, 109067 (2024)
2. Bazin, A., Gros, N., Bertaux, A., Nicolle, C.: Condensed representations of association rules in n-ary relations. IEEE Trans. Knowl. Data Eng. **35**(5), 4598–4607 (2022)
3. Ganter, B., Wille, R.: Formal Concept Analysis - Mathematical Foundations. Springer, Cham (1999). https://doi.org/10.1007/978-3-031-63422-2
4. Luxenburger, M.: Implications partielles dans un contexte. Mathématiques informatique et sciences humaines **113**, 35–55 (1991)
5. Parida, L., Ramakrishnan, N.: Redescription mining: structure theory and algorithms. In: AAAI, vol. 5, pp. 837–844 (2005)
6. Pasquier, N., Bastide, Y., Taouil, R., Lakhal, L.: Discovering frequent closed itemsets for association rules. In: Beeri, C., Buneman, P. (eds.) ICDT 1999. LNCS, vol. 1540, pp. 398–416. Springer, Heidelberg (1999). https://doi.org/10.1007/3-540-49257-7_25
7. Rouane-Hacene, M., Huchard, M., Napoli, A., Valtchev, P.: Relational concept analysis: mining concept lattices from multi-relational data. Ann. Math. Artif. Intell. **67**(1), 81–108 (2013)
8. Voutsadakis, G.: Polyadic concept analysis. Order **19**(3), 295–304 (2002)

Real Talk, Virtual Faces: A Formal Concept Analysis of Personality and Sentiment in Influencer Audiences

Shahram Chaudhry(✉), Sidahmed Benabderrahmane, and Talal Rahwan

Division of Science, Computer Science Department, New York University (NYUAD), Abu Dhabi, United Arab Emirates
sc9425@nyu.edu

Abstract. Virtual influencers (VIs)—digitally synthetic social-media personas—attract audiences whose discourse appears qualitatively different from discourse around human influencers (HIs). Existing work characterises this difference through surveys or aggregate engagement statistics, which reveal *what* audiences say but not *how* multiple signals co-occur. We propose a two-layer, structure-first framework grounded in Formal Concept Analysis (FCA) and association rule mining. The first layer applies FCA with support-based iceberg filtering to weekly-aggregated comment data, extracting discourse profiles—weekly co-occurrence bundles of sentiment, Big Five personality cues, and topic tags. The second layer mines association rules at the comment level, revealing personality–sentiment–topic dependencies invisible to frequency-table analysis.

Applied to YouTube comments from three VI–HI influencer pairs, the two-layer analysis reveals a consistent structural divergence: HI discourse concentrates into a single, emotionally regulated (stability-centred) regime (low neuroticism anchoring positivity), while VI discourse supports three structurally distinct discourse modes, including an appearance-discourse cluster absent from HI despite near-equal marginal prevalence. Topic-specific analyses further show that VI contexts exhibit negative sentiment in psychologically sensitive domains (mental health, body image, artificial identity) relative to HI contexts. Our results position FCA as a principled tool for multi-signal discourse analysis and demonstrate that virtuality reshapes not just what audiences say, but the underlying grammar of how signals co-occur in their reactions.

Keywords: Formal Concept Analysis · virtual influencers · sentiment analysis · psycholinguistic features · social media discourse

1 Introduction

Formal Concept Analysis (FCA) provides a principled framework for analyzing co-occurrence structure in binary objectâĂŞattribute data [3]. Unlike marginal frequency analysis, FCA identifies closed sets of attributes that recur jointly

M. Croitoru et al. (Eds.): CONCEPTS 2026, LNAI 16811, pp. 306–317, 2027.
https://doi.org/10.1007/978-3-032-34742-8_20

across subsets of objects, making it well suited for studying how discourse signals co-occur rather than how frequently they appear individually. While FCA has been widely applied in knowledge discovery and text analysis, its use as a structural diagnostic for large-scale social discourse remains underexplored.

We ask whether the digitally synthetic nature of virtual influencers (VIs) leaves a detectable imprint on the structure of audience discourse beyond what marginal statistics reveal. Virtual influencers such as LilMiquela, APOKI, and MillaSofia attract emotionally complex audience reactions ranging from admiration to skepticism, particularly on sensitive topics such as mental health and body image [4,10]. Capturing these interactions requires methods that model structural relations between sentiment, personality, and topical signals rather than isolated distributions.

Contributions. We introduce a two-layer framework combining (i) weekly FCA with iceberg filtering to identify recurring discourse profiles and (ii) comment-level association rule mining to extract personality–sentiment–topic regularities.

Using YouTube comments from matched VI–HI influencer pairs, we show that:

1. VI and HI discourse exhibit qualitatively different FCA concept structures;
2. VI discourse generates substantially denser and more diverse association-rule structures than HI discourse;
3. similar marginal attribute prevalences can mask important structural differences in co-occurrence organization;
4. VI discourse contains more negative sentiment in psychologically sensitive topics such as body image and mental health.

Research Questions

RQ1. How do weekly FCA discourse profiles differ between VI and HI conditions?
RQ2. What association rules characterize VI versus HI comment-level discourse, and how do the resulting rule structures differ?
RQ3. How do sentiment and personality patterns differ between VI and HI audiences across psychologically sensitive topics?

FCA Perspective. Beyond the empirical analysis of influencer discourse, this work illustrates how FCA can serve as a structural diagnostic for multi-signal social data. In particular, conditions with similar marginal attribute frequencies may still exhibit substantially different closed-set and association-rule structures.

2 Related Work

Formal Concept Analysis and association rules. Formal Concept Analysis (FCA) models data as binary object–attribute relations and extracts closed attribute sets organised in a concept lattice [3]. FCA is closely related to frequent closed itemset mining [7,11] and has been applied in knowledge discovery, text mining, and social analytics [8]. Association rule mining [1] complements FCA by summarising directional co-occurrence regularities through support, confidence, and lift. We use these tools to identify interpretable sentiment–personality–topic structures in audience discourse.

Virtual Influencer Audiences. Prior work on virtual influencers highlights authenticity, parasocial ties, realism, and identity ambiguity as central to audience response [2,5,9,10,14,15]. Recent work on Lil Miquela further shows polarised reactions around artificial identity [4]. Most studies rely on surveys, experiments, or aggregate engagement metrics. We instead analyse large-scale comment text and ask how multiple discourse signals co-occur structurally.

Psycholinguistic Discourse Features. Text-derived Big Five cues have been used as computational proxies for language style and social behaviour [6]. We do not interpret these cues as psychological measurements of individuals; rather, we use them as aggregate psycholinguistic indicators combined with sentiment and topic tags inside FCA contexts.

3 Data

3.1 Dataset and Influencer Pairing

We collect top-level YouTube comments via the YouTube Data API (v3) from three VIâĂŞHI influencer pairs matched on content niche, subscriber scale, and posting frequency. We retain English-language comments (`langdetect`), remove duplicates and empty strings, and strip HTML.

Table 1. Selected VI–HI influencer pairs. HI counterparts are chosen by automated API search within a ±10% subscriber window, then qualitatively aligned on content niche.

Virtual Influencer	Subscribers	Human Counterpart	Niche
Lil Miquela	~271k	Samantha Nicole	Fashion/lifestyle
APOKI	~329k	YOUNG POSSE	K-pop/performance
Milla Sofia	~28k	Lydia Stoner	Fashion lookbooks

Table 1 summarises the pairings. The final dataset contains 29,327 VI comments and 40,171 HI comments (69,498 total). We frame the analysis as a pair-matched structural comparison rather than a causal analysis of virtuality.

3.2 Comment Enrichment

Each comment is enriched with three attribute families:

Sentiment. Three-class (positive/neutral/negative) classification via a fine-tuned RoBERTa classifier.

Big Five personality cues. Openness, Conscientiousness, Extraversion, Agreeableness, and Neuroticism scores are inferred using a transformer-based regressor [6] and discretized into `high`/`low` binary attributes using group-level means. These scores are treated as psycholinguistic style proxies rather than ground-truth personality measurements.

Topics. Twelve-class taxonomy assigned by Gemini Flash-Lite via zero-shot NLI: `positivity`, `appearance`, `authenticity_critique`, `artificial_identity`, `parasocial`, `brand_ads`, `criticism`, `humor`, `performance`, `mental_health`, `body_image`, `social_comparison`. The resulting vocabulary contains $|M| = 25$

binary attributes: 3 sentiment attributes, 12 topic attributes, and 10 personality-bin attributes. Table 2 reports selected marginal attribute prevalences. Table 2 reports *marginal* attribute prevalence (how often each signal appears in isolation). In Sect. 4.1, we quantify the resulting *concept space* under FCA iceberg filtering, capturing how signals *co-occur* structurally rather than individually.

Table 2. Attribute prevalence (selected attributes), sorted by Δ. The near-equal appearance prevalence (0.011 gap) contrasts sharply with its structural asymmetry in rule mining (Sect. 5.2).

Attribute	HI	VI	Δ (VI−HI)
`topic_artificial_identity`	0.005	0.184	+0.179
`sentiment_Negative`	0.067	0.125	+0.058
`topic_authenticity_critique`	0.037	0.062	+0.025
`topic_appearance`	0.159	0.170	+0.011
`topic_social_comparison`	0.007	0.007	0.000
`sentiment_Positive`	0.766	0.669	−0.097
`topic_positivity`	0.677	0.472	−0.205

4 Methodology

Our pipeline has two analytical layers plus a complementary topic-level analysis. Figure 1 summarizes the main structural contrast identified between HI and VI discourse.

4.1 Layer 1: Weekly FCA with Support-Based Iceberg Filtering

Aggregation. Comments are grouped by calendar week. Within each week, sentiment and topic are summarised by modal label; Big Five traits are averaged

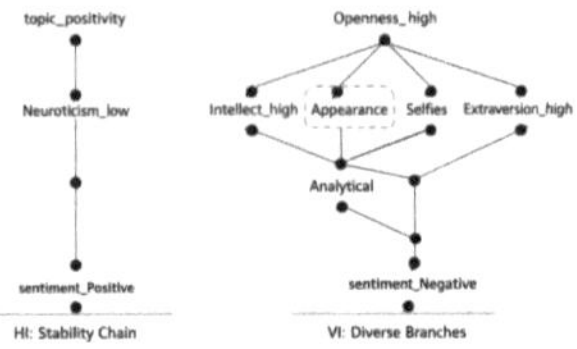

Fig. 1. Schematic concept lattice comparison. **Left (HI):** discourse converges to a single stability-centred chain (`topic_positivity` → `Neuroticism_low` → `sentiment_Positive`); 8 filtered rules, 1 discourse mode. **Right (VI):** discourse fans into three branches from an `Openness_high` backbone; 51 filtered rules, 3 discourse modes. The dashed orange border marks the appearance-discourse cluster absent from HI despite near-equal appearance prevalence (VI: 0.170 vs. HI: 0.159)—the core "when frequencies lie" result.

across comments and then binarised against the group-level weekly mean. Each week becomes one binary object in the formal context.

Formal Context and Concept Extraction. We build one binary formal context $\mathbb{K}_c = (G_c, M, I_c)$ per condition $c \in \{\text{HI}, \text{VI}\}$, where G_c is the set of weeks and M is the shared attribute vocabulary. FCA extracts formal concepts; a *formal concept* (A, B) satisfies $A = B'$ and $B = A'$, where $B' = \{g \in G_c \mid \forall m \in B : (g, m) \in I_c\}$ and symmetrically. We order concepts by $\subseteq$ on extents to form the concept lattice $\mathcal{L}(\mathbb{K}_c)$ [3].

Iceberg Filtering. To improve interpretability, we retain only concepts with temporal support $\geq 20\%$ and intent size ≥ 3. Thresholds were selected empirically to balance coverage and noise reduction. Under the selected configuration, the VI concept space is reduced from 1,895 raw concepts to 10 filtered concepts, while HI is reduced from 864 to 24. Similar qualitative asymmetries were observed across nearby threshold settings.

Cross-Group Comparison. Concepts with identical intents across conditions are labelled *shared*; those unique to one condition are labelled *VI-only* or *HI-only*. We visualise attribute prevalence within each category using horizontal bar charts.

4.2 Layer 2: Comment-Level Association Rule Mining

Context Construction. We construct a second formal context where objects are individual comments and attributes are the same 25 binary signals. Personality traits are discretized globally at the comment level, whereas weekly FCA uses locally averaged weekly traits.

Rule Generation. Association rules are generated using the Galicia implementation of Valtchev et al.'s approximate algorithm [12,13]. Candidate rules $X \Rightarrow Y$ are filtered using minimum support ($\geq 1\%$), confidence (≥ 0.8), and lift (> 1.2).

We report association rules as statistical regularities rather than logical implications.

Rule Clustering. Retained rules are grouped by the main topic appearing in their antecedents to identify recurring discourse patterns.

4.3 Complementary Topic-Level Analysis

To capture psychologically salient topics that may not form stable weekly concepts, we additionally analyze four topics at the comment level: artificial identity, authenticity critique, body image, and mental health. For each topic and condition, we compute sentiment distributions and average Big Five personality profiles, visualized as radar charts.

5 Results

5.1 RQ1: Weekly FCA Discourse Profiles

(a) HI-only stable concepts

(b) VI-only stable concepts

Fig. 2. Dominant attributes in group-specific (HI-only vs. VI-only).

Figure 2 shows a clear structural contrast between HI-only and VI-only stable concepts. HI concepts are dominated by positive sentiment, topic positivity, low neuroticism, and high conscientiousness, indicating emotionally stable evaluative discourse. In contrast, VI concepts emphasize high openness, agreeableness, and extraversion, with greater neuroticism and weaker positivity signals. Overall, HI discourse appears sentiment-centered, whereas VI discourse is more personality-centered and exploratory. This structural distinction—sentiment-centred HI vs. personality-centred VI—constitutes a qualitative difference not visible from Table 2.

5.2 RQ2: Comment-Level Rule Grammar

Overall density. Under identical filtering thresholds, VI discourse yields 51 association rules compared to only 8 for HI, a 6.4-fold difference. VI rules also exhibit

Table 3. Rule summary statistics (minsup = 1%, minconf = 0.8, lift > 1.2).

Metric	Mean	Median	Max
HI rules (8 total)			
Support	0.062	0.065	0.090
Confidence	0.92	0.94	0.96
Lift	1.23	1.23	1.25
VI rules (51 total)			
Support	0.146	0.080	0.420
Confidence	0.88	0.88	0.96
Lift	1.32	1.32	1.43

higher average lift (1.32 vs. 1.23) and substantially higher maximum support (0.42 vs. 0.09), indicating denser and more recurrent co-occurrence structure (Table 3).

HI Rule Structure. All HI rules belong to a single positivity-centered cluster in which `topic_positivity` and `Neuroticism_low` predict `sentiment_Positive` (conf. 0.92-0.96, lift 1.20-1.25). This indicates a relatively narrow, stability-centered discourse structure.

VI Rule Structure. VI rules form three distinct premise clusters:

Table 4. All 8 HI rules. Single cluster: `topic_positivity` ∧ `Neuroticism_low` anchors all rules.

Premise X	Consequent Y	supp	conf	lift
Agreeableness_high ∧ Neuroticism_low ∧ topic_positivity	sentiment_Positive	0.060	0.96	1.25
Extraversion_high ∧ Neuroticism_low ∧ topic_positivity	sentiment_Positive	0.080	0.95	1.24
Conscientiousness_low ∧ Neuroticism_low ∧ topic_positivity	sentiment_Positive	0.070	0.95	1.24
Neuroticism_low ∧ topic_positivity	sentiment_Positive	0.090	0.94	1.23
Neuroticism_low ∧ Openness_high ∧ topic_positivity	sentiment_Positive	0.090	0.94	1.23
Agreeableness_high ∧ Neuroticism_low ∧ sentiment_Positive	topic_positivity	0.060	0.82	1.21
Agreeableness_low ∧ Neuroticism_low ∧ topic_positivity	sentiment_Positive	0.030	0.92	1.20
Conscientiousness_high ∧ Neuroticism_low ∧ topic_positivity	sentiment_Positive	0.020	0.92	1.20

1. **Positivity-Framing** (40 rules): `topic_positivity` acts as the main topic anchor and co-occurs with diverse Big Five configurations, including `Neuroticism_high`, which is absent from HI. Unlike HI, positive VI discourse persists under emotionally intense configurations.
2. **Appearance-Discourse** (7 rules): `topic_appearance` predicts `sentiment_Positive`. This cluster is entirely absent from HI despite near-equal marginal prevalence, and remains VI-specific across tested thresholds.

3. **Personality-Only** (4 rules): No topic attribute appears in the premise; personality configurations alone predict positive sentiment.

Tables 4–5 list the full HI rule set and the top VI rules by cluster.

5.3 Rule Extraction Robustness

Table 5. Selected VI rules. Top positivity-framing rules include Neuroticism_high—absent from HI. Appearance-discourse rules have no HI counterpart despite equal marginal prevalence.

Premise X	Consequent Y	supp	conf	lift
Positivity-framing cluster (top rules by lift)				
`Agreeableness_high` ∧ `Neuroticism_low` ∧ `topic_positivity`	`sentiment_Positive`	0.050	0.96	1.43
`Neuroticism_low` ∧ `topic_positivity`	`sentiment_Positive`	0.080	0.94	1.40
`Agreeableness_high` ∧ `Neuroticism_high` ∧ `topic_positivity`	`sentiment_Positive`	0.200	0.92	1.37
`topic_positivity`	`sentiment_Positive`	0.420	0.89	1.33
Appearance-discourse cluster (absent from HI)				
`Agreeableness_high` ∧ `Conscientiousness_low` ∧ `topic_appearance`	`sentiment_Positive`	0.070	0.88	1.32
`Agreeableness_high` ∧ `Neuroticism_high` ∧ `topic_appearance`	`sentiment_Positive`	0.070	0.87	1.30
`Agreeableness_high` ∧ `topic_appearance`	`sentiment_Positive`	0.090	0.85	1.27

Table 6. Rule counts vs. extraction thresholds (lift > 1.2) for selected configurations.

minsup	minconf	#HI rules	#VI rules
0.005	0.8	22	114
0.005	0.9	14	68
0.010	0.8	8	51
0.010	0.9	6	29
0.020	0.8	3	18

To confirm that the 6.4-fold difference in rule counts (and the specific presence of appearance rules in VI) is not an artifact of the chosen thresholds (minsup=1%, minconf=0.8), we tested a grid of parameters. Table 6 demonstrates that VI consistently generates substantially more rules than HI, and that `topic_appearance` rules remain exclusively found in VI discourse across all tested configurations.

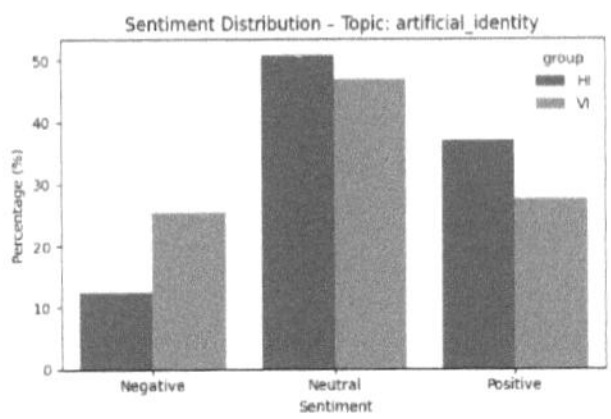

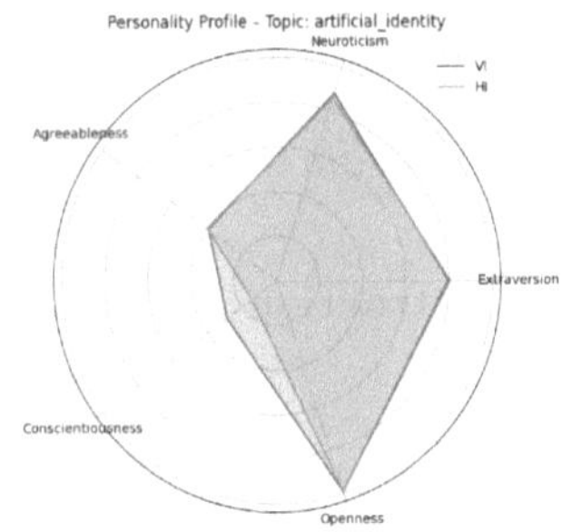

Fig. 3. Sentiment distribution: *artificial identity.* VI shows ≈25% negative vs. ≈12% for HI.

Fig. 4. Big Five profile: *artificial identity.* VI commenters score lower on Agreeableness.

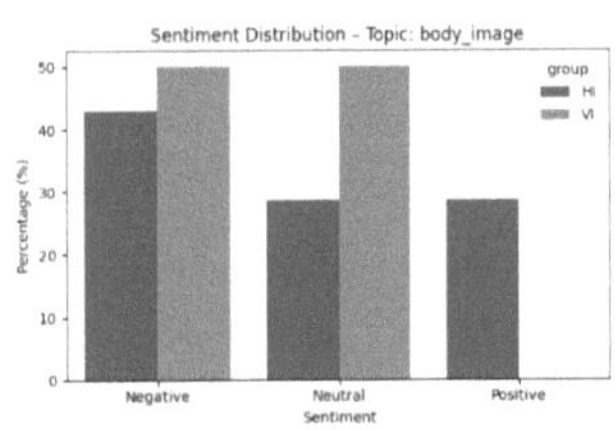

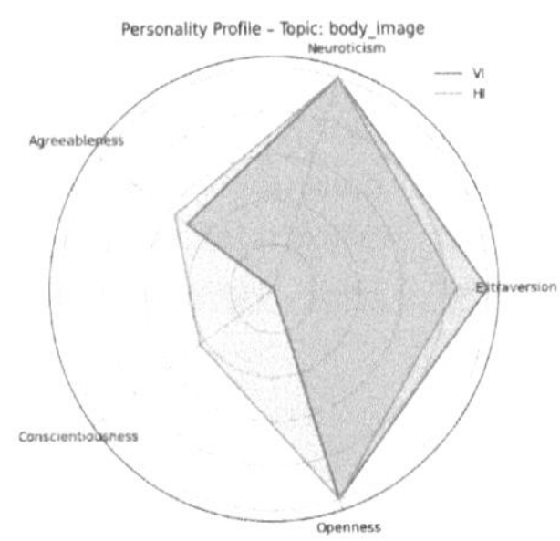

Fig. 5. Sentiment: *body image.* VI is overwhelmingly negative/neutral; HI retains ≈28% positive.

Fig. 6. Big Five profile: *body image.* HI shows higher agreeableness and conscientiousness.

5.4 RQ3: Topic-Level Sentiment and Personality Patterns

Artificial Identity. Both groups are predominantly neutral on this topic (47.2% VI, 50.8% HI). However, VI comments show more negative sentiment (24.8% vs. 12.3%) and less positive sentiment (28.0% vs. 36.9%). Figure 4 shows similar openness and neuroticism across groups, but lower agreeableness and conscientiousness in VI discourse, indicating a more critical tone (Fig. 3).

Authenticity Critique. Both groups are predominantly neutral (41.6% VI, 39.4% HI), but VI threads show more negative sentiment (36.1% vs. 24.8%) and less positive sentiment (22.3% vs. 35.8%). Personality profiles are broadly similar (Fig. 2), with high openness and neuroticism in both groups, but VI audiences respond more skeptically to authenticity-related discourse.

Body Image. VI body-image comments are predominantly negative or neutral, with almost no positive sentiment, whereas HI threads contain 28.4% positive sentiment (Fig. 5). HI profiles show higher agreeableness and conscientiousness, while VI profiles show higher extraversion and lower conscientiousness (Fig. 6), indicating more expressive but less moderated VI discourse.

Mental Health. The mental health topic shows the most extreme divergence: 80.6% of VI-associated comments are negative, versus 42.1% for HI; HI retains 31.4% positive and 26.5% neutral (Fig. 7). VI personality profiles show higher neuroticism and lower conscientiousness than HI (Fig. 8), consistent with more emotionally reactive and less structured discourse.

Sentiment–Trait Cross-Section. Table 7 shows that openness is uniformly high across all conditions, while sentiment-specific differences emerge in agreeableness, neuroticism, and conscientiousness. Positive VI comments show the highest agreeableness (affiliative, warm); negative VI comments show the lowest agreeableness and highest conscientiousness (critical, deliberate). This reinforces the two-architecture interpretation: VI audiences oscillate between warm expressiveness and structured critique, whereas HI discourse is more uniformly regulated.

6 Discussion

The results reveal two distinct discourse architectures. HI discourse is compact and stability-centred: positive sentiment is anchored by low neuroticism and topic positivity. VI discourse is more diverse and personality-centred, with positivity persisting even under emotionally intense configurations. The most important finding is the appearance-discourse cluster: although `topic_appearance` occurs at similar rates in VI and HI comments, it becomes structurally embedded only in VI rules. This demonstrates why closed-set and rule-based analysis can reveal patterns hidden from marginal frequency tables.

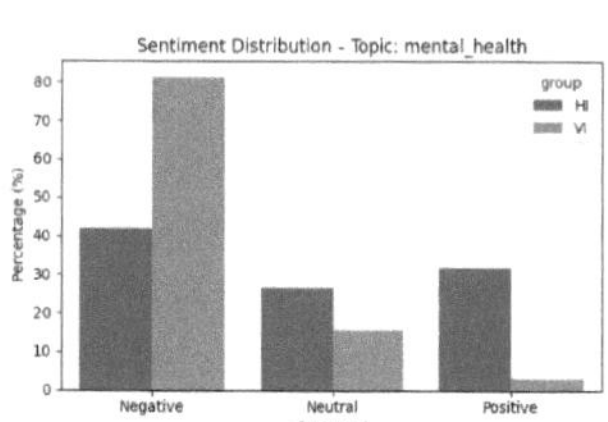

Fig. 7. Sentiment: *mental health.* VI: ≈81% negative. HI: ≈42% negative, ≈31% positive.

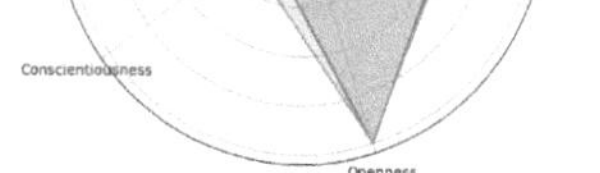

Fig. 8. Big Five profile: *mental health.* VI shows higher neuroticism and lower conscientiousness.

VI comments also show higher negativity in sensitive domains such as mental health, body image, and artificial identity. These results are associative, not causal, but they suggest that synthetic embodiment may create additional audience scrutiny and affective tension. The findings are consistent with uncanny-valley accounts [14, 15], while providing large-scale comment-level evidence.

Table 7. Average Big Five personality trait profiles by sentiment category and influencer type. Traits are abbreviated as follows: E = Extraversion, N = Neuroticism, A = Agreeableness, C = Conscientiousness, O = Openness.

Group	Sentiment	E	N	A	C	O
HI	Positive	0.89	0.84	0.53	0.20	0.99
VI	Positive	0.88	0.82	0.61	0.18	0.99
HI	Neutral	0.84	0.93	0.43	0.20	0.99
VI	Neutral	0.84	0.89	0.42	0.22	0.99
HI	Negative	0.81	0.87	0.44	0.23	0.99
VI	Negative	0.81	0.88	0.33	0.27	0.99

Limitations. The study is limited to English YouTube comments from three matched VI–HI pairs. Topic, sentiment, and personality labels are automatically inferred, and personality scores should be interpreted only as psycholinguistic proxies. Association rules are statistical regularities rather than causal or logical claims. Future work should extend the analysis across platforms, languages, and longitudinal audience trajectories.

7 Conclusion

Using weekly FCA and comment-level association rule mining on ≈70,000 YouTube comments from matched VIâĂŞHI influencer pairs, we identify a clear structural divergence between virtual and human influencer discourse. HI discourse forms a compact, stability-centered structure, whereas VI discourse is more personality-centered and structurally diverse. Most notably, appearance-related discourse emerges as a stable rule cluster only in VI despite near-equal marginal prevalence across conditions, illustrating how FCA reveals structural differences invisible to frequency analysis alone. More broadly, our results demonstrate the value of FCA as a structural diagnostic for complex social discourse data.

References

1. Agrawal, R., Srikant, R.: Fast algorithms for mining association rules in large databases. In: Proceedings of the 20th International Conference on Very Large Data Bases (VLDB 1994), pp. 487–499. Morgan Kaufmann (1994)

2. Arsenyan, J., Mirowska, A.: Almost human? A comparative experiment on the effectiveness of human and virtual influencers. Psychol. Mark. **39**(12), 2273–2287 (2022). https://doi.org/10.1002/mar.21720
3. Ganter, B., Wille, R.: Formal concept analysis: mathematical foundations. Springer, Heidelberg (1999). https://doi.org/10.1007/978-3-642-59830-2
4. Looi, J., Kim, E.A., E, Z.: Sponsorship disclosure in virtual influencer marketing: assessing users' sentiment and engagement toward virtual influencer endorsements. J. Advertising Res. 1–23 (2025)
5. Lou, C., et al.: Authentically fake? HOW consumers respond to the influence of virtual influencers. J. Advert. **52**(4), 540–557 (2022). https://doi.org/10.1080/00913367.2022.2149641
6. Mairesse, F., Walker, M.A., Mehl, M.R., Moore, R.K.: Using linguistic cues for the automatic recognition of personality in conversation and text. J. Artif. Intell. Res. **30**, 457–500 (2007). https://doi.org/10.1613/jair.2349
7. Pasquier, N., Bastide, Y., Taouil, R., Lakhal, L.: Discovering frequent closed itemsets for association rules. In: Proceedings of the 7th International Conference on Database Theory (ICDT 1999), pp. 398–416. Springer (1999). https://doi.org/10.1007/3-540-49257-7_25
8. Poelmans, J., Kuznetsov, S.O., Ignatov, D.I., Dedene, G.: Formal concept analysis in knowledge processing: a survey on models and techniques. Expert Syst. Appl. **40**(16), 6601–6623 (2013). https://doi.org/10.1016/j.eswa.2013.05.007
9. Sands, S., Ferraro, C., Campbell, C., Kietzmann, J.: Unreal influence: leveraging AI in influencer marketing. Eur. J. Mark. **56**(6), 1721–1747 (2022)
10. da Silva Oliveira, A.B., Chimenti, P.: "Humanized robots": a proposition of categories to understand virtual influencers. Australas. J. Inf. Syst. **25** (2021)
11. Stumme, G., Taouil, R., Bastide, Y., Pasquier, N., Lakhal, L.: Computing iceberg concept lattices with TITANIC. Data Knowl. Eng. **42**(2), 189–222 (2002)
12. Valtchev, P., Missaoui, R., Godineau, R.: GALICIA: An open platform for lattices. In: Priss, U., Corbett, D.R., Angelova, G. (eds.) Working with Conceptual Structures: Contributions to ICCS 2002, pp. 241–254. Shaker Verlag, Aachen (2002)
13. Valtchev, P., Missaoui, R., Lebrun, P.: A partition-based approach towards building the Hasse diagram of a concept lattice. J. Exp. Theor. Artif. Intell. **16**, 107–113. Taylor & Francis (2004)
14. Xie-Carson, L., Benckendorff, P., Hughes, K.: Keep it #unreal: exploring Instagram users' engagement with virtual influencers in tourism contexts. J. Hospitality Tourism Res. **48**(6), 1006–1019 (2024)
15. Yan, J., Xia, S., Jiang, A., Lin, Z.: The effect of different types of virtual influencers on consumers' emotional attachment. J. Bus. Res. **177**, 114646 (2024)

Alternative Diagrams for Concept Lattices

Uta Priss(✉)

Fakultät Informatik, Ostfalia University, Wolfenbüttel, Germany
upriss@gmail.com
https://www.upriss.org.uk

Abstract. This paper presents several types of diagrams for visualising concept lattices: tabular Euler diagrams with additional features, such as icons, nesting, factorisation and object frequencies, and also Repeated Attribute Lattice diagrams and diagrams for AFOC-posets and Relation Algebraic Concept Analysis. The aim is to provide a variety of means for visualising conceptual structures with carefully designed but easy to interpret diagrammatic representations.

1 Introduction

This paper continues previous research on using Euler diagrams for representing concept lattices (Priss and Dürrschnabel 2024) in the sense of Formal Concept Analysis (FCA) as defined by Ganter & Wille (1999). But it also presents other diagrams for concept lattices and related structures in order to showcase a variety of FCA related visualisations. It is not claimed that everything presented here is fundamentally novel considering that the literature on diagrams spans more than 100 years (e.g. Neurath (1936) as an older example). But in our opinion, FCA still does not achieve its full potential for its diagrammatic representations. While Hasse diagrams[1] are favoured by mathematicians, they are not self-evident because, for example, their edges can be misread as vectors[2]. Because FCA is often applied to complex data structures, which are by nature challenging to represent, there is a danger for FCA software visualisations to contain an overload of features, sliders, buttons, windows and other options with a steep learning curve. In this paper a selection of diagram types is introduced that are intended to be less complex but self-explanatory and, furthermore, a few diagram types (AFOC-posets, APT, RAL and RaCA diagrams) that are novel at least for FCA.

Introductions to FCA and Euler diagrams are not included in this paper but can be found in Ganter & Wille (1999) and Priss & Dürrschnabel (2024),

[1] The diagrams should not be named after Hasse because he did not invent them but the name is established in the literature.

[2] Based on personal observations while teaching mathematics to first year university students.

M. Croitoru et al. (Eds.): CONCEPTS 2026, LNAI 16811, pp. 318–328, 2027.
https://doi.org/10.1007/978-3-032-34742-8_21

respectively. As a compromise between FCA and Euler diagram terminology, elements of sets are called *objects* and the sets themselves are called *attributes.* Elements of lattices are called *concepts* and correspond to *zones* of an Euler diagram. FCA contexts are called *matrices.* All sets are finite. A Boolean lattice with 2^n elements or, in other words, n attributes is abbreviated as Bn in this paper.

2 Euler Diagrams

Euler diagrams are a means for visualising sets and their partial orders. Each set, or attribute, is represented by a closed curve, such as a circle or rectangle. Elements, or objects, can be written into the *zones*, which are the smallest areas that are surrounded by some curve segments. In particular, *tabular diagrams* are easy to read because they are essentially tables where row or column headings are allowed to extend to more than one neighbouring row or column. A tabular diagram should have as many non-shaded zones as there are concepts in a lattice but not all lattices are drawable as Euler diagrams of a certain type. For example, a B2 is drawable as a linear diagram, a B3 with rectangles or circles and a B4 with rectangles or ellipses but not with circles. Mechanisms exist for increasing the drawability such as shading areas which are not meant to exist, omitting the bottom concept, *splitting attributes* into more than one curve, using curves of other shapes or other visual cues, for example, colours and icons.

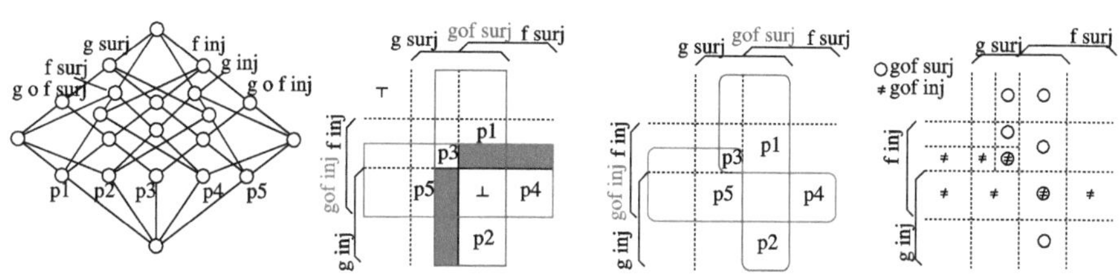

Fig. 1. A Hasse diagram of a lattice and three versions of a corresponding tabular diagram

The example in Fig. 1 is based on a lattice of properties of functions from Ganter (2013, p. 76) and contains some objects (p1, p2, ... p5) inserted into zones. The top concept can be notated by $\top$ and the bottom concept by $\perp$. If the bottom concept is omitted its neighbours can instead be marked with $\perp$. In a tabular diagram, containment indicates a subset relationship, such as 'g $\circ$ f surj' being contained in'g surj', which according to FCA means that 'g $\circ$ f surj' implies 'g surj'. Presumably, such containment is more intuitive to read from Euler diagrams. Most likely only experienced users will immediately observe that the structure in Fig. 1 is a B4 with 2 further attributes ('g $\circ$ f surj' and 'g $\circ$ f inj'), which however, is even more difficult to see in the Hasse diagram.

The tabular diagrams on the right in Fig. 1 showcase other visual cues such as other shapes and icons in order to avoid shading. Figure 2 displays a well-known example from Ganter & Wille (1999) converted into an Euler diagram. In general, tabular Euler diagrams are feasible for many kinds of lattices and in particular for those that are a nominal scale, crown-like or tree-like where parts of the tree can be B2s, B3s or even B4s and the bottom concept may be omitted.

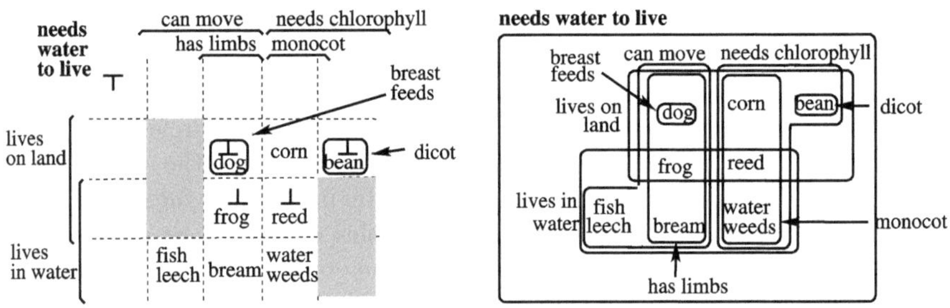

Fig. 2. 'Live in water' as a tabular diagram and a standard Euler diagram

3 Geometrical Diagrams, Nesting and Factorisation

This section discusses several different types of FCA diagrams. Ganter & Wille (1999) describe a special type of diagram called *geometrical diagram*, which is essentially a view from above or below onto a lattice. The bottom left of Fig. 3 shows a geometrical diagram of a nominal scale in Ganter & Wille (GW) notation. In GW notation the top and bottom concepts should be omitted but because any lattice can be a substructure of another lattice, top and bottom concepts must be drawable as well and are included in Fig. 3. In GW notation concepts with a single upper neighbour are drawn adjacent but slightly behind the neighbour as shown for the concepts 2, 3 and 4. Concepts with more than one upper neighbour are drawn as n-simplexes (lines, triangles and so on). In the nominal scale concept 5 must be connected to concepts 2, 3 and 4, which is only possible with a distorted triangle (shown as a shape that is striped).

Clearly already a nominal scale is almost impossible to draw if the top and bottom concepts are included because of the directly adjacent concepts. Therefore we are introducing an *arrow notation* as graphs with arrows between concepts and their direct upper neighbours as in the other examples in Fig. 3. The set of arrows pointing away from a single concept corresponds to a simplex in GW notation. The GW notation can be translated into the arrow notation with the exact same positioning of the concepts but the arrow notation can also represent lattices which are challenging in GW notation. Figure 3 shows further examples including the Forum Romanum of Ganter &Wille (1999) which is further discussed in Fig. 6 below. A B3 can be drawn in a triangular layout with the

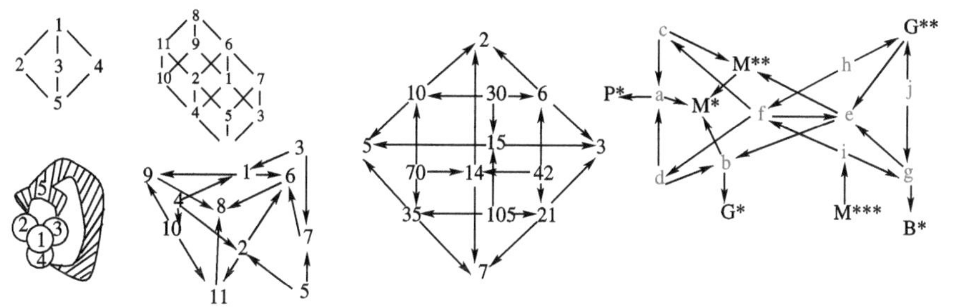

Fig. 3. Geometrical diagrams: nominal scale, two connected B3s, B4 and Forum Romanum

top and bottom concepts in the middle. A B4 without top and bottom concept can be drawn as a square with triangles for its B3 sublattices.

The layout of a geometrical diagram is not the same as for an Euler diagram because, in the former, higher and lower concepts can both be placed between other concepts whereas in the latter higher concepts are placed outside of and lower concepts between other concepts. As a result, geometrical diagrams are better than Euler diagrams at showing which concepts are neighbours whereas such information can be lost for some zones in an Euler diagram. But both types of diagrams suffer from the challenges caused by forcing complex structures into a 2-dimensional representation. The top and bottom concepts of the Forum Romanum in Fig. 3 are missing because otherwise P*, M*, G* and B* would need to be connected to it leading to more line crossings if the top concept is placed in the middle or curved lines if the top concept is placed on the outside. In summary, geometrical diagrams display interesting symmetries and patterns but also have drawing limitations.

If a lattice is not drawable as an Euler diagram, nesting and factorisation provide means for compacting or splitting a diagram. Figure 4 displays different versions of a B7 where an inner B3 with split attributes is *nested* into an outer B4. In the tabular diagrams, circles are used for the inner B3 for better visual differentiation. Each attribute of the inner lattice is split 16 times. The tabular diagrams provide significantly more space for adding objects than the Hasse diagram. Ideally, the selection of which attributes to use in the inner and outer lattice and their left-right, top-down sequence should be based on some semantic difference or to highlight patterns, for example, if colouring is used for object frequencies.

A *factorisation* of a concept lattice is a selection of factor concepts that carry sufficient information to construct the lattice because the union of the factor concept matrices equals the matrix of the lattice (and so does a product of 2 matrices which have the factors as columns/rows (Kim 1982)). Determining a minimal factorisation is an NP-complete problem (Belohlavek & Vychodil 2010).

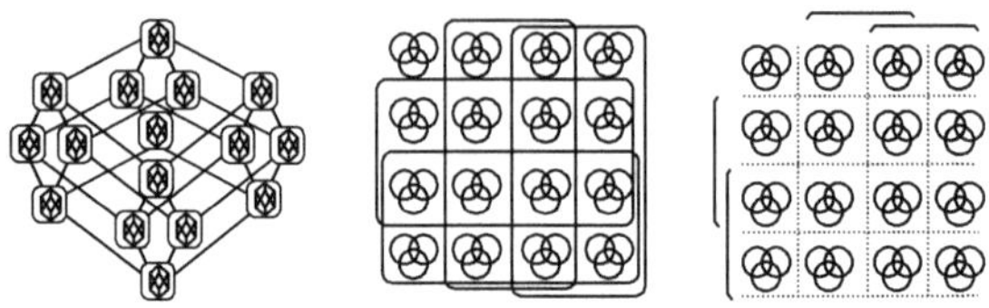

Fig. 4. A Boolean lattice with 7 attributes as a nested diagram and two types of Euler diagrams

Figure 5 shows an example[3] of a minimal factorisation of B6 as a union of 4 factor concept matrices.

$$\begin{array}{c}111110\\111101\\110111\\111011\\101111\\011111\end{array} = \begin{array}{c}110100\\110100\\110100\\000000\\000000\\000000\end{array} \cup \begin{array}{c}101010\\000000\\000000\\101010\\101010\\000000\end{array} \cup \begin{array}{c}000000\\011001\\000000\\011001\\000000\\011001\end{array} \cup \begin{array}{c}000000\\000000\\000111\\000000\\000111\\000111\end{array}$$

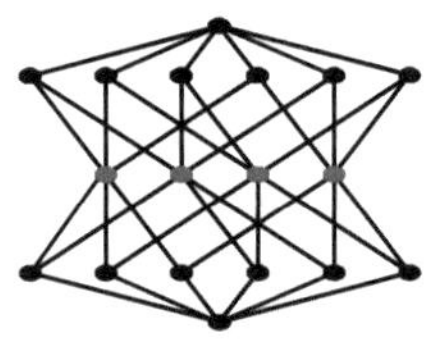

Fig. 5. Factorisation of a B6 and its AFOC-poset

An *AOC-poset* is a subset of a lattice consisting of attribute and object concepts and their connections (Osswald & Petersen 2002). An AOC-poset contains sufficient information to reconstruct a lattice but usually has many edge crossing, which are difficult to visually discern. We are suggesting to create an *AFOC-poset* instead by including factors in addition to attribute and object concepts. The factors chosen can be those of a minimal factorisation, such as the blue concepts in the middle layer in Fig. 5. Or all factors can be selected that cover a given threshold number of objects and attributes under the condition that the union of the factor concept matrices equals the lattice matrix.

In the AFOC-poset in Fig. 6 each of the 3 factors covers at least 3 objects and 3 attributes. Figures 5 and 6 demonstrate that an AFOC-poset constitutes a compromise between a lattice and an AOC-poset because it contains fewer elements than a lattice and fewer edge crossing than an AOC-poset thus reducing the visual complexity while still maintaining sufficient information about the object-attribute relationships. While Hasse diagrams of lattices might contain more potentially visually appealing parallel edges, it can be questioned in how far such patterns are meaningful for an application. AFOC-posets may be less 'pretty' but will be more concise.

For discussing factorisations Ganter & Wille (1999) utilise the Digits example, which is divided in Fig. 7 into the concepts above and below the factors,

[3] Thanks to Dmitry I. Ignatov for sending me the factorisation of this example. His algorithm (Ignatov & Yakovleva 2021) provides a factorisation, however, not always minimal.

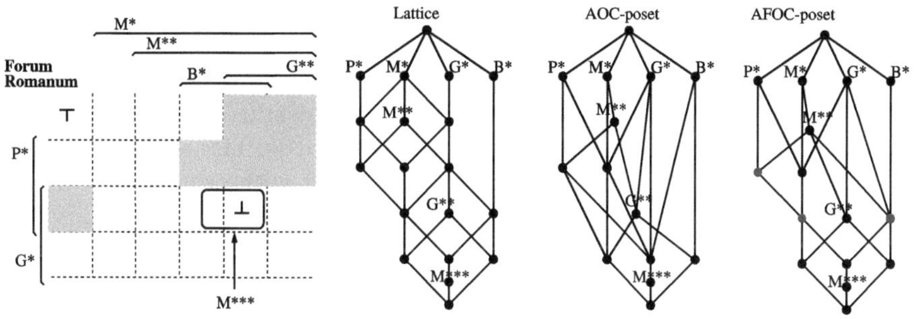

Fig. 6. Forum Romanum as a tabular diagram, lattice, AOC- and AFOC-poset

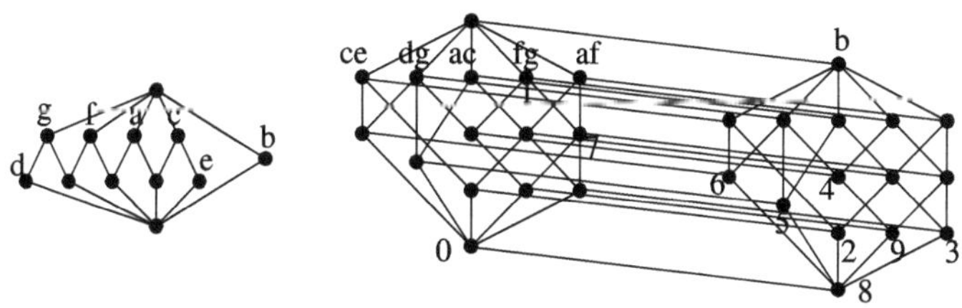

Fig. 7. Factorisation of the Digits example

because its lattice is quite complex. The bottom half is probably best presented by separating the concepts with and without attribute 'b' as shown in Fig. 7 as a Hasse diagram and in Fig. 8 as an Euler diagram. While we would argue that the Hasse and Euler diagrams in Figs. 7 and 8 are both well readable, the AFOC-poset (of top and bottom combined) is probably more informative for most application purposes and more concise.

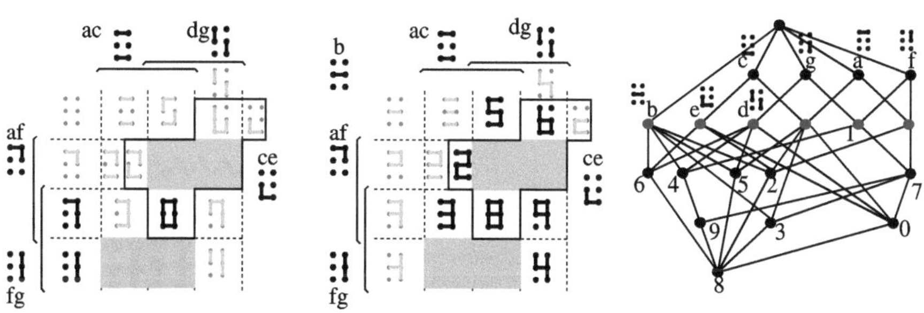

Fig. 8. Digits: bottom half as a 2-part Euler diagram and complete as an AFOC-poset

4 Object Frequency and Repeated Attributes

In some applications only object frequencies are of relevance. Euler diagrams are called *area-proportional* if zone sizes correspond to object frequencies as shown in the middle of Fig. 9 although not exactly drawn to scale. The contingency table on the left of Fig. 9 shows the object frequencies but with ordinal row and column headers. Unfortunately, area-proportionality provides another constraint on drawability. Therefore one of the shapes in the middle diagram is not a rectangle. Furthermore, area-proportionality requires visual size comparisons, which can be misleading if the shapes are different (Neurath 1936). Therefore, we are introducing *axis-proportional tabular diagrams with icons (APT diagrams)* as on the right in Fig. 9. so that the width of the columns and the height of the rows are proportional to the frequencies along the two axes. Each icon (here: circle) represents a certain number of objects (here: 10) so that object frequencies can be compared. If the distribution of the objects is statistically independent then cell percentages are a product of the row and column percentages and an APT diagram is area-proportional. Otherwise it is easy to see which combinations are lower or higher than expected by evaluating how empty or crowded the zones are. APT diagrams are not an entirely new invention because they are related to Mosaic plots as explained below and somewhat similar displays have also been utilised in existing FCA software.

		a	a, b	b	
c	0	20	50	40	110
c	20	40	10	20	90
	20	60	60	60	200

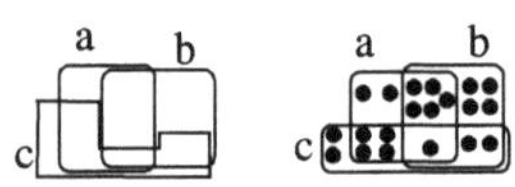

Fig. 9. Contingency table, area-proportional diagram and APT diagram

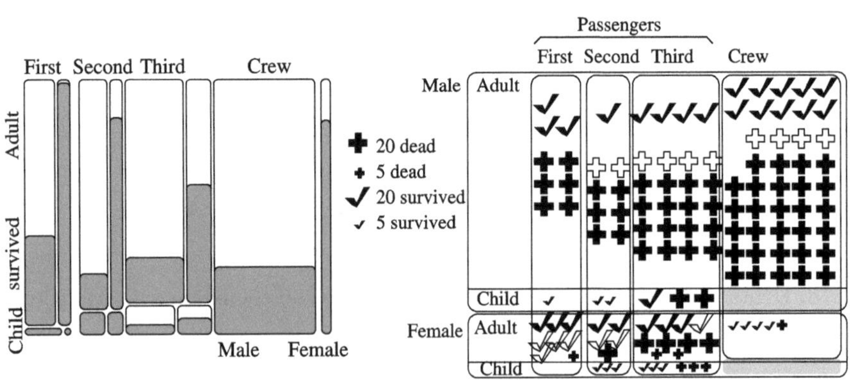

Fig. 10. Survival on the Titanic as a mosaic plot (left) and as an APT diagram (right)

Mosaic plots as invented by Hartigan and Kleiner (1981) and extended by Friendly (1994) for visualising contingency tables are essentially area-proportional Euler diagrams with split attributes. The left side of Fig. 10 displays a mosaic plot of the well-known Titanic data for the many-valued attributes class, gender, age and survival. The diagram shows for example the better chance of survival for women and children. But it is basically impossible to compare percentages across attributes because of the different shapes. The APT diagram on the right side of Fig. 10 with four split attributes (adult, child, dead and survived) displays the same data but with more information. Icons for survival and death have two sizes (for groups of 20 and groups of 5) and a white colour for higher counts than expected. Only the APT diagram shows clearly that the survival rate of first class male adults and third class male children corresponds exactly to the 30% survival rate of all passengers. Males had higher survival chances if they were crew members than second or third class passengers. Zones for the adult female passengers are crowded because of small numbers of female crew and zones for crew children are shaded because there were none.

Apart from objects, attributes can also occur with higher frequencies in some applications. Hasse diagrams of concept lattices are sometimes drawn to contain parallel edges, which might improve readability but carry no further meaning. In some applications attributes can apply more than once to an object in which case all parallel edges can represent a single attribute. We are calling such diagrams *Repeated Attribute Lattice diagrams (RAL diagram)* and each attribute a *vector*. The far left of Fig. 11 displays a RAL diagram of numbers and divisors where one vector represents 'multiply 2' and the other 'multiply 3'. The length of a vector does not carry any meaning but vector addition corresponds to multiplication, such as $2 \cdot 2 \cdot 3 = 12$. Unfortunately, only small parts of RAL diagrams can be drawn for more than 2 vectors because eventually crossing will occur that are not valid multiples. Espinosa-Aldama and Mendoza (2024) construct lattices for physical units without considering how often units are used. We are suggesting to use RAL diagrams instead. Figure 11 displays parts of a RAL diagram for physical units that simultaneously show valid products, such as $F \cdot \Omega = s$, $\Omega \cdot A = V$, $A \cdot s = C$, $V \cdot s = Wb$, $A \cdot V \cdot s = J$ and many more.

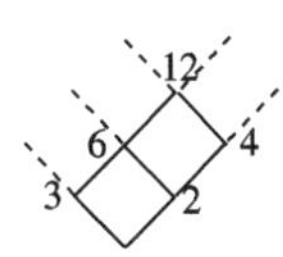

	m	Ω	F	A	Pa	T
s		1	1			
V		1		1		
Wb		2	1	1		
Wb	2					1
C		1	1	1		
J		2	1	2		
kg	1	2	2		1	
W		1		2		

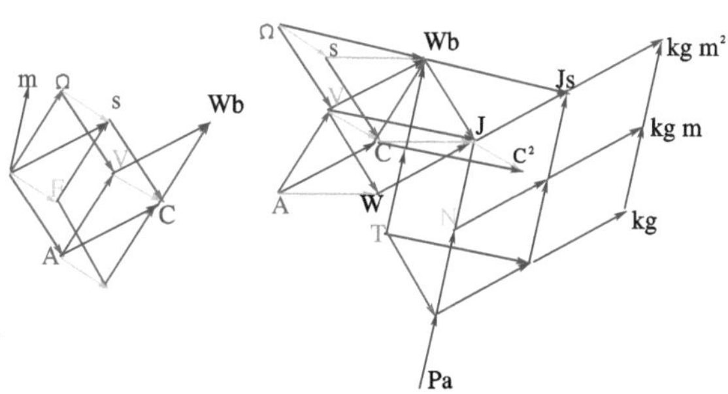

Fig. 11. RAL diagrams: multiples, matrix and parts of a RAL diagram for physical units

5 Relation Algebraic Concept Analysis

If a concept lattice is combined with a relation, many additional concepts can be defined in an ad-hoc manner. For example, attributes 'male' and 'female' together with a parent-child relationship yield concepts such as 'male parent' and 'parent of at least one female child'. Relational concepts are either lexicalised ('father', 'daughter') or can be described ad hoc, such as 'has parent who has daughter', which might be renamed to 'has or is sister'. Together with quantifiers this leads to many possibilities. Extensions of FCA such as RCA (Dolques, Le Ber & Huchard 2013) and GFCA (Ferre & Cellier 2019) exist, which study the formation of relational concepts. They were preceded by what used to be called RCA (Priss 1999) but is renamed into Relation Algebraic Concept Analysis (RaCA) in order to avoid confusion with the unrelated later RCA. While RCA and GFCA compute all possibilities for some relation and develop algorithms, the focus of RaCA is on deriving diagrams in a flexible manner using standard Relation Algebra and matrix operations (Priss 2006). In this paper RaCA is demonstrated using an example of some members of the British royal family (Fig. 12) originally from GFCA (Ferre & Cellier 2019).

Table P:

name	gender	birth
Charles	male	1948
Diana	female	1961
William	male	1982
Harry	male	1984
Kate	female	1982
George	male	2013
Charlotte	female	2015
Louis	male	2018

Table PC:

parent	child
Charles	William
Charles	Harry
Diana	William
Diana	Harry
William	George
William	Charlotte
William	Louis
Kate	George
Kate	Charlotte
Kate	Louis

I	m f
Charles	1 0
Diana	0 1
William	1 0
Kate	0 1

J	m f
William	1 0
Harry	1 0
George	1 0
Charlotte	0 1
Louis	1 0

R	WHGCL
C	1 1 0 0 0
D	1 1 0 0 0
W	0 0 1 1 1
K	0 0 1 1 1

$I \cup (R \circ J)$

	m f m f
C	1 0 1 0
D	0 1 1 0
W	1 0 1 1
K	0 1 1 1

Scale:
< 1950, < 1980
< 2000, ≥ 2000

S	
1948	1 1 1 0
1961	0 1 1 0
1982	0 0 1 0
1984	0 0 1 0
2013	0 0 0 1
2015	0 0 0 1
2018	0 0 0 1

Fig. 12. A parent-child relationship amongst some members of the British royal family

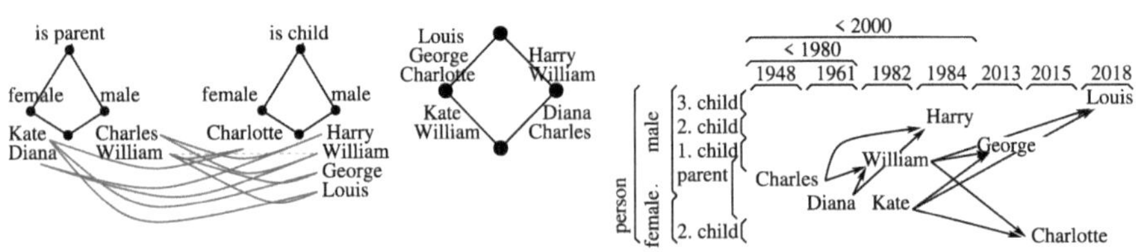

Fig. 13. A relation amongst objects in lattices and an Euler diagram

The data of the example is contained in the tables P and PC in Fig. 12, which are modelled as binary matrices I and J, R and a scale S for 4 different ranges of the time of birth. The left side of Fig. 13 displays a modelling of the primary data as lattices where the lines that connect parents and children are difficult to visually trace. The dashed line is meant to indicate that 'William' refers to the same person. The right side of Fig. 13 shows the relationships amongst individual objects with arrows, which are easier to observe. The attributes '1. child', '2. child', '3. child' are computed from background information for temporal data but can also be visually inferred from the diagram because the two generations, married couples and birth sequence form visual patterns. The attribute '2. child' is split.

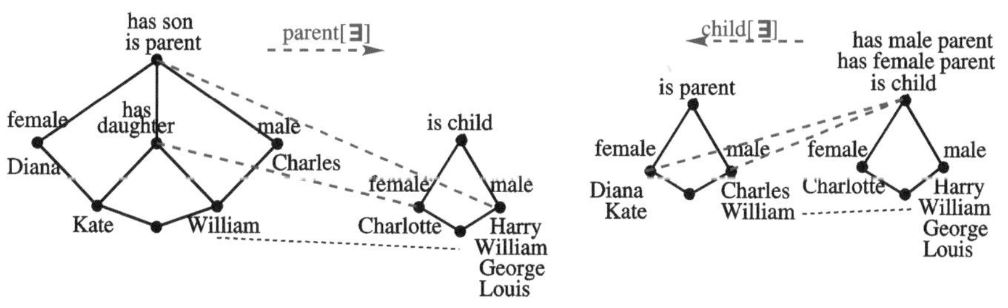

Fig. 14. RaCA diagrams: conceptual parent-child[∃] relation

In RaCA a relation amongst objects leads to relations amongst concepts based on quantifiers (Priss 1999). While tabular Euler diagrams may be more suitable for relations amongst objects, Hasse diagrams are more suited for relations amongst concepts. The data for the following diagrams is produced by binary matrix multiplication with complementation depending on the quantifiers as explained by Priss (1999). For example, in order to add the attributes of the children to the lattice of the parents the operation $I \cup (R \circ J)$ is performed on the matrices from Fig. 12 with a disjoint union so that attributes get renamed ('female' for children becomes 'has female child' for adults) resulting in the lattices in Fig. 14. The corresponding matrix operation for the children is $(I \circ R)^d \cup J$ where ^{d} indicates the dual matrix. Priss (1999) suggests that a relation amongst concepts can be visualised via a basis where ∀-quantifiers are inherited by subconcepts and ∃-quantifiers by superconcepts so that ∀-quantifiers only need to be shown for the largest concepts and ∃-quantifiers only for the smallest concepts. In Fig. 14 *all* parents have *at least 1* son but only Kate and William have *at least 1* daughter. *All* children have *at least 1* male and female parent. Obviously, as soon as more attributes are added to the lattice of the parents these lead to more attributes of the children resulting in $((I \cup (R \circ J))^d \circ R)^d \cup J$ and so on. Repeated multiplication of a binary matrix will reach a fixed state once the product does not change anymore or has a period (Kim 1982). Together with a union this will lead to the lattices stabilising after a few iterations. The scale S of Fig. 12 is only displayed in the Euler diagram in Fig. 13 but applying a scale is also just a matter of matrix multiplication.

In conclusion, this paper presents a variety of diagrams for lattices with or without additional structures such as relations or repeated objects and attributes. It is argued that Euler diagrams are easier to read for untrained users and are suitable for nesting and some RaCA diagrams but without nesting only feasible for fairly small lattices which are mostly tree-like or crown-like. A certain type of Euler diagram called APT diagram is presented as an improvement over Mosaic plots. Euler diagrams provide more space for representing objects whereas Hasse diagrams are more suitable for some applications where individual objects are less relevant. Factorisation leads to a type of Hasse diagram called AFOC-poset, which is a compromise between a lattice and its minimal representation as an AOC-poset. RaCA diagrams are Hasse diagrams with additional relations amongst lattices and RAL diagrams are Hasse diagrams with repeated attributes. Last but not least, geometrical diagrams are neither Hasse, nor Euler diagrams but a type of graph and are interesting but most likely of limited practical use.

References

Belohlavek, R., Vychodil, V.: Discovery of optimal factors in binary data via a novel method of matrix decomposition. J. Comput. Syst. Sci. **76**(1), 3–20 (2010)

Dolques, X., Le Ber, F., Huchard, M.: AOC-posets: a scalable alternative to Concept Lattices for Relational Concept Analysis. CLA: Concept Lattices and their Applications (2013)

Espinosa-Aldama, M., Mendoza, S.: Multidimensional representation of semantic relations between physical theories, fundamental constants and units of measurement with formal concept analysis. Symmetry **16**, 7 (2024)

Ferre, S., Cellier, P.: Graph-FCA: an extension of formal concept analysis to knowledge graphs. Discret. Appl. Math. **273**, 81–102 (2019)

Friendly, M.: Mosaic displays for multi-way contingency tables. J. Amer. Stat. Assoc. **89**(425), 190–200 (1994)

Ganter, B., Wille, R.: Formal Concept Analysis. Mathematical Foundations. Springer (1999)

Ganter, B.: Diskrete Mathematik: Geordnete Mengen. Springer (2013)

Hartigan, J.A., Kleiner, B.: Mosaics for contingency tables. In: Eddy, W.F. (ed.) Computer Science and Statistics: Proceedings of the 13th Symposium on the Interface, pp. 268–273. Springer, New York (1981)

Ignatov, D.I., Yakovleva, A.: On suboptimality of GreConD for boolean matrix factorisation of contranominal scales. In: FCA4AI@IJCAI 2021, pp. 87–98 (2021)

Kim, K.H.: Boolean Matrix Theory and Applications. Marcel Dekker, New York (1982)

Neurath, O.: International Picture Language. Kegan Paul, London (1936)

Osswald, R., Petersen, W.: Induction of classifications from linguistic data. In: Proc. of the ECAI-Workshop on Advances in FCA for KDD (2002)

Priss, U.: Efficient implementation of semantic relations in lexical databases. Comput. Intell. **15**(1), 79–87 (1999)

Priss, U.: An FCA interpretation of relation algebra. In: Missaoui, R., Schmidt, J. (eds.) ICFCA 2006. LNCS (LNAI), vol. 3874, pp. 248–263. Springer, Heidelberg (2006). https://doi.org/10.1007/11671404_17

Priss, U., Dürrschnabel, D.: Rectangular Euler diagrams and order theory. In: Proceedings of Diagrams 2024. LNAI, vol. 14981, pp. 165–181. Springer (2024)

Advancing Metadata-Driven Enterprise Architecture Management Tools Using Conceptual Structures

Mahpara Saleem[1(✉)], Simon Polovina[2,3], and Richard Fallon[4]

[1] Mahaz Tech Enterprise Limited (MTE), Manchester, UK
mahpara@mahaztechenterprise.com
[2] Department of Computing and Digital Technologies, Sheffield Hallam University, Sheffield, UK
S.Polovina@shu.ac.uk
[3] Simile Logics Limited, Sheffield, UK
simon@similelogics.ltd
[4] Red Rooster IT, Vienna, Austria
richard@fallon.at

Abstract. Metadata-driven Enterprise Architecture (EA) is critical for aligning business strategy with digital execution, yet metadata often remains fragmented across systems and tools. Moregraph uses Conceptual Graphs as its formal specification and SAP Graph as an exemplar, visualising 4,560 clean-core data objects—but visualisation alone does not ensure governance. This paper extends Moregraph with a formal *Metadata-to-Governance Transformation* (MGT): a principled, deterministic mapping from OData entity type metadata to structured *Data Object* governance records, grounded in five design principles and delivered via two pathways (real-time API and Excel bulk import). Demonstrated using SAP LeanIX across four SAP Graph namespaces, functional validation confirms correctness, completeness, and efficiency gains over manual documentation. The approach generalises to any OData-compliant source and any EA platform supporting programmatic or bulk import.

Keywords: Enterprise Architecture Management · Conceptual Graphs · SAP Graph · SAP LeanIX · Metadata Management · Clean Core · Design Science

1 Introduction

Enterprise Architecture (EA) management aligns an organisation's technology landscape with its business strategy [3,18]. A persistent challenge is *metadata fragmentation*: data objects and their properties are distributed across disparate documentation, making it difficult for architects to maintain a coherent model of the data landscape [2]. SAP Graph—a unified API layer providing cross-system

M. Croitoru et al. (Eds.): CONCEPTS 2026, LNAI 16811, pp. 329–339, 2027.
https://doi.org/10.1007/978-3-032-34742-8_22

access to SAP business data objects via OData v4 (a standard, machine-readable format for data entities and relationships) and implementing the SAP Clean Core strategy [10, 11]—exposes 4,560 clean-core data objects programmatically. However, translating this metadata into a governed EA model remains largely manual: at 30–60 min per entity, documenting the full clean-core landscape represents weeks of architect effort [6].

Moregraph [8] addresses part of this gap through interactive visualisation. EA governance platforms such as SAP LeanIX [12]—an Enterprise Architecture Management (EAM) tool that stores architecture information as typed *fact sheets*—require structured *Data Object* records capturing identity, properties, relationships, and lifecycle [16, 17]. No automated mechanism currently bridges SAP Graph metadata to such records. This paper closes that gap with the formal *Metadata-to-Governance Transformation* (MGT): a deterministic function from OData entity type nodes to EA Data Object governance records, grounded in five design principles. Its novelty lies in (i) formal platform-independent specification, (ii) complete coverage of governance-required fields, and (iii) automated, auditable execution.

The contributions are:

1. A formal, platform-independent MGT mapping Moregraph's OData-derived metadata graph to structured EA Data Object governance records, grounded in five explicit design principles.
2. Two complementary delivery pathways—real-time API export (Pathway 1) and governance-friendly Excel bulk export (Pathway 2)—demonstrated using SAP LeanIX.
3. Functional validation across four SAP Graph namespaces (five entities) confirming correctness, completeness, consistency, and robust error handling.

2 Background

2.1 SAP Graph, Clean Core, and Design Science

SAP Graph provides consistent access to SAP business data objects via OData v4, spanning SAP S/4HANA (1,479), SAP Sales Cloud (2,027), SAP SuccessFactors (999), and 55 cross-system objects—4,560 clean-core data objects in total [8]. The Clean Core strategy positions SAP Graph as the preferred integration pattern, discouraging direct system modifications [10]. Governing these artefacts within a dedicated EA platform is essential for architectural clarity [2], yet no automated bridge exists. This paper follows Design Science Research (DSR) [1]: the *artefact* is the MGT; the *relevance cycle* established the automation gap; the *design cycle* iterated over transformation rules and pathway designs; the *rigor cycle* grounds the design in OData semantics [5], the LeanIX metamodel [4], and EA governance literature [3].

2.2 Conceptual Structures and EA Alignment

Moregraph's requirements and conceptual structure were captured in Conceptual Graphs (CGs) [7,13,14]—a formal knowledge representation in which concept nodes (blue rectangles) denote entities and relation nodes (yellow ovals) denote relationships, designed to be both human-readable and computationally precise. Figure 1 shows Moregraph's prior CG specification [8], built using CharGer[1], proceeding from `[Application: Moregraph]` through `[Business Data Graph]` to `[Enterprise Architecture]`. Figure 2 enhances this by adding `[MGT]`, formalising how Moregraph transforms SAP Graph metadata into governed `[Data Object]` fact sheets in `[EAM Tool: SAP LeanIX]`.

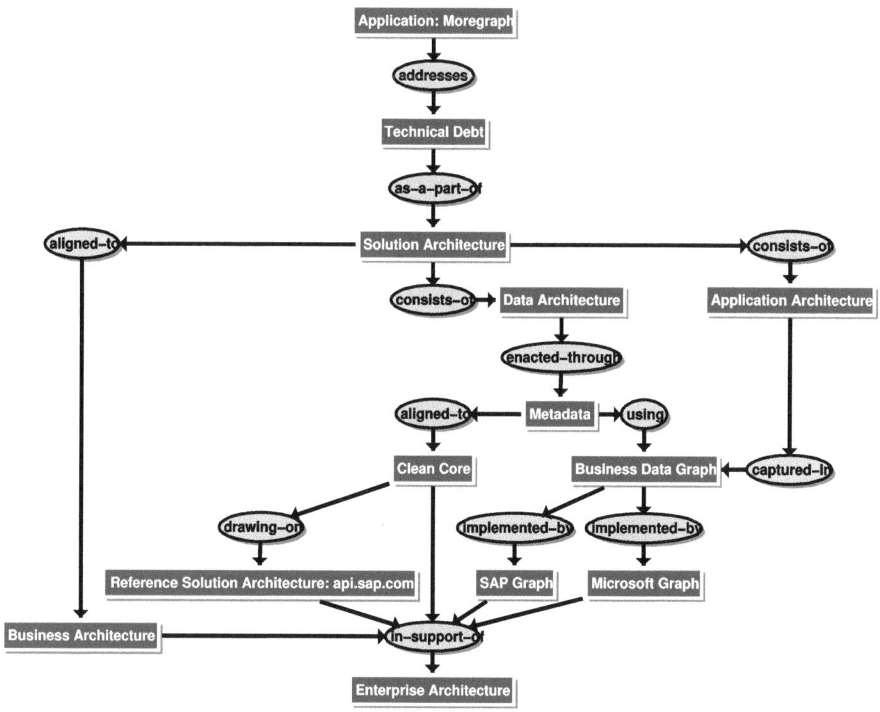

Fig. 1. Prior CG specification of Moregraph [8].

In Moregraph's internal graph, OData entity-type nodes correspond to CG concept nodes and navigation-property edges to CG relation nodes. Table 1 formalises the structural alignment between OData and LeanIX models that grounds the MGT: a *Data Object* in EA practice captures a business data entity's identifier, properties, relationships, lifecycle status, and provenance [16,17], and SAP LeanIX realises this as a Data Object fact sheet ingested via REST/GraphQL API or Excel bulk import [4].

[1] https://github.com/Conceptual-Graphs/CharGer.

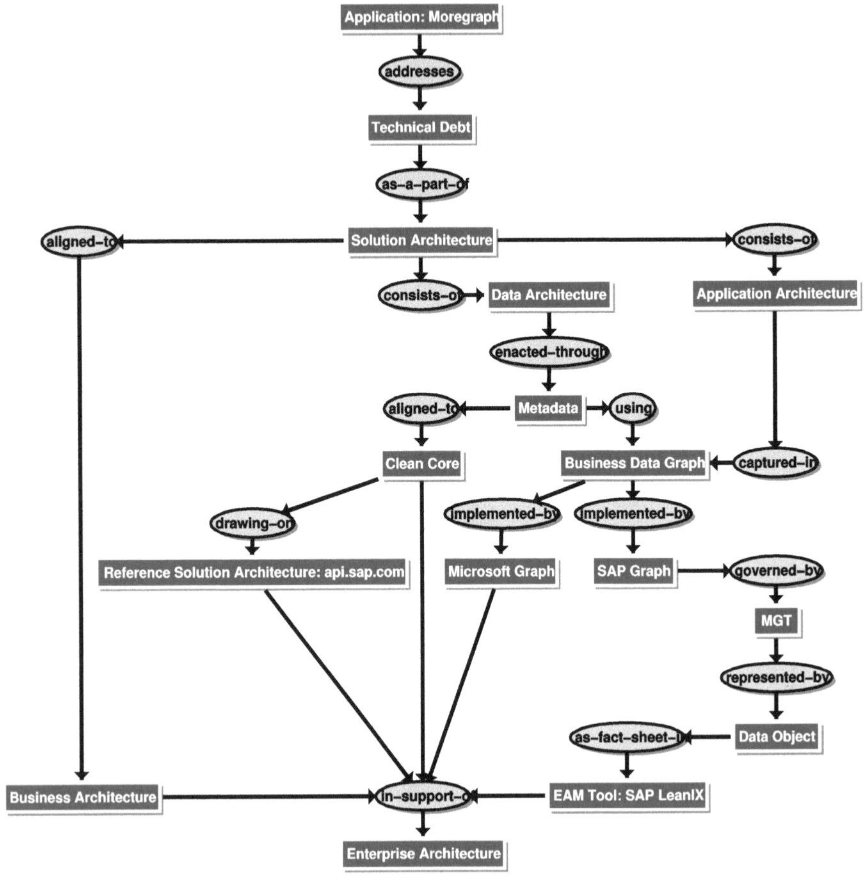

Fig. 2. MGT-enhanced CG specification of Moregraph.

3 The Metadata-to-Governance Transformation

3.1 Research Question and Architecture

Building on Moregraph's visualisation [8]: *How can Moregraph's metadata visualisation be integrated with SAP LeanIX to improve EA governance?* The framework has three stages (Fig. 3): (1) **Metadata Extraction**—Moregraph parses OData v4 documents and builds an internal conceptual graph; (2) **Transformation**—the MGT converts graph nodes into LeanIX-compatible structures; (3) **Synchronisation**—Pathway 1 (API) or Pathway 2 (Excel) delivers artefacts to LeanIX.

3.2 Metadata Extraction

Moregraph parses OData v4 metadata across the `sap.s4`, `sap.c4c`, `sap.hcm`, and `sap.graph` namespaces, building $G = (N, E, \lambda)$: node set N (entity types),

Table 1. Conceptual alignment between OData v4 entity type and LeanIX Data Object fact sheet models.

OData v4 Entity Type	LeanIX Data Object Fact Sheet
Qualified entity type name	Fact sheet name and external identifier
Property definitions	Custom fields (StringValue typed)
Navigation properties	Relationships to other fact sheets
Namespace/service origin	Provenance description
API documentation URL	Resource link

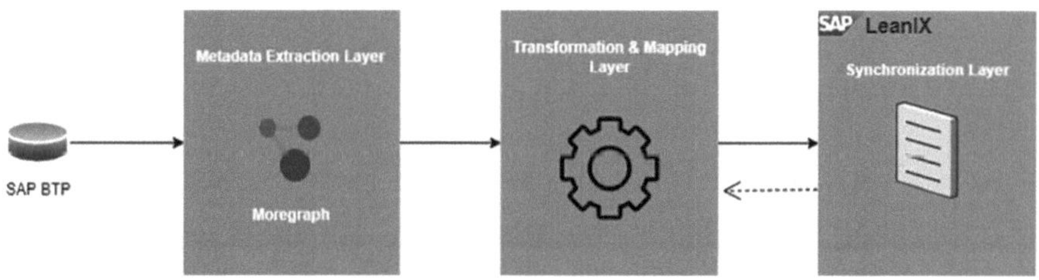

Fig. 3. Three-stage integration architecture (left to right).

directed edges E (navigation properties), and labelling function $\lambda : N \to A$. For each node $n \in N$:

$$\lambda(n) = \langle id,\ properties,\ service,\ adj(n)\rangle$$

where id is the fully qualified identifier (e.g. `sap.c4c.ServiceRequest`), *properties* is the list of OData property definitions, *service* is the system of origin, and $adj(n) = \{m \in N \mid (n, m) \in E\}$ is the set of outgoing navigation-property neighbours.

3.3 Formal MGT Definition

The MGT is $T : N \times M \to F$, where F is the set of EA Data Object governance records and $M = \{API, Excel\}$:

$$T(n, \mu) = \langle\, name(n, \mu),\ type,\ description,\ fields,\ resource\,\rangle \tag{1}$$

Components are derived deterministically from $\lambda(n)$: $name(n, \mu)$ is $localName(id)$ in API mode (display clarity) or the full id in Excel mode (namespace uniqueness); $type$ = *Data Object*; $description = \delta(service, id)$ (template-derived provenance); $fields = \{(p.name, \texttt{StringValue}) \mid p \in properties\}$; $resource$ = SAP Graph documentation URL. For Excel, $T^+(n) = \{T(n, Excel)\} \cup \{T(m, Excel) \mid m \in adj(n)\}$ captures the entity and its outgoing neighbourhood in one batch.

Five **design principles** ground the MGT: **DP1 Canonical Identity** (fully qualified id as external reference); **DP2 Semantic Fidelity** (auto-populate derivable fields; reserve governance fields for human review); **DP3 Bidirectional Traceability** (resource link to SAP Graph documentation); **DP4 Governance Mode Flexibility** (μ separates transformation from delivery); **DP5 Structural Completeness** (T^+ captures entity and neighbourhood). Table 2 summarises the field mapping.

Table 2. Field mapping implementing the MGT (DP = design principle realised).

$\lambda(n)$ Component	LeanIX Field	Mode	DP
localName(*id*)	Name, Display Name	API	DP1
Full *id*	Name, Display Name	Excel	DP1
Full *id*	External reference	Both	DP1
service + *id*	Description	Both	DP2
properties	Custom fields	Both	DP2
SAP Graph URL	Resource link	API (auto)	DP3
adj(*n*) (Excel only)	Neighbour rows	Excel	DP5

3.4 Delivery Pathways

Pathway 1 (API) realises $T(n, API)$: (1) obtain OAuth 2.0 bearer token server-side (DP4); (2) POST to `/pathfinder/v1/factSheets` (DP1, DP2); (3) attach SAP Graph documentation link via GraphQL mutation (DP3); (4) return duplicates and API errors as structured inline feedback; (5) navigate user to the new fact sheet on success.

Pathway 2 (Excel) realises $T^+(n)$, generating a workbook formatted to the LeanIX bulk import template. Columns A–H map to: ID (empty for new records), Type (*Data Object*), Name and Display Name (full *id*, DP1), and governance-reserved fields for Description, Level, Status, and Quality Seal (DP2). The workbook is timestamped for audit traceability (DP3).

4 Case Study and Demonstration

Scenario. A manufacturing organisation runs SAP S/4HANA, SAP Sales Cloud, and SAP SuccessFactors under a clean-core compliance programme with SAP LeanIX as its EA governance platform. Five entities were selected across all four SAP Graph namespaces to evaluate the MGT across the full clean-core landscape.

`sap.c4c`—**ServiceRequest**: With 18 outgoing navigation properties, this entity tests both pathways comprehensively. Figure 4 shows the Moregraph graph view with ServiceRequest selected (red outline) and the context menu offering *View on SAP Graph*, *Export to SAP LeanIX* (Pathway 1), and *Export to*

Excel (Pathway 2). Pathway 1 ($T(\mathit{ServiceRequest}, \mathit{API})$) produces a fact sheet in under five seconds. Pathway 2 ($T^+(\mathit{ServiceRequest})$) generates a 20-row workbook: one row for ServiceRequest plus 19 rows for its outgoing neighbours, each row populating Name and Display Name with the fully qualified `sap.c4c.*` identifier (DP1) and leaving governance-reserved columns (Description, Level, Status, Quality Seal) blank for EA team enrichment (DP2). The workbook is timestamped at generation for audit traceability (DP3).

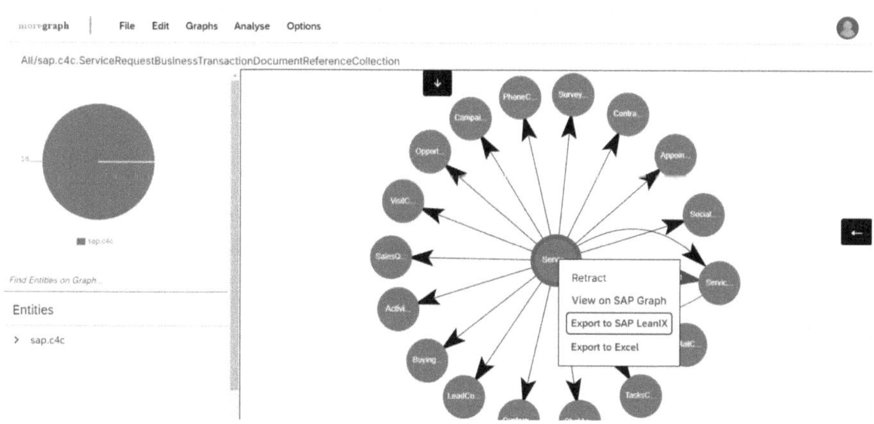

Fig. 4. Moregraph context menu for `sap.c4c.ServiceRequest` (Pathway 1 and 2 options visible).

`sap.s4` and `sap.hcm`: $T(\mathit{A\_SalesOrder}, \mathit{API})$ and $T(\mathit{Employee}, \mathit{API})$ each produce fact sheets with namespace-specific provenance descriptions and SAP Graph documentation links, confirming the MGT applies uniformly (Table 3).

Pathway 1 Fact Sheet: Figure 5 shows the LeanIX fact sheet for `sap.c4c.LeadBusinessTransactionDocumentReferenceCollection`: $\mathit{localName}(\mathit{id})$ provides the name (DP1); $\delta(\mathit{service}, \mathit{id})$ the description (DP2); the Resources tab the documentation link (DP3). Status *Check needed* indicates pending governance review (DP2).

Duplicate Detection: Re-applying Pathway 1 to *BusinessPartner* already in LeanIX returns a structured inline error with no silent failure. Table 3 summarises Pathway 1 coverage across all four namespaces.

5 Functional Validation

The validation assessed the MGT against five functional criteria within the DSR evaluation cycle [1]. For each of the five entities, both pathways were applied independently: Pathway 1 outputs were compared field-by-field against $\lambda(n)$ to verify all derivable fields were correctly populated and governance-reserved

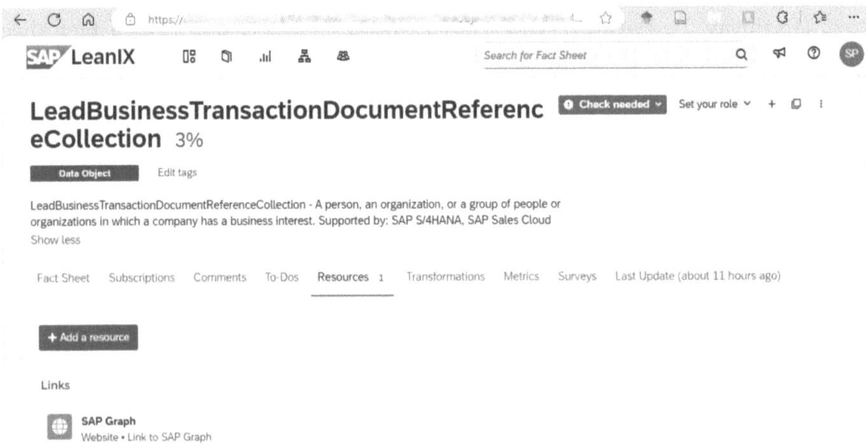

Fig. 5. The `sap.c4c.LeadBusinessTransactionDocumentReferenceCollection` LeanIX Data Object fact sheet for Pathway 1.

Table 3. Data Object fact sheets created via Pathway 1 across all four SAP Graph namespaces.

SAP Graph Entity	Namespace	Fact Sheet Name
sap.c4c.ServiceRequest	`sap.c4c`	ServiceRequest
sap.graph.BusinessPartner	`sap.graph`	BusinessPartner
sap.s4.A_SalesOrder	`sap.s4`	A_SalesOrder
sap.hcm.Employee	`sap.hcm`	Employee
sap.c4c.CorporateAccount	`sap.c4c`	CorporateAccount

fields (DP2) intentionally blank; Pathway 2 workbooks were inspected against the LeanIX import template for structural completeness; duplicate detection was tested by re-applying Pathway 1 to an already-imported entity. This is a *functional validation*—an internal artefact assessment—rather than a controlled empirical study; practitioner user studies constitute future work. Table 4 summarises the findings.

As a directional indicator, Pathway 1 produced a complete fact sheet in under five seconds versus 30–60 min for manual entry; controlled time-on-task studies constitute future work.

Table 4. Functional validation results across five criteria and both pathways.

Criterion	Pathway 1 (API)	Pathway 2 (Excel)	Finding
Correctness	All 5 entities verified	All 20 rows verified	Outputs match $\lambda(n)$
Completeness	All derivable fields set	Full template populated	DP2 fields reserved
Mode consistency	*localName*(*id*)	Full *id* used	Intentional per DP1
Cross-entity	4 namespaces consistent	Batch output consistent	MGT applied uniformly
Error handling	Duplicate surfaced	Import report visible	No silent failures

6 Discussion and Related Work

Contribution and Generalisability. The MGT formalises the previously implicit alignment between OData entity types and EA Data Object fact sheets (Table 1), eliminating interpretation variability. DP4's dual-pathway design accommodates governance models from agile direct API access to formal change-management workflows. Grounding the MGT in OData v4 [5] rather than SAP-specific constructs means its rules apply to any OData v4-compliant source, including Microsoft Graph [8], and DP4's separation of transformation from delivery enables adaptation to other EA platforms—Ardoq, Essential Project [9], or ServiceNow CMDB—without altering the core mapping. The main limitation is the one-time snapshot: a future incremental synchronisation mechanism monitoring SAP Graph delta changes is the highest-priority extension.

Related Work. CGs [7,13,14] serve as Moregraph's formal specification (Fig. 1); this paper extends that specification to capture the MGT (Fig. 2). TOGAF [17], Zachman [15,18], and ArchiMate 3.1 [16] provide normative EA structures; Lankhorst et al. [3] survey EA tools comprehensively. Commercial EAM tools such as Ardoq and ServiceNow CMDB support manual metadata entry and limited API population, but lack a formally specified, deterministic transformation from OData v4 sources. Inmon et al. [2] establish metadata governance as prerequisite for EA clarity; Olesen-Bagneux [6] addresses the enterprise data catalogue. Schema.org-based cataloguing and ad-hoc ETL scripts are used for data integration but lack the formal conceptual structure grounding of the MGT. The challenge of bridging OData metadata to EA governance platforms via a formally defined transformation has not been addressed in prior literature.

7 Conclusion

This paper presented the Metadata-to-Governance Transformation (MGT): a formal, platform-independent, deterministic mapping from OData entity-type metadata to structured EA Data Object governance records, grounded in Moregraph's updated CG specification and five design principles. Two pathways operationalise it: real-time API export (Pathway 1) and governance-friendly Excel export (Pathway 2). Functional validation across four SAP Graph namespaces confirms correctness, completeness, consistency, and robust error handling.

The key insight—that the properties used to describe a data object in metadata are precisely those needed to govern it in an EA platform—is not LeanIX-specific: it holds wherever EA platforms implement the Data Object concept. The framework's OData-neutral rules generalise to any OData v4-compliant source (e.g. Microsoft Graph), and DP4 enables adaptation to other EA platforms. Future work will close the synchronisation gap and conduct practitioner user studies.

References

1. Hevner, A.R., March, S.T., Park, J., Ram, S.: Design science in information systems research. MIS Q. **28**(1), 75–105 (2004)
2. Inmon, W.H., O'Neil, B., Fryman, L.: Business Metadata: Capturing Enterprise Knowledge. Morgan Kaufmann (2010)
3. Lankhorst, M.: Enterprise Architecture at Work: Modelling, Communication and Analysis, 4th edn. Springer, Berlin, Heidelberg (2017)
4. LeanIX: LeanIX Meta Model (2025). https://docs-eam.leanix.net/docs/meta-model. Accessed 28 Feb 2026
5. OASIS: OData Version 4.0 Part 1: Protocol (2014). https://docs.oasis-open.org/odata/odata/v4.0/odata-v4.0-part1-protocol.html. Accessed 28 Feb 2026
6. Olesen-Bagneux, O.: The Enterprise Data Catalog. O'Reilly Media (2023)
7. Polovina, S.: An introduction to conceptual graphs. In: Priss, U., Polovina, S., Hill, R. (eds.) Conceptual Structures: Knowledge Architectures for Smart Applications, pp. 1–14. Springer Berlin Heidelberg, Berlin, Heidelberg (2007). https://shura.shu.ac.uk/1175/
8. Polovina, S., Fallon, R., Saleem, M.: Moregraph: metadata-driven enterprise architecture using conceptual structures. In: Conceptual Knowledge Structures. CONCEPTS 2025. Lecture Notes in Computer Science, pp. 91–106. Springer Nature Switzerland (2025). https://shura.shu.ac.uk/36156/
9. Saleem, M., Polovina, S.: Towards metadata-driven enterprise architecture by integrating sap graph and essential project. In: Proceedings of MOVE2024. Springer CCIS (2026). in press
10. SAP SE: RISE with SAP—ERP Clean Core Strategy (2024). https://www.sap.com/products/erp/rise/methodology/clean-core.html. Accessed 28 Feb 2026
11. SAP SE: SAP Graph: Unified Business Data Access (2024). https://api.sap.com/graph. Accessed 28 Feb 2026
12. SAP SE: SAP LeanIX Enterprise Architecture Management (2024). https://www.leanix.net. Accessed 28 Feb 2026
13. Sowa, J.F.: Conceptual Structures: Information Processing in Mind and Machine. Addison-Wesley, Reading, Massachusetts (1984)
14. Sowa, J.F.: Conceptual graphs for representing conceptual structures. In: Conceptual Structures in Practice. Chapman and Hall/CRC (2009). num Pages: 36

15. Sowa, J.F., Zachman, J.A.: Extending and formalizing the framework for information systems architecture. IBM Syst. J. **31**(3), 590–616 (1992)
16. The Open Group: ArchiMate 3.1 Specification. The Open Group (2019)
17. The Open Group: TOGAF Standard, Version 10. The Open Group (2025)
18. Zachman, J.A.: A framework for information systems architecture. IBM Syst. J. **26**(3), 276–292 (1987)

Using Storytelling for Knowledge Acquisition in Child-Robot Interaction

Hadil Ladj[1], Nathalie Blanc[2], and Madalina Croitoru[1(✉)]

[1] University of Montpellier, Montpellier, France
croitoru@lirmm.fr
[2] University Paul Valery, Montpellier, France

Abstract. In this paper we place ourselves in the setting of child robot interaction and investigate the problem of knowledge representation and reasoning about the above mentioned interaction. In this context we are interested in how to elicit knowledge about the interaction in various scenarios. The scenario we address is a particularily challenging scenario due to its data scarcity and namely young children (i.e. 3-5 of age) interacting with robots. We explain the architecture of our proposal and how this allows for the aquisition phase.

Keywords: Knowledge Representation · Human Robot Interaction · Knowledge Aquisition

1 Introduction

In Knowledge Representation and Reasoning (KR) [12], a central challenge is to integrate heterogeneous forms of knowledge and reasoning within a unified formal framework [13]. In particular, the interaction between structured, rule-based inference and weaker, associative forms of knowledge remains insufficiently explored. While logical formalisms provide precise mechanisms for inference, they typically assume that the underlying knowledge base is already well-formed. In contrast, associative knowledge-often arising from interaction or experience lacks an explicit representation and is not directly amenable to reasoning.

In previous work [3–6] we introduced a dual-process cognitive model that combines logical inference with associative reasoning within a unified formal setting. In that model, knowledge is represented through beliefs, preferences, and associations, and reasoning is defined as the construction of inference paths combining logical rules and association rules. A key aspect of this framework is the distinction between different types of inference and their associated effort, allowing agents to rely on associations when logical reasoning is too costly.

However, in that formulation, associations are defined at the level of abstract formulas and are not grounded in a structured representation of knowledge. As a result, the interaction between associative knowledge and structured representations remains implicit. In particular, the model does not specify how associative

M. Croitoru et al. (Eds.): CONCEPTS 2026, LNAI 16811, pp. 340–350, 2027.
https://doi.org/10.1007/978-3-032-34742-8_23

knowledge can be integrated into a relational representation, nor how it can support the construction of explicit knowledge structures.

This paper addresses this limitation by proposing a conceptual graph-based [16] formalisation of associative and rule-based knowledge. Conceptual Graphs (CG) [7] provide a well-established formalism for representing structured knowledge through concepts and relations, together with a semantics grounded in logic. We extend this formalism by introducing associative knowledge directly within the graph, enabling a unified representation in which both associative and logical components coexist. More precisely, we represent associative knowledge through a dedicated ternary relation *associatedWith* that links two concepts and a third concept representing the strength or value of the association. This design allows associative information to be encoded explicitly as part of the knowledge base, rather than as an external annotation. The use of a third argument for association strength ensures that this information remains accessible to reasoning and can be manipulated using standard KR mechanisms. Within this framework, we distinguish two types of relations. Associative relations capture weak, experience-driven links between concepts. In contrast, structured relations capture explicit knowledge that can be used for inference. The transition between these two levels is governed by inference rules. In particular, rules can promote strong associations into structured relations, detect conflicts between competing associations, and support query answering over the graph. This provides a formal mechanism for integrating associative and rule-based reasoning within a single representation.

The proposed model thus instantiates the dual-process perspective introduced in our previous work within a relational KR setting. Associative relations correspond to the weaker inference mechanisms captured by association rules, while structured relations and logical rules correspond to standard inference. By embedding both within conceptual graphs, we obtain a uniform representation in which reasoning paths can combine associative and logical steps in a principled way. We apply this framework to a knowledge acquisition setting based on human-robot interaction. In this setting, a robot interacts with children to teach associations between concepts, such as emotions and colors. The interaction generates associative links whose strength depends on the modality of interaction. These associations are represented using the *associatedWith* relation, and their evolution over time reflects the acquisition process.

Reasoning rules are then applied to the resulting conceptual graphs to derive explicit knowledge and evaluate its consistency. For instance, strong associations can be promoted to structured relations, while conflicting associations can be identified and analyzed. Query answering over the graph provides a formal account of task performance, linking observed responses to the underlying knowledge representation. We evaluate the proposed approach using experimental data collected from child-robot interaction studies. The data captures the effect of different interaction modalities on knowledge acquisition. Within our framework, these effects are interpreted as differences in the structure and strength of associative relations, which in turn influence the outcomes of rule-based reasoning.

This provides an explicit connection between interaction design, knowledge representation, and reasoning performance.

2 Associative and Rule-Based Knowledge

In this section, we formalise the representation of associative and structured knowledge using Conceptual Graphs (CG), and define the interaction between associative relations and rule-based inference. We assume a vocabulary defined by a set of concept types $\mathcal{T}_C$ and a set of relation types $\mathcal{T}_R$. A conceptual graph is a bipartite graph composed of concept nodes and relation nodes.

Definition 1. (Conceptual Graph) *A conceptual graph G is a tuple $G = (C, R, \iota)$ where:*

- *C is a finite set of concept nodes,*
- *R is a finite set of relation nodes,*
- *$\iota : R \to C^*$ is a function that assigns to each relation node an ordered tuple of concept nodes.*

Each concept node $c \in C$ is typed by a concept type $\tau(c) \in \mathcal{T}_C$, and may be labelled by an individual marker. Each relation node $r \in R$ is typed by a relation type $\tau(r) \in \mathcal{T}_R$. We consider in particular concept types such as *Emotion*, *Color*, and *AssociationValue*, and relation types including *associatedWith* and domain-specific structured relations such as *hasColor*. Projection is the standard homomorphism-based mapping between conceptual graphs and it is sound and complete with respect to deduction in the existential positive fragment of FOL [9]. Reasoning is defined as the iterative application of inference rules over a conceptual graph. Query answering corresponds to checking the existence of a projection from a query graph into the knowledge graph.

Definition 2. (Query Answering). *Given a query graph Q and a knowledge graph G, Q is satisfied by G if there exists a projection from Q to G.*

Associative knowledge is represented through a dedicated ternary relation.

Definition 3. (Associative Relation). *The relation type associatedWith $\in \mathcal{T}_R$ is a quaternary relation linking a relation type, two concept nodes, and an association value. A fact of the form:*

$$associatedWith(r, c_1, c_2, v)$$

indicates that the relation r holds associatively between concept c_1 and concept c_2 with strength v, where:

- *$r \in \mathcal{T}_R$ is a relation type,*
- *$c_1, c_2 \in C$ are concept nodes,*
- *v is a concept node of type AssociationValue.*

The association value encodes the strength of the association and belongs to a finite and complete ordered set (e.g., *Low*, *Medium*, *High*). Associative relations capture weak, experience-driven links between concepts. They are directly constructed from interaction data and do not necessarily satisfy logical consistency constraints. Structured knowledge is represented through standard binary relations (e.g., *hasColor*) and is subject to logical inference. We define inference rules over conceptual graphs as graph transformation rules.

Definition 4. (Inference Rule). *An inference rule is a pair* (L, R) *where* L *and* R *are conceptual graphs. A rule can be applied to a graph* G *if there exists a projection* π *from* L *to* G*. The application of the rule adds to* G *the image of* R *under* π*.*

We define inference rules that connect associative knowledge to structured knowledge. Strong associative relations are promoted to structured relations:

$$\mathit{associatedWith}(r, c_1, c_2,\ \mathrm{v}) \wedge \mathit{High}(v)\ \Rightarrow\ r(c_1, c_2)$$

This rule states that when an associative relation reaches a sufficiently high strength, the corresponding structured relation can be inferred. Competing strong associations for the same relation are detected as ambiguity:

$$\begin{aligned}&\mathit{associatedWith}(r, c_1, c_2, v_1) \wedge \mathit{associatedWith}(r, c_1, c_3, v_2)\\ &\wedge\ \mathit{High}(v_1) \wedge \mathit{High}(v_2) \wedge c_2 \neq c_3\\ &\Rightarrow\ \mathit{Ambiguous}(r, c_1)\end{aligned}$$

This rule identifies situations in which multiple competing associations are simultaneously strong enough to support incompatible structured inferences.

The proposed framework differs from existing approaches for representing annotated or uncertain knowledge, such as RDF reification, named graphs, and quadruple-based representations. In RDF reification and named graphs, additional information is typically attached to statements externally, for example through metadata describing provenance, confidence, or context. Similarly, quadruple-based approaches extend triples with contextual identifiers or annotations. Conceptual graphs provide a relational and projection-based semantics that naturally supports graph transformation rules and query answering. The proposed framework therefore combines relational structure, associative strength, and symbolic inference in a unified representation rather than separating annotations from reasoning. However, please note that many works looked into the relation between RDF/S semantics and Conceptual Graphs [1,2].

3 Child-Robot Interaction Study

This section presents the experimental study conducted to support knowledge acquisition through child-robot interaction. The experiment was carried out in a preschool environment with children aged 3 to 6 years. The activity was structured around four phases: (1) familiarization with the robot, (2) collective storytelling (bimodal condition), (3) individual emotion interaction (multimodal condition), and (4) an interactive quiz to assess acquired associations. A total of 40 children participated in the study, equally divided into two age groups: 20 children aged 3-4 and 20 children aged 5-6. The main material used was the humanoid robot Pepper, developed by SoftBank Robotics.[1] Pepper was equipped with the application we built that includes storytelling, emotion-based interaction, a conversational module, and an interactive quiz (Fig. 1).

Fig. 1. Pepper robot in the preschool classroom, displaying the application's interface.

The experimental session followed the steps below:

1. **Familiarization phase** The children entered the room in small groups (maximum 10) and met the robot. Pepper introduced itself and invited the children to interact. Using the conversational module, the children were encouraged to ask questions. This phase was designed to reduce hesitation and prepare the children for the interaction.
2. **Narration phase – Bimodal condition** The robot narrated the story *The Color Monster* by Anna Llenas. The story introduces six basic emotions: joy, sadness, fear, anger, love, and calm. The narration was performed collectively using speech and gesture animations, without physical interaction. This phase corresponds to the bimodal condition.
3. **Emotion interaction phase – Multimodal condition** Each child then interacted individually with Pepper. The robot expressed four emotions (joy, sadness, anger, fear) and invited the child to respond through touch (e.g.,

[1] https://aldebaran.com/en/pepper/.

"Could you gently touch my head?"). These interactions combined speech, gestures, and tactile input, defining the multimodal condition.

4. **Emotion recognition quiz** At the end of the session, each child completed a short quiz on Pepper's tablet. The quiz assessed the ability to associate emotions with the corresponding colors introduced during the story. An adult was present to assist when necessary (Fig. 2).

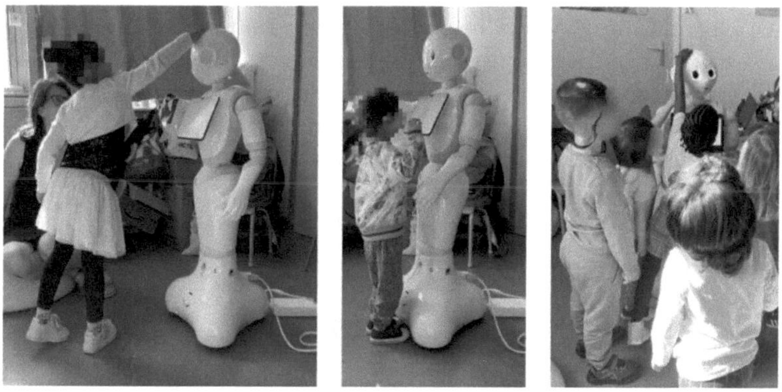

Fig. 2. Children interacting with the Pepper robot during the experimental sessions.

For each child, the quiz provides responses indicating whether the correct association between an emotion and a color has been identified. The collected data consists of the interaction modality (bimodal or multimodal) and the responses of each child to the quiz.

4 From Interaction Data to Conceptual Graphs

In this section, we describe how the interaction traces collected during the child–robot experiment are translated into conceptual graph structures. Rather than considering quiz responses only as performance scores, we interpret them as observable manifestations of underlying associative knowledge acquired during the interaction. For each child, the interaction generates a set of associations between emotions and colors introduced during the storytelling activity. These associations are represented using the relation:

$$associatedWith(r, c_1, c_2, v)$$

- r represents the target relation type,
- c_1 is an emotion concept,
- c_2 is a color concept,
- v is an association value representing the strength of the acquired association.

In the context of this experiment, the target relation corresponds to r = *hasColor*. A correct identification of the relation between sadness and blue gives:

$$associatedWith(hasColor, Sadness, Blue, High)$$

Association strengths are assigned from the interaction traces collected during the experiment. Correct and stable responses correspond to stronger association values, while hesitant, inconsistent, or incorrect responses correspond to weaker or competing associations. A conceptual graph is constructed for each participant from the quiz responses collected after the interaction phase. Each answer contributes new associative relations to the graph. Repeated correct answers reinforce the corresponding association strength, while conflicting answers generate competing associative structures. For example, if a child consistently identifies sadness with blue, the resulting graph contains:

$$associatedWith(hasColor, Sadness, Blue, High)$$

Applying the promotion rule:

$$associatedWith(r, c_1, c_2, v) \wedge High(v) \Rightarrow r(c_1, c_2)$$

allows the inference:

$$hasColor(Sadness, Blue)$$

This corresponds to the acquisition of structured knowledge from interaction-driven associative knowledge. Conversely, if a child alternates between two responses, for example blue and red for sadness, the graph may contain:

$$associatedWith(hasColor, Sadness, Blue, Low)$$

and

$$associatedWith(hasColor, Sadness, Red, Low)$$

In this situation, neither association is sufficiently strong to trigger the promotion rule, resulting in unstable or incomplete structured knowledge. The framework also allows for the explicit representation of ambiguity. When multiple competing associations become simultaneously strong, ambiguity relations can be inferred. For example:

$$associatedWith(hasColor, Sadness, Blue, High)$$

and

$$associatedWith(hasColor, Sadness, Red, High)$$

lead to:

$$Ambiguous(hasColor, Sadness)$$

This corresponds to situations where the child maintains multiple competing strong associations simultaneously.

5 Results and Discussion

In the previous section, we illustrated how interaction traces can be translated into formal rules within the conceptual graph framework. However, the interaction data does not only support rule construction; it also provides insights into the behaviour of the children during the learning process. The empirical results reported in this section capture these behavioural patterns through statistical analysis, highlighting differences across interaction modalities, age groups, and emotion types. These observations complement the formal model by grounding the associative structures in observed performance, thereby linking interaction, knowledge acquisition, and behavioural outcomes.

The data used in this study was collected through a dedicated application developed for the Pepper robot. The application orchestrates the full interaction sequence, including the narration of the story The Color Monster by Anna Llenas, which provides a structured mapping between emotions and colors. The storytelling module is integrated with a database that encodes the target associations (e.g., emotion-color pairs) and drives the robot's behaviour throughout the interaction. The robot expresses each emotion through coordinated speech, gestures, and, in the multimodal condition, tactile prompts that invite the child to respond physically. The application manages the sequencing, timing, and repetition of these elements, ensuring that each child is exposed to the same interaction structure under the assigned condition. It also logs the responses given during the quiz phase, resulting in a consistent and structured dataset that directly reflects the associations formed during the interaction. We then compared the answers obtained under the bimodal and multimodal conditions to assess the impact of interaction modality on the acquisition of these associations.

Children achieved a mean score of $M = 5.05$ ($SD = 1.50$) out of 6, corresponding to over 84% correct responses on average. Out of the 40 participants, 25 achieved the maximum score of 6. A statistical analysis comparing bimodal (voice + animation) and multimodal (voice + animation + touch) conditions revealed a significant effect of modality. Multimodal interaction significantly improved emotion recognition performance compared to bimodal interaction. Age was a significant predictor of performance ($OR = 2.45$, $p < .001$). Children aged 5–6 outperformed children aged 3–4 across conditions. Using binomial logistic regression we compared the effectiveness of both conditions: bimodal (voice + animation) and multimodal (voice + animation + touch). The analysis revealed a significant effect of modality. Specifically, children were more likely to correctly identify emotions when they had experienced the emotion through multimodal interaction. The odds ratio for this effect was $OR = 3.34$, with a p-value of .014, indicating that the odds of a correct response were more than three times higher in the multimodal condition.

A Generalized Linear Model (GLM) was trained to predict correct responses based on modality, age, and emotion type. The dataset was split into training and testing sets. The model achieved an accuracy of 81.2% on the test set, with an Area Under the Curve (AUC) of 0.742. This predictive model can be used to identify which interaction configurations are most effective, to anticipate potential learning difficulties, and to guide the design of adaptive interaction strategies that reinforce weak or ambiguous associations (Table 1).

Table 1. Coefficients from the Generalized Linear Model for emotion recognition performance.

Variable	Coefficient	P-value
Constant	1.5586	<0.001
Age (z-score)	0.8558	< 0.001
Modality (multimodal)	1.0384	0.040
Emotion (fear)	−0.2911	0.727
Emotion (sadness)	−1.2288	0.114

If we place ourselves in the context of human-robot interaction [17] recently social robotics has gained considerable attention in the field of education. Humanoid robots, such as Pepper [14], are increasingly used to support children's learning in playful, interactive, and personalized settings [10]. One promising direction involves using robots as storytellers, particularly through storytelling with emotional content, to capture children's attention, foster emotional understanding and verbalization, and promote appropriate responses in emotionally charged situations. The ethical considerations of how children perceive robots have been long debated in the literature [11]. Unfortunately, these studies often lack objective data to measure the actual effect on various cognitive aspects of the interaction. Moreover, young children of pre-school age (between 3 and 5) have limited interaction skills (i.e. cannot fill questionnaires, they have short attention span etc.) and, therefore, objective data concerning such age is even more difficult to collect [11].

With the advancement of Artificial Intelligence (AI) in general and Large Language models (LLMs) in particular [18], it is becoming obvious that the human-AI interaction study has to be placed within a richer setting that accounts for multi-modal interactions (i.e. text, voice, touch, feedback loops etc.) [15]. This is specifically important in practical applications where AI software is physically embodied in devices that interact in a multi-modal manner with the human (such as autonomous vehicles or robots). However, as shown by current literature, the impact of the different interaction modalities is difficult to quantify (either independently or interdependently) [19].

This paper introduced a unified Knowledge Representation and Reasoning (KR) framework for modelling knowledge acquisition in child-robot interaction. The central objective was to bridge associative and rule-based reasoning within a single formalism, grounded in empirical data. This formalisation builds on our previous work on dual-process cognitive models, where reasoning was defined as the combination of logical and associative inference paths. In the present paper, we provide a concrete instantiation of this model within a relational KR setting.

Conceptual graphs offer a natural support for this integration, as they allow both relational structure and inference to be expressed in a uniform way.

Several directions for future work can be identified. A first direction concerns the refinement of the representation of association values. In the current model, association strength is captured through a finite set of qualitative values (e.g., low, medium, high). Extending this to a more fine-grained or dynamic representation would allow a more precise modelling of the acquisition process. In particular, incorporating temporal aspects of interaction could enable the tracking of how associations evolve over repeated exposures. Argumentation theory and appropiate argumentation semantics could be used here in order to model how arguments are varying over time [20].

A second direction is the development of adaptive interaction strategies. The current study uses a fixed interaction protocol, but the framework naturally supports adaptation. By analysing the structure of associative relations, it is possible to identify weak or ambiguous knowledge and to design targeted interventions. For example, additional multimodal cues could be introduced to reinforce specific associations, or alternative interaction patterns could be used to resolve ambiguity. This would transform the system from a passive teaching tool into an adaptive learning agent.

Last but not least please note that this work follows a line of work combining symbolic and sub symbolic approches to Artificial Intelligence for transdisciplinary research in Computer Science and Psychology [8].

Acknolowedgements. The work of the last two authors has been supported by the PROMOTE-S project funded by the Occitanie Region (France).

References

1. Atencia, M., et al.: Defining key semantics for the RDF datasets: experiments and evaluations. In: International Conference on Conceptual Structures, pp. 65–78. Springer (2014)
2. Baget, J.F., Croitoru, M., Gutierrez, A., Leclère, M., Mugnier, M.L.: Translations between RDF (s) and conceptual graphs. In: International Conference on Conceptual Structures, pp. 28–41. Springer (2010)
3. Bisquert, P., Croitoru, M., de Saint-Cyr, F.D.: Four ways to evaluate arguments according to agent engagement. In: Brain Informatics and Health (BIH), pp. 445–456 (2015)
4. Bisquert, P., Croitoru, M., de Saint-Cyr, F.D.: Towards a dual process cognitive model for argument evaluation. In: Scalable Uncertainty Management (SUM), pp. 298–313 (2015)
5. Bisquert, P., Croitoru, M., de Saint-Cyr, F.D., Hecham, A.: Substantive irrationality in cognitive systems. In: Proceedings of ECAI, pp. 1642–1643 (2016)
6. Bisquert, P., Croitoru, M., de Saint-Cyr, F.D., Hecham, A.: Formalizing cognitive acceptance of arguments: durum wheat selection interdisciplinary study. Mind. Mach. **27**(1), 233–252 (2017)
7. Chein, M., Mugnier, M.L., Croitoru, M.: Visual reasoning with graph-based mechanisms: the good, the better and the best. Knowl. Eng. Rev. **28**(3), 249–271 (2013)

8. Croitoru, M., Blanc, N., Anders, R.: Symbolic artificial intelligence for schema therapy using knowledge graphs. In: International Joint Conference on Conceptual Knowledge Structures, pp. 327–333. Springer (2024)
9. Croitoru, M., Compatangelo, E.: A combinatorial approach to conceptual graph projection checking. In: International Conference on Innovative Techniques and Applications of Artificial Intelligence, pp. 130–143. Springer, London (2004)
10. Croitoru, M., et al.: A child-robot interaction experiment to analyze gender stereotypes in the perception of mathematical abilities. In: Proceedings of the SGAI Conference (2), pp. 232–237 (2024)
11. Langer, A., Marshall, P., Levy-Tzedek, S.: Ethical considerations in child-robot interactions. Neurosci. Biobehav. Rev. (2023). https://doi.org/10.1016/j.neubiorev.2023.105230
12. Levesque, H.J., Brachman, R.J.: Expressiveness and tractability in knowledge representation and reasoning 1. Comput. Intell. **3**(1), 78–93 (1987)
13. Levy, A.Y.: Logic-based techniques in data integration. In: Logic-Based Artificial Intelligence, pp. 575–595. Springer, Boston, MA (2000)
14. Roštšinskaja, A., et al.: Unlocking the potential of social robot pepper: a comprehensive evaluation of child-robot interaction. J. Pediatr. Health Care (2025). https://doi.org/10.1016/j.pedhc.2025.01.010
15. Saktheeswaran, A., Srinivasan, A., Stasko, J.T.: Touch? Speech? or touch and speech? Investigating multimodal interaction for visual network exploration and analysis. IEEE Trans. Visual Comput. Graph. (2020). https://doi.org/10.1109/tvcg.2020.2970512
16. Sowa, J.F.: Conceptual graphs. Found. Artif. Intell. **3**, 213–237 (2008)
17. Wainer, J., Feil-Seifer, D.J., Shell, D.A., Mataric, M.J.: Embodiment and human-robot interaction: a task-based perspective. In: RO-MAN 2007-The 16th IEEE International Symposium on Robot and Human Interactive Communication, pp. 872–877. IEEE (2007)
18. Wang, J., et al.: Large language models for robotics: opportunities, challenges, and perspectives. arXiv preprint arXiv:2401.04334 (2024)
19. Wróbel, A., Źróbek, K., Schaper, M.M., Zguda, P., Indurkhya, B.: Age-appropriate robot design: In-the-wild child-robot interaction studies of perseverance styles and robot's unexpected behavior. In: IEEE International Symposium on Robot and Human Interactive Communication (2023). https://doi.org/10.1109/ro-man57019.2023.10309332
20. Yun, B., Vesic, S., Croitoru, M.: Ranking-based semantics for sets of attacking arguments. In: Proceedings of the AAAI Conference on Artificial Intelligence, vol. 34, pp. 3033–3040 (2020)

Conceptual Views of Neural Networks: A Framework for Neuro-Symbolic Analysis

Johannes Hirth[1] and Tom Hanika[2(✉)]

[1] Knowledge & Data Engineering, University of Kassel, Kassel, Germany
hirth@cs.uni-kassel.de
[2] Information Systems and Machine Learning Lab, University of Hildesheim, Hildesheim, Germany
hanika@uni-hildesheim.de

Abstract. We introduce *conceptual views* as a formal framework grounded in Formal Concept Analysis for globally explaining neural networks. Experiments on twenty-four ImageNet models and Fruits-360 show that these views faithfully represent the original models, enable architecture comparison via Gromov–Wasserstein distance, and support abductive learning of human-comprehensible rules from neurons.

1 Introduction

Neural networks (NNs) are known for their strong performance across a wide range of learning problems. However, these results are almost always achieved at the cost of human explainability. This tension is addressed from different standpoints in the literature. On the one hand, there are calls to refrain from using NNs for high-stakes decisions and to rely on inherently interpretable methods, even at the cost of accuracy [16]. On the other hand, a substantial body of research aims to develop methods for explaining NN models. Such explanations can be broadly classified as *local explanations*, which address why a particular input was treated in a specific way [15], and *global explanations*, which seek to characterize the model as a whole. While local methods such as saliency maps or activation highlighting [4] are effective for flat data like images, they are less applicable to high-dimensional or complex data where human visual inspection is infeasible. Global approaches, by contrast, are inherently more challenging and therefore less explored, yet they are essential for comprehensive understanding of NNs.

In this work, we propose *conceptual views* as a formal framework for the global analysis of NNs. Our approach targets the embedding space of a NN, specifically the outputs at the last hidden layer. We introduce two complementary representations: 1. A *many-valued conceptual view* that captures the real-valued activation and weight structure as a pair of matrices, inducing a pseudo-metric space on objects and classes. 2. A *symbolic conceptual view* that

M. Croitoru et al. (Eds.): CONCEPTS 2026, LNAI 16811, pp. 351–361, 2027.
https://doi.org/10.1007/978-3-032-34742-8_24

discretizes this structure via conceptual scaling [5] from Formal Concept Analysis (FCA) [6], yielding a binary relational representation.

The key advantage of our framework is its composability: multiple neuro-symbolic explanation procedures can be integrated, their results merged within a concept lattice structure, and additional parts of the representation decoded using background knowledge. The concept lattice further enables various forms of symbolic reasoning, including the extraction of propositional implications.

We demonstrate through extensive experiments that: (i) many-valued conceptual views achieve high fidelity as surrogates for the original models; (ii) the Gromov-Wasserstein distance applied to conceptual views yields meaningful similarity measures between architectures; (iii) symbolic conceptual views, particularly with Tanh activation, enable decision-tree based surrogates with competitive fidelity; and (iv) background knowledge can be integrated via subgroup discovery to derive human-comprehensible rules about neurons.

2 Related Work

Explanation methods for NNs are commonly grouped into local approaches that highlight input-level evidence [4,15], concept-based approaches that quantify user- or auto-discovered concepts [9], and concept bottleneck models [10,12] that bake interpretable concepts into the architecture. Mechanistic interpretability [1] pursues circuit-level reverse-engineering, and representational similarity is typically assessed via CKA [11]. Our framework is post-hoc, global, and algebraic: it does not constrain the architecture, does not require pre-defined concepts, and analyses the pseudo-metric space induced by the last hidden layer instead of activations directly, using the Gromov–Wasserstein distance [13]. The algebraic backbone is Formal Concept Analysis [6] with conceptual scaling [5]; FCA has previously been used for decision tree induction [2], and our scale-measure machinery [7] underlies the symbolic translation, contributing a bridge to neuro-symbolic reasoning [18].

3 The Views of Neural Networks

To extract the inherent knowledge captured by a neural network, we propose a two-staged approach. First, we derive a formal relational structure that describes how the data is represented by the last hidden layer of a neural network. For this, we employ conceptual scaling from Formal Concept Analysis ([6]), which provides a formal and comprehensible method to transform data into a symbolic space. The derived symbolic attributes are user defined and depend on the data. A key idea here is that these attributes are simple, allowing the analyst to relate symbolic deductions to subspaces of the real-valued data. Throughout the remainder of this section, we propose the use of thresholds δ for individual neuron activations. This introduces two symbolic attributes $n_{\leq\delta}$ and $n_{\geq\delta}$ that are in relation to entities that have an activation above or below that threshold. While this process is intentionally straightforward, we show in the following section empirically that the choice of δ is a difficult problem that depends on the learning problem. We illustrate this approach in Fig. 1. In the second step, we decode the symbolic space using background knowledge and symbolic features derived from concept-based explanations. We elaborate on this in greater detail in Sect. 5.

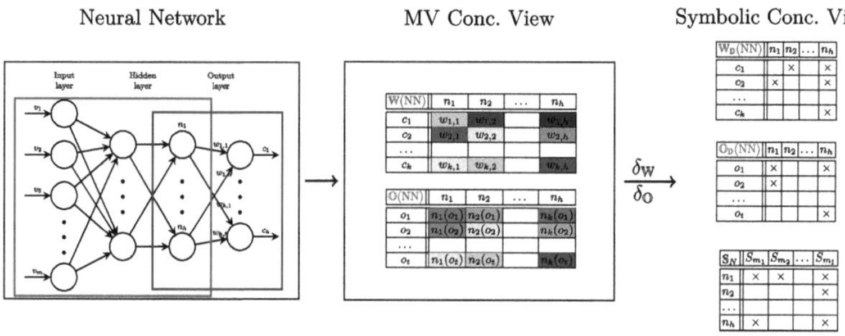

Fig. 1. A simplified neural network drawing (left), its many-valued conceptual view (middle), and its symbolic conceptual view (right).

3.1 Many-Valued Conceptual View

We introduce two notions of conceptual view of a neural network: a *many-valued* and a *symbolic* view. Both provide novel methods to enable a human AI analyst to grasp deeper insights into the knowledge captured by the neurons. In addition, the symbolic view facilitates the application of abductive learning procedures. This results in rules that allow explaining a NN by means of human-comprehensible terminology, as well as in terms of the neurons.

Let N be the set of neurons of the last hidden layer of a NN. We interpret NNs as a map from input objects $g \in G$, represented as $g = (v_1, \dots, v_m) \in \mathbb{R}^m$, to outputs in $[0,1]^{|C|}$ for classes C. The parameter m specifies the number of input features (see Fig. 1). Naturally, we interpret each $n \in N$ as a function by itself from the input layer up to the activation of n, i.e., $n : \mathbb{R}^m \to \mathbb{R}$. The output neurons can be characterized analogously by $c : \mathbb{R}^{|N|} \to \mathbb{R}$. With $w_{i,j}$ we address the weights connecting the output neuron $c_i \in C$ with hidden neuron $n_j \in N$.

Definition 1. (Many-Valued Conceptual View). *For a neural network NN, C its output classes and $N = \{n_1, \dots, n_h\}$ the neurons of the last hidden layer. We define the* many-valued conceptual view *as $\mathcal{V} = (\mathbb{O}, \mathbb{W})$, where $\mathbb{O} \in \mathbb{R}^{|G| \times |N|}$ with value at (i,j) equal to the activation $n_j(g_i)$, called* Object View, *and $\mathbb{W} \in \mathbb{R}^{|C| \times |N|}$ with value at (i,j) equal to the weight $w_{i,j}$, called* Class View.

A short motivation: with the object view $\mathbb{O}$, we study the activation of the neurons N given an object g. Complementarily, with the class view $\mathbb{W}$, we investigate the relation of the neurons N to the outputs $c \in C$ by their corresponding weights $w_{i,j}$. For example, given Fig. 1, which depicts the object and class view (right) of the network (left). We find that $n_k(o_t)$ is greater than $n_1(o_t)$, from which we infer that the relation of o_t to n_k is greater than n_1.

We employ the introduced views to comprehend the complete classification captured by a NN model. We can represent any object g as a row in the object view matrix, i.e., $O(g) := (n_1(g), \ldots, n_h(g))$. Analogously, we can represent any class c_i as a row in the class view matrix, i.e., $W(c_i) := (w_{i,1}, \ldots, w_{i,h})$. The outputs of the NN for class c_i follow from the term $O(g) \cdot W(c_i) + b$, where b is a bias. This can be rewritten as $\left|O(g)\right| \cdot \left|W(c_i)\right| \cos(O(g), W(c_i)) + b$ where $\cos(O(g), W(c_i))$ is the cosine value of the angle between $O(g)$ and $W(c_i)$.

Thus, to understand the inner representation of the classes C within the NN, it is reasonable to grasp the objects and classes in the same space and classify objects using similarity measures. Using this we can introduce an *object-class distance map* $d_{\mathcal{V}} : G \times C \to \mathbb{R}, (g, c) \mapsto d(O(g), W(c))$, where a sensible choice for d is *cosine similarity* or the *Euclidean distance*. We investigate both in Sect. 4.1.

Hence, using $d_{\mathcal{V}}$ and similar distance maps for $G \times G$ and $C \times C$, one can derive a pseudo-metric space $(G \cup C, \hat{d}_{\mathcal{V}})$. From this representation of G and C one can infer a simple classification map, e.g., by applying 1-NN classification.

Similarity of Neural Networks. Conceptual views enable a direct comparison of NNs. We employ the Gromov-Wasserstein (GW) distance [13], as experimentally demonstrated in Sect. 4.2. The GW distance solves an underlying optimization problem that seeks isometric mappings of the pseudo-metric spaces of two neural networks into a common third space, minimizing the deviation of object representations. In contrast to the Gromov-Hausdorff distance, the GW distance allows for matchings instead of one-to-one mappings between objects. The GW distance is moreover invariant with respect to permutations of the many-valued conceptual views.

3.2 Symbolic View

We employ *conceptual scaling* [5] from FCA using standard notation for *formal contexts* $\mathbb{K} = (G, M, I)$ and the *derivation operators* $(\cdot)^I : \mathcal{P}(G) \to \mathcal{P}(M)$, with $A^I = \{m \in M \mid \forall g \in A : (g, m) \in I\}$ and analogously $(\cdot)^I : \mathcal{P}(M) \to \mathcal{P}(G)$. We employ *dichotomic scaling*, using thresholds for the object view $\delta_{\mathbb{O}}$ and the class view $\delta_{\mathbb{W}}$ (see Fig. 1). The resulting relational structure is invariant with respect to row- or column permutations in the many-valued conceptual view.

Definition 2. (Symbolic Conceptual View). *Let $\mathcal{V} = (\mathbb{O}, \mathbb{W})$ the many-valued conceptual view of a NN and let $\delta_{\mathbb{O}}, \delta_{\mathbb{W}}$ be threshold values. We define the* symbolic conceptual view $\mathcal{V}_{\mathbb{D}} = (\mathbb{O}_{\mathbb{D}}, \mathbb{W}_{\mathbb{D}})$ *via the* Symbolic Object/Class Views*:*

$$\mathbb{O}_{\mathbb{D}} := (G, N \cup \bar{N}, I_{\mathbb{O}}), \text{ with } (g, n_j) \in I_{\mathbb{O}} :\Longleftrightarrow n_j(g) > \delta_{\mathbb{O}} \text{ and} \\ (g, \bar{n}_j) \in I_{\mathbb{O}} :\Longleftrightarrow n_j(g) \le \delta_{\mathbb{O}} \tag{1}$$

$$\mathbb{W}_{\mathbb{D}} := (C, N \cup \bar{N}, I_{\mathbb{W}}), \text{ with } (c_i, n_j) \in I_{\mathbb{W}} :\Longleftrightarrow w_{i,j} > \delta_{\mathbb{W}} \text{ and } (c_i, \bar{n}_j) \in I_{\mathbb{W}} :\Longleftrightarrow w_{i,j} \leq \delta_{\mathbb{W}}. \quad (2)$$

with artificial symbols $\bar{N} := \{\bar{n} \mid n \in N\}$ *used as defined above.*

This definition allows for constructing human-comprehensible explanations given a background ontology, e.g., from human annotations, ontological databases, or from concept-based explanations. We exemplify this in Fig. 1 using the formal context $\mathbb{S}_N$ that employs interpretable features $S_{m_1}, \ldots, S_{m_l}$. We provide more details in Sect. 5. Suitable threshold values $\delta_{\mathbb{W}}, \delta_{\mathbb{O}}$ depend on the architecture of the NN model under analysis. For example, if the activation function is ReLU, the neuron's co-domain is positive. Thus it becomes difficult to determine a reasonable δ for negative symbols $\bar{N}$, as studied in Sect. 4.3. **Evaluating Symbolic Conceptual Views:** Crucial for the quality of the derived symbolic representations are two criteria. First, classes need to be uniquely represented in $\mathbb{W}_{\mathbb{K}D}$. Second, the symbolic features should allow for straightforward descriptions for each class in C. This can be measured by the performance of interpretable classifiers such as decision trees or nearest-neighbor classifiers.

4 Experimental Study

We support our formal framework of conceptual views through an experimental study using common and well-known data sets and NN models. Our experimental design follows a principled evaluation strategy where each transformation step (from the original model through the many-valued view to the symbolic view) is separately validated. First, we evaluate the fidelity of the many-valued conceptual view by a classification task (Sect. 4.1). Second, we show how to compare many-valued conceptual views of different NN models (Sect. 4.2). Third, we derive human-comprehensible representations via symbolic views, conducting a parameter study to identify reasonable threshold values before validating them via classification (Sect. 4.3). The code and trained models are publicly available.[1]

Although the scaling procedure is conceptually simple, it is not trivially effective. The quality of the resulting views depends on the activation function, the distribution of activations and weights, and the number of neurons. Each step must therefore be carefully evaluated, which explains the staged design.

4.1 Many-Valued Conceptual Views on ImageNet

We demonstrate that many-valued conceptual views are capable of capturing a large share of a NN model's behavior. For this, we use all twenty-four NN models from TensorFlow that are trained on the ImageNet [3] data set (as of July 2022).

[1] https://github.com/FCA-Research/Formal-Conceptual-Views-in-Neural-Networks.

The object view is calculated using the test set, i.e., 100k images, of *ImageNet* used in the ILSVRC [17] challenge. In the extended version[2] we compile basic statistics on these networks and our views. The models span a variety of architectures and employ either ReLU or Swish activation functions in the last hidden layer. The number of neurons ranges from 1,024 (MobileNet) to 4,096 (VGG). Weight means are near zero across all models, while activation distributions vary considerably depending on the architecture.

Evaluating ImageNet Views. To evaluate the quality of our views, we compare a one-nearest-neighbor (1-NN) classifier on the pseudo-metric space $(G \cup C, \hat{d}_{\mathcal{V}})$ introduced in Sect. 3 directly with the NN classification function on all 100,000 test images. We use model fidelity as the evaluation criterion, i.e., we count instances where the 1-NN outputs the same class label as the NN and normalize by the cardinality of the test set. We differentiate between using cosine similarity and Euclidean distance within $\hat{d}_{\mathcal{V}}$.

Table 1. Fidelity between a NN model and its many-valued conceptual view using 1-NN. All twenty-four results are in the extended version.

	VGG16	DenseNet201	MobilNetV1	ResNet152V2	EffB0	EffB7
Euclidean	0.945	0.972	0.575	0.999	0.944	0.985
Cosine	0.841	0.728	0.449	0.314	0.933	0.979

Observations. We find that the many-valued conceptual view achieves high fidelity across the majority of models (see Table 1). The MobileNetV1 model is the only notable exception, which we attribute to its compact architecture and aggressive dimensionality reduction. Euclidean distance is consistently superior to cosine similarity, with particularly large gaps for ResNet models (up to 0.6 difference). For the EfficientNet family, we observe a near-monotone relationship between the number of neurons $|N|$ in the last hidden layer and fidelity. These results suggest that the many-valued conceptual view is a meaningful representation and that classification functions based on the resulting pseudo-metric space can serve as faithful surrogates for the NN model.

We acknowledge that the choice of distance metric is a design decision that may not generalize uniformly across all architectures. However, the consistently strong performance of Euclidean distance provides a practical default. Future work could investigate learned distance metrics to further improve fidelity, particularly for compact architectures where the simple metrics show limitations.

4.2 Similarity of Neural Networks

From the many-valued conceptual view we derive for all NN models a pseudo-metric space as introduced in Sect. 3, comparing them via the GW distance [13]

[2] The extended version with all supporting figures and tables is available on arXiv https://arxiv.org/abs/2209.13517v2.

on ten percent of the test set under a uniform probability measure. Pairwise fidelity serves as a baseline. From the pairwise fidelity diagram (extended version[4]) we infer that almost all models are distinct, with the exception of VGG16, VGG19, ResNet50, and the EfficientNet instances, where later models become more similar with increasing neuron count. The GW-based similarity reveals a richer structure: visually identifiable clusters of models often correspond to similar architectures, and the class view yields a finer clustering than the object view, suggesting that the weight structure captures architecture-specific patterns more effectively. CKA [11] operates on activations directly; our GW-based approach instead works on the full pseudo-metric space and is invariant under neuron permutations, complementing rather than replacing CKA.

4.3 Symbolic Conceptual View

We study the influence of activation functions and the number of neurons on the determination of threshold values for meaningful symbolic conceptual views.

Parameter Study. To evaluate the influence of the activation function and the number of neurons, we trained one NN architecture multiple times on the *Fruits-360* [14] data set, which contains 67,692 images of 131 types of fruits or vegetables (plus 22,688 test images). We used the architecture from the Fruits-360 experiment[3] with parameters from [14], modifying the last two hidden layers. For the last hidden layer N we vary its size 2^n between 2^4 and 2^9. For the penultimate layer we use $2^{\lfloor \frac{10+n}{2} \rfloor}$ for dimensional reduction. We studied the impact of *ReLU*, *Linear*, *Swish*, and *Tanh* activation functions across all layers. For each parameter setting we trained ten models and computed their respective conceptual views.

Table 2. Parameter study results for Tanh: influence of activation function and neuron count on view quality. V-Fid and SV-Fid denote the fidelity of 1-NN to the original model for the MV- and symbolic view, respectively. Full results in the extended version.

	2^4	2^5	2^6	2^7	2^8	2^9
Tanh						
$\delta_{\mathbb{O}} = 0$ Split	49.7/50.3	49.7/50.3	49.8/50.2	49.9/50.1	50.0/50.0	49.9/50.1
$\delta_{\mathbb{W}} = 0$ Split	49.9/50.1	49.8/50.2	49.8/50.2	50.0/50.0	49.9/50.1	50.0/50.0
Model Acc	90.5± 0.8	94.3± 0.5	94.7± 0.5	94.9± 0.4	95.0± 0.4	94.8± 0.3
V-Fid	98.3± 0.5	99.5± 0.1	99.7± 0.0	99.7± 0.0	99.8± 0.0	99.8± 0.0
SV-Fid	94.3± 1.4	97.4± 0.4	97.7± 0.4	97.6± 0.1	97.8± 0.2	97.6± 0.2

Observations. The distributions for the object views differ substantially among activation functions. We found that Tanh produces the most notable separation

[3] https://github.com/Horea94/Fruit-Images-Dataset.

of positive and negative values (see Fig. 2). Splitting with $\delta_{\mathbb{O}} = 0$ is meaningful for all examples with respect to separation and symmetry, yielding two sets of almost equal size. The same holds for $\delta_{\mathbb{W}}$. We experimented with alternative threshold determination methods, including mean values, median values, per-neuron medians, and kernel-density estimation for bivariate Gaussians, but the split at zero was consistently favorable with respect to model fidelity. We report scores for Tanh in Table 2; results for all activation functions are in the extended version.

We conclude from our parameter study that Tanh is the recommended activation function, with $\delta_{\mathbb{O}}, \delta_{\mathbb{W}} = 0$.

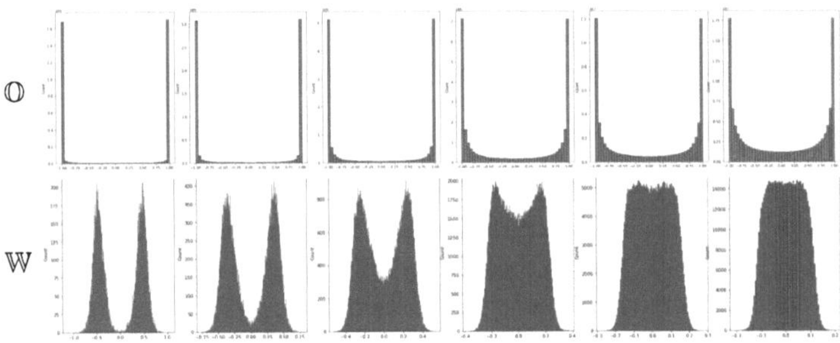

Fig. 2. Value distributions for the object ($\mathbb{O}$) and class ($\mathbb{W}$) view for ten runs using Fruits-360 and **Tanh** activation. Last hidden layer sizes from 2^4 (1st col.) to 2^9 (last col.). Note that the absolute values are not important; the relevant aspect is the distributional behavior shown in the plots. All activation functions are in the extended version.

Symbolic Conceptual Views of ImageNet. Based on the parameters identified above, we computed the symbolic conceptual views for the ImageNet models (results in Table 3). We found that the classes are uniquely represented (class separation equals 1), meaning a perfect classification procedure is theoretically possible using the symbolic view. However, a direct application of 1-NN using the binary vectors from the symbolic view yields very poor classification performance for ReLU-based models. In contrast, the Swish-based models achieve mediocre to good results, with performance improving for larger architectures. A reason for the unfavorable ReLU results is its positive co-domain, which hinders the construction of meaningful negated attributes $\bar{N}$; selected distributions and a discussion of architecture-specific scaling strategies are in the extended version (see Footnote 2) .

Symbolic Conceptual Views on Fruits-360. The twenty-four ImageNet models employ only ReLU and Swish activation functions. To complement our study with Tanh, we trained five models on Fruits-360: the baseline from [14], VGG16, ResNet50, IncV3, and EffB0 (transfer-learned with Tanh dense lay-

Table 3. Fidelity between six NN models and their symbolic conceptual view using 1-NN. All values are in the extended version.

	VGG16	DenseNet201	MobilNetV1	ResNet152V2	EffB0	EffB7
Euclidean	0.552	0.000	0.036	0.000	0.758	0.957
Cos	0.552	0.000	0.036	0.000	0.758	0.957
Class Sep	1.0	1.0	1.0	1.0	1.0	1.0
Activation	ReLU	ReLU	ReLU	ReLU	Swish	Swish

ers; full training details in the extended version[4]). The results in Table 4 show that all models achieve high accuracy, with the transfer-learned models outperforming the baseline. Crucially, while a decision tree classifier could not learn within the many-valued view, the same procedure applied to the symbolic view yields competitive classification, demonstrating that the symbolic translation produces representations amenable to inherently interpretable classifiers.

Table 4. Five NNs (Tanh) and their (symbolic) conceptual views captured by different surrogates (decision tree, 1-NN). IncV3 could not distinguish *Cherry 1* and *Plum*; EffB0 could not distinguish *Apple Red 1* and *Apple Pink Lady* in the symbolic view.

Model	Model	DTree		Euclidean		Cos		
	ACC	ACC	Fid	ACC	Fid	ACC	Fid	
Baseline	0.936	0.017	0.017	0.935	0.989	0.935	0.988	
VGG16	0.988	0.017	0.018	0.988	0.998	0.988	0.997	
ResNet50	0.989	0.018	0.018	0.989	0.998	0.989	0.997	
IncV3	0.983	0.013	0.013	0.983	0.999	0.984	0.999	
EffB0	0.984	0.007	0.007	0.984	0.998	0.983	0.984	
Symbolic								Class Sep
Baseline	0.936	0.857	0.879	0.927	0.964	0.927	0.964	1.0
VGG16	0.988	0.972	0.977	0.988	0.994	0.988	0.994	1.0
ResNet50	0.989	0.952	0.957	0.988	0.996	0.988	0.996	1.0
IncV3	0.983	0.975	0.988	0.984	0.997	0.984	0.997	0.992
EffB0	0.984	0.938	0.934	0.984	0.996	0.984	0.996	0.992

5 Beyond Views: Reasoning and Abductive Interpretation

Because the symbolic view is a formal context, its concept lattice $\mathfrak{B}(\mathbb{K})$ is directly available, exposing the conceptual hierarchy learned by the network and

[4] The extended version with all supporting figures and tables is available on arXiv https://arxiv.org/abs/2209.13517v2.

bounding the number of encoded concepts. Equally, given background knowledge $\mathbb{C} = (C, S_M, I_{\mathbb{C}})$ and a reflexive symmetric similarity $\sim$ on classes, the *symbolic interpretation* $\mathbb{S} = (N, S_M, R)$ with $(n, S_m) \in R :\Leftrightarrow \{n\}^{I_{\mathbb{W}}} \sim \{S_m\}^{I_{\mathbb{C}}}$ expresses neurons in terms of human-interpretable features, and (via subgroup discovery [8]) as propositional statements over S_M. In the extended version we instantiate both: lattice-based structural analysis of the indistinguishable classes *Apple Red*, *Pink Lady*, *Plum*, *Cherry* across five Fruits-360 models, and a subgroup-discovery decoding of the Tanh views with visual and taxonomic features, yielding rules such as "if neurons $\bar{13}, \bar{14}, \bar{9}$ are active, the fruit is orange" with confidence ≈ 0.54.

6 Discussion and Limitations

We introduced *conceptual views* as a global, post-hoc framework for analysing NN, grounded in Formal Concept Analysis. The framework jointly treats activations and output weights, requires neither auxiliary opaque models nor predefined concepts, and is architecture-agnostic in the sense that any model with a distinguishable last hidden layer admits a view. Across twenty-four ImageNet models and controlled Fruits-360 experiments, the many-valued view attains fidelity up to 0.999, the symbolic view separates classes uniformly, and the resulting representations are amenable to interpretable surrogates and to rule extraction. Three limitations should guide follow-up work: the formalisation currently targets feed-forward architectures with a well-defined last hidden layer, leaving recurrent and attention-based models open; dichotomic scaling is highly sensitive to the activation function, with Tanh clearly preferred and non-symmetric activations calling for data-driven thresholding; and concept lattices grow exponentially in the number of attributes, which constrains direct human inspection even though implications can be computed without materialising the lattice.

References

1. Bereska, L., Gavves, E.: Mechanistic interpretability for AI safety—a review. Trans. Mach. Learn. Res. (2024). https://doi.org/10.48550/arxiv.2404.14082
2. Bělohlávek, R., De Baets, B., Outrata, J., Vychodil, V.: Inducing decision trees via concept lattices. In: Eklund, P.W., Diatta, J., Liquiere, M. (eds.) CLA. CEUR Workshop Proceedings, vol. 331, pp. 1–12. CEUR-WS.org (2007)
3. Deng, J., Dong, W., Socher, R., Li, L.J., Li, K., Fei-Fei, L.: Imagenet: A large-scale hierarchical image database. In: CVPR, pp. 248–255. IEEE (2009). https://doi.org/10.1109/cvprw.2009.5206848
4. Fong, R., Vedaldi, A.: Net2vec: quantifying and explaining how concepts are encoded by filters in deep neural networks. In: CVPR, pp. 8730–8738. IEEE (2018). https://doi.org/10.1109/cvpr.2018.00910
5. Ganter, B., Wille, R.: Conceptual scaling. In: Roberts, F. (ed.) Applications of Combinatorics and Graph Theory to the Biological and Social Sciences, pp. 139–167. Springer (1989). https://doi.org/10.1007/978-1-4684-6381-1_6

6. Ganter, B., Wille, R.: Formal Concept Analysis - Mathematical Foundations, Second Edition. Springer (2024)
7. Hanika, T., Hirth, J.: On the lattice of conceptual measurements. Inf. Sci. **613**, 453–468 (2022). https://doi.org/10.1016/j.ins.2022.09.005
8. Herrera, F., Carmona, C., González, P., del Jesus, M.: An overview on subgroup discovery: foundations and applications. Knowl. Inf. Syst. **29**(3), 1–31 (2010). https://doi.org/10.1007/s10115-010-0356-2
9. Kim, B., Wattenberg, M., Gilmer, J., Cai, C., Wexler, J., Viegas, F., Sayres, R.: Interpretability beyond feature attribution: quantitative testing with concept activation vectors (TCAV). In: Dy, J.G., Krause, A. (eds.) ICML. Proceedings of Machine Learning Research, pp. 2668–2677. PMLR (2018)
10. Koh, P., et al.: Concept bottleneck models. In: ICML. Proceedings of Machine Learning Research, vol. 119, pp. 5338–5348. PMLR (2020). https://doi.org/10.48550/arxiv.2007.04612
11. Kornblith, S., Norouzi, M., Lee, H., Hinton, G.: Similarity of neural network representations revisited. In: Chaudhuri, K., Salakhutdinov, R. (eds.) ICML. Proceedings of Machine Learning Research, vol. 97, pp. 3519–3529. PMLR (2019).https://doi.org/10.48550/arxiv.1905.00414
12. Mangal, R., Narodytska, N., Gopinath, D., Hu, B., Roy, A., Jha, S., Pasareanu, C.: Concept-based analysis of neural networks via vision-language models. In: ECAI, pp. 49–77. LNCS, Springer (2024). https://doi.org/10.1007/978-3-031-65112-0_3
13. Mémoli, F.: Gromov–wasserstein distances and the metric approach to object matching. Found. Comput. Math. **11**(4), 417–487 (2011). https://doi.org/10.1007/s10208-011-9093-5
14. Mureşan, H., Oltean, M.: Fruit recognition from images using deep learning. arXiv preprint arXiv:1712.00580 (2017). https://arxiv.org/pdf/1712.00580
15. Ribeiro, M., Singh, S., Guestrin, C.: "why should I trust you?": explaining the predictions of any classifier. In: Krishnapuram, B., Shah, M., Smola, A.J., Aggarwal, C., Shen, D., Rastogi, R. (eds.) KDD. pp. 1135–1144. ACM (2016). https://doi.org/10.48550/arxiv.1602.04938
16. Rudin, C.: Stop explaining black box machine learning models for high stakes decisions and use interpretable models instead. Nat. Mach. Intell. **1**(5), 206–215 (2019). https://doi.org/10.1038/s42256-019-0048-x
17. Russakovsky, O., et al.: ImageNet large scale visual recognition challenge. Int. J. Comput. Vis. **115**(3), 211–252 (2015). https://doi.org/10.1007/s11263-015-0816-y
18. Sarker, M., Zhou, L., Eberhart, A., Hitzler, P.: Neuro-symbolic artificial intelligence. AI Commun. **34**(3), 197–209 (2022).https://doi.org/10.3233/aic-210084

Exploring Metadata in Enterprise Architecture by Applying Conceptual Graphs—Formal Concept Analysis (CGFCA) to Moregraph

Mahpara Saleem[1(✉)], Simon Polovina[2,3], and Richard Fallon[4]

[1] Mahaz Tech Enterprise Limited (MTE), Manchester, UK
mahpara@mahaztechenterprise.com

[2] Department of Computing and Digital Technologies, Sheffield Hallam University, Sheffield, UK
S.Polovina@shu.ac.uk

[3] Simile Logics Limited, Sheffield, UK
simon@similelogics.ltd

[4] Red Rooster IT, Vienna, Austria
richard@fallon.at

Abstract. Enterprise Architecture (EA) is increasingly driven by heterogeneous metadata drawn from cloud-based APIs, ERP systems, and platform reference architectures. This paper revisits Moregraph, a metadata-driven EA platform that combines OData API metadata parsing, force-directed graph visualisation, and extends its specification with Conceptual Graph – Formal Concept Analysis (CGFCA). Moregraph's specification is expressed as a Conceptual Graph (CG), which captures the overarching architectural concepts of metadata-driven EA. The CG is expressed in the Conceptual Graph Interchange Format (CGIF), which is part of the interoperable family of logics in the ISO/IEC 24707:2018 Common Logic standard. The CGIF encodes thirteen architectural concepts that include `[Application: Moregraph]`, `[Solution Architecture]`, `[Business Data Graph]`, `[SAP Graph]`, and `[Microsoft Graph]`, connected by seventeen relational triples. The CGFCA algorithm transforms these triples into a 13×17 binary Formal Concept Analysis (FCA) context in Burmeister format, identifies seven direct pathways from the single input concept `[Application: Moregraph]` to the single output concept `[Enterprise Architecture]`, all mediated by `[Technical Debt]`. We show that the combination of CG and FCA in CGFCA provides a principled foundation for navigating, validating, and analysing complex EA metadata landscapes.

Keywords: Enterprise Architecture · Conceptual Graphs · Formal Concept Analysis · Metadata · OData · CGIF · CGFCA · SAP Graph · Microsoft Graph

M. Croitoru et al. (Eds.): CONCEPTS 2026, LNAI 16811, pp. 362–372, 2027.
https://doi.org/10.1007/978-3-032-34742-8_25

1 Introduction

Enterprise architects managing large SAP or Microsoft deployments face a fundamental challenge: thousands of data entities are published as machine-readable OData metadata through SAP Graph [17] and Microsoft Graph [7], yet the architecturally significant relationships among them—Technical Debt, Solution Architecture alignment, Clean Core compliance [16,22,26]—remain undocumented in any formal, machine-readable form [20]. Bridging this gap requires a formal knowledge representation capable of encoding typed architectural relationships and an automated means of deriving structural insights from it.

Conceptual Graphs (CGs) [10,18,19] provide a logic-based notation with direct first-order semantics, standardised in CGIF (ISO/IEC 24707:2018 [5]). Formal Concept Analysis (FCA) [4,23] derives hierarchical concept lattices from binary cross-tables. CGFCA builds on Wille's Concept Graphs [24] to bring CG and FCA together [1,2], enabling lattice-based structural classification beyond conventional graph traversal. This paper revisits Moregraph [11], a metadata-driven EA platform, and extends its specification with CGFCA. Moregraph's specification is expressed as a CG in CGIF, enabling interoperability between CGs and other logics [3].

To demonstrate the end-to-end workflow, we convert Moregraph's CG to CGIF and translate it into a Burmeister FCA context using the open-source CharGer tool[1], whose CGFCA source code is also demonstrated in Moregraph. The analysis identifies a single input concept `[Application: Moregraph]`, a single output concept `[Enterprise Architecture]`, and seven direct pathways between them, all passing through `[Technical Debt]` and `[Solution Architecture]`. The derived 13×17 FCA binary context exposes the full transitive reachability structure of the CG.

Beyond [11], this paper contributes: (i) the complete 13×17 FCA formal context; (ii) five structural observations identifying input/output concepts, root and leaf attributes as formal invariants not derivable by graph traversal alone; and (iii) a concept lattice confirming the top/bottom ordering—all of direct practical value to enterprise architects validating metadata traceability.

2 Background

A **Conceptual Graph** (CG) [10,18,19] consists of `[concept]` nodes and `(relation)` nodes with first-order semantics; CGIF [5] serialises them as typed tokens, enabling interoperability with other logics [3]. **Formal Concept Analysis** (FCA) [4,23] derives concept lattices from binary formal contexts (G, M, I) ordered by extent inclusion [25], supporting ontology construction and information retrieval [12–14,21]; **CGFCA** [1,2] formalises the CG-to-FCA mapping, building on Wille's Concept Graphs [24]. **OData** [8,9] is an OASIS standard for REST-based data services; SAP Graph and Microsoft Graph expose large API estates via OData [7,17]. **Enterprise Architecture** (EA) disciplines [6,22]

[1] https://github.com/Conceptual-Graphs/CharGer.

decompose information systems into Business, Application, and Data Architecture layers forming the Solution Architecture; SAP's **Clean Core** strategy [16] mandates customisations within approved extension points, making metadata traceability essential for Technical Debt control.

3 The Moregraph Platform

Moregraph is a Next.js web application backed by PostgreSQL via the Prisma ORM [11], comprising four subsystems: the *OData Parser* (accepts EDMX, auto-detects V2/V4, extracts entity types and typed navigation properties in four categories: containment, external reference, internal navigation, and referential constraint); the *Graph Store*; the *Force-directed Visualiser* (physics simulation grouped by service, with entity panel and pie chart); and the *CGFCA Tool* (three-tab browser interface to upload CGIF/CSV/draw.io XML, run the algorithm client-side, and download `.cxt` and pathway `.txt` files).

4 CG Representation of the Moregraph EA

We used Moregraph's CG specification [11], authored in CharGer and exported to CGIF [5], as the EA knowledge base for CGFCA. The CG encodes thirteen architectural concepts and seventeen relational triples (Fig. 1), with `[Application: Moregraph]` as the unique input and `[Enterprise Architecture]` as the unique output.

Table 1 lists the thirteen concept types (left) and seventeen relational triples (right). Two concepts carry individual referents—`[Application: Moregraph]` and `[Ref. Solution Architecture: api.sap.com]`—while the remaining eleven are generic. In the CGIF encoding, `in-support-of` is n-ary (last referent = target EA, preceding referents = sources), compressing five triples into one token; `drawing-on` grounds Clean Core compliance in the SAP reference architecture at api.sap.com.

5 CGFCA: Triples to Binaries

5.1 Binary Context Generation

The CGFCA Tool accepts CGIF, CSV triples, or draw.io XML; for CGIF it scans `[Type: referent]` tokens then `(relation refs...)` tokens, treating the last referent as target and all preceding as sources. After parsing, *input concepts* (never a target) and *output concepts* (never a source) are identified. The formal context is then constructed as follows:

- **Objects** G: all CG concepts (13 for the Moregraph CG).

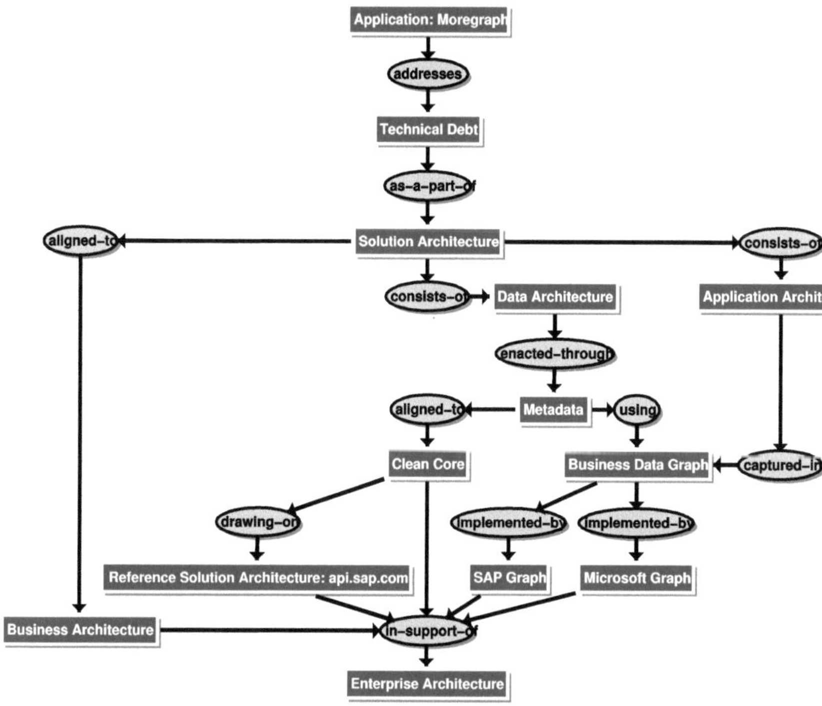

Fig. 1. CG representation of the Moregraph specification.

- **Attributes** M: all triples, labelled `''source relation''`. The 17 triples yield 17 attribute columns. Two pairs share the same source–relation label with distinct targets; these are disambiguated by appending the target in parentheses (e.g., *SA consists-of (AA)* and *SA consists-of (DA)*). ConExp treats column headers as unique strings; the appended targets ensure all 17 attribute labels are distinct in the exported `.cxt` file.
- **Incidence** I: $g\ I\ m$ iff concept g is reachable as a target from triple m through the transitive relational closure.

Transitivity is computed by the AddBinary procedure, called once per triple: starting from the triple's direct target, it follows outgoing triples recursively, marking each visited concept as reachable; a path-membership check prevents revisiting nodes, giving worst-case $O(|G| \cdot |M|)$ complexity. The result is written as a Burmeister `.cxt` file: header `B`, object and attribute counts, names, and a binary matrix of `X/.` symbols.

5.2 FCA Context for the Moregraph CG

Table 2 shows the complete 13×17 binary FCA context generated from the Moregraph CGIF, matching the `.cxt` file produced by the CGFCA Tool. Rows

Table 1. Concept types (left) and relational triples (right) in the Moregraph CG. Abbreviations in the right half are introduced in the left.

Concept	Referent
Application (MG)	Moregraph
Ref. Solution Arch. (RSA)	api.sap.com
Enterprise Architecture (EA)	(generic)
Solution Architecture (SA)	(generic)
Application Architecture (AA)	(generic)
Business Architecture (BA)	(generic)
Data Architecture (DA)	(generic)
Metadata (M)	(generic)
Business Data Graph (BDG)	(generic)
Microsoft Graph (MS)	(generic)
SAP Graph (SAP)	(generic)
Technical Debt (TD)	(generic)
Clean Core (CC)	(generic)

Relation	Source	Target
`addresses`	MG	TD
`as-a-part-of`	TD	SA
`consists-of`	SA	DA
`consists-of`	SA	AA
`aligned-to`	SA	BA
`enacted-through`	DA	M
`captured-in`	AA	BDG
`using`	M	BDG
`aligned-to`	M	CC
`drawing-on`	CC	RSA
`implemented-by`	BDG	MS
`implemented-by`	BDG	SAP
`in-support-of`	MS	EA
`in-support-of`	SAP	EA
`in-support-of`	BA	EA
`in-support-of`	RSA	EA
`in-support-of`	CC	EA

are concepts (objects); columns are triples (attributes) labelled by source and relation. **X** marks reachability—direct or transitive. Five structural observations follow: (1) Row 1 (Application: Moregraph) no X—unique **input**; (2) Row 13 (EA) X in every column—unique **output**; (3) Col. 1 (MG addresses) covers all twelve other rows—**root attribute**; (4) Cols. 3, 9, 15–17 (*in-support-of*) cover only Row 13—five **leaf attributes**; (5) Col. 12 (CC drawing-on) covers only Rows 12–13, confirming RSA reachable exclusively via *drawing-on*.

6 Experimental Results

6.1 Pathway Analysis

Table 3 lists the seven direct pathways from *Application: Moregraph* to *Enterprise Architecture*. Every pathway traverses MG $\xrightarrow{\text{addresses}}$ TD $\xrightarrow{\text{as-a-part-of}}$ SA, making *Technical Debt* and *Solution Architecture* mandatory mediators. Pathway 4 (via `drawing-on`) confirms Clean Core compliance traceability to the SAP reference architecture; no cyclic dependencies were detected.

6.2 Structural Observations from the Binary Context

Table 2 supports lattice observations without full lattice computation. Under the Ganter–Wille ordering [4], *Enterprise Architecture* (Row 13, all X) generates the

Table 2. Complete 13 × 17 FCA formal context from the Moregraph CGIF.

Object	Application: Moregraph addresses	Technical Debt as-a-part-of	Business Architecture in-support-of	Solution Architecture aligned-to	Application Architecture captured-in	Data Architecture enacted-through	Metadata aligned-to	Metadata using	Clean Core in-support-of	Solution Architecture consists-of (AA)	Solution Architecture consists-of (DA)	Clean Core drawing-on	Business Data Graph implemented-by (SAP)	Business Data Graph implemented-by (MS)	SAP Graph in-support-of	Microsoft Graph in-support-of	Reference Solution Architecture: api.sap.com in-support-of
Application: Moregraph																	
Technical Debt	×																
Business Architecture	×	×		×													
Solution Architecture	×	×															
Application Architecture	×	×								×							
Data Architecture	×	×									×						
Metadata	×	×				×					×						
Clean Core	×	×				×	×				×						
Business Data Graph	×	×			×	×		×		×	×						
SAP Graph	×	×			×	×		×		×	×		×				
Microsoft Graph	×	×			×	×		×		×	×			×			
Reference Solution Architecture: api.sap.com	×	×				×	×				×	×					
Enterprise Architecture	×	×	×	×	×	×	×	×	×	×	×	×	×	×	×	×	×

bottom concept; *Application: Moregraph* (Row 1, all dot) generates the **top** concept. Cols. 3, 9, 15–17 (*in-support-of* leaf attributes) have extent $\{EA\}$ only; Cols. 1–2 cover the most objects and are the most generative. *Reference Solution Architecture* (Row 12) is reachable exclusively via *Clean Core drawing-on*, giving it the smallest non-empty intent. Figure 2, computed in ConExp[2], confirms this ordering: EA at the bottom node, Application: Moregraph at the top, with the seven pathways visible in the branching structure. The lattice additionally

[2] https://conexp.sourceforge.net/.

Table 3. Seven direct pathways from *Application: Moregraph* to *Enterprise Architecture* (CGFCA output).

#	Pathway (relation labels omitted for brevity)
1	MG → TD → SA → DA → M → BDG → MS → EA
2	MG → TD → SA → DA → M → BDG → SAP → EA
3	MG → TD → SA → DA → M → CC → EA
4	MG → TD → SA → DA → M → CC → RSA → EA
5	MG → TD → SA → BA → EA
6	MG → TD → SA → AA → BDG → MS → EA
7	MG → TD → SA → AA → BDG → SAP → EA

reveals which concepts share identical structural positions (same lattice node), a classification not expressible as a formal invariant by directed-graph traversal.

7 Related Work

The theoretical relationship between CGs and FCA was studied by Andrews and Polovina [1], who provided a foundational mapping from CG triples to FCA formal contexts and compared the approach to Wille's Concept Graphs [24]—a distinct diagrammatic reasoning system grounded directly in FCA, which Wille intentionally named to distinguish it from Sowa's Conceptual Graphs. CGFCA was further described in [2]. Rudolph and Stumme [14] showed that concept lattices can be constructed from CG projection graphs; Priss and Old [13] modelled semantic aspects of CGs using FCA incidence structures. The CGFCA algorithm is complementary: it constructs a formal context directly from the triple structure, capturing transitive reachability and pathway topology rather than via projection. While pathway analysis from input to output concept is achievable through conventional directed-graph traversal, the FCA formal context additionally enables lattice-based structural classification: the concept lattice identifies each architectural element's structural role—input/output concepts, leaf and root attributes, and relative generativity—as formal invariants of the knowledge representation, beyond what graph traversal alone provides [4,25].

The Moregraph platform was introduced in [11]. The present paper adds: (1) the complete 13 × 17 FCA formal context in Burmeister format; (2) five structural observations identifying root/leaf attributes and input/output concepts as formal invariants; and (3) a concept lattice confirming the top/bottom ordering. A companion paper [15] extends the platform with a Metadata-to-Governance Transformation (MGT), mapping OData metadata to governed EA artefacts in SAP LeanIX.

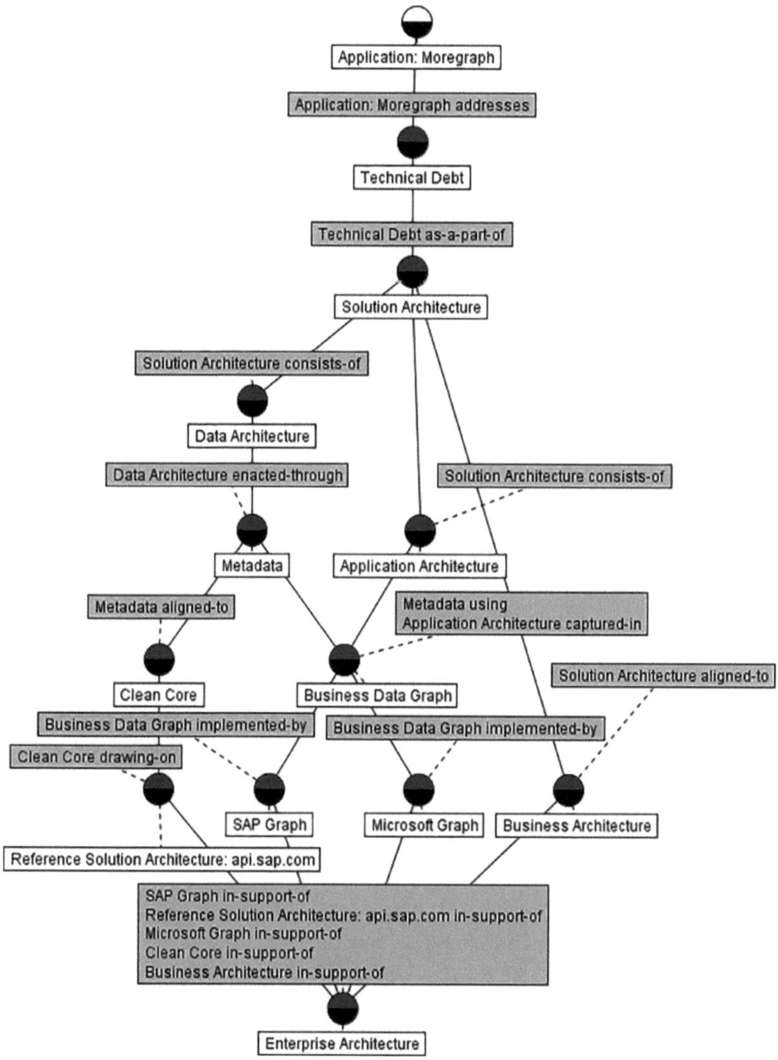

Fig. 2. Moregraph CG formalised as a concept lattice (CGFCA and ConExp).

In EA tooling, Lankhorst [6] advocates for model-driven EA using ArchiMate; Moregraph differs in grounding its model in machine-readable OData metadata rather than manually authored diagrams. Priss [12] surveys FCA in information science, underscoring its value for hierarchical knowledge organisation—a central requirement in EA.

8 Conclusion

We have presented Moregraph, a metadata-driven EA platform combining OData metadata parsing, force-directed visualisation, and a browser-based CGFCA tool, applied to a thirteen-concept, seventeen-triple CG in CGIF. The resulting 13×17 Burmeister FCA context identifies seven direct pathways from *Application: Moregraph* to *Enterprise Architecture*, all mediated by *Technical Debt* and *Solution Architecture*, with no cyclic dependencies. The formal context reveals EA is transitively reachable from every triple and that *addresses* is the root attribute—non-trivial invariants that emerge automatically, beyond what directed-graph traversal alone exposes. A companion paper [15] extends this into a Metadata-to-Governance Transformation (MGT) for SAP LeanIX; future work will render the concept lattice interactively within Moregraph.

Disclosure of Interests. The authors have no competing interests to declare that are relevant to the content of this article.

References

1. Andrews, S., Polovina, S.: A mapping from conceptual graphs to formal concept analysis. In: Andrews, S., Polovina, S., Hill, R., Akhgar, B. (eds.) Conceptual Structures for Discovering Knowledge, The 19th International Conference on Conceptual Structures, ICCS 2011, Derby, UK, pp. 63–76. Springer, Heidelberg (2011)
2. Andrews, S., Polovina, S.: Exploring, reasoning with and validating directed graphs by applying formal concept analysis to conceptual graphs. In: Croitoru, M., Marquis, P., Rudolph, S., Stapleton, G. (eds.) Graph Structures for Knowledge Representation and Reasoning, 5th International Workshop, GKR 2017, Melbourne, VIC, Australia, August 21, 2017, Revised Selected Papers, pp. 3–28. No. 10775 in Lecture Notes in Artificial Intelligence, Springer (2018)
3. Bridges, S., Schiffel, J., Polovina, S.: OpenSEA: a framework for semantic interoperation between enterprises. In: Bessis, N., Xhafa, F. (eds.) Next Generation Data Technologies for Collective Computational Intelligence, pp. 61–86. No. 352 in Studies in Computational Intelligence, Springer (2011). https://doi.org/10.1007/978-3-642-20344-2, https://shura.shu.ac.uk/3819/
4. Ganter, B., Wille, R.: Formal Concept Analysis: Mathematical Foundations. Springer, Berlin, Heidelberg (1999)
5. ISO/IEC: Information technology—common logic (CL): A framework for a family of logic-based languages. ISO/IEC 24707:2018. Tech. rep., International Organization for Standardization (2018)
6. Lankhorst, M.: Enterprise Architecture at Work: Modelling, 4th edn. Communication and Analysis. Springer, Berlin, Heidelberg (2017)

7. Microsoft Corporation: Microsoft Graph REST API v1.0 reference. Tech. rep., Microsoft Corporation (2024). https://learn.microsoft.com/en-us/graph/api/overview
8. OASIS: Open data protocol (OData) version 2.0. Tech. rep., OASIS Open (2014). oASIS Standard
9. OASIS: OData version 4.01. part 1: Protocol. Tech. rep., OASIS Open (2020). oASIS Standard
10. Polovina, S.: An introduction to conceptual graphs. In: Priss, U., Polovina, S., Hill, R. (eds.) Conceptual Structures: Knowledge Architectures for Smart Applications, pp. 1–14. Springer, Berlin Heidelberg, Berlin, Heidelberg (2007)
11. Polovina, S., Fallon, R., Saleem, M.: Moregraph: metadata-driven enterprise architecture using conceptual structures. In: Conceptual Knowledge Structures: CONCEPTS 2025. Lecture Notes in Computer Science, vol. 15941. Springer (2025)
12. Priss, U.: Formal concept analysis in information science. Ann. Rev. Inf. Sci. Technol. **40**(1), 521–543 (2006)
13. Priss, U., Old, L.J.: Modelling semantic aspects of conceptual graphs with FCA. In: Conceptual Structures: Leveraging Semantic Technologies, 17th International Conference on Conceptual Structures, ICCS 2009. Lecture Notes in Artificial Intelligence, vol. 5662, pp. 193–206. Springer (2009)
14. Rudolph, S., Stumme, G.: Constructing lattices from conceptual graphs. In: Conceptual Structures at Work: 12th International Conference on Conceptual Structures, ICCS 2004. Lecture Notes in Artificial Intelligence, vol. 3127, pp. 139–155. Springer, Berlin, Heidelberg (2004)
15. Saleem, M., Polovina, S.: Advancing metadata-driven enterprise architecture management tools using conceptual structure. In: Conceptual Knowledge Structures: CONCEPTS 2026, Springer (2026). In press
16. SAP SE: Clean core strategy for SAP S/4HANA. SAP Community (2023). available at community.sap.com
17. SAP SE: SAP Graph: A unified API for SAP data. Tech. rep., SAP SE (2024). available at api.sap.com
18. Sowa, J.F.: Conceptual Structures: Information Processing in Mind and Machine. Addison-Wesley, Reading, MA (1984)
19. Sowa, J.F.: Conceptual graphs for representing conceptual structures. In: Conceptual Structures in Practice. Chapman and Hall/CRC (2009). num Pages: 36
20. Sowa, J.F., Zachman, J.A.: Extending and formalizing the framework for information systems architecture. IBM Syst. J. **31**(3), 590–616 (1992)
21. Stumme, G., Maedche, A.: FCA-MERGE: bottom-up merging of ontologies. In: Proceedings of the 17th International Joint Conference on Artificial Intelligence (IJCAI 2001), pp. 225–230. Morgan Kaufmann (2001)
22. The Open Group: TOGAF standard, version 10 (2025). Tech. rep., The Open Group latest
23. Wille, R.: Restructuring lattice theory: An approach based on hierarchies of concepts. In: Rival, I. (ed.) Ordered Sets, pp. 445–470. Reidel, Dordrecht (1982)
24. Wille, R.: Conceptual graphs and formal concept analysis. In: Conceptual Structures: Fulfilling Peirce's Dream: Fifth International Conference on Conceptual Structures, ICCS 1997. Lecture Notes in Computer Science, vol. 1257, pp. 290–303. Springer, Berlin, Heidelberg (1997)

25. Wille, R.: Formal concept analysis as mathematical theory of concepts and concept hierarchies. In: Formal Concept Analysis: Foundations and Applications. Lecture Notes in Computer Science, vol. 3626, pp. 1–33. Springer, Berlin, Heidelberg (2005)
26. Zachman, J.A.: A framework for information systems architecture. IBM Syst. J. **26**(3), 276–292 (1987)

Nectar Papers

Multidimensional Representation of Physical Theories, Constants and Units Using Formal Concept Analysis
Originally Published at "Symmetry"

Mariana Espinosa-Aldama[1(✉)] and Sergio Mendoza-Ramos[2]

[1] IIMAS-UNAM-SECIHTI, Mexico City, Mexico
eamariana@yahoo.com
[2] IA-UNAM, Mexico City, Mexico

This contribution recalls results published in Symmetry on the use of Formal Concept Analysis (FCA) to represent semantic relations between physical theories, fundamental constants, and systems of units. The starting point is Bronstein's diagrams classifying physical theories and Zelmanov's cube of fundamental constants (gravitation constant G, speed of light c, Plank's constant $\hbar$). Their classification is formalized as a context whose concept lattice makes explicit the hierarchical relations between classical physics, relativity and quantum physics. The lattice representation clarifies inclusion relations and structural dependencies between theories in a way that complements traditional diagrammatic presentations.

The analysis is then extended by incorporating some other constants, such as the electron's charge e, Boltzmann's constant k, and Milgroms critical acceleration a_0, proposed in the context of Modified Newtonian Dynamics (MoND). The resulting structure illustrates how the addition of a constant reorganizes the lattice and generates new formal concepts corresponding to modified or intermediate theoretical frameworks and application regimes. The lattice thus provides a precise way of tracking structural differentiation in theory space.

A further dimension of the study examines the relation between fundamental constants and the International System of Units. By constructing contexts relating constants to base magnitudes and derived units, the analysis reveals how dimensional dependencies and definitional structures can also be represented within FCA.

Espinosa-Aldama, M., Mendoza, S.: Multidimensional Representation of Physical Theories, Constants and Units Using Formal Concept Analysis. *Symmetry* 16(7), 899 (2024).

M. Croitoru et al. (Eds.): CONCEPTS 2026, LNAI 16811, pp. 375–376, 2027.
https://doi.org/10.1007/978-3-032-34742-8

This work provides a case study of FCA applied to metatheoretical structures as a tool for organizing and visualizing relations at multiple levels: theoretical, dimensional, and metrological. The concept lattices derived from these contexts are interpreted as hierarchical semantic networks, where each formal concept corresponds to a class of theories sharing specific structural features.

Formal Context Transforms and Their Affordances for Exploratory Data Analysis
Originally Published at "Mathematics MDPI"

Francisco J. Valverde-Albacete[1(✉)], Carmen Peláez-Moreno[2], Inma P. Cabrera[3], Pablo Cordero[3], and Manuel Ojeda-Aciego[3]

[1] Depto. Teoría de Señal y Comunicaciones, Sistemas Telemáticos y Computación, Univ. Rey Juan Carlos, Madrid, Spain
francisco.valverde@urjc.es
[2] Depto. Teoría de Señal y Comunicaciones, Univ. Carlos III de Madrid, Madrid, Spain
[3] Depto. de Matemática Aplicada, Univ. de Málaga, Málaga, Spain

We introduce an approach to investigating the information content of a formal context using very generic concepts from the Philosophy of Information. The analysis-synthesis process of the information in data-bearing structures cryptomorphic to formal contexts is called in this work a *Formal Context Transform (FCT)*, instances of which are, e.g., Formal Concept Analysis, Logical Concept Analysis, Formal Independence Analysis, among others.

To try and explain the different types of qualitative information afforded by using each particular type of FCT as a data analysis procedure, we posit the concept of *formal qualia*, minimal differences in data-bearing items that provide cognitive affordances to understand and manipulate the results of analyses.

We provide a pattern for discerning how new types of FCT might appear:

- They should adopt the guise of an analysis-synthesis theorem, like the standard theorem of FCA does.
- For that purpose, specific, basic mathematical "entities" capable of capturing information should be identified, that is a formal quale RES should be chosen.
- A formal context should be cryptomorphic to a relational structure based on the order of such mathematical entities. This amounts, perhaps, to finding a new representation theorem.
- The rest of formal qualia proposed in this text should be identified, chosen or otherwise engineered: formal qualia BIAS and COLOURING.
- After the fact, we should analyse what type of RELATEDNESS the construction provides and what its relation to previous types of FCT is.

From this we introduce a pseudo-algorithm for obtaining new such data-analysis procedures and use this pseudo-algorithm to obtain a new type of FCT that we call Formal Object Neighbourhood Analysis.

F. J. Valverde-Albacete, C. Peláez-Moreno, I. P. Cabrera, P. Cordero, and M. Ojeda-Aciego, "Formal Context Transforms and Their Affordances for Exploratory Data Analysis," Mathematics, 14(1), 32, 2026, https://doi.org/10.3390/math14010032.

M. Croitoru et al. (Eds.): CONCEPTS 2026, LNAI 16811, pp. 377–378, 2027.
https://doi.org/10.1007/978-3-032-34742-8

The possibility of other FCT extracting new information from formal contexts depends on our capability to perceive other formal qualia in the epistemological framework of formal contexts. Our proposal can serve as a guide for discovering such transforms.

Towards Ordinal Data Science
Originally Published in the Transactions on Graph Data and Knowledge

Gerd Stumme[1(✉)], Dominik Dürrschnabel[2], and Tom Hanika[3]

[1] Research Center for Information System Design, University of Kassel, Kassel, Germany
stumme@cs.uni.kassel.de

[2] Baden-Wuerttemberg Cooperative State University Mosbach, Mosbach, Germany

[3] Information Systems and Machine Learning Lab, University of Hildesheim, Hildesheim, Germany

Along with proximity/distance, order is one of the two fundamental types of relation between objects in (empirical) data. Yet far fewer analysis methods exist for ordinal than for proximity data, and they cover a narrower range of tasks. This is partly because of limited computational resources in the last century, and partly because order-based methods are seen as too mathematically rigorous for real-world data. As a consequence, many analysts resort to methods designed for other relation types. We therefore call on interested researchers to join us in establishing the new field of *Ordinal Data Science*, revisiting existing research with ordinal methods and developing new ones within a comprehensive framework, drawing heavily on order theory and Formal Concept Analysis (FCA) to provide solid mathematical foundations. Contributions are sought in two areas: theoretical foundations for analyzing ordinal structures, especially for knowledge extraction and representation; and algorithmic methods to efficiently measure and calculate with ordinal and algebraic structures in real-world data.

In our work*, we propose different means for measuring and calculating with ordinal structures and show how to infer knowledge from them. Besides cross-fertilization with other machine learning and knowledge representation methods, a broad range of disciplines will benefit from this endeavor, including psychology, economics, sociology, web science, knowledge engineering, and scientometrics. Ordinal data is a part of the large family of relational data, which has received high interest of the computer science community in recent years. This is due to developments in fields such as sociology ("relational turn"), online social networks or knowledge graphs, genetics or epidemiology.

We expect Ordinal Data Science to become a scientific field with many ramifications. In the full article*, we discuss in an exemplary fashion five out of many potential subfields as programmatic research tasks: (*i*) *ordinal measurement theory*, an order-theoretic extension of the Representational Theory of Measurement

G. Stumme, D. Dürrschnabel, T. Hanika. Towards Ordinal Data Science. TGDK, Vol. 1, Issue 1, Pp. 6:1–6:39, Schloss Dagstuhl (2023). DOI: https://doi.org/10.4230/TGDK.1.1.6.

M. Croitoru et al. (Eds.): CONCEPTS 2026, LNAI 16811, pp. 379–380, 2027.
https://doi.org/10.1007/978-3-032-34742-8

to non-numerical scales; *(ii) ordered metric spaces*, which study the compatibility of an order relation and a metric on the same data; *(iii) algebraic constructions and decompositions* for complexity reduction, made robust enough for noisy data; *(iv) ordinal factor analysis*, an ordinal counterpart to classical factor analysis; and *(v) visualization, exploration, and browsing* of ordinal data.

Distances Between FCA Structures Originally Published in "Transactions on Graph Data and Knowledge (TGDK)"

Alexandre Bazin[1] and Giacomo Kahn[2](✉)

[1] LIRMM, CNRS, Université de Montpellier, Montpellier, France
[2] Univ Lumière Lyon 2, INSA Lyon, Université Lyon 1, Université Jean Monnet Saint-Etienne, DISP UR4570, Lyon, France
giacomo.kahn@univ-lyon2.fr

Given two data tables on the same objects and attributes, how far apart are the structures that are extracted from them? We define three families of distances: between formal contexts, between implication bases, and between concept lattices. For formal contexts, we consider the incidence relation and use set-based analogues of Minkowski distances to define the *factual distance*. For concept lattices and implication bases, we consider the structures as representations of, respectively, the derivation operators and the closure operator of the corresponding context and propose Minkowski-like distances: the *conceptual distance* and the *logical distance*. We experimentally study the correlations between those distances on formal contexts that are *closer* or *farther apart* and observe that these correlations depend on the factual distance.

An application would be the comparison of concept lattices or implication bases on very similar data, *e.g.* in the variability in different software product lines [2]. This contribution would allow for the study of the trajectory of a given software collection between versions – how much a new version differs from older versions. The notion of trajectory can also be used for iterative processes such as attribute exploration or Relational Concept Analysis [1, 3], to quantify the variation between concept lattices between steps. In those applications, the objects and attributes are basically the same during the process, and the labels of objects carry some significance, which is why our distances consider contexts with the same object and attributes sets.

Bazin, A. and Kahn, G., 2025. Distances Between Formal Concept Analysis Structures. Transactions on Graph Data and Knowledge, 3(2), pp.2–1.

M. Croitoru et al. (Eds.): CONCEPTS 2026, LNAI 16811, pp. 381–382, 2027.
https://doi.org/10.1007/978-3-032-34742-8

References

1. Bazin, A., Galasso, J., Kahn, G.: Polyadic relational concept analysis. Int. J. Approximate Reasoning **164**, 109067 (2024)
2. Bazin, A., Huchard, M., Martin, P.: Towards analyzing variability in space and time of products from a product line using triadic concept analysis. In: Proceedings of the 27th ACM International Systems and Software Product Line Conference-Volume B, pp. 85–89 (2023)
3. Rouane-Hacene, M., Huchard, M., Napoli, A., Valtchev, P.: Relational concept analysis: mining concept lattices from multi-relational data. Ann. Math. Artif. Intell. **67**, 81–108 (2013)

Interactive Exploration of Concept Lattices with Lattice.js: A Web-Based Visualization Library
Originally Published at "SGSOACS 2025"

Fabiola Hodo[1,2(✉)], Sara Balderas-Díaz[2], Gabriel Guerrero-Contreras[2], and Barış Sertkaya[1]

[1] Computer Science and Engineering, Frankfurt University of Applied Sciences, Frankfurt am Main, Germany
sertkaya@fra-uas.de

[2] Department of Computer Science and Engineering, University of Cadiz, Cádiz, Spain
fabiola.hodo@alum.uca.es, sara.balderas@uca.es, gabriel.guerrero@uca.es

Concept lattice visualization plays a central role in Formal Concept Analysis (FCA), supporting knowledge discovery and the interpretation of structured data [3, 5]. Over the years, several FCA tools have been developed for concept lattice construction and visualization, including ConExp [6], ToscanaJ [7], Galicia [8], Conexp-clj [10], LatViz [11], FCA4J [12], RCAviz [13] and DimDraw [14, 15]. While these tools have made important contributions to the FCA community and some remain actively maintained, others rely on older technologies, provide limited interactivity or extensibility, or are no longer actively developed.

To address these limitations, we present *lattice.js*, a lightweight, open-source JavaScript library for interactive and extensible concept lattice visualization, built on top of the D3.js framework [9]. The library combines hierarchical layout generation with user-driven exploration functionalities, enabling scalable and high-quality concept lattice representations through SVG rendering. The project is publicly available on GitHub.[1] The library is designed for easy installation, efficient execution, and user-friendly interaction.

lattice.js supports several functionalities for concept lattice exploration, including zooming, node dragging, node selection, filtering, shortest-path computation, customizable labeling strategies, and tooltip-based interaction. The library additionally computes structural metrics such as extent and intent sizes, stability, neighborhood size, lattice density, and the total number of concepts, objects, and attributes. To improve readability in dense lattices, the system supports both full and reduced labeling strategies.

To improve visual clarity and reduce edge crossings, *lattice.js* combines a heuristic variant of the Coffman–Graham layering algorithm [1] with barycentric reordering techniques [2]. Furthermore, the library supports export in multiple

11th Spanish German Symposium on Applied Computer Science, SGSOACS 2025, Vienna, Austria, June 30 – July 3, 2025, DOI: https://doi.org/10.1007/978-3-032-14816-2, Pages: 59–70.

[1] https://github.com/fabiolahodo/Concept-Lattice-Visualization-Tool..

M. Croitoru et al. (Eds.): CONCEPTS 2026, LNAI 16811, pp. 383–384, 2027.
https://doi.org/10.1007/978-3-032-34742-8

formats, including JSON, PNG, PDF, CSV, and CXT. The proposed system provides a flexible and accessible environment for both research and educational applications in FCA.

References

1. Coffman, E.G., Jr., Graham, R.L.: Optimal scheduling for two-processor systems. Acta Informatica **1**, 200–213 (1972)
2. Sugiyama, K., Tagawa, S., Toda, M.: Methods for visual understanding of hierarchical system structures. IEEE Trans. Syst. Man Cybern. **11**(2), 109–125 (1981)
3. Wille, R.: Concept lattices and conceptual knowledge systems. Comput. Math. Appl. **23**(6–9), 493–515 (1992)
4. Eades, P., Wormald, N.C.: Edge crossings in drawings of bipartite graphs. Algorithmica **11**, 379–403 (1994)
5. Ganter, B., Wille, R.: Formal Concept Analysis. Springer, Heidelberg (1999). https://doi.org/10.1007/978-3-642-59830-2
6. Yevtushenko, S.A.: System of data analysis "Concept Explorer" (in Russian). In: 7th National Conference on Artificial Intelligence, pp. 127–134, Russia (2000)
7. Becker, P., Hereth, J., Stumme, G.: ToscanaJ - an open source tool for qualitative data analysis. In: Workshop FCAKDD of the 15th ECAI, Lyon, France (2002)
8. Valtchev, P., Grosser, D., Roume, C., Rouane Hacene, M.: Galicia: an open platform for lattices. In: ICCS Workshop on FCA Applications (2003)
9. Bostock, M., Ogievetsky, V., Heer, J.: D3 data-driven documents. IEEE Trans. Visual Comput. Graphics **17**(12), 2301–2309 (2011)
10. Borchmann, D.: Exploratory programming for FCA - an introduction to conexp-clj. In: Workshop for FCA Tools and Applications, FCA-Tools (2013)
11. Alam, M., Napoli, A., Lévy, N., Toussaint, Y.: LatViz - a new practical tool for performing interactive exploration over concept lattices. In: 13th International Conference on Concept Lattices and Their Applications (CLA 2016), vol. 1624, pp. 9–20 (2016)
12. Gutierrez, A., Huchard, M., Martin, P.: FCA4J: a java library for relational concept analysis and formal concept analysis. In: ETAFCA 2022, pp. 207–212 (2022)
13. Muller, E., Huchard, M., Martin, P., Poncelet, P., Sallaberry, A.: RCAviz: visualizing and exploring relational conceptual structures. In: CLA 2022, pp. 135–148 (2022)
14. Dürrschnabel, D.: Explaining and visualizing structural knowledge in bipartite graphs. Ph.D. Dissertation. University of Kassel, Germany (2023)
15. Dürrschnabel, D., Hanika, T., Stumme, G., Dürrschnabel, D.: DimDraw - a novel tool for drawing concept lattices. In: Supplementary Proceedings of ICFCA 2019 Conference and Workshops, pp. 60–64. CEUR Workshop Proceedings (2019)

Computing the D-Base and D-Relation in Finite Closure Systems

Originally Published at "Theoretical Computer Science"

Kira Adaricheva[1], Lhouari Nourine[2], and Simon Vilmin[3(✉)]

[1] Department of Mathematics, Hofstra University, Hempstead, NY 11549, USA
Kira.Adaricheva@hoftsra.edu

[2] Université Clermont-Auvergne, CNRS, Clermont-Auvergne-INP, LIMOS, Clermont-Ferrand, France
lhouari.nourine@uca.fr

[3] Aix-Marseille Université, CNRS, LIS, Marseille, France
simon.vilmin@lis-lab.fr

Abstract. Implicational bases (IBs) are a common representation of finite closure systems and lattices, along with meet-irreducible elements. They appear in a wide variety of fields ranging from logic and databases to Knowledge Space Theory.

Different IBs can represent the same closure system. Therefore, several IBs have been studied, such as the canonical and canonical direct bases. In this paper, we investigate the D-base, a refinement of the canonical direct base. It is connected with the D-relation, an essential tool in the study of free lattices. The D-base demonstrates desirable algorithmic properties, and together with the D-relation, it conveys essential properties of the underlying closure system. Hence, computing the D-base and the D-relation of a closure system from another representation is crucial to enjoy its benefits. However, complexity results for this task are lacking.

In this paper, we give algorithms and hardness results for the computation of the D-base and D-relation. Specifically, we establish the NP-completeness of finding the D-relation from an arbitrary IB; we give an output-quasi-polynomial time algorithm to compute the D-base from meet-irreducible elements; and we obtain a polynomial-delay algorithm computing the D-base from an arbitrary IB. These results complete the picture regarding the complexity of identifying the D-base and D-relation of a closure system.

Keywords: closure systems · D-base · D-relation · minimal join covers · algorithmic enumeration · distributive lattice dualization · solution-graph traversal

---

Published version: https://www.sciencedirect.com/science/article/abs/pii/S0304397525003974. Manuscript available at https://arxiv.org/abs/2404.07037.

M. Croitoru et al. (Eds.): CONCEPTS 2026, LNAI 16811, p. 385, 2027.
https://doi.org/10.1007/978-3-032-34742-8

Enumerating the Irreducible Closed Sets of an Acyclic Implicational Base of Bounded Degree

Originally Published at "International Symposium on Algorithms and Computation (ISAAC 2025)"

Oscar Defrain(✉), Arthur Ohana, and Simon Vilmin(✉)

Aix-Marseille Université, CNRS, LIS, Marseille, France
Oscar.Defrain@lis-lab.fr, Arthur.Ohana@lis-lab.fr, Simon.Vilmin@lis-lab.fr

Abstract. We consider the problem of enumerating the irreducible closed sets of a closure system given by an implicational base. To date, the complexity status of this problem is widely open, and it is further known to generalize the notorious hypergraph dualization problem, even in the case of acyclic convex geometries, i.e., closure systems admitting an acyclic implicational base. This paper studies this case with a focus on the degree, which corresponds to the maximal number of implications in which an element occurs. We show that the problem is tractable for bounded values of this parameter, even when relaxed to the notions of premise- and conclusion-degree. Our algorithms rely on a sequential approach leveraging from acyclicity, combined with the solution graph traversal technique for the case of premise-degree. They are shown to perform in incremental-polynomial time. These results are complemented in the long version of this document by showing that the dual problem of constructing the implicational base can be solved in polynomial time. Finally, we argue that our running times cannot be improved to polynomial delay using the standard framework of flashlight search.

Keywords: Algorithmic enumeration · closure systems · acyclic convex geometries · implications · solution graph traversal · flashlight search · extension · hypergraph dualization

Published version: https://drops.dagstuhl.de/entities/document/10.4230/LIPIcs.ISAAC.2025.24. The long version is available on arXiv at the following address: https://arxiv.org/abs/2506.24052. The authors have been supported by the ANR project PARADUAL (ANR-24-CE48-0610-01).

M. Croitoru et al. (Eds.): CONCEPTS 2026, LNAI 16811, p. 386, 2027.
https://doi.org/10.1007/978-3-032-34742-8

Computing Bonds Between Formal Contexts
Originally Published at "Mathematical Methods in the Applied Sciences"

Roberto G. Aragón, Jesús Medina, and Samuel Molina-Ruiz(✉)

University of Cádiz, Cádiz, Spain
jesus.medina@uca.es

Computing bonds between formal contexts is a fundamental problem in Formal Concept Analysis (FCA), particularly in the study of information aggregation from multiple datasets without altering their structure. While the notion of bond has been widely investigated in both classical and fuzzy settings, its computational aspects have received comparatively less attention. In this work, we talk about our recent paper where we address this issue by developing a mechanism for the computation of all bonds between two formal contexts in both the crisp and fuzzy setting based on residuated lattices.

Given two disjoint contexts, bonds can be understood as relations whose rows and columns correspond to intents and extents of the original contexts, respectively. This observation allows us to reinterpret the problem of computing bonds as the construction of relations satisfying compatibility conditions with respect to these families of sets. Building on this idea, we propose a recursive algorithm that generates all possible relations whose columns are extents of the first context and whose rows are intents of the second, ensuring consistency at each step of the construction.

We prove that the proposed algorithm is both sound and complete in the crisp setting, in the sense that every relation it produces is a bond and every bond between the given contexts can be obtained through this procedure. Furthermore, we extend the method to the fuzzy framework based on residuated lattices, where checking the rows and columns of a relation also suffices to characterize bonds between contexts, allowing for a natural generalization of the algorithm.

These results provide a computational tool for the study of bonds in both classical and fuzzy FCA. Moreover, they open the door to further research on optimized implementations, as well as on the study of bonds in more general

Partially supported by the project PID2022-137620NB-I00 funded by MICIU/AEI/10.13039/501100011033 and FEDER, UE, Project FEDER-UCA-2024-A2-04 funded by Programa Operativo FEDER Andaluca 2021–2027 and by Consejera de Universidad, Investigacin e Innovacin, Junta de Andaluca and DGP_PRED_2024_01455 funded by the Junta de Andaluca/CUII and by FSE+.
R. G. Aragón, J. Medina, and S. Molina-Ruiz. Computing bonds between formal contexts.*Mathematical Methods in the Applied Sciences*, 2026.

M. Croitoru et al. (Eds.): CONCEPTS 2026, LNAI 16811, pp. 387–388, 2027.
https://doi.org/10.1007/978-3-032-34742-8

fuzzy frameworks, such as the multi-adjoint concept lattice framework, and their applications to real-world data aggregation problems.

Attribute Implication Bases from Galois Connection Structures
Originally Published at "Mathematical Methods in the Applied Sciences"

M. Eugenia Cornejo, Jesús Medina, and Francisco José Ocaña(✉)

Department of Mathematics, University of Cádiz, Cádiz, Spain
mariaeugenia.cornejo@uca.es, jesus.medina@uca.es,
franciscojose.ocana@uca.es

Modeling of knowledge systems through the identification of relationships among relevant variables remains a fundamental and challenging problem in many real-world scenarios. In this context, attribute implications, introduced within the framework of Formal Concept Analysis, provide a rigorous mathematical tool for representing dependencies between attributes. Since the number of valid implications extracted from formal contexts is usually very large, effective methodologies for their reduction and management are required. One of the main challenges is the determination of a non-redundant subset of valid attribute implications from which all others can be derived, namely, a basis of attribute implications. Several approaches have been proposed in both the classical and fuzzy residuated settings, although the mechanisms underlying these procedures are not equivalent in general.

In this work, we present a new procedure inspired by the methodology of Guigues and Duquenne for computing bases of attribute implications. The proposal is based on the notion of Galois connection and characterizes the validity of an implication through the degree of inclusion of the consequent set in the closure of the antecedent set. A mechanism for determining the most informative implications is introduced together with a sound and complete operational semantics based on Armstrong's axioms. In addition, the notions of non-redundant attribute implication and basis are studied in a general framework, extending the original notion of minimal non-redundant node to facilitate the computation of implication bases associated with a context. Finally, three alternative notions of bases are analyzed from different perspectives, highlighting their role in knowledge representation and dependency modeling.

Partially supported by the project PID2022-137620NB-I00 funded by MICIU/AEI/10.13039/501100011033 and FEDER, UE, by the grant TED2021-129748B-I00 funded by MCIN/AEI/10.13039/501100011033 and European Union NextGeneration EU/PRTR.

M. Eugenia Cornejo, Jesús Medina, Francisco José Ocaña. Attribute implication bases from Galois connection structures. Mathematical Methods in the Applied Sciences, 49:2729–2753, 2026. DOI: https://doi.org/10.1002/mma.70279.

M. Croitoru et al. (Eds.): CONCEPTS 2026, LNAI 16811, p. 389, 2027.
https://doi.org/10.1007/978-3-032-34742-8

Author Index

M. Croitoru et al. (Eds.): CONCEPTS 2026, LNAI 16811, pp. 391–392, 2027.
https://doi.org/10.1007/978-3-032-34742-8

MIX
Papier aus verantwortungsvollen Quellen
Paper from responsible sources
FSC® C105338

If you have any concerns about our products,
you can contact us on
ProductSafety@springernature.com

In case Publisher is established outside the EU,
the EU authorized representative is:
Springer Nature Customer Service Center GmbH
Europaplatz 3, 69115 Heidelberg, Germany

Printed by Libri Plureos GmbH
in Hamburg, Germany